Beginning
Microsoft® Visual Basic® 2008

W9-AHA-223

(Continued)

Beginning
Microsoft® Visual Basic® 2008

Thearon Willis
and
Bryan Newsome

Wiley Publishing, Inc.

Beginning Microsoft® Visual Basic® 2008

Published by
Wiley Publishing, Inc.
10475 Crosspoint Boulevard
Indianapolis, IN 46256
www.wiley.com

Copyright © 2008 by Wiley Publishing, Inc., Indianapolis, Indiana

Published simultaneously in Canada

ISBN: 978-0-470-19134-7

Manufactured in the United States of America

10 9 8 7 6 5 4 3 2 1

Library of Congress Cataloging-in-Publication Data

Willis, Thearon.
   Beginning Microsoft Visual basic 2008 / Thearon Willis and Bryan Newsome.
      p. cm.
   Includes index.
   ISBN 978-0-470-19134-7 (paper/website)
      1. Microsoft Visual BASIC   2. BASIC (Computer program language)
I. Newsome, Bryan, 1971-   II. Title.
QA76.73.B3W45556   2008
005.2'762—dc22

                                          2008004982

For my daughter, Stephanie, my most precious gift from God.
For Wendy, my love and friend in Christ.
—Thearon

To Jennifer and Katelyn.
—Love, Bryan

About the Authors

Thearon Willis currently works as a senior developer and builds Windows applications and add-ins for Microsoft Office products using Microsoft Visual Basic 2008. Over the years, Thearon has worked on a variety of systems from mainframe to client-server development.

Bryan Newsome works as a director for a custom software solutions company specializing in Microsoft applications. Since starting his career building Visual Basic 5 solutions, he has embraced each new version Visual Basic and now creates all new solutions leveraging the .NET platform and VB.NET. He provides clients with solutions and mentoring on leading-edge Microsoft technologies. For VB.NET, Bryan is a Microsoft Certified Application Developer.

Credits

Acquisitions Editor
Katie Mohr

Development Editors
Sara Shlaer
Sydney Jones

Technical Editor
Mark Lavoie

Production Editor
Kathryn Duggan

Copy Editor
Travis Henderson

Editorial Manager
Mary Beth Wakefield

Production Manager
Tim Tate

Vice President and Executive Group Publisher
Richard Swadley

Vice President and Executive Publisher
Joseph B. Wikert

Project Coordinator, Cover
Lynsey Stanford

Proofreader
Jeremy Bagai, Word One New York Editing & Proofreading

Indexer
Johnna VanHoose Dinse

Acknowledgments

First and foremost I want to thank God for giving me the wisdom and knowledge to share with others and for the many talents that he has blessed me with. I would also like to thank Katie Mohr for giving me the opportunity to write this book and Sara Shlaer and Sydney Jones for their hard work in editing. Also thanks to all the other people at Wiley who work so hard to bring this book to market. I'd be remiss if I didn't thank my good friend and co-author Bryan Newsome; thanks for your hard work and dedication.

—*Thearon*

So many people put so much effort into publishing this work. Thank you all; this would not be possible without your hard work and dedication. Special thanks to Katie Mohr, Sara Shlaer, Sydney Jones, and Mark Lavoie for making my work readable and technically sound. It was a pleasure to work with you all over the past months. Thank you Thearon; you were a terrific mentor for me and the reason I ever had the opportunity to write.

—*Bryan*

Contents

Contents

Contents

Contents

Contents

Contents

Contents

Introduction

Visual Basic 2008 is Microsoft's latest version of the highly popular Visual Basic .NET programming language, one of the many languages supported in Visual Studio 2008. Visual Basic 2008's strength lies in its ease of use and the speed at which you can create Windows Forms applications, WPF Windows applications, web applications, WPF Browser applications, mobile device applications, and web services.

In this book, we introduce you to programming with Visual Basic 2008 and show you how to create these types of applications and services. Along the way you'll also learn about object-oriented techniques and learn how to create your own business objects and Windows controls.

Microsoft .NET Framework provides Visual Basic 2008 programmers with the capability to create full object-oriented programs, just like the ones created using C# or C++. The .NET Framework provides a set of base classes that are common to all programming languages in Visual Studio 2008, which provides you with the same capability to create object-oriented programs as a programmer using C# or C++.

This book will give you a thorough grounding in the basics of programming using Visual Basic 2008; from there the world is your oyster.

Who Is This Book For?

This book is designed to teach you how to write useful programs in Visual Basic 2008 as quickly and easily as possible.

There are two kinds of beginners for whom this book is ideal:

❑ You're a beginner to programming and you've chosen Visual Basic 2008 as the place to start. That's a great choice! Visual Basic 2008 is not only easy to learn, it's also fun to use and very powerful.

❑ You can program in another language but you're a beginner to .NET programming. Again, you've made a great choice! Whether you've come from Fortran or Visual Basic 6, you'll find that this book quickly gets you up to speed on what you need to know to get the most from Visual Basic 2008.

What Does This Book Cover?

Visual Basic 2008 offers a great deal of functionality in both tools and language. No one book could ever cover Visual Basic 2008 in its entirety — you would need a library of books. What this book aims to do is to get you started as quickly and easily as possible. It shows you the roadmap, so to speak, of what there is and where to go. Once we've taught you the basics of creating working applications (creating the windows and controls, how your code should handle unexpected events, what object-oriented

Introduction

programming is, how to use it in your applications, and so on), we'll show you some of the areas you might want to try your hand at next. To this end, the book is organized as follows:

❑ Chapters 1 through 9 provide an introduction to Visual Studio 2008 and Windows programming.

❑ Chapter 6 provides an introduction to XAML and Windows Presentation Foundation (WPF) programming.

❑ Chapter 10 provides an introduction to application debugging and error handling.

❑ Chapters 11 through 13 provide an introduction to object-oriented programming and building objects.

❑ Chapter 14 provides an introduction to creating Windows Forms user controls.

❑ Chapter 15 provides an introduction to graphics in Windows applications.

❑ Chapters 16 and 17 provide an introduction to programming with databases and covers Access, SQL Server, ADO.NET and LINQ.

❑ Chapters 18 and 19 provide an introduction to ASP.NET and show you how to write applications for the Web.

❑ Chapter 20 provides a brief introduction to XML, a powerful tool for integrating your applications—regardless of the language they were written in.

❑ Chapter 21 introduces you to web services and the Windows Communication Foundation (WCF).

❑ Chapter 22 introduces you to sequential workflows using the Windows Workflow Foundation (WF).

❑ Chapter 23 introduces you to building applications for mobile devices using the Compact Framework classes.

❑ Chapter 24 introduces you to deploying applications using ClickOnce technology.

❑ Chapter 25 provides some insight on where to go next in your journey to learn about Visual Basic 2008.

❑ Appendix A provides the answers to chapter exercises.

❑ Appendix B introduces the Microsoft Solution Framework.

❑ Appendix C provides some background on security.

❑ Appendix D provides insight into Windows CardSpace.

❑ Appendix E compares the differences between the latest versions of the .NET Framework.

What Do I Need to Run Visual Basic 2008?

Apart from a willingness to learn, all you'll need for the first 13 chapters are a PC running Windows Vista (preferred), Windows XP (Home or Professional Edition), or Windows Server 2003; Internet Explorer; and of course, one of the following:

❑ Microsoft Visual Basic 2008 Express

❑ Microsoft Visual Basic 2008 Profession Edition

❑ Microsoft Visual Basic 2008 Team System

As the later chapters cover more advanced subject areas, you will need other software to get the most out of them. Also note that Visual Basic 2008 Express does not support creating web applications, mobile applications, or deployment projects.

❑ Chapter 14 requires Microsoft Visual Basic 2008 Professional Edition or above in order to create Windows Forms User Controls.

❑ Chapter 16 requires Microsoft Access 2000.

❑ For Chapter 17, you will need to have access to SQL Server 2005, SQL Server 2005 Express Edition, or SQL Server 2008.

Don't worry if you don't have these products yet and want to wait a while before you purchase them. You should still find that you get a lot out of this book.

Conventions

We've used a number of different styles of text and layout in this book to help differentiate between the different kinds of information. Here are examples of the styles we used and an explanation of what they mean.

Try It Out   How Do They Work?

1. Each step has a number.

2. Follow the steps in sequence.

How It Works

If there's more that you need to understand about what's going on as you complete the steps, you will find a subsequent "How It Works" section that explains what's going on behind the scenes.

Background information, asides, and references appear in text like this.

Code has several styles. If it's a word that we're talking about in the text — for example, when discussing a For...Next loop, it's in this font. If it's a block of code that can be typed as a program and run, it looks like this:

```
Private Sub btnAdd_Click(ByVal sender As System.Object, _
            ByVal e As System.EventArgs) Handles btnAdd.Click
    Dim n As Integer
    n = 27
    MessageBox.Show(n)
End Sub
```

Sometimes you'll see code in a mixture of styles, like this:

```
Private Sub btnAdd_Click(ByVal sender As System.Object, _
            ByVal e As System.EventArgs) Handles btnAdd.Click
    Dim n As Integer
    n = 27
    n = n + 2
    MessageBox.Show(n)
End Sub
```

In cases like this, the code with a white background is code that Visual Studio 2008 has automatically generated (in a Try It Out) or code you are already familiar with (in a How It Works); the lines highlighted in gray show a change or a new addition to the code.

Source Code

As you work through the examples in this book, you may choose either to type in all the code manually or to use the source code files that accompany the book. All of the source code used in this book is available for download at www.wrox.com. When at the site, locate the book's title (either by using the Search box or by using one of the title lists) and click the Download Code link on the book's detail page to obtain all the source code for the book.

> *Because many books have similar titles, you may find it easiest to search by ISBN; this book's ISBN is 978-0-470-19134-7.*

After you have downloaded the code, decompress it with your favorite compression tool. Alternately, you can go to the main Wrox code download page at www.wrox.com/dynamic/books/download.aspx to see the code available for this book and all other Wrox books.

Errata

We make every effort to ensure that there are no errors in the text or in the code. However, no one is perfect, and mistakes do occur. If you find an error in one of our books, like a spelling mistake or faulty piece of code, we would be very grateful for your feedback. By sending in errata you may save another reader hours of frustration and at the same time you will be helping us provide even higher quality information.

To find the errata page for this book, go to www.wrox.com and locate the title using the Search box or one of the title lists. Then, on the book details page, click the Book Errata link. On this page you can view all errata that have been submitted for this book and posted by Wrox editors. A complete book list including links to each book's errata is also available at www.wrox.com/misc-pages/booklist.shtml.

If you don't spot your error on the Book Errata page, go to www.wrox.com/contact/techsupport .shtml and complete the form there to send us the error you have found. We'll check the information and, if appropriate, post a message to the book's errata page and fix the problem in subsequent editions of the book.

p2p.wrox.com

For author and peer discussion, join the P2P forums at p2p.wrox.com. The forums are a web-based system for you to post messages relating to Wrox books and related technologies and interact with other readers and technology users. The forums offer a subscription feature to e-mail you topics of interest of your choosing when new posts are made to the forums. Wrox authors, editors, other industry experts, and your fellow readers are present on these forums.

At p2p.wrox.com you will find a number of different forums that will help you not only as you read this book, but also as you develop your own applications. To join the forums, just follow these steps:

1. Go to p2p.wrox.com and click the Register link.
2. Read the terms of use and click Agree.
3. Complete the required information to join as well as any optional information you wish to provide and click Submit.
4. You will receive an e-mail with information describing how to verify your account and complete the joining process.

    You can read messages in the forums without joining P2P but in order to post your own messages, you must join.

After you've joined, you can post new messages and respond to messages other users post. You can read messages at any time on the Web. If you would like to have new messages from a particular forum e-mailed to you, click the Subscribe to this Forum icon by the forum name in the forum listing.

For more information about how to use the Wrox P2P, be sure to read the P2P FAQs for answers to questions about how the forum software works as well as many common questions specific to P2P and Wrox books. To read the FAQs, click the FAQ link on any P2P page.

Welcome to
Visual Basic 2008

This is an exciting time to enter the world of programming with Visual Basic 2008 and Windows Vista. Windows Vista represents the first Windows operating system upgrade since Windows XP was first released in 2002. A lot has changed in the Windows user interface and Visual Basic 2008 makes it easy to write professional-looking Windows applications as well as web applications and web services. Haven't upgraded to Windows Vista yet? No worries, Visual Basic 2008 also allows you to write professional-looking applications for Windows XP as well.

The goal of this book is to help you use the Visual Basic 2008 programming language, even if you have never programmed before. You will start slowly and build on what you have learned in subsequent chapters. So take a deep breath, let it out slowly, and tell yourself you can do this. No sweat! No kidding!

Programming a computer is a lot like teaching a child to tie his shoes. Until you find the correct way of giving the instructions, not much is accomplished. Visual Basic 2008 is a language you can use to tell your computer how to do things. But, like a child, the computer will understand only if you explain things very clearly. If you have never programmed before, this sounds like an arduous task, and sometimes it can be. However, Visual Basic 2008 gives you an easy-to-use language to explain some complex tasks. Although it never hurts to have an understanding of what is happening at the lowest levels, Visual Basic 2008 frees the programmer from having to deal with the mundane complexities of writing Windows applications. You are free to concentrate on solving real problems.

Visual Basic 2008 helps you create solutions that run on the Microsoft Windows operating systems, such as Windows Vista, Windows Server 2008, and Windows Mobile 6. If you are looking at this book, you might have already felt the need or desire to create such programs. Even if you have never written a computer program before, as you progress through the Try It Out exercises in this book, you will become familiar with the various aspects of the Visual Basic 2008 language, as well as its foundations in the Microsoft .NET Framework. You will find that it is not nearly as difficult as you had imagined. Before you know it, you will feel quite comfortable creating a variety of different types of programs with Visual Basic 2008.

Visual Basic 2008 can also be used to create web applications and web services as well as mobile applications that can run on Pocket PCs or SmartPhones. However, you will begin by focusing on Windows applications before extending your boundaries to other platforms.

This chapter covers the following topics:

❑ Event-driven programming

❑ The installation of Visual Basic 2008

❑ A tour of the Visual Basic 2008 Integrated Development Environment (IDE)

❑ How to create a simple Windows program

❑ How to use the integrated Help system

Event-Driven Programming

A Windows program is quite different from yesteryear's MS-DOS program. A DOS program follows a relatively strict path from beginning to end. Although this does not necessarily limit the functionality of the program, it does limit the road the user has to take to get to it. A DOS program is like walking down a hallway; to get to the end you have to walk down the hallway, passing any obstacles that you may encounter. A DOS program would only let you open certain doors along your stroll.

Windows, on the other hand, opened up the world of *event-driven programming*. *Events* in this context include clicking a button, resizing a window, or changing an entry in a text box. The code that you write responds to these events. In terms of the hallway analogy: In a Windows program, to get to the end of the hall, you just click the end of the hall. The hallway can be ignored. If you get to the end and realize that is not where you wanted to be, you can just set off for the new destination without returning to your starting point. The program reacts to your movements and takes the necessary actions to complete your desired tasks.

Another big advantage in a Windows program is the *abstraction of the hardware*; which means that Windows takes care of communicating with the hardware for you. You do not need to know the inner workings of every laser printer on the market just to create output. You do not need to study the schematics for graphics cards to write your game. Windows wraps up this functionality by providing generic routines that communicate with the drivers written by hardware manufacturers. This is probably the main reason that Windows has been so successful. The generic routines are referred to as the Windows *application programming interface* (API), and the classes in the .NET Framework take care of communicating with those APIs.

Before Visual Basic 1.0 was introduced to the world in 1991, developers had to be well versed in C and C++ programming, as well as the building blocks of the Windows system itself, the Windows API. This complexity meant that only dedicated and properly trained individuals were capable of turning out software that could run on Windows. Visual Basic changed all of that, and it has been estimated that there are now as many lines of production code written in Visual Basic as in any other language.

Visual Basic changed the face of Windows programming by removing the complex burden of writing code for the user interface (UI). By allowing programmers to *draw* their own UI, it freed them to concentrate on the business problems they were trying to solve. When the UI is drawn, the programmer can then add the code to react to events.

Visual Basic has also been *extensible* from the very beginning. Third-party vendors quickly saw the market for reusable modules to aid developers. These modules, or *controls*, were originally referred to as VBXs (named after their file extension). Prior to Visual Basic 5.0, if you did not like the way a button behaved, you could either buy or create your own, but those controls had to be written in C or C++. Database access utilities were some of the first controls available. Version 5 of Visual Basic introduced the concept of *ActiveX*, which allowed developers to create their own *ActiveX controls*.

When Microsoft introduced Visual Basic 3.0, the programming world changed significantly. Now you could build database applications directly accessible to users (so-called *front-end applications*) completely with Visual Basic. There was no need to rely on third-party controls. Microsoft accomplished this task with the introduction of *Data Access Objects* (DAO), which allowed programmers to manipulate data with the same ease as manipulating the user interface.

Versions 4.0 and 5.0 extended the capabilities of Version 3.0 to allow developers to target the new Windows 95 platform. They also made it easier for developers to write code, which could then be manipulated to make it usable to other language developers. Version 6.0 provided a new way to access databases with the integration of *ActiveX Data Objects* (ADO). The ADO feature was developed by Microsoft to aid web developers using Active Server Pages (ASP) to access databases. All of the improvements to Visual Basic over the years have ensured its dominant place in the programming world — it helps developers write robust and maintainable applications in record time.

With the release of Visual Basic .NET in February 2002, most of the restrictions that used to exist have been obliterated. In the past, Visual Basic was criticized and maligned as a "toy" language, because it did not provide all of the features of more sophisticated languages such as C++ and Java. Now, Microsoft has removed these restrictions and made Visual Basic .NET a very powerful development tool. This trend has continued with the release of Visual Basic 2003, Visual Basic 2005, and the latest release, Visual Basic 2008. Each new release of the Visual Basic .NET programming language brings about many new trends, features, and improvements, making it a great choice for programmers of all levels.

Installing Visual Basic 2008

You may own Visual Basic 2008 in one of the following forms:

❑ As part of Visual Studio 2008, a suite of tools and languages that also includes C# (pronounced *C-sharp*) and Visual C++. The Visual Studio 2008 product line includes Visual Studio Professional Edition or Visual Studio Tools Team Editions. The Team Edition versions come with progressively more tools for building and managing the development of larger, enterprise-wide applications.

❑ As Visual Basic 2008 Express Edition, which includes the Visual Basic 2008 language, and a reduced set of the tools and features that are available with Visual Studio 2008.

Both of these products enable you to create your own applications for the Windows platform. The installation procedure is straightforward. In fact, the Visual Studio Installer is smart enough to figure out exactly what your computer requires to make it work.

The descriptions in the following Try It Out exercise are based on installing Visual Studio 2008 Professional Edition. Most of the installation processes are straightforward, and you can accept the default installation options for most environments. So, regardless of which edition you are installing, the installation process should be smooth when accepting the default installation options.

Try It Out   **Installing Visual Basic 2008**

1. The Visual Studio 2008 DVD has an auto-run feature, but if the Setup screen does not appear after inserting the DVD, you need to run Setup.exe from the root directory of the DVD. To do this, click the Windows Start menu at the bottom left of your screen and then select the Run start menu item or browse to the Setup program on the DVD. In the Run dialog box, you can click the Browse button to locate the `setup.exe` program on your DVD. Then click the OK button in the Run dialog box to start the setup program. After the setup program initializes, you will see the initial screen as shown in Figure 1-1.

Figure 1-1

2. The dialog box shown in Figure 1-1 shows the order in which the installation will occur. To function properly, Visual Studio 2008 requires various updates to be installed depending on the operating system that you have (for example, Service Pack 2 on Windows XP). The setup program will automatically inform you of these updates if they are not installed. You should install those updates first and then return to the Visual Studio 2008 setup program. The individual updates required are different from the service releases listed as the third option in Figure 1-1. Step 1 of the setup program will install Visual Studio 2008 so click the Install Visual Studio 2008 link shown in Figure 1-1.

3. The next step in the installation process asks you if you want to send the setup information from the installation of Visual Studio 2008 to Microsoft. This is a good idea to help streamline the installation process of future editions of Visual Studio, and no personal information will be sent. You can click the Next button at this screen after you have selected or cleared the check box indicating whether or not you want this information sent.

4. The third step in the installation process is the license agreement. Read the license agreement and then select the option button indicating your acceptance of the licensing terms. Then click the Next button to continue.

5. As with most setup programs, you are presented with a choice of options to be installed as shown in Figure 1-2. The default installation installs the recommended product features as determined by Microsoft. You have the option to choose the default installation, a full installation, or to customize the installation. When choosing the custom installation feature, you will be presented with a dialog box allowing you to choose the languages and features of each language to be installed. If disk space allows, it is recommended that you choose a full installation. However, if you choose to customize the installation and omit some features from being installed, you can always install those features later by rerunning the setup program. After choosing your installation option, click the Install button to have those features installed.

Figure 1-2

6. The first component that is installed is the Microsoft .NET Framework version 3.5. During the installation of this component you will be required to restart your computer. After your computer has restarted and you log back in, the setup program will continue. Note to Windows Vista users: you will be prompted that the setup program needs to run and will need to grant permission to let the setup program continue. After the setup program continues, you can sit back and relax while all of the features are being installed. The setup program can take anywhere from 20 minutes on up depending on the installation features chosen and the speed of your computer.

7. Once the installation has been completed, you will be presented with a dialog box informing you of the status of the installation. Here you can see any problems that the setup program encountered. At this point you are encouraged to update your computer with the latest security patches and a link is provided in the notes to Windows Update. When you have finished reviewing the setup status, click the Finish button to move on to the next step.

8. If you chose to have your setup information sent to Microsoft, the next step will be a dialog box sending the setup information. This dialog box requires no action on your part and it will automatically close when finished. The next dialog box is the one shown earlier in Figure 1-1 with the option to install the production documentation enabled. Click the Install Product Documentation link to install the MSDN library.

9. The first step in installing the MSDN library is choosing whether to send the setup information to Microsoft. Make the appropriate choice and then click the Next button to continue. Again, it is recommended to send this information to help streamline future MSDN library installations.

10. Next, read and accept the license agreement. After you click the option button to accept the license agreement, click the Next button to continue.

11. Like the installation of Visual Studio 2008, the MSDN library installation provides you with the options to choose the installation that best suits your needs, as shown in Figure 1-3. If you chose to install the complete Visual Studio 2008 product set then you'll most likely want to choose the full installation of the MSDN library. After making your installation option choice, click the Install button to begin the installation.

Figure 1-3

If you have the spare hard drive space, it is a very good idea to install the full documentation. That way you have access to the full library, which will be important if you choose a limited set of options during the install and later add more features.

12. After the MSDN documentation has been installed, you are presented with a dialog box informing you of the status of the installation. Click the Finish button to be returned to the initial setup screen again. The Check for Service Releases option is now available.

It is a good idea to select Service Releases to check for updates. Microsoft has done a good job of making software updates available through the Internet. These updates can include anything from additional documentation to bug fixes. You will be given the choice to install any updates through a Service Pack CD or the Internet. Obviously, the Internet option requires an active connection. Since updates can be quite large, a fast connection is highly recommended.

After you have performed the update process, Visual Studio 2008 is ready to use. Now the real fun can begin! So get comfortable, relax, and enter the world of Visual Basic 2008.

The Visual Basic 2008 IDE

You don't need Visual Basic 2008 to write applications in the Visual Basic .NET language. The ability to run Visual Basic .NET code is included with the .NET Framework. You could write all of your Visual Basic .NET code using a text editor such as Notepad. You could also hammer nails using your shoe as a hammer, but that slick pneumatic nailer sitting there is a lot more efficient. In the same way, by far the easiest way to write in Visual Basic .NET code is by using the Visual Studio 2008 IDE. This is what you see when working with Visual Basic 2008 — the windows, boxes, and so on. The IDE provides a wealth of features unavailable in ordinary text editors — such as code checking, visual representations of the finished application, and an explorer that displays all of the files that make up your project.

The Profile Setup Page

An IDE is a way of bringing together a suite of tools that makes developing software a lot easier. Fire up Visual Studio 2008 and see what you've got. If you used the default installation, go to your Windows Start menu and then select All Programs ➪ Microsoft Visual Studio 2008 ➪ Microsoft Visual Studio 2008. A splash screen will briefly appear, and then you see the Choose Default Environment Settings dialog box. Select the Visual Basic Development Settings option and click Start Visual Studio. After Visual Studio configures the environment based on the chosen settings, the Microsoft Development Environment will appear, as shown in Figure 1-4.

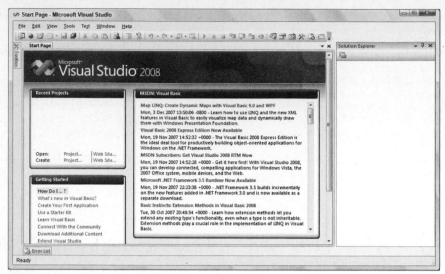

Figure 1-4

The Menu

By now, you may be eager to start writing some code. Begin your exploration of the IDE by looking at the menu and toolbar, which are not really all that different from the toolbars and menus you have seen in Microsoft Office 2003 (although they differ from the ribbon bars in Microsoft Office 2007).

The Visual Studio 2008 menu is *dynamic*, which means items will be added or removed depending on what you are trying to do. When looking at the blank IDE, the menu bar consists only of the File, Edit, View, Tools, Window, and Help menus. When you start working on a project, however, the full Visual Studio 2008 menu appears as shown in Figure 1-5.

Figure 1-5

At this point, there is no need to cover each menu topic in detail. You will become familiar with each of them as you progress through the book. Here is a quick rundown of what activities each menu item pertains to:

❑ **File:** Most software programs have a File menu. It has become the standard where you should find, if nothing else, a way to exit the application. In this case, you can also find ways of opening and closing single files and whole projects.

❑ **Edit:** The Edit menu provides access to the common items you would expect: Undo, Redo, Cut, Copy, Paste, and Delete.

❑ **View:** The View menu provides quick access to the windows that exist in the IDE, such as the Solution Explorer, Properties window, Output window, Toolbox, and so on.

- ❑ **Project:** The Project menu allows you to add various files to your application such as forms and classes.

- ❑ **Build:** The Build menu becomes important when you have completed your application and want to run it without the use of the Visual Basic 2008 environment (perhaps running it directly from your Windows Start menu, as you would any other application such as Word or Access).

- ❑ **Debug:** The Debug menu allows you to start and stop running your application within the Visual Basic 2008 IDE. It also gives you access to the Visual Studio 2008 debugger. The debugger allows you to step through your code while it is running to see how it is behaving.

- ❑ **Data:** The Data menu enables you to use information that comes from a database. It allows you to view and add data sources, and preview data. Chapters 16 and 17 will introduce you to working with databases.

- ❑ **Tools:** The Tools menu has commands to configure the Visual Studio 2008 IDE, as well as links to other external tools that may have been installed.

- ❑ **Test:** The Test menu provides options that allow you to create and view unit tests for your application to exercise the source code in various scenarios.

- ❑ **Window:** The Window menu has become standard for any application that allows more than one window to be open at a time, such as Word or Excel. The commands on this menu allow you to switch between the windows in the IDE.

- ❑ **Help:** The Help menu provides access to the Visual Studio 2008 documentation. There are many different ways to access this information (for example, through the help contents, an index, or a search). The Help menu also has options that connect to the Microsoft web site to obtain updates or report problems.

The Toolbars

Many toolbars are available within the IDE, including Formatting, Image Editor, and Text Editor, which you can add to and remove from the IDE through the View ➪ Toolbars menu option. Each one provides quick access to often-used commands, preventing you from having to navigate through a series of menu options. For example, the leftmost icon (New Project) on the default toolbar (called the Standard toolbar), shown in Figure 1-6, is available from the menu by navigating to File ➪ New ➪ Project.

Figure 1-6

The toolbar is segmented into groups of related options, which are separated by vertical bars. The first six icons provide access to the commonly used project and file manipulation options available through the File and Project menus, such as opening and saving files.

The next group of icons is for editing (Cut, Copy, and Paste). The next icon is for finding and replacing items in your code.

The third group of icons is used for commenting out and un-commenting sections of code. This can be useful in debugging when you want to comment out a section of code to determine what results the program might produce by not executing those lines of code.

The fourth group of icons is for undoing and redoing edits and for navigating through your code.

The fifth group of icons provides the ability to start (via the green triangle), pause, and stop your application. You can also use the last three icons in this group to step into your code line by line, step over entire sections of code, and step out of a procedure. These icons will be covered in depth in Chapter 10.

The final group of icons provides quick links to the Solution Explorer, Properties window, Object Browser, Toolbox, Error List, and the Immediate window. If any of these windows is closed, clicking the appropriate icon will bring it back into view.

> *If you forget what a particular icon does, you can hover your mouse pointer over it so that a tooltip appears displaying the name of the toolbar option.*

You could continue to look at each of the windows in the IDE by clicking on the View menu and choosing the appropriate window. But, as you can see, they are all empty at this stage and therefore not too revealing. The best way to look at the capabilities of the IDE is to use it while writing some code.

Creating a Simple Application

To finish your exploration of the IDE, you need to create a project, so that the windows shown earlier in Figure 1-4 have some interesting content for you to look at. In the following Try It Out exercise, you are going to create a very simple application called HelloUser that will allow you to enter a person's name and display a greeting to that person in a message box.

Try It Out   Creating a HelloUser Project

1.   Click the New Project button on the toolbar.

2.   In the the New Project dialog box, select Visual Basic in the Project Types tree-view box to the left and then select Windows beneath it. The Templates box on the right will display all of the available templates for the project type chosen. Select the Windows Forms Application template. Finally, type **Hello User** in the Name text box and click OK. Your New Project dialog box should look like Figure 1-7.

Figure 1-7

Visual Studio 2008 allows you to target your application to a specific version of the Microsoft .NET Framework. The combo box in the upper right corner of the New Project dialog box has version 3.5 selected, but you can target your application to version 3.0 or even version 2.0 of the .NET Framework.

The IDE will then create an empty Windows application for you. So far, your Hello User program consists of one blank window, called a Windows Form (or sometimes just a form), with the default name of Form1.vb, as shown in Figure 1-8.

Whenever Visual Studio 2008 creates a new file, either as part of the project creation process or when you create a new file, it will use a name that describes what it is (in this case, a form) followed by a number.

Windows in the Visual Studio 2008 IDE

At this point, you can see that the various windows in the IDE are beginning to show their purposes, and you should take a brief look at them now before you come back to the Try It Out exercise. Note that if any of these windows are not visible on your screen, you can use the View menu to show them. Also, if you do not like the location of any particular window, you can move it by clicking its title bar (the blue bar at the top) and dragging it to a new location. The windows in the IDE can *float* (stand out on their own) or be *docked* (as they appear in Figure 1-8). The following list introduces the most common windows:

Figure 1-8

❑ **Toolbox:** The Toolbox contains reusable controls and components that can be added to your application. These range from buttons to data connectors to customized controls that you have either purchased or developed.

❑ **Design window:** The Design window is where a lot of the action takes place. This is where you will draw your user interface on your forms. This window is sometimes referred to as the Designer.

❑ **Solution Explorer:** The Solution Explorer window contains a hierarchical view of your solution. A *solution* can contain many projects, whereas a *project* contains forms, classes, modules, and components that solve a particular problem.

❑ **Data Sources:** The Data Sources window allows you to connect to a database and choose the database objects for your application.

❑ **Properties:** The Properties window shows what *properties* the selected object makes available. Although you can set these properties in your code, sometimes it is much easier to set them while you are designing your application (for example, drawing the controls on your form). You will notice that the `File Name` property has the value `Form1.vb`. This is the physical file name for the form's code and layout information.

Try It Out   **Creating a HelloUser Project (cont.)**

Next you'll give your form a name and set a few properties for it.

1.   Change the name of your form to something more indicative of what your application is. Click `Form1.vb` in the Solution Explorer window. Then, in the Properties window, change the `File Name` property from `Form1.vb` to **HelloUser.vb** and press Enter, as shown in Figure 1-9. When changing properties you must either press Enter or click on another property for it to take effect.

Figure 1-9

2.   Note that the form's file name has also been updated in the Solution Explorer to read `HelloUser.vb`.

3.   Click the form displayed in the Design window. The Properties window will change to display the form's `Form` properties (instead of the `File` properties, which you have just been looking at). You will notice that the Properties window is dramatically different. The difference is the result of two different views of the same file. When the form name is highlighted in the Solution Explorer window, the physical file properties of the form are displayed. When the form in the Design window is highlighted, the visual properties and logical properties of the form are displayed.

The Properties window allows you to set a control's properties easily. Properties are a particular object's set of internal data; they usually describe appearance or behavior. In Figure 1-10 you can see that properties are displayed alphabetically. The properties can also be grouped together in categories — Accessibility, Appearance, Behavior, Data, Design, Focus, Layout, Misc, and Window Style.

Figure 1-10

4. Right now, the title (Text property) of your form (displayed in the bar at the top) is Form1. This is not very descriptive, so change it to reflect the purpose of this application. Locate the Text property in the Properties window. Change the Text property's value to **Hello from Visual Basic 2008** and press Enter. Note that the form's title has been updated to reflect the change.

    If you have trouble finding properties, click the little AZ icon on the toolbar toward the top of the Properties window. This changes the property listing from being ordered by category to being ordered by name.

5. You are now finished with the procedure. Click the Start button on the Visual Studio 2008 toolbar (the green triangle) to run the application. As you work through the book, whenever we say "run the project" or "start the project," just click the Start button. An empty window with the title Hello from Visual Basic 2008 is displayed.

That was simple, but your little application isn't doing much at the moment. Let's make it a little more interactive. To do this, you are going to add some controls — a label, a text box, and two buttons to the form. This will let you see how the Toolbox makes adding functionality quite simple. You may be wondering at this point when you will actually look at some code. Soon! The great thing about Visual Basic 2008 is that you can develop a fair amount of your application *without* writing any code. Sure, the code is still there, behind the scenes, but, as you will see, Visual Basic 2008 writes a lot of it for you.

The Toolbox

The Toolbox is accessed through the View ➪ Toolbox menu option, by clicking the Toolbox icon on the Standard menu bar, or by pressing Ctrl+Alt+X. Alternatively, the Toolbox tab is displayed on the left of the IDE; hovering your mouse over this tab will cause the Toolbox window to fly out, partially covering your form.

The Toolbox contains a Node type view of the various controls and components that can be placed onto your form. Controls such as text boxes, buttons, radio buttons, and combo boxes can be selected and then *drawn* onto your form. For the HelloUser application, you will be using only the controls in the Common Controls node. Figure 1-11 shows a listing of common controls for Windows Forms.

Figure 1-11

Controls can be added to your forms in any order, so it does not matter if you add the label control after the text box or the buttons before the label. In the following Try It Out exercise, you start adding controls.

Try It Out   Adding Controls to the HelloUser Application

1. Stop the project if it is still running, because you now want to add some controls to your form. The simplest way to stop your project is to click the close (X) button in the top-right corner of the form. Alternatively, you can click the blue square on the toolbar (which displays a ToolTip that says "Stop Debugging" if you hover over it with your mouse pointer).

2. Add a Label control to the form. Click Label in the Toolbox, drag it over to the form's Designer and drop it in the desired location. (You can also place controls on your form by double-clicking the required control in the Toolbox or clicking the control in the Toolbox and then drawing it on the form.)

3. If the Label control you have just drawn is not in the desired location, it really isn't a problem. When the control is on the form, you can resize it or move it around. Figure 1-12 shows what

the control looks like after you place it on the form. To move it, click the dotted border and drag it to the desired location. The label will automatically resize itself to fit the text that you enter in the `Text` property.

Figure 1-12

4. After drawing a control on the form, you should at least configure its name and the text that it will display. You will see that the Properties window to the right of the Designer has changed to `Label1`, telling you that you are currently examining the properties for the label. In the Properties window, set your new label's `Text` property to **Enter Your Name**. Note that, once you press Enter or click on another property, the label on the form has automatically resized itself to fit the text in the `Text` property. Now set the `Name` property to **lblName**.

5. Now, directly beneath the label, you want to add a text box, so that you can enter a name. You are going to repeat the procedure you followed for adding the label, but this time make sure you select the TextBox control from the toolbar. After you have dragged and dropped (or double-clicked) the control into the appropriate position as shown in Figure 1-13, use the Properties window to set its `Name` property to **txtName**.

Notice the sizing handles on the left and right side of the control. You can use these handles to resize the text box horizontally.

Figure 1-13

6. In the bottom left corner of the form, add a Button control in exactly the same manner as you added the label and text box. Set its `Name` property to **btnOK** and its `Text` property to **&OK**. Your form should now look similar to the one shown in Figure 1-14.

The ampersand (&) is used in the `Text` property of buttons to create a keyboard shortcut (known as a hot key). The letter with the & sign placed in front of it will become underlined (as shown in Figure 1-14) to signal users that they can select that button by pressing the Alt+letter key combination, instead of using the mouse (on some configurations the underline doesn't appear until the user presses Alt). In this particular instance, pressing Alt+O would be the same as clicking the OK button. There is no need to write code to accomplish this.

Figure 1-14

7. Now add a second Button control to the bottom right corner of the form by dragging the Button control from the Toolbox onto your form. Notice that, as you get close to the bottom right of the form, a blue snap line appears, as shown in Figure 1-15. This snap line allows you to align this new Button control with the existing Button control on the form. The snap lines assist you in aligning controls to the left, right, top, or bottom of each other, depending on where you are trying to position the new control. The light blue line provides you with a consistent margin between the edge of your control and the edge of the form. Set the `Name` property to **btnExit** and the `Text` property to **E&xit**. Your form should look similar to Figure 1-16.

Figure 1-15   **Figure 1-16**

Now before you finish your sample application, let us briefly discuss some coding practices that you should be using.

Modified Hungarian Notation

You may have noticed that the names given to the controls look a little funny. Each name is prefixed with a shorthand identifier describing the type of control it is. This makes it much easier to understand what type of control you are working with when you are looking through the code. For example, say you had a control called simply Name, without a prefix of `lbl` or `txt`. You would not know whether you were working with a text box that accepted a name or with a label that displayed a name. Imagine if, in the previous Try It Out exercise, you had named your label Name1 and your text box Name2 — you would very quickly become confused. What if you left your application for a month or two and then came back to it to make some changes?

When working with other developers, it is very important to keep the coding style consistent. One of the most commonly used styles for control names within application development in many languages was designed by Dr. Charles Simonyi, who worked for the Xerox Palo Alto Research Center (XPARC) before joining Microsoft. He came up with short prefix mnemonics that allowed programmers to easily identify the type of information a variable might contain. Because Simonyi is from Hungary, and the prefixes make the names look a little foreign, the name *Hungarian Notation* came into use for this system. Because the original notation was used in C/C++ development, the notation for Visual Basic 2008 is termed Modified. Table 1-1 shows some of the commonly used prefixes that you will be using in this book.

Table 1-1: Common Prefixes in Visual Basic 2008

Control	Prefix
Button	btn
ComboBox	cbo
CheckBox	chk
Label	lbl
ListBox	lst
MainMenu	mnu
RadioButton	rdb
PictureBox	pic
TextBox	txt

Hungarian Notation can be a real time-saver when you are looking at code someone else wrote or at code that you wrote months earlier. However, by far the most important thing is to be consistent in your naming. When you start coding, choose a convention for your naming. It is recommended that you use the de facto standard Modified-Hungarian for Visual Basic 2008, but it is not required. After you pick a convention, stick to it. When modifying others' code, use theirs. A standard naming convention followed throughout a project will save countless hours when the application is maintained. Now let's get back to the application. It's now time to write some code.

The Code Editor

Now that you have the HelloUser form defined, you have to add some code to make it actually do something interesting. You have already seen how easy it is to add controls to a form. Providing the functionality behind those on-screen elements is no more difficult. To add the code for a control, you just double-click the control in question. This opens the code editor in the main window, shown in Figure 1-17.

Figure 1-17

Note that an additional tab has been created in the main window. Now you have the Design tab and the Code tab, each containing the name of the form you are working on. You draw the controls on your form in the Design tab, and you write code for your form in the Code tab. One thing to note here is that Visual Studio 2008 has created a separate file for the code. The visual definition and the code behind it exist in separate files: `HelloUser.Designer.vb` and `HelloUser.vb`. This is actually the reason why building applications with Visual Basic 2008 is so slick and easy. Using the Design view you can visually lay out your application, and then, using Code view, you add just the bits of code to implement your desired functionality.

Note also that there are two combo boxes at the top of the window. These provide shortcuts to the various parts of your code. Hover your mouse on the combo box on the left, and you'll see a tooltip appear, telling you that it is the Class Name combo box. If you expand this combo box, you will see a list of all the objects within your application. If you hover your mouse on the combo box on the right, you'll see a tooltip telling you that this is the Method Name combo box. If you expand this combo box, you will see a list of all defined functions and subroutines for the object selected in the Class Name combo box. If this particular form had a lot of code behind it, these combo boxes would make navigating to the desired code area very quick — jumping to the selected area in your code. However, since all of the code for this project so far fits in the window, there are not a lot of places to get lost.

Try It Out   **Adding Code to the HelloUser Project**

1.   To begin adding the necessary code, click the Design tab to show the form again. Then double-click the OK button. The code window will open with the following code. This is the shell of the button's `Click` event and is the place where you enter the code that you want to run when you click the button. This code is known as an *event handler* and sometimes is also referred to as *an event procedure*:

```
Private Sub btnOK_Click(ByVal sender As System.Object, _
    ByVal e As System.EventArgs) Handles btnOK.Click

End Sub
```

As a result of the typographic constraints in publishing, it is not possible to put the Sub *declaration on one line. Visual Basic 2008 allows you to break up lines of code by using the underscore character (_) to signify a line continuation. The space before the underscore is required. Any whitespace preceding the code on the following line is ignored.*

Sub is an example of a *keyword*. In programming terms, a keyword is a special word that is used to tell Visual Basic 2008 to do something special. In this case, it tells Visual Basic 2008 that this is a *subroutine,* a procedure that does not return a value. Anything that you type between the lines Private Sub and End Sub will make up the event procedure for the OK button.

2. Now add the highlighted code into the procedure:

```
Private Sub btnOK_Click(ByVal sender As System.Object, _
    ByVal e As System.EventArgs) Handles btnOK.Click
    'Display a message box greeting to the user
    MessageBox.Show("Hello, " & txtName.Text & _
        "! Welcome to Visual Basic 2008.", _
        "Hello User Message")
End Sub
```

Throughout this book, you will be presented with code that you should enter into your program if you are following along. Usually, we will make it pretty obvious where you put the code, but as we go, we will explain anything that looks out of the ordinary. The code with the gray background is code that you should enter.

3. After you have added the preceding code, go back to the Design tab, and double-click the Exit button. Add the following highlighted code to the btnExit_Click event procedure:

```
Private Sub btnExit_Click(ByVal sender As System.Object, _
    ByVal e As System.EventArgs) Handles btnExit.Click
    'End the program and close the form
    Me.Close()
End Sub
```

You may be wondering what Me is. Me is a keyword that refers to the form. Just like the pronoun *me*, it is just shorthand for referring to one's self.

4. Now that the code is finished, the moment of truth has arrived and you can see your creation. First, however, save your work by using File ➾ Save All from the menu or by clicking the Save All button on the toolbar. The Save Project dialog box is displayed as shown in Figure 1-18, prompting you for a name and location for saving the project.

By default, a project is saved in a folder with the project name; in this case Hello User. Since this is the only project in the solution, there is no need to create a separate folder for the solution which contains the same name as the project, thus the Create directory for solution check box has been unchecked.

Figure 1-18

5. Now click the Start button on the toolbar. You will notice a lot of activity in the Output window at the bottom of your screen. Provided that you have not made any mistakes in entering the code, this information just lets you know which files are being loaded to run your application.

At this point Visual Studio 2008 will *compile* the code. Compiling is the activity of taking the Visual Basic 2008 source code that you have written and translating it into a form that the computer understands. After the compilation is complete, Visual Studio 2008 runs (also known as *executes*) the program, and you'll be able to see the results.

Any errors that Visual Basic 2008 encounters will be displayed as tasks in the Task List window. Double-clicking a task transports you to the offending line of code. You will learn more about how to debug the errors in your code in Chapter 10.

6. When the application loads, you see the main form. Enter a name and click OK or press the Alt+O key combination (see Figure 1-19).

Figure 1-19

A window known as a message box appears as shown in Figure 1-20, welcoming the person whose name was entered in the text box on the form — in this case Stephanie.

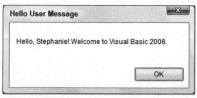

Figure 1-20

7. After you close the message box by clicking the OK button, click the Exit button on your form. The application closes and you will be returned to the Visual Basic 2008 IDE.

How It Works

The code that you added to the `Click` event for the OK button will take the name that was entered in the text box and use it as part of the message that was displayed in Figure 1-20.

The first line of text you entered in this procedure (`'Display a message box greeting to the user`) is actually a *comment*, text that is meant to be read by the human programmer who is writing or maintaining the code, not by the computer. Comments in Visual Basic 2008 begin with a single quote (`'`), and everything following on that line is considered a comment and ignored by the compiler. Comments will be discussed in detail in Chapter 3.

The `MessageBox.Show` method displays a message box that accepts various parameters. As used in your code, you have passed the string text to be displayed in the message box. This is accomplished through the *concatenation* of string constants defined by text enclosed in quotes. Concatenation of strings into one long string is performed through the use of the ampersand (`&`) character.

The code that follows concatenates a string constant of `"Hello, "` followed by the value contained in the `Text` property of the `txtName` text box control followed by a string constant of `"! Welcome to Visual Basic 2008."`. The second parameter being passed to the `MessageBox.Show` method is the caption to be used in the title bar of the Message Box dialog box.

Finally, the underscore (_) character used at the end of the lines in the following code enables you to split your code onto separate lines. This tells the compiler that the rest of the code for the parameter is continued on the next line. This is really useful when building long strings, because it allows you to view the entire code fragment in the Code Editor without having to scroll the Code Editor window to the right to view the entire line of code.

```
Private Sub btnOK_Click(ByVal sender As System.Object, _
    ByVal e As System.EventArgs) Handles btnOK.Click

    'Display a message box greeting to the user
    MessageBox.Show("Hello," & txtName.Text & _
      "! Welcome to Visual Basic 2008.", _
      "Hello User Message")
End Sub
```

The next procedure that you added code for was the Exit button's `Click` event. Here you simply enter the code: `Me.Close()`. As explained earlier, the `Me` keyword refers to the form itself. The `Close` method of the form closes the form and releases all resources associated with it, thus ending the program.

```
Private Sub btnExit_Click(ByVal sender As System.Object, _
    ByVal e As System.EventArgs) Handles btnExit.Click

    'End the program and close the form
    Me.Close()
End Sub
```

Using the Help System

The Help system included in Visual Basic 2008 is an improvement over the Help systems in earlier versions. As you begin to learn Visual Basic 2008, you will probably become very familiar with the Help system. However, it is worthwhile to give you an overview, just to help speed your searches for information.

The Help menu contains the items shown in Figure 1-21.

Figure 1-21

As you can see, this menu contains a few more items than the typical Windows application. The main reason for this is the vastness of the documentation. Few people could keep it all in their heads — but luckily, that is not a problem, because you can always quickly and easily refer to the Help system. Think of it as a safety net for your brain.

One really fantastic feature is Dynamic Help. When you select the Dynamic Help menu item from the Help menu, the Dynamic Help window is displayed as a tab behind the Properties window, with a list of relevant topics for whatever you may be working on.

Suppose you are working with a text box (perhaps the text box in the HelloUser application) and want to find out some information; you just select the text box on your form or in the code window and then use Dynamic Help to see all the help topics that pertain to text boxes, as shown in Figure 1-22.

Figure 1-22

The other help commands in the Help menu (Search, Contents, and Index), function just as they would in any other Windows application. The How Do I menu item displays the Visual Studio Help collection with a list of common tasks that are categorized. This makes finding help on common tasks fast and efficient.

Summary

Hopefully, you are beginning to see that developing basic applications with Visual Basic 2008 is not that difficult. You have taken a look at the IDE and have seen how it can help you put together software very quickly. The Toolbox enables you to add controls to your form and design a user interface very quickly and easily. The Properties window makes configuring those controls a snap, while the Solution Explorer gives you a bird's eye view of the files that make up your project. You even wrote a little code.

In the coming chapters, you will go into even more detail and get comfortable writing code. Before you go too far into Visual Basic 2008 itself, the next chapter will give you an introduction to the Microsoft .NET Framework. This Framework is what gives all of the .NET languages their ease of use, ease of interoperability, and simplicity in learning.

To summarize, you should now be familiar with:

- ❑ The integrated development environment (IDE)
- ❑ Adding controls to your form in the Designer
- ❑ Setting the properties of your controls
- ❑ Adding code to your form in the code window

Exercise

The answers for this exercise and those at the end of each chapter in this book can be found in Appendix A.

1. Create a Windows Application with a Textbox and Button control that will display whatever is typed in the text box when the user clicks on the button.

The Microsoft .NET Framework

The .NET Framework provides an unprecedented platform for building Windows, web, and mobile applications with one or more languages. It is a definitive guide, encompassing and encapsulating where we have come from as a development community and, of course, where we are going.

.NET has been a success in many respects. Within the .NET Framework, new languages (C# and J#) have been born, and the well-established Visual Basic language has been reborn. The .NET Framework even supports legacy languages such as C++.

The .NET Framework provides the base for all development using Visual Studio 2008. It provides base classes, available to all Visual Studio 2008 languages for such functions as accessing databases, parsing XML, displaying and processing Windows and Web forms, and providing security for your applications. All languages in Visual Studio 2008 share and use the same base classes, making your choice of a programming language in Visual Studio 2008 a matter of personal preference and syntax style.

In this chapter, you will examine the following topics:

- ❑ What the .NET Framework is
- ❑ The .NET vision
- ❑ Why Microsoft dared to spend $2 billion on a single development project

Microsoft's Reliance on Windows

In terms of the great corporations of the world, Microsoft is still a new kid on the block. It is a fabulously rich and successful business. Nonetheless, the company has grown from nothing to a corporate superpower in a very short time.

What is perhaps more interesting is that although the origins of Microsoft can be traced to the mid-1970s, it is really the Windows family of operating systems that has brought the company great success. Based on Presentation Manager for OS/2, Windows has seen many incarnations from Windows/286 to Windows Vista, but the essential way that you use Windows and Windows applications has not changed in all that time. (Granted, there have been advances in the user interface and the hardware, but you still use the version of Excel included with Office 2007 in roughly the same way that you used the first version.)

The scary thing to Microsoft and its investors is that the pace of technological change means that they cannot be sure that Windows is going to be as relevant in 2011 as it is today. All it takes is one change in the way that people want to use computers, and the Windows platform's current incarnation may become obsolete.

It is unfair to say that Microsoft has been extremely lucky over the past several years in the way that it has reacted to the opportunities offered by the Internet. Do not underestimate the number of smart people working for that company. When they discovered that companies like Netscape were making money with the Internet and identified the risk, they turned a large corporation on a dime and went after an unexplored market with teeth bared. Their gambles paid off, and with the invention of the .NET Framework, corporations and users are leveraging the power of the Internet in new ways.

Luckily for Microsoft, the applications that drove the adoption of the Internet worked well on a desktop operating system. Microsoft managed to adapt the Windows platform to provide the two killer Internet applications (e-mail and the Web browser) to the end user with a minimum of hassle, securing the Windows platform for another few years. It also delivered several powerful tools for developers, such as Active Server Pages Extended (ASPX), web services, and Internet Information Server (IIS), and improved existing tools such as Visual Basic and SQL Server, all of which made it easier for developers to build advanced Internet applications.

MSN 1.0

When the Internet started to become popular in the early 1990s, Microsoft was trying to push the original incarnation of Microsoft Network (MSN). Rather than the successful portal that it is today, MSN was originally a proprietary dial-up service much like CompuServe. In the beginning, MSN did not provide access to the rich world of the Internet as we know today; it was a closed system. Let us call the original MSN "MSN 1.0."

MSN 1.0 provided an opportunity for innovative companies to steal a march on Microsoft, which was already seen as an unshakable behemoth thanks to the combination of Windows and Office. As it turned out, it was a missed opportunity.

Imagine an alternative 1995 in which Microsoft stuck to its guns with MSN 1.0, rather than plotting the course that brought it where it is today. Imagine that a large computer manufacturer, such as Dell, identified this burgeoning community of forward-thinking business leaders and geeks called the Internet. Also suppose Dell predicted that Microsoft's strategy was to usurp this community with MSN 1.0 — in other words, rather than cooperating with this community, Microsoft would decide to crush it at all costs.

Now Dell needs to find a way to build this community. It predicts that home users and small businesses will love the Internet and so puts together a very low-cost PC. They need software to run on it and, luckily, they predict that the Web and e-mail will be the killer applications of this new community. They find Linus Torvalds, who has been working on this thing called Linux since 1991, and they find Sun, which is keen to start pushing Java as a programming language to anyone who will listen. Another business partner builds a competent, usable suite of productivity applications for the platform using Java. Another business partner builds easy-to-use connectivity solutions that allow the computers to connect to the Internet and other computers in the LAN, easily and cheaply.

Dell, Sun, and their selected business partners start pushing this new computer to anyone and everyone. The concept is a success and, for the first time since 1981, the dominance of the IBM-compatible PC is reduced, and sales of Microsoft products plummet. All because Microsoft did not move on a critical opportunity.

We all know that this did not happen, but there is nothing outlandish or crazy about this scenario. It could have happened, and that is what scared Microsoft. It came very close to losing everything, and .NET is its insurance against this happening again.

The .NET Vision

To understand .NET, you have to ignore the marketing hype from Microsoft and really think about what it is doing. With the first version of the .NET Framework and indeed even now, Microsoft appears to be pushing .NET as a platform for building web services and large-scale enterprise systems. Although we cover web services in Chapter 21, it is a tiny, tiny part of what .NET is all about. In simple terms, .NET splits an operating system's platform (be it Windows, Linux, Mac OS, or any other OS) into two layers: a programming layer and an execution layer.

All computer platforms are trying to achieve roughly the same effect: to provide applications to the user. If you wanted to write a book, you would have the choice of using the word processor in StarOffice under Linux, or Word under Windows. However, you would be using the computer in the same way; in other words, the application remains the same irrespective of the platform.

It is a common understanding that software support is a large part of any platform's success. Typically, the more high-quality the available software is for a given platform, the larger the consumer adoption of that platform will be. The PC is the dominant platform because, back in the early 1980s, it was the predominant target for software writers. That trend has continued to this day, and people are writing applications that run on Windows, which targets the 32-bit and 64-bit Intel processors. The Intel processor harks back to the introduction of the Intel 8086 processor in 1979 and today includes the Intel Core 2 Duo, Intel Core 2 Quad, and Intel Xeon processors, and competitors like AMD's Athlon and Turion.

So without .NET, developers are still reliant on Windows, and Windows is still reliant on Intel. Although the relationship between Microsoft and Intel is thought to be fairly symbiotic, it is reasonable to assume that the strategists at Microsoft, who are feeling (rightly) paranoid about the future, might want to lessen the dependence on a single family of chips too.

The Windows/Intel combination (sometimes known as *Wintel*) is also known as the *execution layer*. This layer takes the code and runs it — simple as that.

Although .NET originally targeted and still targets only the Windows platform, you are seeing development communities using open-source projects to convert .NET to run on other platforms such as Linux and Unix. What this means is that a program written by a .NET developer on Windows could run unchanged on Linux. In fact, the Mono project (www.mono-project.com) has already released several versions of its product. This project has developed an open source version of a C# and VB.NET compiler, a runtime for the Common Language Infrastructure (CLI, also known as the Common Intermediate Language or CIL), a subset of the .NET classes, and other .NET goodies independent of Microsoft's involvement.

.NET is a *programming layer*. It is totally owned and controlled by Microsoft. By turning all developers into .NET programmers rather than Windows programmers, software is written as .NET software, not Windows software.

To see the significance of this, imagine that a new platform is launched and starts eating up market share like crazy. Imagine that, like the Internet, this new platform offers a revolutionary way of working and living that offers real advantages. With the .NET vision in place, all Microsoft has to do to gain a foothold on this platform is develop a version of .NET that works on it. All of the .NET software now runs on the new platform, lessening the chance that the new platform will usurp Microsoft's market share.

This Sounds like Java

Some of this does sound a lot like Java. In fact, Java's mantra of "write once, run anywhere" fits nicely into the .NET doctrine. However, .NET is not a Java clone. Microsoft has a different approach.

To write in Java, developers were expected to learn a new language. This language was based on C++, and although C++ is a popular language, it is not the most popular language. In fact, the most popular language in terms of number of developers is Visual Basic, and, obviously, Microsoft owns it. Some estimates put the number of Visual Basic developers at approximately three million worldwide, but bear in mind that this number includes both Visual Basic professionals and people who tinker with macros in the various Office products.

Whereas Java is "one language, many platforms," .NET is "many languages, one platform, for now." Microsoft wants to remove the barrier to entry for .NET by making it accessible to anyone who has used pretty much any language. The two primary languages for .NET are Visual Basic 2008 and C#. Visual Studio 2008 comes supplied with both of these. Although C# is not C++, the developers of C++ applications should be able to migrate to C# with about the same amount of relearning that a Visual Basic 6 developer will have to do in order to move to Visual Basic 2008. Of course the .NET Framework supports developers using C++ and allows them to write C++ applications using the .NET Framework.

With Java, Sun attempted to build from the ground-up something so abstracted from the operating system that when you compare an application written natively in something like Visual C++ with a Java equivalent, it becomes fairly obvious that the Java version will run slower and not look as good in terms of user interface. Sun tried to take too big a bite out of the problem by attempting to support everything, so in the end it did not support one single thing completely. That's probably why you see so many third party and open source tools for Java developers, like Eclipse and Ruby.

Microsoft's .NET strategy is more like a military campaign. First, it will use its understanding of the Windows platform to build .NET into something that will stand against a native C++ application. After it wins over the voters on Windows, it may invade another platform, most likely Linux. This second stage will prove the concept that .NET applications can be ported from one platform to the next. After invading and conquering Linux, it may move to another platform. Microsoft has been attempting to shake Solaris from the top spot in the server market for a long time, so it's likely that it'll go there next.

Where Now?

Microsoft has bet its future on .NET and rightly so with its ever-increasing adoption by developers and businesses alike. With developers writing software for the programming layer rather than an execution layer, it really does not matter whether Windows or Linux or some other software is the dominant platform in 2011. The remainder of this chapter drills into the mechanics of .NET and takes a detailed look at how the whole thing works.

Writing Software for Windows

To understand how .NET works, you need to look at how developers used to write software for Windows. The general principle was the same as with .NET, only they had to do things in different ways to work with different technologies — the Component Object Model (COM), ActiveX Data Objects (ADO), and so forth.

Any software that you write has to interact with various parts of the operating system to do its job. If the software needs a block of memory to store data in, it interacts with the memory manager. To read a file from disk, you use the disk subsystem. To request a file from the network, you use the network subsystem. To draw a window on the screen, you use the graphics subsystem, and so on.

This *subsystems* approach breaks down as far as .NET is concerned, because there is no commonality between the ways you use the subsystems on different platforms, despite the fact that platforms tend to have things in common. For example, even if you are writing an application for Linux, you may still need to use the network, disk, and screen subsystems. However, because different organizations developed these platforms, the way you open a file using the Linux platform may be different from the way you do it on Windows. If you want to move code that depends on one platform to another, you will probably have to rewrite portions of the code. You will also have to test the code to ensure it still works as intended.

Windows software communicates with the operating system and various subsystems using something called the Windows 32-bit Application Programming Interface (Win32 API). Although object-orientation in programming was around at the time, this API was designed to be an evolution of the original Windows API, which predates the massive adoption of object-oriented techniques that are discussed in Chapter 11.

It is not easy to port the Win32 API to other platforms, which is why there is no version of the Win32 API for Linux even though Linux has been around for over a decade. There is a cut-down version of the Win32 API for the Mac, but this has never received much of an industry following.

The Win32 API provides all basic functionality, but now and again, Microsoft extends the capabilities of Windows with a new API. A classic example is the Windows Internet API, also known as the *WinInet API*. This API allows an application to download resources from a web server, upload files to an FTP server, discover proxy settings, and so on. Again, it is not object oriented, but it does work. Another example of this is the Win32 API that is part of the Windows Vista operating system. Since so many of the core components of the operating system have changed, a new version of the Win32 API had to be developed for this operating system.

A large factor in the success of early versions of Visual Basic is that it took the tricky-to-understand Win32 API calls and packaged them in a way that could be easily understood. Using the native Win32 API, it takes about a hundred lines of code to draw a window on the screen. The same effect can be achieved in Visual Basic with a few gestures of the mouse. Visual Basic represents an abstraction layer on top of the Win32 API that makes it easier for developers to use.

A long-time frustration for C++ developers was that a lot of the things that were very easy to do in Visual Basic remained not so much hard as laborious in C++. Developers like C++ because it gives them an amazing amount of control over how a program works, but their programs take longer to write. Microsoft introduced the Microsoft Foundation Classes (MFC) because of this overhead, which, along with the IDE of Visual Studio, brought the ease of Visual C++ development closer to that of Visual Basic.

The .NET Framework Classes

Unlike the Win32 API, .NET is totally object-oriented. Anything you want to do in .NET, you are going to be doing with an object. If you want to open a file, you create an object that knows how to do this. If you want to draw a window on the screen, you create an object that knows how to do this. When you get to Chapter 11, you will discover that this is called *encapsulation*; the functionality is encapsulated in an object, and you don't really care how it's done behind the scenes.

Although there is still the concept of subsystems in .NET, these subsystems are never accessed directly — instead they are abstracted away by the Framework classes. Either way, your .NET application never has to talk directly to the subsystem (although you can do so if you really need or want to). Rather, you talk to objects, which then talk to the subsystem. In Figure 2-1, the box marked System.IO.File is a class defined in the .NET Framework.

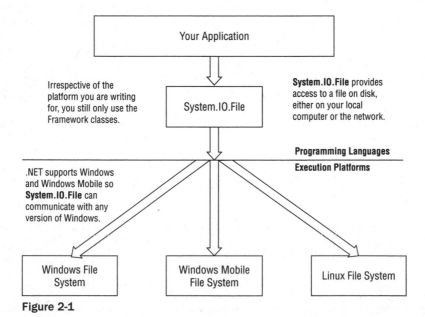

Figure 2-1

If you are talking to objects that talk to subsystems, do you really care what the subsystem looks like? Thankfully the answer is "no," and this is how Microsoft removes your reliance on Windows. If you know the name of a file, you use the same objects to open it whether you are running on a Windows Vista machine, a Pocket PC, or even, the Mono Project version of the .NET Framework, Linux. Likewise, if you need to display a window on the screen, you do not care whether it is on a Windows operating system or on a Mac.

The .NET Framework is actually a set of classes called *base classes*. The base classes in the .NET Framework are rather extensive and provide the functionality for just about anything that you need to do in a Windows or Web environment, from working with files to working with data to working with forms and controls.

The class library itself is vast, containing several thousand objects available to developers, although in your day-to-day development you will only need to understand a handful of these to create powerful applications.

Another really nice thing about the base classes in the .NET Framework is that they are the same irrespective of the language used. So, if you are writing a Visual Basic 2008 application, you use the same object as you would from within a C# application. That object will have the same methods, properties, and events, meaning that there is very little difference in capabilities between the languages, since they all rely on the framework.

Executing Code

The base class library is only half the equation. After you have written the code that interacts with the classes, you still need to run it. This poses a tricky problem; to remove the reliance on the platform is to remove the reliance on the processor.

Whenever you write software for Windows, you are guaranteed that this code will run on an Intel chip. With .NET, Microsoft does not want to make this guarantee. It might be that the dominant chip in 2011 is a Transmeta chip, or something you have never yet seen. What needs to be done is to abstract .NET from the processor, in a similar fashion to the way .NET is abstracted from the underlying subsystem implementations.

Programming languages are somewhere in between the languages that people speak every day and the language that the computer itself understands. The language that a computer uses is the *machine code* (sometimes called *machine instructions* or *machine language*) and consists entirely of zeros and ones, each corresponding to electrical current flowing or not flowing through this or that part of the chip. When you are using a PC with an Intel or competing processor, this language is more specifically known as *x86* machine instructions.

If you wrote an application with Visual Basic 6, you had to *compile* it into a set of *x86* machine instructions before you could deploy it. This machine code would then be installed and executed on any machine that supported *x86* instructions and was also running Windows.

If you write an application with Visual Basic 2008, you still have to compile the code. However, you do not compile the Visual Basic 2008 code directly into *x86* machine instructions, because that would mean that the resulting program would run only on processors that support this language — in other words, the program would run only on Intel chips and their compatible competitors. Instead, compilation creates something called *Microsoft Intermediate Language* (MSIL). This language is not dependent on any processor. It is a layer above the traditional machine code.

MSIL code will not just run on any processor, because processors do not understand MSIL. To run the code, it has to be further compiled, as shown in Figure 2-2, from MSIL code into the native code that the processor understands.

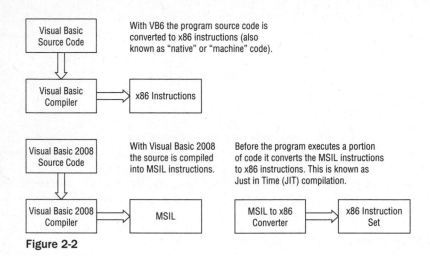

Figure 2-2

However, this approach also provides the industry with a subtle problem. In a world where .NET is extremely popular (some might say dominant), who is responsible for developing an MSIL-to-native compiler when a new processor is released? Is the new processor at the mercy of Microsoft's willingness to port .NET to the chip? Time will tell.

Next, take a look at the thing that makes .NET work: the Common Language Runtime.

Common Language Runtime

The Common Language Runtime (CLR) is the heart of .NET. CLR takes your .NET application, compiles it into native processor code, and runs it. It provides an extensive range of functionalities for helping applications run properly:

❑   Code loading and execution

❑   Application isolation

❑   Memory management

❑   Security

❑   Exception handling

❑   Interoperation

Do not worry if you do not understand what all these are — the following sections discuss all of them except for memory management. Memory management is quite a complex subject and is discussed in Chapter 12.

Code Loading and Execution

The code loading and execution part of the CLR deals with reading the MSIL code from the disk and running it. It compiles the code from MSIL into the native language (machine code) that the processor understands.

> *Java also has a concept similar to MSIL, known as* byte code, *which the Java runtime loads and executes.*

Application Isolation

One important premise of modern operating systems like Windows and Linux is that applications are isolated from one another. This is critically important from both security and stability standpoints.

Imagine that you have a badly written program and it crashes the PC. Should this happen? No, you want only the badly behaved program to crash, as you do not want other applications or the operating system itself to be affected by a program running on it. For example, if your e-mail program crashes, you do not want to lose any unsaved changes in your word processor. With proper application isolation, one application crashing should not cause others to crash.

In some instances, even under Windows XP, a badly behaved program can do something so horrendous that the entire machine crashes. This is commonly known as a *Blue Screen of Death* (BSOD), so called because your attractive Windows desktop is replaced with a stark blue screen with a smattering of white text explaining the problem. This problem should be alleviated in .NET, but it is unlikely to be completely solved.

The other aspect to application isolation is one of security. Imagine that you are writing a personal and sensitive e-mail. You do not want other applications running on your computer to be able to grab, or even stumble across, the contents of the e-mail and pass it on to someone else. Applications running in an isolated model cannot just take what they want. Instead, they have to ask whether they can have something, and they are given it only if the operating system permits it.

This level of application isolation is already available in Windows. .NET extends and enhances this functionality by further improving it.

Security

.NET has powerful support for the concept of code security. The Framework was designed to give system administrators, users, and software developers a fine level of control over what a program can and cannot do.

Imagine that you have a program that scans your computer's hard disk looking for Word documents. You might think this is a useful program if it is the one that you run to find documents that are missing. Now imagine that this program is delivered through e-mail and it automatically runs and e-mails copies of any "interesting" documents to someone else. You are less likely to find that useful.

This is the situation you find yourself in today with old-school Windows development. To all intents and purposes, Windows applications have unrestricted access over your computer and can do pretty much anything they want. That is why the Melissa and I Love You–type viruses are possible — Windows does not understand the difference between a benign script file you write that, say, looks through your address book and sends e-mails to everyone, and those written by others and delivered as viruses.

Windows Vista solves this problem by locking down the security aspects of Windows applications. If an application is not properly signed, Vista will prompt you for permission to let the program run. Likewise, Vista will prompt you for any program needing administrative permission to do operating system tasks. You then have the option of letting these programs run or canceling them, thus protecting your computer from these rogue viruses.

With .NET this situation changes because of the security features built into the CLR. Under the CLR, code requires *evidence* to run. This evidence can consist of policies set by you and your system administrator, as well as the origin of the code (for example, whether it came off your local machine, off a machine on your office network, or over the Internet).

Security is a very involved topic and is addressed only briefly in Appendix C of this book. However, you can find many books that cover only the topic of .NET security and it is worthwhile to find the book that best meets your needs.

Interoperation

Interoperation in the .NET Framework is achieved on various levels not covered here. However, we must point out some of the types of interoperation that it provides. One kind of interoperation is at the core of the framework, where data types are shared by all managed languages. This is known as the Common Type System (CTS). This is a great improvement for language interoperability (see the section "The Common Type System and Common Language Specification" later in this chapter).

The other type of interoperation is that of communicating with existing Component Object Model (COM) interfaces. Because a large application-software base is written in COM, it was inevitable that .NET should be able to communicate with existing COM libraries. This is also known as *COM interop*.

Exception Handling

Exception handling is the concept of dealing with exceptional happenings when you are running the code. Imagine that you have written a program that opens a file on disk. What if that file is not there? Well, the fact that the file is not there is exceptional, and you need to handle it in some way. It could be that you crash, or you could display a window asking the user to supply a new file name. Either way, you have a fine level of control over what happens when an error does occur.

.NET provides a powerful exception handler that can catch exceptions when they occur and give your programs the opportunity to react and deal with the problem in some way. Chapter 10 talks about exception handling in more detail, but for now, think of exception handling as something provided by the CLR to all applications.

The Common Type System and Common Language Specification

One of the most important aspects of .NET that Microsoft had to get right is inter-language operation. Remember, Microsoft's motivation was to get any developer using any language to use .NET, and for this to happen, all languages had to be treated equally. Likewise, applications created in one language have to be understood by other languages. For example, if you create a class in Visual Basic 2008, a C# developer should be able to use and extend that class. Alternatively, you may need to define a string in C#, pass that string to an object built in Visual Basic 2008, and make that object understand and manipulate the string successfully.

The Common Type System (CTS) allows software written in different languages to work together. Before .NET, Visual Basic and C++ handled strings in completely differently ways, and you had to go through a conversion process each time you went from one to the other. With the CTS in place, all .NET languages use strings, integers, and so on in the same way, and therefore no conversion needs to take place.

In addition, the Common Language Specification (CLS) was introduced by Microsoft to make it easier for language developers to adapt their languages to make them compatible with .NET.

> *The Common Type System and Common Language Specification are the foundation for this interoperation, but detailed discussion is, unfortunately, beyond the scope of this book.*

When talking to other .NET developers, you will likely hear the term *managed code*. This simply describes code that runs inside the CLR. In other words, you get all of the advantages of the CLR, such as the memory management and all of the language interoperability features previously mentioned.

Code written in Visual Basic 2008 and C# is automatically created as managed code. C++ code is not automatically created as managed code, because C++ does not fit well into the memory management scheme implemented by the CLR. You can, if you are interested, turn on an option to create managed code from within C++, in which case you use the term *managed C++*.

Hand-in-hand with managed code is *managed data*. As you can probably guess, this is data managed by the CLR, although in nearly all cases this data actually consists of objects. Objects managed by the CLR can easily be passed between languages.

Summary

This chapter introduced the Microsoft .NET Framework and explained why Microsoft chose to radically change the way programs were written for Windows. You also saw that part of Microsoft's motivation for this was to move the dependence of developers from the execution platform (Windows, Linux, whatever) over to a new programming platform that it would always own.

After learning about why Microsoft developed .NET, you saw how writing for it is not much different from writing for Windows. You still have a layer that you program against; it is just that now, rather than being flat like the Win32 API, it is a rich set of classes that allows you to write true object-oriented programs no matter what .NET language you choose to develop in. This chapter also discussed how these classes could be ported to other platforms and how your applications could transfer across.

Finally, you looked at some of the more technical aspects of the .NET Framework, specifically the Common Language Runtime.

To summarize, you should now understand:

- ❑ Microsoft's new business venture
- ❑ The goals of the .NET Framework
- ❑ The abstractions that the .NET Framework provides
- ❑ An introduction to the core of the .NET Framework

Writing Software

Now that you have Visual Basic 2008 up and running and even written a simple program, you're going to look at the fundamentals behind the process of writing software and start putting together some exciting programs of your own.

In this chapter, you will:

- ❏ Learn about algorithms
- ❏ Learn to use variables
- ❏ Explore different data types, including integers, floating-point numbers, strings, and dates
- ❏ Study scope
- ❏ Learn about debugging applications
- ❏ Learn more about how computers store data in memory

Information and Data

Information describes facts and can be presented or found in any format, whether that format is optimized for humans or for computers. For example, if you send four people to different intersections to survey traffic, at the end of the process you will end up with four handwritten tallies of the number of cars that went past (say, a tally for each hour).

The term *data* is used to describe information that has been collated, ordered, and formatted in such a way that it can be used by a piece of computer software. The information you have (several notebooks full of handwritten scribbles) cannot be directly used by a piece of software. Rather, someone has to work with it to convert it into usable data the computer can understand. For example, the scribbles can be transferred to an Excel spreadsheet that can be directly used by a piece of software designed to analyze the results.

Algorithms

The computer industry changes at an incredible speed. Most professionals constantly retrain and re-educate themselves to keep their skills sharp and up-to-date. However, some aspects of computing haven't really changed since they were first invented and perhaps won't change within our lifetimes. The process and discipline of software development is a good example of an aspect of computer technology whose essential nature hasn't changed since the beginning.

For software to work, you need to have some data to work with. The software then takes this data and manipulates it into another form. For example, software may take your customer database stored as ones and zeros on your computer's hard drive and make it available for you to read on your computer's monitor. The on-board computer in your car constantly examines environmental and performance information and continually adjusts the fuel mix to make the car run more efficiently. Your telephone service provider records the phone number of each call and the length of the call that you make and generates bills based on this information.

The base underpinning of all software is the *algorithm*. Before you can write software to solve a problem, you have to break it down into a step-by-step description of how the problem is going to be solved. An algorithm is independent of the programming language, so, if you like, you can describe it to yourself either as a spoken language, with diagrams, or with whatever helps you visualize the problem.

Imagine that you work for a wireless telephone company and need to produce bills based on calls that your customers make. Here's an algorithm that describes a possible solution:

1. On the first day of the month, you need to produce a bill for each customer you have.

2. For each customer, you have a list of calls that the customer has made in the previous month.

3. You know the duration of each call, and the time of day when the call was made. Based on this information, you can determine the cost of each call.

4. For each bill, you total the cost of each call.

5. If a customer exceeds a preset time limit, you charge the customer a certain rate for each minute that exceeds the allotted time.

6. You apply sales tax to each bill.

7. After you have the final bill, you need to print it and mail it.

Those seven points describe, fairly completely, an algorithm for a piece of software that generates bills for a wireless telephone company. At the end of the day, it doesn't matter whether you build this solution in C++, Visual Basic 2008, C#, Java, or whatever — the basic algorithms of the software never change. (However, it's important to realize that each of those seven parts of the algorithm may well be made up of smaller, more detailed algorithms.)

The good news for a newcomer to programming is that algorithms are usually easy to construct. There shouldn't be anything in the preceding algorithm that you don't understand. Algorithms always follow common-sense reasoning, although you may have to code algorithms that contain complex mathematical or scientific reasoning. It may not seem like common sense to you, but it will to someone else! The bad news is that the process of turning the algorithm into code can be arduous. As a programmer, learning how to construct algorithms is the most important skill you will ever obtain.

All good programmers respect the fact that the preferred language of the programmer is largely irrelevant. Different languages are good at doing different things. C++ gives the developer a lot of control over the way a program works; however, it's harder to write software in C++ than it is in Visual Basic 2008. Likewise, building the user interface for desktop applications is far easier to do in Visual Basic 2008 than it is in C++. (Some of these problems do go away when you use managed C++ with .NET, so this statement is less true today than it was years ago.) What you need to learn to do as a programmer is to adapt different languages to achieve solutions to a problem in the best possible way. Although when you begin programming you'll be hooked on one language, remember that different languages are focused toward developing different kinds of solutions. At some point, you may have to take your basic skills as an algorithm designer and coder to a new language.

What Is a Programming Language?

A programming language is anything capable of making a decision. Computers are very good at making decisions, but they have to be fairly basic, for example: "Is this number greater than three?" or "Is this car blue?"

If you have a complicated decision to make, the process of making that decision has to be broken down into simple parts that the computer can understand. You use algorithms to determine how to break down a complicated decision into simpler ones.

A good example of a problem that's hard for a computer to solve is recognizing peoples' faces. You can't just say to a computer, "Is this a picture of Dave?" Instead, you have to break the question down into a series of simpler questions that the computer can understand.

The decisions that you ask computers to make will have one of two possible answers: yes or no. These possibilities are also referred to as true and false and also as 1 and 0. In software terms, you cannot make a decision based on the question, "How much bigger is 10 compared to 4?" Instead, you have to make a decision based on the question, "Is 10 bigger than 4?" The difference is subtle, yet important — the first question does not yield an answer of yes or no, whereas the second question does. Of course, a computer is more than capable of answering the first question, but this is actually done through an operation; in other words, you have to actually subtract 4 from 10 to use the result in some other part of your algorithm.

You might be looking at the requirement for yes/no answers as a limitation, but it isn't really. Even in our everyday lives the decisions we make are of the same kind. Whenever you decide something, you accept (yes, true, 1) something and reject (no, false, 0) something else.

You are using Visual Basic 2008 for a language, but the important aspects of programming are largely language independent of the language. Understanding that any software, no matter how flashy it is, or which language it is written in, is made up of *methods* (functions and subroutines: the lines of code that actually implement the algorithm) and *variables* (place holders for the data the methods manipulate) is key.

Working with Variables

A variable is something that you store a value in as you work through your algorithm. You can then make a decision based on that value (for example, "Is it equal to 7?" or "Is it more than 4?"), or you can perform operations on that value to change it into something else (for example, "Add 2 to the value", "Multiply it by 6", and so on).

Before you get bogged down in code, take a moment to look at another algorithm:

1. Create a variable called `intNumber` and store in it the value 27.

2. Add 1 to the value of the variable called `intNumber` and store the new value in the same variable.

3. Display the value of the variable called `intNumber` to the user.

This algorithm, creates a variable called `intNumber` and stores in it the value 27. This means that there's a part of the computer's memory that is being used by the program to store the value 27. That piece of memory keeps storing that value until you change it or tell the program that you don't need it any more.

In the second step, an add operation is performed. You're taking the value contained in `intNumber` and adding 1 to its value. After you've performed this operation, the piece of memory given over to storing `intNumber` contains the value 28.

In the final point, you want to tell the user what the value of `intNumber` is. So you read the current value from memory and write it out to the screen.

Again, there's nothing about the algorithm there that you can't understand. It's just common sense! However, the Visual Basic 2008 code looks a little more cryptic. In the following Try It Out, you learn more about working with variables first hand.

Try It Out   **Working with Variables**

1. Create a new project in Visual Studio 2008 by selecting File ⇨ New Project from the menu bar. In the New Project dialog box, select Windows Forms Application from the right-hand pane and enter the project name as **Variables** and click OK (see Figure 3-1).

Figure 3-1

2. Make Form1 a little smaller and add a Button control from the Toolbox to it. Set the button's Text property to **Add 1 to intNumber** and its Name property to **btnAdd.** Your form should look similar Figure 3-2.

Figure 3-2

3. Double-click the button to open the btnAdd_Click event handler. Add the following highlighted code to it:

```
Private Sub btnAdd_Click(ByVal sender As System.Object, _
    ByVal e As System.EventArgs) Handles btnAdd.Click
    Dim intNumber As Integer
    intNumber = 27
    intNumber = intNumber + 1
    MessageBox.Show("Value of intNumber + 1 = " & intNumber.ToString, _
        "Variables")
End Sub
```

4. Click the Save All button on the toolbar, verify the information in the Save Project dialog box, and then click the Save button to save your project.

5. Run the project, click the Add 1 to intNumber button, and you'll see a message box like the one in Figure 3-3.

Figure 3-3

How It Works

The program starts at the top and works its way down, one line at a time, to the bottom. The first line defines a new variable, called intNumber:

```
Dim intNumber As Integer
```

Dim is a keyword. As stated in Chapter 1, a keyword has a special meaning in Visual Basic 2008 and is used for things such as commands. Dim tells Visual Basic 2008 that what follows is a variable definition.

Its curious name harks back to the original versions of the BASIC language. BASIC has always needed to know how much space to reserve for an array (discussed in Chapter 5), so it had a command to tell it the dimensions of the array — Dim for short. Visual Basic extends that command to all other kinds of variables as well to mean make some space for in general.

The variable name comes next and is `intNumber`. Note that the variable name uses the Modified Hungarian notation discussed in Chapter 1. In this case the prefix `int` is short for Integer, which represents the data type for this variable, as described in the following paragraph. Then a name was chosen for this variable; in this case the name is `Number`. Whenever you see this variable throughout your code, you know that this variable will represent a number that is of the Integer data type.

`As Integer` tells Visual Basic 2008 what kind of value you want to store in the variable. This is known as the *data type*. For now, all you need to know is that this is used to tell Visual Basic 2008 that you expect to store an integer (whole number) value in the variable.

The next line sets the value of `intNumber`:

```
intNumber = 27
```

In other words, it stores the value `27` in the variable `intNumber`.

The next statement simply adds `1` to the variable `intNumber`:

```
intNumber = intNumber + 1
```

What this line actually means is: Keep the current value of `intNumber` and add `1` to it.

The final line displays a message box with the text `Value of intNumber + 1 =` and the current value of `intNumber`. You've also set the title of the message box to `Variables` to match the project name. When using numeric variables in text, it is a good idea to use the `ToString` method to cast the numeric value to a string. This prevents the compiler from having to figure out that this is a number and then converting that number to a string so it can be displayed:

```
MessageBox.Show("Value of intNumber + 1 = " & intNumber.ToString, _
    "Variables")
```

Comments and Whitespace

When writing software code, you must be aware that you or someone else may have to change that code in the future. Therefore, you should try to make it as easy to understand as possible.

Comments

Comments are parts of a program that are ignored by the Visual Basic 2008 compiler, which means you can write whatever you like in them, be it English, C#, Perl, FORTRAN, Chinese, whatever. What they're supposed to do is help the human developer reading the code understand what each part of the code is supposed to be doing.

All languages support comments, not just Visual Basic 2008. If you're looking at C# code, for example, you'll find that comments start with a double forward slash (//).

What's a good way of knowing when you need a comment? Well, it's different for different situations, but a good rule of thumb is to think about the algorithm. The program in the previous Try It Out exercise had this algorithm:

1. Define a value for `intNumber`.

2. Add 1 to the value of `intNumber`.

3. Display the new value of `intNumber` to the user.

You can add comments to the code from that example to match the steps in the algorithm:

```
'Define a variable for intNumber
Dim intNumber As Integer

'Set the initial value
intNumber = 27

'Add 1 to the value of intNumber
intNumber = intNumber + 1

'Display the new value of intNumber
MessageBox.Show("Value of intNumber + 1 = " & intNumber.ToString, _
    "Variables")
```

In Visual Basic 2008, you begin your comments with an apostrophe ('). Anything on the same line following that apostrophe is your comment. You can also add comments onto a line that already has code, like this:

```
intNumber = intNumber + 1 'Add 1 to the value of intNumber
```

This works just as well, because only comments (not code) follow the apostrophe. Note that the comments in the preceding code, more or less, match the algorithm. A good technique for adding comments is to write a few words explaining the stage of the algorithm that's being expressed as software code.

You can also use the built-in XML Documentation Comment feature of Visual Studio 2008 to create comment blocks for your methods. To use this feature, place your cursor on the blank line preceding your method definition and type three consecutive apostrophes. The comment block is automatically inserted as shown in the code here.

```
''' <summary>
''' 
''' </summary>
''' <param name="sender"></param>
''' <param name="e"></param>
''' <remarks></remarks>
    Private Sub btnAdd_Click(ByVal sender As System.Object, _
        ByVal e As System.EventArgs) Handles btnAdd.Click
```

What's really cool about this feature is that Visual Studio 2008 automatically fills in the name values of the parameters in the comment block based on the parameters defined in your method. If your method does not have any parameters, the <param> tag will not be inserted into the comment block.

Once a comment block has been inserted, you can provide a summary of what the method does and any special remarks that may need to be noted before this method is called or any other special requirements of the method. If the method returns a value, then a <returns> tag will also be inserted, and you can insert the return value and description.

Comments are primarily used to make the code easier to understand, either to a new developer who's never seen your code before or to you when you haven't reviewed your code for a while. The purpose of a comment is to point out something that might not be immediately obvious or to summarize code to enable the developer to understand what's going on without having to ponder each and every line.

You'll find that programmers have their own guidelines about how to write comments. If you work for a larger software company, or your manager/mentor is hot on coding standards, they'll dictate which formats your comments should take and where you should and should not add comments to the code.

Whitespace

Another important aspect of writing readable code is to leave lots of *whitespace*. Whitespace (space on the screen or page not occupied by characters) makes code easier to read, just as spaces do in English. In the previous example, there is a blank line before each comment. This implies to anyone reading the code that each block is a unit of work, which it is.

You'll be coming back to the idea of whitespace in the next chapter, which discusses controlling the flow through your programs using special code blocks, but you'll find that the use of whitespace varies between developers. For now, remember not to be afraid to space out your code — it'll greatly improve the readability of your programs, especially as you write long chunks of code.

The compiler ignores whitespace and comments, so there are no performance differences between code with lots of whitespace and comments, and code with none.

Data Types

When you use variables, it's a good idea to know ahead of time the things that you want to store in them. So far in this chapter, you've seen a variable that holds an integer number.

When you define a variable, you must tell Visual Basic 2008 the type of data that should be stored in it. As you might have guessed, this is known as the *data type*, and all meaningful programming languages have a vast array of different data types to choose from. The data type of a variable has a great impact on how the computer will run your code. In this section, you'll take a deeper look at how variables work and how their types affect the performance of your program.

Working with Numbers

When you work with numbers in Visual Basic 2008, you'll be working with two kinds of numbers: *integers* and *floating-point numbers*. Both have very specific uses. Integers are usually not much use for calculations of quantities, for example, calculating how much money you have left on your mortgage or calculating how long it would take to fill a swimming pool with water. For these kinds of calculations, you're more likely to use floating-point variables because they can be used to represent numbers with fractional parts, whereas integer variables can hold only whole numbers.

On the other hand, oddly, you'll find that in your day-to-day activities you're far more likely to use integer variables than floating-point variables. Most of the software that you write will use numbers to keep track of what is going on by counting, rather than to calculate quantities.

For example, suppose you are writing a program that displays customer details on the screen. Furthermore, suppose you have 100 customers in your database. When the program starts, you'll display the first customer on the screen. You also need to keep track of which customer is being displayed, so that when the user says, "Next, please," you'll actually know which one is next.

Because a computer is more comfortable working with numbers than with anything else, you'll usually find that each customer has been given a unique number. This unique number will, in most cases, be an integer. What this means is that each of your customers will have a unique integer number between 1 and 100 assigned to them. In your program, you'll also have a variable that stores the ID of the customer that you're currently looking at. When the user asks to see the next customer, you add one to that ID (a.k.a. *increment by one*) and display the new customer.

You'll see how this works as you move on to more advanced topics, but for now, rest assured that you're more likely to use integers than floating-point numbers. Take a look now at some common operations.

Common Integer Math Operations

In this section, you create a new project for your math operations.

Try It Out   **Common Integer Math**

1. Create a new project in Visual Studio 2008 by selecting File ⇨ New Project from the menu. In the New Project dialog box, select Windows Forms Application from the right pane (refer to Figure 3-1), and enter the project name as **Integer Math** and click OK.

2. Using the Toolbox, add a new Button control to Form1 as before. Set its Name property to **btnIntMath** and its Text property to **Math Test**. Double-click it and add the following highlighted code to the new Click event handler that will be created:

```
Private Sub btnIntMath_Click(ByVal sender As System.Object, _
    ByVal e As System.EventArgs) Handles btnIntMath.Click
    'Declare variable
    Dim intNumber As Integer

    'Set number, add numbers, and display results
    intNumber = 16
```

```
        intNumber = intNumber + 8
        MessageBox.Show("Addition test... " & intNumber.ToString, _
            "Integer Math")

        'Set number, subtract numbers, and display results
        intNumber = 24
        intNumber = intNumber - 2
        MessageBox.Show("Subtraction test... " & intNumber.ToString, _
            "Integer Math")

        'Set number, multiply numbers, and display results
        intNumber = 6
        intNumber = intNumber * 10
        MessageBox.Show("Multiplication test... " & intNumber.ToString, _
            "Integer Math")

        'Set number, divide numbers, and display results
        intNumber = 12
        intNumber = CType(intNumber / 6, Integer)
        MessageBox.Show("Division test... " & intNumber.ToString, _
            "Integer Math")
    End Sub
```

3. Save your project by clicking the Save All button on the toolbar.

4. Run the project and click the Math Test button. You'll be able to click through four message box dialog boxes, as shown in Figure 3-4.

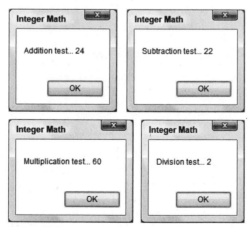

Figure 3-4

How It Works

None of the code you've seen should be too baffling. You've already seen the addition operator before. Here it is again:

```
        'Set number, add numbers, and display results
        intNumber = 16
        intNumber = intNumber + 8
        MessageBox.Show("Addition test... " & intNumber.ToString, _
            "Integer Math")
```

So, all you're saying is this:

1. Let `intNumber` be equal to the value of 16.

2. Then, let `intNumber` be equal to the current value of `intNumber` (which is 16) plus 8.

As you can see from the message dialog box shown in Figure 3-4, you get a result of 24, which is correct.

The subtraction operator is a minus (–) sign. Here it is in action:

```
'Set number, subtract numbers, and display results
intNumber = 24
intNumber = intNumber - 2
MessageBox.Show("Subtraction test... " & intNumber.ToString, _
    "Integer Math")
```

Again, same deal as before:

1. Let `intNumber` be equal to the value 24.

2. Let `intNumber` be equal to the current value of `intNumber` (which is 24) minus 2.

The multiplication operator is an asterisk (*). Here it is in action:

```
'Set number, multiply numbers, and display results
intNumber = 6
intNumber = intNumber * 10
MessageBox.Show("Multiplication test... " & intNumber.ToString, _
    "Integer Math")
```

Here your algorithm states:

1. Let `intNumber` be equal to the value 6.

2. Let `intNumber` be equal to the current value of `intNumber` (which is 6) times 10.

Finally, the division operator is a forward slash (/). Here it is in action:

```
'Set number, divide numbers, and display results
intNumber = 12
intNumber = CType(intNumber / 6, Integer)
MessageBox.Show("Division test... " & intNumber.ToString, _
    "Integer Math")
```

Again, all you're saying is:

1. Let `intNumber` be equal to the value of 12.

2. Let `intNumber` be equal to the current value of `intNumber` (which is 12) divided by 6.

The division of `intNumber` *by the value of 6 has been enclosed in the* `CType` *function. The* `CType` *function returns the result of explicitly converting an expression to a specified data type, which in this case is an Integer number as indicated by the Integer type name. Because the division of two numbers could result in a floating-point number, you should use the* `CType` *function to force the results to an integer number.*

This explicit conversion is not necessary when the Option Strict setting is set to Off but is required when this setting is set to On. The Option Strict setting ensures compile-time notification of narrowing conversion of numeric operations so they can be avoided and prevent run-time errors.

To access the settings for Option Strict, click the Tools menu in Visual Studio 2008 and then click the Options menu item. In the Options dialog box, expand the Projects and Solutions node and then click VB Defaults. From here you can turn the Option Strict setting on and off.

Integer Math Shorthand

In the next Try It Out, you'll see how you can perform the same operations without having to write as much code by using *shorthand operators* (assignment operators). Although they look a little less logical than their more verbose counterparts, you'll soon learn to love them.

Try It Out   Using Shorthand Operators

1. Go back to Visual Studio 2008 and open the code for `Form1.vb` again. Change the highlighted lines:

```
Private Sub btnIntMath_Click(ByVal sender As System.Object, _
    ByVal e As System.EventArgs) Handles btnIntMath.Click

    'Declare variable
    Dim intNumber As Integer

    'Set number, add numbers, and display results
    intNumber = 16
    intNumber += 8
    MessageBox.Show("Addition test... " & intNumber.ToString, _
        "Integer Math")

    'Set number, subtract numbers, and display results
    intNumber = 24
    intNumber -= 2
    MessageBox.Show("Subtraction test... " & intNumber.ToString, _
        "Integer Math")

    'Set number, multiply numbers, and display results
    intNumber = 6
    intNumber *= 10
```

```
MessageBox.Show("Multiplication test... " & intNumber.ToString, _
    "Integer Math")

'Set number, divide numbers, and display results
intNumber = 12
intNumber = CType(intNumber / 6, Integer)
MessageBox.Show("Division test... " & intNumber.ToString, _
    "Integer Math")
End Sub
```

2. Run the project and click the Math Test button. You'll get the same results as in the previous Try It Out exercise.

How It Works

To use the shorthand version you just drop the last `intNumber` variable and move the operator to the left of the equals sign. Here is the old version:

```
intNumber = intNumber + 8
```

... and here's the new version:

```
intNumber += 8
```

The Problem with Integer Math

The main problem with integer math is that you can't do anything that involves a number with a fractional part. For example, you can't do this:

```
'Try multiplying numbers...
intNumber = 6
intNumber = intNumber * 10.23
```

Or, rather, you can actually run that code, but you won't get the result you were expecting. Because `intNumber` has been defined as a variable designed to accept an integer only; the result is rounded up or down to the nearest integer. In this case, although the actual answer is 61.38, `intNumber` will be set to the value 61. If the answer were 61.73, `intNumber` would be set to 62.

> With the Option Strict setting set to On, the preceding code would produce an error in the IDE and the program would not compile. With the Option Strict setting set to Off, this code is allowed.

A similar problem occurs with division. Here's another piece of code:

```
'Try dividing numbers...
intNumber = 12
intNumber = intNumber / 7
```

This time the answer is 1.71. However, because the result has to be rounded up in order for it to be stored in `intNumber`, you end up with `intNumber` being set equal to 2. As you can imagine, if you were trying to write programs that actually calculated some form of value, you'd be in big trouble, as every step in the calculation would be subject to rounding errors.

In the next section, you'll look at how you can do these kinds of operations with floating-point numbers.

Floating-Point Math

You know that integers are not good for most mathematical calculations because most calculations of these types involve a fractional component of some quantity. Later in this chapter, you'll see how to use floating-point numbers to calculate the area of a circle. In the following Try It Out, we'll introduce the concepts.

Try It Out   Floating-Point Math

1. Create a new Windows Forms Application project in Visual Studio 2008 called **Floating Point Math**. As before, place a button on the form, setting its name to **btnFloatMath** and its text to **Double Test**.

2. Double-click btnFloatMath and add the following highlighted code:

```
Private Sub btnFloatMath_Click(ByVal sender As System.Object, _
    ByVal e As System.EventArgs) Handles btnFloatMath.Click

        'Delcare variable
        Dim dblNumber As Double

        'Set number, multiply numbers, and display results
        dblNumber = 45.34
        dblNumber *= 4.333
        MessageBox.Show("Multiplication test... " & dblNumber.ToString, _
            "Floating Points")

        'Set number, divide numbers, and display results
        dblNumber = 12
        dblNumber /= 7
        MessageBox.Show("Division test... " & dblNumber.ToString, _
            "Floating Points")
    End Sub
```

3. Save your project by clicking the Save All button on the toolbar.

4. Run the project and you'll see the results shown in Figure 3-5.

Figure 3-5

How It Works

Perhaps the most important change in this code is the way you're defining your variable:

```
'Declare variable
Dim dblNumber As Double
```

Rather than saying As Integer at the end, you're saying As Double. This tells Visual Basic 2008 that you want to create a variable that holds a double-precision floating-point number, rather than an integer number. This means that any operation performed on dblNumber will be a floating-point operation, rather than an integer operation. Also note that you have used a different Modified Hungarian notation prefix to signify that this variable contains a number that is of the Double data type.

However, there's no difference in the way either of these operations is performed. Here, you set dblNumber to be a decimal number and then multiply it by another decimal number:

```
'Set number, multiply numbers, and display results
dblNumber = 45.34
dblNumber *= 4.333
MessageBox.Show("Multiplication test... " & dblNumber.ToString, _
    "Floating Points")
```

When you run this, you get a result of 196.45822, which, as you can see, has a decimal component, and therefore you can use this in calculations.

Of course, floating-point numbers don't have to have an explicit decimal component:

```
'Set number, divide numbers, and display results
dblNumber = 12
dblNumber /= 7
MessageBox.Show("Division test... " & dblNumber.ToString, _
    "Floating Points")
```

This result still yields a floating-point result, because dblNumber has been set up to hold such a result. You can see this by your result of 1.71428571428571, which is the same result you were looking for when you were examining integer math.

This time, the code allows you to use the math shorthand to divide two numbers as the variable that holds the results will accept a floating-point number. Thus you do not have to use the CType function to convert the results to an integer value.

A floating-point number gets its name because it is stored like a number written in scientific notation on paper. In scientific notation, the number is given as a power of 10 and a number between 1 and 10 that is multiplied by that power of 10 to get the original number. For example, 10,001 is written 1.0001×10^4, and 0.0010001 is written 1.0001×10^{-3}. The decimal point "floats" to the position after the first digit in both cases. The advantage is that large numbers and small numbers are represented with the same degree of precision (in this example, one part in 10,000). A floating-point variable is stored in the same way inside the computer, but in base two instead of base 10 (see "Storing Variables," later in this section).

Other States

Floating-point variables can hold a few other values besides decimal numbers. Specifically, these are:

❑ NaN — which means *not a number*

❑ Positive infinity

❑ Negative infinity

We won't show how to get all of the results here, but the mathematicians among you will recognize that .NET caters to your advanced math needs.

Single-Precision Floating-Point Numbers

We've been saying "double-precision floating-point." In .NET, there are two main ways to represent floating-point numbers, depending on your needs. In certain cases the decimal fractional components of numbers can zoom off to infinity (pi being a particularly obvious example), but the computer does not have an infinite amount of space to hold digits, so there has to be some limit at which the computer stops keeping track of the digits to the right of the decimal point. The limit is related to the size of the variable, which is a subject discussed in much more detail toward the end of this chapter. There are also limits on how large the component to the left of the decimal point can be.

A double-precision floating-point number can hold any value between -1.7×10^{308} and $+1.7 \times 10^{308}$ to a great level of accuracy (one penny in 45 trillion dollars). A single-precision floating-point number can only hold between -3.4×10^{38} and $+3.4 \times 10^{38}$. Again, this is still a pretty huge number, but it holds decimal components to a lesser degree of accuracy (one penny in only \$330,000) — the benefits being that single-precision floating-point numbers require less memory and calculations involving them are faster on some computers.

You should avoid using double-precision numbers unless you actually require more accuracy than the single-precision type allows. This is especially important in very large applications, where using double-precision numbers for variables that only require single-precision numbers could slow your program significantly.

The calculations you're trying to perform will dictate which type of floating-point number you should use. If you want to use a single-precision number, use As Single rather than As Double, like this:

```
Dim sngNumber As Single
```

Working with Strings

A *string* is a sequence of characters, and you use double quotes to mark its beginning and end. You've seen how to use strings to display the results of simple programs on the screen. Strings are commonly used for exactly this function — telling the user what happened and what needs to happen next. Another common use is storing a piece of text for later use in an algorithm. You'll see lots of strings throughout the rest of the book. So far, you've used strings like this:

```
MessageBox.Show("Multiplication test... " & dblNumber.ToString, _
    "Floating Points")
```

"Multiplication test..." and "Floating Points" are strings; you can tell because of the double quotes ("). However, what about dblNumber? The value contained within dblNumber is being converted to a string value that can be displayed on the screen by use of the ToString method of the Double class, which defines the variable type. For example, if dblNumber represents the value 27, to display it on the screen it has to be converted into a quoted string two characters in length, and this is what the ToString method does. In the next Try It Out, you look at some of the things you can do with strings.

Try It Out   Using Strings

1. Create a new Windows Forms Application using the File ⇨ New Project menu option. Call it **Strings**.

2. Using the Toolbox, draw a button with the Name property **btnStrings** on the form and set its Text property to **Using Strings**. Double-click it and then add the highlighted code:

```
Private Sub btnStrings_Click(ByVal sender As System.Object, _
    ByVal e As System.EventArgs) Handles btnStrings.Click

    'Declare variable
    Dim strResults As String

    'Set the string value
    strResults = "Hello World!"

    'Display the results
    MessageBox.Show(strResults, "Strings")
End Sub
```

3. Save your project by clicking the Save All button on the toolbar.

4. Run the project and click the Using Strings button. You'll see a message like the one in Figure 3-6.

Figure 3-6

How It Works

You can define a variable that holds a string using a similar notation to that used with the number variables, but this time using As String:

```
'Declare variable
Dim strResults As String
```

You can also set that string to have a value, again as before:

```
'Set the string value
strResults = "Hello World!"
```

You need to use double quotes around the string value to *delimit* the string, meaning to mark where the string begins and where the string ends. This is an important point, because these double quotes tell the Visual Basic 2008 compiler not to try to compile the text that is contained within the string. If you don't include the quotes, Visual Basic 2008 treats the value stored in the variable as part of the program's code, tries to compile it and can't, causing the whole program to fail to compile.

With the value `Hello World!` stored in a string variable called `strResults`, you can pass that variable to the message box whose job it is to extract the value from the variable and display it. So, you can see that strings can be defined and used in the same way as the numeric values you saw before. Now look at how to perform operations on strings.

Concatenation

Concatenation means linking things together in a chain or series; to join them. If you have two strings that you join together, one after the other, you say they are concatenated. You can think of concatenation as addition for strings. In the next Try It Out, you work with concatenation.

Try It Out   Concatenation

1. Using the same Strings project, view the Designer for Form1 and add a new button. Set its **Name** property to **btnConcatenation** and its **Text** property to **Concatenation.** Double-click the button and add the following highlighted code:

```
Private Sub btnConcatenation_Click(ByVal sender As System.Object, _
    ByVal e As System.EventArgs) Handles btnConcatenation.Click

        'Declare variables
        Dim strResults As String
        Dim strOne As String
        Dim strTwo As String

        'Set the string values
        strOne = "Hello"
        strTwo = " World!"

        'Concatenate the strings
        strResults = strOne & strTwo

        'Display the results
        MessageBox.Show(strResults, "Strings")
    End Sub
```

2. Run the project and click the Concatenation button. You'll see the same results that were shown in Figure 3-6.

How It Works

In this Try It Out, you start by declaring three variables that are String data types:

```
'Declare variables
Dim strOne As String
Dim strTwo As String
Dim strResults As String
```

Then you set the values of the first two strings.

```
'Set the string values
strOne = "Hello"
strTwo = " World!"
```

After you've set the values of the first two strings, you use the & operator to concatenate the two previous strings, setting the results of the concatenation in a new string variable called strResults:

```
'Concatenate the strings
strResults = strOne & strTwo
```

What you're saying here is, "Let strResults be equal to the current value of strOne followed by the current value of strTwo." By the time you call MessageBox.Show, strResults will be equal to "Hello World!", so you get the same value as before.

```
'Display the results
MessageBox.Show(strResults, "Strings")
```

Using the Concatenation Operator Inline

You don't have to define variables to use the concatenation operator. You can use it on the fly, as you saw in the Floating-Point Math, Integer Math, and Variables projects. You've already seen the concatenation operator being used like this in previous examples. What this is actually doing is converting the value stored in dblNumber to a string so that it can be displayed on the screen. Look at this code:

```
MessageBox.Show("Division test... " & dblNumber.ToString, _
    "Floating Points")
```

The portion that reads, "Division test... " is actually a string, but you don't have to define it as a string variable. In Visual Basic 2008 parlance, this is called a *string literal*, meaning that it's exactly as shown in the code and doesn't change. When you use the concatenation operator on this string together with dblNumber.ToString, the value contained in the dblNumber variable is converted into a string and tacked onto the end of "Division test... ". Remember that the ToString method converts the value contained in a variable to a string value. The result is one string that is passed to MessageBox .Show and that contains both the base text and the current value of dblNumber.

More String Operations

You can do plenty more with strings! Take a look at some examples in the next Try It Out. The first thing you'll do is look at a property of the string that can be used to return its length.

Returning the Length of a String

1. Using the Strings project, return to the designer for Form1. Add a TextBox control to the form and set its Name property to **txtString.** Add another Button control and set its Name property to **btnLength** and its Text property to **Length.** Rearrange the controls so that they look like Figure 3-7:

Figure 3-7

2. Double-click the Length button to open its Click event handler. Add the following highlighted code:

```
Private Sub btnLength_Click(ByVal sender As System.Object, _
    ByVal e As System.EventArgs) Handles btnLength.Click

    'Declare variable
    Dim strResults As String

    'Get the text from the TextBox
    strResults = txtString.Text

    'Display the length of the string
    MessageBox.Show(strResults.Length.ToString & " characters(s)", _
        "Strings")
End Sub
```

3. Run the project and enter some text into the text box.

4. Click the Length button and you'll see results similar to those shown in Figure 3-8.

Figure 3-8

How It Works

The first thing that you do is to declare a variable to contain string data. Then you extract the text from the text box and store it in your string variable called `strResults`:

```
'Declare variable
Dim strResults As String

'Get the text from the TextBox
strResults = txtString.Text
```

When you have the string, you can use the `Length` property to get an integer value that represents the number of characters in it. Remember, as far as a computer is concerned, characters include things like spaces and other punctuation marks. Since the `Length` property returns the number of characters as an `Integer` data type you want to convert that number to a string using the `ToString` method:

```
'Display the length of the string
MessageBox.Show(strResults.Length.ToString & " characters(s)", _
    "Strings")
```

Substrings

Common ways to manipulate strings in a program include using a set of characters that appears at the start, a set that appears at the end, or a set that appears somewhere in between. These are known as *substrings*.

In the following Try It Out, you build on your previous application and get it to display the first three, middle three, and last three characters.

Try It Out   Working with Substrings

1. Using the Strings project, return to the designer for Form1. Add another Button control to Form1 and set its `Name` property to **btnSubStrings** and its `Text` property to **SubStrings**. Double-click the button and add the code highlighted here:

```
Private Sub btnSubStrings_Click(ByVal sender As System.Object, _
    ByVal e As System.EventArgs) Handles btnSubStrings.Click

    'Declare variable
    Dim strResults As String

    'Get the text from the TextBox
    strResults = txtString.Text

    'Display the first three characters
    MessageBox.Show(strResults.Substring(0, 3), "Strings")
```

```
        'Display the middle three characters
        MessageBox.Show(strResults.Substring(3, 3), "Strings")

        'Display the last three characters
        MessageBox.Show(strResults.Substring(strResults.Length - 3), "Strings")
    End Sub
```

2. Run the project. Enter the word **Cranberry** in the text box.

3. Click the Split button and you'll see three message boxes one after another as shown in Figure 3-9.

Figure 3-9

How It Works

The Substring method lets you grab a set of characters from any position in the string. The method can be used in one of two ways. The first way is to give it a starting point and a number of characters to grab. In the first instance, you're telling it to start at character position 0 — the beginning of the string — and grab three characters:

```
        'Display the first three characters
        MessageBox.Show(strResults.Substring(0, 3), "Strings")
```

In the next instance, you to start three characters in from the start and grab three characters:

```
        'Display the middle three characters
        MessageBox.Show(strResults.Substring(3, 3), "Strings")
```

In the final instance, you're providing only one parameter. This tells the Substring method to start at the given position and grab everything right up to the end. In this case, you're using the Substring method in combination with the Length method, so you're saying, "Grab everything from three characters in from the right of the string to the end."

```
        'Display the last three characters
        MessageBox.Show(strResults.Substring(strResults.Length - 3), "Strings")
```

Formatting Strings

Often when working with numbers, you'll need to alter the way they are displayed as a string. Figure 3-5 shows how a division operator works. In this case, you don't really need to see 14 decimal places — two or three would be fine! What you need is to format the string so that you see everything to the left of the decimal point, but only three digits to the right, which is what you do in the next Try It Out.

Try It Out **Formatting Strings**

1. Open the Floating-Point Math project that you created earlier in this chapter.

2. Open the Code Editor for Form1 and make the following changes:

   ```
   'Set number, divide numbers, and display results
   dblNumber = 12
   dblNumber /= 7
   ```

   ```
   'Display the results without formatting
   MessageBox.Show("Division test without formatting... " & _
       dblNumber.ToString, "Floating Points")

   'Display the results with formatting
   MessageBox.Show("Division test with formatting... " & _
       String.Format("{0:n3}", dblNumber), "Floating Points")
   End Sub
   ```

3. Run the project. After the message box dialog box for the multiplication test is displayed you'll see two more message boxes as shown in Figure 3-10.

Figure 3-10

How It Works

The magic here is in the call to `String.Format`. This powerful method allows the formatting of numbers. The key is all in the first parameter, as this defines the format the final string will take:

```
MessageBox.Show("Division test with formatting... " & _
    String.Format("{0:n3}", dblNumber), "Floating Points")
```

You passed `String.Format` two parameters. The first parameter, `"{0:n3}"`, is the format that you want. The second parameter, `dblNumber`, is the value that you want to format. Note that since you are formatting a number to a string representation, you do not need to provide the `ToString` method after `dblNumber` as in the previous call to the `Show` method of the `MessageBox` class. This is because the `String.Format` method is looking for a number and not a string.

The `0` in the format tells `String.Format` to work with the zeroth data parameter, which is just a cute way of saying "the second parameter", or `dblNumber`. What follows the colon is how you want `dblNumber` to be formatted. You said n3, which means "floating-point number, three decimal places." You could have said n2 for "floating-point number, two decimal places."

Localized Formatting

When building .NET applications, it's important to realize that the user may be familiar with cultural conventions that are uncommon to you. For example, if you live in the United States, you're used to seeing the decimal separator as a period (.). However, if you live in France, the decimal separator is actually a comma (,).

Windows can deal with such problems for you based on the locale settings of the computer. If you use the .NET Framework in the correct way, by and large you'll never need to worry about this problem.

Here's an example — if you use a formatting string of n3 again, you are telling .NET that you want to format the number with thousands separators and also that you want the number displayed to three decimal places (1,714.286).

The equation changed from 12 / 7 to 12000 / 7 to allow the display of the thousands separator (,).

Now, if you tell your computer that you want to use the French locale settings, and you run the *same code* (you make no changes whatsoever to the application itself), you'll see 1 714,286.

You can change your language options by going to the Control Panel and clicking the Regional and Language Options icon and changing the language to French.

In France, the thousands separator is a space, not a comma, while the decimal separator is a comma, not a period. By using `String.Format` appropriately, you can write one application that works properly regardless of how the user has configured the locale settings on the computer.

Replacing Substrings

Another common string manipulation replaces occurrences of one string with another. To demonstrate this, in the next Try It Out you'll modify your Strings application to replace the string `"Hello"` with the string `"Goodbye"`.

Try It Out   **Replacing Substrings**

1. Open the Strings project that you were working with earlier.

2. Return to the Forms Designer for Form1, add another Button control and set its Name property to **btnReplace** and set its Text property to **Replace**. Double-click the button and add the following highlighted code to its Click event handler:

```
Private Sub btnReplace_Click(ByVal sender As System.Object, _
    ByVal e As System.EventArgs) Handles btnReplace.Click

        'Declare variables
        Dim strData As String
        Dim strResults As String

        'Get the text from the TextBox
        strData = txtString.Text

        'Replace the string occurance
        strResults = strData.Replace("Hello", "Goodbye")

        'Display the new string
        MessageBox.Show(strResults, "Strings")
    End Sub
```

3. Run the project and enter **Hello World!** into the text box (using this exact capitalization).

4. Click the Replace button. You should see a message box that says Goodbye World!

How It Works

Replace works by taking the substring to look for as the first parameter and the new substring to replace it with as the second parameter. After the replacement is made, a new string is returned that you can display in the usual way.

```
        'Replace the string occurance
        strResults = strData.Replace("Hello", "Goodbye")
```

You're not limited to a single search and replace within this code. If you enter Hello twice into the text box and click the button, you'll notice two Goodbye returns. However, the case is important — if you enter hello, it will not be replaced. You'll take a look at case-insensitive string comparisons in the next chapter.

Using Dates

Another data type that you'll often use is Date. This data type holds, not surprisingly, a date value. You learn to display the current date in the next Try It Out.

Try It Out   **Displaying the Current Date**

1.   Create a new Windows Forms Application project called **Date Demo**.

2.   In the usual way, use the Toolbox to draw a new Button control on the form. Call it **btnShowDate** and set its `Text` property to **Show Date**.

3.   Double-click the button to bring up its `Click` event handler and add this code:

```
Private Sub btnShowDate_Click(ByVal sender As System.Object, _
    ByVal e As System.EventArgs) Handles btnShowDate.Click

        'Declare variable
        Dim dteResults As Date

        'Get the current date and time
        dteResults = Now

        'Display the results
        MessageBox.Show(dteResults.ToString, "Date Demo")
End Sub
```

4.   Save your project by clicking the Save All button on the toolbar.

5.   Run the project and click the button. You should see something like Figure 3-11 depending on the locale settings on your machine.

Figure 3-11

How It Works

The `Date` data type can be used to hold a value that represents any date and time. After creating the variable, you initialized it to the current date and time using the `Now` property. Then you display the date in a message box dialog box. Note that since you want to display a `Date` data type as a string, that you once again use the `ToString` method to convert the results to a string format.

```
        'Declare variable
        Dim dteResults As Date

        'Get the current date and time
        dteResults = Now

        'Display the results
        MessageBox.Show(dteResults.ToString, "Date Demo")
```

Date data types aren't any different from other data types, although you can do more with them. In the next couple of sections, you'll see ways to manipulate dates and control the way they are displayed on the screen.

Formatting Date Strings

You've already seen one way in which dates can be formatted. By default, if you pass a Date variable to MessageBox.Show, the date and time are displayed as shown in Figure 3-11.

Because this machine is in the United States, the date is shown in m/d/yyyy format and the time is shown using the 12-hour clock. This is another example of how the computer's locale setting affects the formatting of different data types. For example, if you set your computer to the United Kingdom locale, the date is in dd/mm/yyyy format and the time is displayed using the 24-hour clock, for example, 07/08/2004 07:02:47.

Although you can control the date format to the nth degree, it's best to rely on .NET to ascertain how the user wants strings to look and automatically display them in their preferred format. In the next Try It Out, you'll look at four useful methods that enable you to format dates.

Try It Out   **Formatting Dates**

1. Return to the Code Editor for Form1, find the Click event handler for the button, and add the following highlighted code:

    ```
    'Display the results
    MessageBox.Show(dteResults.ToString, "Date Demo")

    'Display dates
    MessageBox.Show(dteResults.ToLongDateString, "Date Demo")
    MessageBox.Show(dteResults.ToShortDateString, "Date Demo")

    'Display times
    MessageBox.Show(dteResults.ToLongTimeString, "Date Demo")
    MessageBox.Show(dteResults.ToShortTimeString, "Date Demo")
    End Sub
    ```

2. Run the project. You'll be able to click through five message boxes. You have already seen the first message box dialog box; it displays the date and time according to your computers locale settings. The next message dialog box displays the long date, and the next message dialog box displays the short date. The fourth message box displays the long time, and the last message box displays the short time.

How It Works

You're seeing the four basic ways that you can display dates and times in Windows applications, namely long date, short date, long time, and short time. The names of the formats are self-explanatory!

```
                    'Display dates
                    MessageBox.Show(dteResults.ToLongDateString, "Date Demo")
                    MessageBox.Show(dteResults.ToShortDateString, "Date Demo")

                    'Display times
                    MessageBox.Show(dteResults.ToLongTimeString, "Date Demo")
                    MessageBox.Show(dteResults.ToShortTimeString, "Date Demo")
```

Extracting Date Properties

When you have a variable of type Date, there are several properties that you can call to learn more about the date; let's look at them.

Try It Out   **Extracting Date Properties**

1. Return to the Forms Designer for the Date Demo project and add another Button control to Form1 and set its Name property to **btnDateProperties** and its Text property to **Date Properties**. Double-click the button and add the following highlighted code to the Click event:

    ```
    Private Sub btnDateProperties_Click(ByVal sender As System.Object, _
        ByVal e As System.EventArgs) Handles btnDateProperties.Click

            'Declare variable
            Dim dteResults As Date

            'Get the current date and time
            dteResults = Now

            'Display the various date properties
            MessageBox.Show("Month: " & dteResults.Month, "Date Demo")
            MessageBox.Show("Day: " & dteResults.Day, "Date Demo")
            MessageBox.Show("Year: " & dteResults.Year, "Date Demo")
            MessageBox.Show("Hour: " & dteResults.Hour, "Date Demo")
            MessageBox.Show("Minute: " & dteResults.Minute, "Date Demo")
            MessageBox.Show("Second: " & dteResults.Second, "Date Demo")
            MessageBox.Show("Day of week: " & dteResults.DayOfWeek, "Date Demo")
            MessageBox.Show("Day of year: " & dteResults.DayOfYear, "Date Demo")
    End Sub
    ```

2. Run the project. If you click the button, you'll see a set of fairly self-explanatory message boxes.

How It Works

Again, there's nothing here that's rocket science. If you want to know the hour, use the Hour property. To get at the year, use Year, and so on.

Date Constants

In the preceding Try It Out, when you called `DayOfWeek` property, you were actually given an integer value, as shown in Figure 3-12.

Figure 3-12

The date that we're working with, September 3, 2007, is a Monday, and, although it may not be immediately obvious, Monday is 1. Because the first day of the week is Sunday in the United States, you start counting from Sunday, with Sunday being 0. However, there is a possibility that you're working on a computer whose locale setting starts the calendar on a Monday, in which case `DayOfWeek` would return 0. Complicated? Perhaps, but just remember that you can't guarantee that what you think is `"Day 1"` is always going to be Monday. Likewise, what's Wednesday in English is Mittwoch in German.

If you need to know the name of the day or the month in your application, a better approach is to get .NET to get the name for you, again from the particular locale settings of the computer, as you do in the next Try It Out.

Try It Out   **Getting the Names of the Weekday and the Month**

1. Return to the Form Designer in the Date Demo project, add a new Button control and set its Name property to **btnDateNames** and its Text property to **Date Names**. Double-click the button and add the following highlighted code to the `Click` event handler:

```
Private Sub btnDateNames_Click(ByVal sender As System.Object, _
    ByVal e As System.EventArgs) Handles btnDateNames.Click

    'Declare variable
    Dim dteResults As Date

    'Get the current date and time
    dteResults = Now

    MessageBox.Show("Weekday name: " & dteResults.ToString("dddd"), _
        "Date Demo")
    MessageBox.Show("Month name: " & dteResults.ToString("MMMM"), _
        "Date Demo")
End Sub
```

2. Run the project and click the button. You will see a message box that tells you the weekday name (Monday, for example) and a second one that tells you the month (September, for example).

How It Works

When you used your `ToLongDateString` method and its siblings, you were basically allowing .NET to look in the locale settings for the computer for the date format the user preferred. In this example, you're using the `ToString` method but supplying your own format string.

```
MessageBox.Show("Weekday name: " & dteResults.ToString("dddd"), _
    "Date Demo")
MessageBox.Show("Month name: " & dteResults.ToString("MMMM"), _
    "Date Demo")
```

Usually, it's best practice not to use the `ToString` method to format dates to different string values, because you should rely on the built-in formats in .NET, but here you're using the `"dddd"` string to get the weekday name and `"MMMM"` to get the month name. (The case is important here — `"mmmm"` won't work.)

To show this works, if the computer is set to use Italian locale settings, you get one message box telling you the weekday name is `Lunedì` and another telling you the month name is `Settembre`.

Defining Date Literals

You know that if you want to use a string literal in your code, you can do this:

```
Dim strResults As String
strResults = "Woobie"
```

Date literals work in more or less the same way. However, you use pound signs (#) to delimit the start and end of the date. You learn to define date literals in the next Try It Out.

Try It Out   Defining Date Literals

1. Return to the Forms Designer for the Date Demo project and add another Button control to the form and set its `Name` property to **btnDateLiterals** and its `Text` property to **Date Literals**. Double-click the button and add the following highlighted code to the `Click` event handler:

```
Private Sub btnDateLiterals_Click(ByVal sender As System.Object, _
    ByVal e As System.EventArgs) Handles btnDateLiterals.Click

    'Declare variable
    Dim dteResults As Date

    'Set a date and time
    dteResults = #1/1/2010 8:01:00 AM#

    'Display the date and time
    MessageBox.Show(dteResults.ToLongDateString & " " & _
        dteResults.ToLongTimeString, "Date Demo")
End Sub
```

2. Run the project and click the button. You should see the message box shown in Figure 3-13.

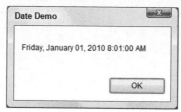

Figure 3-13

How It Works

When defining a date literal, it *must* be defined in the mm/dd/yyyy format, regardless of the actual locale settings of the computer. You may or may not see an error if you try to define the date in the format dd/mm/yyyy. This is because you could put in a date in the format dd/mm/yyyy (for example, 06/07/2008) that is also a valid date in the required mm/dd/yyyy format. This requirement reduces ambiguity: Does 6/7/2008 mean July 6 or June 7?

> *In fact, this is a general truth of programming as a whole: There are no such things as dialects when writing software. It's usually best to conform to North American standards. As you'll see through the rest of this book, this includes variables and method names, for example* GetColor *rather than* GetColour.

It's also worth noting that you don't have to supply both a date *and* a time. You can supply one, the other, or both.

Manipulating Dates

One thing that's always been pretty tricky for programmers to do is manipulate dates. Most of you will remember New Year's Eve 1999, waiting to see whether computers could deal with tipping into a new century. Also, dealing with leap years has always been a bit of a problem.

The next turn of the century that also features a leap year will be 2399 to 2400. In the next Try It Out, you'll take a look at how you can use some of the methods available on the Date data type to adjust the date around that particular leap year.

Try It Out   Manipulating Dates

1. Return to the Forms Designer for the Date Demo project and add another Button control to the form and set its Name property to **btnDateManipulation** and its Text property to **Date Manipulation**. Double-click the button and add the following highlighted code to the Click event handler:

```
Private Sub btnDateManipulation_Click(ByVal sender As System.Object, _
    ByVal e As System.EventArgs) Handles btnDateManipulation.Click
```

```
                    'Declare variables
                    Dim dteStartDate As Date
                    Dim dteChangedDate As Date

                    'Start in the year 2400
                    dteStartDate = #2/28/2400#

                    'Add a day and display the results
                    dteChangedDate = dteStartDate.AddDays(1)
                    MessageBox.Show(dteChangedDate.ToLongDateString, "Date Demo")

                    'Add some months and display the results
                    dteChangedDate = dteStartDate.AddMonths(6)
                    MessageBox.Show(dteChangedDate.ToLongDateString, "Date Demo")

                    'Subtract a year and display the results
                    dteChangedDate = dteStartDate.AddYears(-1)
                    MessageBox.Show(dteChangedDate.ToLongDateString, "Date Demo")
              End Sub
```

2. Run the project and click the button. You'll see three message boxes, one after another. The first message box displays the long date for 2/29/2400, whereas the second message box displays the long date for 8/28/2400. The final message box displays the long date for 2/28/2399.

How It Works

The Date data type supports several methods for manipulating dates. Here are three of them:

```
                    'Add a day and display the results
                    dteChangedDate = dteStartDate.AddDays(1)
                    MessageBox.Show(dteChangedDate.ToLongDateString, "Date Demo")

                    'Add some months and display the results
                    dteChangedDate = dteStartDate.AddMonths(6)
                    MessageBox.Show(dteChangedDate.ToLongDateString, "Date Demo")

                    'Subtract a year and display the results
                    dteChangedDate = dteStartDate.AddYears(-1)
                    MessageBox.Show(dteChangedDate.ToLongDateString, "Date Demo")
```

It's worth noting that when you supply a negative number to any of the Add methods when working with Date variables, the effect is subtraction (demonstrated by going from 2400 back to 2399). The other important Add methods are AddHours, AddMinutes, AddSeconds, and AddMilliseconds.

Boolean

So far, you've seen the Integer, Double, Single, String, and Date data types. The other one you need to look at is Boolean. After you've done that, you've seen all of the simple data types that you're most likely to use in your programs.

A `Boolean` variable can be either `True` or `False`. It can never be anything else. `Boolean` values are really important when it's time for your programs to start making decisions, which is something you look at in more detail in Chapter 4.

Storing Variables

The most limited resource on your computer is typically its memory. It is important that you try to get the most out of the available memory. Whenever you create a variable, you are using a piece of memory, so you must strive to use as few variables as possible and use the variables that you do have in the most efficient manner.

Today, absolute optimization of variables is not something you need to go into a deep level of detail about, for two reasons. First, computers have far more memory these days, so the days when programmers tried to cram payroll systems into 32KB of memory are long gone. Second, the compilers themselves have a great deal of intelligence built into them these days, to help generate the most optimized code possible.

Binary

Computers use binary to represent everything. That means that whatever you store in a computer must be expressed as a binary pattern of ones and zeros. Take a simple integer, 27. In binary code, this number is actually 11011, each digit referring to a power of two. The diagram in Figure 3-14 shows how you represent 27 in the more familiar base-10 format, and then in binary.

10^7	10^6	10^5	10^4	10^3	10^2	10^1	10^0
10,000,000	1,000,000	100,000	10,000	1,000	100	10	1
0	0	0	0	0	0	2	7

In base-10, each digit represents a power of 10. To find what number the "pattern of base-10 digits" represents, you multiply the relevant number by the power of 10 that the digit represents and add the results.

$$2 \times 10 + 7 \times 1 = 27$$

2^7	2^6	2^5	2^4	2^3	2^2	2^1	2^0
128	64	32	16	8	4	2	1
0	0	0	1	1	0	1	1

In base-2, or binary, each digit represents a power of two. To find what number the "pattern of binary" represents, you multiply the relevant number by the power of two that the digit represents and add the results.

$$1 \times 16 + 1 \times 8 + 1 \times 2 + 1 \times 1 = 27$$

Figure 3-14

Although this may appear to be a bit obscure, look what's happening. In base-10, the decimal system that you're familiar with, each digit fits into a *slot*. This slot represents a power of 10 — the first representing 10 to the power zero, the second 10 to the power one, and so on. If you want to know what number the pattern represents, you take each slot in turn, multiply it by the value it represents, and add the results.

The same applies to binary — it's just that you're not familiar with dealing with base-2. To convert the number back to base-10, you take the digit in each slot in turn and multiply that power of *two* by the number that the slot represents (zero or one). Add all of the results together and you get the number.

Bits and Bytes

In computer terms, a binary slot is called a *bit*. It is the smallest possible unit of information, the answer to a single yes/no question, represented by a part of the computer's circuitry that either has electricity flowing in it or not. The reason why there are eight slots/bits on the diagram in Figure 3-14 is that there are eight bits in a *byte*. A byte is the unit of measurement that you use when talking about computer memory.

A *kilobyte* or KB is 1,024 bytes. You use 1,024 rather than 1,000 because 1,024 is the 10th power of 2, so as far as the computer is concerned it's a round number. Computers don't tend to think of things in terms of 10s like you do, so 1,024 is more natural to a computer than 1,000 is.

Likewise, a *megabyte* is 1,024 kilobytes, or 1,048,576 bytes. Again, that is another round number because this is the 20th power of 2. A *gigabyte* is 1,024 megabytes, or 1,073,741,824 bytes. (Again, think 2 to the power of 30 and you're on the right track.) Finally, a *terabyte* is 2 to the 40th power, and a *petabyte* is 2 to the 50th power.

So what's the point of all this? Well, having an understanding of how computers store variables helps you design your programs better. Suppose your computer has 256MB of memory. That's 262,144KB or 268,435,456 bytes or (multiply by 8) 2,147,483,648 bits. As you write your software, you have to make the best possible use of this available memory.

Representing Values

Most desktop computers in use today are 32-bit, which means that they're optimized for dealing with integer values that are 32 bits in length. The number you just saw in the example was an 8-bit number. With an 8-bit number, the largest value you can store is:

```
1x128 + 1x64 + 1x32 + 1x16 + 1x8 + 1x4 + 1x2 + 1x1 = 255
```

A 32-bit number can represent any value between –2,147,483,648 and 2,147,483,647. Now, if you define a variable like this:

```
Dim intNumber As Integer
```

you want to store an integer. In response to this, .NET will allocate a 32-bit block of memory in which you can store any number between 0 and 2,147,483,647. Also, remember you have only a finite amount of memory, and on your 256MB computer; you can store only a maximum of 67,108,864 long numbers. Sounds like a lot, but remember that memory is for sharing. You shouldn't write software that deliberately tries to use as much memory as possible. Be frugal!

You also defined variables that were double-precision floating-point numbers, like this:

```
Dim dblNumber As Double
```

To represent a double-precision floating point number, you need 64 bits of memory. That means you can store only a maximum of 33,554,432 double-precision floating-point numbers.

Single-precision floating-point numbers take up 32 bits of memory — in other words half as much as a double-precision number and the same as an integer value.

If you do define an integer, whether you store 1, 3, 249, or 2,147,483,647, you're always using exactly the same amount of memory, 32 bits. The size of the number has no bearing on the amount of memory required to store it. This might seem incredibly wasteful, but the computer relies on numbers of the same type taking the same amount of storage. Without this, it would be unable to work at a decent speed.

Now look at how you define a string:

```
Dim strResults As String
strResults = "Hello World!"
```

Unlike integers and doubles, strings do not have a fixed length. Each character in the string takes up two bytes, or 16 bits. So, to represent this 12-character string, you need 24 bytes, or 192 bits. That means that your computer is able to store only a little over two million strings of that length. Obviously, if the string is twice as long, you can hold half as many, and so on.

A common mistake that new programmers make is not taking into consideration the impact the data type has on storage. If you have a variable that's supposed to hold a string, and you try to hold a numeric value in it, like this:

```
Dim strData As String
strData = "65536"
```

you're using 10 bytes (or 80 bits) to store it. That's less efficient than storing the value in an `Integer` data type. To store this numerical value in a string, each character in the string has to be converted into a numerical representation. This is done according to something called *Unicode*, which is a standard way of defining the way computers store characters. Each character has a unique number between 0 and 65,535, and it's this value that is stored in each byte allocated to the string.

Here are the Unicode codes for each character in the string:

❑ **6:** Unicode 54, binary 0000000000110110

❑ **5:** Unicode 53, binary 0000000000110101

❑ **5:** Unicode 53, binary 0000000000110101

❑ **3:** Unicode 51, binary 0000000000110011

❑ **6:** Unicode 54, binary 0000000000110110

Each character requires 16 bits, so to store a 5-digit number in a string requires 80 bits — five 16 bit numbers. What you should do is this:

```
Dim intNumber As Integer
intNumber = 65536
```

This stores the value as a single number binary pattern. An Integer uses 32 bits, so the binary representation will be 00000000000000010000000000000000, far smaller than the space needed to store it as a string.

Converting Values

Although strings seem natural to us, they're unnatural to a computer. A computer wants to take two numbers and perform some simple mathematical operation on them. However, a computer can perform such a vast number of these simple operations each second that you, as humans, get the results you want.

Let's imagine that a computer wants to add 1 to the value 27. You already know that you can represent 27 in binary as 11011. Figure 3-15 shows what happens when you want to add 1 to the value 27.

As you can see, binary math is no different from decimal (base-10) math. If you try to add one to the first bit, it won't fit, so you revert it to zero and carry the one to the next bit. The same happens, and you carry the one to the third bit. At this point, you've finished, and if you add up the value you get 28, as intended.

2^7	2^6	2^5	2^4	2^3	2^2	2^1	2^0
128	64	32	16	8	4	2	1
0	0	0	1	1	0	1	1

$$1 \times 16 + 1 \times 8 + 1 \times 2 + 1 \times 1 = 27$$

2^7	2^6	2^5	2^4	2^3	2^2	2^1	2^0
128	64	32	16	8	4	2	1
0	0	0	1	1	1	0	0

← add 1

carry 1 carry 1

Just like the math you're familiar with, if you hit the "ceiling" value for the base (in this case "2"), you set the digit to "0" and carry "1".

$$1 \times 16 + 1 \times 8 + 1 \times 4 = 28$$

Figure 3-15

Any value that you have in your program ultimately has to be converted to simple numbers for the computer to do anything with them. To make the program run more efficiently, you have to keep the number of conversions to a minimum. Here's an example:

```
Dim strResults As String
strResults = "27"
strResults = strResults + 1
MessageBox.Show(strResults)
```

Let's look at what's happening:

1. You create a string variable called `strResults`.

2. You assign the value `27` to that string. This uses 4 bytes of memory.

3. To add `1` to the value, the computer has to convert `27` to an internal, hidden `Integer` variable that contains the value `27`. This uses an additional 4 bytes of memory, taking the total to 8. However, more importantly, this conversion takes time!

4. When the string is converted to an integer, `1` is added to it.

5. The new value then has to be converted into a string.

6. The string containing the new value is displayed on the screen.

To write an efficient program, you don't want to be constantly converting variables between different types. You want to perform the conversion only when it's absolutely necessary.

Here's some more code that has the same effect:

```
Dim intNumber As Integer
intNumber = 27
intNumber += 1
MessageBox.Show(intNumber.ToString)
```

1. You create an integer variable called `intNumber`.

2. You assign the value `27` to the variable.

3. You add `1` to the variable.

4. You convert the variable to a string and display it on the screen.

In this case, you have to do only one conversion, and it's a logical one; use the `ToString` method on the `Integer` data type. `MessageBox.Show` works in terms of strings and characters, so that's what it's most comfortable with.

What you have done is cut the conversions from two (string to integer, integer to string) down to one. This will make your program run more efficiently and use less memory. Again, it's a small improvement, but imagine this improvement occurring hundreds of thousands of times each minute — you'll get an improvement in the performance of the system as a whole.

> It is absolutely vital that you work with the correct data type for your needs. In simple applications like the ones you've created in this chapter, a performance penalty is not really noticeable. However, when you write more complex, sophisticated applications, you'll really want to optimize your code by using the right data type.

Methods

A *method* is a self-contained block of code that does something. Methods, also called *procedures,* are essential for two reasons. First, they break a program up and make it more understandable. Second, they promote code *reuse* — a topic you'll be spending most of your time on throughout the rest of this book.

As you know, when you write code you start with a high-level algorithm and keep refining the detail of that algorithm until you get the software code that expresses all of the algorithms up to and including the high-level one. A method describes a line in one of those algorithms, for example "open a file", "display text on screen", "print a document", and so on.

Knowing how to break up a program into methods is something that comes with experience. To add to the frustration, it's far easier to understand why you need to use methods when you're working on far more complex programs than the ones you've seen so far. In the rest of this section, we'll endeavor to show you how and why to use methods.

Why Use Methods?

In day-to-day use, you need to pass information to a method for it to produce the expected results. This might be a single integer value, a set of string values, or a combination of both. These are known as *input values*. However, some methods don't take input values, so having input values is not a requirement of a method. The method uses these input values and a combination of environmental information (for instance, facts about the current state of the program that the method knows about) to do something useful.

We say that when you give information to a method, you *pass* it data. You can also refer to that data as *parameters*. Finally, when you want to use a method, you *call* it.

> To summarize, you call a method, passing data in through parameters.

The reason for using methods is to promote this idea of code reuse. The principle behind using a method makes sense if you consider the program from a fairly high level. If you have an understanding of all the algorithms involved in a program, you can find commonality. If you need to do the same thing more than once, you should wrap it up into a method that you can reuse.

Imagine you have a program that comprises many algorithms. Some of those algorithms call for the area of a circle to be calculated. Because *some* of those algorithms need to know how to calculate the area of a circle, it's a good candidate for a method. You write code that knows how to find the area of a circle given its radius, *encapsulate* it (wrap it up) into a method, which you can reuse when you're coding the other algorithms. This means that you don't have to keep writing code that does the same thing — you do it once and reuse it as often as needed.

It might be the case that one algorithm needs to work out the area of a circle with 100 for its radius, and another needs to work out one with a radius of 200. By building the method in such a way that it takes the radius as a parameter, you can use the method from wherever you want.

> With Visual Basic 2008, you can define a method using the Sub keyword or using the Function keyword. Sub, short for subroutine, is used when the method doesn't return a value, as mentioned in Chapter 1. Function is used when the method returns a value.

Methods You've Already Seen

The good news is that you've been using methods already. Consider the following code that you wrote at the beginning of this chapter:

```
Private Sub btnAdd_Click(ByVal sender As System.Object, _
    ByVal e As System.EventArgs) Handles btnAdd.Click

        'Define a variable for intNumber
        Dim intNumber As Integer

        'Set the initial value
        intNumber = 27

        'Add 1 to the value of intNumber
        intNumber = intNumber + 1

        'Display the new value of intNumber
        MessageBox.Show("Value of intNumber + 1 = " & intNumber.ToString, _
            "Variables")
End Sub
```

That code is a method — it's a self-contained block of code that does something. In this case, it adds 1 to the value of `intNumber` and displays the result in a message box.

This method does not return a value (that is, it's a subroutine, so it starts with the `Sub` keyword and ends with the `End Sub` statement). Anything between these two statements is the code assigned to the method. Let's take a look at how the method is defined (this code was automatically created by Visual Basic 2008):

```
Private Sub btnAdd_Click(ByVal sender As System.Object, _
    ByVal e As System.EventArgs) Handles btnAdd.Click
```

1. First of all, you have the word `Private`. The meaning of this keyword is discussed in later chapters. For now, think of it as ensuring that this method cannot be called up by anything other than the user clicking the Add button.

2. Second, you have the keyword `Sub` to tell Visual Basic 2008 that you want to define a subroutine.

3. Third, you have `btnAdd_Click`. This is the name of the subroutine.

4. Fourth, you have `ByVal sender As System.Object, ByVal e As System.EventArgs`. This tells Visual Basic 2008 that the method takes two parameters — `sender` and e. We'll talk about this more later.

5. Finally, you have `Handles btnAdd.Click`. This tells Visual Basic 2008 that this method should be called whenever the `Click` event on the control `btnAdd` is fired.

In the next Try It Out, you take a look at how you can build a method that displays a message box and call the same method from three separate buttons.

Using Methods

1. Create a new Windows Forms Application project called **Three Buttons**.

2. Use the Toolbox to draw three buttons on the form.

3. Double-click the first button (Button1) to create a new `Click` event handler. Add the highlighted code:

```
Private Sub Button1_Click(ByVal sender As System.Object, _
    ByVal e As System.EventArgs) Handles Button1.Click

        'Call your method
        SayHello()
End Sub

Private Sub SayHello()
    'Display a message box
    MessageBox.Show("Hello World!", "Three Buttons")
End Sub
```

4. Save your project by clicking the Save All button on the toolbar.

5. Run the project and you'll see the form with three buttons appear. Click the topmost button and you'll see "Hello World!" displayed in a message box.

How It Works

As you know now, when you double-click a Button control in the Designer, a new method is automatically created:

```
Private Sub Button1_Click(ByVal sender As System.Object, _
    ByVal e As System.EventArgs) Handles Button1.Click

End Sub
```

The `Handles Button1.Click` statement at the end tells Visual Basic 2008 that this method should automatically be called when the `Click` event on the button is fired. As part of this, Visual Basic 2008 provides two parameters, which you don't have to worry about for now. Outside of this method, you've defined a new method:

```
Private Sub SayHello()
    'Display a message box
    MessageBox.Show("Hello World!", "Three Buttons")
End Sub
```

The new method is called `SayHello`. Anything that appears between the `Sub` and `End Sub` keywords is part of the method and when that method is called, the code is executed. In this case, you've asked it to display a message box.

So you know that when the button is clicked, Visual Basic 2008 will call the `Button1_Click` method. You then call the `SayHello` method. The upshot of all this is that when the button is clicked, the message box is displayed:

```
Private Sub Button1_Click(ByVal sender As System.Object, _
    ByVal e As System.EventArgs) Handles Button1.Click

    'Call your method
    SayHello()
End Sub
```

That should make the general premise behind methods a little clearer, but why did you need to break the code into a separate method to display the message box? You learn more about that in the next Try It Out.

Try It Out   Reusing the Method

1. If your project is still running, stop it.

2. Return to the Forms Designer, and double-click the second button and add the highlighted code to the new event handler:

```
Private Sub Button2_Click(ByVal sender As System.Object, _
    ByVal e As System.EventArgs) Handles Button2.Click

    'Call your method
    SayHello()
End Sub
```

3. Switch back to the Forms Designer and double-click the third button and add the highlighted code:

```
Private Sub Button3_Click(ByVal sender As System.Object, _
    ByVal e As System.EventArgs) Handles Button3.Click

    'Call your method
    SayHello()
End Sub
```

4. Now run the project. You'll notice that when you click each of the buttons, they all bring up the same message box.

5. Stop the project and find the `SayHello` method definition. Change the text to be displayed, like this:

```
Private Sub SayHello()
    'Display a message box
    MessageBox.Show("I have changed!", "Three Buttons")
End Sub
```

6. Run the project again and click each of the three buttons. You'll notice that the text displayed on the message boxes has changed.

How It Works

Each of the event handlers calls the same `SayHello()` method:

```
Private Sub Button1_Click(ByVal sender As System.Object, _
    ByVal e As System.EventArgs) Handles Button1.Click

    'Call your method
    SayHello()
End Sub

Private Sub Button2_Click(ByVal sender As System.Object, _
    ByVal e As System.EventArgs) Handles Button2.Click

    'Call your method
    SayHello()
End Sub

Private Sub Button3_Click(ByVal sender As System.Object, _
    ByVal e As System.EventArgs) Handles Button3.Click

    'Call your method
    SayHello()
End Sub
```

You'll also notice that the `Handles` keyword on each of the methods ties the method to a different control — Button1, Button2, or Button3.

What's really important (and clever) here is that when you change the way that `SayHello` works, the effect you see on each button is the same. This is a really important programming concept. You can centralize code in your application so that when you change it in once place, the effect is felt throughout the application. Likewise, this saves you from having to enter the same or very similar code repeatedly.

Building a Method

In the next Try It Out, you'll build a method that's capable of returning a value. Specifically, you'll build a method that can return the area of a circle if its radius is given. You can do this with the following algorithm:

1. Square the radius.
2. Multiply it by pi.

Try It Out   Building a Method

1. To try out this exercise, reuse the Three Buttons project and return to the Code Editor.

2. Add this code to define a new method (which will be a function, because it returns a value):

```
'CalculateAreaFromRadius - find the area of a circle
Private Function CalculateAreaFromRadius(ByVal radius As Double) As Double
    'Declare variables
    Dim dblRadiusSquared As Double
    Dim dblResult As Double

    'Square the radius
    dblRadiusSquared = radius * radius

    'Multiply it by pi
    dblResult = dblRadiusSquared * Math.PI

    'Return the result
    Return dblResult
End Function
```

3. Now delete the existing code from the Button1_Click event handler, and add the highlighted code:

```
Private Sub Button1_Click(ByVal sender As System.Object, _
    ByVal e As System.EventArgs) Handles Button1.Click

    'Declare variable
    Dim dblArea As Double

    'Calculate the area of a circle with a radius of 100
    dblArea = CalculateAreaFromRadius(100)

    'Display the results
    MessageBox.Show(dblArea.ToString, "Area of 100")
End Sub
```

4. Run the project and click Button1. You'll see results like the one shown in Figure 3-16:

Figure 3-16

How It Works

First, you build a separate method called `CalculateAreaFromRadius`. You do this by using the `Private Function ... End Function` block.

```
Private Function CalculateAreaFromRadius(ByVal radius As Double) As Double
...
End Function
```

Anything between `Private Function` and `End Function` is the *body* of the method and will be executed only when the method is called.

The `ByVal radius As Double` portion defines a parameter for the method. When a parameter is passed *by value*, as indicated here by the keyword `ByVal`, .NET in effect creates a new variable and stores the passed parameter information in it. Even if the method is called with a variable given for the parameter, the contents of that original variable are not modified by the method. In this case, you're telling .NET that you want to pass a parameter into the method called `radius`. In effect, this statement creates a variable called `radius`, just as if you had done this:

```
Dim radius As Double
```

In fact, there's a little more. The variable will be automatically set to the value passed through as a parameter, so if you pass `200` through as the value of the parameter, what you're effectively doing is this:

```
Dim radius As Double = 200
```

If you passed `999` as the value of the parameter, you'd have this:

```
Dim radius As Double = 999
```

Another way of passing a parameter is by reference, using the keyword `ByRef` *instead of* `ByVal`*. When a parameter is passed by reference, the parameter name used within the method body effectively becomes another name for the variable specified when the method is called, so that anything the method does that modifies the parameter value modifies the original variable value as well.*

The `As Double` sitting at the end of the method declaration tells Visual Basic 2008 that this method will return a double-precision floating-point number back to whoever called it:

```
Private Function CalculateAreaFromRadius(ByVal radius As Double) As Double
```

Now you can look at the method properly. First off, you know that to find the area of a circle you have this algorithm:

1. Get a number that represents the radius of a circle.

2. Square the number.

3. Multiply it by pi (π).

And that's precisely what you've done:

```
'Declare variables
Dim dblRadiusSquared As Double
Dim dblResult As Double

'Square the radius
dblRadiusSquared = radius * radius

'Multiply it by pi
dblResult = dblRadiusSquared * Math.PI
```

The `Math.PI` in the previous code is a constant defined in .NET that defines the value of pi (π) for us. After the last line, you need to return the result to whatever code called the method. This is done with this statement:

```
'Return the result
Return dblResult
```

The code you added in `Button1_Click` calls the method and tells the user the results:

```
'Declare variable
Dim dblArea As Double

'Calculate the area of a circle with a radius of 100
dblArea = CalculateAreaFromRadius(100)

'Display the results
MessageBox.Show(dblArea.ToString, "Area of 100")
```

The first thing to do is define a variable called `dblArea` that will contain the area of the circle. You set this variable to whatever value `CalculateAreaFromRadius` returns. Using parentheses at the end of a method name is how you send the parameters. In this case, you're passing just one parameter and you're passing the value 100.

After you call the method, you wait for the method to finish calculating the area. This area is returned from the method (the `Return` result line defined within `CalculateAreaFromRadius`) and stored in the variable `dblArea`. You can then display this on the screen in the usual way.

Choosing Method Names

The .NET Framework has a few standards for how things should be named. These conventions help developers move between languages — a topic discussed in Chapter 2. We recommend that whenever you create a method, you use *Pascal casing*. This is a practice in which the first letter in each word in the method is uppercase but nothing else is. This is merely a suggestion for best coding practices and is not a requirement of Visual Basic 2008. An example of this is as follows:

❑   `CalculateAreaFromRadius`

❑   `OpenXmlFile`

❑   `GetEnvironmentValue`

Note that even when an abbreviation is used (in this case, XML), it *isn't* written in uppercase. This alleviates confusion for developers, who may or may not know how something should be capitalized.

We recommend that you always write parameter names in *camel casing*. (If you've ever seen Java code, you'll be familiar with this.) To get camel casing, you do the same as Pascal casing, but you don't capitalize the very first letter:

❑ `myAccount`

❑ `customerDetails`

❑ `updatedDnsRecord`

Again, abbreviations (such as DNS) are not treated as a special case, so they appear as a mix of upper and lowercase letters, just like in Pascal casing.

> *The name* camel casing *comes from the fact that the identifier has a hump in the middle, for example,* `camelCasing`. *Pascal casing comes from the fact that the convention was invented for use with the programming language Pascal.*

In Chapter 2, you saw that .NET isn't tied to a particular language. Because some languages are *casesensitive* and others are not, it's important that you define standards to make life easier for programmers who may be coming from different programming language backgrounds.

The term *case-sensitive* means that the positions of uppercase and lowercase letters are important. In a case-sensitive language, `MYACCOUNT` is not the same as `myAccount`. However, Visual Basic 2008 is *not* a case-sensitive language, meaning that for all intents and purposes you can do whatever you like with respect to capitalization; in other words `MYACCOUNT` would be the same as `mYacCounT`.

> *Note that languages such as Java, C#, and C++ are case-sensitive.*

Scope

When introducing the concept of methods, we described them as *self-contained*. This has an important effect on the way that variables are used and defined in methods. Imagine you have these two methods, both of which define a variable called `strName`:

```
Private Sub DisplaySebastiansName()
    'Declare variable and set value
    Dim strName As String
    strName = "Sebastian Blackwood"

    'Display results
    MessageBox.Show(strName, "Scope Demo")
End Sub

Private Sub DisplayBalthazarsName()
    'Declare variable and set value
```

```
        Dim strName As String
        strName = "Balthazar Keech"

        'Display results
        MessageBox.Show(strName, "Scope Demo")
    End Sub
```

Even though both of these methods use a variable with the same name (`strName`), the self-contained feature of methods means that this is perfectly practicable and the variable names won't affect each other. Try it out next.

Try It Out   **Scope**

1.   Create a new Windows Forms Application project called **Scope Demo**.

2.   Add a Button control to the form and set its `Name` property **btnScope** and its `Text` property to **Scope**. Double-click the button and add the following highlighted code to the `Click` event handler and add the other two methods:

```
Private Sub btnScope_Click(ByVal sender As System.Object, _
    ByVal e As System.EventArgs) Handles btnScope.Click

    'Call a method
    DisplayBalthazarsName()
End Sub

Private Sub DisplaySebastiansName()
    'Declare variable and set value
    Dim strName As String
    strName = "Sebastian Blackwood"

    'Display results
    MessageBox.Show(strName, "Scope Demo")
End Sub

Private Sub DisplayBalthazarsName()
    'Declare variable and set value
    Dim strName As String
    strName = "Balthazar Keech"

    'Display results
    MessageBox.Show(strName, "Scope Demo")
End Sub
```

3.   Save your project by clicking the Save All button on the toolbar.

4.   Run the project and you'll see the message box displaying the name `Balthazar Keech` when you click the button.

How It Works

What this exercise illustrates is that even though you've used the same variable name in two separate places, the program still works as intended:

```
Private Sub DisplaySebastiansName()
    'Declare variable and set value
    Dim strName As String
    strName = "Sebastian Blackwood"

    'Display results
    MessageBox.Show(strName, "Scope Demo")
End Sub

Private Sub DisplayBalthazarsName()
    'Declare variable and set value
    Dim strName As String
    strName = "Balthazar Keech"

    'Display results
    MessageBox.Show(strName, "Scope Demo")
End Sub
```

When a method starts running, the variables that are defined within that method (in other words, between Sub and End Sub, or between Function and End Function) are given *local scope*. The *scope* defines which parts of the program can see the variable, and *local* specifically means *within the current method*.

The strName variable technically doesn't exist until the method starts running. At this point, .NET and Windows allocate memory to the variable so that it can be used in the code. First, you set the value and then you display the message box. Therefore, in this case as you're calling the method DisplayBalthazarsName, the variable is created the moment the method is called, you run the code in the method that alters the newly created version of strName, and when the method has finished, the variable is deleted.

You will see in Chapter 4 that scope can even be limited to loops within your subroutines and functions.

Summary

This chapter introduced the concept of writing software not just for Visual Basic 2008 but also for all programming languages. We started by introducing the concept of an algorithm — the underpinnings of all computer software. We then introduced the concept of variables, and looked closely at the most commonly used data types: Integer, Double, String, Date, and Boolean. You saw how you could use these data types to perform operations such as mathematical operations, concatenating strings, returning the length of a string, splitting text into substrings, retrieving the current date, and extracting date properties. You then looked at how variables are stored in the computer.

After this, you looked at methods — what they are, why you need them, how to create them, and how the variables you declare within your methods have local scope within that method and do not apply outside of it. We also described the difference between a function and a subroutine.

To summarize, you should know:

❑   What an algorithm is and how it applies to software development

❑   How to declare and use the most common types of variables

❑   How to use the most common string functions when working with the String data type

❑   How to use the Date data type and display dates and times so that they are automatically localized to the user's computer settings

❑   How to create and use simple methods

Exercises

1.   Create a Windows application with two button controls. In the Click event for the first button, declare two Integer variables and set their values to any number that you like. Perform any math operation on these variables and display the results in a message box.

In the Click event for the second button, declare two String variables and set their values to anything that you like. Perform a string concatenation on these variables and display the results in a message box.

2.   Create a Windows application with a text box and a button control. In the button's Click event, display three message boxes. The first message box should display the length of the string that was entered into the text box. The second message box should display the first half of the string, and the third message box should display the last half of the string.

Controlling the Flow

In Chapter 3, you learned about algorithms and their role in programming. In this chapter, you're going to look at how you can control the flow through your algorithms so that you can make decisions like, "If X is the case, go and do A; otherwise do B." This ability to make decisions is known as *branching*. You'll also see how you can repeat a section of code (a process known as *looping*) a specified number of times, or while a certain condition applies.

Specifically, you'll learn more about:

- ❏ The If statement
- ❏ Select Case
- ❏ For loops
- ❏ Do loops

Making Decisions

Algorithms often include decisions. It's this decision-making ability that makes computers do what they do so well. When you're writing code, you make two kinds of decisions. The first kind is used to find out what part of an algorithm you're currently working on or to cope with problems. For example, imagine you have a list of 10 people and need to write a piece of code to send an e-mail to each of them. To do this, after sending each e-mail, you ask, "Have I finished?" If so, you quit the algorithm; otherwise you get the next person in the list. As another example, you might need to open a file, so you ask, "Does the file exist?" You have to deal with both possible answers to that question.

The second kind of decision is used to perform a different part of the algorithm depending on one or more facts. Imagine you're going through your list of 10 people so that you can send an e-mail to those who own a computer but telephone those who don't. As you look at each person, you use the fact that the person does or doesn't own a computer to choose what you should do.

These decisions are all made in the same way, and it doesn't matter whether you have more of the first kind, more of the second kind, or whatever. Now, let's take a look at how to make a decision using the If statement.

The If Statement

The simplest way to make a decision in a Visual Basic 2008 program is to use the If . . . Then statement. You learn to use an If . . . Then statement in the following Try It Out exercise.

Try It Out   **A Simple If . . . Then Statement**

1. Create a Windows Forms Application project called **Simple If**. Add a Button control, set its Name property to **btnIf**, and set its Text property to **If**. Double-click the button and add the following highlighted code:

```
Private Sub btnIf_Click(ByVal sender As System.Object, _
    ByVal e As System.EventArgs) Handles btnIf.Click

        'Declare and set a variable
        Dim intNumber As Integer = 27

        'Here's where you make a decision,
        'and tell the user what happened
        If intNumber = 27 Then
            MessageBox.Show("'intNumber' is, indeed, 27!", "Simple If")
        End If

End Sub
```

2. Save your project and then run it. Click the If button and you'll see the message box shown in Figure 4-1.

Figure 4-1

How It Works

First you declare an Integer variable called intNumber and set its value to 27, all in the same line of code, as shown here:

```
        'Declare and set a variable
        Dim intNumber As Integer = 27
```

Then you use an If . . . Then statement to determine what you should do next. In this case, you say, "If intNumber is equal to 27...":

```
'Here's where you make a decision,
'and tell the user what happened
If intNumber = 27 Then
    MessageBox.Show("'intNumber' is, indeed, 27!", "Simple If")
End If
```

The code block that follows this will be executed only if intNumber equals 27. You end the code block with End If. Anything between If and End If is called only if the expression you're testing for is true.

So, as you walk through the code, you get to the If statement, and it's true. You drop into the code block that runs if the expression is true, and the text is displayed in a message box.

Notice that the code within the If . . . End If block is automatically indented for you. This is to increase readability so that you can tell what code will run in the event of the condition being true. It's also good to add some white space before the If . . . Then statement and after the End If statement to enhance readability further.

A simple If block like the previous one may also be written on one line, without an End If statement, for example:

```
If intNumber = 27 Then MessageBox.Show("'intNumber' is, indeed, 27!", "Simple If")
```

This works equally well — although you are limited to only one line of code within the If statement. So now you know what happens if your condition is true. But what happens if you fail the test and the result is false? You find out in the next Try It Out.

Failing the Test

1. Return to the Forms Designer for the Simple If program. Add another Button control to the form and set its Name property to **btnAnotherIf** and its Text property to **Another If**. Double-click the button and add the following highlighted code:

```
Private Sub btnAnotherIf_Click(ByVal sender As System.Object, _
    ByVal e As System.EventArgs) Handles btnAnotherIf.Click

    'Declare and set a variable
    Dim intNumber As Integer = 27

    'Here's where you make a decision,
    'and tell the user what happened
    If intNumber = 1000 Then
        MessageBox.Show("'intNumber' is, indeed, 1000!", "Simple If")
    End If
End Sub
```

2. Run your project and click the Another If button; nothing will happen.

How It Works

In this case, the question "Is intNumber equal to 1000?" comes out false. The code block executes only if the statement is true, so it's skipped. If the statement were true, the line between the If and End If lines would have executed. However, in this instance the statement was false, so the next line to be executed was the first line directly following the End If line (which is End Sub). In effect, the true code block is skipped.

The Else Statement

If you want to run one piece of code if the condition is true and another piece if the condition is false, you use the Else statement. Expand on the previous Try It Out to see how it works.

Try It Out **The Else Statement**

1. Return to the Code Editor in the Simple If project and modify the code in the btnAnotherIf_Click procedure so that it looks like this:

```
Private Sub btnAnotherIf_Click(ByVal sender As System.Object, _
    ByVal e As System.EventArgs) Handles btnAnotherIf.Click

    'Declare and set a variable
    Dim intNumber As Integer = 27

    'Here's where you make a decision,
    'and tell the user what happened
    If intNumber = 1000 Then
        MessageBox.Show("'intNumber' is, indeed, 1000!", "Simple If")
    Else
        MessageBox.Show("'intNumber' is not 1000!", "Simple If")
    End If
End Sub
```

2. Run the project and you'll see the message box shown in Figure 4-2.

Figure 4-2

How It Works

The code following the `Else` statement runs if the condition in the `If` statement is not met. In this case, the value of `intNumber` is 27, but the condition being tested for is `intNumber = 1000`, so the code after the `Else` statement is run:

```
Else
    MessageBox.Show("'intNumber' is not 1000!", "Simple If")
End If
```

Allowing Multiple Alternatives with ElseIf

If you want to test for more than one condition, you need to make use of the `ElseIf` statement. Now take your Simple If program as an example to see how you can test for the value of `intNumber` being 27 and 1000.

Try It Out **The ElseIf Statement**

1. Return to the Code Editor and change the code in the `btnAnotherIf_Click` procedure so that it looks like this:

```
Private Sub btnAnotherIf_Click(ByVal sender As System.Object, _
    ByVal e As System.EventArgs) Handles btnAnotherIf.Click

    'Declare and set a variable
    Dim intNumber As Integer = 27

    'Here's where you make a decision,
    'and tell the user what happened
    If intNumber = 1000 Then
        MessageBox.Show("'intNumber' is, indeed, 1000!", "Simple If")
    ElseIf intNumber = 27 Then
        MessageBox.Show("'intNumber' is 27!", "Simple If")
    Else
        MessageBox.Show("'intNumber' is neither 1000 nor 27!", "Simple If")
    End If
End Sub
```

2. Run the project and you'll see the message box shown in Figure 4-3.

Figure 4-3

How It Works

This time the code in the `ElseIf` statement ran because `intNumber` met the condition `intNumber = 27`. Note that you can still include the `Else` statement at the end to catch instances where `intNumber` is neither 27 nor 1000, but something else entirely:

```
ElseIf intNumber = 27 Then
    MessageBox.Show("'intNumber' is 27!", "Simple If")
Else
    MessageBox.Show("'intNumber' is neither 1000 nor 27!", "Simple If")
End If
```

You can add as many `ElseIf` statements as you need to test for conditions. However, bear in mind that each `ElseIf` statement is executed as Visual Basic 2008 attempts to discover whether the condition is true. This slows your program if you have a lot of conditions to be tested. If this is the case, you should try to put the statements in the order they are most likely to be executed, with the most common one at the top. Alternatively, you should use a `Select Case` block, which you will be looking at later in the chapter.

Nested If Statements

It's possible to nest an `If` statement inside another:

```
If intX = 3 Then
    MessageBox.Show("intX = 3")

    If intY = 6 Then
        MessageBox.Show("intY = 6")
    End If

End If
```

There's no real limit to how far you can nest your `If` statements. However, the more levels of nesting you have, the harder it is to follow what's happening in your code. So try to keep the nesting of `If` statements to a minimum.

Single-Line If Statement

The single-line form is typically used for short, simple tests, and it saves space in the text editor. However, it doesn't provide the structure and flexibility of the multiline form and is usually harder to read:

```
If intX = 3 Then MessageBox.Show("intX = 3") Else MessageBox.Show("intX is not 3")
```

You don't need an `End If` at the end of a single-line `If ... Then` statement.

Multiple statements can also be executed within a single line If . . . Then statement. All statements must be on the same line and must be separated by colons, as in the following example:

```
If intX = 3 Then MessageBox.Show("intX = 3") : intX = intX + 1 : Total += intX
```

Comparison Operators

You know how to check whether a particular variable is equal to some value and execute code if this is the case. In fact, If is far more flexible than this. You can ask questions such as these, all of which have yes/no answers.

- ❑   Is intNumber greater than 49?

- ❑   Is intNumber less than 49?

- ❑   Is intNumber greater than or equal to 49?

- ❑   Is intNumber less than or equal to 49?

- ❑   Is strName not equal to Ben?

When working with string values, most of the time you'll use the Equal To or Not Equal To operator. When working with numeric values (both integer and floating-point), you can use all of these arithmetic operators discussed in the previous chapter.

Using Not Equal To

You have not used Not Equal To yet, so test the Not Equal To operator with strings.

Try It Out   Using Not Equal To

1. Create a Windows Forms Application project called **If Demo**. Add a TextBox control and a Button control. Set the Name property for TextBox1 to **txtName** and the Text property to **Stephanie**. Set the Name property for Button1 to **btnCheck** and the Text property to **Check**.

2. Double-click the Button control to create its Click event handler. Add the highlighted code:

```
Private Sub btnCheck_Click(ByVal sender As System.Object, _
    ByVal e As System.EventArgs) Handles btnCheck.Click

        'Declare a variable and get the name from the text box
        Dim strName As String
        strName = txtName.Text

        'Is the name Wendy?
        If strName <> "Wendy" Then
            MessageBox.Show("The name is *not* Wendy.", "If Demo")
        End If
End Sub
```

3. Save your project and then run it. When the form is displayed, click the Check button and you will see a message box indicating that the name is not Wendy.

How It Works

The Not Equal To operator looks like this: <>. When the button is clicked, the first thing you do is to retrieve the name from the text box by looking at its Text property:

```
'Declare a variable and get the name from the text box
Dim strName As String
strName = txtName.Text
```

After you have the name, you use an If statement. This time, however, you use the Not Equal To operator rather than the Equal To operator. Also note that you are comparing two string values.

```
'Is the name Wendy?
If strName <> "Wendy" Then
    MessageBox.Show("The name is *not* Wendy.", "If Demo")
End If
```

The code between Then and End If executes only if the answer to the question asked in the If statement is True. You'll probably find this a bit of a heady principle, because the question you're asking is, "Is strName not equal to Wendy?" to which the answer is "Yes, the strName is *not* equal to Wendy." As the answer to this question is yes, or True, the code runs and the message box displays. However, if you enter Wendy into the text box and click Check, nothing happens, because the answer to the question is "No, the strName *is* equal to Wendy"; therefore you have a no, or False, answer.

If you try this, be sure to enter Wendy *with an uppercase* W *and with the rest of the letters in lowercase; otherwise the application won't work properly. You'll see why later.*

An alternative way of checking that something does not equal something else is to use the Not keyword. The condition in the If statement could have been written:

```
If Not strName = "Wendy" Then
```

Using the Numeric Operators

In this section, you take a look at the four other comparison operators you can use. These are all fairly basic, so you'll go through this quite fast.

Try It Out   **Using Less Than**

1. Return to the Forms Designer for the If Demo project. Add another TextBox control and set its Name property to **txtValue**. Add another Button control and set its Name property to **btnCheckNumbers** and its Text property to **Check Numbers**.

2. Double-click the Check Numbers button and add the following highlighted code to its Click event handler:

```
Private Sub btnCheckNumbers_Click(ByVal sender As System.Object, _
    ByVal e As System.EventArgs) Handles btnCheckNumbers.Click

    'Declare variable
    Dim intNumber As Integer

    Try
        'Get the number from the text box
        intNumber = CType(txtValue.Text, Integer)
    Catch
    End Try

    'Is intNumber less than 27?
    If intNumber < 27 Then
        MessageBox.Show("Is 'intNumber' less than 27? Yes!", "If Demo")
    Else
        MessageBox.Show("Is 'intNumber' less than 27? No!", "If Demo")
    End If
End Sub
```

3. Run the project. Enter a number into the text box and click the Check Numbers button. You'll be told whether the number entered is less than or greater than 27 as shown in Figure 4-4.

Figure 4-4

How It Works

First, you get the value back from the text box. However, there is a slight wrinkle. Because this is a text box, the end users are free to enter anything they like into it, and if a series of characters that cannot be converted into an integer is entered, the program will crash. Therefore, you add an *exception handler* to make sure that you always get a value back. Also, with the Option Strict option turned on, you'll need to convert the string value in the text box to an `Integer` data type using the `CType` function as you did in the last chapter. If the user enters something invalid, `intNumber` remains 0 (the default value), otherwise it will be whatever is entered:

```
'Declare variable
Dim intNumber As Integer

Try
    'Get the number from the text box
    intNumber = CType(txtValue.Text, Integer)
Catch
End Try
```

You'll be introduced to exception handling properly in Chapter 10. For now, you can safely ignore it!

The Less Than operator looks like this: <. Here, you test to check whether the number entered was less than 27, and if it is, you say so in a message box; otherwise you say No:

```
'Is intNumber less than 27?
If intNumber < 27 Then
    MessageBox.Show("Is 'intNumber' less than 27? Yes!", "If Demo")
Else
    MessageBox.Show("Is 'intNumber' less than 27? No!", "If Demo")
End If
```

Here's something interesting though. If you actually enter 27 into the text box and click the button, you'll see a message box that tells you `intNumber` is not less than 27. The `If` statement said No, and it's right; `intNumber` is actually equal to 27 and the cutoff point for this operator is anything up to *but not including* the value itself. You can get around this problem with a different operator, as you'll see in the next Try It Out.

Try It Out   **Using the Less Than Or Equal To Operator**

1. Return to the Code Editor and change the `If` statement in the `btnCheckNumbers_Click` event handler as shown here:

```
Try
    'Get the number from the text box
    intNumber = CType(txtValue.Text, Integer)
Catch
End Try
```

```
'Is intNumber less than or equal to 27?
If intNumber <= 27 Then
    MessageBox.Show("Is 'intNumber' less than or equal to 27? Yes!", _
        "If Demo")
Else
    MessageBox.Show("Is 'intNumber' less than or equal to 27? No!", _
        "If Demo")
End If
```

2. Now run the project and enter **27** into the text box. Click the Check Numbers button and you should see the results shown in Figure 4-5.

Figure 4-5

How It Works

The Less Than Or Equal To operator looks like this: <=. In this situation, you're extending the possible range of values up to and including the value you're checking. So, in this case when you enter 27, you get the answer, `Yes, n is less than or equal to 27`. This type of operator is known as an *inclusive operator*.

The final two operators look really similar to this, so let's look at them now.

Try It Out   Using Greater Than and Greater Than Or Equal To

1. Return to the Code Editor and add two additional `If` statements in the `btnCheckNumbers_Click` event handler as shown here:

```
'Is intNumber less than or equal to 27?
If intNumber <= 27 Then
    MessageBox.Show("Is 'intNumber' less than or equal to 27? Yes!", _
        "If Demo")
Else
    MessageBox.Show("Is 'intNumber' less than or equal to 27? No!", _
        "If Demo")
End If
```

```
        'Is intNumber greater than 27?
        If intNumber > 27 Then
            MessageBox.Show("Is 'intNumber' greater than 27? Yes!", _
                "If Demo")
        Else
            MessageBox.Show("Is 'intNumber' greater than 27? No!", _
                "If Demo")
        End If

        'Is intNumber greater than or equal to 27?
        If intNumber = 27 Then
            MessageBox.Show("Is 'intNumber' greater than or equal to 27? Yes!", _
                "If Demo")
        Else
            MessageBox.Show("Is 'intNumber' greater than or equal to 27? No!", _
                "If Demo")
        End If
    End Sub
```

2. Run the program. This time enter a value of **99** and click the Check Numbers button. You'll see three message boxes one after the other. The first message box will indicate that intNumber is not less than or equal to 27, while the second message box will indicate that intNumber is greater than 27. The final message box will indicate that intNumber is greater than or equal to 27.

How It Works

The Greater Than and Greater Than Or Equal To operators are basically the opposite of their Less Than counterparts. This time, you're asking, "Is intNumber greater than 27?" and, "Is intNumber greater than or equal to 27?" The results speak for themselves.

The And and Or Operators

What happens when you need your If statement to test more than one condition? For example, if you want to make sure that "intNumber is less than 27 *and* greater than 10"? Or, how about checking that strName is "Wendy" or "Stephanie"? You can combine operators used with an If statement with the And and Or operators, as you do in the next Try It Out.

Try It Out   **Using the Or Operator**

1. Create a new Windows Forms Application called **And Or Demo**.

2. In the Form Designer for Form1, add two TextBox controls and a Button control. Set the Name properties of the text boxes to **txtName1** and **txtName2** and the Name property of the button to **btnOrCheck**.

3. Set the `Text` property for txtName1 to **Wendy** and the `Text` property for txtName2 to **Stephanie**. Finally, set the `Text` property for btnOrCheck to **Or Check**. Your completed form should look similar to the one shown in Figure 4-6.

Figure 4-6

4. Double-click the Or Check button and add the following code to its `Click` event handler:

```
Private Sub btnOrCheck_Click(ByVal sender As System.Object, _
    ByVal e As System.EventArgs) Handles btnOrCheck.Click
```

```
    'Declare variables
    Dim strName1 As String, strName2 As String

    'Get the names
    strName1 = txtName1.Text
    strName2 = txtName2.Text

    'Is one of the names Wendy?
    If strName1 = "Wendy" Or strName2 = "Wendy" Then
        MessageBox.Show("One of the names is Wendy.", _
            "And Or Demo")
    Else
        MessageBox.Show("Neither of the names is Wendy.", _
            "And Or Demo")
    End If
End Sub
```

5. Run the project and click the button. You should see the results as shown in Figure 4-7.

Figure 4-7

6. Click OK to dismiss the message box dialog box and flip the names around so that the top one (txtName1) is **Stephanie** and the bottom one (txtName2) is **Wendy**. Click the button again and you'll see a message box indicating that one of the names is Wendy.

7. Now, click OK to dismiss the message box again and this time change the names so that neither of them is Wendy. Click the button and you should see a message box indicating that neither of the names is Wendy.

How It Works

The Or operator is a great way of building If statements that compare two different values in a single hit. In your Click event handler, the first thing you do is declare your variables and then retrieve both names and store them in variables strName1 and strName2:

```
'Declare variables
Dim strName1 As String, strName2 As String

'Get the names
strName1 = txtName1.Text
strName2 = txtName2.Text
```

You'll notice that you've defined two variables on the same line. This is perfectly legitimate coding practice, although it can sometimes make the code look congested. The variables are separated with commas; note that it's still important to use the As keyword to tell Visual Basic 2008 what data type each of the variables is.

Once you have both names, you use the Or operator to combine two separate If statements. The question you're asking here is, "Is strName1 equal to Wendy or is strName2 equal to Wendy?" The answer to this question (provided that one of the text boxes contains the name Wendy) is, "Yes, either strName1 is equal to Wendy or strName2 is equal to Wendy." Again, it's a yes/no or true/ false answer, even though the question is seemingly more complex:

```
'Is one of the names Wendy?
If strName1 = "Wendy" Or strName2 = "Wendy" Then
    MessageBox.Show("One of the names is Wendy.", _
        "And Or Demo")
Else
    MessageBox.Show("Neither of the names is Wendy.", _
        "And Or Demo")
End If
```

Using the And Operator

The And operator is conceptually similar to Or, except that both parts of the condition need to be satisfied, as you will see in the next Try It Out.

Try It Out   **Using the And Operator**

1.   Return to the Forms Designer in the And Or Demo project and add another Button control to
     the form. Set its Name property to **btnAndCheck** and its Text property to **And Check**.
     Double-click the button and add the following highlighted code to its Click event handler:

```
Private Sub btnAndCheck_Click(ByVal sender As System.Object, _
    ByVal e As System.EventArgs) Handles btnAndCheck.Click

        'Declare variables
        Dim strName1 As String, strName2 As String

        'Get the names
        strName1 = txtName1.Text
        strName2 = txtName2.Text

        'Are both names Wendy?
        If strName1 = "Wendy" And strName2 = "Wendy" Then
            MessageBox.Show("Both names are Wendy.", _
                "And Or Demo")
        Else
            MessageBox.Show("One of the names is not Wendy.", _
                "And Or Demo")
        End If
End Sub
```

2.   Run the program. Click the And Check button, and a message box tells you that one of the
     names is not Wendy.

3.   However, if you change both names so that they are both Wendy and click the button, you'll
     see the results shown in Figure 4-8.

Figure 4-8

How It Works

After you've retrieved both names from the text boxes, you compare them. In this case, you're asking the question, "Is strName1 equal to Wendy *and* is strName2 equal to Wendy?" In this case, both parts of the If statement must be satisfied in order for the "Both names are Wendy" message box to be displayed:

```
'Are both names Wendy?
If strName1 = "Wendy" And strName2 = "Wendy" Then
    MessageBox.Show("Both names are Wendy.", _
        "And Or Demo")
Else
    MessageBox.Show("One of the names is not Wendy.", _
        "And Or Demo")
End If
```

More on And and Or

You've seen And and Or used with strings. But they can be used with numeric values, like this:

```
If intX = 2 And intY = 2.3 Then
    MessageBox.Show("Hello, both of the conditions has been satisfied!")
End If
```

or

```
If intX = 2 Or intY = 2.3 Then
    MessageBox.Show("Hello, one of the conditions have been satisfied!")
End If
```

Also, in Visual Basic 2008, there's no realistic limit to the number of And operators or Or operators that you can include in a statement. It's perfectly possible to do this:

```
If intA = 1 And intB = 2 And intC = 3 And intD = 4 And intE = 5 And _
    intF = 6 And intG = 7 And intH = 1 And intI = 2 And intJ = 3 And _
    intK = 4 And intL = 5 And intM = 6 And intN = 7 And intO = 1 And _
    intP = 2 And intQ = 3 And intR = 4 And intS = 5 And intT = 6 And _
    intU = 7 And intV = 1 And intW = 2 And intX = 3 And intY = 4 And _
    intZ = 5 Then
    MessageBox.Show("That's quite an If statement!")
End If
```

... although why you'd want to do so is beyond us!

Finally, it's possible to use parentheses to group operators and look for a value within a range. For example, say you want to determine whether the value of intX is between 12 and 20 exclusive or between 22 and 25 exclusive. You can use the following If ... Then statement:

```
If (intX > 12 And intX < 20) Or (intX > 22 And intX < 25) Then
```

There are many other combinations of operators, far more than we have room to go into here. Rest assured that if you want to check for a condition, there is a combination to suit your needs.

String Comparison

When working with strings and If statements, you often run into the problem of uppercase and lowercase letters. A computer treats the characters "A" and "a" as separate entities, even though people consider them to be similar. This is known as *case sensitivity* — meaning that the case of the letters does matter when comparing strings. For example, if you run the following code, the message box would *not* be displayed.

```
Dim strName As String
strName = "Winston"
If strName = "WINSTON" Then
    MessageBox.Show("Aha! You are Winston.")
End If
```

Because WINSTON is not strictly speaking the same as Winston, this If statement will not return a message. However, in many cases you don't actually care about the case, so you have to find a way of comparing strings and ignoring the case of the characters. In the next Try It Out, you work with case-insensitive strings.

Try It Out   Using Case-Insensitive String Comparisons

1. Return to the Forms Designer in the And Or Demo project and add another TextBox and Button control to the form.

2. Set the Name property of the TextBox to **txtName3** and the Text property to **Bryan**. Set the Name property of the Button to **btnStringCompare** and the Text property to **String Compare**.

3. Double-click the String Compare button to open its Click event handler and add the highlighted code:

```
Private Sub btnStringCompare_Click(ByVal sender As System.Object, _
    ByVal e As System.EventArgs) Handles btnStringCompare.Click

    'Declare variable
    Dim strName As String

    'Get the name
    strName = txtName3.Text

    'Compare the name
    If String.Compare(strName, "BRYAN", True) = 0 Then
        MessageBox.Show("Hello, Bryan!", "And Or Demo")
    End If
End Sub
```

4. Run the project and click the button. You should see results like the ones shown in Figure 4-9.

Figure 4-9

5. Now, dismiss the message box and enter the name in the last text box as **BrYaN**, or some other combination of upper- and lowercase letters, and click the button. You should still see a message box that says "Hello, Bryan!"

6. However, if you enter a name that isn't Bryan, the message box will not be displayed when you click the button.

How It Works

After you get the name back from the text box, you have to use a function to compare the two values rather than use the basic Equal To operator. In this instance, you're using the Compare method on System.String and giving it the two strings you want to compare. The first string is the value stored in strName (which is the value entered into the text box), with the second string being "BRYAN". The last parameter that you supply is True, which tells Compare to perform a case-insensitive match; in other words, it should ignore the differences in case. If you had supplied False for this parameter, the comparison would have been case sensitive, in which case you would have been no better off than using the vanilla Equal To operator:

```
'Compare the name
If String.Compare(strName, "BRYAN", True) = 0 Then
    MessageBox.Show("Hello, Bryan!", "And Or Demo")
End If
```

String.Compare returns a fairly curious result. It actually returns an integer, rather than a True or False value. This is because String.Compare can be used to determine *how* two strings are different rather than just a straightforward, "Yes, they are" or, "No, they're not." If the method returns 0, the strings match. If the method returns a value that is not 0, the strings do not match.

> String.Compare *returns an indication of how different two strings are in order to help you build sorting algorithms.*

Select Case

On occasion, you need to make a set of similar decisions like this:

❏   Is the customer called Bryan? If so, do this.

❏   Is the customer called Stephanie? If so, do this.

❏   Is the customer called Cathy? If so, do this.

❏   Is the customer called Betty? If so, do this.

❏   Is the customer called Edward? If so, do this.

You can obviously do this with a set of `If ... Then` statements. In fact, it would look a little like this:

```
If Customer.Name = "Bryan" Then
       (do something)
ElseIf Customer.Name = "Stephanie" Then
       (do something)
ElseIf Customer.Name = "Cathy" Then
       (do something)
ElseIf Customer.Name = "Betty" Then
       (do something)
ElseIf Customer.Name = "Edward" Then
       (do something)
End If
```

What happens if you decide you want to check `Customer.FirstName` instead of `Customer.Name`? You'd have to change every `If` statement, which is a pain. Also, if `Customer.Name` turns out to be `"Edward"`, you still have to go through the other four `If` statements, which is very inefficient. In the next Try It Out, you learn a better way!

Try It Out   **Using Select Case**

1.   Create a new Windows Forms Application project. Call it **Select Demo**. Set the `Text` property of the form to **Select Case**.

2.   From the Toolbox, add a ListBox control to the form and set its `Name` property to **lstData**, its `Dock` property to **Fill**, and its `IntegralHeight` property to **False**.

3.   With lstData selected in the Form Designer, look at the Properties window and select the `Items` property. Click the ellipses button to the right of the property, and in the String Collection Editor that appears, add the five names on separate lines as shown in Figure 4-10.

Figure 4-10

4. Click OK to save the changes, and the names are added to your list box.

5. Now double-click lstData to create a new `SelectedIndexChanged` event handler and add the highlighted code:

```
Private Sub lstData_SelectedIndexChanged(ByVal sender As System.Object, _
    ByVal e As System.EventArgs) Handles lstData.SelectedIndexChanged

    'Declare variables
    Dim strName As String
    Dim strFavoriteColor As String

    'Get the selected name
    strName = lstData.Items(lstData.SelectedIndex).ToString

    'Use a Select Case statement to get the favorite color
    'of the selected name
    Select Case strName
        Case "Bryan"
            strFavoriteColor = "Madras Yellow"

        Case "Stephanie"
            strFavoriteColor = "Sea Blue"

        Case "Cathy"
            strFavoriteColor = "Morning Mist"

        Case "Betty"
            strFavoriteColor = "Passionate Purple"

        Case "Edward"
            strFavoriteColor = "Battleship Gray"
    End Select

    'Display the favorite color of the selected name
    MessageBox.Show(strName & "'s favorite color is " & strFavoriteColor, _
        "Select Demo")
End Sub
```

6. Save your project and then run it. Whenever you click one of the names, a message box will appear as shown in Figure 4-11.

Figure 4-11

How It Works

The first thing you need to do in the `SelectedIndexChanged` event handler is declare your variables and work out which name was selected. You do this by finding the item in the list that matches the current value of the `SelectedIndex` property. The `Items` collection of the `ListBox` class returns an `Object` data type so you use the `ToString` method to convert the object to a `String` data type for the `strName` variable:

```
'Declare variables
Dim strName As String
Dim strFavoriteColor As String

'Get the selected name
strName = lstData.Items(lstData.SelectedIndex).ToString
```

When you have that, you start a `Select Case...End Select` block. To do this, you need to supply the variable that you're matching against; in this case, you're using the name that was selected in the list.

Inside the `Select Case...End Select` block, you define separate `Case` statements for each condition to be checked against. In this example, you have five, and each one is set to respond to a different name. If a match can be found, Visual Basic 2008 executes the code immediately following the relevant `Case` statement.

For example, if you clicked Betty, the message box would display Passionate Purple as her favorite color, because Visual Basic 2008 would execute the line, `strFavoriteColor = "Passionate Purple"`. If you clicked Stephanie, the message box would display Sea Blue as her favorite color, because Visual Basic 2008 would execute `strFavoriteColor = "Sea Blue"`.

```
'Use a Select Case statement to get the favorite color
'of the selected name
Select Case strName
    Case "Bryan"
        strFavoriteColor = "Madras Yellow"

    Case "Stephanie"
        strFavoriteColor = "Sea Blue"
```

```
        Case "Cathy"
            strFavoriteColor = "Morning Mist"

        Case "Betty"
            strFavoriteColor = "Passionate Purple"

        Case "Edward"
            strFavoriteColor = "Battleship Gray"
    End Select
```

After the `Select Case...End Select` block, you display a message box:

```
        'Display the favorite color of the selected name
        MessageBox.Show(strName & "'s favorite color is " & strFavoriteColor, _
                        "Select Demo")
```

So how do you get out of a `Select Case...End Select` block? Well, as you're processing code that's beneath a `Case` statement, if you meet another `Case` statement, Visual Basic 2008 jumps out of the block and down to the line immediately following the block. Here's an illustration:

1. The user clicks Betty. The `SelectedIndexChanged` event is activated, and you store `"Betty"` in `strName`.

2. You reach the `Select Case` statement. This is set to compare the value in `strName` with one of the five supplied names.

3. Visual Basic 2008 finds a `Case` statement that satisfies the request and immediately moves to `strFavoriteColor = "Passionate Purple"`.

4. Visual Basic 2008 moves to the next line. This is another `Case` statement, and, seeing that you're already in one, you move to the first line after the `Select Case...End Select` block and display the message box.

`Select Case` is a powerful and easy-to-use technique for making a choice from several options. However, you must leave the block as soon as another `Case` statement is reached.

Case-Insensitive Select Case

Just like `If`, `Select Case` is case sensitive; prove it in the next Try It Out.

Try It Out   **Using Case-Sensitive Select Case**

1. Return to the Select Demo project and open the Forms Designer. Locate the `Items` property for the list box and open the String Collection Editor again.

2. Change all the names so that they appear in all uppercase letters as shown in Figure 4-12.

Figure 4-12

3. Click OK to save your changes and run the project. You'll notice that when you click a name, the message box doesn't specify a favorite color as shown in Figure 4-13.

Figure 4-13

How It Works

`Select Case` performs a case-sensitive match, just like `If`. This means that if you provide the name `CATHY` or `BETTY` to the statement, there won't be a corresponding `Case` statement because you're trying to say:

```
If "CATHY" = "Cathy"
```

or

```
If "BETTY" = "Betty"
```

Earlier in this chapter, you took a look at how you can use the `String.Compare` method to perform case-insensitive comparisons with `If` statements. With `Select Case`, you can't use this method, so if you want to be insensitive towards case, you need to employ a different technique — the one you learn in the next Try It Out.

Try It Out   Case-Insensitive Select Case

1. Return to the Select Demo project and open the Code Editor for Form1 and make these changes to the event handler for `SelectedIndexChanged`. Pay special attention to the `Case` statements — the name that you're trying to match *must* be supplied in all lowercase letters:

```
Private Sub lstData_SelectedIndexChanged(ByVal sender As System.Object, _
    ByVal e As System.EventArgs) Handles lstData.SelectedIndexChanged

    'Declare variables
    Dim strName As String
    Dim strFavoriteColor As String

    'Get the selected name
    strName = lstData.Items(lstData.SelectedIndex).ToString

    'Use a Select Case statement to get the favorite color
    'of the selected name
    Select Case strName.ToLower
        Case "bryan"
            strFavoriteColor = "Madras Yellow"

        Case "stephanie"
            strFavoriteColor = "Sea Blue"

        Case "cathy"
            strFavoriteColor = "Morning Mist"

        Case "betty"
            strFavoriteColor = "Passionate Purple"

        Case "edward"
            strFavoriteColor = "Battleship Gray"
    End Select

    'Display the favorite color of the selected name
    MessageBox.Show(strName & "'s favorite color is " & strFavoriteColor, _
        "Select Demo")
End Sub
```

2. Run the project and try selecting a name again. This time you will see that the message box includes the favorite color of the person you clicked as shown in Figure 4-14.

Figure 4-14

How It Works

To make the selection case insensitive, you have to convert the `strName` variable into all lowercase letters. This is done using the `ToLower` method:

```
Select Case strName.ToLower
```

This means that whatever string you're given (whether it's `"BETTY"` or `"Betty"`) you always convert it to all lowercase (`"betty"`). However, when you do this, you have to make sure that you're comparing apples to apples (and not to Apples), which is why you had to convert the values you're checking against in the `Case` statements to all lowercase too. Therefore, if you are given `"BETTY"`, you convert this to `"betty"`, and then try to find the `Case` that matches `"betty"`:

```
        Case "bryan"
            strFavoriteColor = "Madras Yellow"

        Case "stephanie"
            strFavoriteColor = "Sea Blue"

        Case "cathy"
            strFavoriteColor = "Morning Mist"

        Case "betty"
            strFavoriteColor = "Passionate Purple"

        Case "edward"
            strFavoriteColor = "Battleship Gray"
    End Select
```

Finally, once you have the favorite color, you display a message box as usual.

You could have done the opposite of this and converted all the names to uppercase and used `strName.ToUpper` *instead of* `strName.ToLower`.

Multiple Selections

You're not limited to matching one value inside a `Select Case...End Select` block. You can also match multiple items. In the next Try It Out, you'll modify the application so that you also report the sex of whoever you click on.

Multiple Selections

1. Return to the Select Demo project, open the Code Editor for Form1, and add the code in the `SelectedIndexChanged` handler as highlighted here:

    ```
    'Display the favorite color of the selected name
    MessageBox.Show(strName & "'s favorite color is " & strFavoriteColor, _
        "Select Demo")

    'Use a Select Case statement to display a person's gender
    Select Case strName.ToLower
        Case "bryan", "edward"
            MessageBox.Show("This person's gender is male.", "Select Demo")
        Case "stephanie", "cathy", "betty"
            MessageBox.Show("This person's gender is female.", "Select Demo")
    End Select
    End Sub
    ```

2. Run the project and click one of the female names. You will see results as shown in Figure 4-15 after the message box indicating the person's favorite color.

Figure 4-15

How It Works

The code you use to get back the name and initialize the `Select Case` block remains the same. However, in each `Case` statement you can provide a list of possible values separated with commas. In the first one, you look for `bryan` *or* `edward`. If either of these matches, you run the code under the `Case` statement:

```
    Case "bryan", "edward"
        MessageBox.Show("This person's gender is male.", "Select Demo")
```

In the second one, you look for `stephanie` *or* `cathy` *or* `betty`. If any of these three matches, you again run the code under the `Case` statement:

```
Case "stephanie", "cathy", "betty"
    MessageBox.Show("This person's gender is female.", "Select Demo")
```

It's important to realize that these are all *or* matches. You're saying "one *or* the other," not "one *and* the other."

The Case Else Statement

So what happens if none of the `Case` statements that you've included is matched? You saw this before when demonstrating the case-sensitive nature of `Select Case`. In the next Try It Out, you see it with the `Case Else` statement.

Try It Out   **Using Case Else**

1. Return to the Forms Designer, locate the `Items` property for the list box, and open the String Collection Editor again. Add another name in all uppercase letters to the collection and then click the OK button.

2. In the `lstData_SelectedIndexChanged` event handler, add the highlighted code:
    ```
    'Use a Select Case statement to display a person's gender
    Select Case strName.ToLower
        Case "bryan", "edward"
            MessageBox.Show("This person's gender is male.", "Select Demo")
        Case "stephanie", "cathy", "betty"
            MessageBox.Show("This person's gender is female.", "Select Demo")
        Case Else
            MessageBox.Show("I don't know this person's gender.", _
                "Select Demo")
    End Select
    End Sub
    ```

3. Run the project and click the last name that you just added, and you will see results similar to those shown in Figure 4-16.

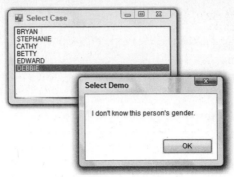

Figure 4-16

How It Works

The `Case Else` statement is used if none of the other supplied `Case` statements match what you're looking for. There isn't a `Case "debbie"` defined within the block, so you default to using whatever is underneath the `Case Else` statement. In this instance, you display a message box indicating that you do not know the gender of the person who's been selected.

Different Data Types with Select Case

In this chapter, you used `Select Case` with variables of type `String`. However, you can use `Select Case` with all basic data types in Visual Basic 2008, such as `Integer`, `Double`, and `Boolean`.

In day-to-day work, the most common types of `Select Case` are based on `String` and `Integer` data types. However, as a general rule, if a data type can be used in an `If` statement with the Equals (=) operator, it will work with `Select Case`.

Loops

When writing computer software, you often need to perform the same task several times to get the effect you want. For example, you might need to create a telephone bill for *all* customers, or read in 10 files from your computer's disk.

To accomplish this, you use a *loop*, and in this section, you'll take a look at the two main types of loops available in Visual Basic 2008:

❑   **For loops** — These loops occur a certain number of times (for example, exactly 10 times).

❑   **Do loops** — These loops keep running until a certain condition is reached (for example, until all of the data is processed).

The For . . . Next Loop

The simplest loop to understand is the For . . . Next loop, which you learn to build in the next Try It Out.

1. Create a new Windows Forms Application project called **Loops**.

2. Add a ListBox and a Button control to the form.

3. Change the Name property of the list box to **lstData** and its IntegralHeight property to False.

4. Change the Name property of the button to **btnForNextLoop**. Also, set its Text property to **For Next Loop**. You'll be adding more buttons later so make this button a little wider as shown in Figure 4-17.

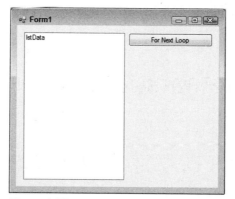

Figure 4-17

5. Double-click the button to create its Click event handler and add the highlighted code:

```
Private Sub btnForNextLoop_Click(ByVal sender As System.Object, _
    ByVal e As System.EventArgs) Handles btnForNextLoop.Click

        'Declare variable
        Dim intCount As Integer

        'Clear the list
        ClearList()

        'Perform a loop
        For intCount = 1 To 5
            'Add the item to the list
            lstData.Items.Add("I'm item " & intCount.ToString & _
                " in the list!")
        Next
    End Sub
```

6. Now create the following method:

```
Private Sub ClearList()
    'Clear the list
    lstData.Items.Clear()
End Sub
```

7. Save and run the project and then click the For Next Loop button. You should see results like those in Figure 4-18.

Figure 4-18

How It Works

First, inside the `Click` event handler, you define a variable:

```
'Declare variable
Dim intCount As Integer
```

Next you clear the list box by calling the `ClearList` method. Although the list is empty at this point, you'll be adding more buttons to this project in the following Try It Out exercises and may want to compare the results of the each of the buttons.

```
'Clear the list
ClearList()
```

Then you start the loop by using the `For` keyword. This tells Visual Basic 2008 that you want to create a loop. Everything that follows the `For` keyword is used to define how the loop should act. In this case, you're giving it the variable you just created and then telling it to count *from* 1 *to* 5:

```
'Perform a loop
For intCount = 1 To 5
```

The variable that you give the loop (in this case, intCount) is known as the *control variable*. When you first enter the loop, Visual Basic 2008 sets the control variable to the initial count value — in this case, 1. After the loop starts, Visual Basic 2008 moves to the first line within the For loop — in this case, the line that adds a string to the list box:

```
'Add the item to the list
lstData.Items.Add("I'm item " & intCount.ToString & _
    " in the list!")
```

This time, this line of code adds I'm item 1 in the list! to the list box. Visual Basic 2008 then hits the Next statement, and that's where things start to get interesting:

```
Next
```

When the Next statement is executed, Visual Basic 2008 increments the control variable by one. The first time Next is executed, the value in intCount changes from 1 to 2. Providing that the value of the control variable is less than or equal to the "stop" value (in this case, 5), Visual Basic 2008 moves back to the first line after the For statement, in this case:

```
'Add the item to the list
lstData.Items.Add("I'm item " & intCount.ToString & _
    " in the list!")
```

This time, this line of code adds I'm item 2 in the list! to the list box. Again, after this line is executed, you run the Next statement. The value of intCount is now incremented from 2 to 3 and, because 3 is less than or equal to 5, you move back to the line that adds the item to the list. This happens until intCount is incremented from 5 to 6. As 6 is greater than the stop value for the loop, the loop stops.

> When you're talking about loops, you tend to use the term iteration. *One iteration includes one movement from the* For *statement to the* Next *statement. Your loop has five iterations.*

The method you define contains only one line of code but its reuse becomes apparent in the next Try It Out. This method merely clears the Items collection of the list box.

```
Private Sub ClearList()
    'Clear the list
    lstData.Items.Clear()
End Sub
```

Step

You don't have to start your loop at 1 — you can pick any value you like. You also don't have to increment the control value by 1 on each iteration — again, you can increment by any value you like. In the next Try It Out, you learn about the flexibility of the Step keyword.

Try It Out   **Using Step**

1. Return to the Forms Designer for the Loops project and add another Button control to your form. Set its `Name` property to **btnForNextLoopWithStep** and its `Text` property to **For Next Loop w/Step**.

2. Double-click the button and add the following highlighted code in the `Click` event handler:

```
Private Sub btnForNextLoopWithStep_Click(ByVal sender As System.Object, _
    ByVal e As System.EventArgs) Handles btnForNextLoopWithStep.Click

        'Clear the list
        ClearList()

        'Perform a loop
        For intCount As Integer = 4 To 62 Step 7
            'Add the item to the list
            lstData.Items.Add(intCount.ToString)
        Next
    End Sub
```

3. Run the project and click the For Next Loop w/Step button. You will see results like those in Figure 4-19.

Figure 4-19

How It Works

The magic in this example all happens with this statement:

```
'Perform a loop
For intCount As Integer = 4 To 62 Step 7
```

First, note that you didn't declare the `intCount` variable using a `Dim` statement. This has been done as part of the `For` statement and makes this variable local to this loop. Using the `As` keyword and the data type for the variable (in this case `Integer`), you have effectively declared an inline variable.

Next, instead of using 1 as the start value, you're using 4. This means that on the first iteration of the loop, `intCount` is set to 4, and you can see this by the fact that the first item added to the list is indeed 4.

Also, you've used the `Step` keyword to tell the loop to increment the control value by 7 on each iteration rather than by the default of 1. This is why, by the time you start running the second iteration of the loop, `intCount` is set to 11 and not 5.

Although you gave `For` a stop value of 62, the loop has actually stopped at 60 because the stop value is a *maximum*. After the ninth iteration, `intCount` is actually 67, which is more than 62, and so the loop stops.

Looping Backwards

By using a `Step` value that's less than 0 (or a negative number), you can make the loop go backwards rather than forward, as you see in the next Try It Out.

Try It Out   Looping Backwards

1. Return to the Forms Designer and add another Button control to your form and set its `Name` property to **btnBackwardsForNextLoop** and its `Text` property to **Backwards For Next Loop**.

2. Double-click the button and add the following highlighted code in the `Click` event handler:

```
Private Sub btnBackwardsForNextLoop_Click(ByVal sender As System.Object, _
    ByVal e As System.EventArgs) Handles btnBackwardsForNextLoop.Click

        'Clear the list
        ClearList()

        'Perform a loop
        For intCount As Integer = 10 To 1 Step -1
            'Add the item to the list
            lstData.Items.Add(intCount.ToString)
        Next
    End Sub
```

3. Run the project and click the Backwards for Next Loop button. You should see results like those shown in Figure 4-20.

Figure 4-20

How It Works

If you use a negative number, like −1, For tries to add −1 to the current control value. Adding a negative number has the effect of subtracting the number, so intCount goes from its start value of 10 to its new value of 9 and so on until the stop value is reached.

The For Each . . . Next Loop

In practical, day-to-day work, it's unlikely that you'll use For . . . Next loops as illustrated here. Because of way the .NET Framework typically works, you'll usually use a derivative of the For . . . Next loop called the For Each . . . Next loop.

In the algorithms you design, whenever a loop is necessary, you'll have a collection of things to work through, and usually this set is expressed as an *array*. For example, you might want to look through all of the files in a folder, looking for those that are over a particular size. When you ask the .NET Framework for a list of files, you are returned an array of strings, each string in that array describing a single file. In the next Try It Out, you'll modify your Loops application so that it returns a list of folders contained at the root of your C drive.

Try It Out   **For Each Loop**

1. Return to the Forms Designer, add another Button control to your form, and set its Name property to **btnForEachLoop** and its Text property to **For Each Loop**.

2. Double-click the button and add the following highlighted code to the Click event handler:

```
Private Sub btnForEachLoop_Click(ByVal sender As System.Object, _
    ByVal e As System.EventArgs) Handles btnForEachLoop.Click

        'Clear the list
        ClearList()

        'List each folder at the root of your C drive
        For Each strFolder As String In _
            My.Computer.FileSystem.GetDirectories("C:\")

            'Add the item to the list
            lstData.Items.Add(strFolder)
        Next
    End Sub
```

3. Run the project and click the For Each Loop button. You should see a list of folders that are at the root of your C drive.

How It Works

The `My` namespace in the .NET Framework exposes several classes that make it easy for you to find the information that you'll use on a daily basis. In particular, the `Computer` class provides several other classes related to the computer that your program is running on. Since you want to find out about files and folders, you use the `FileSystem` class, which provides methods and properties for working with files and folders.

The `GetDirectories` method returns a *collection* of strings representing names of directories (or folders) on your computer. In this case, you use it to return a collection of names of folders in the root of the computer's C drive.

The principle with a `For Each...Next` loop is that for each iteration you'll be given the "thing" that you're supposed to be working with. You need to provide a source of things (in this case, a collection of strings representing folder names) and a control variable into which the current thing can be put. The `GetDirectories` method provides the collection, and the inline variable `strFolder` provides the control variable:

```
'List each folder at the root of your C drive
For Each strFolder As String In _
    My.Computer.FileSystem.GetDirectories("C:\")
Next
```

What this means is that on the first iteration, `strFolder` is equal to the first item in the string collection (in this case, `"C:\$Recycle.Bin"`). You then add that item to the list box:

```
'Add the item to the list
lstData.Items.Add(strFolder)
```

As with normal `For...Next` loops, for every iteration of the loop you're given a string containing a folder name, and you add that string to the list. When there are no more folders to be returned, execution automatically drops out of the loop.

The Do . . . Loop Loops

The other kind of loop you can use is one that keeps happening until a certain condition is met. These are known as `Do...Loop` loops, and there are a number of variations.

The first one you'll learn about is the `Do Until...Loop`. This kind of loop keeps going until something happens. For this Try It Out, you're going to use the random number generator that's built into the .NET Framework and create a loop that will keep generating random numbers *until* it produces the number 10. When you get the number 10, you'll stop the loop.

Try It Out   **Using the Do Until . . . Loop**

1. Return to the Forms Designer in the Loops project, add another Button control to your form, and set its Name property to **btnDoUntilLoop** and its Text property to **Do Until Loop**.

2. Double-click the button and add the following highlighted code to its Click event handler:

```
Private Sub btnDoUntilLoop_Click(ByVal sender As System.Object, _
    ByVal e As System.EventArgs) Handles btnDoUntilLoop.Click

        'Declare variables
        Dim objRandom As New Random
        Dim intRandomNumber As Integer = 0

        'Clear the list
        ClearList()

        'Process the loop until intRandomNumber = 10
        Do Until intRandomNumber = 10
            'Get a random number between 0 and 24
            intRandomNumber = objRandom.Next(25)
            'Add the number to the list
            lstData.Items.Add(intRandomNumber.ToString)
        Loop
End Sub
```

3. Run the project and click the Do Until Loop button. You'll see results similar to the results shown in Figure 4-21. Keep clicking the button. You'll see that the number of elements in the list is different each time.

Figure 4-21

How It Works

A Do Until...Loop keeps running the loop until the given condition is met. When you use this type of loop, there isn't a control variable *per se*; rather, you have to keep track of the current position of the loop yourself — let's see how you do this. You begin by declaring a variable (also known as an object) for the Random class, which provides methods for generating random numbers. This object has been prefixed with obj to specify that this is an object derived from a class. The next variable that you declare is the intRandomNumber, and this variable will be used to receive the random number generated by your objRandom object:

```
'Declare variables
Dim objRandom As New Random()
Dim intRandomNumber As Integer = 0
```

Then you clear the list of any previous items that may have been added:

```
'Clear the list
ClearList()
```

Next, you set up the loop and tell it that you want to keep running the loop until intRandomNumber is equal to 10:

```
'Process the loop until intRandomNumber = 10
Do Until intRandomNumber = 10
```

With each iteration of the loop, you ask the random number generator for a new random number and store it in intRandomNumber. This is done by calling the Next method of objRandom to get a random number. In this case, you've passed 25 as a parameter to Next, meaning that any number returned should be between 0 and 24 inclusive — that is, the number you supply must be one larger than the biggest number you ever want to get. In other words, the bounds that you ask for are noninclusive. You then add the number that you got to the list:

```
'Get a random number between 0 and 24
intRandomNumber = objRandom.Next(25)
'Add the number to the list
lstData.Items.Add(intRandomNumber.ToString)
Loop
```

The magic happens when you get to the Loop statement. At this point, Visual Basic 2008 returns not to the first line within the loop, but instead to the Do Until line. When execution returns to Do Until, the expression is evaluated. Provided it returns False, the execution pointer moves to the first line within the loop. However, if intRandomNumber is 10, the expression returns True, and instead of moving to the first line within the loop, you continue at the first line immediately after Loop. In effect, the loop is stopped.

Do While . . . Loop

The conceptual opposite of a `Do Until . . . Loop` is a `Do While . . . Loop`. This kind of loop keeps iterating while a particular condition is `True`. Let's see it in action.

Using the Do While . . . Loop

1. Return to the Forms Designer once again and add another Button control to your form and set its `Name` property to **btnDoWhileLoop** and its `Text` property to **Do While Loop**.

2. Double-click the button and add the following highlighted code to the `Click` event handler:

```vb
Private Sub btnDoWhileLoop_Click(ByVal sender As System.Object, _
    ByVal e As System.EventArgs) Handles btnDoWhileLoop.Click

        'Declare variables
        Dim objRandom As New Random
        Dim intRandomNumber As Integer = 0

        'Clear the list
        ClearList()

        'Process the loop while intRandomNumber < 15
        Do While intRandomNumber < 15
            'Get a random number between 0 and 24
            intRandomNumber = objRandom.Next(25)
            'Add the number to the list
            lstData.Items.Add(intRandomNumber.ToString)
        Loop
    End Sub
```

3. Run the project and click the Do While Loop button. You'll see something similar to the results shown in Figure 4-22.

Figure 4-22

Every time you press the button, the loop executes until the random number generator produces a number greater than or equal to 15.

How It Works

A Do While ... Loop keeps running so long as the given expression remains True. As soon as the expression becomes False, the loop quits. When you start the loop, you check to make sure that intRandomNumber is less than 15. If it is, the expression returns True, and you can run the code within the loop:

```
'Process the loop while intRandomNumber < 15
Do While intRandomNumber < 15
    'Get a random number between 0 and 24
    intRandomNumber = objRandom.Next(25)
    'Add the number to the list
    lstData.Items.Add(intRandomNumber.ToString)
Loop
```

Again, when you get to the Loop statement, Visual Basic 2008 moves back up to the Do While statement. When it gets there, it evaluates the expression again. If it's True, you run the code inside the loop once more. If it's False (because intRandomNumber is greater than or equal to 15), you continue with the first line after Loop, effectively quitting the loop.

Acceptable Expressions for a Do . . . Loop

You might be wondering what kind of expressions you can use with the two variations of Do ... Loop. If you can use it with an If statement, you can use it with a Do ... Loop. For example, you can write this:

```
Do While intX > 10 And intX < 100
```

or

```
Do Until (intX > 10 And intX < 100) Or intY = True
```

or

```
Do While String.Compare(strA, strB) > 0
```

In short, it's a pretty powerful loop!

Other Versions of the Do . . . Loop

It's possible to put the Until or While statements after Loop rather than after Do. Consider these two loops:

```
Do While intX < 3
    intX += 1
Loop
```

and

```
Do
    intX += 1
Loop While intX < 3
```

At first glance, it looks like the While intX < 3 has just been moved around. You might think that these two loops are equivalent — but there's a subtle difference. Suppose the value of intX is greater than 3 (4 say) as these two Do loops start. The first loop will not run at all. However, the second loop will run *once*. When the Loop While intX < 3 line is executed, the loop will be exited. This happens despite the condition saying that intX must be less than 3.

Now consider these two Do Until loops:

```
Do Until intX = 3
    intX += 1
Loop
```

and

```
Do
    intX += 1
Loop Until intX = 3
```

Again, although at first glance it looks like these two loops are equivalent, they're not and they behave slightly differently. Let's say that intX is 3 this time. The first loop isn't going to run, as intX already meets the exit condition for this loop. However, the second loop will run *once*. Then when you execute Loop Until intX = 3 the first time, intX is now 4. So you go back to the start of the loop and increment intX to 5, and so on. In fact, this is a classic example of an *infinite loop* (which is discussed later in this chapter) and will not stop.

> *When you use* Loop While *or* Loop Until, *you are saying that, no matter what, you want the loop to execute at least once. In general, it's best to stick with* Do While *and* Do Until, *rather than use* Loop While *and* Loop Until.

You may also come across a variation of Do While ... Loop called the While ... End While. This convention is a throwback to previous versions of Visual Basic, but old-school developers may still use it with .NET code, so it's important that you can recognize it. These two are equivalent, but you should use the first one.

```
Do While intX < 3
    intX += 1
Loop
```

and

```
While intX < 3
    intX += 1
End While
```

Nested Loops

You might need to start a loop even though you're already working through another loop. This is known as *nesting*, and is similar in theory to the nesting that you saw when you looked at `If` statements. In this Try It Out, you'll see how you can create and run through a loop, even though you're already working through another one.

Try It Out   Using Nested Loops

1. In the Forms Designer, add another Button control to your form and set its `Name` property to **btnNestedLoops** and its `Text` property to **Nested Loops**.

2. Double-click the button and add the following highlighted code to its `Click` event handler:

```vb
Private Sub btnNestedLoops_Click(ByVal sender As System.Object, _
    ByVal e As System.EventArgs) Handles btnNestedLoops.Click

        'Clear the list
        ClearList()

        'Process an outer loop
        For intOuterLoop As Integer = 1 To 2
            'Process a nested (inner) loop
            For intInnerLoop As Integer = 1 To 3
                lstData.Items.Add(intOuterLoop.ToString & _
                    ", " & intInnerLoop.ToString)
            Next
        Next
    End Sub
```

3. Run the program and click the Nested Loops button. You should see results that look like those shown in Figure 4-23.

Figure 4-23

How It Works

This code is really quite simple. Your first loop (outer loop) iterates `intOuterLoop` from 1 to 2, and the nested loop (inner loop) iterates `intInnerLoop` from 1 to 3. Within the nested loop, you have a line of code to display the current values of `intOuterLoop` and `intInnerLoop`:

```
'Process an outer loop
For intOuterLoop As Integer = 1 To 2
    'Process a nested (inner) loop
    For intInnerLoop As Integer = 1 To 3
        lstData.Items.Add(intOuterLoop.ToString & _
            ", " & intInnerLoop.ToString)
    Next
Next
```

Each `For` statement must be paired with a `Next` statement, and each `Next` statement that you reach always "belongs" to the last created `For` statement. In this case, the first `Next` statement you reach is for the `1 To 3` loop, which results in `intInnerLoop` being incremented. When the value of `intInnerLoop` gets to be 4, you exit the inner loop.

After you've quit the inner loop, you hit another `Next` statement. This statement belongs to the first `For` statement, so `intOuterLoop` is set to 2 and you move back to the first line within the first, outer loop — in this case, the other `For` statement. Once there, the inner loop starts once more. Although in this Try It Out you've seen two `For . . . Next` loops nested together, you can nest `Do . . . While` loops and even mix them, so you can have two `Do . . . Loop` statements nested inside a `For` loop and vice versa.

Quitting Early

Sometimes you don't want to see a loop through to its natural conclusion. For example, you might be looking through a list for something specific, and when you find it, there's no need to go through the remainder of the list.

In this Try It Out, you'll look through folders on your local drive, but this time, when you get to `c:\ Program Files`, you'll display a message and quit.

Try It Out   Quitting a Loop Early

1. Return to the Forms Designer and add another Button control to your form and set its `Name` property to **btnQuittingAForLoop** and its `Text` property to **Quitting a For Loop**.

2. Double-click the button and add the following highlighted code to the `Click` event handler:

```
Private Sub btnQuittingAForLoop_Click(ByVal sender As System.Object, _
    ByVal e As System.EventArgs) Handles btnQuittingAForLoop.Click
```

```
       'Clear the list
       ClearList()

       'List each folder at the root of your C drive
       For Each strFolder As String In _
           My.Computer.FileSystem.GetDirectories("C:\")

           'Add the item to the list
           lstData.Items.Add(strFolder)

           'Do you have the folder C:\Program Files?
           If String.Compare(strFolder, "c:\program files", True) = 0 Then

               'Tell the user
               MessageBox.Show("Found it, exiting the loop now.", "Loops")

               'Quit the loop early
               Exit For

           End If
       Next
   End Sub
```

3. Run the program and click the Quitting a For Loop button. You'll see something similar to the results shown in Figure 4-24.

Figure 4-24

How It Works

This time, with each iteration, you use the `String.Compare` method that was discussed earlier to check the name of the folder to see whether it matches `C:\Program Files`:

```
'Do you have the folder C:\Program Files?
If String.Compare(strFolder, "c:\program files", True) = 0 Then
```

If it does, the first thing you do is display a message box:

```
'Tell the user
MessageBox.Show("Found it, exiting the loop now.", "Loops")
```

After the user has clicked OK to dismiss the message box, you use the `Exit For` statement to quit the loop. In this instance, the loop is short-circuited, and Visual Basic 2008 moves to the first line after the `Next` statement.

```
'Quit the loop early
Exit For
```

Of course, if the name of the folder doesn't match the one you're looking for, you keep looping. Using loops to find an item in a list is one of their most common uses. Once you've found the item you're looking for, using the `Exit For` statement to short-circuit the loop is a very easy way to improve the performance of your application.

Imagine you have a list of a thousand items to look through. You find the item you're looking for on the tenth iteration. If you don't quit the loop after you've found the item, you're effectively asking the computer to look through another 990 useless items. If, however, you do quit the loop early, you can move on and start running another part of the algorithm.

Quitting Do . . . Loops

As you might have guessed, you can quit a `Do . . . Loop` in more or less the same way, as you see in the next Try It Out.

Try It Out   **Quitting a Do . . . Loop**

1. Return to the Forms Designer one last time and add another Button control to your form and set its `Name` property to **btnQuittingADoLoop** and its `Text` property to **Quitting a Do Loop**.

2. Double-click the button and add the following highlighted code to the `Click` event handler:

```
Private Sub btnQuittingADoLoop_Click(ByVal sender As System.Object, _
    ByVal e As System.EventArgs) Handles btnQuittingADoLoop.Click

    'Declare variable
    Dim intCount As Integer = 0
```

```
            'Clear the list
            ClearList()

            'Process the loop
            Do While intCount < 10

                'Add the item to the list
                lstData.Items.Add(intCount.ToString)

                'Increment the count by 1
                intCount += 1

                'Should you quit the loop
                If intCount = 3 Then
                    Exit Do
                End If

            Loop
        End Sub
```

3. Run the project and click the Quitting a Do Loop button. You'll see a list containing the values 0, 1, and 2.

How It Works

In this case, because you're in a Do ... Loop, you have to use Exit Do rather than Exit For. However, the principle is exactly the same. Exit Do will work with both the Do While ... Loop and Do Until ... Loop loops.

Infinite Loops

When building loops, you can create something called an *infinite loop*. What this means is a loop that, once started, will never finish. Consider this code:

```
Dim intX As Integer = 0
Do
    intX += 1
Loop Until intX = 0
```

This loop will start and run through the first iteration. Then when you execute Loop Until intX = 0 the first time, intX is 1. So you go back to the start of the loop again and increment intX to 2, and so on. What's important here is that it will never get to 0. The loop becomes infinite, and the program won't crash (at least not instantly), but it may well become unresponsive.

If you suspect a program has dropped into an infinite loop, you'll need to force the program to stop. With Windows Vista, this is pretty easy. If you are running your program in Visual Studio 2008, flip over to it, and select Debug ⇨ Stop Debugging from the menu. This will immediately stop the program. If you are running your compiled program, you'll need to use the Windows Task Manager. Press Ctrl+Alt+Del and select Task Manager. Your program should show as Not Responding. Select your program in the Task Manager and click End Task. Eventually this opens a dialog box saying that the program is not responding (which you knew already) and asking whether you want to kill the program stone dead, so click End Task again.

In some extreme cases, the loop can take up so much processing power or other system resources that you won't be able to open Task Manager or flip over to Visual Studio. In these cases, you can persevere and try to use either of these methods; or you can reset your computer and chalk it up to experience.

Visual Studio 2008 does not automatically save your project before running the application the first time, so you're likely to lose all of your program code if you have to reset. Therefore, it would be wise to save your project before you start running your code.

Summary

In this chapter, you took a detailed look at the various ways that programs can make decisions and loop through code. You first saw the alternative operators that can be used with If statements and examined how multiple operators could be combined by using the And and Or keywords. Additionally, you examined how case-insensitive string comparisons could be performed.

You then looked at Select Case, an efficient technique for choosing one outcome out of a group of possibilities. Next you examined the concept of looping within a program and were introduced to the two main types of loops: For loops and Do loops. For loops iterate a given number of times, and the derivative For Each loop can be used to loop automatically through a list of items in a collection. Do While loops iterate while a given condition remains True, whereas Do Until loops iterate until a given condition becomes True.

In summary, you should know how to use:

❑   If, ElseIf, and Else statements to test for multiple conditions

❑   Nested If statements

❑   Comparison operators and the String.Compare method

❑   The Select Case statement to perform multiple comparisons

❑   For ... Next and For ... Each loops

❑   Do ... Loop and Do While ... Loop statements

Exercises

1.   Create a Windows Forms Application with a text box and a Button control. In the Click event of the Button, extract the number from the text box and use a Select Case statement with the numbers 1 through 5. In the Case statement for each number, display the number in a message box. Ensure that you provide code to handle numbers that are not in the range of 1 through 5.

2.   Create a Windows Forms Application that contains a ListBox control and a Button control. In the Click event for the button, create a For ... Next loop that will count from 1 to 10 and display the results in the list box. Then create another For ... Next loop that will count backwards from 10 to 1 and display those results in the list box.

Working with Data Structures

In the previous chapters, you worked with simple data types, namely `Integer` and `String` variables. Although these data types are useful in their own rights, more complex programs call for working with *data structures*; that is, groups of data elements that are organized in a single unit. In this chapter, you learn about the various data structures available in Visual Basic 2008. You also will see some ways in which you can work with complex sets of data. Finally, you learn how you can build powerful collection classes for working with, maintaining, and manipulating lists of complex data.

In this chapter, you learn about:

❑ Arrays

❑ Enumerations

❑ Constants

❑ Structures

Understanding Arrays

A fairly common requirement in writing software is the need to hold lists of similar or related data. You can provide this functionality by using an *array*. Arrays are just lists of data that have a single data type. For example, you might want to store a list of your friends' ages in an integer array or their names in a string array.

In this section, you take a look at how to define, populate, and use arrays in your applications.

Defining and Using Arrays

When you define an array, you're actually creating a variable that has more than one dimension. For example, if you define a variable as a string you can only hold a single string value in it:

```
Dim strName As String
```

However, with an array you create a kind of multiplier effect with a variable, so you can hold more than one value in a single variable. An array is defined by entering the size of the array after the variable name. So, if you wanted to define a string array with 10 elements, you'd do this:

```
Dim strName(9) As String
```

The reason you use (9) *instead of* (10) *to get an array with 10 elements is explained in detail later. The basic explanation is simply that because numbering in an array starts at zero, the first element in an array is zero, the second element in an array is one, and so on.*

When you have an array, you can access individual elements in it by providing an index value between 0 and a maximum possible value — this maximum possible value happens to be one less than the total size of the array.

So, to set the element with index 2 in the array, you'd do this:

```
strName(2) = "Katie"
```

To get that same element back again, you'd do this:

```
MessageBox.Show(strName(2))
```

What's important is that other elements in the array are unaffected when you set their siblings. So, if you do this:

```
strName(3) = "Betty"
```

`strName(2)` remains set to `"Katie"`.

Perhaps the easiest way to understand what an array looks like and how it works is to write some code.

Try It Out   **Defining and Using a Simple Array**

1. In Visual Studio 2008, click the File menu and choose New ⇨ Project. In the New Project dialog box, create a new Windows Forms Application called **Array Demo**.

2. When the Designer for Form1 appears, add a ListBox control to the form. Using the Properties window set its Name property to **lstFriends** and its IntegralHeight property to **False**.

3. Add a Button control to the form, set its Name property to **btnArrayElement**, and set its Text property to **Array Element**. Arrange your controls so that your form looks similar to Figure 5-1 as you'll be adding more Button controls to this project later.

Figure 5-1

4. Double-click the button and add the following highlighted code to its Click event handler. You'll receive an error message that the ClearList procedure is not defined. You can ignore this error because you'll be adding that procedure in the next step:

```
Private Sub btnArrayElement_Click(ByVal sender As System.Object, _
    ByVal e As System.EventArgs) Handles btnArrayElement.Click
```

```
        'Clear the list
        ClearList()

        'Declare an array
        Dim strFriends(4) As String

        'Populate the array
        strFriends(0) = "Wendy"
        strFriends(1) = "Harriet"
        strFriends(2) = "Jay"
        strFriends(3) = "Michelle"
        strFriends(4) = "Richard"

        'Add the first array item to the list
        lstFriends.Items.Add(strFriends(0))
    End Sub
```

5. Now create the following procedure:

```
Private Sub ClearList()
    'Clear the list
    lstFriends.Items.Clear()
End Sub
```

6. Save your project by clicking the Save All button on the toolbar and then run it. When the form displays, click the Array Element button and the list box on your form will be *populated* with the name Wendy.

How It Works

First you clear the list box by calling the `ClearList` method. Although the list is empty at this point, you'll be adding more buttons to this project in the following Try It Out exercises and may want to compare the results of the each of the buttons.

```
'Clear the list
ClearList()
```

When you define an array, you have to specify a data type and a size. In this case, you're specifying an array of type `String` and also defining an array size of 5. The way the size is defined is a little quirky. You have to specify a number one less than the final size you want (you'll learn why shortly). So here, you have used the line:

```
'Declare an array
Dim strFriends(4) As String
```

In this way, you end up with an array of size 5. Another way of expressing this is to say that you have an array consisting of 5 *elements*.

When done, you have your array, and you can access each item in the array by using an *index*. The index is given as a number in parentheses after the name of the array. Indexes start at zero and go up to one less than the number of items in the array. The following example sets all five possible items in the array to the names:

```
'Populate the array
strFriends(0) = "Wendy"
strFriends(1) = "Harriet"
strFriends(2) = "Jay"
strFriends(3) = "Michelle"
strFriends(4) = "Richard"
```

Just as you can use an index to set the items in an array, you can use an index to get items back out. In this case, you're asking for the item at position 0, which returns the first item in the array, namely `Wendy`:

```
'Add the first array item to the list
lstFriends.Items.Add(strFriends(0))
```

The reason the indexes and sizes seem skewed is that the indexes are zero-based, whereas humans tend to number things beginning at 1. When putting items into or retrieving items from an array, you have to adjust the position you want down by one to get the actual index; for example, the fifth item is actually at position 4, the first item is at position 0, and so on. When you define an array, you do not actually specify the size of the array but rather the upper *index bound* — that is, the highest possible value of the index that the array will support.

Why should the indexes be zero-based? Remember that to the computer, a variable represents the address of a location in the computer's memory. Given an array index, Visual Basic 2008 just multiplies the index by the size of one element and adds the product to the address of the array as a whole to get the address of the specified element. The starting address of the array as a whole is also the starting address of the first element in it. That is, the first element is zero times the size of an element away from the start of the whole array; the second element is 1 times the size of an element away from the start of the whole array; and so on.

The method you define contains only one line of code but its reuse becomes apparent in the next Try It Out. This method merely clears the Items collection of the list box.

```
Private Sub ClearList()
    'Clear the list
    lstFriends.Items.Clear()
End Sub
```

Using For Each . . . Next

One common way to work with arrays is by using a For Each...Next loop. This loop is introduced in Chapter 4, when you used it with a string collection returned from the My.Computer.FileSystem .GetDirectories method. In the following Try It Out, you look at how you use For Each...Next with an array.

Try It Out   Using For Each . . . Next with an Array

1. Close your program if it is still running and open the Code Editor for Form1. Add the following highlighted variable declaration at the top of your form class:

```
Public Class Form1

    'Declare a form level array
    Private strFriends(4) As String
```

2. In the Class Name combo box at the top left of your Code Editor, select (Form1 Events). In the Method Name combo box at the top right of your Code Editor, select the Load event. This causes the Form1_Load event handler to be inserted into your code. Add the following highlighted code to this procedure:

```
Private Sub Form1_Load(ByVal sender As Object, _
    ByVal e As System.EventArgs) Handles Me.Load

    'Populate the array
    strFriends(0) = "Wendy"
    strFriends(1) = "Harriet"
    strFriends(2) = "Jay"
    strFriends(3) = "Michelle"
    strFriends(4) = "Richard"
End Sub
```

3. Switch to the Form Designer and add another Button control. Set its Name property to **btnEnumerateArray** and its Text property to **Enumerate Array**.

4. Double-click this new button and add the following highlighted code to its `Click` event handler:

```
Private Sub btnEnumerateArray_Click(ByVal sender As System.Object, _
    ByVal e As System.EventArgs) Handles btnEnumerateArray.Click

        'Clear the list
        ClearList()

        'Enumerate the array
        For Each strName As String In strFriends
            'Add the array item to the list
            lstFriends.Items.Add(strName)
        Next
End Sub
```

5. Run the project and click the button. You'll see results like those in Figure 5-2.

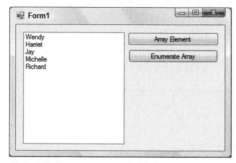

Figure 5-2

How It Works

You start this exercise by declaring an array variable that is local to the form, meaning that the variable is available to all procedures in the form class. Whenever variables are declared outside a method in the form class, they are available to all methods in the form.

```
'Declare a form level array
Private strFriends(4) As String
```

Next you added the `Load` event handler for the form and then added code to populate the array. This procedure will be called whenever the form loads, ensuring that your array always gets populated.

```
Private Sub Form1_Load(ByVal sender As Object, _
    ByVal e As System.EventArgs) Handles Me.Load

        'Populate the array
        strFriends(0) = "Wendy"
```

```
              strFriends(1) = "Harriet"
              strFriends(2) = "Jay"
              strFriends(3) = "Michelle"
              strFriends(4) = "Richard"
       End Sub
```

Chapter 4 shows the For Each...Next loop iterate through a string collection; in this example, it is used in an array. The principle is similar; you have to create a control variable that is of the same type as an element in the array and gives this to the loop when it starts. This has all been done in one line of code. The control variable, strName, is declared and used in the For Each statement by using the As String keyword.

The internals behind the loop move through the array starting at element 0 until it reaches the last element. For each iteration, you can examine the value of the control variable and do something with it; in this case, you add the name to the list.

```
              'Enumerate the array
              For Each strName As String In strFriends
                  'Add the array item to the list
                  lstFriends.Items.Add(strName)
              Next
```

Also, note that the items are added to the list in the same order that they appear in the array. That's because For Each...Next proceeds from the first item to the last item as each item is defined.

Passing Arrays as Parameters

It's extremely useful to be able to pass an array (which could be a list of values) to a function as a parameter. In the next Try It Out, you'll look at how to do this.

Try It Out   **Passing Arrays as Parameters**

1. Return to the Forms Designer in the Array Demo project and add another Button control. Set its Name property to **btnArraysAsParameters** and its Text property to **Arrays as Parameters**.

2. Double-click the button and add the following highlighted code to its Click event handler. You'll receive an error message that the AddItemsToList procedure is not defined. You can ignore this error because you'll be adding that procedure in the next step:

```
Private Sub btnArraysAsParameters_Click(ByVal sender As System.Object, _
    ByVal e As System.EventArgs) Handles btnArraysAsParameters.Click

        'Clear the list
        ClearList()

        'List your friends
        AddItemsToList(strFriends)
End Sub
```

3. Add the `AddItemsToList` procedure as follows:

```
Private Sub AddItemsToList(ByVal arrayList() As String)
    'Enumerate the array
    For Each strName As String In arrayList
        'Add the array item to the list
        lstFriends.Items.Add(strName)
    Next
End Sub
```

4. Run the project and click the button. You'll see the same results that were shown in Figure 5-2.

How It Works

The trick here is to tell the `AddItemsToList` method that the parameter it's expecting is an array of type `String`. You do this by using empty parentheses, like this:

```
Sub AddItemsToList(ByVal arrayList() As String)
```

If you specify an array but don't define a size (or upper-bound value), you're telling Visual Basic 2008 that you don't know or care how big the array is. That means that you can pass an array of any size through to `AddItemsToList`. In the `btnArraysAsParameters_Click` procedure, you're sending your original array:

```
'List your friends
AddItemsToList(strFriends)
```

But what happens if you define another array of a different size? In the next Try It Out, you'll find out.

Try It Out **Adding More Friends**

1. Return to the Forms Designer of the Array Demo project. Add another Button control and set its `Name` property to **btnMoreArrayParameters** and its `Text` property to **More Array Parameters**.

2. Double-click the button and add the following highlighted code to its `Click` event handler:

```
Private Sub btnMoreArrayParameters_Click(ByVal sender As System.Object, _
    ByVal e As System.EventArgs) Handles btnMoreArrayParameters.Click

    'Clear the list
    ClearList()

    'Declare an array
    Dim strMoreFriends(1) As String

    'Populate the array
```

```
        strMoreFriends(0) = "Elaine"
        strMoreFriends(1) = "Debra"

        'List your friends
        AddItemsToList(strFriends)
        AddItemsToList(strMoreFriends)
End Sub
```

3. Run the project and click the button. You will see the form shown in Figure 5-3.

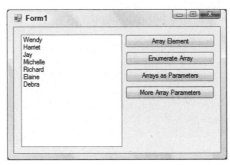

Figure 5-3

How It Works

What you have done here is prove that the array you pass as a parameter does not have to be of a fixed size. You created a new array of size 2 and passed it through to the same `AddItemsToList` function.

As you're writing code, you can tell whether a parameter is an array type by looking for empty parentheses in the IntelliSense pop-up box, as illustrated in Figure 5-4.

Figure 5-4

Not only are you informed that arrayList *is an array type, but you also see that the data type of the array is* String.

Sorting Arrays

It is sometimes useful to be able to sort an array. In this Try It Out, you see how you can take an array and sort it alphabetically.

Try It Out   Sorting Arrays

1. Return to the Forms Designer in the Array Demo project and add another Button control. Set its Name property to **btnSortingArrays** and its Text property to **Sorting Arrays.**

2. Double-click the button and add the following highlighted code to its Click event handler:

```
Private Sub btnSortingArrays_Click(ByVal sender As System.Object, _
    ByVal e As System.EventArgs) Handles btnSortingArrays.Click

        'Clear the list
        ClearList()

        'Sort the array
        Array.Sort(strFriends)

        'List your friends
        AddItemsToList(strFriends)
    End Sub
```

3. Run the project and click the button. You'll see the list box on your form populated with the names from your array sorted alphabetically.

How It Works

All arrays are internally implemented in a class called System.Array. In this case, you use a method called Sort on that class. The Sort method takes a single parameter — namely, the array you want to sort. The method then does as its name suggests and sorts it for you into an order appropriate to the data type of the array elements. In this case you are using a string array, so you get an alphanumeric sort. If you were to attempt to use this technique on an array containing integer or floating-point values, the array would be sorted in numeric order.

```
        'Sort the array
        Array.Sort(strFriends)
```

The ability to pass different parameter types in different calls to the same method name and to get behavior that is appropriate to the parameter types actually passed is called *method overloading*. Sort is referred to as an overloaded method.

Going Backwards

For Each...Next will go through an array in only one direction. It starts at position 0 and loops through to the end of the array. If you want to go through an array backwards (from the length –1 position to 0), you have two options.

First, you can step through the loop backwards by using a standard For...Next loop to start at the upper index bound of the first dimension in the array and work your way to 0 using the Step -1 keyword, as shown in the following example:

```
For intIndex As Integer = strFriends.GetUpperBound(0) To 0 Step -1
    'Add the array item to the list
    lstFriends.Items.Add(strFriends(intIndex))
Next
```

You can also call the Reverse method on the Array class to reverse the order of the array and then use your For Each...Next loop, as shown in the next Try It Out.

Try It Out   Reversing an Array

1.   Return to the Forms Designer and add another Button control. Set its Name property to **btnReversingAnArray** and its Text property to **Reversing an Array**.

2.   Double-click the button and add the following highlighted code to its Click event handler:

```
Private Sub btnReversingAnArray_Click(ByVal sender As System.Object, _
    ByVal e As System.EventArgs) Handles btnReversingAnArray.Click

        'Clear the list
        ClearList()

        'Reverse the order - elements will be in descending order
        Array.Reverse(strFriends)

        'List your friends
        AddItemsToList(strFriends)
End Sub
```

3.   Run the project and click the button. You'll see the friends listed in reverse order as shown in Figure 5-5.

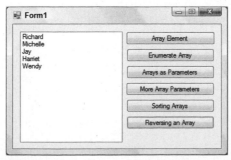

Figure 5-5

How It Works

The Reverse method reverses the order of elements in a one-dimensional array, which is what you are working with here. By passing the strFriends array to the Reverse method, you are asking the Reverse method to re-sequence the array from bottom to top:

```
'Reverse the order - elements will be in descending order
Array.Reverse(strFriends)
```

After the items in your array have been reversed, you simply call the AddItemsToList procedure to have the items listed:

```
'List your friends
AddItemsToList(strFriends)
```

If you want to list your array in descending sorted order, you would call the Sort method on the Array class to have the items sorted in ascending order and then call the Reverse method to have the sorted array reversed, putting it into descending order.

Initializing Arrays with Values

It is possible to create an array in Visual Basic 2008 and populate it in one line of code, rather than having to write multiple lines of code to declare and populate the array as shown here:

```
'Declare an array
Dim strFriends(4) As String

'Populate the array
strFriends(0) = "Wendy"
strFriends(1) = "Harriet"
strFriends(2) = "Jay"
strFriends(3) = "Michelle"
strFriends(4) = "Richard"
```

You learn more about initializing arrays with values in the next Try It Out.

Try It Out   Initializing Arrays with Values

1. Return to the Forms Designer in the Array Demo project and add one last Button control. Set its Name property to **btnInitializingArraysWithValues** and its Text property to **Initializing Arrays with Values**.

2. Double-click the button and add the following highlighted code to its Click event handler:

```
Private Sub btnInitializingArraysWithValues_Click( _
    ByVal sender As System.Object, ByVal e As System.EventArgs) _
    Handles btnInitializingArraysWithValues.Click
```

```
        'Clear the list
        ClearList()

        'Declare and populate an array
        Dim strMyFriends() As String = {"Elaine", "Richard", "Debra", _
            "Wendy", "Harriet"}
        'List your friends
        AddItemsToList(strMyFriends)
    End Sub
```

3. Run the project and click the button. Your list box is populated with the friends listed in this array.

How It Works

The pair of braces { } allows you to set the values that should be held in an array directly. In this instance, you have five values to enter into the array, separated with commas. Note that when you do this, you don't specify an upper bound for the array; instead, you use empty parentheses. Visual Basic 2008 prefers to calculate the upper bound for you based on the values you supply.

```
        'Declare and populate an array
        Dim strMyFriends() As String = {"Elaine", "Richard", "Debra", _
            "Wendy", "Harriet"}
```

This technique can be quite awkward to use when populating large arrays. If your program relies on populating large arrays, you might want to use the method illustrated earlier: specifying the positions and the values. This is especially true when populating an array with values that change at runtime.

Understanding Enumerations

So far, the variables you've seen had virtually no limitations on the kinds of data you can store in them. Technical limits notwithstanding, if you have a variable defined As Integer, you can put any number you like in it. The same holds true for String and Double. You have seen another variable type, however, that has only two possible values: Boolean variables can be either True or False and nothing else.

Often, when writing code, you want to limit the possible values that can be stored in a variable. For example, if you have a variable that stores the number of doors that a car has, do you really want to be able to store the value 163,234?

Using Enumerations

Enumerations allow you to build a new type of variable, based on one of these data types: Integer, Long, Short, or Byte. This variable can be set to one value of a set of possible values that you define, and ideally prevent someone from supplying invalid values. It is used to provide clarity in the code, as it can describe a particular value. In the following Try It Out, you'll look at how to build an application that looks at the time of day and, based on that, can record a `DayAction` of one of these possible values:

❑ Asleep

❑ Getting ready for work

❑ Traveling to work

❑ At work

❑ At lunch

❑ Traveling from work

❑ Relaxing with friends

❑ Getting ready for bed

Try It Out   Using Enumerations

1. Create a new Windows Forms Application in Visual Studio 2008 called **Enum Demo**.

2. Set the Text property of Form1 to **What's Richard Doing?**

3. Now add a DateTimePicker control and set the following properties:

    ❑ Set Name to **dtpHour**.

    ❑ Set Format to **Time**.

    ❑ Set ShowUpDown to **True**.

    ❑ Set Value to **00:00** AM.

    ❑ Set Size to **90, 20**.

4. Add a Label control to the form, set its Name property to **lblState**, and set its Text property to **State Not Initialized**. Resize your form so it looks similar to Figure 5-6.

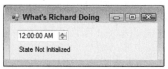

Figure 5-6

5. View the Code Editor for the form by right-clicking the form and choosing View Code from the context menu. At the top of the class add the following highlighted enumeration:

```
Public Class Form1

    'DayAction Enumeration
    Private Enum DayAction As Integer
        Asleep = 0
        GettingReadyForWork = 1
        TravelingToWork = 2
        AtWork = 3
        AtLunch = 4
        TravelingFromWork = 5
        RelaxingWithFriends = 6
        GettingReadyForBed = 7
    End Enum
```

6. With an enumeration defined, you can create new member variables that use the enumeration as their data type. Add this member:

```
    'Declare variable
    Private CurrentState As DayAction
```

7. Add the following code below the variable you just added:

```
    'Hour property
    Private Property Hour() As Integer
        Get
            'Return the current hour displayed
            Return dtpHour.Value.Hour
        End Get
        Set(ByVal value As Integer)
            'Set the date using the hour passed to this property
            dtpHour.Value = _
                New Date(Now.Year, Now.Month, Now.Day, value, 0, 0)
            'Set the display text
            lblState.Text = "At " & value & ":00, Richard is "
        End Set
    End Property
```

8. In the Class Name combo box at the top of the Code Editor, select (Form1 Events), and in the Method Name combo box, select the Load event. Add the following highlighted code to the event handler:

```
    Private Sub Form1_Load(ByVal sender As System.Object, _
        ByVal e As System.EventArgs) Handles MyBase.Load

        'Set the Hour property to the current hour
        Me.Hour = Now.Hour
    End Sub
```

9. In the Class Name combo box at the top of the Code Editor, select dtpHour, and in the Method Name combo box, select the `ValueChanged` event. Add the following highlighted code to the event handler:

```
Private Sub dtpHour_ValueChanged(ByVal sender As Object, _
    ByVal e As System.EventArgs) Handles dtpHour.ValueChanged

        'Update the Hour property
        Me.Hour = dtpHour.Value.Hour
    End Sub
```

10. Save your project and then run it. You will be able to click the up and down arrows in the date and time picker control and see the text updated to reflect the hour selected as shown in Figure 5-7.

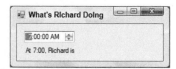

Figure 5-7

How It Works

In this application, the user will be able to use the date-time picker to choose the hour. You then look at the hour and determine which one of the eight states Richard is in at the given time. To achieve this, you have to keep the hour around somehow. To store the hour, you have created a property for the form in addition to the properties it already has, such as Name and Text. The new property is called `Hour`, and it is used to set the current hour in the DateTimePicker control and the label control. The property is defined with a `Property...End Property` statement:

```
Private Property Hour() As Integer
    Get
        'Return the current hour displayed
        Return dtpHour.Value.Hour
    End Get
    Set(ByVal value As Integer)
        'Set the date using the hour passed to this property
        dtpHour.Value = _
            New Date(Now.Year, Now.Month, Now.Day, value, 0, 0)
        'Set the display text
        lblState.Text = "At " & value & ":00, Richard is "
    End Set
End Property
```

Note the `Get...End Get` and `Set...End Set` blocks inside the `Property...End Property` statement. The `Get` block contains a `Return` statement and is called automatically to return the property value when the property name appears in an expression. The data type to be returned is not specified in the `Get` statement, because it was already declared `As Integer` in the `Property` statement. The `Set` block is called automatically when the value is set, such as by putting the property name to the left of an equals sign.

When the application starts, you set the `Hour` property to the current hour on your computer. You get this information from `Now`, a `Date` variable containing the current date and time:

```
Private Sub Form1_Load(ByVal sender As System.Object, _
    ByVal e As System.EventArgs) Handles MyBase.Load

    'Set the Hour property to the current hour
    Me.Hour = Now.Hour
End Sub
```

You also set the `Hour` property when the `Value` property changes in the DateTimePicker control:

```
Private Sub dtpHour_ValueChanged(ByVal sender As Object, _
    ByVal e As System.EventArgs) Handles dtpHour.ValueChanged

    'Update the Hour property
    Me.Hour = dtpHour.Value.Hour
End Sub
```

When the `Hour` property is set, you have to update the value of the DateTimePicker control to show the new hour value, and you have to update the label on the form as well. The code to perform these actions is put inside the `Set` block for the `Hour` property.

The first update that you perform is to update the `Value` property of the DateTimePicker control. The `Value` property of the date-time picker is a `Date` data type; thus, you cannot simply set the hour in this control, although you can retrieve just the hour from this property. To update this property, you must pass it a `Date` data type.

You do this by calling `New` (see Chapter 11) for the `Date` class, passing it the different date and time parts as shown in the code: year, month, day, hour, minute, second. You get the year, month, and day by extracting them from the `Now` variable. The hour is passed using the `value` parameter that was passed to this `Hour` property, and the minutes and seconds are passed as `0`, since you do not want to update the specific minutes or seconds.

```
'Set the date using the hour passed to this property
dtpHour.Value = _
    New Date(Now.Year, Now.Month, Now.Day, value, 0, 0)
```

The second update performed by this `Hour` property is to update the label on the form using some static text and the hour that is being set in this property.

```
'Set the display text
lblState.Text = "At " & value & ":00, Richard is "
```

You have not evaluated the Hour property to determine the state using the DayAction enumeration, but you do that next.

Determining the State

In the next Try It Out, you look at determining the state when the Hour property is set. You can take the hour returned by the DateTimePicker control and use it to determine which value in your enumeration it matches. This section demonstrates this and displays the value on your form.

Try It Out   Determining State

1. Open the Code Editor for Form1 and modify the Hour property as follows:

```
Set(ByVal value As Integer)
    'Set the date using the hour passed to this property
    dtpHour.Value = _
        New Date(Now.Year, Now.Month, Now.Day, value, 0, 0)

    'Determine the state
    If value >= 6 And value < 7 Then
        CurrentState = DayAction.GettingReadyForWork
    ElseIf value >= 7 And value < 8 Then
        CurrentState = DayAction.TravelingToWork
    ElseIf value >= 8 And value < 13 Then
        CurrentState = DayAction.AtWork
    ElseIf value >= 13 And value < 14 Then
        CurrentState = DayAction.AtLunch
    ElseIf value >= 14 And value < 17 Then
        CurrentState = DayAction.AtWork
    ElseIf value >= 17 And value < 18 Then
        CurrentState = DayAction.TravelingFromWork
    ElseIf value >= 18 And value < 22 Then
        CurrentState = DayAction.RelaxingWithFriends
    ElseIf value >= 22 And value < 23 Then
        CurrentState = DayAction.GettingReadyForBed
    Else
        CurrentState = DayAction.Asleep
    End If

    'Set the display text
    lblState.Text = "At " & value & ":00, Richard is " & _
        CurrentState
End Set
```

2. Run the project. You'll see something like Figure 5-8.

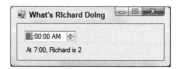

Figure 5-8

3. Here's the problem: The user doesn't know what 2 means. Close the project and find the following section of code at the end of the `Hour` property:

```
'Set the display text
lblState.Text = "At " & value & ":00, Richard is " & _
    CurrentState
End Set
```

4. Change the last line to read as follows:

```
'Set the display text
lblState.Text = "At " & value & ":00, Richard is " & _
    CurrentState.ToString
End Set
```

5. Now run the project and you'll see something like Figure 5-9.

Figure 5-9

How It Works

As you typed the code, you might have noticed that whenever you tried to set a value against `CurrentState`, you were presented with an enumerated list of possibilities as shown in Figure 5-10.

Figure 5-10

Visual Studio 2008 knows that `CurrentState` is of type `DayAction`. It also knows that `DayAction` is an enumeration and that it defines eight possible values, each of which is displayed in the IntelliSense pop-up box. Clicking an item in the enumerated list causes a tooltip to be displayed with the actual value of the item; for example, clicking `DayAction.RelaxingWithFriends` will display a tooltip with a value of 6.

Fundamentally, however, because DayAction is based on an integer, CurrentState is an integer value. That's why, the first time you ran the project with the state determination code in place, you saw an integer at the end of the status string. At 7 A.M., you know that Richard is traveling to work, or rather CurrentState equals DayAction.TravelingToWork. You defined this as 2, which is why 2 is displayed at the end of the string.

What you've done in this Try It Out is to tack a call to the ToString method onto the end of the CurrentState variable. This results in a string representation of DayAction being used, rather than the integer representation

---

Enumerations are incredibly useful when you want to store one of a possible set of values in a variable. As you start to drill into more complex objects in the Framework, you'll find that they are used all over the place!

Setting Invalid Values

One of the limitations of enumerations is that it is possible to store a value that technically isn't one of the possible defined values of the enumeration. For example, you can change the Hour property so that rather than setting CurrentState to Asleep, you can set it to 999:

```
ElseIf value >= 22 And value < 23 Then
    CurrentState = DayAction.GettingReadyForBed
Else
    CurrentState = 999
End If
```

If you build the project, you'll notice that Visual Basic 2008 doesn't flag this as an error if you have the Option Strict option turned off. When you run the project, you'll see that the value for CurrentState is shown on the form as 999.

So, you can see that you can set a variable that references an enumeration to a value that is not defined in that enumeration and the application will still "work" (as long as the value is of the same type as the enumeration). If you build classes that use enumerations, you have to rely on the consumer of that class being well behaved. One technique to solve this problem would be to disallow invalid values in any properties that used the enumeration as their data type.

Understanding Constants

Another good programming practice that you need to look at is the *constant*. Imagine you have these two methods, each of which does something with a given file on the computer's disk. (Obviously, we're omitting the code here that actually manipulates the file.)

```
Public Sub DoSomething()
    'What's the filename?
    Dim strFileName As String = "c:\Temp\Demo.txt"
    'Open the file
    ...
End Sub
Public Sub DoSomethingElse()
    'What's the filename?
    Dim strFileName As String = "c:\Temp\Demo.txt"
    'Do something with the file
    ...
End Sub
```

Using Constants

The code defining a string literal gives the name of a file twice. This is poor programming practice because if both methods are supposed to access the same file, and if that file name changes, this change has to be made in two separate places.

In this instance, both methods are next to each other and the program itself is small. However, imagine you had a massive program in which a separate string literal pointing to the file is defined in 10, 50, or even 1,000 places. If you needed to change the file name, you'd have to change it many times. This is exactly the kind of thing that leads to serious problems for maintaining software code.

What you need to do instead is define the file name globally and then use that global symbol for the file name in the code, rather than using a string literal. This is what a constant is. It is, in effect, a special kind of variable that cannot be varied when the program is running. In the next Try It Out, you learn to use constants.

Try It Out   **Using Constants**

1. Create a new Windows Forms Application in Visual Studio 2008 called **Constants Demo**.

2. When the Forms Designer appears, add three Button controls. Set the Name property of the first button to **btnOne**, the second to **btnTwo**, and the third to **btnThree**. Change the Text property of each to **One**, **Two**, and **Three**, respectively. Arrange the controls on your form so it looks similiar Figure 5-11.

Figure 5-11

3. View the Code Editor for the form by right-clicking the form and choosing View Code from the context menu. At the top of the class definition, add the following highlighted code:

```
Public Class Form1

    'File name constant
    Private Const strFileName As String = "C:\Temp\Hello.txt"
```

4. In the Class Name combo box at the top of the editor, select btnOne, and in the Method Name combo box select the Click event. Add the following highlighted code to the Click event handler:

```
Private Sub btnOne_Click(ByVal sender As Object, _
    ByVal e As System.EventArgs) Handles btnOne.Click

    'Using a constant
    MessageBox.Show("1: " & strFileName, "Constants Demo")
End Sub
```

5. Select btnTwo in the Class Name combo box and select its Click event in the Method Name combo box. Add the highlighted code:

```
Private Sub btnTwo_Click(ByVal sender As Object, _
    ByVal e As System.EventArgs) Handles btnTwo.Click

    'Using the constant again
    MessageBox.Show("2: " & strFileName, "Constants Demo")
End Sub
```

6. Select btnThree in the Class Name combo box and the Click event in the Method Name combo box. Add this code to the Click event handler:

```
Private Sub btnThree_Click(ByVal sender As Object, _
    ByVal e As System.EventArgs) Handles btnThree.Click

    'Reusing the constant one more time
    MessageBox.Show("3: " & strFileName, "Constants Demo")
End Sub
```

7. Save and run your project and then click button One. You'll see the message box shown in Figure 5-12.

Figure 5-12

Likewise, you'll see the same file name when you click buttons Two and Three.

How It Works

A constant is actually a type of value that cannot be changed when the program is running. It is defined as a variable, but you add `Const` to the definition indicating that this variable is constant and cannot change.

```
'File name constant
Private Const strFileName As String = "C:\Temp\Hello.txt"
```

You'll notice that it has a data type, just like a variable, and you have to give it a value when it's defined — which makes sense, because you can't change it later.

When you want to use the constant, you refer to it just as you would refer to any variable:

```
Private Sub btnOne_Click(ByVal sender As Object, _
    ByVal e As System.EventArgs) Handles btnOne.Click

    'Using a constant
    MessageBox.Show("1: " & strFileName, "Constants Demo")
End Sub
```

As mentioned before, the appeal of a constant is that it allows you to change a value that's used throughout a piece of code by altering a single piece of code. However, note that you can change constants only at design time; you cannot change their values at runtime. Look at how this works.

Different Constant Types

In this section, you've seen how to use a string constant, but you can use other types of variables as constants. There are some rules: Basically, a constant must not be able to change, so you should not store an object data type (which we will discuss in Chapter 11) in a constant.

Integers are very common types of constants. They can be defined like this:

```
Public Const intHoursAsleepPerDay As Integer = 8
```

Also, it's fairly common to see constants used with enumerations, like this:

```
Public Const intRichardsTypicalState As DayAction = DayAction.AtWork
```

Structures

Applications commonly need to store several pieces of information of different data types that all relate to one thing and must be kept together in a group, such as a customer's name and address (strings) and balance (a number). Usually, an object of a class is used to hold such a group of variables, as you'll discover in Chapter 11, but you can also use a *structure*. Structures are similar to class objects but are somewhat simpler, so they're discussed here.

Later on, as you design applications, you need to be able to decide whether to use a structure or a class. As a rule of thumb, we suggest that if you end up putting a lot of methods on a structure, it should probably be a class. It's also relatively tricky to convert from a structure to a class later on, because structures and objects are created using different syntax rules, and sometimes the same syntax produces different results between structures and objects. So choose once and choose wisely!

Building Structures

Take a look at how you can build a structure.

Try It Out   Building a Structure

1. Create a new Windows Forms Application in Visual Studio 2008 called **Structure Demo**.

2. When the Forms Designer appears add four Label controls, four TextBox controls, and a Button control. Arrange your controls so that they look similar to Figure 5-13.

3. Set the Name properties as follows:

❑ Set Label1 to **lblName**.

❑ Set TextBox1 to **txtName**.

❑ Set Label2 to **lblFirstName**.

❑ Set TextBox2 to **txtFirstName**.

❑ Set Label3 to **lblLastName**.

❑ Set TextBox3 to **txtLastName**.

❑ Set Label4 to **lblEmail**.

❑ Set TextBox4 to **txtEmail**.

❑ Set Button1 to **btnListCustomer**.

4. Set the Text properties of the following controls:

❑ Set lblName to **Name**.

❑ Set lblFirstName to **First Name**.

❑ Set lblLastName to **Last Name**.

❑ Set lblEmail to **E-mail**.

❑ Set btnListCustomer to **List Customer**.

Figure 5-13

5. Right-click the project name in the Solution Explorer, choose the Add menu item from the context menu, and then choose the Class submenu item. In the Add New Item – Structure Demo dialog box, enter **Customer** in the Name field and then click the Add button to have this item added to your project.

6. When the Code Editor appears, replace all existing code with the following code:

```
Public Structure Customer
    'Public members
    Public FirstName As String
    Public LastName As String
    Public Email As String
End Structure
```

Note that you must make sure to replace the `Class` *definition with the* `Structure` *definition!*

7. View the Code Editor for the form and add this procedure:

```
Public Class Form1

    Public Sub DisplayCustomer(ByVal customer As Customer)
        'Display the customer details on the form
        txtFirstName.Text = customer.FirstName
        txtLastName.Text = customer.LastName
        txtEmail.Text = customer.Email
    End Sub
```

8. In the Class Name combo box at the top of the editor, select btnListCustomer, and in the Method Name combo box select the `Click` event. Add the following highlighted code to the `Click` event handler:

```
    Private Sub btnListCustomer_Click(ByVal sender As System.Object, _
        ByVal e As System.EventArgs) Handles btnListCustomer.Click

        'Create a new customer
        Dim objCustomer As Customer
        objCustomer.FirstName = "Michael"
        objCustomer.LastName = "Dell"
        objCustomer.Email = "mdell@somecompany.com"

        'Display the customer
        DisplayCustomer(objCustomer)

    End Sub
```

9. Save and run your project. When the form appears, click the List Customer button and you should see results similar to those shown in Figure 5-14.

Figure 5-14

How It Works

You define a structure using a `Structure...End Structure` statement. Inside this block, the variables that make up the structure are declared by name and type: These variables are called *members* of the structure.

```
Public Structure Customer
    'Public members
    Public FirstName As String
    Public LastName As String
    Public Email As String
End Structure
```

Notice the keyword `Public` in front of each variable declaration as well as in front of the `Structure` statement. You have frequently seen `Private` used in similar positions. The `Public` keyword means that you can refer to the member (such as `FirstName`) outside of the definition of the `Customer` structure itself.

In the `btnListCustomer_Click` procedure, you define a variable of type `Customer` using the `Dim` statement. (If `Customer` were a class, you would also have to initialize the variable by setting `objCustomer` equal to `New Customer`, as will be discussed in Chapter 11.)

```
Private Sub btnListCustomer_Click(ByVal sender As System.Object, _
    ByVal e As System.EventArgs) Handles btnListCustomer_Click.Click

    'Create a new customer
    Dim objCustomer As Customer
```

Then you can access each of the member variables inside the `Customer` structure `objCustomer` by giving the name of the structure variable, followed by a dot, followed by the name of the member:

```
    objCustomer.FirstName = "Michael"
    objCustomer.LastName = "Dell"
    objCustomer.Email = "mdell@somecompany.com"

    'Display the customer
    DisplayCustomer(objCustomer)
End Sub
```

The `DisplayCustomer` procedure simply accepts a `Customer` structure as its input parameter and then accesses the members of the structure to set the `Text` properties of the text boxes on the form:

```
Public Sub DisplayCustomer(ByVal customer As Customer)
    'Display the customer details on the form
    txtFirstName.Text = customer.FirstName
    txtLastName.Text = customer.LastName
    txtEmail.Text = customer.Email
End Sub
```

Adding Properties to Structures

You can add properties to a structure, just as you did to the form in the Enum Demo project earlier in the chapter. You learn how in the next Try It Out.

Try It Out   **Adding a Name Property**

1. Open the Code Editor for `Customer` and add this highlighted code to create a read-only property `Name`:

```
'Public members
Public FirstName As String
Public LastName As String
Public Email As String

'Name property
Public ReadOnly Property Name() As String
    Get
        Return FirstName & " " & LastName
    End Get
End Property
```

2. Open the Code Editor for Form1. Modify the `DisplayCustomer` method with the highlighted code:

```
Public Sub DisplayCustomer(ByVal customer As Customer)
    'Display the customer details on the form
    txtName.Text = customer.Name
    txtFirstName.Text = customer.FirstName
    txtLastName.Text = customer.LastName
    txtEmail.Text = customer.Email
End Sub
```

3. Run the project and click the List Customer button. You'll see that the Name text box, which was empty in Figure 5-14, is now populated with the customer's first and last name.

Working with ArrayLists

Suppose you need to store a set of `Customer` structures. You could use an array, but in some cases the array might not be so easy to use.

❑   If you need to add a new `Customer` to the array, you need to change the size of the array and insert the new item in the new last position in the array. (You'll learn how to change the size of an array later in this chapter.)

❑   If you need to remove a `Customer` from the array, you need to look at each item in the array in turn. When you find the one you want, you have to create another version of the array one element smaller than the original array and copy every item except the one you want to delete into the new array.

❑   If you need to replace a `Customer` in the array with another customer, you need to look at each item in turn until you find the one you want and then replace it manually.

The `ArrayList` provides a way to create an array that can be easily manipulated as you run your program.

Using an ArrayList

Look at using an `ArrayList` in this next Try It Out.

Try It Out   **Using an ArrayList**

1.   Return to the Structure Demo project in Visual Studio 2008. Make the form larger, move the existing controls down, and then add a new ListBox control as shown in Figure 5-15. Set the `Name` property of the list box to **lstCustomers** and its `IntegralHeight` property to False.

You can click the form and press Ctrl+A to select all of the controls and then drag them to their new location.

Figure 5-15

2. Open the Code Editor for Form1 and add the member highlighted here to the top of the class definition:

```
Public Class Form1

    'Form level members
    Private objCustomers As New ArrayList
```

3. Add this method to Form1 to create a new customer:

```
Public Sub CreateCustomer(ByVal firstName As String, _
    ByVal lastName As String, ByVal email As String)

    'Declare a Customer object
    Dim objNewCustomer As Customer

    'Create the new customer
    objNewCustomer.FirstName = firstName
    objNewCustomer.LastName = lastName
    objNewCustomer.Email = email

    'Add the new customer to the list
    objCustomers.Add(objNewCustomer)

    'Add the new customer to the ListBox control
    lstCustomers.Items.Add(objNewCustomer)
End Sub
```

4. Modify the btnListCustomer_Click method next, making these code changes:

```
Private Sub btnListCustomer_Click(ByVal sender As System.Object, _
    ByVal e As System.EventArgs) Handles btnListCustomer.Click

    'Create some customers
    CreateCustomer("Darrel", "Hilton", "dhilton@somecompany.com")
    CreateCustomer("Frank", "Peoples", "fpeoples@somecompany.com")
    CreateCustomer("Bill", "Scott", "bscott@somecompany.com")
End Sub
```

5. Run the project and click the List Customer button. You'll see results like those shown in Figure 5-16.

Figure 5-16

You are adding `Customer` structures to the list, but they are being displayed by the list as `Structure_Demo.Customer`; this is the full name of the structure. The ListBox control accepts string values, so, by specifying that you wanted to add the `Customer` structure to the list box, Visual Basic 2008 called the `ToString` method of the `Customer` structure. By default, the `ToString` method for a structure returns the structure name, not the contents that you wanted to see. So what you want to do is tweak the `Customer` structure so that it can display something more meaningful. When you do that in the next Try It Out, you'll see how the `ArrayList` works.

Overriding ToString

1. Return to the Structure Demo project and open the Code Editor for `Customer` and add the following method to the structure, ensuring that it is below the member declarations. Remember from Chapter 3 that to insert an XML Document Comment block, you type three apostrophes above the method name:

```
''' <summary>
''' Overrides the default ToString method
''' </summary>
''' <returns>String</returns>
''' <remarks>Returns the customer name and email address</remarks>
    Public Overrides Function ToString() As String
        Return Name & " (" & Email & ")"
    End Function
End Structure
```

2. Run the project and click the List Customer button. You'll see the same results as shown in Figure 5-17.

Figure 5-17

How It Works

Whenever a `Customer` structure is added to the list, the list box calls the `ToString` method on the structure to get a string representation of that structure. With this code, you *override* the default functionality of the `ToString` method so that, rather than returning just the name of the structure, you get some useful text:

```
''' <summary>
''' Overrides the default ToString method
''' </summary>
''' <returns>String</returns>
''' <remarks>Returns the customer name and email address</remarks>
    Public Overrides Function ToString() As String
        Return Name & " (" & Email & ")"
    End Function
```

An `ArrayList` can be used to store a list of objects/structures of any type (in contrast to a regular array). In fact, you can mix the types within an `ArrayList` — a topic we'll be talking about in a little while. In this example, you created a method called `CreateCustomer` that initializes a new `Customer` structure based on parameters that were passed to the method:

```
Public Sub CreateCustomer(ByVal firstName As String, _
    ByVal lastName As String, ByVal email As String)

    'Declare a Customer object
    Dim objNewCustomer As Customer

    'Create the new customer
    objNewCustomer.FirstName = firstName
    objNewCustomer.LastName = lastName
    objNewCustomer.Email = email
```

After the structure has been initialized, you add it to the `ArrayList` stored in `objCustomers`:

```
    'Add the new customer to the list
    objCustomers.Add(objNewCustomer)
```

You also add it to the list box itself, like this:

```
    'Add the new customer to the ListBox control
    lstCustomers.Items.Add(objNewCustomer)
```

With `CreateCustomer` defined, you can call it to add new members to the `ArrayList` and to the List-Box control when the user clicks the List Customer button:

```
Private Sub btnListCustomer_Click(ByVal sender As System.Object, _
    ByVal e As System.EventArgs) Handles btnListCustomer.Click

    'Create some customers
    CreateCustomer("Darrel", "Hilton", "dhilton@somecompany.com")
    CreateCustomer("Frank", "Peoples", "fpeoples@somecompany.com")
    CreateCustomer("Bill", "Scott", "bscott@somecompany.com")
End Sub
```

Deleting from an ArrayList

OK, so now you know the principle behind an `ArrayList`. You use it to do something that's traditionally hard to do with arrays but is pretty easy to do with an `ArrayList`, such as dynamically adding new values. Now let's look at how easy it is to delete items from an `ArrayList`.

Deleting Customers

1. Return to the Code Editor in the Structure Demo project and add the `SelectedCustomer` property to the form as follows:

```
Public ReadOnly Property SelectedCustomer() As Customer
    Get
        If lstCustomers.SelectedIndex <> -1 Then
            'Return the selected customer
            Return CType(objCustomers(lstCustomers.SelectedIndex), Customer)
        End If
    End Get
End Property
```

2. Now switch to the Forms Designer and add a new Button control to the bottom of the form and set its `Name` property to **btnDeleteCustomer** and its `Text` property to **Delete Customer.**

3. Double-click the button and add the highlighted code:

```
Private Sub btnDeleteCustomer_Click(ByVal sender As System.Object, _
    ByVal e As System.EventArgs) Handles btnDeleteCustomer.Click

        'If no customer is selected in the ListBox then...
        If lstCustomers.SelectedIndex = -1 Then

            'Display a message
            MessageBox.Show("You must select a customer to delete.", _
                "Structure Demo")

            'Exit this method
            Exit Sub
        End If

        'Prompt the user to delete the selected customer
        If MessageBox.Show("Are you sure you want to delete " & _
            SelectedCustomer.Name & "?", "Structure Demo", _
            MessageBoxButtons.YesNo, MessageBoxIcon.Question) = _
            DialogResult.Yes Then

            'Get the customer to be deleted
            Dim objCustomerToDelete As Customer = SelectedCustomer

            'Remove the customer from the ArrayList
```

```
                    objCustomers.Remove(objCustomerToDelete)

                    'Remove the customer from the ListBox
                    lstCustomers.Items.Remove(objCustomerToDelete)
        End If
    End Sub
```

4. Run the project and click the List Customer button. *Do not* select a customer in the list box and then click the Delete Customer button. You'll see a message box indicating that you must select a customer.

5. Now select a customer and click Delete Customer. You'll see a confirmation dialog box similar to the one shown in Figure 5-18.

6. Click Yes, and the customer you selected will be removed from the list.

Figure 5-18

How It Works

The trick here is to build a read-only property that returns the Customer structure that's selected in the list box back to the caller on demand. The SelectedIndex property of the list box returns a value of -1 if no selection has been made. Otherwise it returns the zero-based index of the selected customer. Since the Items collection of the list box contains a collection of Object data types, you must convert the object returned to a Customer object, which you do by using the CType function.

```
    Public ReadOnly Property SelectedCustomer() As Customer
        Get
            If lstCustomers.SelectedIndex <> -1 Then
                'Return the selected customer
                Return CType(objCustomers(lstCustomers.SelectedIndex), Customer)
            End If
        End Get
    End Property
```

Like the Name property that you added to the Customer structure, this property is identified as read-only by the keyword ReadOnly. It contains a Get block but no Set block. The reason for making it read-only is that it constructs the value it returns from other information (the contents of the Customer structures in the list) that can be set and changed by other means.

Inside the Click event handler for the Delete Customer button, you first test to see whether a customer has been selected in the list box. If no customer has been selected, you display a message box indicating that a customer must be selected. Then you exit the method allowing the user to select a customer and try again:

```
'If no customer is selected in the ListBox then...
If lstCustomers.SelectedIndex = -1 Then

    'Display a message
    MessageBox.Show("You must select a customer to delete.", _
        "Structure Demo")

    'Exit this method
    Exit Sub
End If
```

If a customer has been selected, you prompt the user to confirm the deletion:

```
'Prompt the user to delete the selected customer
If MessageBox.Show("Are you sure you want to delete " & _
    SelectedCustomer.Name & "?", "Structure Demo", _
    MessageBoxButtons.YesNo, MessageBoxIcon.Question) = _
    DialogResult.Yes Then
```

If the user does want to delete the customer, you get a return value from MessageBox.Show equal to DialogResult.Yes. Then you declare a customer structure to save the customer to be deleted and populate that structure with the selected customer:

```
'Get the customer to be deleted
Dim objCustomerToDelete As Customer = SelectedCustomer
```

The Remove method of the ArrayList can then be used to remove the selected customer:

```
'Remove the customer from the ArrayList
objCustomers.Remove(objCustomerToDelete)
```

You also use a similar technique to remove the customer from the list box:

```
'Remove the customer from the ListBox
lstCustomers.Items.Remove(objCustomerToDelete
```

Showing Items in the ArrayList

For completeness, you'll want to add one more piece of functionality to enhance the user interface of your application. In the next Try It Out, you add code in the `SelectedIndexChanged` event for the Customers list box. Every time you select a new customer, the customer's details will be displayed in the text boxes on the form.

Try It Out   Showing Details of the Selected Item

1. Return to the Forms Designer in the Structure Demo project and double-click the list box. This creates a new `SelectedIndexChanged` event handler. Add the highlighted code:

    ```
    Private Sub lstCustomers_SelectedIndexChanged( _
        ByVal sender As System.Object, ByVal e As System.EventArgs) _
        Handles lstCustomers.SelectedIndexChanged

            'Display the customer details
            DisplayCustomer(SelectedCustomer)
    End Sub
    ```

2. Run the project and click the List Customer button to populate the list box. Now when you select a customer in the list box, that customer's information will appear in the fields at the bottom of the form, as shown in Figure 5-19.

Figure 5-19

Working with Collections

The `ArrayList` is a kind of *collection*, which the .NET Framework uses extensively. A collection is a way of easily creating ad hoc groups of similar or related items. If you take a look back at your Structure Demo code and peek into the `CreateCustomer` method, you'll notice that when adding items to the `ArrayList` and to the list box, you use a method called `Add`:

```
'Add the new customer to the list
objCustomers.Add(objNewCustomer)

'Add the new customer to the ListBox control
lstCustomers.Items.Add(objNewCustomer)
```

The code that deletes a customer uses a method called `Remove` on both objects:

```
'Remove the customer from the ArrayList
objCustomers.Remove(objCustomerToDelete)

'Remove the customer from the ListBox
lstCustomers.Items.Remove(objCustomerToDelete)
```

Microsoft is very keen to see developers use the collection paradigm whenever they need to work with a list of items. They are also keen to see collections work in the same way, irrespective of what they actually hold — which is why you use `Add` to add an item and `Remove` to remove an item, even though you're using a `System.Collections.ArrayList` object in one case and a `System.Windows.Forms .ListBox.ObjectCollection` object in another. Microsoft has taken a great deal of care with this feature when building the .NET Framework.

Consistency is good — it allows developers to map an understanding of one thing and use that same understanding with a similar thing. When designing data structures for use in your application, you should take steps to follow the conventions that Microsoft has laid down. For example, if you have a collection class and want to create a method that removes an item, call it `Remove`, not `Delete`. Developers using your class will have an intuitive understanding of what `Remove` does because they're familiar with it. On the other hand, developers would do a double-take on seeing `Delete`, because that term has a different connotation.

One of the problems with using an `ArrayList` is that the developer who has an array list cannot guarantee that every item in the list is of the same type. For this reason, each time an item is extracted from the `ArrayList`, the type should be checked to avoid causing an error.

The solution is to create a *strongly typed* collection, which contains only elements of a particular type. Strongly typed collections are very easy to create. According to .NET best programming practices as defined by Microsoft, the best way to create one is to derive a new class from `System.Collections .CollectionBase` (discussed in the How It Works for the next Try It Out) and add two methods (`Add` and `Remove`) and one property (`Item`):

- ❑ `Add` adds a new item to the collection.
- ❑ `Remove` removes an item from the collection.
- ❑ `Item` returns the item at the given index in the collection.

Creating CustomerCollection

In this Try It Out, you create a `CustomerCollection` designed to hold a collection of `Customer` structures.

Creating CustomerCollection

1. Return to the Structure Demo project in Visual Studio 2008 and in the Solution Explorer, right-click the project and choose Add from the context menu and then choose the Class submenu item. In the Add New Item – Structure Demo dialog box, enter **CustomerCollection** in the Name field and then click the Add button to have the class added to your project.

2. Add the following highlighted line in the Code Editor:

    ```
    Public Class CustomerCollection
        Inherits CollectionBase

    End Class
    ```

3. You'll need to add an `Add` method to add a customer to the collection. Add the following code:

    ```
    'Add a customer to the collection
    Public Sub Add(ByVal newCustomer As Customer)
        Me.List.Add(newCustomer)
    End Sub
    ```

4. Next, you need to add a `Remove` method to remove a customer from the collection, so add this method:

    ```
    'Remove a customer from the collection
    Public Sub Remove(ByVal oldCustomer As Customer)
        Me.List.Remove(oldCustomer)
    End Sub
    ```

5. Open the Code Editor for the form and find the definition for the `objCustomers` member. Change its type from `ArrayList` to `CustomerCollection` as highlighted here:

    ```
    Public Class Form1

        'Form level members
        Private objCustomers As New CustomerCollection
    ```

6. Finally, run the project. You'll notice that the application works as before.

How It Works

Your `CustomerCollection` class is the first occasion for you to create a *class* explicitly (although you have been using them implicitly from the beginning). Classes and objects are discussed in Chapter 11 and later chapters. For now, note that, like a structure, a class represents a data type that groups one or more members that can be of different data types, and it can have properties and methods associated with it. Unlike a structure, a class can be *derived* from another class, in which case it *inherits* the members, properties, and methods of that other class (which is known as the *base class*) and can have further members, properties, and methods of its own.

Your `CustomerCollection` class inherits from the `System.Collections.CollectionBase` class, which contains a basic implementation of a collection that can hold any object. In that respect it's very similar to an `ArrayList`. The advantage comes when you add your own methods to this class.

Since you provided a version of the `Add` method that has a parameter type of `Customer`, it can accept and add only a `Customer` structure. Therefore, it's impossible to put anything into the collection that isn't a `Customer`. You can see there that IntelliSense is telling you that the only thing you can pass through to `Add` is a `Structure_Demo.Customer` structure.

Internally, `CollectionBase` provides you with a property called `List`, which in turn has `Add` and `Remove` methods that you can use to store items. That's precisely what you use when you need to add or remove items from the list:

```
'Add a customer to the collection
Public Sub Add(ByVal newCustomer As Customer)
    Me.List.Add(newCustomer)
End Sub

'Remove a customer from the collection
Public Sub Remove(ByVal oldCustomer As Customer)
    Me.List.Remove(oldCustomer)
End Sub
```

Building collections this way is a .NET best practice. As a newcomer to .NET programming, you may not appreciate just how useful this is, but trust us — it is. Whenever you need to use a collection of classes, this technique is the right way to go and one that you'll be familiar with.

Adding an Item Property

At the beginning of this section, you read that you were supposed to add two methods and one property. You've seen the methods but not the property, so take a look at it in the next Try It Out.

Try It Out   Adding an Item Property

1. Return to Visual Studio 2008, open the Code Editor for the `CustomerCollection` class, and add this code:

```
'Item property to read or update a customer at a given position
'in the list
Default Public Property Item(ByVal index As Integer) As Customer
    Get
        Return CType(Me.List.Item(index), Customer)
    End Get
```

```
                       Set(ByVal value As Customer)
                           Me.List.Item(index) = value
                       End Set
                   End Property
```

2. To verify that this works, open the Code Editor for Form1. Modify the `SelectedCustomer` property with this code:

```
Public ReadOnly Property SelectedCustomer() As Customer
    Get
        If lstCustomers.SelectedIndex <> -1 Then
            'Return the selected customer
            Return objCustomers(lstCustomers.SelectedIndex)
        End If
    End Get
End Property
```

3. Run the project. Click the Test button and note that when you select items in the list, the details are shown in the fields as they were before.

How It Works

The `Item` property is actually very important; it gives the developer direct access to the data stored in the list but maintains the strongly typed nature of the collection.

If you look at the code again for `SelectedCustomer`, you'll notice that when you wanted to return the given item from within `objCustomers`, you didn't have to provide the property name of `Item`. Instead, `objCustomers` behaved as if it were an array:

```
            If lstCustomers.SelectedIndex <> -1 Then
                'Return the selected customer
                Return objCustomers(lstCustomers.SelectedIndex)
            End If
```

IntelliSense tells you to enter the index of the item that you require and that you should expect to get a `Customer` structure in return.

The reason you don't have to specify the property name of `Item` is that you marked the property as the default by using the `Default` keyword:

```
            'Item property to read or update a customer at a given position
            'in the list
            Default Public Property Item(ByVal index As Integer) As Customer
                Get
                    Return CType(Me.List.Item(index), Customer)
                End Get
                Set(ByVal value As Customer)
                    Me.List.Item(index) = value
                End Set
            End Property
```

A given class can have only a single default property, and that property must take a parameter of some kind. This parameter must be an index or search term of some description. The one used here provides an index to an element in a collection list. You can have multiple overloaded versions of the same property so that, for example, you could provide an e-mail address rather than an index. This provides a great deal of flexibility to enhance your class further.

What you have at this point is the following:

❏ A way of storing a list of Customer structures, and just Customer structures

❏ A way of adding new items to the collection on demand

❏ A way of removing existing items from the collection on demand

❏ A way of accessing members in the collection as if it were an ArrayList

Building Lookup Tables with Hashtable

So far, whenever you want to find something in an array or in a collection, you have to provide an integer index representing the position of the item. It's common to end up needing a way of being able to look up an item in a collection when you have something other than an index. For example, you might want to find a customer when you provide an e-mail address.

In this section you'll take a look at the Hashtable. This is a special kind of collection that works on a *key-value* principle.

Using Hashtables

A Hashtable is a collection in which each item is given a *key*. This key can be used at a later time to unlock the value. So, if you add Darrel's Customer structure to the Hashtable, you'll be given a key that matches his e-mail address of dhilton@somecompany.com. If at a later time you come along with that key, you'll be able to find his record quickly.

Whenever you add an object to the Hashtable, it calls a method System.Object.GetHashCode, which provides a unique integer value for that object that is the same every time it is called, and uses this integer ID as the key. Likewise, whenever you want to retrieve an object from the Hashtable, it calls GetHashCode on the object to get a lookup key and matches that key against the ones it has in the list. When it finds it, it returns the related value to you.

Lookups from a Hashtable are very, very fast. Irrespective of the object you pass in, you're only matching on a relatively small integer ID. You learn to use a Hashtable in the following Try It Out.

An integer ID takes up 4 bytes of memory, so if you pass in a 100-character string (which is 200 bytes long), the lookup code only needs to compare 4 bytes, which makes everything run really quickly.

Try It Out   Using a Hashtable

1.   Return to Visual Studio 2008 and open the Code Editor for the `CustomerCollection` class. Add the highlighted member to the top of the class definition:

```
Public Class CustomerCollection
    Inherits CollectionBase

        'Private member
        Private objEmailHashtable As New Hashtable
```

2.   Next, add this read-only property to the class:

```
        'EmailHashtable property to return the Email Hashtable
        Public ReadOnly Property EmailHashtable() As Hashtable
            Get
                Return objEmailHashtable
            End Get
        End Property
```

3.   Now, make this change to the `Add` method:

```
        'Add a customer to the collection
        Public Sub Add(ByVal newCustomer As Customer)
            Me.List.Add(newCustomer)

            'Add the email address to the Hashtable
            EmailHashtable.Add(newCustomer.Email, newCustomer)
        End Sub
```

4.   Next, add this overloaded version of the `Item` property that allows you to find a customer by e-mail address:

```
        'Overload Item property to find a customer by email address
        Default Public ReadOnly Property Item(ByVal email As String) As Customer
            Get
                Return CType(EmailHashtable.Item(email), Customer)
            End Get
        End Property
```

5.   Open the Forms Designer for Form1, resize the controls on your form, and add a new Button control next to the E-mail text box as shown in Figure 5-20. Set the `Name` property of the button to **btnLookup** and the `Text` property to **Lookup**.

Figure 5-20

6. Double-click the Lookup button and add the following highlighted code to its `Click` event handler:

```
Private Sub btnLookup_Click(ByVal sender As System.Object, _
    ByVal e As System.EventArgs) Handles btnLookup.Click

    'Declare a customer object and set it to the customer
    'with the email address to be found
    Dim objFoundCustomer As Customer = objCustomers(txtEmail.Text)

    If Not IsNothing(objFoundCustomer.Email) Then
        'Display the customers name
        MessageBox.Show("The customers name is: " & _
            objFoundCustomer.Name, "Structure Demo")
    Else
        'Display an error
        MessageBox.Show("There is no customer with the e-mail" & _
            " address " & txtEmail.Text & ".", "Structure Demo")
    End If
End Sub
```

7. Run the project and click the List Customer button to populate the list of customers. If you enter an e-mail address that does not exist into the E-mail text box and click the Lookup button, you'll see a message box similar to the one shown in Figure 5-21.

Figure 5-21

If you enter an e-mail address that does exist, for example, `dhilton@somecompany.com`, the name of the customer is shown in the message box.

How It Works

You've added a new member to the `CustomerCollection` class that can be used to hold a `Hashtable`:

```
'Private member
Private objEmailHashtable As New Hashtable
```

Whenever you add a new `Customer` to the collection, you also add it to the `Hashtable`:

```
'Add a customer to the collection
Public Sub Add(ByVal newCustomer As Customer)
    Me.List.Add(newCustomer)

    'Add the email address to the Hashtable
    EmailHashtable.Add(newCustomer.Email, newCustomer)
End Sub
```

However, unlike the kinds of `Add` methods that you saw earlier, the `EmailHashtable.Add` method takes two parameters. The first is the key, and you're using the e-mail address as the key. The key can be any object you like, but it must be unique. You cannot supply the same key twice. (If you try to, an exception will be thrown.) The second parameter is the value that you want to link the key to, so whenever you give that key to the `Hashtable`, you get that object back.

The next trick is to create an overloaded version of the default `Item` property. This one, however, takes a string as its only parameter. IntelliSense displays the overloaded method as items 1 and 2 when you access it from your code.

This time you can provide either an index or an e-mail address. If you use an e-mail address, you end up using the overloaded version of the Item property, and this defers to the Item property of the Hashtable object. This takes a key and returns the related item, provided that the key can be found:

```
'Overload Item property to find a customer by email address
Default Public ReadOnly Property Item(ByVal email As String) As Customer
    Get
        Return EmailHashtable.Item(email)
    End Get
End Property
```

At this point, you have a collection class that not only enables you to look up items by index but also allows you to look up customers by e-mail address.

Cleaning Up: Remove, RemoveAt, and Clear

It isn't possible to use the same key twice in a Hashtable. Therefore, you have to take steps to ensure that what's in the Hashtable matches whatever is in the list itself.

Although you implemented the Remove method in your CustomerCollection class, the CollectionBase class also provides the RemoveAt and Clear methods. Whereas Remove takes an object, RemoveAt takes an index. In the next Try It Out, you need to provide new implementations of these methods to adjust the Hashtable.

Try It Out   Cleaning Up the List

1. Return to Visual Studio 2008 and open the Code Editor for Form1. Locate the btnListCustomer_Click method and add the highlighted code to clear the two lists:

```
Private Sub btnListCustomer_Click(ByVal sender As System.Object, _
    ByVal e As System.EventArgs) Handles btnListCustomer.Click

    'Clear the lists
    objCustomers.Clear()
    lstCustomers.Items.Clear()

    'Create some customers
    CreateCustomer("Darrel", "Hilton", "dhilton@somecompany.com")
    CreateCustomer("Frank", "Peoples", "fpeoples@somecompany.com")
    CreateCustomer("Bill", "Scott", "bscott@somecompany.com")
End Sub
```

2. To demonstrate how a `Hashtable` cannot use the same key twice, run your project and click the List Customer button to have the customer list loaded. Now click the List Customer button again and you'll see the error message shown in Figure 5-22:

Figure 5-22

3. Click the Stop Debugging button on the toolbar in Visual Studio 2008 to stop the program.

4. Add the following method to the `CustomerCollection` class:

```
'Provide a new implementation of the Clear method
Public Shadows Sub Clear()
    'Clear the CollectionBase
    MyBase.Clear()
    'Clear your hashtable
    EmailHashtable.Clear()
End Sub
```

5. Modify the `Remove` method as follows:

```
'Remove a customer from the collection
Public Sub Remove(ByVal oldCustomer As Customer)
    Me.List.Remove(oldCustomer)

    'Remove customer from the Hashtable
    EmailHashtable.Remove(oldCustomer.Email.ToLower)
End Sub
```

6. Add the `RemoveAt` method to override the default method defined in the `CollectionBase` class:

```
'Provide a new implementation of the RemoveAt method
Public Shadows Sub RemoveAt(ByVal index As Integer)
    Remove(Item(index))
End Sub
```

7. Run the project and click the List Customer button to load the customers. Click the List Customer button again to have the existing list of customers cleared before the customers are added again. Note that this time no exception has been thrown.

How It Works

The exception isn't thrown the second time around, because you are now making sure that the `Hashtable` and the internal list maintained by `CollectionBase` are properly synchronized. Specifically, whenever your `CustomerCollection` list is cleared using the `Clear` method, you make sure that the `Hashtable` is also cleared.

To clear the internal list maintained by `CollectionBase`, you ask the base class to use its own `Clear` implementation rather than try to provide your own implementation. You do this by calling `MyBase.Clear()`. Right after that, you call `Clear` on the `Hashtable`:

```
'Provide a new implementation of the Clear method
Public Shadows Sub Clear()
    'Clear the CollectionBase
    MyBase.Clear()
    'Clear your hashtable
    EmailHashtable.Clear()
End Sub
```

You'll also find that when you delete items from the collection by using `Remove`, the corresponding entry is also removed from the `Hashtable`, because of this method that you added:

```
'Provide a new implementation of the RemoveAt method
Public Shadows Sub RemoveAt(ByVal index As Integer)
    Remove(Item(index))
End Sub
```

The `Shadows` keyword indicates that this `Clear` procedure and `RemoveAt` procedure should be used instead of the `Clear` procedure and `RemoveAt` procedure in the base class. The arguments and the return type do not have to match those in the base class procedure, even though they do here.

> *You don't need to worry too much about the details of* `Shadows` *and* `Overrides` *at this point, as they are discussed in detail in Chapter 11.*

Case Sensitivity

It's about this time that case sensitivity rears its ugly head again. If you run your project and click the List Customer button and then enter a valid e-mail address in all uppercase letters, you'll see a message box indicating that there is no customer with that e-mail address.

You need to get the collection to ignore case sensitivity on the key. In the next Try It Out, you do this by making sure that whenever you save a key, you transform the e-mail address into all lowercase characters. Whenever you look up based on a key, you transform whatever you search for into lowercase characters too.

Try It Out   **Case Sensitivity**

1. Return to Visual Studio 2008, open the Code Editor for the `CustomerCollection` class, and make the highlighted change to the `Add` method:

```
'Add a customer to the collection
Public Sub Add(ByVal newCustomer As Customer)
    Me.List.Add(newCustomer)

    'Add the email address to the Hashtable
    EmailHashtable.Add(newCustomer.Email.ToLower, newCustomer)
End Sub
```

2. Find the overloaded `Item` property that takes an e-mail address and modify the code as shown here:

```
'Overload Item property to find a customer by email address
Default Public ReadOnly Property Item(ByVal email As String) As Customer
    Get
        Return CType(EmailHashtable.Item(email.ToLower), Customer)
    End Get
End Property
```

3. Find the Remove method and modify the code as shown here:

```
'Remove a customer from the collection
Public Sub Remove(ByVal oldCustomer As Customer)
    Me.List.Remove(oldCustomer)

    'Remove customer from the Hashtable
    EmailHashtable.Remove(oldCustomer.Email.ToLower)
End Sub
```

4. Run the project and click the List Customer button. Now if you enter a valid e-mail address in all uppercase, the lookup will still work.

How It Works

In Chapter 4 you saw how you could perform case-insensitive string comparisons using the `String.Compare` method. You can't use this technique here because the `Hashtable` is handling the comparison and, ideally, you don't want to produce your own version of the comparison code that the `Hashtable` uses just to do a case-insensitive match.

You can use the `ToLower` method available on strings. This creates a new string in which all of the characters are transformed into the lowercase equivalent, so whether you pass `DHILTON@SOMECOMPANY.COM` or `DHilton@SomeCompany.com` in, you always get `dhilton@somecompany.com` out.

When you add an item to the collection, you can get `ToLower` to convert the e-mail address stored in the `Customer` structure so that it is always in lowercase:

```
'Add the email address to the Hashtable
EmailHashtable.Add(newCustomer.Email.ToLower, newCustomer)
```

Likewise, when you actually do the lookup, you also turn whatever value is passed in as a parameter into all lowercase characters:

```
Return CType(EmailHashtable.Item(email.ToLower), Customer)
```

When you're consistent with it, this action makes uppercase characters "go away" — in other words, you'll never end up with uppercase characters being stored in the key or being checked against the key.

> *This technique for removing the problem of uppercase characters can be used for normal string comparisons, but* `String.Compare` *is more efficient.*

Advanced Array Manipulation

Being able to manipulate the size of an array from code, and being able to store complex sets of data in an array is important, but with .NET it's far easier to achieve both of these using the collection functionality that the majority of this chapter has discussed. The following two sections are included for completeness and so that you can make the comparisons between the two for yourself.

Dynamic Arrays

When using an array, if you want to change its size in order to add items, or clean up space when you remove items, you need to use the `ReDim` keyword to make it a dynamic array. This is a short form of, not surprisingly, *redimension*. In the next Try It Out, you'll reuse the Array Demo project you created at the start of the chapter and tweak it so that you can add new friends to the array after the initial array has been created.

Try It Out   Using ReDim

1. Find and open the Array Demo project in Visual Studio 2008. Open the Code Editor for `Form1` and modify the code in the `AddItemsToList` method so that it looks like this:

```
Private Sub AddItemsToList(ByVal arrayList() As String)
    'Enumerate the array
    For Each strName As String In arrayList
        'Add the array item to the list
        lstFriends.Items.Add("[" & strName & "]")
    Next
End Sub
```

2. Run the project and click the Initializing Arrays with Values button. Your form should look like Figure 5-23; note the square brackets around each name.

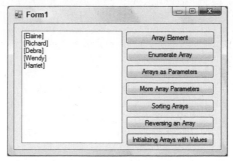

Figure 5-23

3. Stop the project and make the highlighted change to the `btnInitializingArraysWithValues_Click` method:

```
Private Sub btnInitializingArraysWithValues_Click( _
    ByVal sender As System.Object, ByVal e As System.EventArgs) _
    Handles btnInitializingArraysWithValues.Click

    'Clear the list
    ClearList()

    'Declare and populate an array
    Dim strMyFriends() As String = {"Elaine", "Richard", "Debra", _
        "Wendy", "Harriet"}

    'Make the strMyFriends array larger
    ReDim strMyFriends(6)
    strMyFriends(5) = "Lane"
    strMyFriends(6) = "Joel"

    'List your friends
    AddItemsToList(strMyFriends)
End Sub
```

4. Run the project again and click the Initializing Arrays with Values button. Your form should look like the one shown in Figure 5-24.

Figure 5-24

How It Works

After defining an array of five items, you use the ReDim keyword to redimension the array to have an upper boundary of 6, which, as you know, gives it a size of 7. After you do that, you have two new items in the array to play with — items 5 and 6:

```
'Make the strMyFriends array larger
ReDim strMyFriends(6)
strMyFriends(5) = "Lane"
strMyFriends(6) = "Joel"
```

Then, you can pass the resized array through to AddItemsToList:

```
'List your friends
AddItemsToList(strMyFriends)
```

But, as you can see from the results, the values for the first five items have been lost. (This is why you wrapped brackets around the results — if the name stored in the array is blank, you still see something appear in the list.) ReDim does indeed resize the array, but when an array is redimensioned, by default all of the values in the array are cleared, losing the values you defined when you initialized the array in the first place.

You can solve this problem by using the Preserve keyword.

Using Preserve

By including the Preserve keyword with the ReDim keyword, you can instruct Visual Basic 2008 to not clear the existing items. One thing to remember is that if you make an array smaller than it originally was, data will be lost from the eliminated elements even if you use Preserve. In the next Try It Out, you use Preserve.

Try It Out   **Using Preserve**

1. Return to Visual Studio 2008, open the Code Editor for Form1, and modify the
`btnInitializingArraysWithValues_Click` method as follows:

```
'Make the strMyFriends array larger
ReDim Preserve strMyFriends(6)
strMyFriends(5) = "Lane"
strMyFriends(6) = "Joel"
```

2. Run the project again and click the Initializing Arrays with Values button. You should now
find that the existing items in the array are preserved, as shown in Figure 5-25.

Figure 5-25

Summary

In this chapter, you saw some ways in which you could manage complex groups of data. You started by
looking at the concept of an array, or rather, defining a special type of variable that's configured to hold a
one-dimensional list of similar items rather than a single item.

You then looked at the concepts behind enumerations and constants. Both of these can be used to great
effect in making more readable and manageable code. An enumeration lets you define human-readable,
common-sense titles for basic variable types. So rather than saying `"CurrentState = 2"`, you can say
`"CurrentState = DayAction.TravelingToWork"`. Constants allow you to define literal values
globally and use them elsewhere in your code.

You then looked at structures. These are similar to classes and are well suited for storing groups of items
of information that all pertain to a particular thing or person. After looking at these, you moved on to
look at various types of collections, including the basic `ArrayList` and then saw how you could build
your own powerful collection classes inherited from `CollectionBase`. Finally, you looked at the
`Hashtable` class and covered some of the less commonly used array functionality.

To summarize, you should know how to:

- ❑ Define and redimension fixed and dynamic string arrays
- ❑ Enumerate through arrays and find their upper dimension
- ❑ Define an enumeration of values using the Enum class
- ❑ Create and use structures to manipulate sets of related data
- ❑ Use an ArrayList to hold any type of object
- ❑ Use collections to manage sets of related data

Exercises

1. Create a Windows Forms Application that contains three buttons. Add an enumeration of three names to your code. For the Click event for each button, display a message box containing a member name and value from the enumeration.

2. Create a Windows Forms Application that contains a TextBox control and a Button control. At the form level, create a names array initialized with a single name. In the Click event for the button control, add the code to redimension the array by one element while preserving the existing data, add the new name from the text box to the array, and display the last name added to the array in a message box.

Hint: To determine the upper boundary of the array, use the GetUpperBound(0) method.

6

Extensible Application Markup Language (XAML)

In the past, user interface (UI) designers have often relied on tools like Adobe Dreamweaver and Photoshop to develop screen mockups of Windows applications and HTML for web applications. Although these tools do provide designers with cutting-edge tools to create graphics, they are limited to creating graphics and have limited ability to create actual Windows forms and web forms. Up to this point, these limited tools have hindered UI designers from creating rich user interfaces, forcing them to rely on developers who have access to tools like Visual Studio.

Microsoft has recognized the separation of duties between UI designers and developers and has created a new language and a new set of tools to assist UI designers, allowing them to create the Windows forms and web forms that will be used by developers to create world-class applications.

This new language comes in the form of the Extensible Application Markup Language (XAML), pronounced *Zammel*. Because XAML is an extensible application markup language, the language defines the elements of the user interface. This allows not only Microsoft to create tools for designing user interfaces such as Expression Blend and Expression Design, but other companies as well. One such example of this is the Aurora XAML Designer from Mobiform Software, which enables UI designers to create user interfaces for Windows and web applications.

In this chapter, you will learn:

- ❑ What XAML is and how it applies to the .NET Framework
- ❑ How XAML relates to the Windows Presentation Foundation (WPF)
- ❑ How to create WPF applications in Visual Studio 2008

What Is XAML?

As previously mentioned, XAML is an Extensible Application Markup Language. But what exactly does this mean? Wikipedia (www.wikipedia.org) defines XAML as a declarative XML-based language used to initialize structured values and objects. Others define XAML as a declarative XML-based language that defines objects and their properties.

Given these definitions you can begin to understand how the acronym for this new language was formed. You can see that this new language is based on XML, which has become the industry standard for sharing structured data between applications. The A in XAML is the application part of the acronym, and the declarative part of the definition refers to the language's ability to declare objects that represent controls on a form.

So you can start to visualize that this new language defines an application's UI in an XML-type language by defining the controls on a form. The controls that XAML defines map to classes in the .NET Framework. Keep in mind that XAML is an application markup language used to define a user interface and should not be confused with a programming language such as Visual Basic 2008.

To illustrate this point, take a look at a basic Windows application defined in XAML and the output that it produces as shown in Figure 6-1. You can see that XAML looks a lot like XML because is an XML-based language and adheres to the XML standard. You can also see that the controls defined in the sample in Figure 6-1 map to classes in the .NET Framework and that the output looks like a standard windows application that you've already created in previous chapters.

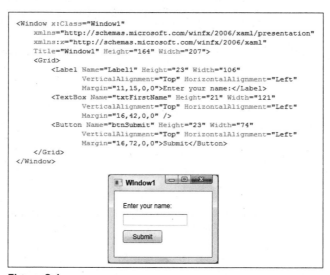

```
<Window x:Class="Window1"
    xmlns="http://schemas.microsoft.com/winfx/2006/xaml/presentation"
    xmlns:x="http://schemas.microsoft.com/winfx/2006/xaml"
    Title="Window1" Height="164" Width="207">
    <Grid>
        <Label Name="Label1" Height="23" Width="106"
            VerticalAlignment="Top" HorizontalAlignment="Left"
            Margin="11,15,0,0">Enter your name:</Label>
        <TextBox Name="txtFirstName" Height="21" Width="121"
            VerticalAlignment="Top" HorizontalAlignment="Left"
            Margin="16,42,0,0" />
        <Button Name="btnSubmit" Height="23" Width="74"
            VerticalAlignment="Top" HorizontalAlignment="Left"
            Margin="16,72,0,0">Submit</Button>
    </Grid>
</Window>
```

Figure 6-1

Given the nature of XAML and the output that it produces, you can start to visualize how XAML can more completely separate the duties of the UI designer from the developer. The UI designer would create the XAML code shown in the figure typically using a tool such as Expression Blend, Expression Design, or Aurora XAML Designer by visually creating the Windows form and having the tool create the XAML.

The next step would be for the UI designer to give the developer the XAML, which is stored in a file with a .xaml extension. The developer would import that XAML file into Visual Studio 2008 and then write the code to make the form shown in Figure 6-1 have functional meaning so that when the user clicks the button something useful happens.

You should now start to visualize the bigger picture and concept behind XAML and can see what role you might play in this picture in the future. In larger organizations that have a person or team dedicated to creating user interfaces this scenario may soon become a reality. Your job in that organization might then be to write the code to make these user interfaces functional.

XAML Syntax

The best way to learn about XAML syntax and how it all works is to take an in-depth look at an actual example. Using the XAML code shown in Figure 6-1, this section breaks down the pieces so you have an understanding of how it all fits together and how it relates to the .NET Framework, and explains the syntax along the way.

Every element in a XAML file maps to a .NET Framework class, thus creating a corresponding object at runtime. XAML files can be parsed at runtime although it is more typical that they are part of an application and are compiled into an executable file.

The following code defines the basic Windows form that you have dealt with in the previous chapters. Here you notice that the element name is Window, which corresponds to the Window class in the .NET Framework instead of the typical Form class that you've been dealing with. The Window element is the root element in this XAML document, and like every well-formed XML document it must contain only one root element.

The attributes of the Window element define the namespaces used in this XAML document and map to properties of the Window class. The XML standard xmlns attribute, typical of most XML documents, defines the schema used with this XAML document. The xmlns:x attribute defines a custom namespace within the document with the name of x, and custom namespaces can also be found in other complex XML documents.

The x:Class attribute provides a name for the Window class and in this example the class name is Window1. The Title attribute maps to the Title property of the Window class and sets the title that is displayed in the window, as shown in the form in Figure 6-1.

The Height and Width attributes map to the Height and Width properties of the Window class. These attributes are used to define the height and width of the window as was seen in Figure 6-1.

```
<Window x:Class="Window1"
    xmlns="http://schemas.microsoft.com/winfx/2006/xaml/presentation"
    xmlns:x="http://schemas.microsoft.com/winfx/2006/xaml"
    Title="Window1" Height="164" Width="207">
</Window>
```

Unlike the Windows forms that you've been using in the previous chapters, the Window class does not have a design surface that allows you to just start drawing controls on; it needs to have a container control that will in turn host other controls. There are several different container controls available for use in XAML, each with its own purpose. The Grid class, however, is the default container that gets added to XAML when using Visual Studio 2008 to design a XAML window. This is represented in the following code by the Grid element.

The Grid element allows you to precisely position controls in the window using columns and rows. Basically, it behaves in the same manner as the forms that you've been using up to this point.

```
<Window x:Class="Window1"
    xmlns="http://schemas.microsoft.com/winfx/2006/xaml/presentation"
    xmlns:x="http://schemas.microsoft.com/winfx/2006/xaml"
    Title="Window1" Height="164" Width="207">
    <Grid>
    </Grid>
</Window>
```

The first control that you see in the window in Figure 6-1 is a label that contains the text Enter your name:. This is represented in XAML by the Label element, which maps to the Label class in the .NET Framework.

The Name attribute on the Label element maps back to the Name property of the Label class and is the name that you would reference in code should you choose to the change the text displayed in the label. The Height and Width attributes map to the Height and Width attributes of the Label class and specify the height and width of the label in the window.

The VerticalAlignment attribute maps to its corresponding property in the Label class and sets the label's vertical alignment within the Grid. This attribute has a value of Top indicating that this control should align to the top of the Grid. Other possible values are Center, Bottom, and Stretch.

The HorizontalAlignment attribute specifies the horizontal alignment of the Label within the Grid and maps to the same named property in the Label class. Possible values for this attribute are Left, Right, Center, and Stretch.

The Margin attribute maps to the Margin property of the Label class and specifies the outer margin of the element. The Margin property defines a Thickness structure that contains Double values for the Left, Top, Right, and Bottom sides of the rectangle.

To put this into perspective, the Enter your name: label has a Left margin of 11 and a Top margin of 15. If you set both of these margins to a value of 0, it would cause the label to be aligned to the very left and very top of the Grid.

The inner text of the Label element is the text that gets displayed on the form. In a label on a Windows form that you've been using up to this point, the text in the label would be set using the Text property. The inner text of the Label element in XAML instead maps back to the Content property in the Label class in the .NET Framework. This is a little confusing and is worth keeping in the back of your mind in case you ever want to change the text of a label in code.

At this point you can start to see how a complete window is starting to take shape with the various XAML elements and their attributes.

```
<Window x:Class="Window1"
    xmlns="http://schemas.microsoft.com/winfx/2006/xaml/presentation"
    xmlns:x="http://schemas.microsoft.com/winfx/2006/xaml"
    Title="Window1" Height="164" Width="207">
    <Grid>
```

```
        <Label Name="Label1" Height="23" Width="106"
               VerticalAlignment="Top" HorizontalAlignment="Left"
               Margin="11,15,0,0">Enter your name:</Label>
    </Grid>
</Window>
```

Let's continue building out the code for this simple form to see how the next element, a text box control, aligns using the Margin attribute. In the following code you can see that the text box control is represented by the TextBox element, which maps to the TextBox class in the .NET Framework. The Name attribute also maps to the Name property of the class and again, this is the property that you will use to access the text contained in this control in your code.

The Height and Width attributes also map to their named counterparts in the TextBox class in the .NET Framework and specify the height and width of the text box. Again the VerticalAlignment and HorizontalAlignment attributes set the vertical and horizontal alignment in the grid specifying that this control should be aligned to the left and top of the Grid.

The Margin attribute is what is really interesting here. This attribute maps to the Margin property in the TextBox class and behaves in the same manner as it does for the Label element. Remember that the Margin property defines a Thickness structure that contains Double values for the Left, Top, Right, and Bottom sides of the rectangle.

The Left attribute, as you would guess, specifies the distance from the left side of the Grid. Similarly, the Top margin specifies the top of this control from the top of the Grid, not from the bottom of the previous control as you might expect.

If you wanted to specify some initial text for the TextBox element, you would create an ending tag of </TextBox> and place the text between the beginning tag and ending tag just as it was specified in the Label element. You can also access the text entered by the user in your code by querying the Text property of the TextBox class.

```
<Window x:Class="Window1"
    xmlns="http://schemas.microsoft.com/winfx/2006/xaml/presentation"
    xmlns:x="http://schemas.microsoft.com/winfx/2006/xaml"
    Title="Window1" Height="164" Width="207">
    <Grid>
        <Label Name="Label1" Height="23" Width="106"
               VerticalAlignment="Top" HorizontalAlignment="Left"
               Margin="11,15,0,0">Enter your name:</Label>
        <TextBox Name="txtFirstName" Height="21" Width="121"
               VerticalAlignment="Top" HorizontalAlignment="Left"
               Margin="16,42,0,0" />
    </Grid>
</Window>
```

The final control in this sample XAML code is a Button control. The Button element in the following code maps to the Button class in the .NET Framework, and all of the attributes specified map to their counterparts in the Button class and behave as already discussed.

The text that is displayed on the button lies between the beginning and ending tags of the `Button` element. Like the `Label` element, this text is accessed through code via the `Content` property.

```
<Window x:Class="Window1"
    xmlns="http://schemas.microsoft.com/winfx/2006/xaml/presentation"
    xmlns:x="http://schemas.microsoft.com/winfx/2006/xaml"
    Title="Window1" Height="164" Width="207">
    <Grid>
        <Label Name="Label1" Height="23" Width="106"
                VerticalAlignment="Top" HorizontalAlignment="Left"
                Margin="11,15,0,0">Enter your name:</Label>
        <TextBox Name="txtFirstName" Height="21" Width="121"
                VerticalAlignment="Top" HorizontalAlignment="Left"
                Margin="16,42,0,0" />
        <Button Name="btnSubmit" Height="23" Width="74"
                VerticalAlignment="Top" HorizontalAlignment="Left"
                Margin="16,72,0,0">Submit</Button>
    </Grid>
</Window>
```

At this point, you've seen what XAML looks like and the results that it can produce. You should have a basic understanding of XAML and how it relates to XML and the .NET Framework. The one piece that is missing is how XAML relates to Windows Presentation Foundation, which is the next topic of conversation.

Windows Presentation Foundation

Windows Presentation Foundation, better known as WPF, is a presentation technology built into the .NET Framework and used to build rich user interfaces in WPF Windows and WPF Web applications. WPF Windows applications differ from the Windows Forms applications that you've built thus far as it separates the user interface code from the application's business logic code in much the same way that web forms in a web application do. The user interface code, as you might have guessed, is XAML. You'll learn more about web forms and its code separation in Chapter 18.

WPF is represented in the .NET Framework in the PresentationFramework.dll and contains its own set of classes for building controls in WPF. For instance, if you display the Button Class topic in the MSDN Library that gets installed with Visual Studio 2008, you'll get a index result prompting you to select the appropriate class: Web, WPF, or Windows.

You'll find most of the common controls (such as Label, TextBox, ComboBox, and Button) that exist for Windows Forms also exist in WPF. Although most of the properties, events, and methods are the same, there are some subtle differences as you will soon discover.

At this point you may be wondering what you can do in WPF applications that you can't do in a Windows Forms application. Most everything that can be done in a WPF application can be done in a Windows Forms application. However, WPF applications make it easier to do more complex tasks such as working with and manipulating images.

Figure 6-2 demonstrates some of the power of Windows Presentation Foundation in a WPF application. Notice that the image displayed on the form is skewed at an angle and contains a partial shadow of the image that fades out. The presentation code for this entire form is represented in XAML and you will walk through the steps to create this form in the next Try It Out.

Figure 6-2

Creating a Rich WPF User Interface

One of the strong points of WPF Windows applications is the ease with which you can create rich three-dimensional images in a user interfaces such as the one shown in Figure 6-2. You can take a two-dimensional image, skew it at an angle, and add a drop shadow of the image that fades out. You will start to create the user interface shown in Figure 6-2 in the next Try It Out.

If you want to use the same credit card image as shown in Figure 6-2, you can download the code for this chapter at the Wrox web site at www.wrox.com. The download includes this image as well as the code for this application.

Try It Out   Creating a Rich WPF User Interface

1. Open Visual Studio 2008 and from the File menu select New Project. In the New Project dialog box, select Visual Basic in the Project Types list and WPF Application in the Templates list. Enter **Credit Card** in the Name field and click OK.

2. Note that the Forms Designer is divided into two sections. The top section contains the visual representation of the form while the bottom section contains the XAML code used to create the visual representation. You can modify the form contents by clicking on the form or form controls and setting their properties in the Properties window or you can modify the properties directly in the XAML code.

Modify the properties for the Window element in the XAML editor by setting the Height property to **600** and the Width property to **800**.

3. Before adding any controls to the form, you want to add the credit card image to your project. Right-click the Credit Card project in the Solution Explorer and select Add ⇨ Existing Item. Browse to the downloaded credit card image or an image of your choice and then click Add in the Add Existing Item dialog box.

4. Click in the middle of the window in the Forms Designer which is the Grid control. Now drag a Label control from the Toolbox and align it at the top of the window and center it from left to right. In the Properties window, set the Content property to **Apply for Your Card Today**.

Scroll down in the Properties window until you find the FontFamily property and then set it to **Segoe UI**. Set the FontSize property to **18** and the FontWeight property to **Bold**.

Now resize the Label control in the window until all of the text appears and then reposition it so it is centered in the form.

5. A Border control will be used to apply the various effects to the image. Drag a Border from the Toolbox and drop it on your window. In the XAML Code Editor, set the Margin property to **0,60,0,0**. Set the following properties in the Properties window:

❑   Set Width to **380**.

❑   Set Height to **200**.

6. Drag an Image control from the Toolbox and drop it in the Border control in the window. Set the following properties in the Properties window:

❑   Set Source to **CreditCard.jpg**.

❑   Set Height to **185**.

❑   Set Width to **300**.

❑   Set Height to **200**.

7. In the XAML Code Editor, click the Border element. In the Properties window, change the BitmapEffect property to DropShadowBitmapEffect.

8. Beneath the `BitmapEffect` property in the Properties window are the sub-properties for this property. Change the following sub-properties:

❑ Set `Opacity` to **0.5**.

❑ Set `ShadowDepth` to **8**.

❑ Set `Softness` to **1**.

9. At this point your image has a shadow around the bottom and right edges. In order to skew the image you will need to modify the XAML code in the XAML Code Editor. After adding the following code, your image should look similar to the one shown in Figure 6-3.

```
</Border.BitmapEffect>
<Border.RenderTransform>
    <SkewTransform CenterX="0" CenterY="0" AngleX="0" AngleY="-3" />
</Border.RenderTransform>
```

Figure 6-3

10. Now you need to create a second border to contain the upside-down faded reflection of the credit card. Drag a Border control from the Toolbox and place it beneath the first Border control. Set the following properties in the Properties window:

❑ Set `Margin` to **41,251,0,110**.

❑ Set `Width` to **300**.

11. In the XAML Code Editor, modify the second `Border` element by adding an ending `Border` element and removing the forward slash from the end of the `Border` element. Then add the following code:

```
<Border Margin="41,259,0,102" Name="Border2" HorizontalAlignment="Left"
    Width="300">
    <Border.Background>
        <VisualBrush Visual="{Binding ElementName=Image1}">
            <VisualBrush.Transform>
                <ScaleTransform CenterX="300" CenterY="100" ScaleX="1"
                    ScaleY="-1" />
            </VisualBrush.Transform>
        </VisualBrush>
    </Border.Background>
</Border>
```

12. Now you want to make the image fade out from top to bottom. Add the following code:

```
        </VisualBrush>
    </Border.Background>
    <Border.OpacityMask>
        <LinearGradientBrush StartPoint="0,0" EndPoint="0,1">
            <GradientStop Offset="0" Color="Black"></GradientStop>
            <GradientStop Offset="0.7" Color="Transparent"></GradientStop>
        </LinearGradientBrush>
    </Border.OpacityMask>
```

13. The last thing that you want to do is to skew the image shown in the second Border control. Add the following code:

```
        </LinearGradientBrush>
    </Border.OpacityMask>
    <Border.RenderTransform>
        <SkewTransform CenterX="0" CenterY="0" AngleX="30" AngleY="-3.3" />
    </Border.RenderTransform>
```

14. Save your project by clicking the Save All button on the toolbar. After your project has been saved, go ahead and run it. Your window should look similar to the one shown in Figure 6-4.

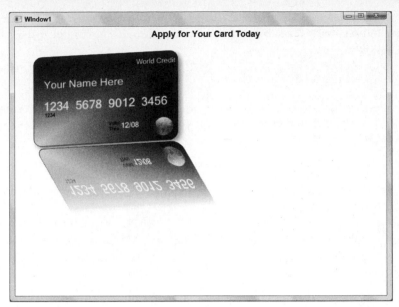

Figure 6-4

How It Works

You start by modifying the size of the form and you have a choice of setting the Height and Width properties in the Properties window or using the XAML editor. You selected to modify the Height and Width properties in the XAML editor and as you changed the Height property you saw the form resized immediately.

Next, you add an existing image to the project to be used in the Image control. You then add the Label control for the title and modify the properties for that control to have it centered in the window and to display the Segoe UI font.

The Border control has numerous built-in properties that allow you to render various effects on the objects contained in the Border control. You add an Image control inside the Border control in order to apply the effects available in the Border control to the image.

The BitmapEffect property allows you to create a shadow effect around the bottom and right edges of the image by setting this property to DropShadowBitmapEffect. You fine-tune the shadow created by the BitmapEffect property by setting the sub-property Opacity to control the darkness of the shadow, the ShadowDepth sub-property to control the width of the shadow, and the Softness sub-property to control the softness of the shadow from one edge to the other. After applying the BitmapEffect property your image has a shadow around the bottom and right edges.

In order to skew the image at an angle, you add the following code. The RenderTransform property sets the transformation that affects the rendering of the contents contained in the Border control. The SkewTransform element is used to transform a two-dimensional object into a three-dimensional object, in this case the image of the credit card.

The CenterX and CenterY attributes specify the center coordinates of the transform and have been set to a value of 0 to specify the center of the image. The AngleX attribute specifies the X coordinate of the skew angle, which in this case is the starting point. The `AngleY` attribute specifies the `Y` coordinate of the skew and in this case has been set to a value of `-3`:

```
<Border.RenderTransform>
    <SkewTransform CenterX="0" CenterY="0" AngleX="0" AngleY="-3" />
</Border.RenderTransform>
```

The second Border control that you added to the window provides the upside-down faded reflection of the credit card. When you add the following code, you immediately see an upside-down image of the credit card contained in the `Image` element.

The `Background` property of the border sets the brush that will fill the inside area of the border. However, instead of using a solid color to fill the area inside the border you use a `VisualBrush`. A `VisualBrush` paints an area with a visual image, in this case the image of the credit card. The `Visual` attribute shown in the following code is used to set the visual content of the `VisualBrush` and is bound to the `Image` element whose `Name` property is set to `Image1`. You specify the `Binding ElementName` keywords to bind the Image to the `Visual` attribute.

The `Transform` property is used to apply a transformation to the image contained in the `VisualBrush`. The `ScaleTransform` element is used to rotate the image upside-down. The `CenterX` and `CenterY` attributes are used to specify the center point of the transform and the `ScaleX` and `ScaleY` attributes are used to specify the X and Y axis for scaling.

The `CenterX` attribute has been set to the width of the image and the `CenterY` attribute has been set to a value of `100` to show only a portion of the credit card contained in the `Image` element. `ScaleX` has been set to a value of `1` to indicate that the image should be scaled to a one-to-one ratio, in other words its normal size. The `ScaleY` value has been set to a value of `-1` in order to rotate the image upside-down:

```
<Border.Background>
    <VisualBrush Visual="{Binding ElementName=Image1}">
        <VisualBrush.Transform>
            <ScaleTransform CenterX="300" CenterY="100" ScaleX="1"
                ScaleY="-1" />
        </VisualBrush.Transform>
    </VisualBrush>
</Border.Background>
```

The `OpacityMask` element uses a `Brush` element to set the opacity of a UI element, in this case the image of the credit card contained in the second Border control. The `LinearGradientBrush` element specifies a brush that paints an area with a linear gradient (for example, horizontal). The `StartPoint` attribute specifies the two-dimensional starting point to begin the gradient and the `EndPoint` attribute specifies the two-dimensional ending point to end the gradient.

The `GradientStop` elements are used to specify the location and color of a transition point in a gradient. The first `GradientStop` element is used to specify the color `Black` with an offset of `0` indicating the gradient vector should stop at offset 0. The second `GradientStop` element uses the color `Transparent` and specifics an offset of `0.7`. This provides the faded look starting at the top of the image where it is darker to the bottom of the image where it is barely visible:

```
<Border.OpacityMask>
    <LinearGradientBrush StartPoint="0,0" EndPoint="0,1">
        <GradientStop Offset="0" Color="Black"></GradientStop>
        <GradientStop Offset="0.7" Color="Transparent"></GradientStop>
```

```
        </LinearGradientBrush>
    </Border.OpacityMask>
```

The `RenderTransform` property and the `SkewTransform` element have already been covered during the creation of the first Border control. Here you set the `AngleX` attribute to a value of `30` indicating the angle of the transform starting at the upper left corner. The `AngleY` attribute controls the angle of the upper right corner and has been set to a value of `-3.3`:

```
<Border.RenderTransform>
    <SkewTransform CenterX="0" CenterY="0" AngleX="30" AngleY="-3.3" />
</Border.RenderTransform>
```

Using WPF Common Controls

You worked with the Label, TextBox, and Button controls in the Windows Forms applications that you built in the previous chapters. At this point you should be quite familiar with the more common properties of these controls, namely the `Name` and `Text` properties.

In the following Try It Out you will complete the user interface in the WPF Credit Card application that you have started building by adding Label, TextBox, Button, and ComboBox controls. As you add these controls to your window and set their properties, you will start to see how they differ from their Windows Forms counterparts.

Try It Out   **Using WPF Common Controls**

1. If your project is still running, stop it and return to the Forms Designer. Drag a Label control from the Toolbox and drop it on your window towards the upper right corner. Set the following properties for this control in the Properties window:

- ❏ Set `Content` to **Personal Information**.
- ❏ Set `Margin` to **0,38,89,0**.
- ❏ Set `FontFamily` to **Segoe UI**.
- ❏ Set `FontSize` to **11**.
- ❏ Set `FontWeight` to **Bold**.

2. Drag another Label control from the Toolbox and position it slightly beneath and to the left of the previous Label control. Set the following properties for this label:

- ❏ Set `Content` to **First Name**.
- ❏ Set `Width` to **95**.
- ❏ Set `Margin` to **0,69,225,0**.
- ❏ Set `FontFamily` to **Segoe UI**.

❑   Set FontSize to **11**.

3.   Drag a TextBox control from the Toolbox and position it to the right of the second label. The Name property is in the top border area of the Properties window. Set the following properties:

❑   Set Name to **txtFirstName**.

❑   Set Width to **185**.

❑   Set Margin to **0,71,35,0**.

❑   Set FontFamily to **Segoe UI**.

❑   Set FontSize to **11**.

4.   Drag a Label control from the Toolbox and align it beneath the second Label control. Set the following properties:

❑   Set Content to **Last Name**.

❑   Set Width to **95**.

❑   Set Margin to **0,99,225,0**.

❑   Set FontFamily to **Segoe UI**.

❑   Set FontSize to **11**.

5.   Drag a TextBox control from the Toolbox and position it beneath the previous TextBox control. Set the following properties:

❑   Set Name to **txtLastName**.

❑   Set Width to **185**.

❑   Set Margin to **0,101,35,0**.

❑   Set FontFamily to **Segoe UI**.

❑   Set FontSize to **11**.

6.   Drag a Label control from the Toolbox and align it beneath the previous Label control. Set the following properties:

❑   Set Content to **Address**.

❑   Set Width to **95**.

❑   Set Margin to **0,129,225,0**.

❑   Set FontFamily to **Segoe UI**.

❑   Set FontSize to **11**.

7. Drag a TextBox control from the Toolbox and position it beneath the previous TextBox control. Set the following properties:

❏ Set `Name` to **txtAddress**.

❏ Set `Width` to **185**.

❏ Set `Margin` to **0,131,35,0**.

❏ Set `FontFamily` to **Segoe UI**.

❏ Set `FontSize` to **11**.

8. Drag a Label control from the Toolbox, align it beneath the previous Label control, and set the following properties:

❏ Set `Content` to **City**.

❏ Set `Width` to **95**.

❏ Set `Margin` to **0,159,225,0**.

❏ Set `FontFamily` to **Segoe UI**.

❏ Set `FontSize` to **11**.

9. Drag a TextBox control from the Toolbox, position it beneath the previous TextBox control, and set the following properties:

❏ Set `Name` to **txtCity**.

❏ Set `Width` to **185**.

❏ Set `Margin` to **0,161,35,0**.

❏ Set `FontFamily` to **Segoe UI**.

❏ Set `FontSize` to **11**.

10. Drag a Label control from the Toolbox, align it beneath the previous Label control, and set the following properties:

❏ Set `Content` to **State**.

❏ Set `Width` to **95**.

❏ Set `Margin` to **0,189,225,0**.

❏ Set `FontFamily` to **Segoe UI**.

❏ Set `FontSize` to **11**.

11. Drag a ComboBox control from the Toolbox, position it beneath the previous TextBox control, and set the following properties:

❏ Set `Name` to **cboState**.

❏ Set `Width` to **95**.

❏ Set `Margin` to **0,191,125,0**.

❑   Set `FontFamily` to **Segoe UI**.

❑   Set `FontSize` to **11**.

12.   Drag a Label control from the Toolbox, align it beneath the previous Label control, and set the following properties:

❑   Set `Content` to **Postal Code**.

❑   Set `Width` to **95**.

❑   Set `Margin` to **0,219,225,0**.

❑   Set `FontFamily` to **Segoe UI**.

❑   Set `FontSize` to **11**.

13.   Drag a TextBox control from the Toolbox, position it beneath the previous ComboBox control, and set the following properties:

❑   Set `Name` to **txtPostalCode**.

❑   Set `Width` to **95**.

❑   Set `Margin` to **0,221,125,0**.

❑   Set `FontFamily` to **Segoe UI**.

❑   Set `FontSize` to **11**.

14.   Drag a Label control from the Toolbox, align it beneath the previous TextBox control, and set the following properties:

❑   Set `Content` to **Employment Information**.

❑   Set `Width` to **145**.

❑   Set `Margin` to **0,261,75,273**.

❑   Set `FontFamily` to **Segoe UI**.

❑   Set `FontSize` to **11**.

❑   Set `FontWeight` to **Bold**.

15.   Drag a Label control from the Toolbox, position it below and to the left of the previous Label control, and set the following properties:

❑   Set `Content` to **Company Name**.

❑   Set `Width` to **95**.

❑   Set `Margin` to **0,0,225,242**.

❑   Set `FontFamily` to **Segoe UI**.

❑   Set `FontSize` to **11**.

16. Drag a TextBox control from the Toolbox, position it to the right of the previous Label control, and set the following properties:

- ❑ Set `Name` to **txtCompanyName**.
- ❑ Set `Width` to **185**.
- ❑ Set `Margin` to **0,0,35,245**.
- ❑ Set `FontFamily` to **Segoe UI**.
- ❑ Set `FontSize` to **11**.

17. Drag a Label control from the Toolbox, position it below the previous Label control, and set the following properties:

- ❑ Set `Content` to **Address**.
- ❑ Set `Width` to **95**.
- ❑ Set `Margin` to **0,0,225,212**.
- ❑ Set `FontFamily` to **Segoe UI**.
- ❑ Set `FontSize` to **11**.

18. Drag a TextBox control from the Toolbox, position it below the previous TextBox control, and set the following properties:

- ❑ Set `Name` to **txtCompanyAddress**.
- ❑ Set `Width` to **185**.
- ❑ Set `Margin` to **0,0,35,215**.
- ❑ Set `FontFamily` to **Segoe UI**.
- ❑ Set `FontSize` to **11**.

19. Drag a Label control from the Toolbox, position it below the previous Label control, and set the following properties:

- ❑ Set `Content` to **City**.
- ❑ Set `Width` to **95**.
- ❑ Set `Margin` to **0,0,225,182**.
- ❑ Set `FontFamily` to **Segoe UI**.
- ❑ Set `FontSize` to **11**.

20. Drag a TextBox control from the Toolbox, position it below the previous TextBox control, and set the following properties:

- ❑ Set `Name` to **txtCompanyCity**.
- ❑ Set `Width` to **185**.
- ❑ Set `Margin` to **0,0,35,185**.

- ❑ Set `FontFamily` to **Segoe UI**.
- ❑ Set `FontSize` to **11**.

21. Drag a Label control from the Toolbox, position it below the previous Label control, and set the following properties:

- ❑ Set `Content` to **State**.
- ❑ Set `Width` to **95**.
- ❑ Set `Margin` to **0,0,225,152**.
- ❑ Set `FontFamily` to **Segoe UI**.
- ❑ Set `FontSize` to **11**.

22. Drag a ComboBox control from the Toolbox, position it below the previous TextBox control, and set the following properties:

- ❑ Set `Name` to **cboCompanyState**.
- ❑ Set `Width` to **95**.
- ❑ Set `Margin` to **0,0,125,155**.
- ❑ Set `FontFamily` to **Segoe UI**.
- ❑ Set `FontSize` to **11**.

23. Drag a Label control from the Toolbox, position it below the previous Label control, and set the following properties:

- ❑ Set `Content` to **Postal Code**.
- ❑ Set `Width` to **95**.
- ❑ Set `Margin` to **0,0,225,122**.
- ❑ Set `FontFamily` to **Segoe UI**.
- ❑ Set `FontSize` to **11**.

24. Drag a TextBox control from the Toolbox, position it below the previous TextBox control, and set the following properties:

- ❑ Set `Name` to **txtCompanyPostalCode**.
- ❑ Set `Width` to **95**.
- ❑ Set `Margin` to **0,0,125,125**.
- ❑ Set `FontFamily` to **Segoe UI**.
- ❑ Set `FontSize` to **11**.

25. Drag a Label control from the Toolbox, position it below the previous Label control, and set the following properties:

- ❑ Set `Content` to **Years of Service**.
- ❑ Set `Width` to **95**.
- ❑ Set `Margin` to **0,0,225,92**.
- ❑ Set `FontFamily` to **Segoe UI**.
- ❑ Set `FontSize` to **11**.

26. Drag a TextBox control from the Toolbox, position it below the previous TextBox control, and set the following properties:

- ❑ Set `Name` to **txtCompanyYearsOfService**.
- ❑ Set `Width` to **35**.
- ❑ Set `Margin` to **0,0,185,95**.
- ❑ Set `FontFamily` to **Segoe UI**.
- ❑ Set `FontSize` to **11**.

27. Drag a Label control from the Toolbox, position it below the previous Label control, and set the following properties:

- ❑ Set `Content` to **Annual Income**.
- ❑ Set `Width` to **95**.
- ❑ Set `Margin` to **0,0,225,62**.
- ❑ Set `FontFamily` to **Segoe UI**.
- ❑ Set `FontSize` to **11**.

28. Drag a TextBox control from the Toolbox, position it below the previous TextBox control, and set the following properties:

- ❑ Set `Name` to **txtCompanyAnnualIncome**.
- ❑ Set `Width` to **95**.
- ❑ Set `Margin` to **0,0,125,65**.
- ❑ Set `FontFamily` to **Segoe UI**.
- ❑ Set `FontSize` to **11**.

29. Drag a Button control from the Toolbox, position it in the bottom right corner of the window, and set the following properties:

- ❑ Set `Name` to **btnApplyNow**.
- ❑ Set `Content` to **Apply Now**.
- ❑ Set `Margin` to **0,0,35,16**.

❏ Set `FontFamily` to **Segoe UI**.

❏ Set `FontSize` to **11**.

30. Save your project and then run it. Your completed form should look similar to Figure 6-5.

Figure 6-5

How It Works

Adding controls to a WPF window is no different than adding controls to a Windows form, as you discovered. You simply drag the control from the Toolbox and drop it on the window. The difference comes when you try to position a control and align it to other controls.

In a Windows Forms application, you can drag a control from the Toolbox and align it to other controls with snap lines before releasing the left mouse button. In a WPF application you drag the control and place it on the form first and then reposition the control before you see any snap lines when aligning it with other controls.

A TextBox control in a WPF application has a `Text` property to specify the text displayed in the control as it does in a Windows Form application. However, the Label and Button control do not use the `Text` property to specify the text displayed in the control as they do in a Windows Forms application; instead, they use the `Content` property.

You'll undoubtedly have noticed that you must use the `Margin` property to reposition controls from within the Properties Window unlike using the `Location` property in a Windows Forms application. The differences in the properties do not stop at being named differently. The `Location` property uses a set of X,Y coordinates that position a control relative to the upper left corner of the form.

The `Margin` property of a WPF control specifies the outer margins of the control as `Left`, `Top`, `Right`, and `Bottom`. Where the control is placed on a window will determine which of the margins are used to position the control relative to the window bounds. For example, placing a control toward the upper left corner of the window will cause the `Left` and `Top` margins to be set with values relative to the upper left corner of the window. Placing a control toward the upper right of the window will cause the `Top` and `Right` margin values to be set relative to the upper right of the window.

You may also have noticed that the Properties Window does not provide as rich of an interface as the Properties Windows in a Windows Forms application. Case in point is the `FontFamily` property. In a Windows Forms application the `Font` property provides the Font dialog that allows you to choose the font, style, and size desired. In a WPF application, you must type the actual name of the font in the box provided for the `FontFamily` property.

With these differences and limitations aside, WPF applications do allow you to create some stunning graphics in your applications. Although WPF may not be the norm for most applications, it does have a growing presence in desktop and browser applications.

Wiring Up Events

In the following Try It Out you will wire up some event handlers in the code to load the combo boxes on the form and to handle the button being clicked. This will allow you to see firsthand how similar events in WPF applications are compared to Window Forms applications and how to add code to make your WPF application functional.

Try It Out   Wiring Up Events

1. If your project is still running, stop it. Right-click Window1.xaml in the Solution Explorer and choose View Code in the context menu. Add the following `Imports` statement at the top of the class:

```
Imports System.Text

Class Window1
```

2. Declare a string array to hold the abbreviations of the states that will be loaded in the combo boxes. To keep the code short, we've only included the first six state abbreviations in alphabetical order. Add the following highlighted code to your class:

```
Class Window1

    'Private variables
    Private strStates() As String = {"AL", "AK", "AZ", "AR", "CA", "CO"}
```

3. You want to load the combo boxes with the data from the `strStates` array. The best time to do this is when the window is loaded and after all the controls have been initialized. Select `(Windows1 Events)` in the Class Name combo box at the top of the Code Editor and then select the `Loaded` event in the Method Name combo box. Add the following highlighted code to the event handler:

```
Private Sub Window1_Loaded(ByVal sender As Object, _
    ByVal e As System.Windows.RoutedEventArgs) Handles Me.Loaded

        'Bind the combo boxes to the strStates array
        cboState.ItemsSource = strStates
        cboCompanyState.ItemsSource = strStates

    End Sub
```

4. When the user clicks the button on the window, you want the application to perform some action. To keep the code simple, display a message box with some information from the window. Select `btnApplyNow` in the Class Name combo box and the `Click` event in the Method Name combo box. Add the following highlighted code to the event handler:

```
Private Sub btnApplyNow_Click(ByVal sender As Object, _
    ByVal e As System.Windows.RoutedEventArgs) Handles btnApplyNow.Click

        'Declare and instantiate a StringBuilder object
        Dim objStringBuilder As New StringBuilder

        'Add the question
        objStringBuilder.AppendLine("Is your personal " & _
            "information listed here correct?")
        objStringBuilder.AppendLine(String.Empty)

        'Add the personal information
        objStringBuilder.AppendLine(txtFirstName.Text & " " & _
            txtLastName.Text)
        objStringBuilder.AppendLine(txtAddress.Text)
        objStringBuilder.AppendLine(txtCity.Text & ", " & _
            cboState.SelectedItem & " " & txtPostalCode.Text)

        'Display a message box to verify the information
        If MessageBox.Show(objStringBuilder.ToString, _
            My.Application.Info.Title, MessageBoxButton.YesNo, _
            MessageBoxImage.Question) = MessageBoxResult.Yes Then
            'Do some processing here
        Else
            'Return to the window and let the user correct
            'their information
        End If

    End Sub
```

5. Save your project and then run it. Enter some data in the Personal Information section of the window and click the Apply Now button. You should see results similar to the ones shown in Figure 6-6.

Figure 6-6

How It Works

You start the code by adding the `Imports` statement below. This `Imports` statement is needed for the `StringBuilder` class:

```
Imports System.Text
```

The `strStates` variable is declared as a `String` array because of the parenthesis after the variable name. Next you set the array values in the string, enclosing each string value in double quotes and separating each value with a comma. The entire list of values is enclosed in curly brackets.

```
'Private variables
Private strStates() As String = {"AL", "AK", "AZ", "AR", "CA", "CO"}
```

The code in the `Window1_Loaded` event handles loading the combo boxes with the items contained in the `strStates` string array. The `ItemsSource` property of the `ComboBox` class is used to set the `Items` collection to a list of items. You use the `ItemsSource` property when you want to bind a list of items to a combo box, such as items in a `String` array, a `DataSet`, or a `DataView`. You'll learn about the `DataSet` and `DataView` in Chapter 16.

```
Private Sub Window1_Loaded(ByVal sender As Object, _
    ByVal e As System.Windows.RoutedEventArgs) Handles Me.Loaded

    'Bind the combo boxes to the strStates array
    cboState.ItemsSource = strStates
    cboCompanyState.ItemsSource = strStates
End Sub
```

When a user clicks the Apply Now button, the Click event handler for this control is fired. The first thing that you do here is to declare and instantiate a StringBuilder object. The StringBuilder object is an efficient way to build large strings using less system resources than simply appending text to a String variable.

The AppendLine method of the StringBuilder class appends the text to the string and then automatically appends a line terminator after the data. The first line of text that you specify is a question for the user, and then you append a blank line by supplying an empty string. This will provide a separation between the question in the message box and the data that is displayed.

```
Private Sub btnApplyNow_Click(ByVal sender As Object, _
    ByVal e As System.Windows.RoutedEventArgs) Handles btnApplyNow.Click

    'Declare and instantiate a StringBuilder object
    Dim objStringBuilder As New StringBuilder

    'Add the question
    objStringBuilder.AppendLine("Is your personal " & _
        "information listed here correct?")
    objStringBuilder.AppendLine(String.Empty)
```

Next you start appending the information entered in the window to the string. First you append the first and last name on a single line, and then append the address information on the next line. The city, state, and postal code are added to the next line.

```
    'Add the personal information
    objStringBuilder.AppendLine(txtFirstName.Text & " " & _
        txtLastName.Text)
    objStringBuilder.AppendLine(txtAddress.Text)
    objStringBuilder.AppendLine(txtCity.Text & ", " & _
        cboState.SelectedItem & " " & txtPostalCode.Text)
```

Next, you want to display the results of the string in a message box. Just as you've done before, you use the MessageBox class and call the Show method. The first parameter to the Show method uses the ToString method of the StringBuilder class to output the string that has been built. The caption for the message box is set in the next parameter to the Show method. Here you use the Title property from the My.Application.Info object. This object contains useful information about your application. You'll learn more about the My namespace in Chapter 10.

The next parameter to the Show method is the buttons that should be displayed on the message box. Here you specify the YesNo constant from the MessageBoxButton enumeration. The last parameter to the Show method is the icon that should be displayed in the message box. In this parameter you specify the Question icon since you are asking the user a question.

The Show method will return a dialog result based on the buttons that you specify. Because you specify that the Yes and No buttons be displayed, the Show method will return a dialog result of either Yes or No. You handle this in an If...Then statement checking for a dialog result of Yes.

The appropriate comments have been added in the following code to indicate where you provide your own code to perform some processing. You'll learn more about the `MessageBox` and how to use its buttons and icons in If...Then statement blocks in Chapter 8.

```
'Display a message box to verify the information
If MessageBox.Show(objStringBuilder.ToString, _
    My.Application.Info.Title, MessageBoxButton.YesNo, _
    MessageBoxImage.Question) = MessageBoxResult.Yes Then
    'Do some processing here
Else
    'Return to the window and let the user correct
    'their information
End If
End Sub
```

Summary

In this chapter you took a look at what XAML is and how it can be used to build WPF applications in Visual Studio 2008. You have also seen firsthand the power of XAML and WPF in building applications with interfaces that provide rich graphic manipulation which is not easily done with Windows Forms applications.

In building the Credit Card application, you not only learned how to create a WPF application that provides rich graphic manipulation, but you also learned how to wire events to the controls in a window. At this point you should start to realize the potential of WPF applications and also start to understand how they differ from Windows Forms applications. You'll learn more about Windows Forms applications in the next chapter, which will help to tie all this information together.

To summarize, you should now know:

❑ What XAML is

❑ What WPF is and how XAML relates to it

❑ How to build a WPF application using Visual Studio 2008

❑ How to work with graphics in a WPF application

❑ How to work with control event handlers in a WPF application

Exercise

1. Add code to the Credit Card application to display a message box containing the user's state selection when they select a state in the State combo box. *Hint:* To access a control's default event handler, double-click the control in the Forms Designer.

Building Windows Applications

When Microsoft first released Visual Basic 1.0, developers fell in love with it, because it made building the user interface components of an application very simple. Instead of having to write thousands of lines of code to display windows — the very staple of a Windows application — developers could simply draw the window on the screen.

In Visual Basic (any version), a window is known as a *form*. With the .NET Framework, this form design capability has been brought to all of the managed languages as *Windows Forms* in Windows Forms Applications and as *Windows* in WPF Applications. You've been using Windows Forms over the course of the previous chapters and in the last chapter you learned about Windows in WPF Applications. However, you haven't really given that much thought to them — focusing instead on the code that you've written inside them.

In this chapter, you'll look in detail at Windows Forms and Windows and learn how you can use Visual Basic 2008 to put together fully featured Windows applications using Windows Forms Application projects and WPF Application projects. In particular, you will look at:

❑   Adding more features using buttons, text boxes, and radio buttons

❑   Creating a simple toolbar and toolbar buttons to respond to events

❑   Creating additional forms and windows in your applications

   Note that in this chapter Windows Forms refers to Windows Forms Application projects, while Windows refers to WPF Application projects.

Responding to Events

Building a user interface using Windows Forms or Windows is all about responding to *events* (such as the Click event), so programming for Windows is commonly known as *event-driven programming*. To build a form, you paint controls onto a blank window called the Forms Designer using the mouse. Each of these controls is able to tell you when an event happens. For example, if you run your program and click a button that's been painted onto a form, that button will say, "Hey, I've been clicked!" and give you an opportunity to execute some code that you provide to respond to that event. You have already been using this feature.

Setting Up a Button Event

A good way to illustrate the event philosophy is to wire up a button to an event. An example would be the Click event, which is *fired* whenever the button is clicked. You have more events than just the Click event, although in day-to-day practice it's unlikely you'll use more than a handful of these. Even though you've already seen the Click event in action, this next Try It Out will go into some of the details of Code Editor and some more Button events that you have not seen up until this point.

In the real world, you'll more than likely be tasked to work on multiple projects at the same time. When you have down time in one project you'll switch to the other project and work on it. That's what you'll be doing in the next Try It Out, working on multiple projects at one time; one Windows Forms Application project and one WPF Application project. This will allow you to see firsthand how button events are handled in each type of Windows application.

Try It Out — Using Button Events

1. Start two separate instances of Visual Studio 2008. In the first instance of Visual Studio 2008, select File ⇨ New Project from the menu. In the New Project dialog box, select Visual Basic as the Project Type and Windows Forms Application as the Templates type. Enter a project name, **Windows Forms Button Events**, in the Name field and then click the OK button.

2. Click the form in the Forms Designer and then in the Properties window, change the Text property from Form1 to **Windows Button Events**.

3. From the Toolbox, drag a Button control onto the form. Change its Text property to **Hello World!** and its Name property to **btnSayHello**. Resize your button and form so that it looks similar to the one shown in Figure 7-1.

Figure 7-1

4. Save your project by clicking the Save All button on the toolbar.

5. In the second instance of Visual Studio 2008, select File ⇨ New Project from the menu. In the New Project dialog box, select Visual Basic as the Project Type and WPF Application as the Templates type. Enter the project name **WPF Button Events** in the Name field and then click the OK button.

6. In the WPF Button Events project, click the top of the window in the Forms Designer. In the Properties window, change the Title property from Window1 to **WPF Button Events**.

7.   From the Toolbox, drag a Button control onto the form. Change its `Content` property to **Hello World!** and its `Name` property to **btnSayHello**. Resize your button and form so that it looks similar to the one shown in Figure 7-2.

Figure 7-2

8.   Save your project by clicking the Save All button on the toolbar.

9.   At this point, run both projects to get an idea of how both application types look very similar as shown in Figure 7-3.

Figure 7-3

10.   Stop both projects and return to the Forms Designer in the Windows Forms Button Events project.

11.   Double-click the button and add the following highlighted code to the `Click` event handler:

```
Private Sub btnSayHello_Click(ByVal sender As System.Object, _
    ByVal e As System.EventArgs) Handles btnSayHello.Click

    MessageBox.Show("Hello World!", Me.Text)
End Sub
```

12.   Drop down the list in the Class Name combo box at the top of the code window. You'll see the options shown in top portion of Figure 7-4. The bottom portion of Figure 7-4 shows the class members from the WPF Button Events project.

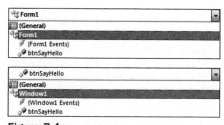

Figure 7-4

Visual Basic 2008 adds a small icon to the left of everything it displays in these lists. These can tell you what the item in the list actually is. A small purple box represents a method, a small blue box represents a member, four books stacked together represent a library, three squares joined together with lines represent a class, and a yellow lightning bolt represents an event.

Visual Studio may also decorate these icons with other icons to indicate the way they are defined. For example, next to Finalize in Figure 7-5 you'll see a small key, which tells you the method is protected. The padlock icon tells you the item is private. It's not really important to memorize all of these now, but Visual Basic 2008 is fairly consistent with its representations, so if you do learn them over time they will help you understand what's going on.

Notice that the last two items in the list are slightly indented. This tells you that (Form1 Events) and btnSayHello are all related to Form1. That is, the btnSayHello class is a member of Form1. As you add more members to the form, they will appear in this list.

In the WPF Button Events project this indentation tells you that (Window1 Events) and btnSayHello are all related to Window1. Again, as you add more members to the form, they will appear in this list.

Now select Form1 in this list.

13. Open the drop-down list from the Method Name combo box to the right of the Class Name combo box and you'll see the options shown in Figure 7-5; the top portion of the figure lists the events in the Windows Form Button Events project and the bottom portion of the figure lists the events in the WPF Button Events project. These options are described in the list that follows the figure.

Figure 7-5

❑ The contents of the Method Name combo box change depending on the item selected in the Class Name combo box. This list lets you navigate through the methods related to the selected class. In this case, its main job is to show you the methods and properties related to the class. This applies to both Windows Forms Applications and WPF Applications.

❑ The (Declarations) entry takes you to the top of the class where you can change the definition of the class and add member variables.

❑ The New method will create a new constructor for the class that you are working with. The constructor should contain any initialization code that needs to be executed for the class.

❑ The Finalize method will create a new method called Finalize and add it to the class and will be called when your program ends to release any unmanaged resources.

❑ The `Dispose` method (not available in WPF Applications) takes you to the `Dispose` method for the class that you are working with and allows you to add any addition clean up code for your class.

❑ The `InitializeComponent` method takes you to the code that initializes the controls for the class that you are working with. You should not modify this method directly. Instead, you should use the Form Designer to modify the properties of the controls on your form.

14. Select `btnSayHello` in the Class Name combo box. Now, drop down the Method Name combo box, as shown in Figure 7-6. The list on the left is from the Windows Forms Button Events project and the list on the right is from the WPF Button Events project.

Figure 7-6

Since you selected `btnSayHello` in the Class Name combo box, the Method Name combo box now contains items that are exclusively related to that control. In this case, you have a huge list of events. One of those events, `Click`, is shown in bold because you provided a definition for that event. If you select `Click`, you'll be taken to the method in the form that provides an event handler for this method.

15. Now add another event handler to the Button control. With `btnSayHello` still selected in the Class Name combo box, select the `MouseEnter` event in the Method Name combo box. A new event handler method will be created, and you need to add the following code to it as highlighted:

```
Private Sub btnSayHello_MouseEnter(ByVal sender As Object, _
    ByVal e As System.EventArgs) Handles btnSayHello.MouseEnter

    'Change the Button text
    btnSayHello.Text = "The mouse is here!"
End Sub
```

The MouseEnter event will be fired whenever the mouse pointer enters the control, in other words, crosses its boundary.

16. To complete this exercise, you need to add another event handler. With btnSayHello still selected in the Class Name combo box, select the MouseLeave event in the Method Name combo box. Again, a new event will be created, so add the highlighted code here:

```
Private Sub btnSayHello_MouseLeave(ByVal sender As Object, _
    ByVal e As System.EventArgs) Handles btnSayHello.MouseLeave

    'Change the Button text
    btnSayHello.Text = "The mouse has gone!"
End Sub
```

The MouseLeave event will be fired whenever the mouse pointer moves back outside of the control.

17. Switch over to the Forms Designer in the WPF Button Events project. Double-click the button and add the following highlighted code to the Click event handler:

```
Private Sub btnSayHello_Click(ByVal sender As System.Object, _
    ByVal e As System.Windows.RoutedEventArgs) Handles btnSayHello.Click

    MessageBox.Show("Hello World!", Me.Title)
End Sub
```

18. Now add another event handler to the Button control. With btnSayHello still selected in the Class Name combo box, select the MouseEnter event in the Method Name combo box. A new event handler method will be created, and you need to add the following code to it as highlighted:

```
Private Sub btnSayHello_MouseEnter(ByVal sender As Object, _
    ByVal e As System.Windows.Input.MouseEventArgs) _
    Handles btnSayHello.MouseEnter

    'Change the Button text
    btnSayHello.Content = "The mouse is here!"
End Sub
```

19. To complete this project, you'll need to add an event handler for the MouseLeave event. With btnSayHello still selected in the Class Name combo box, select the MouseLeave event in the Method Name combo box. Add the highlighted code to the event handler as shown:

```
Private Sub btnSayHello_MouseLeave(ByVal sender As Object, _
    ByVal e As System.Windows.Input.MouseEventArgs) _
    Handles btnSayHello.MouseLeave

    'Change the Button text
    btnSayHello.Content = "The mouse has gone!"
End Sub
```

20. Run both projects to compare how they look and perform. Note that both forms look very similar and that both forms behave exactly the same way.

The two forms in the upper left hand corner of Figure 7-7 show the Windows Buttons Events form and the WPF Button Events form. The Windows Buttons Events form has focus and the mouse has been hovered over the button.

The two forms in the upper right-hand corner of Figure 7-7 show that the mouse has left the region of the button in the Windows Buttons Events form and has entered the button region in the WPF Button Events form.

The last two forms at the bottom of Figure 7-7 show that the mouse has left the button region of the WPF Button Events form. As you compare the minor differences in how the forms look, you should realize that both forms behave exactly the same way.

Figure 7-7

How It Works

Most of the controls that you use will have a dazzling array of events, although in day-to-day programming only a few of them will be consistently useful. For the Button control, the most useful event is usually the `Click` event.

Visual Basic 2008 knows enough about the control to create the default event handlers for you automatically. This makes your life a lot easier and saves on typing!

You've seen the `Click` event handler for buttons in Windows forms in Chapters 1, 3, 4, and 5. The one parameter that I want to point out in the `btnSayHello_Click` method is the parameter defined as a `System.EventArgs`. The `EventArgs` class is defined in the System namespace and is used for most common controls in Windows Forms Applications.

The `EventArgs` class will contain various data depending on the event being raised. For example, when the button is clicked and the `Click` event is raised, `EventArgs` will contain `MouseEventArgs`, allowing you to determine which mouse button was clicked and the X and Y coordinates of the mouse within the button.

```
Private Sub btnSayHello_Click(ByVal sender As System.Object, _
    ByVal e As System.EventArgs) Handles btnSayHello.Click

    MessageBox.Show("Hello World!", Me.Text)
End Sub
```

Did you notice the class that was specified in the Click event handler in your WPF application that corresponds to the EventArgs class is defined in a Windows Forms application? The parameter defined in the Click event handler for the button in your WPF application is defined as System.Windows.RoutedEventArgs. The RoutedEventArgs class is part of the System.Windows namespace, which is a namespace for the Windows Presentation Foundation.

In a WPF application, this class does not provide any useful information about the mouse button that was clicked. This is one of the major differences between Windows Forms applications and WPF applications.

```
Private Sub btnSayHello_Click(ByVal sender As System.Object, _
    ByVal e As System.Windows.RoutedEventArgs) Handles btnSayHello.Click

    MessageBox.Show("Hello World!", Me.Title)
End Sub
```

If you'll look at the end of the btnSayHello_MouseEnter method definition for both application types, you'll notice the Handles keyword. This ties the method definition into the btnSayHello.MouseEnter event. When the button fires this event, your code will be executed.

```
Private Sub btnSayHello_MouseEnter(ByVal sender As Object, _
    ByVal e As System.EventArgs) Handles btnSayHello.MouseEnter

    'Change the Button text
    btnSayHello.Text = "The mouse is here!"
End Sub

Private Sub btnSayHello_MouseEnter(ByVal sender As Object, _
    ByVal e As System.Windows.Input.MouseEventArgs) _
    Handles btnSayHello.MouseEnter

    'Change the Button text
    btnSayHello.Content = "The mouse is here!"
End Sub
```

Although you set the button's Text property (for the Windows Forms Button Event project) and the button's Content property (for the WPF Button Events project) at design time using the Properties window, here you can see that you can change those properties at run time too.

As a quick reminder here, design time is the term used to define the period of time that you actually writing the program, in other words, working with the Designer or adding code. Run time is the term used to define the period of time when the program is running.

Likewise, the `MouseLeave` event works in a very similar way for both applications:

```
Private Sub btnSayHello_MouseLeave(ByVal sender As Object, _
    ByVal e As System.EventArgs) Handles btnSayHello.MouseLeave

    'Change the Button text
    btnSayHello.Text = "The mouse has gone!"
End Sub

Private Sub btnSayHello_MouseLeave(ByVal sender As Object, _
    ByVal e As System.Windows.Input.MouseEventArgs) _
    Handles btnSayHello.MouseLeave

    'Change the Button text
    btnSayHello.Content = "The mouse has gone!"
End Sub
```

Building a Simple Application

Visual Studio 2008 comes with a comprehensive set of controls that you can use in your projects. For the most part, you'll be able to build all of your applications using just these controls, but in Chapter 14 you look at how you can create your own controls.

Take a look at how you can use some of these controls to put together a basic application. In the following Try It Out, you build a basic Windows Forms application that lets the user enter text into a form. The application will count the number of words and letters in the block of text that they enter.

Building the Form

The first job in creating your application is to start a new project and build a form. This form will contain a multi-line text box where you can enter text. It will also contain two radio buttons that will give you the option of counting either the words or the number of characters in the text box.

Try It Out   **Building the Form**

1.   Select File ⇨ New Project from the Visual Studio 2008 menu and create a new Windows Forms Application project. Enter the project name **Windows Forms Word Counter** and click OK.

2.   Click on Form1 in the Forms Designer and in the Properties window, set the `Size` property to **442, 300**, the `StartPosition` property to **CenterScreen**, and the `Text` property to **Word Counter**.

3.   To instruct the user what to do with the form, add a label. Select the Label control from the Toolbox, drag it to the top left-hand corner of the form. Use the snap lines to align this control in the upper left of the form as shown in Figure 7-8 before releasing the mouse button. Change the Text property to **Enter some text for counting:**.

Strictly speaking, unless you have to talk to the control from your code, you don't need to change its Name property. With a text box, you need to use its properties and methods in code to make the application work. However, a label is just there for esthetics, so you don't need to change the name for Label1.

If you are referring to a control from code, it's a good coding practice to give the control a name. Developers should be able to determine what the control represents based on its name even if they've never seen your code before. Refer to the section on Modified Hungarian Notation in Chapter 1 for prefixes to use with your control names.

Figure 7-8

4. Drag a TextBox control from the Toolbox and use the snap lines as shown in Figure 7-9 to align it beneath the Label control that you just added. Once the snap lines show the position of the control as shown in Figure 7-9, release the mouse button to have the control created and positioned.

Now change the properties of the text box as shown in the following list:

❑ Set Name to **txtWords**.

❑ Set Multiline to **True.**

❑ Set ScrollBars to **Vertical**.

❑ Set Size to **390, 190**.

Figure 7-9

5. Your application will be capable of counting either the characters the user entered or the number of words. To allow the user to select the preferred count method, you use two *radio buttons*. Draw two RadioButton controls onto the form next to each other below the text box. You need to refer to the radio buttons from your code, so change the properties as shown in the following lists:

   For the first radio button:

   ❑ Set Name to **radCountChars**.

   ❑ Set Checked to **True.**

   ❑ Set Text to **Chars**.

   For the second radio button:

   ❑ Set Name to **radCountWords**.

   ❑ Set Text to **Words**.

6. As the user types, you'll take the characters that the user enters and count the words or characters as appropriate. You want to pass your results to the user, so add two new Label controls next to the RadioButton controls that you just added.

7. The first Label control is just for esthetics, so leave the Name property as is and change its Text property to **The results are:**. The second Label control will report the results, so you need to give it a name. Set the Name property as **lblResults** and clear the Text property. Your completed form should look similar to the one shown in Figure 7-10.

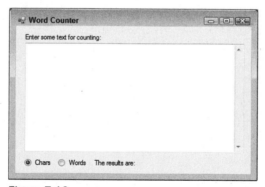

Figure 7-10

8. Now that you have the controls laid out on your form the way you want it, you can make sure you keep it that way. Select one of the controls and not the actual form, and then select Format ⇨ Lock Controls from the menu. This sets the Locked property of each of the controls to True and prevents them from accidentally being moved, resized, or deleted.

9. Finally, save your project by clicking the Save All button on the toolbar.

10. Start another instance of Visual Studio 2008. Select File ⇨ New Project from the Visual Studio 2008 menu and create a new WPF Application project. Enter the project name **WPF Word Counter** and click OK.

11. Click on Window1 in the Forms Designer and in the Properties window, set the `Width` property to **442**, the `WindowStartupLocation` property to **CenterScreen**, and the `Title` property to **Word Counter**.

12. The Forms Designer for WPF applications does not have the same rich support as the Forms Designer for Windows Forms applications thus there are no snap lines to help you align controls. Drag a Label control from the Toolbox and drop it on the window.

Now change the properties of the label as shown in the following list:

❑ Set `Content` to **Enter some text for counting:**.

❑ Set `Width` to **165**.

❑ Set `Margin` to **8,8,0,0**.

13. Drag a TextBox control from the Toolbox and drop it on the form. Using the list below, set the properties of the text box:

❑ Set `Name` to **txtWords**.

❑ Set `Width` to **390**.

❑ Set `Height` to **190**.

❑ Set `Margin` to **13,34,13,0**.

❑ Set `VerticalScrollBarVisibility` to **Visible**.

❑ Check the check box for **AcceptsReturn**.

❑ Set `TextWrapping` to **Wrap**.

14. Draw two RadioButton controls onto the form next to each other below the text box. You need to refer to the radio buttons from your code, so change the properties as shown in the following lists:

For the first radio button:

❑ Set `Name` to **radCountChars**.

❑ Set `Content` to **Chars**.

❑ Set `IsChecked` to **True**.

❑ Set `Width` to **55**.

❑ Set `Height` to **16**.

❑ Set `Margin` to **14,0,0,11**.

For the second radio button:

❑ Set `Name` to **radCountWords**.

❑ Set `Content` to **Words**.

❑ Set `Width` to **55**.

❑ Set `Height` to **16**.

❑ Set `Margin` to **75,0,0,11**.

15.   Draw a Label control on the form and set it properties as follows:

❑   Set Content to **The results are:**.

❑   Set Width to **95.**

❑   Set Height to **23.**

❑   Set Margin to **135,0,190,0.**

16.   Draw another Label control on the form and set its properties as follows:

❑   Set Name to **lblResults.**

❑   Clear Content.

❑   Set Width to **175.**

❑   Set Height to **23.**

❑   Set Margin to **230,0,0,9.**

17.   There are no lock control features for a WPF window so just save your project by clicking the Save All button on the toolbar.

Counting Characters

With your forms designed, you'll want to build some event handlers to count the number of characters in a block of text that the user types. Since your application will be able to count words and characters, you build separate functions for each. In this Try It Out, you write the code to count characters.

Try It Out   **Counting Characters**

1.   Return to the Windows Forms Word Counter project and view the code for Form1. Add the following code to count characters. Remember, to insert an XML Document Comment block, you need to type three apostrophes above the function after you have written the code:

```
'''  <summary>
'''  Count the characters in a block of text
'''  </summary>
'''  <param name="text">The string containing the text to count
'''  characters in</param>
'''  <returns>The number of characters in the string</returns>
'''  <remarks></remarks>
Private Function CountCharacters(ByVal text As String) As Integer
    Return text.Length
End Function
```

2. Now you need to build an event handler for the text box. Select `txtWords` in the Class Name combo box and, in the Method Name combo box, select the `TextChanged` event. Add the following highlighted code to the event handler:

```
Private Sub txtWords_TextChanged(ByVal sender As Object, _
    ByVal e As System.EventArgs) Handles txtWords.TextChanged

    'Count the number of characters
    Dim intChars As Integer = CountCharacters(txtWords.Text)

    'Display the results
    lblResults.Text = intChars & " characters"
End Sub
```

3. Run the project. Enter some text into the text box and you'll see a screen like the one in Figure 7-11.

Figure 7-11

4. Now return to the WPF Word Counter project and view the code for Window1. Add the following code to count characters:

```
''' <summary>
''' Count the characters in a block of text
''' </summary>
''' <param name="text">The string containing the text to count</param>
''' <returns>The number of characters in the string</returns>
''' <remarks></remarks>
Private Function CountCharacters(ByVal text As String) As Integer
    Return text.Length
End Function
```

5. To build the `TextChanged` event handler, select `txtWords` in the Class Name combo box and, in the Method Name combo box, select the `TextChanged` event. Add this highlighted code:

```
Private Sub txtWords_TextChanged(ByVal sender As Object, _
    ByVal e As System.Windows.Controls.TextChangedEventArgs) _
    Handles txtWords.TextChanged
```

```
                'Count the number of characters
                Dim intChars As Integer = CountCharacters(txtWords.Text)

                'Display the results
                lblResults.Content = intChars & " characters"
        End Sub
```

6. Now run the WPF Word Counter project and enter some text. You'll see a screen similar to the one shown in Figure 7-12.

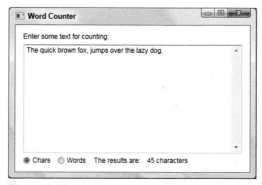

Figure 7-12

How It Works

Whenever you type a character into the text box, the label at the bottom of the form reports the current number of characters. That's because the TextChanged event is fired whenever the user changes the text in the box. This happens when new text is entered, when changes are made to existing text, and when old text is deleted. You are listening for this event, and whenever you hear it (or rather receive it), you call CountCharacters and pass in the block of text from the text box. As the user types text into the txtWords text box, the Text property is updated to reflect the text that has been entered. You can get the value for this property (in other words, the block of text) and pass it to CountCharacters:

```
                'Count the number of characters
                Dim intChars As Integer = CountCharacters(txtWords.Text)
```

The CountCharacters function in return counts the characters and passes back an integer representing the number of characters that it has counted:

```
                Return text.Length
```

After you have the number of characters, you update the lblResults control for your Windows form using:

```
                'Display the results
                lblResults.Text = intChars & " characters"
```

and for the WPF window using:

```
                'Display the results
                lblResults.Content = intChars & " characters"
```

Counting Words

Although building a Visual Basic 2008 application is actually very easy, building an elegant solution to a problem requires a combination of thought and experience.

Take your application, for example. When the Words radio button is checked, you want to count the number of words, whereas when Chars is checked, you want to count the number of characters. This has two implications.

First, when you respond to the TextChanged event, you need to call a different method that counts the words, rather than your existing method for counting characters. This isn't too difficult. Second, whenever you select a different radio button, you need to change the text in the results from "characters" to "words" or back again. Again, this isn't that difficult.

Now you'll add some more event handlers to your code, and when you finish, examine the logic behind the techniques you used.

Try It Out   Counting Words

1. Return to the Windows Forms Word Counter project and stop it if is still running. The first thing you want to do is add another function that will count the number of words in a block of text. Add this code to create the CountWords function:

```
''' <summary>
''' Count the number of words in a block of text
''' </summary>
''' <param name="text">The string containing the text to count</param>
''' <returns>The number of words in the string</returns>
''' <remarks></remarks>
Private Function CountWords(ByVal text As String) As Integer
    'Is the text empty?
    If text.Trim.Length = 0 Then Return 0

    'Split the words
    Dim strWords() As String = text.Split(" "c)

    'Return the number of words
    Return strWords.Length
End Function
```

2. The UpdateDisplay procedure handles getting the text from the text box and updating the display. It also understands whether it's supposed to find the number of words or number of characters by looking at the Checked property on the radCountWords radio button. Add this code to create the procedure:

```
Private Sub UpdateDisplay()
    'Do we want to count words?
    If radCountWords.Checked Then
        'Update the results with words
        lblResults.Text = CountWords(txtWords.Text) & " words"
```

```
        Else
            'Update the results with characters
            lblResults.Text = CountCharacters(txtWords.Text) & " characters"
        End If
    End Sub
```

3. Now, instead of calling `CountCharacters` from within your `TextChanged` handler, you want to call `UpdateDisplay`. Make the following change:

```
Private Sub txtWords_TextChanged(ByVal sender As Object, _
    ByVal e As System.EventArgs) Handles txtWords.TextChanged

    'Something changed so display the results
    UpdateDisplay()
End Sub
```

4. Next, you want the display to change when you change the radio button from Chars to Words and vice versa. To add the `CheckedChanged` event, select `radCountWords` in the Class Name combo box at the top of the code window and the `CheckedChanged` event in the Method Name combo box. Add the following highlighted code to the event handler procedure:

```
Private Sub radCountWords_CheckedChanged(ByVal sender As Object, _
    ByVal e As System.EventArgs) Handles radCountWords.CheckedChanged

    'Something changed so display the results
    UpdateDisplay()
End Sub
```

5. Repeat the previous step for the `radCountChars` radio button:

```
Private Sub radCountChars_CheckedChanged(ByVal sender As Object, _
    ByVal e As System.EventArgs) Handles radCountChars.CheckedChanged

    'Something changed so display the results
    UpdateDisplay()
End Sub
```

6. Run the project and enter some text. Then check the Words radio button and notice that the display changes to show the number of words as shown in Figure 7-13.

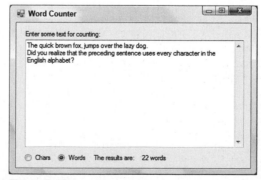

Figure 7-13

227

7. Return to the WPF Word Counter project and stop it if it is still running. Add this code to create the `CountWords` function:

```
''' <summary>
''' Count the number of words in a block of text
''' </summary>
''' <param name="text">The string containing the text to count</param>
''' <returns>The number of words in the string</returns>
''' <remarks></remarks>
Private Function CountWords(ByVal text As String) As Integer
    'Is the text empty?
    If text.Trim.Length = 0 Then Return 0

    'Split the words
    Dim strWords() As String = text.Split(" "c)

    'Return the number of words
    Return strWords.Length
End Function
```

8. Add the following code to create the `UpdateDisplay` procedure:

```
Private Sub UpdateDisplay()
    'If the window has not completed initialization then exit
    'this procedure as the radCountWords radio button has not
    'been created yet
    If Not Me.IsInitialized Then Exit Sub

    'Do we want to count words?
    If radCountWords.IsChecked Then
        'Update the results with words
        lblResults.Content = CountWords(txtWords.Text) & " words"
    Else
        'Update the results with characters
        lblResults.Content = CountCharacters(txtWords.Text) & " characters"
    End If
End Sub
```

9. Modify the `txtWords_TextChanged` event handler as follows:

```
Private Sub txtWords_TextChanged(ByVal sender As Object, _
    ByVal e As System.Windows.Controls.TextChangedEventArgs) _
    Handles txtWords.TextChanged

    'Something changed to display the results
    UpdateDisplay()
End Sub
```

10. Select `radCountWords` in the Class Name combo box at the top of the code window and the `Checked` event in the Method Name combo box. Add the following highlighted code to the event handler procedure:

```
Private Sub radCountWords_Checked(ByVal sender As Object, _
    ByVal e As System.Windows.RoutedEventArgs) _
    Handles radCountWords.Checked

        'Update the display
        UpdateDisplay()
End Sub
```

11. Repeat the previous step for the `radCountChars` radio button:

```
Private Sub radCountChars_Checked(ByVal sender As Object, _
    ByVal e As System.Windows.RoutedEventArgs) _
    Handles radCountChars.Checked

        'Update the display
        UpdateDisplay()
End Sub
```

12. Run the project and enter some text. Then select the Words radio button and notice that the display changes to show the number of words as shown in Figure 7-14.

Figure 7-14

How It Works

Before you look at the technique that you used to put the form together, take a quick look at the CountWords function:

```
''' <summary>
''' Count the number of words in a block of text
''' </summary>
''' <param name="text">The string containing the text to count</param>
''' <returns>The number of words in the string</returns>
''' <remarks></remarks>
Private Function CountWords(ByVal text As String) As Integer
    'Is the text empty?
    If text.Trim.Length = 0 Then Return 0

    'Split the words
    Dim strWords() As String = text.Split(" "c)

    'Return the number of words
    Return strWords.Length
End Function
```

You start by checking to see whether the string passed to this function is empty by first trimming the blank spaces from the end of the string using the Trim method of the String class and then comparing the Length property of the String class to a value of 0. If no text has been passed to this procedure, you immediately return from the function with a value of 0 indicating zero words counted.

The Split method of the String class is used to take a string and turn it into an array of string objects. There are several overloaded methods of the Split method and the parameter you passed here is a Char data type. You want to split the string using the space character, so you specify a space in double quotes and put a lower case c following the quotes to let the compiler know that this is a Char data type and to let it convert the space. This means that Split returns an array containing each of the words in the string. You then return the length of this array; in other words, the number of words back to the caller.

Note that because this code uses a single space character to split the text into words, you'll get unexpected behavior if you separate your words with more than one space character or use the Return key to start a new line.

One of the golden rules of programming is that you never write more code than you absolutely have to. In particular, when you find yourself in a position where you are going to write the same piece of code twice, try to find a workaround that requires that you write it only once. In this example, you have to change the value displayed in lblResults from two different places. The most sensible way to do this is to split the code that updates the label into a separate method; UpdateDisplay. You can then easily set up the TextChanged and CheckedChanged event handlers to call this method in your Windows Forms Word Counter project or the TextChanged and Checked event handlers in your WPF Word Counter project. The upshot of this is that you only have to write the tricky get the text, find the results, and update them routine once. This technique also creates code that is easier to change in the future and easier to debug when a problem is found. Here is the code for the `UpdateDisplay` method:

```
Private Sub UpdateDisplay()
    'Do we want to count words?
    If radCountWords.Checked Then
        'Update the results with words
        lblResults.Text = CountWords(txtWords.Text) & " words"
    Else
        'Update the results with characters
        lblResults.Text = CountCharacters(txtWords.Text) & " characters"
    End If
End Sub
```

A WPF application starts a little differently from a Windows Forms application. A Windows Forms application calls an `InitializeComponent` procedure, which is responsible for creating all of the controls on the form. This procedure is executed before the code that you write so that all controls on the form are built and initialized before your code accesses those controls.

A WPF application builds and initializes the controls from the top down as defined in the XAML. This causes a problem because events start to get fired on those controls as they are built. For example, when the `radCountChars` radio button is built and initialized, it fires the `Checked` event which in turn causes the `UpdateDisplay` method to be called when the `IsChecked` property is set to `True` on this control.

At this point, the `radCountWords` radio button has not been built by the application and a `NullReferenceException` is thrown when your code tries to access the `radCountWords` control. To handle this behavior, you'll want to check the `IsInitialized` property of the window. This property returns a `Boolean` value indicating if the window has been completely initialized, and by using this property you can exit this method if the controls in the window are still be built and initialized.

```
Private Sub UpdateDisplay()
    'If the window has not completed initialization then exit
    'this procedure as the radCountWords radio button has not
    'been created yet
    If Not Me.IsInitialized Then Exit Sub

    'Do we want to count words?
    If radCountWords.IsChecked Then
        'Update the results with words
        lblResults.Content = CountWords(txtWords.Text) & " words"
    Else
        'Update the results with characters
        lblResults.Content = CountCharacters(txtWords.Text) & " characters"
    End If
End Sub
```

You'll find as you build applications that this technique of breaking out the code for an event handler is something you'll do quite often.

Creating More Complex Applications

Normal applications generally have a number of common elements. Among these are toolbars and status bars. Putting together an application that has these features is a fairly trivial task in Visual Basic 2008.

In the next Try It Out, you build an application that allows you to make changes to the text entered into a text box, such as changing its color and making it all uppercase or lowercase. You'll be using a ToolBar control to change the color of the text in your text box and also to change the case of the text to either all uppercase letters or all lowercase letters.

The StatusBar control will also be used in your project to display the status of your actions as a result of clicking a button on the toolbar.

The Text Editor Project

Your first step on the road to building your application is to create a new project. You will be building the Text Editor project using both Windows Forms and WPF.

Try It Out   Creating the Text Editor Project

1. Create a new Windows Forms Application project and name it **Windows Forms Text Editor**.

2. Most of the time, Form1 isn't a very appropriate name for a form, as it's not very descriptive. Right-click the form in the Solution Explorer, select Rename, and change its name to **TextEditor.vb** as shown in Figure 7-15. Then press Enter to save the changes.

Figure 7-15

3. Now click the form in the Forms Designer, and in the Properties window change the Text property to **Text Editor**.

4. In the screenshots, we're going to show the design window as quite small to save paper. You should explicitly set the size of the form by going to the Properties window of the form and setting the Size property to **600, 460**.

5. Save your project by clicking the Save All button on the toolbar.

6. Start a new instance of Visual Studio 2008. Create a new WPF Application project and name it **WPF Text Editor**.

7. In the Solution Explorer, rename Window1.xaml to **TextEditor.xaml** as shown in Figure 7-16 and press enter to save the changes.

Figure 7-16

8. Now click the form in the Forms Designer, and in the Properties window change the Title property to **Text Editor**.

9. Set the Width property to **600** and the Height property to **460**.

10. Save your project by clicking on the Save All button on the toolbar.

In the next section, you start building the user interface part of the application.

Creating the Toolbar

The toolbar you are building will contain a collection of buttons, like the toolbar in Visual Studio 2008. In the following Try It Out, you will create the toolbar and add the buttons to it.

Try It Out   Adding the Toolbar

1. Return to the Forms Designer in the Windows Forms Text Editor project. Select the ToolStrip control from the Toolbox and drag and drop it on the form. It will automatically dock at the top of the form. Set the Stretch property to True to cause the toolbar to stretch across the entire form at run time.

2. To add buttons to the toolbar you use a built-in editor. Find the Items property in the Properties window, select it, and left-click the ellipsis (...) to the right of (Collection).

3. You're going to add six buttons to the toolbar: Clear, Red, Blue, Uppercase, Lowercase, and About.

4. To add the first button, click the Add button in the Items Collection Editor. The Items Collection Editor displays a properties palette much like the one that you're used to using. For each button you need to change its name, change its display style, give it an icon, clear its text, and provide some explanatory tool tip text. Change the Name property to **tbrClear** as shown in Figure 7-17.

Figure 7-17

5. Locate the Image property and select it. Then click the ellipsis button for this property to invoke the Select Resource editor. In the Select Resource editor, click the Import button. In the Open dialog box, browse to the installation folder where Visual Studio 2008 was installed (the default installation path is shown here) and locate the following folder:

```
C:\Program Files\Microsoft Visual Studio 9.0\Common7\ VS2008ImageLibrary\1033
```

If you have not previously extracted the contents of the VS2008ImageLibrary.zip file you will need to do so now.

From the installation folder, browse to the VS2008ImageLibary\Actions\32bitcolor bitmaps\16x16 folder. Select the New_DocumentHS.bmp file and then click the Open button to import the resource. Next, click the OK button in Select Resource editor and you'll be returned to the Items Collection Editor.

6. The background color of the bitmap is black so you'll need to adjust the image transparency color so the image displays correctly in the toolbar. Locate the ImageTransparentColor property and click the drop-down arrow next the text Magenta. Then locate the color black near the top of the list and select it.

7. Now set the ToolTipText property to **New**. This completes the steps necessary to create the first button.

8. You want to create a separator between the Clear button and the Red button. In the combo box in the Items Collection Editor, select Separator and then click the Add button. You can accept all default properties for this button.

9. Repeat steps 4 through 7 to create the Red button and use the following properties for this button. Before clicking the Add button, ensure you select Button in the combo box:

    ❑ Set `Name` to **tbrRed**.

    ❑ Use `VS2008ImageLibary\Actions\32bitcolor bitmaps\16x16 \ Color_fontHS.bmp` for the Image property.

    ❑ Set `ImageTransparentColor` to **Black**.

    ❑ Set the `ToolTipText` property to **Red**.

10. Repeat steps 4 through 7 to create the Blue button and use the following properties for this button:

    ❑ Set `Name` to **tbrBlue**.

    ❑ Use `VS2008ImageLibary\Actions\32bitcolor bitmaps\16x16 \ Color_lineHS.bmp` for the `Image` property.

    ❑ Set `ImageTransparentColor` to **Black**.

    ❑ Set the `ToolTipText` property to **Blue**.

11. You want to create a separator between the Blue button and the Uppercase button. In the combo box in the Items Collection Editor, select Separator and then click the Add button. You can accept all default properties for this button.

12. Repeat steps 4 through 7 to create the Uppercase button and use the following properties for this button. Before clicking the Add button, ensure you select Button in the combo box:

    ❑ Set `Name` to **tbrUpperCase**.

    ❑ Use `VS2008ImageLibary\Actions\32bitcolor bitmaps\16x16 \ FillUpHS.bmp` for the Image property.

    ❑ Set `ImageTransparentColor` to **Black**.

    ❑ Set the `ToolTipText` property to **Upper Case**.

13. Repeat steps 4 through 7 to create the Lowercase button and use the following properties for this button:

    ❑ Set `Name` to **tbrLowerCase**.

    ❑ Use `VS2008ImageLibary\Actions\32bitcolor bitmaps\16x16 \ FillDownHS.bmp` for the Image property.

    ❑ Set `ImageTransparentColor` to **Black**.

    ❑ Set the `ToolTipText` property to **Lower Case**.

14. You want to create a separator between the Lowercase button and the Help button. In the combo box in the Items Collection Editor, select Separator and then click the Add button. You can accept all default properties for this button.

15. Repeat steps 4 through 7 to create the Help button and use the following properties for this button. Note the different image path for the help image. Before clicking the Add button, ensure you select Button in the combo box:

❑ Set Name to **tbrHelpAbout**.

❑ Use VS2008ImageLibary\Annotation&Buttons\bmp_format\ Help.bmp for the Image property.

❑ Set ImageTransparentColor to **Magenta**.

❑ Set the ToolTipText property to **About**.

16. Click the OK button in the Items Collection Editor to close it.

17. Save your project by clicking the Save All button on the toolbar.

18. Switch to the WPF Text Editor project and click the Grid control in window in the Forms Designer. Next, select the ToolBarPanel control from the Toolbox and drag it and drop it on the Grid. Reposition the ToolBarPanel control to the upper left hand corner of the Grid. Drag the right edge of the ToolBarPanel control to the right hand side of the Grid until it snaps into place. The ToolBarPanel is now set to expand with the width of the window at runtime.

19. Drag a ToolBar control from the toolbox and drop it on the ToolBarPanel control. Expand its width until it completely fills the ToolBarPanel control.

20. Click in the XAML editor on the definition for the ToolBar control and modify the code for this control as follows:

```
<ToolBar Height="26" Name="ToolBar1" Width="575">
</ToolBar>
```

21. Add the following XAML code to create the toolbar buttons:

```
<ToolBar Height="26" Name="ToolBar1" Width="575">
        <Button Name="tbrClear" ToolTip="Clear">
            <Image Source="file:///C:/Program Files/Microsoft
Visual Studio 9.0/Common7/VS2008ImageLibrary/1033/VS2008ImageLibrary/
Actions/32bitcolor bitmaps/16x16/NewDocumentHS.BMP"></Image>
        </Button>
        <Separator Padding="1" />
        <Button Name="tbrRed" ToolTip="Red">
            <Image Source="file:///C:/Program Files/Microsoft
Visual Studio 9.0/Common7/VS2008ImageLibrary/1033/VS2008ImageLibrary/
Actions/32bitcolor bitmaps/16x16/Color_fontHS.bmp"></Image>
        </Button>
        <Button Name="tbrBlue" ToolTip="Blue">
            <Image Source="file:///C:/Program Files/Microsoft
Visual Studio 9.0/Common7/VS2008ImageLibrary/1033/VS2008ImageLibrary/
Actions/32bitcolor bitmaps/16x16/Color_lineHS.bmp"></Image>
        </Button>
        <Separator/>
        <Button Name="tbrUpperCase" ToolTip="Upper Case">
            <Image Source="file:///C:/Program Files/Microsoft
```

```
Visual Studio 9.0/Common7/VS2008ImageLibrary/1033/VS2008ImageLibrary/
Actions/32bitcolor bitmaps/16x16/FillUpHS.BMP"></Image>
                  </Button>
                  <Button Name="tbrLowerCase" ToolTip="Lower Case">
                      <Image Source="file:///C:/Program Files/Microsoft
Visual Studio 9.0/Common7/VS2008ImageLibrary/1033/VS2008ImageLibrary/
Actions/32bitcolor bitmaps/16x16/FillDownHS.BMP"></Image>
                  </Button>
                  <Separator/>
                  <Button Name="tbrHelpAbout" ToolTip="About">
                      <Image Source="file:///C:/Program Files/Microsoft
Visual Studio 9.0/Common7/VS2008ImageLibrary/1033/VS2008ImageLibrary/
Annotations&amp;Buttons/bmp_format/Help.BMP"></Image>
                  </Button>
          </ToolBar>
```

22. Save your project by clicking the Save All button on the toolbar.

How It Works

For Windows Forms Application projects, the ToolStrip control docks to a particular position on the form. In this case, it docks itself to the top edge of the form.

The six buttons and three separators that you added to the toolbar actually appear as full members of the `TextEditor` class and have the usual events that you are accustomed to seeing. Later, you'll see how you can respond to the `Click` event for the various buttons.

A toolbar button can display text only, an image only, or both text and an image. Your project displays an image that is the default display style for toolbar buttons. Normally you would create your own images or have a graphics designer create the images, but for this Try It Out you used images that ship with Visual Studio 2008. At this point, your toolbar should look similar to the one shown in Figure 7-18.

Figure 7-18

The `ToolTipText` property enables Visual Basic 2008 to display a tool tip for the button whenever the user hovers the mouse over it. You don't need to worry about actually creating or showing a tool tip; Visual Basic 2008 does this for you.

For WPF Application projects, you use the ToolBarPanel and ToolBar controls to create a toolbar. You have to position these controls manually and adjust their width in order to have the toolbar expand to fill the top of the window. Then you have to add some XAML control to create the tool bar buttons and images as shown in the partial code fragment below.

The ToolBarPanel control determines which buttons will fit in the toolbar and which buttons will need to go into the overflow area as the form is resized smaller and larger. The ToolBarPanel and ToolBar control work hand in hand to display a toolbar in a WPF application.

Each button on the toolbar is created using the `Button` class as shown in the partial code listing below. The `Button` class contains the `Name` and `ToolTip` properties to set the name of the button that is used to access the button from code and to display the tooltip when the user hovers a mouse over the button. The separator control is created using the `Separator` class and contains no properties that need to be set. The remaining buttons for the toolbar are created in the same manner as the Clear button.

```
<Button Name="tbrClear" ToolTip="Clear">
        <Image Source="file:///C:/Program Files/Microsoft
Visual Studio 9.0/Common7/VS2008ImageLibrary/1033/VS2008ImageLibrary/
Actions/32bitcolor bitmaps/16x16/NewDocumentHS.BMP"></Image>
        </Button>
        <Separator />
```

The toolbar in your WPF Text Editor project looks very similar to the one shown previously in Figure 7-18.

Creating the Status Bar

The status bar is a panel that sits at the bottom of an application window and tells the user what's going on. You create the status bar in the next Try It Out.

Try It Out   **Adding a Status Bar**

1. Return to your Windows Forms Text Editor project, drag a StatusStrip control from the Toolbox, and drop it onto your form. You'll notice that it automatically docks itself to the bottom edge of the form and you'll only be able to change the height portion of its `Size` property if desired.

2. You need to add one StatusStripLabel to the Items collection of the StatusStrip so that you can display text on the status bar. Click the ellipsis button in the `Items` property to invoke the Items Collection Editor dialog box. In the Items Collection Editor dialog box, click the Add button to add a StatusLabel.

3. Set the following properties for the StatusStripLabel:

    ❑   Set `Name` to **sslStatus**.

    ❑   Set `DisplayStyle` to Text.

    ❑   Set `Text` to **Ready**.

4. Click the OK button to close the Items Collection Editor dialog box.

5. Open the Code Editor for the form and add the following code. You can quickly view the Code Editor by right-clicking the form and choosing View Code from the context menu:

```
'Get or set the text on the status bar
Public Property StatusText() As String
    Get
        Return sslStatus.Text
    End Get
    Set(ByVal value As String)
        sslStatus.Text = value
    End Set
End Property
```

6. Switch over to your WPF Text Editor project. Drag a StatusBar control from the toolbox onto the window. Position the control to the bottom left of the window and then expand the width of the control until it snaps to the right margin of the Grid.

7. In the properties window, click the ellipsis button in the `Items` property to invoke the Items Collection Editor dialog box. In the Collection Editor: Items dialog box, click the Add button to add a StatusBarItem.

8. Set the `Content` property to **Ready** and then click the OK button to close the Collection Editor: Items dialog box.

9. Click the StatusBarItem in the window and then in the Properties window set the `Name` property to **sbiStatus**.

10. Right-click the window and choose View Code from the context menu and add the following code:

```
'Get or set the text on the status bar
Public Property StatusText() As String
    Get
        Return sbiStatus.Content.ToString
    End Get
    Set(ByVal value As String)
        sbiStatus.Content = value
    End Set
End Property
```

There's no need to run the projects at this point, so let's just talk about what you've done here.

How It Works

Visual Studio 2008 has some neat features for making form design easier. One thing that was always laborious in previous versions of Visual Basic and Visual C++ was to create a form that would automatically adjust itself when the user changed its size.

In Visual Studio 2008, controls have the capability to dock themselves to the edges of the form. By default, the StatusStrip control sets itself to dock to the bottom of the form, but you can change the docking location if so desired. So, when someone resizes the form, either at design time or at run time, the status bar (StatusStrip control) stays where you put it.

The StatusBar control in a WPF application behaves a little differently and does not automatically dock itself to the bottom of the window. You have to manually drag and position the control to the bottom left corner of the window and then expand the width of the control in order to have it automatically stretch to fill the size of the window as it gets resized.

You may be wondering why you built a StatusText property to get and set the text on the status bar. This comes back to abstraction. Ideally, you want to make sure that anyone using this class doesn't have to worry about how you've implemented the status bar. You might want to replace the .NET-supplied status bar with another control, and if you did, any users wanting to use your TextEditor class in their own applications (or developers wanting to add more functionality to this application later) would have to change their code to make sure it continued to work properly.

That's why you defined this property as Public. This means that others creating an instance of TextEditor class to use its functionality in their own applications can change the status bar text if they want. If you don't want them to be able to change the text themselves, relying instead on other methods and properties on the form to change the text on their behalf, you would mark the property as Private.

As you work through this example, you'll see definitions of Public and Private. From this you'll be able to infer what functionality might be available to a developer using your TextEditor class.

Creating an Edit Box

The first thing you do in the next Try It Out is create a text box that can be used to edit the text entered. The text box has a MultiLine property, which by default is set to False. This property determines whether the text box should have only one line or can contain multiple lines. When you change this property to True, the text box control can be resized to any size that you want, and you can enter multiple lines of text in this control.

Try It Out   Creating an Edit Box

1. Return to the Forms Designer in the Windows Forms Text Editor project and drag a TextBox control from the ToolBox, and drop it onto your form.

2. Change the following properties of the TextBox control:

    ❑   Set Name to **txtEdit**.

    ❑   Set Dock to Fill.

    ❑   Set MultiLine to Truc.

    ❑   Set ScrollBars to Vertical.

    Your form should now look like Figure 7-19.

Figure 7-19

3. Switch over to the Forms Designer in your WPF Text Editor project and drag a TextBox control from the ToolBox, and drop it onto your form.

4. Align the text box to the left margin of the Grid directly beneath the toolbar. Now expand the width of the text box until it snaps to the right border of the Grid. Then expand the height of the text box until it touches the status bar.

5. Change the following properties of the TextBox control:

   ❑ Set Name to **txtEdit**.

   ❑ Set VerticalAlignment to **Stretch**.

   ❑ Set VerticalScrollBarVisbility to **Visible**.

   ❑ Check AcceptsReturn.

   ❑ Set TextWrapping to **Wrap**.

   Your form should now look like Figure 7-20.

Figure 7-20

Clearing the Edit Box

In the following Try It Out, you're going to create a property called EditText that will get or set the text you're going to edit. Then, clearing the edit box will simply be a matter of setting the EditText property to an empty string.

Try It Out   **Clearing txtEdit**

1. Switch to the Code Editor in your Windows Forms Text Editor project and add this code:

```
'Gets or sets the text that you're editing
Public Property EditText() As String
    Get
        Return txtEdit.Text
    End Get
    Set(ByVal value As String)
        txtEdit.Text = value
    End Set
End Property
```

As you have done earlier, when you created a property to abstract away the action of setting the status bar text, you created this property to give developers using the TextEditor form the ability to get or set the text of the document irrespective of how you actually implement the editor.

2. You can now build ClearEditBox, the method that actually clears your text box. Add the following code:

```
'Clears the txtEdit control
Public Sub ClearEditBox()
    'Set the EditText property
    EditText = String.Empty

    'Reset the font color
    txtEdit.ForeColor = Color.Black

    'Set the status bar text
    StatusText = "Text box cleared"
End Sub
```

3. Select txtEdit in the Class Name combo box and the TextChanged event in the Method Name combo box at the top of the code editor. Add this code:

```
Private Sub txtEdit_TextChanged(ByVal sender As Object, _
    ByVal e As System.EventArgs) Handles txtEdit.TextChanged

    'Reset the status bar text
    StatusText = "Ready"
End Sub
```

4. Switch to the Code Editor in your WPF Text Editor project and add this code:

```
'Gets or sets the text that you're editing
Public Property EditText() As String
    Get
        Return txtEdit.Text
    End Get
    Set(ByVal value As String)
        txtEdit.Text = value
    End Set
End Property
```

5. Add the following code to create the `ClearEditBox` method:

```
'Clears the txtEdit control
Public Sub ClearEditBox()
    'Set the EditText property
    EditText = String.Empty

    'Reset the font color
    txtEdit.Foreground = Brushes.Black

    'Set the status bar text
    StatusText = "Text box cleared"
End Sub
```

6. Finally, select `txtEdit` in the Class Name combo box and the `TextChanged` event in the Method Name combo box at the top of the code editor. Add this code:

```
Private Sub txtEdit_TextChanged(ByVal sender As Object, _
    ByVal e As System.Windows.Controls.TextChangedEventArgs) _
    Handles txtEdit.TextChanged

    'Reset the status bar text
    StatusText = "Ready"
End Sub
```

How It Works

The first thing you want to do is clear your text box. In the next Try It Out, you see how you can call `ClearEditBox` from the toolbar.

All this procedure does is set the `EditText` property to an empty string by using the `Empty` field of the `String` class. Then it sets the `ForeColor` property of the text box (which is the color of the actual text) to black and places the text `Text box cleared` in the status bar.

```
'Clears the txtEdit control
Public Sub ClearEditBox()
    'Set the EditText property
    EditText = String.Empty
    'Reset the font color
    txtEdit.ForeColor = Color.Black
    'Set the status bar text
    StatusText = "Text box cleared"
End Sub
```

The code in the `EditText` property of your WPF Text Editor project is slightly different in that you need to set the `Foreground` property of the text box using the `Black` property from the `Brushes` class.

```
'Reset the font color
txtEdit.Foreground = Brushes.Black
```

As mentioned, `EditText` abstracts the action of getting and setting the text in the box away from your actual implementation. This makes it easier for other developers down the line to use your `TextEditor` form class in their own applications. This code is the same for both projects:

```
'Gets or sets the text that you're editing
Public Property EditText() As String
    Get
        Return txtEdit.Text
    End Get
    Set(ByVal value As String)
        txtEdit.Text = value
    End Set
End Property
```

As you type, the `TextChanged` event handler will be repeatedly called. The actual code is the same in both projects although the event handler is slightly different in the WPF Text Editor from the code from the Windows Forms Text Editor shown below:

```
Private Sub txtEdit_TextChanged(ByVal sender As Object, _
    ByVal e As System.EventArgs) Handles txtEdit.TextChanged

    'Reset the status bar text
    StatusText = "Ready"
End Sub
```

Changing the status bar text at this point resets any message that might have been set in the status bar. For example, if the user has to type a lot of text and looks down to see *Text box cleared*, he or she may be a little concerned. Setting it to Ready is a pretty standard way of informing the user that the computer is doing something or waiting. It does not mean anything specific.

Responding to Toolbar Buttons

In the following Try It Out, you'll start implementing the `Click` events for the various toolbar buttons on your toolbar. When you look at building application menus in Chapter 9, you'll notice that most menus provide the same functionality as your toolbar buttons, and thus you'll want to implement the code in your menu item `Click` event procedures and have the corresponding toolbar button procedures call the menu item `Click` event procedures.

Try It Out   Responding to Toolbar Button Click Events

1.   Return to the Code Editor in your Windows Forms Text Editor project and select `tbrClear` from the Class Name combo box, and in the Method Name combo box, select the `Click` event. Add the following highlighted code to the `Click` event handler:

```
Private Sub tbrClear_Click(ByVal sender As Object, _
    ByVal e As System.EventArgs) Handles tbrClear.Click

    'Clear the edit box
    ClearEditBox()
End Sub
```

2.   You need to create a procedure that will change the text in the edit box to red and update the status bar. Add the following code:

```
Public Sub RedText()
    'Make the text red
    txtEdit.ForeColor = Color.Red

    'Update the status bar text
    StatusText = "The text is read"
End Sub
```

3.   Next, select `tbrRed` in the Class Name combo box, select the `Click` event in the Method Name combo box, and add the following highlighted to the `Click` event handler:

```
Private Sub tbrRed_Click(ByVal sender As Object, _
    ByVal e As System.EventArgs) Handles tbrRed.Click

    'Make the text red
    RedText()
End Sub
```

4.   Run the project and enter some text. Click the Red button, and the text's color will change from black to red. Note that if you continue typing in the edit box, the new text will also be red. Click the Clear button to remove the text and revert the color of any new text to black.

5.   Switch to the Code Editor in your WPF Text Editor project. Select `tbrClear` from the Class Name combo box, and in the Method Name combo box, select the `Click` event and add the following highlighted code:

```
Private Sub tbrClear_Click(ByVal sender As Object, _
    ByVal e As System.Windows.RoutedEventArgs) _
    Handles tbrClear.Click

    'Clear the edit box
    ClearEditBox()
End Sub
```

6. Add the following code to change the text in the edit box to red and update the status bar:

```
Public Sub RedText()
    'Make the text red
    txtEdit.Foreground = Brushes.Red

    'Update the status bar text
    StatusText = "The text is red"
End Sub
```

7. Select tbrRed in the Class Name combo box, select the Click event in the Method Name combo box, and add the following highlighted code:

```
Private Sub tbrRed_Click(ByVal sender As Object, _
    ByVal e As System.Windows.RoutedEventArgs) _
    Handles tbrRed.Click

        'Make the text red
        RedText()
End Sub
```

8. Run the project and enter some text. Click the Red button, and the text's color will change from black to red. Again, if you continue typing in the edit box, the new text will also be red. Click the Clear button to remove the text and revert the color of any new text to black.

9. Stop both projects if they are still running.

10. Return to the Code Editor in the Windows Forms Text Editor project and add the following BlueText procedure to change the text in the edit box to blue:

```
Public Sub BlueText()
    'Make the text blue
    txtEdit.ForeColor = Color.Blue

    'Update the status bar text
    StatusText = "The text is blue"
End Sub
```

11. Select tbrBlue in the Class Name combo box and the Click event in the Method Name combo box. Add the following highlighted code to the Click event handler:

```
Private Sub tbrBlue_Click(ByVal sender As Object, _
    ByVal e As System.EventArgs) Handles tbrBlue.Click

        'Make the text blue
        BlueText()
End Sub
```

12. You now need to create a procedure to change the text in the edit box to all uppercase. Add the following code to your project:

```
Public Sub UpperCaseText()
    'Make the text uppercase
    EditText = EditText.ToUpper

    'Update the status bar text
    StatusText = "The text is all uppercase"
End Sub
```

13. Select tbrUpperCase in the Class Name combo box and the Click event in the Method Name combo box. Add the following highlighted code to the Click event handler:

```
Private Sub tbrUpperCase_Click(ByVal sender As Object, _
    ByVal e As System.EventArgs) Handles tbrUpperCase.Click

    'Make the text uppercase
    UpperCaseText()
End Sub
```

14. Add the following procedure to change the text to all lowercase:

```
Public Sub LowerCaseText()
    'Make the text lowercase
    EditText = EditText.ToLower

    'Update the status bar text
    StatusText = "The text is all lowercase"
End Sub
```

15. Select tbrLowerCase in the Class Name combo box and the Click event in the Method Name combo box. Add the following code to the Click event handler:

```
Private Sub tbrLowerCase_Click(ByVal sender As Object, _
    ByVal e As System.EventArgs) Handles tbrLowerCase.Click

    'Make the text lowercase
    LowerCaseText()
End Sub
```

16. Run the project and enter some text into the box in a mixture of lowercase and uppercase. Then click the Uppercase button to make the text all uppercase, similar to the WPF Text Editor shown in Figure 7-21. Clicking the Lowercase button will convert the text to all lowercase, and clicking on the Red or Blue buttons will cause the text to change color. Finally, clicking the Clear button will cause all text to be cleared and the color and case to be restored to the default.

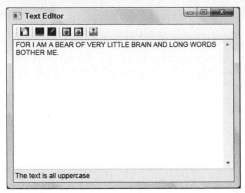

Figure 7-21

17. Return to the Code Editor in the WPF Text Editor project. Add the following `BlueText` procedure to change the text in the edit box to blue:

```
Public Sub BlueText()
    'Make the text blue
    txtEdit.Foreground = Brushes.Blue

    'Update the status bar text
    StatusText = "The text is blue"
End Sub
```

18. Select `tbrBlue` in the Class Name combo box and the `Click` event in the Method Name combo box and add the following highlighted code:

```
Private Sub tbrBlue_Click(ByVal sender As Object, _
    ByVal e As System.Windows.RoutedEventArgs) _
    Handles tbrBlue.Click

    'Make the text blue
    BlueText()
End Sub
```

19. Add the code below to create a procedure to change the text in the edit box to all uppercase:

```
Public Sub UpperCaseText()
    'Make the text uppercase
    EditText = EditText.ToUpper

    'Update the status bar text
    StatusText = "The text is all uppercase"
End Sub
```

20. Select tbrUpperCase in the Class Name combo box and the Click event in the Method Name combo box. Add the following highlighted code to the Click event handler:

```
Private Sub tbrUpperCase_Click(ByVal sender As Object, _
    ByVal e As System.Windows.RoutedEventArgs) _
    Handles tbrUpperCase.Click

    'Make the text uppercase
    UpperCaseText()
End Sub
```

21. Add the following procedure to change the text to all lowercase:

```
Public Sub LowerCaseText()
    'Make the text lowercase
    EditText = EditText.ToLower

    'Update the status bar text
    StatusText = "The text is all lowercase"
End Sub
```

22. Finally, select tbrLowerCase in the Class Name combo box and the Click event in the Method Name combo box. Add the following code to the Click event handler:

```
Private Sub tbrLowerCase_Click(ByVal sender As Object, _
    ByVal e As System.Windows.RoutedEventArgs) _
    Handles tbrLowerCase.Click

    'Make the text lowercase
    LowerCaseText()
End Sub
```

23. Run the project and again enter some text into the box in a mixture of lowercase and uppercase. Then click the Uppercase button to make the text all uppercase as shown in Figure 7-21. Exercise the code by clicking the Lowercase button to convert the text to all lowercase, and clicking on the Red and Blue buttons to change the color of the text.

How It Works

This Try It Out was quite simple. By this time, you are quite adept at creating the Click event handler for buttons on your form, and creating the Click event handler for a toolbar button is no different. The first thing that you did was to create the Click event handler for the Clear toolbar button and added the code to call the ClearEditBox procedure:

```
Private Sub tbrClear_Click(ByVal sender As Object, _
    ByVal e As System.EventArgs) Handles tbrClear.Click

    'Clear the edit box
    ClearEditBox()
End Sub
```

Next, you created the RedText procedure to change the text in the edit box to red and to update the status bar with the appropriate information. To change the color of the text in the edit box, you set the ForeColor property of the edit box using the Red constant from the Color enumeration. (The Color enumeration contains an extensive list of named colors.) The ForeColor property remains red until you set it to something else — so clicking the Clear button turns it back to black:

```
Public Sub RedText()
    'Make the text red
    txtEdit.ForeColor = Color.Red

    'Update the status bar text
    StatusText = "The text is red"
End Sub
```

In your WPF Text Editor project you set the Foreground property to red using the Red property of the Brushes class:

```
'Make the text red
txtEdit.Foreground = Brushes.Red
```

You also change the text in the status bar using the StatusText property to display a message indicating the text color has changed. As soon as you start typing again, the message in the status bar is changed to Ready, as set by the TextChanged event handler for the edit box.

In order to call the RedText procedure you added code to the Click event for the Red button on the toolbar:

```
'Make the text red
RedText()
```

The code for the Blue button on the toolbar works in the same manner. You created the BlueText procedure to set the ForeColor property of the edit box to Blue in your Windows Forms Text Editor project and set the Foreground property to Blue in your WPF Text Editor project. Then update the status bar with the appropriate message. You then call the BlueText procedure from the Click event of the Blue toolbar button.

If the user clicks the Uppercase button on the toolbar, you call UppercaseText, which uses the ToUpper method to convert all the text held in EditText to uppercase text:

```
'Make the text uppercase
EditText = EditText.ToUpper
```

Likewise, if the user clicks the Lowercase button, you call LowercaseText, which uses the ToLower method to convert all the text held in EditText to lowercase text:

```
'Make the text lowercase
EditText = EditText.ToLower
```

Each of these procedures is called from the Click event of the appropriate toolbar buttons, and these procedures also update the message in the status bar to reflect whether the text has been changed to red, blue, uppercase, or lowercase.

Using Multiple Forms

All Windows applications have two types of windows: normal windows and dialog boxes. A normal window provides the main user interface for an application. For example, if you use Microsoft Word, you use a normal window for editing your documents.

On occasion, the application will display a dialog box when you want to access a special feature. This type of window hijacks the application and forces you to use just that window. For example, when you select the Print option in Word, a dialog box appears, and from that point on, until you close the dialog by clicking OK, Cancel, or the close box, you can't go back and change the document — the only thing you can use is the Print dialog box itself. Forms that do this are called *modal*. While they're up, you're in that mode.

Dialog boxes are discussed in more detail in Chapter 8. For now, you can focus on adding additional forms to your application. The form that you add in the next exercise is a simple modal form.

The About Dialog Box

Most applications have an About dialog box that describes the application's name and copyright information. As you already have a toolbar button for this feature, you'll want to create this form now.

Note that a standard About dialog exists for Windows Forms applications but does not exist for WPF applications. Therefore, this next Try It Out will only apply to your Windows Forms Text Editor project.

Try It Out   **Adding an About Box**

1. To add a new form to the project, you need to use the Solution Explorer. Right click the Windows Forms Text Editor project and select Add ⇨ Windows Form. In the Add New Item – Windows Forms Text Editor dialog box, shown in Figure 7-22, select the About Box in the Templates pane, enter **About.vb** in the Name field, and click the Add button to create the new form.

Figure 7-22

2. When the form's Designer appears, you'll notice that all of the normal details that are shown in an About dialog box are already on the form. This includes such items as the product name, version number, copyright information, and so on.

3. Right-click the form and choose View Code from the context menu. You'll notice that the Load event for the form already contains a significant amount of code to populate the details on the About form. There is a TODO comment in the code that informs you that you need to update the assembly information for the application.

4. In the Solution Explorer, double-click My Project. Click the Assembly Information button in the Application pane of the Windows Forms Text Editor properties to display the Assembly Information dialog box. Edit the information in this dialog box as shown in Figure 7-23 and then click OK to close this dialog box.

Figure 7-23

5. You need to write a procedure that will display the About dialog box, so add this code to the TextEditor form:

```
Public Sub ShowAboutBox()
    'Display the About dialog box
    Using objAbout As New About
        objAbout.ShowDialog(Me)
    End Using
End Sub
```

6. Finally, you need to call ShowAboutBox when the Help About button on the toolbar is clicked. In the Class Name combo box at the top of the Code Editor, select tbrHelpAbout and in the Method Name combo box, select the Click event. Add the following highlighted code to the Click event handler:

```
Private Sub tbrHelpAbout_Click(ByVal sender As Object, _
    ByVal e As System.EventArgs) Handles tbrHelpAbout.Click

    'Display the About dialog box
    ShowAboutBox()
End Sub
```

7. Run the project and click the Help About button. You should see the dialog box shown in Figure 7-24.

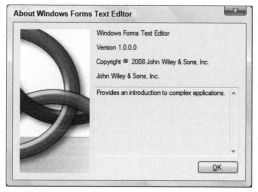

Figure 7-24

How It Works

There are a variety of prebuilt forms provided in Visual Studio 2008, as was shown in Figure 7-22. You choose to add the About Box form to your project to display an About dialog box from your application.

When the About form starts, it will fire the Load event, and this event already has the appropriate code written to load the fields on the form. You'll notice that this code makes efficient use of the My.Application.AssemblyInfo namespace to retrieve the appropriate information from your application's assembly for the About form:

```
Private Sub About_Load(ByVal sender As System.Object, _
    ByVal e As System.EventArgs) Handles MyBase.Load
    ' Set the title of the form.
    Dim ApplicationTitle As String
    If My.Application.Info.Title <> "" Then
        ApplicationTitle = My.Application.Info.Title
    Else
        ApplicationTitle = System.IO.Path.GetFileNameWithoutExtension( _
            My.Application.Info.AssemblyName)
    End If
    Me.Text = String.Format("About {0}", ApplicationTitle)
    ' Initialize all of the text displayed on the About Box.
    ' TODO: Customize the application's assembly information in the
    '"Application" pane of the project
    '    properties dialog (under the "Project" menu).
```

```
        Me.LabelProductName.Text = My.Application.Info.ProductName
        Me.LabelVersion.Text = String.Format("Version {0}", _
            My.Application.Info.Version.ToString)
        Me.LabelCopyright.Text = My.Application.Info.Copyright
        Me.LabelCompanyName.Text = My.Application.Info.CompanyName
        Me.TextBoxDescription.Text = My.Application.Info.Description
    End Sub
```

The assembly information that you modified in the Assembly Information dialog box is used to populate the fields on your About form. If you added the text *John Wiley && Sons, Inc.* to the Company and Copyright fields in the Assembly Information dialog box as shown in Figure 7-23, you'll have noticed that two consecutive ampersands were used in `John Wiley && Sons, Inc.` The reason behind this is that the labels on your About form treat a single ampersand as the start of a code representing a special character. Two consecutive ampersands is then the code for the ampersand character itself.

To display another form, you have to create a new instance of it. That's exactly what you do in the `ShowAboutBox` procedure. A `Using...End Using` block will create a new instance of an object (in this case the `About` form) and allow you to use the `ShowDialog` method to show the About form modally. When you pass the `Me` keyword as a parameter to the `ShowDialog` method, you are specifying that the `TextEditor` form is the owner of the dialog being shown; in this case the `About` form:

```
    Public Sub ShowAboutBox()
        'Display the About dialog box
        Using objAbout As New About
            objAbout.ShowDialog(Me)
        End Using
    End Sub
```

To call the `ShowAboutBox` procedure, you had to add code to the `Click` event of the HelpAbout button on the toolbar:

```
    Private Sub tbrHelpAbout_Click(ByVal sender As Object, _
        ByVal e As System.EventArgs) Handles tbrHelp.Click

        'Display the About dialog box
        ShowAboutBox()
    End Sub
```

So, with very little effort and a minimal amount of code, you have added a lot of functionality to your Windows Form Text Editor project. You can see firsthand how Visual Studio 2008 provides productivity and time-saving features such as prebuilt forms.

Summary

This chapter discussed some of the more advanced features of Windows forms and WPF Windows as well as the commonly used controls. It discussed the event-driven nature of Windows and showed three events that can happen to a button (namely Click, MouseEnter, and MouseLeave).

You created a simple application that allowed you to enter some text and then choose between counting the number of characters or the number of words by using radio buttons.

You then turned your attention to building a more complex application that allowed you to edit text by changing its color or its case. This application showed how easy it was to build an application with toolbars and status bars. You even added an About dialog box to display basic information about your application such as the application title, description, version number, and copyright information.

To summarize, you should now know how to:

❑   Write code to respond to control events

❑   Set properties on controls to customize their look and behavior

❑   Use the ToolStrip and StatusStrip controls

❑   Display other forms in your application

Exercises

1. Create a Windows Forms application with two buttons. Add code to the MouseUp event for the first button to display a MessageBox with a message that the event has fired. Add code to the LostFocus event for the first button to also display a MessageBox with a message that the button has lost focus.

2. Create a Windows Forms application with a toolbar and status bar. Right-click the ToolStrip control and select the Insert Standard Items menu item from the context menu to have the standard buttons added to the control. For the Click event for each of the ToolStripButton controls, display a message in the status bar indicating which button was clicked.

Displaying Dialog Boxes

Visual Basic 2008 provides several built-in dialog boxes that help you provide a rich user interface in your front-end applications. These dialog boxes provide the same common user interface that is found in most Windows applications. They also provide many properties and methods that allow you to customize these dialog boxes to suit your needs while still maintaining the standard look of Windows Forms applications.

In this chapter, you will learn about the following:

- ❑ Creating a message box using different buttons and icons
- ❑ Creating an Open dialog box that enables you to open files
- ❑ Creating a Save dialog box that enables you to save files
- ❑ Creating a Font dialog box that enables you to apply the selected font to text
- ❑ Creating a Color dialog box that enables you to define and select custom colors
- ❑ Creating a Print dialog box that prints text from your application
- ❑ Creating a Browse dialog box that enables you to browse for folders

This chapter explores these dialog boxes in depth and shows how you can use them in your Visual Basic 2008 applications to help you build more professional-looking applications for your users.

The MessageBox Dialog Box

The MessageBox dialog box is one of those dialog boxes that you will use often as a developer. This dialog box enables you to display custom messages to your users and accept their input regarding the choice that they have made. This dialog box is very versatile; you can customize it to display a variety of icons with your messages and choose which buttons to display.

In your day-to-day operation of a computer, you have seen message boxes that display each of the icons shown in Figure 8-1. In this section, you learn how to create and display message boxes that use these icons.

Figure 8-1

The first icon in Figure 8-1 has two names: Asterisk and Information. The second icon also has two names: Exclamation and Warning. The third icon has three names: Error, Hand, and Stop. The final icon in Figure 8-1 has only one name: Question.

When building a Windows application, at times you need to prompt the user for information or display a warning that something expected did not happen or that something unexpected did. For example, suppose the user of your application modified some data and tried to close the application without saving the data. You could display a message box that carries an information or warning icon and an appropriate message — that all unsaved data will be lost. You could also provide OK and Cancel buttons to allow the user to continue or cancel the operation.

This is where the MessageBox dialog box comes in: It enables you to quickly build custom dialog boxes that prompt the user for a decision while displaying your custom message, choice of icons, and choice of buttons. All of this functionality also allows you to display a message box to inform users of validation errors, and to display formatted system errors that are trapped by error handling.

Before you jump into some code, take a look at the `MessageBox` class. The `Show` method is called to display the MessageBox. The title, message, icons, and buttons displayed are determined by the parameters you pass to this method. This may seem complicated, but actually using MessageBox is very simple — as you have seen and will see in the following sections.

Available Icons for MessageBox

You saw the available icons in Figure 8-1. The following table outlines those four standard icons that you can display in a message box. The actual graphic displayed is a function of the operating system constants, and there are four unique symbols with multiple field names assigned to them.

Member Name	Description
Asterisk	Specifies that the message box displays an information icon
Information	Specifies that the message box displays an information icon
Error	Specifies that the message box displays an error icon
Hand	Specifies that the message box displays an error icon
Stop	Specifies that the message box displays an error icon
Exclamation	Specifies that the message box displays an exclamation icon
Warning	Specifies that the message box displays an exclamation icon
Question	Specifies that the message box displays a question mark icon
None	Specifies the message box will not display any icon

Available Buttons for MessageBox

There are several combinations of buttons that you can display in a message box. The following table outlines them.

Member Name	Description
AbortRetryIgnore	Specifies that the message box displays Abort, Retry, and Ignore buttons
OK	Specifies that the message box displays an OK button
OKCancel	Specifies that the message box displays OK and Cancel buttons
RetryCancel	Specifies that the message box displays Retry and Cancel buttons
YesNo	Specifies that the message box displays Yes and No buttons
YesNoCancel	Specifies that the message box displays Yes, No, and Cancel buttons

Setting the Default Button

Along with displaying the appropriate buttons, you can instruct the message box to set a default button for you. This allows the user to read the message and press the Enter key to invoke the action for the default button without having to click the button itself with the mouse. The following table outlines the available default button options.

Member Name	Description
Button1	Specifies that the first button in the message box should be the default button
Button2	Specifies that the second button in the message box should be the default button
Button3	Specifies that the third button in the message box should be the default button

You set the default button relative to the MessageBox buttons, from left to right. Therefore, if you have the Yes, No, and Cancel buttons displayed and you choose the third button to be the default, Cancel will be the default button. Likewise, if you choose the third button to be the default and you have only OK and Cancel buttons, the first button becomes the default. The default button will be highlighted until you hover your mouse over another button.

Miscellaneous Options

A couple of other options are available in the `MessageBoxOptions` enumeration and can be used with the message box. These are shown in the following table.

Member Name	Description
DefaultDesktopOnly	Specifies that the message box be displayed on the active desktop
RightAlign	Specifies that the text in a message box will be right-aligned, as opposed to left-aligned, which is the default
RTLReading	Specifies that the text in a message box be displayed with the RTL (right-to-left) reading order; this applies only to languages that are read from right to left
ServiceNotification	Specifies that the message box be displayed on the active desktop. The caller is a Windows service notifying the user of an event.

The Show Method Syntax

You call the `Show` method to display the message box. The following code example displays the message box shown in Figure 8-2. Notice that the code specifies the text that is displayed in the message box as the first argument, followed by the text that is displayed in the title bar. Then you specify the buttons that should be displayed, followed by the type of icon that should be displayed beside the text. Lastly, you specify the button that you want to set as the default button — in this case `Button1`.

If you want to run this code, start a new Windows Application project, double-click the form in the Designer to generate the `Form1_Load` event, and place the following code inside that procedure:

```
MessageBox.Show("My Text", "My Caption", MessageBoxButtons.OKCancel, _
        MessageBoxIcon.Information, MessageBoxDefaultButton.Button1)
```

Figure 8-2

Now that you have seen the available icons, buttons, and default button fields, take a look at the `Show` method of the `MessageBox` class. You can specify the `Show` method in several ways; the more common syntaxes are shown in the following list:

❑   `MessageBox.Show(`*message text*`)`

❑   `MessageBox.Show(`*message text*`, `*caption*`)`

- ❑   `MessageBox.Show(`*message text*`,` *caption*`,` *buttons*`)`

- ❑   `MessageBox.Show(`*message text*`,` *caption*`,` *buttons*`,` *icon*`)`

- ❑   `MessageBox.Show(`*message text*`,` *caption*`,` *buttons*`,` *icon*`,` *default button*`)`

In the previous examples, *message text* represents the message that displays in the message box. This text can be static text (a literal string value) or supplied in the form of a string variable. The other parameters are optional:

- ❑   *caption* represents either static text or a string variable that will be used to display text in the title bar of the message box. If this parameter is omitted, no text is displayed in the title bar.

- ❑   *buttons* represents a value from the `MessageBoxButtons` enumeration. This parameter enables you to specify which of the available buttons to display in the MessageBox dialog box. If you omit this parameter, the OK button is displayed as the only button in the box.

- ❑   *icon* represents a value from the `MessageBoxIcon` enumeration. This parameter enables you to specify which of the available icons displays in the MessageBox dialog box. If you omit this parameter, no icon is displayed.

- ❑   *default button* represents a value from the `MessageBoxDefaultButton` enumeration. This parameter enables you to specify which of the buttons is set as the default button in the MessageBox dialog box. If you omit this parameter, the first button displayed becomes the default button.

All the syntax examples shown in the previous section return a value from the `DialogResult` enumeration, which indicates which button in the MessageBox dialog box was chosen. The following table shows the available members in the `DialogResult` enumeration.

Member Name	Description
Abort	The return value is Abort and is the result of clicking the Abort button.
Cancel	The return value is Cancel and is the result of clicking the Cancel button.
Ignore	The return value is Ignore and is the result of clicking the Ignore button.
No	The return value is No and is the result of clicking the No button.
None	Nothing is returned, which means the dialog box continues running until a button is clicked.
OK	The return value is OK and is the result of clicking the OK button.
Retry	The return value is Retry and is the result of clicking the Retry button.
Yes	The return value is Yes and is the result of clicking the Yes button.

Example Message Boxes

Because multiple buttons can be displayed in a MessageBox dialog box, there are multiple ways to display a dialog box and check the results. Of course, if you were displaying only one button using the message box for notification, you would not have to check the results at all and could use a very simple syntax. This Try It Out demonstrates how to display two buttons in a message box and then check for the results from the message box to determine which button was clicked.

Try It Out   Creating a Two Button MessageBox

1. Start Visual Studio 2008 and select File ⇨ New Project from the menu. In the New Project dialog box, select Windows Forms Application in the Templates pane and enter a project name of **MessageBox Buttons** in the Name field. Click OK to have this project created.

2. Click the form in the Forms Designer and then set its Text property to **MessageBox Buttons**.

3. Add a Label control to the form to display results on which button in the message box a user clicks. Set the Name property to **lblResults** and the Text property to **Nothing Clicked**.

4. Now add a Button control from the Toolbox to the form that will display a message box. Set its Name property to **btn2Buttons** and its Text property to **2 Buttons**.

5. Double-click the button and add the highlighted code in the Click event handler:

```
Private Sub btn2Buttons_Click(ByVal sender As System.Object, _
    ByVal e As System.EventArgs) Handles btn2Buttons.Click
    If MessageBox.Show("Your Internet connection will now be closed.", _
        "Network Notification", MessageBoxButtons.OKCancel, _
        MessageBoxIcon.Information, MessageBoxDefaultButton.Button1) _
        = Windows.Forms.DialogResult.OK Then

        lblResults.Text = "OK Clicked"
        'Call some method here
    Else
        lblResults.Text = "Cancel Clicked"
        'Call some method here
    End If
End Sub
```

6. Save your project by clicking the Save All button on the toolbar.

7. Run the project and then click the 2 Buttons button. You should see a message box dialog box like the one shown in Figure 8-3.

Figure 8-3

How It Works

The code uses the `Show` method of the `MessageBox` class and uses an `If...End If` statement to see whether the user clicked the OK button:

```
If MessageBox.Show("Your Internet connection will now be closed.", _
        "Network Notification", MessageBoxButtons.OKCancel, _
        MessageBoxIcon.Information, MessageBoxDefaultButton.Button1) _
        = Windows.Forms.DialogResult.OK Then
```

The code specifies that the OK and Cancel buttons are to be displayed in the dialog box and also that the OK button is to be the default button.

You have to specify something for the icon parameter, because this is required when you want to set the default button parameter. If you did not want to display an icon, you could use the `Nothing` keyword for that parameter.

Also notice that you check the results returned from MessageBox using `Windows.Forms .DialogResult.OK`. You could have just as easily have checked for `Windows.Forms.DialogResult .Cancel` and written the `If...End If` statement around that.

This is great if you want to test the results of only one or two buttons. But what happens when you want to test the results from a message box that contains three buttons?

Try It Out   Testing a Three Button MessageBox

1. Stop your project if it is still running and open the Forms Designer for Form1.

2. Add another Button control and set its `Name` property to **btn3Buttons** and its `Text` property to **3 Buttons**. Double-click the button and add the highlighted code to its `Click` event handler:

```
Private Sub btn3Buttons_Click(ByVal sender As System.Object, _
        ByVal e As System.EventArgs) Handles btn3Buttons.Click
    'Declare local variable
    Dim intResult As DialogResult

    'Get the results of the button clicked
    intResult = _
        MessageBox.Show("Do you want to save changes to New Document?", _
        "My Word Processor", MessageBoxButtons.YesNoCancel, _
        MessageBoxIcon.Warning, MessageBoxDefaultButton.Button3)

    'Process the results of the button clicked
    Select Case intResult
        Case Windows.Forms.DialogResult.Yes
            lblResults.Text = "Yes Clicked"
            'Do yes processing here
        Case Windows.Forms.DialogResult.No
            lblResults.Text = "No Clicked"
```

```
            'Do no processing here
        Case Windows.Forms.DialogResult.Cancel
            lblResults.Text = "Cancel Clicked"
            'Do cancel processing here
    End Select

End Sub
```

3. Run the project and click the 3 Buttons button. The message box dialog box shown in Figure 8-4 will be displayed and shows an icon and three buttons. Note that the third button is the default this time around.

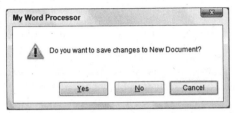

Figure 8-4

How It Works

The Show method returns a DialogResult, which is an Integer value. What you need to do when there are three buttons is capture the DialogResult in a variable and then test that variable.

In the following code, the first thing you do is declare a variable as a DialogResult to capture the DialogResult returned from the message box dialog box. Remember that the results returned from the dialog box are nothing more than an enumeration of Integer values. Next, you set the DialogResult in the variable.

```
    'Declare local variable
    Dim intResult As DialogResult

    'Get the results of the button clicked
    intResult = _
        MessageBox.Show("Do you want to save changes to New Document?", _
        "My Word Processor", MessageBoxButtons.YesNoCancel, _
        MessageBoxIcon.Warning, MessageBoxDefaultButton.Button3)
```

Finally, you test the value of the intResult in a Select Case statement and act on it accordingly:

```
    'Process the results of the button clicked
    Select Case intResult
        Case Windows.Forms.DialogResult.Yes
            lblResults.Text = "Yes Clicked"
            'Do yes processing here
        Case Windows.Forms.DialogResult.No
            lblResults.Text = "No Clicked"
            'Do no processing here
        Case Windows.Forms.DialogResult.Cancel
            lblResults.Text = "Cancel Clicked"
            'Do cancel processing here
    End Select
```

In each of the Case statements, you write the name of the button selected in the label to indicate which button was clicked.

Now you have a better understanding of how the MessageBox dialog box works and you have a point of reference for the syntax. To familiarize yourself further with the MessageBox, try altering the values of the *message text, caption, buttons, icon,* and *default button* parameters in the previous examples.

> *Be careful not to overuse the MessageBox and display a message box for every little event. This can be a real annoyance to the user. You must use common sense and good judgment on when a message box is appropriate. You should display a MessageBox dialog box only when you absolutely need to inform the users that some type of error has occurred or when you need to warn the users that an action that they have requested is potentially damaging. An example of the latter is shutting down the application without saving their work. You would want to prompt the users to let them know that if they continue they will lose all unsaved work, and give them an option to continue or cancel the action of shutting down the application.*

The OpenDialog Control

A lot of Windows applications process data from files, so you need an interface to select files to open and save. The .NET Framework provides the OpenFileDialog and SaveFileDialog classes to do just that. In this section you'll take a look at the OpenFileDialog control, and in the next section you'll look at the SaveFileDialog control.

When you use Windows applications, such as Microsoft Word or Paint, you see the same basic Open dialog box. This does not happen by accident. There is a standard set of application programming interfaces (API) available to every developer that allows you to provide this type of standard interface; however, using the API can be cumbersome and difficult for a beginner. Fortunately, all of this functionality is already built into the .NET Framework, so you can use it as you develop with Visual Basic 2008.

The OpenFileDialog Control

You can use OpenFileDialog as a .NET class by declaring a variable of that type in your code and modifying its properties in code, or as a control by dragging the control from the Toolbox onto the form at design time. In either case, the resulting objects will have the same methods, properties, and events.

You can find the OpenFileDialog control in the Toolbox under the Dialogs tab, where you can drag and drop it onto your form. Then, all you need to do is set the properties and execute the appropriate method. To use OpenFileDialog as a class, you declare your own objects of this type in order to use the dialog box. Then you have control over the scope of the dialog box and can declare an object for it when needed, use it, and then destroy it, thereby using fewer resources.

This section focuses on using OpenFileDialog as a control. Once you have a better understanding of this dialog box and feel comfortable using it, you can then expand your skills and use OpenFileDialog as a class by declaring your own objects for it. Using classes and objects is discussed in greater detail in Chapter 11.

You can use `OpenFileDialog` by simply invoking its `ShowDialog` method, producing results similar to those shown in Figure 8-5.

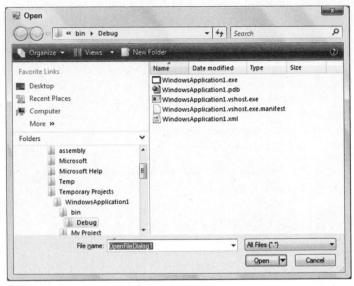

Figure 8-5

The Properties of OpenFileDialog

Although the dialog box shown in Figure 8-5 is the standard Open dialog displayed in Windows Vista, it provides no filtering. You see all file types listed in the window and are unable to specify a file type for filtering, because no filters exist. This is where the properties of OpenFileDialog come in. You can set some of the properties before the Open dialog box is displayed, thereby customizing the dialog box to your needs.

The following table lists some of the available properties for the OpenFileDialog control.

Property	Description
AddExtension	Indicates whether an extension is automatically added to a filename if the user omits the extension. This is mainly used in the SaveFileDialog, which you will see in the next section.
AutoUpgradeEnabled	Indicates whether this dialog should automatically upgrade its appearance and behavior when running on Windows Vista.
CheckFileExists	Indicates whether the dialog box displays a warning if the user specifies a filename that does not exist.

Property	Description
CheckPathExists	Indicates whether the dialog box displays a warning if the user specifies a path that does not exist.
DefaultExt	Indicates the default filename extension.
DereferenceLinks	Used with shortcuts. Indicates whether the dialog box returns the location of the *file referenced by the shortcut* (True) or whether it returns only the location of the *shortcut itself* (False).
FileName	Indicates the path and file name of the selected file in the dialog box.
FileNames	Indicates the path and file names of all selected files in the dialog box. This is a read-only property.
Filter	Indicates the current file name filter string, which determines the choices that appear in the Files of type: combo box in the dialog box.
FilterIndex	Indicates the index of the filter currently selected in the dialog box.
InitialDirectory	Indicates the initial directory displayed in the dialog box.
Multiselect	Indicates whether the dialog box allows multiple files to be selected.
ReadOnlyChecked	Indicates whether the read-only check box is selected.
SafeFileName	Indicates the file name of the selected file in the dialog box.
SafeFileNames	Indicates the file names of all selected files in the dialog box. This is a read-only property.
ShowHelp	Indicates whether the Help button is displayed in the dialog box.
ShowReadOnly	Indicates whether the dialog box contains a read-only check box.
Title	Indicates the title that is displayed in the title bar of the dialog box.
ValidateNames	Indicates whether the dialog box should only accept valid WIN32 file names.

The Methods of OpenFileDialog

Although many methods are available in the OpenFileDialog class, you will be concentrating on the ShowDialog method in these examples. The following list contains some of the other available methods in OpenFileDialog:

❑ Dispose releases the resources used by the Open dialog box.

❑ OpenFile opens the file selected by the user with read-only permission. The file is specified by the FileName property.

❑ Reset resets all properties of the Open dialog box to their default values.

❑ ShowDialog shows the dialog box.

The ShowDialog method is straightforward, because it accepts either no parameters or the owner of the dialog box in the form of the Me keyword. So, before calling the ShowDialog method, you must set all the properties that you want to set. After the dialog box returns, you can query the properties to determine which file was selected, the directory, and the type of file selected. An example of the ShowDialog method is shown in the following code fragment:

```
OpenFileDialog1.ShowDialog()
```

The OpenFileDialog control returns a DialogResult of OK or Cancel, with OK corresponding to the Open button on the dialog box. This control does not actually open and read a file for you; it is merely a common interface that allows a user to locate and specify the file or files to be opened by the application. You need to query the OpenFileDialog properties that have been set by the control after the user clicks the Open button to determine which file or files should be opened.

Using the OpenFileDialog Control

Now that you have had a look at the OpenFileDialog control, you can put this knowledge to use by writing a program that uses this control.

The program in the next Try It Out uses the OpenFileDialog control to display the Open File dialog box. You use the dialog box to locate and select a text file, and then you'll read the contents of the file into a text box on your form using the My.Computer.FileSystem namespace.

Try It Out   Working with OpenFileDialog

1. Create a new Windows Forms Application project called **Windows Forms Dialogs**.

2. To give your form a new name, in the Solution Explorer, right-click Form1.vb and choose Rename from the context menu. Then enter a new name of **Dialogs.vb**. Set the properties of the form as shown in the following list:

    ❑ Set Size to **460, 300**.

    ❑ Set StartPosition to **CenterScreen**.

    ❑ Set Text to **Dialogs**.

3. Because you are going to read the contents of a file into a text box, you want to add a text box to the form. You also want to add a button to the form so that you can invoke the Open File dialog box at will. Add these two controls to the form and set their properties according to the following list:

    ❑ Name the text box **txtFile** and set the following properties: Anchor = **Top,Bottom,Left,Right**; Location = **13, 13**; MultiLine = **True**; ScrollBars = **Vertical**; Size = **330, 232**.

    ❑ Name the Button control **btnOpen** and set the following properties: Anchor = **Top, Right**; Location = **349, 13**; Text = **Open**.

4. When you have finished placing the controls on your form and setting their properties, your form should look similar to Figure 8-6.

Figure 8-6

The reason you anchored your controls in this example is that, when you resize or maximize your form, the text box is resized appropriately to the size of the form, and the button stays in the upper right corner. You can test this at this point by running your project and resizing the form.

5. In the Toolbox, scroll down until you see the OpenFileDialog control in the Dialogs tab and then drag it onto your form and drop it. The control will actually be added to the bottom on the workspace in the IDE.

At this point, you could click the control in the workspace and then set the various properties for this control in the Properties window. However, accept the default name and properties for this control since you'll set the various properties in code later.

6. Switch to the Code Editor for the form. Then declare a string variable that will contain a file name. You set this variable later in your code to the actual path and file name from the Open File dialog box:

```
Public Class Dialogs
    'Declare variable
    Private strFileName As String
```

7. Now you need to write some code in the Click event for the btnOpen button. In the Class Name combo box at the top of the Code Editor, select btnOpen, and in the Method Name combo select the Click event. Add the following highlighted code to the Click event handler:

```
Private Sub btnOpen_Click(ByVal sender As Object, _
    ByVal e As System.EventArgs) Handles btnOpen.Click
    'Set the Open dialog properties
    With OpenFileDialog1
        .Filter = "Text Documents (*.txt)|*.txt|All Files (*.*)|*.*"
        .FilterIndex = 1
        .Title = "Demo Open File Dialog"
    End With

    'Show the Open dialog and if the user clicks the Open button,
```

```
        'load the file
        If OpenFileDialog1.ShowDialog = Windows.Forms.DialogResult.OK Then
            Try
                'Save the file path and name
                strFileName = OpenFileDialog1.FileName


            Catch ex As Exception
                MessageBox.Show(ex.Message, My.Application.Info.Title, _
                    MessageBoxButtons.OK, MessageBoxIcon.Error)
            End Try
        End If
    End Sub
```

8. Now it's time to use some of the prebuilt code snippets that come with Visual Studio 2008. Right-click in the blank space inside the `Try` block statement right before the `Catch` block statement and choose Insert Snippet from the context menu. In the drop-down menu that appears, double-click Fundamentals – Collections, Data Types, File System, Math and then in the new list double-click File System – Processing Drives, Folders, and Files and then finally, scroll down the list and double-click Read Text from a File. Your code should now look like this, and you'll notice that the filename `C:\Test.txt` is highlighted, indicating that this code needs to be changed:

```
Try
    'Save the file path and name
    strFileName = OpenFileDialog1.FileName

    Dim fileContents As String
    fileContents = My.Computer.FileSystem.ReadAllText("C:\Test.txt")
    'Display the file contents in the text box
    txtFile.Text = fileContents
Catch ex As Exception
```

9. Modify the code in the `Try` block as shown here:

```
Try
    'Save the file path and name
    strFileName = OpenFileDialog1.FileName

    Dim fileContents As String
    fileContents = My.Computer.FileSystem.ReadAllText(strFileName)

    'Display the file contents in the text box
    txtFile.Text = fileContents
Catch ex As Exception
```

10. Save your project by clicking the Save All button on the toolbar.

11. Now run your project, and when your form is displayed, click the Open button to have the Open File dialog box displayed. Notice the custom caption in the title bar of the dialog box; you specified this in your code. If you click the file filter combo box, you will see two filters. Click the second filter to see all of the files in the current directory.

12. Now locate a text file on your computer and select it. Then click the Open button to have the file opened and the contents of that file placed in the text box on the form as shown in Figure 8-7.

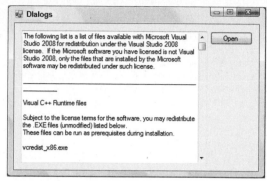

Figure 8-7

13. For the final test, close your application and then start it again. Click the Open button on the form and notice that the Open File dialog box has opened in the same directory from which you selected the last file. There was no code that you had to write to have the Open File dialog box do this.

How It Works

Before displaying the Open File dialog box, you need to set some properties of `OpenFileDialog1` so that the dialog box is customized for your application. You can do this with a `With...End With` statement. The `With...End With` statement allows you to make repeated references to a single object without having to specify the object name over and over. You specify the object name once on the line with the `With` statement and then add all references to the properties of that object before the `End With` statement.

```
With OpenFileDialog1
```

The first property that you set is the `Filter` property. This property enables you to define the filters that are displayed in the file filter combo box at the bottom right hand of the dialog. When you define a file extension filter, you specify the filter description followed by a vertical bar (|) followed by the file extension. When you want the `Filter` property to contain multiple file extensions, as shown in the following code, you separate each file filter with a vertical bar as follows:

```
.Filter = "Text Documents (*.txt)|*.txt|All Files (*.*)|*.*"
```

The next property that you set is the `FilterIndex` property. This property determines which filter is shown in the file filter combo box. The default value for this property is 1, which is the first filter:

```
.FilterIndex = 1
```

Finally, you set the `Title` property. This is the caption that is displayed in the title bar of the dialog box:

```
.Title = "Demo Open File Dialog"
```

To show the Open File dialog box, you use the ShowDialog method. Remember that the ShowDialog method returns a DialogResult value, there are only two possible results, and you can compare the results from the ShowDialog method to Windows.Forms.DialogResult.OK and Windows.Forms.DialogResult.Cancel. If the user clicks the Open button in the dialog box, the ShowDialog method returns a value of OK, and if the user clicks the Cancel button, the ShowDialog method returns Cancel:

```
If OpenFileDialog1.ShowDialog = Windows.Forms.DialogResult.OK Then
```

Next, you add a Try...Catch block to handle any errors that may occur while opening a file. Inside the Try block you retrieve the path and filename that the user has chosen in the Open File dialog box and set it in your strFileName variable. The path and file name are contained in the FileName property of the OpenFileDialog control:

```
'Save the file name
strFileName = OpenFileDialog1.FileName
```

Next, you use the built-in code snippets provided by Visual Studio 2008 to simplify your programming tasks by using the Read Text from a File code snippet. This code snippet contains the necessary code to read the contents from a text file and to place those contents in a string variable.

Then, you modify the code from the code snippet supplying the strFileName variable in the highlighted section of code. This code will read the entire contents of the text file into the fileContents variable:

```
Dim fileContents As String
fileContents = My.Computer.FileSystem.ReadAllText(strFileName)
```

The final line of code that you wrote takes the contents of the allText variable and sets it in the Text property of the TextBox control, thereby populating the text box with the contents of your text file:

```
'Display the file contents in the text box
txtFile.Text = fileContents
```

The code in the Catch block uses the MessageBox class to display the contents of the Message property of the exception thrown should an error occur. The caption parameter of the MessageBox class retrieves the title of your application from the Title property of the My.Application.Info object.

```
Catch ex As Exception
    MessageBox.Show(ex.Message, My.Application.Info.Title, _
        MessageBoxButtons.OK, MessageBoxIcon.Error)
End Try
```

There are many properties in the OpenFileDialog control that haven't been covered in this chapter, and you should feel free to experiment on your own to see all of the possibilities that this dialog box has to offer.

The SaveDialog Control

Now that you can open a file with the OpenFileDialog control, take a look at the SaveFileDialog control so that you can save a file. Like the OpenFileDialog, the SaveFileDialog can be used as a control or a class. Once you have mastered the SaveFileDialog as a control, you will not have any problems using `SaveFileDialog` as a class.

After you open a file, you may need to make some modifications to it and then save it. The SaveFileDialog control provides the same functionality as the OpenFileDialog control, except in reverse. It allows you to choose the location and filename as you save a file. It is important to note that the SaveFileDialog control does not actually save your file; it merely provides a dialog box to allow the user to locate where the file should be saved and to provide a name for the file.

The Properties of SaveFileDialog

The following table lists some of the properties that are available in the SaveFileDialog control. As you can see, this control, or class if you will, contains a wealth of properties that can be used to customize how the dialog box will behave.

Property	Description
AddExtension	Indicates whether an extension is automatically added to a filename if the user omits the extension.
AutoUpgradeEnabled	Indicates whether this dialog box should automatically upgrade its appearance and behavior when running on Windows Vista.
CheckFileExists	Indicates whether the dialog box displays a warning if the user specifies a filename that does not exist. This is useful when you want the user to save a file to an existing name.
CheckPathExists	Indicates whether the dialog box displays a warning if the user specifies a path that does not exist.
CreatePrompt	Indicates whether the dialog box prompts the user for permission to create a file if the user specifies a file that does not exist.
DefaultExt	Indicates the default file extension.
DereferenceLinks	Indicates whether the dialog box returns the location of the *file* referenced by the shortcut or whether it returns the location of the *shortcut itself*.
FileName	Indicates the file name of the selected file in the dialog box. This is a read-only property.
FileNames	Indicates the file names of all selected files in the dialog box. This is a read-only property that is returned as a string array.

(continued)

Property	Description
Filter	Indicates the current file name filter string, which determines the choices that appear in the Files of type: combo box in the dialog box.
FilterIndex	Indicates the index of the filter currently selected in the dialog box.
InitialDirectory	Indicates the initial directory displayed in the dialog box.
OverwritePrompt	Indicates whether the dialog box displays a warning if the user specifies a file name that already exists.
ShowHelp	Indicates whether the Help button is displayed in the dialog box.
SupportMultiDottedExtensions	Indicates whether the dialog box supports displaying and saving files that have multiple file name extensions.
Title	Indicates the title that is displayed in the title bar of the dialog box.
ValidateNames	Indicates whether the dialog box should accept only valid Win32 file names.

The Methods of SaveFileDialog

The SaveFileDialog control exposes the same methods as the OpenFileDialog does. If you want to review these methods, go back to the section "The Methods of OpenFileDialog." All the examples will use the ShowDialog method to show the Save File dialog.

Using the SaveFileDialog Control

To see how to include the SaveFileDialog control in your project, you begin with the Windows Forms Dialogs project from the previous Try It Out as a starting point and build upon it. In this exercise, you want to save the contents of the text box to a file.

You use the SaveFileDialog control to display a Save File dialog box that allows you to specify the location and name of the file. Then you write the contents of the text box on your form to the specified file, again using a built-in code snippet provided by Visual Studio 2008.

Try It Out   Working with SaveFileDialog

1. Return to the Forms Designer in the Windows Forms Dialogs project.

2. Drag another Button control from the Toolbox and drop it beneath the Open button and set its properties as follows:

    ❑   Set Name to **btnSave**.

    ❑   Set Anchor to **Top, Right**.

    ❑   Set Location to **350, 43**.

    ❑   Set Text to **Save**.

3. In the Toolbox, scroll down until you see the SaveFileDialog control and then drag and drop it onto your form. The control will be added to the bottom on the workspace in the IDE.

4. Double-click the Save button to bring up its Click event and add the highlighted code:

```vb
Private Sub btnSave_Click(ByVal sender As System.Object, _
    ByVal e As System.EventArgs) Handles btnSave.Click
    'Set the Save dialog properties
    With SaveFileDialog1
        .DefaultExt = "txt"
        .FileName = strFileName
        .Filter = "Text Documents (*.txt)|*.txt|All Files (*.*)|*.*"
        .FilterIndex = 1
        .OverwritePrompt = True
        .Title = "Demo Save File Dialog"
    End With

    'Show the Save dialog and if the user clicks the Save button,
    'save the file
    If SaveFileDialog1.ShowDialog = Windows.Forms.DialogResult.OK Then
        Try
            'Save the file path and name
            strFileName = SaveFileDialog1.FileName

        Catch ex As Exception
            MessageBox.Show(ex.Message, My.Application.Info.Title, _
                MessageBoxButtons.OK, MessageBoxIcon.Error)
        End Try
    End If
End Sub
```

5. Right-click in the blank space inside the Try block statement right before the Catch block statement and choose Insert Snippet from the context menu. In the drop-down menu that appears, double-click Fundamentals – Collections, Data Types, File System, Math and then in the new list double-click File System – Processing Drives, Folders, and Files and then finally, scroll down the list and double-click Write Text to a File. Your code should now look like this,

and you'll notice that the filename C:\Test.txt is highlighted as is the text string Text, indicating that this code needs to be changed:

```
Try
    'Save the file path and name
    strFileName = SaveFileDialog1.FileName

    My.Computer.FileSystem.WriteAllText("C:\Test.txt",    "Text", True)
Catch ex As Exception
```

6. Modify the code in the Try block as shown here:

```
Try
    'Save the file path and name
    strFileName = SaveFileDialog1.FileName
    My.Computer.FileSystem.WriteAllText(strFileName, txtFile.Text, _False)
Catch ex As Exception
```

7. At this point, you are ready to test this code so run your project. Start with a simple test by opening an existing text file. Type some text into the text box on the form and then click the Save button. The Save dialog box will be displayed. Notice that the File name combo box already has the complete path and file name in it. This is the path file name that was set in the strFileName variable when you declared it in the previous Try It Out.

8. Enter a new file name, but do not put a file extension on it. Then click the Save button and the file will be saved. To verify this, click the Open button on the form to invoke the Open File dialog box; you will see your new file.

9. To test the OverwritePrompt property of the SaveFileDialog control, enter some more text in the text box on the form and then click the Save button. In the Save File dialog box, choose an existing file name and then click the Save button. You will be prompted to confirm replacement of the existing file as shown in Figure 8-8. If you choose Yes, the dialog box will return a DialogResult of OK, and the code inside your If ... End If statement will be executed. If you choose No, you will be returned to the Save File dialog box so that you can enter another file name.

Figure 8-8

When the Open File or Save File dialog box is displayed, the context menu is fully functional and you can cut, copy, and paste files, as well as rename and delete them. There are other options in the context menu that vary depending on what software you have installed. For example, if you have WinZip installed, you will see the WinZip options on the context menu.

How It Works

Before displaying the Save File dialog box, you need to set some properties to customize the dialog box to your application. The first property you set is the `DefaultExt` property. This property automatically sets the file extension if one has not been specified. For example, if you specify a filename of `NewFile` with no extension, the dialog box will automatically add `.txt` to the filename when it returns, so that you end up with a filename of `NewFile.txt`.

```
.DefaultExt = "txt"
```

The `FileName` property is set to the same path and filename as was returned from the Open File dialog. This allows you to open a file, edit it, and then display the same filename when you show the Save File dialog box. Of course, you can override this filename in the application's Save File dialog box.

```
.FileName = strFileName
```

The next two properties are the same as in the OpenFileDialog control. They set the file extension filters to be displayed in the Save as type: combo box and set the initial filter:

```
.Filter = "Text Documents (*.txt)|*.txt|All Files (*.*)|*.*"
.FilterIndex = 1
```

The `OverwritePrompt` property accepts a Boolean value of `True` or `False`. When set to `True`, this property prompts you with a MessageBox dialog box if you choose an existing filename. If you select Yes, the Save File dialog box returns a `DialogResult` of `OK`; if you select No, you are returned to the Save File dialog box to choose another filename. When the `OverwritePrompt` property is set to `False`, the Save File dialog box does not prompt you to overwrite an existing file, and your code will overwrite it without asking for the user's permission.

```
.OverwritePrompt = True
```

The `Title` property sets the caption in the title bar of the Save File dialog box:

```
.Title = "Demo Save File Dialog"
```

After you have the properties set, you want to show the dialog box. The `ShowDialog` method of the SaveFileDialog control also returns a `DialogResult`, so you can use the SaveFileDialog control in an `If...End If` statement to test the return value.

If the user clicks the Save button in the Save File dialog box, the dialog box returns a `DialogResult` of `OK`. If the user clicks the Cancel button in the dialog box, the dialog box returns a `DialogResult` of `Cancel`. The following code tests for `Windows.Forms.DialogResult.OK`:

```
If SaveFileDialog1.ShowDialog = Windows.Forms.DialogResult.OK Then
```

The first thing that you do here is save the path and filename chosen by the user in your `strFileName` variable. This is done in case the user has chosen a new filename in the dialog box:

```
Try
    'Save the file path and name
    strFileName = SaveFileDialog1.FileName
```

Then you modify the code snippet generated by Visual Studio 2008 by replacing the highlighted text with your variables. First you replace the text "C:\Test.txt" with your variable, strFileName. This line of code opens the file for output. Then you replace the text "Text" with the Text property of the text box on your form. This line of code reads the contents of your text box and writes it to the file. The False parameter at the end of this line of code indicates whether text should be appended to the file. A value of False indicates that the contents of the file should be overwritten.

```
My.Computer.FileSystem.WriteAllText(strFileName, txtFile.Text, _
    False)
```

The final bit of code in this If...End If block merely wraps up the Try...Catch block and the If...End If statement.

```
Catch ex As Exception
    MessageBox.Show(ex.Message, My.Application.Info.Title, _
        MessageBoxButtons.OK, MessageBoxIcon.Error)
End Try
End If
```

The FontDialog Control

Sometimes you may need to write an application that allows the user to choose the font in which they want their data to be displayed or entered. Or perhaps you may want to see all available fonts installed on a particular system. This is where the FontDialog control comes in; it displays a list of all available fonts installed on your computer in a standard dialog that your users have become accustomed to.

Like the OpenFileDialog and SaveFileDialog controls, the FontDialog class can be used as a control by dragging it onto a form, or as a class by declaring it in code.

The FontDialog control is really easy to use; you just set some properties, show the dialog box, and then query the properties that you need.

The Properties of FontDialog

The following table lists some of its available properties.

Property	Description
AllowScriptChange	Indicates whether the user can change the character set specified in the Script drop-down box to display a character set other than the one currently displayed.
Color	Indicates the selected font color.
Font	Indicates the selected font.
FontMustExist	Indicates whether the dialog box specifies an error condition if the user attempts to enter a font or style that does not exist.

Property	Description
MaxSize	Indicates the maximum size (in points) a user can select.
MinSize	Indicates the minimum size (in points) a user can select.
ShowApply	Indicates whether the dialog box contains an Apply button.
ShowColor	Indicates whether the dialog box displays the color choice.
ShowEffects	Indicates whether the dialog box contains controls that allow the user to specify strikethrough, underline, and text color options.
ShowHelp	Indicates whether the dialog box displays a Help button.

The Methods of FontDialog

You will only be using one method (ShowDialog) of FontDialog in the following Try It Out. Other methods available include Reset, which allows you to reset all the properties to their default values.

Using the FontDialog Control

You can display the FontDialog control without setting any properties:

```
FontDialog1.ShowDialog()
```

The dialog box would then look like Figure 8-9.

Figure 8-9

Note that the Font dialog box contains an Effects section that enables you to check the options for Strikeout and Underline. However, color selection of the font is not provided by default. If you want this, you must set the ShowColor property before calling the ShowDialog method on the dialog box:

```
FontDialog1.ShowColor = True
FontDialog1.ShowDialog()
```

The ShowDialog method of this dialog box, like all of the ones that you have examined thus far, returns a DialogResult. This will be either DialogResult.OK or DialogResult.Cancel.

When the dialog box returns, you can query for the Font and Color properties to see what font and color the user has chosen. You can then apply these properties to a control on your form or store them to a variable for later use.

Now that you know what the Font dialog box looks like and how to call it, you can use it in a Try It Out. You need to use the program from the last two Try It Outs to open a file, and have the contents of the file read into the text box on the form. You then use the FontDialog control to display the Font dialog box, which allows you to select a font. Then you change the font in the text box to the font that you have chosen.

Try It Out   Working with FontDialog

1. Return to the Forms Designer in the Windows Forms Dialogs project.

2. Add another button from the Toolbox and set its properties according to the values shown in this list:

    ❑   Set Name to **btnFont**.

    ❑   Set Anchor to **Top, Right**.

    ❑   Set Location to **370, 73**.

    ❑   Set Text to **Font**.

3. You now need to add the FontDialog control to your project, so locate this control in the Toolbox and drag and drop it onto the form or in the workspace below the form; the control will be automatically placed in the workspace below the form if dragged onto the form. Accept all default properties for this control.

4. You want to add code to the Click event of the Font button, so double-click it and add the following highlighted code:

```
Private Sub btnFont_Click(ByVal sender As System.Object, _
    ByVal e As System.EventArgs) Handles btnFont.Click

        'Set the Font dialog properties
        FontDialog1.ShowColor = True

        'Show the Font dialog and if the user clicks the OK button,
        'update the font and color in the text box
```

```
        If FontDialog1.ShowDialog = Windows.Forms.DialogResult.OK Then
            txtFile.Font = FontDialog1.Font
            txtFile.ForeColor = FontDialog1.Color
        End If
    End Sub
```

5. Run your project and once your form has been displayed, click the Font button to display the Font dialog box as shown in Figure 8-10. Choose a new font and color and then click OK.

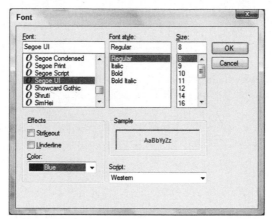

Figure 8-10

6. Add some text in the text box on your form. The text will appear with the new font and color that you have chosen.

7. This same font and color will also be applied to the text that is loaded from a file. To demonstrate this, click the Open button on the form and open a text file. The text from the file is displayed in the same font and color that you chose in the Font dialog box.

How It Works

You know that the Font dialog box does not show a Color box by default, so you begin by setting the `ShowColor` property of the FontDialog control to `True` so that the Color box is displayed:

```
'Set the Font dialog properties
FontDialog1.ShowColor = True
```

Next, you actually show the Font dialog box. Remember the `DialogResult` returns a value of `OK` or `Cancel`, so that you can compare the return value from the FontDialog control to `Windows.Forms .DialogResult.OK`. If the button that the user clicked was OK, you execute the code within the `If...End If` statement:

```
'Show the Font dialog and if the user clicks the OK button,
'update the font and color in the text box
If FontDialog1.ShowDialog = Windows.Forms.DialogResult.OK Then
    txtFile.Font = FontDialog1.Font
    txtFile.ForeColor = FontDialog1.Color
End If
```

You set the `Font` property of the text box (`txtFile`) equal to the `Font` property of the FontDialog control. This is the font that the user has chosen. Then you set the `ForeColor` property of the text box equal to the `Color` property of the FontDialog control, as this will be the color that the user has chosen. After these properties have been changed for the text box, the existing text in the text box is automatically updated to reflect the new font and color. If the text box does not contain any text, any new text that is typed or loaded into the text box will be of the new font and color.

The ColorDialog Control

Sometimes you may need to allow the user to customize the colors on their form. This may be the color of the form itself, a control, or of text in a text box. Visual Basic 2008 provides the ColorDialog control for all such requirements. Once again, the ColorDialog control can also be used as a class — declared in code without dragging a control onto the Form Designer.

The ColorDialog control, shown in Figure 8-11, allows the user to choose from 48 basic colors.

Figure 8-11

Note that the users can also define their own custom colors, adding more flexibility to your applications. When the users click the Define Custom Colors button in the Color dialog box, they can adjust the color to suit their needs (see Figure 8-12).

Having this opportunity for customization and flexibility in your applications gives them a more professional appearance, plus your users are happy because they are allowed to customize the application to meet their own personal tastes.

Figure 8-12

The Properties of ColorDialog

Before you dive into more code, take a look at some of the available properties for the ColorDialog control, shown in the following table.

Property	Description
AllowFullOpen	Indicates whether the user can use the dialog box to define custom colors.
AnyColor	Indicates whether the dialog box displays all available colors in the set of basic colors.
Color	Indicates the color selected by the user.
CustomColors	Indicates the set of custom colors shown in the dialog box.
FullOpen	Indicates whether the controls used to create custom colors are visible when the dialog box is opened.
ShowHelp	Indicates whether a Help button appears in the dialog box.
SolidColorOnly	Indicates whether the dialog box will restrict users to selecting solid colors only.

There aren't many properties that you need to worry about for this dialog box, which makes it even simpler to use than the other dialog boxes that you have examined so far.

As with the other dialog box controls, ColorDialog contains a ShowDialog method. You have already seen this method in the previous examples, and since it is the same, it does not need to be discussed again.

Using the ColorDialog Control

All you need to do to display the Color Dialog box is to execute its ShowDialog method:

```
ColorDialog1.ShowDialog()
```

The ColorDialog control will return a DialogResult of OK or Cancel. Hence, you can use the previous statement in an If...End If statement and test for a DialogResult of OK, as you have done in the previous examples that you have coded.

To retrieve the color that the user has chosen, you simply retrieve the value set in the Color property and assign it to a variable or any property of a control that supports colors, such as the ForeColor property of a text box:

```
txtFile.ForeColor = ColorDialog1.Color
```

In the next Try It Out, you continue using the same project and make the ColorDialog control display the Color dialog box. Then, if the dialog box returns a DialogResult of OK, you change the background color of the form.

Try It Out   Working with the ColorDialog Control

1. Return to the Forms Designer in the Windows Forms Dialogs project.

2. On the form, add another Button control from the Toolbox and set its properties according to the values shown:

    ❑   Set Name to **btnColor**.

    ❑   Set Anchor to **Top, Right**.

    ❑   Set Location to **350, 103**.

    ❑   Set Text to **Color**.

3. Add a ColorDialog control to your project from the Toolbox. It will be added to the workspace below the form, and you will accept all default properties for this control.

4. Double-click the Color button to bring up its Click event handler and add the following highlighted code:

```
Private Sub btnColor_Click(ByVal sender As System.Object, _
    ByVal e As System.EventArgs) Handles btnColor.Click
    'Show the Color dialog and if the user clicks the OK button,
    'update the background color of the form
    If ColorDialog1.ShowDialog = Windows.Forms.DialogResult.OK Then
        Me.BackColor = ColorDialog1.Color
    End If
End Sub
```

5. That's all the code you need to add. Start your project to test your changes.

6. Once the form is displayed, click the Color button to display the Color dialog box. Choose any color that you want, or create a custom color by clicking the Define Custom Colors button. After you have chosen a color, click the OK button in the Color dialog box. The background color of the form will be set to the color that you.

7. As with the Font dialog box, you do not have to set the `Color` property of the ColorDialog control before displaying the Color dialog box again. It automatically remembers the color chosen, and this will be the color that is selected when the dialog box is displayed again. To test this, click the Color button again, and the color that you chose will be selected.

How It Works

This time you did not need to set any properties of the ColorDialog control, so you jumped right in and displayed it in an `If...End If` statement to check the `DialogResult` returned by the `ShowDialog` method of this dialog box:

```
If ColorDialog1.ShowDialog = Windows.Forms.DialogResult.OK Then
```

Within the `If...End If` statement, you added the code necessary to change the `BackColor` property of the form. If the user clicked OK in the Color dialog box, the background color of the form is changed with this line of code:

```
Me.BackColor = ColorDialog1.Color
```

The PrintDialog Control

Any application worth its salt will incorporate some kind of printing capabilities, whether it is basic printing or more sophisticated printing, such as allowing a user to print only selected text or a range of pages. In this next section of the chapter you explore basic printing. You take a look at several classes that help you to print text from a file.

Visual Basic 2008 provides the PrintDialog control. It does not actually do any printing but enables you to select the printer that you want to use and set the printer properties such as page orientation and print quality. It also enables you to specify the print range. You will not be using these features in this next example, but it is worth noting that this functionality is available in the PrintDialog control as shown in Figure 8-13.

Like the previous dialog boxes that you have examined, the Print dialog box provides Print (corresponding to the OK buttons in the other dialogs) and Cancel buttons; thus, its `ShowDialog` method returns a `DialogResult` of `OK` or `Cancel`. You can then use this result in an `If...End If` statement and test for the `DialogResult`. The Apply button merely applies changes made in the Print dialog but does not close the dialog.

Figure 8-13

The Properties of PrintDialog

Take a quick look at some of the properties provided in PrintDialog shown in the following table. Just like the other dialog boxes, PrintDialog exposes a ShowDialog method.

Property	Description
AllowCurrentPage	Indicates whether the Current Page option button is enabled.
AllowPrintToFile	Indicates whether the Print to file check box is enabled.
AllowSelection	Indicates whether the Selection option button is enabled.
AllowSomePages	Indicates whether the Pages option button is enabled.
Document	Indicates the Print Document used to obtain the printer settings.
PrinterSettings	Indicates the printer settings that the dialog box will be modifying.
PrintToFile	Indicates whether the Print to file check box is checked.
ShowHelp	Indicates whether the Help button is displayed.
ShowNetwork	Indicates whether the Network button is displayed.

Using the PrintDialog Control

The only method that you will be using is the ShowDialog method, which will display the Print dialog box shown in Figure 8-13 with only the All page range option button enabled. As mentioned earlier, the PrintDialog control merely displays the Print dialog box; it does not actually do any printing. The following code fragment shows how you display the Print dialog box:

```
PrintDialog1.ShowDialog()
```

The PrintDocument Class

Before you can call the `ShowDialog` method of the PrintDialog control, you have to set the `Document` property of the `PrintDialog` class. This property accepts a `PrintDocument` class, which is used to obtain the printer settings and can send output to the printer. This class requires the `System.Drawing .Printing` namespace, so you must include this namespace before attempting to define an object that uses the `PrintDocument` class.

The Properties of the PrintDocument Class

Before you continue, take a look at some of the important properties of the `PrintDocument` class, listed in the following table.

Property	Description
`DefaultPageSettings`	Indicates the default page settings for the document.
`DocumentName`	Indicates the document name that is displayed while printing the document. This is also the name that appears in the Print Status dialog box and printer queue.
`PrintController`	Indicates the print controller that guides the printing process.
`PrinterSettings`	Indicates the printer that prints the document.

Printing a Document

The `Print` method of the `PrintDocument` class prints a document to the printer specified in the `PrinterSettings` property. When you call the `Print` method of the `PrintDocument` class, the `PrintPage` event is raised for each page as it prints. Therefore, you would need to create a procedure for that event and add an event handler for it. The procedure that you would create for the `PrintPage` event does the actual reading of the data to be printed.

Printing using the `PrintDocument` class requires a lot of coding and knowledge of how actual printing works. Fortunately, the help documentation provides some sample code in the `PrintDocument` class. This can be used as a starting point to help you gain an understanding of the basics of printing. It should be noted that the sample code in the help documentation assumes that a single line in the file to be printed does not exceed the width of a printed page.

The sample code in the help documentation demonstrates how to print from a file. In the next Try It Out, you'll examine how to print the contents of a text box.

Try It Out   **Working with the PrintDialog Control**

1. Return to the Forms Designer in the Windows Forms Dialogs project.

2. Drag a Button control from the Toolbox. Position it beneath the Color button and set the following properties of the new button:

    ❑   Set Name to **btnPrint**.

    ❑   Set Anchor to **Top, Right**.

    ❑   Set Location to **350, 133**.

    ❑   Set Text to **Print**.

3. Now add a PrintDialog control to the project, dragging and dropping it from the Toolbox onto the form. It will be added to the workspace below the form, and you will accept all default properties for this control.

4. Now switch to the Code Editor so that you can add the required namespace for printing. Add this namespace to the top of your class:

```
Imports System.Drawing.Printing


Public Class Dialogs
```

5. Now add the following variable declarations to the top of your class:

```
        'Declare variables and objects
        Private strFileName As String
        Private strPrintRecord As String

        Private WithEvents DialogsPrintDocument As PrintDocument
```

6. Select DialogsPrintDocument in the Class Name combo box and the PrintPage event in the Method Name combo box. Add the following highlighted code to the DialogsPrintDocument_PrintPage event procedure:

```
    Private Sub DialogsPrintDocument_PrintPage(ByVal sender As Object, _
        ByVal e As System.Drawing.Printing.PrintPageEventArgs) _
        Handles DialogsPrintDocument.PrintPage
        'Declare variables
        Dim intCharactersToPrint As Integer
        Dim intLinesPerPage As Integer
        Dim strPrintData As String
        Dim objStringFormat As New StringFormat
        Dim objPrintFont As New Font("Arial", 10)
        Dim objPageBoundaries As RectangleF
        Dim objPrintArea As SizeF

        'Get the page boundaries
```

```
        objPageBoundaries = New RectangleF(e.MarginBounds.Left, _
            e.MarginBounds.Top, e.MarginBounds.Width, e.MarginBounds.Height)

        'Get the print area based on page margins and font used
        objPrintArea = New SizeF(e.MarginBounds.Width, _
            e.MarginBounds.Height - objPrintFont.GetHeight(e.Graphics))

        'Break in between words on a line
        objStringFormat.Trimming = StringTrimming.Word

        'Get the number of characters to print
        e.Graphics.MeasureString(strPrintRecord, objPrintFont, objPrintArea, _
            objStringFormat, intCharactersToPrint, intLinesPerPage)

        'Get the print data from the print record
        strPrintData = strPrintRecord.Substring(0, intCharactersToPrint)

        'Print the page
           e.Graphics.DrawString(strPrintData, objPrintFont, Brushes.Black, _
            objPageBoundaries, objStringFormat)

        'If more lines exist, print another page
        If intCharactersToPrint < strPrintRecord.Length Then
            'Remove printed text from print record
            strPrintRecord = strPrintRecord.Remove(0, intCharactersToPrint)
            e.HasMorePages = True
        Else
            e.HasMorePages = False
        End If
    End Sub
```

7. Select btnPrint in the Class Name combo box and the Click event in the Method Name combo box. Add the following highlighted code to the btnPrint_Click event procedure:

```
Private Sub btnPrint_Click(ByVal sender As System.Object, _
    ByVal e As System.EventArgs) Handles btnPrint.Click
        'Instantiate a new instance of the PrintDocument
        DialogsPrintDocument = New PrintDocument

        'Set the PrintDialog properties
        With PrintDialog1
            .AllowCurrentPage = False
            .AllowPrintToFile = False
            .AllowSelection = False
            .AllowSomePages = False
            .Document = DialogsPrintDocument
            .PrinterSettings.DefaultPageSettings.Margins.Top = 25
            .PrinterSettings.DefaultPageSettings.Margins.Bottom = 25
            .PrinterSettings.DefaultPageSettings.Margins.Left = 25
            .PrinterSettings.DefaultPageSettings.Margins.Right = 25
        End With

        If PrintDialog1.ShowDialog = DialogResult.OK Then
            'Set the selected printer settings in the PrintDocument
```

```
            DialogsPrintDocument.PrinterSettings = _
                PrintDialog1.PrinterSettings

            'Get the print data
            strPrintRecord = txtFile.Text

            'Invoke the Print method on the PrintDocument
            DialogsPrintDocument.Print()
        End If
    End Sub
```

8. You are now ready to test your code, so run the project.

9. Click the Open button to open a file, and then click the Print button to display the Print dialog box shown in Figure 8-14.

Figure 8-14

Note that the Print to file check box as well as the Selection, Current Page, and Pages radio buttons are disabled. This is because you set the `AllowCurrentPage`, `AllowPrintToFile`, `AllowSelection`, and `AllowSomePages` properties in the PrintDialog control to `False`.

If you have more than one printer installed, as shown in Figure 8-14, you can choose the name of the printer that you want to use in the list.

10. Click the Print button in the Print dialog box to have your text printed.

How It Works

You begin by importing the `System.Drawing.Printing` namespace which is needed to support printing. This is the namespace in which the `PrintDocument` class is defined.

You then declare a variable and object needed for printing. The `strPrintRecord` variable is a string variable that will contain the data from the text box to be printed. The `DialogsPrintDocument` object will actually be responsible for printing the text.

Notice the `WithEvents` keyword. This keyword is used to refer to a class that can raise events and will cause Visual Studio 2008 to list those events in the Method Name combo box at the top of the Code Editor:

```
Private strPrintRecord As String

Private WithEvents DialogsPrintDocument As PrintDocument
```

The `DialogsPrintDocument_PrintPage` event handler handles printing a page of output. This event is initially called after you call the `Print` method on the object defined as the `PrintDocument` class; in this case the `DialogsPrintDocument`.

This event handler is where you have to provide the code for actually printing a document and you must determine if more pages exist to be printed. This procedure starts off with a number of variable declarations. The first two variables are `Integer` data types and will contain the number of characters to print to a page and the number of lines that can be printed on a page.

The `strPrintData` variable is a `String` data type that will contain all of the data to be printed on a single page. The `objStringFormat` variable is declared as a `StringFormat` class and this class encapsulates text layout information used to format the data to be printed. The `StringFormat` class is used to trim the data on word boundaries so that the text does not overflow the print area of a page.

The `objPrintFont` object is defined as a `Font` class and sets the font used for the printed text while the `objPageBoundaries` object is defined as a `RectangleF` structure. The `RectangleF` structure contains four floating-point numbers defining the location and size of a rectangle and is used to define the top and left coordinates of a page as well as its width and height. The `objPrintArea` object is defined as a `SizeF` structure and contains the height and width of the print area of a page. This is the actual area that you can print in and not the actual size of the page:

```
Private Sub DialogsPrintDocument_PrintPage(ByVal sender As Object, _
    ByVal e As System.Drawing.Printing.PrintPageEventArgs) _
    Handles DialogsPrintDocument.PrintPage

    'Declare variables
    Dim intCharactersToPrint As Integer
    Dim intLinesPerPage As Integer
    Dim strPrintData As String
    Dim objStringFormat As New StringFormat
    Dim objPrintFont As New Font("Arial", 10)
    Dim objPageBoundaries As RectangleF
    Dim objPrintArea As SizeF
```

The code in this procedure starts off by getting the page boundaries. The `PrintPageEventArgs` passed to this procedure in the `e` parameter contains the top and left coordinates of the page as well as the height and width of the page. These values are used to set the data in the `objPageBoundaries` object.

The print area of the page is contained in the Width and Height properties of the PrintPageEventArgs. The actual height of the page is calculated using the GetHeight method of the Font class in the objPrintFont object as each font size will require more or less vertical space on a page:

```
'Get the page boundaries
objPageBoundaries = New RectangleF(e.MarginBounds.Left, _
        e.MarginBounds.Top, e.MarginBounds.Width, e.MarginBounds.Height)

'Get the print area based on page margins and font used
objPrintArea = New SizeF(e.MarginBounds.Width, _
        e.MarginBounds.Height - objPrintFont.GetHeight(e.Graphics))
```

You now set the Trimming property of the objStringFormat object to instruct it to break the data on a single line using word boundaries. This is done using the StringTrimming enumeration, which contains the Word constant. This ensures that a print line does not exceed the margins of a printed page.

You then need to determine the number of characters that will fit on a page based on the print area of the page, the font size used, and the data to be printed. This is done using the MeasureString method of the Graphics class. This method will take the data to be printed, the font used on the page, the print area of the page and the formatting to be applied and then determine the number of characters that can be printed and the number of lines that will fit on a printed page. The number of print characters and the number of lines will be set in the intCharactersToPrint and intLinesPerPage variables which are passed to the MeasureString method.

Once you know the number of characters that will fit on a page, you get that data from the strPrintRecord variable and set the data to be printed in the strPrintData variable. This is the variable that will contain the data to actually be printed:

```
'Break in between words on a line
objStringFormat.Trimming = StringTrimming.Word

'Get the number of characters to print
e.Graphics.MeasureString(strPrintRecord, objPrintFont, objPrintArea, _
        objStringFormat, intCharactersToPrint, intLinesPerPage)

'Get the print data from the print record
strPrintData = strPrintRecord.Substring(0, intCharactersToPrint)
```

Now that you have the appropriate data to be printed in the strPrintData variable, you are ready to actually send the data to be printed to the printer. This time you are going to use the DrawString method of the Graphics class. This method will actually format and send the data to the printer.

The parameters that you pass to the DrawString method are the data to be printed, the font to be used in printing, a Brushes object representing the font color of the text to print, the page boundaries, and a StringFormat object used to format the printed output:

```
'Print the page
e.Graphics.DrawString(strPrintData, objPrintFont, Brushes.Black, _
        objPageBoundaries, objStringFormat)
```

The last section of code in this procedure determines if more data exist to be printed. You want to compare the value contained in the `intCharactersToPrint` variable to the length of the `strPrintRecord` variable using the `Length` property of the `String` class. The `Length` property returns the number of characters in the string.

If the value contained in the `intCharactersToPrint` variable is less than the length of the `strPrintRecord` variable, then more data exist to be printed. In this case you first want to remove the data from the `strPrintRecord` that has already been printed using the `Remove` method of the `String` class. The `Remove` method accepts the starting position in which to remove data and the amount of data to remove. The amount of data to be removed is contained in the `intCharactersToPrint` variable; the data that have already been printed.

Finally you set the `HasMorePages` property of the `PrintPageEventArgs` parameter to `True` indicating more data exist to be printed. Setting this property to `True` will cause the `PrintPage` event of the `DialogsPrintDocument` object to be raised once more and this event handler will be executed again to continuing printing until all data have been printed.

If no more data exist to be printed you set the `HasMorePages` property to `False`:

```
        'If more lines exist, print another page
        If intCharactersToPrint < strPrintRecord.Length Then
            'Remove printed text from print record
            strPrintRecord = strPrintRecord.Remove(0, intCharactersToPrint)
            e.HasMorePages = True
        Else
            e.HasMorePages = False
        End If
    End Sub
```

The code in the `Click` event of the Print button is less complicated than the code in the `DialogsPrintDocument_PrintPage` event handler. The code in this procedure starts out by instantiating a new instance of the `PrintDocument` class in the `DialogsPrintDocument` object.

You then want to set the properties of the `PrintDialog` control before showing it. Since you have only a simple method to print all pages in a document, you want to disable the features that allow printing only the current page, printing to a file, printing a selection of text and printing specific pages. This is all done by setting the first four properties in the code below to `False`.

Next, you need to set `Document` property of the `PrintDialog` to your `PrintDocument` object so that the dialog can obtain the printer settings. The printer settings are set and retrieved in the `PrintDocument` and can be changed through the `PrintDialog` through its `PrinterSettings` property.

Finally, you set the default margins to be used when printing a document in the `PrinterSettings` property. This can be set before the `PrintDialog` is shown to initially set the print margins for the printer:

```
        'Instantiate a new instance of the PrintDocument
        DialogsPrintDocument = New PrintDocument

        'Set the PrintDialog properties
        With PrintDialog1
            .AllowCurrentPage = False
            .AllowPrintToFile = False
```

```
        .AllowSelection = False
        .AllowSomePages = False
        .Document = DialogsPrintDocument
        .PrinterSettings.DefaultPageSettings.Margins.Top = 25
        .PrinterSettings.DefaultPageSettings.Margins.Bottom = 25
        .PrinterSettings.DefaultPageSettings.Margins.Left = 25
        .PrinterSettings.DefaultPageSettings.Margins.Right = 25
    End With
```

The last thing you want to do in this procedure is to actually display the `PrintDialog` and check for a `DialogResult` of `OK`. If the user clicks the Print button the `PrintDialog` will return a `DialogResult` of `OK` and you want to actually invoke the printing of the data.

The first thing that you do in the `If...Then` block is to capture the printer settings from the `PrintDialog` and set them in the `DialogsPrintDocumnet`. If the user changed any of the margins or other printer settings you want to pass them on to the `PrintDocument` that is used to print the data.

You also want to set the data to be printed from the text box in the `strPrintRecord` variable. Finally, you call the `Print` method on the `DialogsPrintDocument` object to start the printing process. Calling the `Print` method will raise the `PrintPage` event on the `DialogsPrintDocument` object, thus causing your code in the `DialogsPrintDocument_PrintPage` event handler to be executed:

```
    If PrintDialog1.ShowDialog = DialogResult.OK Then
        'Set the selected printer settings in the PrintDocument
        DialogsPrintDocument.PrinterSettings = _
            PrintDialog1.PrinterSettings

        'Get the print data
        strPrintRecord = txtFile.Text

        'Invoke the Print method on the PrintDocument
        DialogsPrintDocument.Print()
    End If
```

The FolderBrowserDialog Control

Occasionally, you'll need to allow your users to select a folder instead of a file. Perhaps your application performs backups, or perhaps you need a folder to save temporary files. The FolderBrowserDialog control displays the Browse For Folder dialog box, which allows your users to select a folder. This dialog box does not display files — only folders, which provides an obvious way to allow your users to select a folder needed by your application.

Like the other dialog boxes that you have examined thus far, the FolderBrowserDialog control can also be used as a class declared in code. The Browse For Folder dialog box, shown in Figure 8-15 without any customization, allows the user to browse for and select a folder. Notice that there is also a Make New Folder button that allows a user to create and select a new folder.

Figure 8-15

The Properties of FolderBrowserDialog

Before you dive into some code, take a look at some of the available properties for the FolderBrowserDialog control, shown in the following table.

Property	Description
Description	Provides a descriptive message in the dialog box.
RootFolder	Indicates the root folder where the dialog box should start browsing from.
SelectedPath	Indicates the folder selected by the user.
ShowNewFolderButton	Indicates whether the Make New Folder button is shown in the dialog box.

This is one dialog control where you'll want to use all of the most common properties, as shown in the preceding table, to customize the dialog box displayed.

As with the other dialog controls, the FolderBrowserDialog contains a ShowDialog method. You have already seen this method in the previous examples, and since it is the same, it does not need to be discussed again.

Using the FolderBrowserDialog Control

Before showing the Browse For Folder dialog box, you'll want to set some basic properties. The three main properties that you are most likely to set are shown in the following code snippet. The first of these properties is the Description property. This property allows you to provide a description or instructions for your users.

The next property is the RootFolder property and specifies the starting folder for the Browse For Folder dialog box. This property uses one of the constants from the Environment.SpecialFolder enumeration. Typically you would use the MyComputer constant to specify that browsing should start at the My Computer level or sometimes you may want to use to the `Personal` constant to start browsing at the My Documents level.

The final property shown in the code snippet is the `ShowNewFolderButton` property. This property has a default value of `True`, which indicates that the Make New Folder button should be displayed. However, if you do not want this button displayed, you need to specify this property and set it to a value of `False`:

```
With FolderBrowserDialog1
    .Description = "Select a backup folder"
    .RootFolder = Environment.SpecialFolder.MyComputer
    .ShowNewFolderButton = False
End With
```

After you have set the necessary properties, you execute the `ShowDialog` method to display the dialog box:

```
FolderBrowserDialog1.ShowDialog()
```

The FolderBrowserDialog control will return a `DialogResult` of `OK` or `Cancel`. Hence, you can use the previous statement in an `If...End If` statement and test for a `DialogResult` of `OK`, as you have done in the previous examples that you have coded.

To retrieve the folder that the user has chosen, you simply retrieve the value set in the `SelectedPath` property and assign it to a variable. The folder that is returned is a fully qualified path name. For example, if you chose a folder named `Temp` at the root of your C drive, the path returned would be `C:\Temp`:

```
strFolder = FolderBrowserDialog1.SelectedPath
```

In the next Try It Out, you continue using the same Windows Forms Dialogs project and have the FolderBrowserDialog control display the Browse For Folder dialog box. Then, if the dialog box returns a `DialogResult` of `OK`, you'll display the selected folder in the text box on your form.

Try It Out   Working with the FolderBrowseDialog Control

1. Return to the Forms Designer in the Windows Forms Dialog project.

2. Add another Button control from the Toolbox to the form beneath the Print button and set its properties as follows:

    ❑   Set `Name` to **btnBrowse**.

    ❑   Set `Anchor` to **Top, Right**.

    ❑   Set `Location` to **350, 163**.

    ❑   Set `Text` to **Browse**.

3. Add a FolderBrowserDialog control to your project from the Toolbox. It will be added to the workspace below the form. Accept all default properties for this control, because you'll set the necessary properties in your code.

4. Double-click the Browse button to bring up its Click event procedure, and add the following code:

```
Private Sub btnBrowse_Click(ByVal sender As System.Object, _
    ByVal e As System.EventArgs) Handles btnBrowse.Click
    'Set the FolderBrowser dialog properties
    With FolderBrowserDialog1
        .Description = "Select a backup folder"
        .RootFolder = Environment.SpecialFolder.MyComputer
        .ShowNewFolderButton = False
    End With

    'Show the FolderBrowser dialog and if the user clicks the
    'OK button, display the selected folder
    If FolderBrowserDialog1.ShowDialog = Windows.Forms.DialogResult.OK Then
        txtFile.Text = FolderBrowserDialog1.SelectedPath
    End If
End Sub
```

5. That's all the code you need to add. To test your changes to your project, click the Start button on the toolbar.

6. When your form displays, click the Browse button, and you'll see a Browse For Folder dialog similar to the one shown in Figure 8-16.

Figure 8-16

7. Now browse your computer and select a folder. When you click the OK button, the selected folder will be displayed in the text box on your form. Notice that the folder returned contains a fully qualified path name.

How It Works

Before displaying the Browse For Folder dialog box, you needed to set some basic properties of the FolderBrowserDialog control to customize the look for this dialog box. You start by setting the `Description` property to provide some basic instructions for your user. Then you select the root folder at which the Browse For Folder dialog box should start browsing. In this instance, you use the `MyComputer` constant, which displayed all drives on your computer, as shown in Figure 8-16. Finally, you set the `ShowNewFolderButton` property to `False` so as not to display the Make New Folder button:

```
'Set the FolderBrowser dialog properties
With FolderBrowserDialog1
    .Description = "Select a backup folder"
    .RootFolder = Environment.SpecialFolder.MyComputer
    .ShowNewFolderButton = False
End With
```

Then you display the dialog box in an `If...End If` statement to check the `DialogResult` returned by the `ShowDialog` method of the FolderBrowserDialog control. Within the `If...End If` statement, you add the code necessary to display the folder selected in the text box on your form, using the `SelectedPath` property:

```
'Show the FolderBrowser dialog and if the user clicks the
'OK button, display the selected folder
If FolderBrowserDialog1.ShowDialog = Windows.Forms.DialogResult.OK Then
    txtFile.Text = FolderBrowserDialog1.SelectedPath
End If
```

Summary

This chapter has taken a look at some of the dialog boxes that are provided in Visual Basic 2008. You examined the MessageBox dialog box, and the OpenFileDialog, SaveFileDialog, FontDialog, ColorDialog, PrintDialog, and FolderBrowserDialog controls. Each of these dialog boxes will help you provide a common interface in your applications for their respective functions. They also hide a lot of the complexities required to perform their tasks, allowing you to concentrate on the logic needed to make your application functional and feature-rich.

Although you used the controls from the Toolbox for all of these dialog boxes, except the MessageBox dialog box, remember that these controls can also be used as normal classes. This means that the classes that these dialog boxes use expose the same properties and methods that you've seen, whether you are selecting a control visually or writing code using the class. You can define your own objects and set them to these classes, and then use the objects to perform the tasks that you performed using the controls. This provides better control over the scope of the objects. For example, you could define an object, set it to the `OpenDialog` class, use it, and then destroy it all in the same procedure. This method uses resources only in the procedure that defines and uses the `OpenDialog` class, and reduces the size of your executable.

To summarize, you should now know how to:

- ❑ Use the MessageBox dialog box to display messages
- ❑ Display icons and buttons in the MessageBox dialog box
- ❑ Use the OpenFileDialog control and read the contents of a file
- ❑ Use the SaveFileDialog control and save the contents of a text box to a file
- ❑ Use the FontDialog control to set the font and color of text in a text box
- ❑ Use the ColorDialog control to set the background color of your form
- ❑ Use the PrintDialog control to print text
- ❑ Use the FolderBrowserDialog control to get a selected folder

Exercises

1. Create a simple Windows application with a TextBox control and two Button controls. Set the buttons to open a file and to save a file. Use the OpenFileDialog class (not the control) and the SaveFileDialog class to open and save your files.

Hint: To use the corresponding classes for the controls use the following statements:

```
Dim objOpenFileDialog As New OpenFileDialog
Dim objSaveFileDialog As New SaveFileDialog
```

2. Create a simple Windows application with a Label control and a Button control. Set the button to display the Browse For Folder dialog box with the Make New Folder button displayed. Use My Documents as the root folder at which the dialog starts browsing. Use the FolderBrowserDialog class (not the control) and display the selected folder in the label on your form.

Creating Menus

Menus are a part of every good application and provide not only an easy way to navigate within an application but also useful tools for working with that application. Take, for example, Visual Studio 2008. It provides menus for navigating the various windows that it displays and useful tools for making the job of development easier through menus and context menus (also called pop-up menus) for cutting, copying, and pasting code. It also provides menu items for searching through code.

This chapter takes a look at creating menus in your Visual Basic 2008 applications. You explore how to create and manage menus and submenus and how to create context menus and override the default context menus. Visual Studio 2008 provides two menu controls in the Toolbox, and you explore both of these.

In this chapter, you will:

- ❑ Create menus
- ❑ Create submenus
- ❑ Create context menus

Understanding Menu Features

The MenuStrip control in Visual Studio 2008 provides several key features. First and foremost, it provides a quick and easy way to add menus, menu items, and submenu items to your application. It also provides a built-in editor that allows you to add, edit, and delete menu items at the drop of a hat.

The menu items that you create may contain images, access keys, shortcut keys, and check marks as well as text labels.

Images

Everyone has seen images on the menus in applications such as Microsoft Outlook or Visual Studio 2008. In earlier versions of Visual Basic, developers were unable to create menu items with images without doing some custom programming or purchasing a third-party control. Visual Basic has come a long way and now provides an Image property for a menu item that makes adding an image to your menu items a breeze.

Access Keys

An *access key* (also known as an *accelerator key*) enables you to navigate the menus using the Alt key and a letter that is underlined in the menu item. When the access key is pressed, the menu appears on the screen, and the user can navigate through it using the arrow keys or the mouse.

Shortcut Keys

Shortcut keys enable you to invoke the menu item without displaying the menus at all. Shortcut keys usually consist of a control key and a letter, such as Ctrl+X to cut text.

Check Marks

A *check mark* symbol can be placed next to a menu item in lieu of an image, typically to indicate that the menu item is being used. For example, if you click the View menu in Visual Studio 2008 and then select the Toolbars menu item, you see a submenu that has many submenu items, some of which have check marks. The submenu items that have check marks indicate the toolbars that are currently displayed.

Figure 9-1 shows many of the available features that you can incorporate into your menus. As you can see, this sample menu provides all the features that were just mentioned plus a *separator*. A separator looks like a raised ridge and provides a logical separation between groups of menu items.

Figure 9-1

Figure 9-1 shows the menu the way it looks when the project is being run. Figure 9-2 shows how the menu looks in Design mode.

Figure 9-2

The first thing that you'll notice when using the MenuStrip control is that it provides a means to add another menu, menu item, or submenu item quickly. Each time you add one of these, another blank text area is added.

The Properties Window

While you are creating or editing a menu, the Properties window displays the available properties that can be set for the menu being edited, as shown in Figure 9-3 which shows the properties for the Toolbars menu item.

Figure 9-3

You can create as many menus, menu items, and submenu items as you need. You can even go as deep as you need to when creating submenu items by creating another submenu within a submenu.

Keep in mind that if the menus are hard to navigate, or if it is hard for users to find the items they are looking for, users will rapidly lose interest in your application.

You should stick with the standard format for menus that you see in most Windows applications today. These are the menus that you see in Visual Studio 2008 or Microsoft Outlook. For example, you always have a File menu and an Exit menu item in the File menu to exit from the application. If your application provides cut, copy, and paste functionality, you would place these menu items in the Edit menu, and so on.

The MSDN library that was installed with Visual Studio 2008 contains a section on Windows Vista User Experience Guidelines. This section contains many topics that address the user interface and the Windows user interface. You can explore these topics for more details on Windows user-interface design-related topics.

The key is to make your menus look and feel like the menus in other Windows applications so that the users can feel comfortable using your application. This way they do not feel like they have to learn the basics of Windows all over again. Some menu items will be specific to your application but the key to incorporating them is to ensure that they fall into a general menu category that users are familiar with or to place them in your own menu category. You would then place this new menu in the appropriate place in the menu bar, generally in the middle.

Creating Menus

Now you move on and see how easy it is to create menus in your applications. In the following Try It Out, you are going to create a form that contains a menu bar, two toolbars, and two text boxes. The menu bar will contain five menus: File, Edit, View, Tools, and Help, and a few menu items and submenu items. This enables you to fully exercise the features of the menu controls. Since there are several steps involved in building this application, this process is broken down into several sections, starting with "Designing the Menus."

Designing the Menus

You will be implementing code behind the menu items to demonstrate the menu and how to add code to your menu items, so let's get started.

Try It Out   **Creating Menus**

1. Start Visual Studio 2008 and click File ➪ New Project. In the New Project dialog box, select Windows Forms Application in the Templates pane and enter the project name **Windows Forms Menus** in the Name field. Click the OK button to have the project created.

2. Click the form in the Forms Designer and set the following properties of the form:

    ❑   Set Font to **Segoe UI** (on Windows Vista only).

    ❑   Set Size to **300, 180**.

    ❑   Set StartPosition to **CenterScreen**.

    ❑   Set Text to **Menu Demo**.

3. Drag a MenuStrip control from the Toolbox and drop it on your form. It is automatically positioned at the top of your form. The control is also added to the bottom of the development environment, just like the dialog box controls discussed in Chapter 8.

4. In the Properties window, set the Font to **Segoe UI**, the Font Style to **Regular**, and the Size to **8** only if you are running on Windows Vista.

5. Right-click the MenuStrip1 control on the form and select the Insert Standard Items context menu item to have the standard menu items automatically inserted.

6. In the Properties window, click the ellipsis dots (…) button next to the Items property or right click on the MenuStrip control in your form and choose Edit Items from the context menu. In the Items Collection Editor dialog box, click the Add button to add a new menu item.

   To be consistent with the current naming standard already in use with the other menu items, set the Name property for this new menu item to **ViewToolStripMenuItem**.

   Now set the Text property to **&View**. An ampersand (&) in the menu name provides an access key for the menu or menu item. The letter before which the ampersand appears is the letter used to access this menu item in combination with the Alt key. So for this menu, you will be able to access and expand the View menu by pressing Alt+V. You'll see this when you run your project later.

   You want to position this menu between the Edit and Tools menu so click the up arrow to the right of the menu items until the View menu is positioned between EditToolStripMenuItem and ToolsToolStripMenuItem in the list.

7. Now locate the DropDownItems property and click the ellipsis dots button next to it so that you can add menu items beneath the View menu. A second Items Collection Editor appears, and its caption reads "Items Collection Editor (ViewToolStripMenuItem.DropDownItems)".

   There is only one menu item under the View menu, and that is Toolbars. Click the Add button in the Item Collections Editor to add a MenuItem.

   Again, you want to be consistent with the naming standard already being used so set the Name property to **ToolbarToolStripMenuItem**. Then set the Text property to **&Toolbars**.

8. You want to add two submenu items under the Toolbars menu item, so locate the DropDownItems property and click the ellipsis button next to it.

   In the Item Collections Editor, click the Add button to add a new menu item. Set the Name property for this submenu item to **MainToolStripMenuItem** and the Text property to **&Main**.

   When you add a toolbar to this project, it is displayed by default, so this submenu item should be checked to indicate that the toolbar is displayed. Set the Checked property to **True** to cause this submenu item to be checked by default and the CheckOnClick property to **True** to allow the check mark next to this submenu item to be toggled on and off.

9. The next submenu item that you add is Formatting. Click the Add button to add a new menu item and set the Name property for this submenu item to **FormattingToolStripMenuItem** and the Text property to **&Formatting**.

Since this toolbar is not shown by default, you need to leave the Checked property set to **False**. You do, however, need to set the CheckOnClick property to **True** so that the submenu item can toggle the check mark on and off.

Keep clicking the OK button in the Items Collection Editors until all of the editors are closed.

10.   Save your project by clicking the Save All button on the toolbar.

11.   If you run your project at this point and then enter Alt+V and ALT+T (without releasing the Alt key), you will see the submenu items as shown in Figure 9-4. You can also click the other menus and see their menu items.

Figure 9-4

How It Works

Visual Studio 2008 takes care of a lot of the details for you by providing the Insert Standard Items context menu item in the MenuStrip control. You click this menu item to have Visual Studio 2008 create the standard menus and menu items found in most common applications. This allows you to concentrate on only the menus and menu items that are custom to your application, which is what you did by adding the View menu, Toolbars menu item, and Main and Formatting submenu items.

Adding Toolbars and Controls

In this section, you add the toolbars and buttons for the toolbars that the application needs. The menus created in the previous section will control the displaying and hiding of these toolbars. You also add a couple of TextBox controls that are used in the application to cut, copy, and paste text using the toolbar buttons and menu items.

Try It Out   **Adding Toolbars and Controls**

1.   Return to the Forms Designer in your Windows Forms Menus project. You need to add two toolbars to the form, so locate the ToolStrip control in the Toolbox and drag and drop it on your form; it automatically aligns itself to the top of the form below the menu. Set the Name property to **tspMain**.

2.   The default toolbar buttons will be fine for this project, so right-click the ToolStrip control on the form and select Insert Standard Items from the context menu to have the standard toolbar buttons added.

3. Next, add a second toolbar to the form in the same manner. It aligns itself below the first toolbar. Set its `Name` property to **tspFormatting** and its `Visible` property to **False**, because you don't want this toolbar to be shown by default.

4. You want to add three buttons to this toolbar, so click the ellipsis dots button next to the Items property in the Properties window or right-click the ToolStrip control on the form and select Edit Items from the context menu.

   In the Items Collection Editor dialog box, click the Add button to add the first button. Since you really won't be using these buttons, you can accept the default name and ToolTip text for these buttons. Ensure the `DisplayStyle` property is set to **Image**, and then click the ellipsis dots button next to the `Image` property.

   In the Select Resource dialog box, click the Import button and browse to `C:\Program Files\ Microsoft Visual Studio 9.0\Common7\VS2008ImageLibrary\1033\ VS2008ImageLibrary\Actions\pngformat` folder. This path assumes a default installation of Visual Studio 2008 and that you extracted the contents of the VS2008ImageLibrary zip file. In the Open dialog box, select `AlignTableCellMiddleLeftJustHS.png` and then click the Open button. Next, click the OK button in the Select Resource dialog box to close it.

5. In the Items Collection Editor dialog box, click the Add button again to add the second button. Ensure the `DisplayStyle` property is set to **Image** and then set the `Image` property to the `AlignTableCellMiddleCenterHS.png` file.

6. In the Items Collection Editor dialog box, click the Add button again to add the next button. Ensure the `DisplayStyle` property is set to **Image** and then set the `Image` property to the `AlignTableCellMiddleRightHS.png` file.

7. Click the OK button in the Items Collection Editor dialog box to close it.

8. Add a Panel control from the toolbox to your form and set its `Dock` property to **Fill**.

9. Add two TextBox controls to the Panel control and accept their default properties. Their location and size are not important, but they should be wide enough to enter text in. Your completed form should look similar to the one shown in Figure 9-5. Notice that your second toolbar is not visible since you set its `Visible` property to `False`.

Figure 9-5

If you run your project at this point you will see the menus, the main toolbar, and two text boxes. The formatting toolbar is not visible at this point because the `Visible` property is set to `False`.

How It Works

You took a look at toolbars in Chapter 7, so review the Text Editor project for details on how the ToolStrip control works. The ToolStrip control, like the MenuStrip control, provides the Insert Standard Items context menu item, which does a lot of the grunt work for you by inserting the standard toolbar buttons, as was shown in Figure 9-5. This without a doubt provides the most efficient means of having the standard toolbar buttons added to the ToolStrip control. You can, of course, rearrange the buttons that have been added and even add new buttons and delete existing buttons.

Because you set the `Visible` property to `False` for the tspFormatting ToolStrip control, that control does not take up any space on your form at design time after the control loses focus.

Coding Menus

Now that you have finally added all of your controls to the form, it's time to start writing some code to make these controls work. First, you have to add functionality to make the menus work. Then you add code to make some of the buttons on the main toolbar work.

Try It Out   Coding the File Menu

1. Start by switching to the Code Editor for the form. In the Class Name combo box at the top of the Code Editor, select NewToolStripMenuItem and select the `Click` event in the Method Name combo box. Add the following highlighted code to the `Click` event handler:

```
Private Sub NewToolStripMenuItem_Click(ByVal sender As Object, _
    ByVal e As System.EventArgs) Handles NewToolStripMenuItem.Click
    'Clear the text boxes
    TextBox1.Text = String.Empty
    TextBox2.Text = String.Empty

    'Set focus to the first text box
    TextBox1.Focus()
End Sub
```

2. Add the procedure for the New button on the toolbar by selecting NewToolStripButton from the Class Name combo box and the `Click` event from the Method Name combo box. Add the following highlighted code to this procedure:

```
Private Sub NewToolStripButton_Click(ByVal sender As Object, _
    ByVal e As System.EventArgs) Handles NewToolStripButton.Click
    'Call the NewToolStripMenuItem_Click procedure
    NewToolStripMenuItem_Click(sender, e)
End Sub
```

3. Select ExitToolStripMenuItem from the Class Name combo box and the `Click` event from the Method Name combo box and add the following highlighted code to the procedure:

```
Private Sub ExitToolStripMenuItem_Click(ByVal sender As Object, _
        ByVal e As System.EventArgs) Handles ExitToolStripMenuItem.Click
    'Close the form and end
    Me.Close()
End Sub
```

How It Works

To clear the text boxes on the form in the `NewToolStripMenuItem_Click` procedure, add the following code. All you are doing here is setting the `Text` property of the text boxes to an empty string. The next line of code sets focus to the first text box by calling the `Focus` method of that text box:

```
'Clear the text boxes
TextBox1.Text = String.Empty
TextBox2.Text = String.Empty

'Set focus to the first text box
TextBox1.Focus()
```

When you click the New menu item under the File menu, the text boxes on the form are cleared of all text, and TextBox1 has the focus and is ready to accept text.

The New button on the toolbar should perform the same function, but you don't want to write the same code twice. You could put the text in the previous procedure in a separate procedure and call that procedure from both the `newToolStripMenuItem_Click` and `newToolStripButton_Click` procedures. Instead, you have the code in the `newToolStripMenuItem_Click` procedure and simply call that procedure from within the `newToolStripButton_Click` procedure. Since both procedures accept the same parameters, you simply pass the parameters received in this procedure to the procedure you are calling:

```
'Call the newToolStripMenuItem_Click procedure
newToolStripMenuItem_Click(sender, e)
```

Now you can click the New button on the toolbar or click the New menu item on the File menu and have the same results, clearing the text boxes on your form.

When you click the Exit menu item, you want the program to end. In the `exitToolStripMenuItem_Click` procedure, you added the following code. The `Me` keyword refers to the class where the code is executing and, in this case, refers to the form class. The `Close` method closes the form, releases all resources, and ends the program:

```
'Close the form and end
Me.Close()
```

That takes care of the code for the File menu and its corresponding toolbar button, so you want to move on to the Edit menu and add the code for those menu items.

Try It Out   Coding the Edit Menu

1.   The first menu item in the Edit menu is the Undo menu item. Select UndoToolStripMenuItem in the Class Name combo box and select the `Click` event in the Method Name combo box. Add the following highlighted code to the `Click` event handler:

```
Private Sub UndoToolStripMenuItem_Click(ByVal sender As Object, _
    ByVal e As System.EventArgs) Handles UndoToolStripMenuItem.Click
    'Undo the last operation
    If TypeOf Me.ActiveControl Is TextBox Then
        CType(Me.ActiveControl, TextBox).Undo()
    End If
End Sub
```

2.   The next menu item that you want to add code for is the Cut menu item. Select CutToolStripMenuItem in the Class Name combo and the `Click` event in the Method Name combo box. Add the highlighted code here:

```
Private Sub CutToolStripMenuItem_Click(ByVal sender As Object, _
    ByVal e As System.EventArgs) Handles CutToolStripMenuItem.Click
    'Copy the text to the clipboard and clear the field
    If TypeOf Me.ActiveControl Is TextBox Then
        CType(Me.ActiveControl, TextBox).Cut()
    End If
End Sub
```

3.   You'll want the Cut button on the toolbar to call the code for the Cut menu item. Select CutToolStripButton in the Class Name combo and the `Click` event in the Method Name combo box. Add the following highlighted code:

```
Private Sub CutToolStripButton_Click(ByVal sender As Object, _
    ByVal e As System.EventArgs) Handles CutToolStripButton.Click
    'Call the CutToolStripMenuItem_Click procedure
    CutToolStripMenuItem_Click(sender, e)
End Sub
```

4.   The next menu item that you need to code is the Copy menu item. Select CopyToolStripMenuItem in the Class Name combo and the `Click` event in the Method Name combo box and then add the following highlighted code:

```
Private Sub CopyToolStripMenuItem_Click(ByVal sender As Object, _
    ByVal e As System.EventArgs) Handles CopyToolStripMenuItem.Click
    'Copy the text to the clipboard
    If TypeOf Me.ActiveControl Is TextBox Then
        CType(Me.ActiveControl, TextBox).Copy()
    End If
End Sub
```

5. You want the Copy button on the toolbar to call the procedure you just added. Select CopyToolStripButton in the Class Name combo and the Click event in the Method Name combo box and then add the following highlighted code:

```
Private Sub CopyToolStripButton_Click(ByVal sender As Object, _
    ByVal e As System.EventArgs) Handles CopyToolStripButton.Click
        'Call the CopyToolStripMenuItem_Click procedure
        CopyToolStripMenuItem_Click(sender, e)
End Sub
```

6. The Paste menu item is next so select PasteToolStripMenuItem in the Class Name combo box and the Click event in the Method Name combo box. Add the following highlighted code to the Click event handler:

```
Private Sub PasteToolStripMenuItem_Click(ByVal sender As Object, _
    ByVal e As System.EventArgs) Handles PasteToolStripMenuItem.Click
        'Copy the text from the clipboard to the text box
        If TypeOf Me.ActiveControl Is TextBox Then
            CType(Me.ActiveControl, TextBox).Paste()
        End If
End Sub
```

7. The Paste toolbar button should execute the code in the PasteToolStripMenuItem_Click procedure. Select PasteToolStripButton in the Class Name combo box and the Click event in the Method Name combo box and add the following highlighted code:

```
Private Sub PasteToolStripButton_Click(ByVal sender As Object, _
    ByVal e As System.EventArgs) Handles PasteToolStripButton.Click
        'Call the PasteToolStripMenuItem_Click procedure
        PasteToolStripMenuItem_Click(sender, e)
End Sub
```

8. The last menu item under the Edit menu that you'll write code for is the Select All menu item. Select SelectAllToolStripMenuItem in the Class Name combo box and the Click event in the Method Name combo box and add the following highlighted code:

```
Private Sub SelectAllToolStripMenuItem_Click(ByVal sender As Object, _
    ByVal e As System.EventArgs) Handles SelectAllToolStripMenuItem.Click
        'Select all the text in the text box
        If TypeOf Me.ActiveControl Is TextBox Then
            CType(Me.ActiveControl, TextBox).SelectAll()
        End If
End Sub
```

How It Works

You added the code for the Edit menu starting with the Undo menu item. Since you have two text boxes on your form, you need a way to determine which text box you are dealing with or a generic way of handling an undo operation for both text boxes. In this example, you go with the latter option and provide a generic way to handle both text boxes.

You do this by first determining whether the active control you are dealing with is a TextBox control. The `ActiveControl` property of the `Form` class returns a reference to the active control on the form, the control that has focus.

Then you want to check the active control to see if it is a TextBox control. This is done using the `TypeOf` operator. This operator compares an object reference to a data type and in the code below you are comparing the object reference returned in the `ActiveControl` property to a data type of `TextBox`.

When you know you are dealing with a TextBox control, you use the `CType` function to convert the object contained in the ActiveControl property to a TextBox control. This exposes the properties and methods of the TextBox control in IntelliSense allowing you to choose the `Undo` method:

```
If TypeOf Me.ActiveControl Is TextBox Then
    CType(Me.ActiveControl, TextBox).Undo()
End If
```

The menu and toolbar are never set as the active control. This allows you to use the menus and toolbar buttons and always reference the active control.

> *The `ActiveControl` property works fine in this small example, because all you are dealing with is two text boxes. However, in a real-world application, you would need to test the active control to see whether it supports the method that you were using (for example, `Undo`).*

You use the same logic for the rest of the menu item procedures as the Undo menu item, checking the type of active control to see if it is a TextBox control. Then you call the appropriate method on the TextBox control to cut, copy, paste, and select all text

Coding the View Menu and Toolbars

Now that you have added the code to make the Edit menu items and the corresponding toolbar buttons functional, the next step is to make the menu items under the View menu functional.

Try It Out   Coding the View Menu

1. Return to the Code Editor in the Windows Forms Menus project and in the Class Name combo box, select MainToolStripMenuItem and in the Method Name combo box select the `Click` event. Add the following highlighted code to the `Click` event handler:

```
Private Sub MainToolStripMenuItem_Click(ByVal sender As Object, _
    ByVal e As System.EventArgs) Handles MainToolStripMenuItem.Click
        'Toggle the visibility of the Main toolbar
        'based on the menu item's Checked property
        If MainToolStripMenuItem.Checked Then
            tspMain.Visible = True
        Else
            tspMain.Visible = False
        End If
End Sub
```

2. You need to add the same type of code that you just added to the Formatting submenu item. Select FormattingToolStripMenuItem in the Class Name combo box and the `Click` event in the Method Name combo box and add the following highlighted code:

```
Private Sub FormattingToolStripMenuItem_Click(ByVal sender As Object, _
    ByVal e As System.EventArgs) Handles FormattingToolStripMenuItem.Click
        'Toggle the visibility of the Formatting toolbar
        'based on the menu item's Checked property
        If FormattingToolStripMenuItem.Checked Then
            tspFormatting.Visible = True
        Else
            tspFormatting.Visible = False
        End If
End Sub
```

How It Works

When the Main submenu item under the Tools menu item is clicked, the submenu item either displays a check mark or removes it based on the current state of the `Checked` property of the submenu item. You add code in the `Click` event of this submenu item to either hide or show the Main toolbar by setting its `Visible` property to `True` or `False`:

```
        'Toggle the visibility of the Main toolbar
        'based on this menu item's Checked property
        If MainToolStripMenuItem.Checked Then
            tspMain.Visible = True
        Else
            tspMain.Visible = False
        End If
```

The same principle works for the Formatting submenu item, and its code is very similar to that of the Main submenu item:

```
        'Toggle the visibility of the Formatting toolbar
        'based on this menu item's Checked property
        If FormattingToolStripMenuItem.Checked Then
            tspFormatting.Visible = True
        Else
            tspFormatting.Visible = False
        End If
```

Testing Your Code

As your applications become more complex, testing your code becomes increasingly important. The more errors that you find and fix during your testing, the better able you will be to implement an application that is both stable and reliable for your users. This translates into satisfied users and earns a good reputation for you for delivering a quality product.

You need not only to test the functionality of your application but also to test various scenarios that a user might encounter or perform. For example, suppose you have a database application that gathers user input from a form and inserts it into a database. A good application validates all user input before trying to insert the data into the database, and a good test plan tries to break the data validation code. This will ensure that your validation code handles all possible scenarios and functions properly.

Try It Out   **Testing Your Code**

1. It's time to test your code. Click the Run toolbar button. When your form loads, the only toolbar that you should see is the main toolbar, as shown in Figure 9-6.

Figure 9-6

2. Click the View menu and then click the Toolbars menu item. Note that the Main submenu item is selected and the main toolbar is visible. Go ahead and click the Formatting submenu item. The Formatting toolbar is displayed along with the main toolbar.

Note also that the controls on your form shifted down when the Formatting toolbar was displayed. The reason that this happened was that you placed a Panel control on your form, set its Dock property to Fill, and then placed your TextBox controls on the Panel control. Doing this allows the controls on your form to be repositioned, either to take up the space when a toolbar is hidden or to make room for the toolbar when it is shown; much like the behavior in Microsoft Outlook or Visual Studio 2008.

3. If you click the View menu again and then click the Toolbars menu item, you will see that both the Main and Formatting submenu items are checked. The selected submenu items indicate that the toolbar is visible, and an unchecked submenu item indicates that the toolbar is not visible.

4. Now test the functionality of the Edit menu. Click in the first text box and type some text. Then click the Edit menu and select the Select All menu item. Once you select the Select All menu item, the text in the text box is highlighted.

5.   You now want to copy the text in the first text box while the text is highlighted. Hover your mouse over the Copy button on the toolbar to view the tool tip. Now either click on the Copy button on the toolbar or select the Edit ➪ Copy menu item.

Place your cursor in the second text box, and then either click the Paste button on the toolbar or select Edit ➪ Paste. The text is pasted into the second text box, as shown in Figure 9-7.

Figure 9-7

6.   Click the first text box and then click Edit ➪ Undo. Note that the changes you made to the first text box have been undone. You might have expected that the text in the second text box would be removed, but Windows keeps track of the cut, copy, and paste operations for each control individually; so there's nothing you need to do.

7.   The last item on the Edit menu to test is the Cut menu item. Type some more text in the first text box, and then highlight the text in the first text box by clicking the Edit menu and selecting the Select All menu item. Then either click the Cut icon on the toolbar or select Edit ➪ Cut. The text is copied to the Clipboard and is then removed from the text box.

Place your cursor in the second text box at the end of the text there. Then paste the text in this text box using the Paste shortcut key Ctrl+V. The text has been placed at the end of the existing text in the text box. This is how Windows' cut, copy, and paste operations work, and, as you can see, there was very little code required to implement this functionality in your program.

8.   Now click the File menu and choose the New menu item. The text in the text boxes is cleared. The only menu item left to test is the Exit menu item under the File menu.

9.   Before testing the Exit menu item, take a quick look at context menus. Type some text in one of the text boxes. Now, right-click in that text box, and you will see a context menu pop up similar to what is shown in Figure 9-8. Notice that this context menu appeared automatically; there was no code that you needed to add to have this done. This is a feature of the Windows operating system, and Visual Studio 2008 provides a way to override the default context menus, as you will see in the next section.

Figure 9-8

10. To test the last bit of functionality of your program, select File ⇨ Exit, and your program ends.

Context Menus

Context menus are menus that pop up when a user clicks the right mouse button on a control or window. They provide the users with quick access to the most commonly used commands for the control that they are working with. As you just saw, the context menu that appeared provides you with a way to manage the text in a text box.

Context menus are customized for the control that you are working with, and in more complex applications, such as Visual Studio 2008 or Microsoft Word, they provide quick access to the commands for the task that is being performed.

You saw that Windows provides a default context menu for the TextBox control that you are working with, and you can override the default context menu if your application's needs dictate that you do so. For example, suppose that you have an application in which you want the user to be able to copy the text in a text box but not actually cut or paste text in that text box. This would be an ideal situation to provide your own context menu to allow only the operations that you want.

Visual Studio 2008 provides a ContextMenuStrip control that you can place on your form and customize, just as you did the MenuStrip control. However, the main difference between the MenuStrip control and the ContextMenuStrip control is that you can create only one top-level menu with the ContextMenuStrip control. You can still create submenu items with the ContextMenuStrip if you need to.

Most controls in the toolbox have a `ContextMenuStrip` property that can be set to the context menu that you define. When you right-click that control, the context menu that you defined is displayed instead of the default context menu.

Some controls, such as the ComboBox and ListBox controls, do not have a default context menu. This is because they contain a collection of items, not a single item like simple controls such as the TextBox. They do, however, have a `ContextMenuStrip` property that can be set to a context menu that you define.

> The ComboBox control does not provide a context menu when its `DropDownStyle` property is set to `DropDownList`, but it does provide a context menu when its `DropDownStyle` property is set to `Simple` or `DropDown`

Creating Context Menus

Now that you know what context menus are, you are ready to learn how to create and use them in your Visual Basic 2008 applications. In the next Try It Out, you expand the code from the previous Try It Out section by adding a context menu to work with your text boxes. You add one context menu and use it for both text boxes. You could just as easily create two context menus, one for each text box, and have the context menus perform different functions.

Try It Out   Creating Context Menus

1. Return to the Forms Designer in your Windows Forms Menus project and then click the toolbox to locate the ContextMenuStrip control. Drag and drop it onto your form. It is added at the bottom of the development environment just as the MenuStrip control was.

2. In the Properties window, click the ellipsis dots button next to the `Items` property. You'll be adding five menu items in your context menu in the next several steps.

3. Click the Add button in the Items Collection Editor dialog box to add the first menu item and set the `Name` property to **ContextUndoToolStripMenuItem**. Click the ellipsis dots button next to the `Image` property and then click the Import button in the Select Resource dialog box. Locate an Undo bitmap or portable network graphics (png) file on your computer and click the Open button. Click OK in the Select Resource dialog box to close it and to return to the Items Collection Editor. Locate the `Text` property and set it to **Undo**.

4. You want to add a separator between the Undo menu item and the next menu item. Select Separator in the List combo box in the Items Collection Editor dialog box and then click the Add button. You'll want to accept all default properties for the separator.

5. Select MenuItem in the combo box and click the Add button again to add the next menu item and set the `Name` property to **ContextCutToolStripMenuItem**. Click the ellipsis dots button next to the `Image` property and, in the Select Resource dialog box, locate a Cut bitmap or png file. Finally, set the `Text` property to **Cut**.

6. Click the Add button again to add the next menu item and set the `Name` property to **ContextCopyToolStripMenuItem**. Click the ellipsis dots button next to the `Image` property and, in the Select Resource dialog box, locate a Copy bitmap or icon file. Finally, set the `Text` property to **Copy**.

7. Click the Add button once again to add the next menu item and set the Name property to **ContextPasteToolStripMenuItem**. Click the ellipse button next to the Image property and in the Select Resource dialog box, import the PASTE.BMP file. Then set the Text property to **Paste**.

8. Now you want to add a separator between the Paste menu item and the next menu item. Select Separator in the combo box in the Items Collection Editor dialog box and then click the Add button. Again, you'll want to accept all default properties for the separator.

9. Now select MenuItem in the combo box and click the Add button to add the final menu item. Set the Name property to **ContextSelectAllToolStripMenuItem** and the Text property to **Select All**. There is no image for this menu item. Finally, click OK in the Items Collection Editor dialog box to close it.

10. When you are done, click any part of the form, and the context menu disappears. (You can always make it reappear by clicking the ContextMenuStrip1 control at the bottom of the development environment.)

11. Click the first text box on your form. In the Properties window, select ContextMenuStrip1 in the drop-down list for the ContextMenuStrip property. Repeat the same action for the second text box to assign a context menu in the ContextMenuStrip property.

12. Test your context menu for look and feel. At this point, you haven't added any code to it, but you can ensure that it looks visually correct. Run the application; then right-click in the first text box, and you will see the context menu that you have just added, as shown in Figure 9-9. The same context menu appears if you also right-click in the second text box.

Figure 9-9

13. Stop your program and switch to the Code Editor for your form so that you can add the code for the context menus. The first procedure that you want to add is that for the Undo context menu item. Select ContextUndoToolStripMenuItem in the Class Name combo box and the Click event in the Method Name combo box and add the following highlighted code:

```
Private Sub ContextUndoToolStripMenuItem_Click(ByVal sender As Object, _
    ByVal e As System.EventArgs) Handles ContextUndoToolStripMenuItem.Click
    'Call the UndoToolStripMenuItem_Click procedure
    UndoToolStripMenuItem_Click(sender, e)
End Sub
```

14. Select ContextCutToolStripMenuItem in the Class Name combo box and the `Click` event in the Method Name combo box. Add the following highlighted code to the `Click` event handler:

```
Private Sub ContextCutToolStripMenuItem_Click(ByVal sender As Object, _
    ByVal e As System.EventArgs) Handles ContextCutToolStripMenuItem.Click
    'Call the CutToolStripMenuItem_Click procedure
    CutToolStripMenuItem_Click(sender, e)
End Sub
```

15. For the Copy context menu item, select ContextCopyToolStripMenuItem in the Class Name combo box and the `Click` event in the Method Name combo box and then add the following highlighted code:

```
Private Sub ContextCopyToolStripMenuItem_Click(ByVal sender As Object, _
    ByVal e As System.EventArgs) Handles ContextCopyToolStripMenuItem.Click
    'Call the CopyToolStripMenuItem_Click procedure
    CopyToolStripMenuItem_Click(sender, e)
End Sub
```

16. Select ContextPasteToolStripMenuItem in the Class Name combo box for the Paste context menu item and the `Click` event in the Method Name combo box. Then add the following highlighted code:

```
Private Sub ContextPasteToolStripMenuItem_Click(ByVal sender As Object, _
    ByVal e As System.EventArgs) Handles ContextPasteToolStripMenuItem.Click
    'Call the PasteToolStripMenuItem_Click procedure
    PasteToolStripMenuItem_Click(sender, e)
End Sub
```

17. The last procedure that you need to perform is for the Select All context menu item. Select ContextSelectAllToolStripMenuItem in the Class Name combo box and the `Click` event in the Method Name combo box and then add the following highlighted code:

```
Private Sub ContextSelectAllToolStripMenuItem_Click(ByVal sender As Object, _
    ByVal e As System.EventArgs) _
    Handles ContextSelectAllToolStripMenuItem.Click
    'Call the SelectAllToolStripMenuItem_Click procedure
    SelectAllToolStripMenuItem_Click(sender, e)
End Sub
```

18. That's all the code that you need to add to implement your own context menu. Pretty simple, huh? Now run your project to see your context menu in action and test it. You can test the context menu by clicking each of the context menu items shown. They perform the same functions as their counterparts in the toolbar and Edit menu.

Do you see the difference in your context menu from the one shown in Figure 9-8? Your context menu has a cleaner look and shows the icons for the various menu items. There is one other subtle difference: Your menu items are all enabled when some of them shouldn't be. You'll rectify this in the next Try It Out.

How It Works

The ContextMenuStrip works in the same manner as the MenuStrip, and you should have been able to follow along and create a context menu with ease. You may have noticed that you use a prefix of `Context` for your context menu names in this exercise. This distinguishes these menu items as context menu items and groups these menu items in the Class Name combo box in the Code Editor, as you probably already noticed.

The code you added here was a no-brainer, as you have already written the code to perform undo, cut, copy, paste, and select all operations. In this exercise, you merely call the corresponding menu item procedures in your `Click` event handlers for the context menu items.

Enabling and Disabling Menu Items and Toolbar Buttons

Now that you have implemented a context menu and have it functioning, you are ready to write some code to complete the functionality in your application. In the following Try It Out, you implement the necessary code to enable and disable menu items, context menu items, and toolbar buttons.

Try It Out   Creating Context Menus

1. You need to create a procedure that can be called to toggle all of the Edit menu items, toolbar buttons, and context menu items, enabling and disabling them as needed. They are enabled and disabled based upon what should be available to the user. You should call this procedure `ToggleMenus`, so stop your program and add the following procedure at the end of your existing code.

```
Private Sub ToggleMenus()
    'Declare a TextBox object and set it to the ActiveControl
    Dim objTextBox As TextBox = CType(Me.ActiveControl, TextBox)

    'Declare and set a Boolean variable
    Dim blnEnabled As Boolean = CType(objTextBox.SelectionLength, Boolean)

    'Toggle the Undo menu items
    UndoToolStripMenuItem.Enabled = objTextBox.CanUndo
    ContextUndoToolStripMenuItem.Enabled = objTextBox.CanUndo

    'Toggle the Cut toolbar button and menu items
    CutToolStripButton.Enabled = blnEnabled
    CutToolStripMenuItem.Enabled = blnEnabled
    ContextCutToolStripMenuItem.Enabled = blnEnabled

    'Toggle the Copy toolbar button and menu items
    CopyToolStripButton.Enabled = blnEnabled
    CopyToolStripMenuItem.Enabled = blnEnabled
    ContextCopyToolStripMenuItem.Enabled = blnEnabled

    'Reset the blnEnabled variable
    blnEnabled = My.Computer.Clipboard.ContainsText

    'Toggle the Paste toolbar button and menu items
    PasteToolStripButton.Enabled = blnEnabled
```

```
PasteToolStripMenuItem.Enabled = blnEnabled
ContextPasteToolStripMenuItem.Enabled = blnEnabled

'Reset the blnEnabled variable
If objTextBox.SelectionLength < objTextBox.TextLength Then
    blnEnabled = True
Else
    blnEnabled = False
End If

'Toggle the Select All menu items
SelectAllToolStripMenuItem.Enabled = blnEnabled
ContextSelectAllToolStripMenuItem.Enabled = blnEnabled
End Sub
```

That's it! All of that code will toggle the Edit menu items, the context menu items, and the toolbar buttons. Now all you need is to figure out when and where to call this procedure.

2. Return to the Forms Designer and locate the Timer control in the Toolbox. Drag this control to your form and drop it. It is positioned at the bottom of the IDE. In the Properties window, set the `Enabled` property to **True** and the `Interval` property to **250**.

3. Double-click the Timer control at the bottom of the IDE to create the `Tick` event handler and add this code:

```
Private Sub Timer1_Tick(ByVal sender As Object, _
    ByVal e As System.EventArgs) Handles Timer1.Tick
    'Toggle toolbar and menu items
    ToggleMenus()
End Sub
```

4. Run your project again. After the form has been displayed, click in the first text box and enter some text. Then, right-click in the text box to display your context menu. Now the context menu has the appropriate menu items enabled as shown in Figure 9-10 as do the toolbar buttons and Edit menu items.

Figure 9-10

How It Works

The first thing that you do in the `ToggleMenus` procedure is to declare an object and set it equal to the active TextBox control. You saw the `ActiveControl` property in the "Coding the Edit Menu" Try It Out exercise:

```
'Declare a TextBox object and set it to the ActiveControl
Dim objTextBox As TextBox = CType(Me.ActiveControl, TextBox)
```

Next you declare a `Boolean` variable that will be used to determine if a property should set to `True` or `False` and initially set it based on the `SelectionLength` property of the active text box. The `SelectionLength` property returns the number of characters selected in a text box. You can use this number to act as a `True` or `False` value because a value of `False` in Visual Basic 2008 is zero and a value of `True` is one. Since the value of `False` is always evaluated first, any number other than zero evaluates to `True`.

In order to make this happen, you need to convert the `SelectionLength` property from an `Integer` data type to a `Boolean` data type using the `CType` function as shown in the code below:

```
'Declare and set a Boolean variable
Dim blnEnabled As Boolean = CType(objTextBox.SelectionLength, Boolean)
```

The first Edit menu item is Undo, so you start with that one. The `TextBox` class has a property called `CanUndo`, which returns a `True` or `False` value indicating whether or not the last operation performed in the text box can be undone.

You use the `CanUndo` property to set the `Enabled` property of the Edit menu item. The `Enabled` property is set using a `Boolean` value, which works out great, because the `CanUndo` property returns a `Boolean` value. The following code shows how you set the `Enabled` property of the Undo menu item and context menu item:

```
'Toggle the Undo menu items
undoToolStripMenuItem.Enabled = objTextBox.CanUndo
contextUndoToolStripMenuItem.Enabled = objTextBox.CanUndo
```

The next menu item in the Edit menu that you wrote code for is the Cut menu item. You have already set the `blnEnabled` variable so the following code merely uses the value contained in that variable to set the `Enabled` property of the Cut menu item, toolbar button, and context menu item:

```
'Toggle the Cut toolbar button and menu items
CutToolStripButton.Enabled = blnEnabled
CutToolStripMenuItem.Enabled = blnEnabled
ContextCutToolStripMenuItem.Enabled = blnEnabled
```

The next menu item in the Edit menu is the Copy menu item. Again, you use the `blnEnabled` variable to set the `Enabled` property appropriately:

```
'Toggle the Copy toolbar button and menu items
CopyToolStripButton.Enabled = blnEnabled
CopyToolStripMenuItem.Enabled = blnEnabled
ContextCopyToolStripMenuItem.Enabled = blnEnabled
```

The next menu item in the Edit menu is the Paste menu item. Setting the `Enabled` property of this menu item requires a little more work. You query the `ContainsText` property of the `My.Computer .Clipboard` object to receive a `Boolean` value indicating whether the Clipboard contains any text. You then set that `Boolean` value in the `blnEnabled` variable which is used to set the `Enabled` property of the Paste toolbar button, Paste menu item, and context menu item as shown in the following code:

```
'Reset the blnEnabled variable
blnEnabled = My.Computer.Clipboard.ContainsText
'Toggle the Paste toolbar button and menu items
PasteToolStripButton.Enabled = blnEnabled
PasteToolStripMenuItem.Enabled = blnEnabled
ContextPasteToolStripMenuItem.Enabled = blnEnabled
```

The last Edit menu item is the Select All menu item. Again, you use the `SelectionLength` property to determine whether any or all text has been selected. If the `SelectionLength` property is less than the `TextLength` property you set the `blnEnabled` variable to `True` as not all text in the text box has been selected, otherwise you set it to `False`. After the `blnEnabled` variable has been appropriately set, you use that variable to set the `Enabled` property of the Select All menu item and context menu item:

```
'Reset the blnEnabled variable
If objTextBox.SelectionLength < objTextBox.TextLength Then
    blnEnabled = True
Else
    blnEnabled = False
End If

'Toggle the Select All menu items
SelectAllToolStripMenuItem.Enabled = blnEnabled
ContextSelectAllToolStripMenuItem.Enabled = blnEnabled
```

To enable and disable the menu items, context menu items and toolbar buttons, you have to call the `ToggleMenus` procedure. The best place to do this is in the `Tick` event of the Timer control that you placed on your form. The `Tick` event is fired using the `Interval` property that you set to a value of 250. The `Interval` property is expressed in milliseconds where 1,000 milliseconds equals one second. So basically, the `Tick` event of the Timer control is fired every quarter second:

```
Private Sub Timer1_Tick(ByVal sender As Object, _
    ByVal e As System.EventArgs) Handles Timer1.Tick

    'Toggle toolbar and menu items
    ToggleMenus()
End Sub
```

Summary

This chapter covered how to implement menus, menu items, and submenu items. You also learned how to implement multiple toolbars, although that was not the focus of the chapter. Through practical hands-on exercises you have seen how to create menus, menu items, and submenu items. You have also seen how to add access keys, shortcut keys, and images to these menu items.

Since you used the Edit menu in the Try It Outs, you have also seen how easy it is to implement basic editing techniques in your application by using the properties of the TextBox control and the Clipboard object. Now you know how easy it is to provide this functionality to your users — something users have come to expect in every good Windows application.

You also explored how to create and implement context menus and to override the default context menus provided by Windows. Since you had already coded the procedure to implement undo, cut, copy, and paste operations, you simply reused that code in your context menus.

Now that you have completed this chapter, you should know how to:

❑ Add a MenuStrip control to your form and add menus, menu items, and submenu items.

❑ Customize the menu items with a check mark.

❑ Add access keys and shortcut keys to your menu items.

❑ Add a ContextMenuStrip control to your form and add menu items.

❑ Use the properties of the TextBox control to toggle the Enabled property of menu items.

Exercise

1. To give your Menus project the standard look of a typical Windows application, add a StatusStrip control to the form and add the necessary code to display a message when text is cut, copied, or pasted.

Debugging and Error Handling

Debugging is an essential part of any development project, as it helps you find errors in your code and in your logic. Visual Studio 2008 has a sophisticated debugger built right into the development environment. This debugger is the same for all languages that Visual Studio 2008 supports. When you have mastered debugging in one language, you can debug in any language that you can write in Visual Studio 2008.

No matter how good your code is, there are always going to be some unexpected circumstances that will cause your code to fail. If you do not anticipate and handle errors, your users will see a default error message about an unhandled exception, which is provided by the common language run-time package. This is not a user-friendly message and usually does not clearly inform the user about what is going on or how to correct it.

This is where error handling comes in. Visual Studio 2008 also provides common structured error-handling functions that are used across all languages. These functions allow you to test a block of code and catch any errors that may occur. If an error does occur, you can display your own user-friendly message that informs the user of what happened and how to correct it, or you can simply handle the error and continue processing.

This chapter looks at some of the debugging features available in Visual Studio 2008 and provides a walk-through of debugging a program. You examine how to set breakpoints in your code to stop execution at any given point, how to watch the value of a variable change, and how to control the number of times a loop can execute before stopping. All of these can help you determine just what is going on inside your code. Finally, this chapter takes a look at the structured error-handling functions provided by Visual Studio 2008.

In this chapter, you will:

- ❏ Examine the major types of errors that you may encounter and how to correct them
- ❏ Examine and walk through debugging a program
- ❏ Examine and implement error handling in a program

Major Error Types

Error types can be broken down into three major categories: syntax, execution, and logic. This section shows you the important differences among these three types of errors and how to correct them.

Knowing what type of errors are possible and how to correct them will significantly speed up the development process. Of course, sometimes you just can't find the error on your own. Don't waste too much time trying to find errors in your code by yourself in these situations. Coming back to a nagging problem after a short coffee break can often help you crack it. Otherwise, ask a colleague to have a look at your code with you; two pairs of eyes are often better than one in these cases.

Syntax Errors

Syntax errors, the easiest type of errors to spot and fix, occur when the code you have written cannot be understood by the compiler because instructions are incomplete, supplied in unexpected order, or cannot be processed at all. An example of this would be declaring a variable of one name and misspelling this name in your code when you set or query the variable.

The development environment in Visual Studio 2008 has a really sophisticated syntax-checking mechanism, making it hard, but not impossible, to have syntax errors in your code. It provides instant syntax checking of variables and objects and lets you know immediately when you have a syntax error.

Suppose you try to declare a variable as `Private` in a procedure. Visual Studio 2008 underlines the declaration with a blue wavy line indicating that the declaration is in error. If the Integrated Development Environment (IDE) can automatically correct the syntax error, you'll see a little orange rectangular box at the end of the blue wavy line, as shown in Figure 10-1, indicating that AutoCorrect options are available for this syntax error. AutoCorrect is a feature of Visual Studio 2008 that provides error correction options that the IDE will suggest to correct the error.

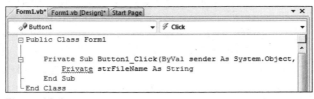

Figure 10-1

When you hover your mouse over the code in error, you'll receive a tooltip, telling you what the error is, and a small gray box with a red circle and a white exclamation point. If you then move your mouse into the gray box, a down arrow appears, as shown in Figure 10-2, to let you know that a dialog box is available with some suggested error correction options.

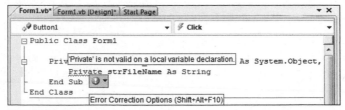

Figure 10-2

Clicking the down arrow or pressing Shift+Alt+F10 causes the Error Correction Options dialog box to appear as shown in Figure 10-3. This dialog box presents one or more choices to you for correcting the error. In this instance, there is only one choice to correct the syntax error as shown in the dialog box in Figure 10-3.

Note that the dialog box shows you how your code can be corrected: by replacing the `Private` keyword with the `Dim` keyword. The sample code displayed in the dialog box has your offending statement in strikethrough and the suggested correction preceding it. Above the code in the dialog box is a hyperlink that will replace the `Private` keyword with the `Dim` keyword. Click this link to apply the fix to your code.

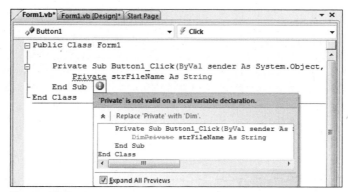

Figure 10-3

Another option available for reviewing all the errors in your code is the Error List window. This window displays a grid with all the errors' descriptions, the files they exist in, and the line numbers and column numbers of the error. If your solution contains multiple projects, it also displays the project that each error exists in.

The Error List can be accessed by clicking the Error List tab at the bottom of the IDE if it is already displayed in the IDE or by clicking the View ⇨ Error List menu item. When the Error List window is displayed, you can double-click any error to be taken to that specific error in your code.

Sometimes you'll receive warnings, displayed with a green wavy line under the code in question. These are just warnings and your code will compile. However, you should heed these warnings and try to correct these errors if possible, because they may produce undesirable results at run time.

As an example, a warning would occur in the line of code shown in Figure 10-3 once the `Private` keyword was replaced with the `Dim` keyword. The IDE would give you a warning that the variable, `strFileName`, is unused in the procedure. Simply initializing the variable or referencing the variable in code would cause this warning to go away.

Keep in mind that you can hover your mouse over errors and warnings in your code to cause the appropriate tooltip to be displayed informing you of the problem. As a reminder, if the IDE can provide the AutoCorrect feature for an error, it will show an orange rectangular box at the end of the blue wavy line.

The IDE also provides IntelliSense to assist in preventing syntax errors. IntelliSense provides a host of features such as providing a drop-down list of members for classes, structures, and namespaces as shown in Figure 10-4. This enables you to choose the correct member for the class, structure, or namespace that you are working with. It also provides tooltip information for the selected member or method, also shown in Figure 10-4. IntelliSense initially displays a list of all members for the object being worked with, and as soon as you start typing one or more letters the list of members is shortened to match the letters that you have typed as shown in Figure 10-4.

Figure 10-4

These IntelliSense features provide two major benefits. First, you do not have to remember all the available members for the class. You simply scroll through the list to find the member that you want to work with or you type the first letter or two of the member to have the list of members reduced to the relevant members. To select the member in the list that you want to work with, you press the Tab or Enter key or double-click the member. Second, the features help you prevent syntax errors because you are less likely to misspell member names or try to use members that do not exist in the given class.

Another great feature of IntelliSense is that it provides a parameter list for the method that you are working with. IntelliSense lists the number, names, and types of the parameters required by the function, as shown in Figure 10-4. This is also a time saver, as you do not have to remember the required parameters for every class member that you work with, or indeed search the product documentation for what you need.

If the method is overloaded — that is, there are several methods with the same name but different parameters — the tooltip indicates this as shown in Figure 10-4 with the text "(+ 1 overloads)". Also, when you start to work with the member, a pop-up list enables you to scroll through the different overloaded methods, as shown in Figure 10-5 for the Substring method of the String class, by simply clicking the up and down arrows to view the different overloaded methods.

Another IntelliSense list appears for the parameter that you are working with and again, this large list of all classes and members is reduced after you start typing one or more letters as indicated in Figure 10.5. Here I started typing the letters my to have the list of available classes and namespaces to reduced to classes and namespaces that begin with the letters my.

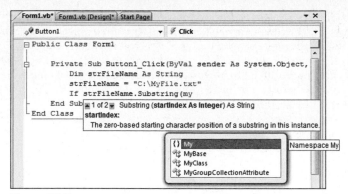

Figure 10-5

Plenty of built-in features in the development environment can help prevent syntax errors. All you need to do is to be aware of these features and take advantage of them to help prevent syntax errors in your code.

Execution Errors

Execution errors (or *run-time errors*) occur while your program is executing. These errors are often caused because something outside of the application, such as a user, database, or hard disk, does not behave as expected.

Developers need to anticipate the possibility of execution errors and build appropriate error-handling logic. Implementing the appropriate error handling does not prevent execution errors, but does allow you to handle them either by gracefully shutting down your application or bypassing the code that failed and giving the user the opportunity to perform that action again. Error handling is covered later in this chapter.

The best way to prevent execution errors is to try anticipating the error before it occurs and to use error handling to trap and handle the error. You must also thoroughly test your code before deploying it.

Most execution errors can be found while you are testing your code in the development environment. This allows you to handle the errors and debug your code at the same time. You can then see what type of errors may occur and implement the appropriate error-handling logic. Debugging, where you find and handle any execution errors that may crop up, is covered later in the "Debugging" section.

Logic Errors

Logic errors (or *semantic errors*) give unexpected or unwanted results because you did not fully understand what the code you were writing did. Probably the most common logic error is an infinite loop:

```
Private Sub PerformLoopExample()
    Dim intIndex As Integer
    Do While intIndex < 10
        ...perform some logic
    Loop
End Sub
```

If the code inside the loop does not set `intIndex` to `10` or above, this loop just keeps going forever. This is a very simple example, but even experienced developers find themselves writing and executing loops whose exit condition can never be satisfied.

Logic errors can be the most difficult to find and troubleshoot, because it is very difficult to be sure that your program is completely free from logic errors.

Another type of logic error occurs when a comparison fails to give the result you expect. Say you made a comparison between a string variable, set by your code from a database field or from the text in a file, and the text entered by the user. You do not want the comparison to be case sensitive, so you might write code like this:

```
If strFileName = txtInput.Text Then
    ...perform some logic
End If
```

However, if `strFileName` is set to `Index.HTML` and `txtInput.Text` is set to `index.html`, the comparison fails. One way to prevent this logic error is to convert both fields being compared to either uppercase or lowercase. This way, the results of the comparison would be `True` if the user entered the same text as that contained in the variable, even if the case was different. The next code fragment shows how you can accomplish this:

```
If strFileName.ToUpper = txtInput.Text.ToUpper Then
    ...perform some logic
End If
```

The `ToUpper` method of the `String` class converts the characters in the string to all uppercase and returns the converted results. Since the `Text` property of a text box is also a string, you can use the same method to convert the text to all uppercase. This would make the comparison in the previous example equal.

An alternative to using either the `ToUpper` or `ToLower` methods of the `String` class is to use the `Compare` method of the `String` class, as shown in the next example. This allows you to compare the two strings ignoring the case of the strings. This is covered in the String Comparison section in Chapter 4.

```
If String.Compare(strFileName, txtInput.Text, True) Then
    ... perform some logic
End If
```

Since logic errors are the hardest errors to troubleshoot and can cause applications to fail or give unexpected and unwanted results, you must check the logic carefully as you code and try to plan for all possible errors that may be encountered by a user. As you become more experienced you will encounter and learn from the common errors that you and your users make.

One of the best ways to identify and fix logic errors is to use the debugging features of Visual Studio 2008. Using these features, you can find loops that execute too many times or comparisons that do not give the expected result.

Debugging

Debugging code is a part of life — even experienced developers will make mistakes and need to debug their code. Knowing how to efficiently debug your code can make the difference between enjoying your job as a developer and hating it.

In the following sections, you'll create and debug a sample project while learning about the Exception Assistant, breakpoints, and how to step through your code and use the Watch and Locals windows to examine variables and objects.

Creating a Sample Project

In this section, you take a look at some of the built-in debugging features in the Visual Studio 2008 development environment through various Try It Out exercises. You write a simple program and learn how to use the most common and useful debugging features available.

You begin this process by creating a program that uses three classes that you create. Classes and objects are covered in greater detail in the next chapter, but by creating and using these classes, you'll be able to learn about some of the other features in Visual Basic 2008 as well as learn how to debug your programs. These classes are used to provide data to be displayed in a list box on your form. These classes introduce two powerful concepts in particular: the generic class with type constraints and the interface. These concepts are explained in the following How It Works.

Try It Out   **Creating a Sample Project to Debug**

1.   Create a new Windows Forms Application project and name it **Debugging**.

2.   In the Solution Explorer window, rename the form to **Debug.vb** by right-clicking the form and choosing Rename from the context menu. Now click the form in the Forms Designer and then set the form's properties in the Properties window as shown:

   ❑   Set Size to **440, 300**.

   ❑   Set StartPosition to **CenterScreen**.

   ❑   Set Text to **Debug Demo**.

3.   Next, you want to add some basic controls to the form and set their properties, as shown in the following list:

   ❑   Create a Button control named **btnStart** and set these properties: Anchor = **Top, Right,** Location = **329, 12**; Text = **Start**.

   ❑   Create a ListBox control named **lstData**, and set these properties: Anchor = **Top, Bottom, Left, Right**; Integral Height = False; Location = **12, 41**; Size = **391, 204**.

4. Right click the Debugging project in the Solution Explorer, choose Add from the context menu, and then choose the Class submenu item. In the Add New Item – Debugging dialog box, enter a class name of **Customer** in the Name field and then click the Add button. Add the following highlighted code to the class:

```
Public Class Customer
    Private intCustomerID As Integer
    Private strName As String

    Public Sub New(ByVal customerID As Integer, ByVal name As String)
        intCustomerID = customerID
        strName = name
    End Sub

    Public ReadOnly Property CustomerID() As Integer
        Get
            Return intCustomerID
        End Get
    End Property

    Public Property CustomerName() As String
        Get
            Return strName
        End Get
        Set(ByVal value As String)
            strName = value
        End Set
    End Property
End Class
```

5. Before moving on to create the next class, take a quick look at the AutoCorrect option in Visual Studio 2008 so that you can get first-hand experience with this feature. The `CustomerName` property that you just created should really be a `ReadOnly` property. Insert the `ReadOnly` keyword between `Public` and `Property` and then click the next line of code.

6. You'll notice that the `Set` statement in this property has a blue wavy line underneath it indicating an error. If you hover your mouse over the line of code in error, you get a ToolTip informing you that a `ReadOnly` property cannot have a `Set` statement.

7. Click the small gray box with a red circle and white exclamation point to display the Error Correction Options dialog box, shown in Figure 10-6.

Figure 10-6

8. You have two options to choose from. The option that you want is the second one, which is to remove the `Set` method. Click the hyperlink to have the AutoCorrect feature remove the `Set` statement from this property.

9. Now add another class to the Debugging project, called **Generics**. Then modify the Class statement as highlighted here:

```
Public Class Generics(Of elementType)

End Class
```

10. Add the following highlighted code to the Generics class:

```
Public Class Generics(Of elementType)
    'This class provides a demonstration of Generics

    'Declare Private variables
    Private strKey() As String
    Private elmValue() As elementType

    Public Sub Add(ByVal key As String, ByVal value As elementType)
        'Check to see if the objects have been initialized
        If strKey IsNot Nothing Then
            'Objects have been initialized
            ReDim Preserve strKey(strKey.GetUpperBound(0) + 1)
            ReDim Preserve elmValue(elmValue.GetUpperBound(0) + 1)
        Else
            'Initialize the objects
            ReDim strKey(0)
            ReDim elmValue(0)
        End If

        'Set the values
        strKey(strKey.GetUpperBound(0)) = key
        elmValue(elmValue.GetUpperBound(0)) = value
    End Sub
```

```
        Public ReadOnly Property Key(ByVal Index As Integer) As String
            Get
                Return strKey(Index)
            End Get
        End Property

        Public ReadOnly Property Value(ByVal Index As Integer) As elementType
            Get
                Return elmValue(Index)
            End Get
        End Property
End Class
```

11. Add one more class to the Debugging project, called **Computer**. This is an example of a class that *implements* the `IDisposable` *interface*, which is explained in the How It Works. Enter the following highlighted code. Once you press the Enter key, Visual Studio 2008 inserts the remaining code listed here automatically.

```
Public Class Computer
    Implements IDisposable

    Private disposedValue As Boolean = False      ' To detect redundant calls

    ' IDisposable
    Protected Overridable Sub Dispose(ByVal disposing As Boolean)
        If Not Me.disposedValue Then
            If disposing Then
                ' TODO: free other state (managed objects).
            End If

            ' TODO: free your own state (unmanaged objects).
            ' TODO: set large fields to null.
        End If
        Me.disposedValue = True
    End Sub

#Region " IDisposable Support "
    ' This code added by Visual Basic to correctly implement
    ' the disposable pattern.
    Public Sub Dispose() Implements IDisposable.Dispose
        ' Do not change this code.  Put cleanup code in
        ' Dispose(ByVal disposing As Boolean) above.
        Dispose(True)
        GC.SuppressFinalize(Me)
    End Sub
#End Region

End Class
```

12. Add the following two properties to the end of the Computer class:

```
Public ReadOnly Property FreeMemory() As String
    Get
        'Using the My namespace
        Return Format(( _
            My.Computer.Info.AvailablePhysicalMemory.ToString \ 1024), _
            "#,###,##0") & " K"
    End Get
End Property

Public ReadOnly Property TotalMemory() As String
    Get
        'Using the My namespace
        Return Format(( _
            My.Computer.Info.TotalPhysicalMemory.ToString \ 1024), _
            "#,###,##0") & " K"
    End Get
End Property
```

13. Switch to the code for the Debug form and add the following highlighted Imports statement:

```
Imports System.Collections.Generic

Public Class Debug
```

14. You need to add a few private variable declarations next. Add the following code:

```
Public Class Debug
    'Using the Generics class
    Private objStringValues As New Generics(Of String)
    Private objIntegerValues As New Generics(Of Integer)

    'Using the List<T> class
    Private objCustomerList As New List(Of Customer)
```

15. Add the following ListCustomer procedure to add customers to the list box on your form:

```
Private Sub ListCustomer(ByVal customerToList As Customer)
    lstData.Items.Add(customerToList.CustomerID & _
        " - " & customerToList.CustomerName)
End Sub
```

16. Next, you need to add the rest of the code to the Start button Click event handler. Select btnStart in the Class Name combo box at the top of the Code Editor and then select the Click event in the Method Name combo box. Add the following highlighted code to the Click event handler:

```
Private Sub btnStart_Click(ByVal sender As Object, _
    ByVal e As System.EventArgs) Handles btnStart.Click
```

```vbnet
'Declare variables
Dim strData As String

lstData.Items.Add("String variable data:")
If strData.Length > 0 Then
    lstData.Items.Add(strData)
End If

'Add an empty string to the ListBox
lstData.Items.Add(String.Empty)

'Demonstrates the use of the List<T> class
lstData.Items.Add("Customers in the Customer Class:")
objCustomerList.Add(New Customer(1001, "Henry For"))
objCustomerList.Add(New Customer(1002, "Orville Wright"))
For Each objCustomer As Customer In objCustomerList
    ListCustomer(objCustomer)
Next

'Add an empty string to the ListBox
lstData.Items.Add(String.Empty)

'Demonstrates the use of Generics
lstData.Items.Add("Generics Class Key/Value Pairs using String Values:")
objStringValues.Add("1001", "Henry Ford")
lstData.Items.Add(objStringValues.Key(0) & " = " & _
    objStringValues.Value(0))

'Add an empty string to the ListBox
lstData.Items.Add(String.Empty)

'Demonstrates the use of Generics
lstData.Items.Add("Generics Class Key/Value Pairs using Integer Values:")
objIntegerValues.Add("Henry Ford", 1001)
lstData.Items.Add(objIntegerValues.Key(0) & " = " & _
    objIntegerValues.Value(0))

'Add an empty string to the ListBox
lstData.Items.Add(String.Empty)

'Demonstrates the use of the Using statement
'Allows acquisition, usage and disposal of the resource
lstData.Items.Add("Computer Class Properties:")
Using objMemory As New Computer
    lstData.Items.Add("FreeMemory = " & objMemory.FreeMemory)
    lstData.Items.Add("TotalMemory = " & objMemory.TotalMemory)
End Using

'Add an empty string to the ListBox
lstData.Items.Add(String.Empty)


'Demonstrates the use of the Continue statement
Dim strPassword As String = "POpPassword"
Dim strLowerCaseLetters As String = String.Empty
'Extract lowercase characters from string
```

```
       For intIndex As Integer = 0 To strPassword.Length - 1
            'Demonstrates the use of the Continue statement
            'If no uppercase character is found, continue the loop
            If Not strPassword.Substring(intIndex, 1) Like "[a-z]" Then
                'No upper case character found, continue loop
                Continue For
            End If
            'Lowercase character found, save it
            strLowerCaseLetters &= strPassword.Substring(intIndex, 1)
       Next

    'Display lowercase characters
    lstData.Items.Add("Password lower case characters:")
    lstData.Items.Add(strLowerCaseLetters)
End Sub
```

17. Before examining how the code works, hover your mouse over the Error List tab at the bottom of the IDE so that the Error List window appears as shown in Figure 10-7. If the Error List tab is not visible, select View ⇨ Error List from the menu bar. You have one warning about a potential error in your code. The line in question causes an error when you run your project; however, this is deliberate and is intended to demonstrate some of the debugging capabilities of Visual Studio 2008. You can ignore this warning for now, because you'll be correcting it shortly.

Error List					
☺ 0 Errors ⚠ 1 Warning ⓘ 0 Messages					
	Description	File	Line	Column	Project
⚠ 1	Variable 'strData' is used before it has been assigned a value. A null reference exception could result at runtime.	Debug.vb	23	12	Debugging

Figure 10-7

18. Save your project by clicking the Save All button on the toolbar.

How It Works

After building the user interface for the Debugging project, you add the Customer class. This class is also straightforward and contains two private variables, a constructor, and two properties.

The two variables in the Customer class are declared as Private, which means that these variables are accessible only to the procedures in the class:

```
Public Class Customer
    Private intCustomerID As Integer
    Private strName As String
```

The *constructor* for this class — a method called whenever a new object of this class is to be created — is defined as a `Public` procedure with a procedure name of `New`. All constructors for classes in the .NET Framework must be declared with a procedure name of `New`.

This constructor accepts two input parameters: `customerID` and `name`. The parameters are used to set the values in the private variables defined for this class:

```
Public Sub New(ByVal customerID As Integer, ByVal name As String)
    intCustomerID = customerID
    strName = name
End Sub
```

Two properties are defined: `CustomerID` and `CustomerName`. These are read-only properties, meaning that the consumer of this class can use these properties only to read the Customer ID and customer name; consumers cannot change them:

```
Public ReadOnly Property CustomerID() As Integer
    Get
        Return intCustomerID
    End Get
End Property

Public Property CustomerName() As String
    Get
        Return strName
    End Get
End Property
End Class
```

The next class that you add to the Debugging project is the `Generics` class. This class will be used to demonstrate the use of Generics in Visual Basic 2008.

The `Collections` class in the .NET Framework allows you to store data in the collection in a key/value pair. The key is always a string value that identifies the value, also known as an *item*. The item is defined as an object, which allows you to use the `Collection` class to store any data type that you want in the item. So, for example, you can use the `Collection` class to store `Integer` values or you can use it to store `String` values. No type checking is performed. This lack of specificity can lead to performance problems as well as run-time problems.

Suppose you intend to use the `Collection` class to store `Integer` values. If (through poor coding practices) you allowed a `String` value to be added to the collection, you would not receive a run-time error when adding the item, but you could receive one when you tried to access the item.

The performance problems that you will encounter are the conversion of the data going into the collection and the data coming out of the collection. When you add an item to the collection, the data must be converted from its native data type to an `Object` data type, since that is how the `Item` property is defined. Likewise, when you retrieve an item from the collection, the item must be converted from an `Object` data type to the data type that you are using.

In Chapter 5, when working with `ArrayLists` (which are a kind of collection), you solved the problem of being able to store items of the wrong type by creating a strongly typed collection class. This did not solve the performance problem. Both problems are solved through Generics and through the introduction of *type constraints*. A type constraint is specified on a class such as `Collection` by using the `Of` keyword followed by a list of type name placeholders that are replaced by actual type names when an object of the class is created. This provides type safety by not allowing you to add an item that is not of the same data type that was defined for the class. It also improves performance because the item does not have to be converted to and from the `Object` data type. The data type for the item is defined using the data type that was defined for the class. You'll see how all of this works in more detail as you explore the rest of the code and as you go through the debugging process.

After adding the Generics class, you modify the class by adding a type constraint using the Of keyword and defining a type list, which in this case contains only one type. This type name is a placeholder that will be used throughout the class to represent the data type that this class is working with. The actual data type is defined when an object of the class is created, as you'll see later in your code:

```
Public Class Generics(Of elementType)

End Class
```

You add two private variables to this class, with both of these variables being defined as an array. The first variable is a defined as a String data type, while the second variable is defined as a generic data type, which is set when an object of the class is created. Note that you have used the type name elementType, which was defined at the class level. This type name is replaced automatically by the data type that is used to create the Generics object.

```
Public Class Generics(Of elementType)
    'This class provides a demonstration of Generics

    'Declare Private variables
    Private strKey() As String
    Private elmValue() As elementType
```

The Add method allows you to add items to your collection. This method accepts two parameters; one for the key and the other for the value, making a key/value pair. The key parameter is always a string value, and the value parameter is defined using the data type that is used when a Generics collection is created.

The first thing that you want to do in this procedure is to see whether the variable arrays have been initialized. You do this by using the IsNot operator and comparing the strKey array to a value of Nothing. If the array is not equal to a value of Nothing, the array has already been initialized, and you simply need to increment the array dimension by one. This is done by first getting the current upper bounds of the array and then adding 1 to it.

If the variable arrays have not been initialized, you need to initialize them using the ReDim statement as shown in the Else statement in the code that follows.

After the arrays have been expanded or initialized, you add the key and value to the arrays:

```
Public Sub Add(ByVal key As String, ByVal value As elementType)
    'Check to see if the objects have been initialized
    If strKey IsNot Nothing Then
        'Objects have been initialized
        ReDim Preserve strKey(strKey.GetUpperBound(0) + 1)
        ReDim Preserve elmValue(elmValue.GetUpperBound(0) + 1)
```

```
            Else
                'Initialize the objects
                ReDim strKey(0)
                ReDim elmValue(0)
            End If

            'Set the values
            strKey(strKey.GetUpperBound(0)) = key
            elmValue(elmValue.GetUpperBound(0)) = value
        End Sub
```

You add two read-only properties to this class to return the key and the value for a key/value pair. Notice that the Value property is defined to return the data type that will be used when a Generics object is created.

```
        Public ReadOnly Property Key(ByVal Index As Integer) As String
            Get
                Return strKey(Index)
            End Get
        End Property

        Public ReadOnly Property Value(ByVal Index As Integer) As elementType
            Get
                Return elmValue(Index)
            End Get
        End Property
    End Class
```

The final class that you added was the Computer class. This class implements the IDisposable interface. An interface in this sense is a set of methods and properties common to all classes that implement it. In this case, the IDisposable interface contains methods for releasing memory resources when an object of the class is disposed of. Methods that use this class should call the Dispose method when they are through with a Computer object.

To implement the interface, you add the Implements statement and specify the IDisposable interface. When you press the Enter key, Visual Studio 2008 adds the code from the IDisposable interface to your class, as shown in the following code:

```
    Public Class Computer
        Implements IDisposable

        Private disposedValue As Boolean = False ' To detect redundant calls

        ' IDisposable
        Protected Overridable Sub Dispose(ByVal disposing As Boolean)
            If Not Me.disposedValue Then
                If disposing Then
                    ' TODO: free other state (managed objects).
                End If

                ' TODO: free your own state (unmanaged objects).
                ' TODO: set large fields to null.
            End If
```

```
                Me.disposedValue = True
        End Sub

#Region " IDisposable Support "
        ' This code added by Visual Basic to correctly implement
        ' the disposable pattern.
        Public Sub Dispose() Implements IDisposable.Dispose
            ' Do not change this code.  Put cleanup code in
            ' Dispose(ByVal disposing As Boolean) above.
            Dispose(True)
            GC.SuppressFinalize(Me)
        End Sub
#End Region

End Class
```

You add two read-only properties to this class; FreeMemory and TotalMemory. These properties return the available memory on your computer as well as the total amount of memory on your computer. These properties use the My.Computer.Info namespace to access the amount of available memory and the total amount of memory.

The AvailablePhysicalMemory and TotalPhysicalMemory properties of the My.Computer.Info namespace return the available and total memory in bytes. However, we as users are used to seeing these numbers in kilobytes. Therefore you convert the number of bytes into kilobytes and then have that number formatted using commas.

Remember that there are 1024 bytes to a kilobyte, 1024 kilobytes to a megabyte, and so on. The number that you pass to the Format function will be in kilobytes after you divide the number of bytes by 1024.

You then add a space to the formatted number and then the letter K indicating that the available and total memory figures are in kilobytes:

```
        Public ReadOnly Property FreeMemory() As String
            Get
                'Using the My namespace
                Return Format(( _
                    My.Computer.Info.AvailablePhysicalMemory.ToString \ 1024), _
                    "#,###,##0") & " K"
            End Get
        End Property

        Public ReadOnly Property TotalMemory() As String
            Get
                'Using the My namespace
                Return Format(( _
                    My.Computer.Info.TotalPhysicalMemory.ToString \ 1024), _
                    "#,###,##0") & " K"
            End Get
        End Property
```

You add code to the Debug form class next. This class uses a class List<T>, which is a generic list class. You'll be using this class to hold a list of Customer objects created from your Customer class. The List<T> class uses a dynamically sized array to hold the objects of the type that you specify: You need to *import* the System.Collections.Generic namespace in order to access the List<T> class. You accomplish that requirement by using an Imports statement.

```
Imports System.Collections.Generic
```

Next you define three private objects at the class level; these objects are available to all procedures in this class. The first two objects use your Generics class. Remember that the Generics class used the Of keyword to define a type list. In the declaration of your objects, you use similar Of clauses to specify that the Generics class should be using a String data type in the type list for the first object and an Integer data type for the second object. The data type specified here will be applied throughout the Generics class.

The last object that you define here is an object that holds an array of Customer objects created from your Customer class:

```
'Using the Generics class
Private objStringValues As New Generics(Of String)
Private objIntegerValues As New Generics(Of Integer)

'Using the List<T> class
Private objCustomerList As New List(Of Customer)
```

The ListCustomer procedure simply accepts a Customer object as input and adds the Customer ID and Customer Name to the list box on your form:

```
Private Sub ListCustomer(ByVal customerToList As Customer)
    lstData.Items.Add(customerToList.CustomerID & _
        " - " & customerToList.CustomerName)
End Sub
```

The Click event handler for the Start button contains the rest of the code for your project. You start this procedure by declaring a local String variable that will be used to demonstrate checking to see whether a variable has been initialized.

The code following the variable declaration checks the length of the variable and then adds the contents of the variable to the list box on the form.

```
Private Sub btnStart_Click(ByVal sender As Object, _
    ByVal e As System.EventArgs) Handles btnStart.Click

    'Declare variables
    Dim strData As String

    lstData.Items.Add("String variable data:")
    If strData.Length > 0 Then
        lstData.Items.Add(strData)
    End If
```

Since you will be writing the various results of your processing to the list box on your form, you'll want to add a blank entry to the list box to separate your results for aesthetic reasons, which is what the next line of code does. Here you simply use the `Empty` method of the `String` class to return an empty string to be added to the list box:

```
'Add an empty string to the ListBox
lstData.Items.Add(String.Empty)
```

This next section of code demonstrates the use of the `List<T>` class, as the comment in the code indicates. You add two new `Customer` objects to the `objCustomerList` object and then display those customers in the list box. Using a `For Each...Next` loop to iterate through the collection of `Customer` objects, you add each customer to the list box by calling the `ListCustomer` function passing that function the `Customer` object:

```
'Demonstrates the use of the List<T> class
lstData.Items.Add("Customers in the Customer Class:")
objCustomerList.Add(New Customer(1001, "Henry For"))
objCustomerList.Add(New Customer(1002, "Orville Wright"))
For Each objCustomer As Customer In objCustomerList
    ListCustomer(objCustomer)
Next
```

Again you add a blank entry to the list box and use the objects that were defined using your `Generics` class. The first object, `objStringValues`, uses the `Generics` class with a `String` data type, as the object name indicates. Remember that the `Add` method in this class accepts a key/value pair and that the `key` parameter is always a `String` value. The `value` parameter uses the data type that was used to initialize this class, which in this case is also a string.

When you add a key/value pair to your `objStringValues` object, you want to display that data in the list box on your form. You do this by accessing the `Key` and `Value` properties in the `Generics` class from which this object was derived:

```
'Add an empty string to the ListBox
lstData.Items.Add(String.Empty)

'Demonstrates the use of Generics
lstData.Items.Add("Generics Class Key/Value Pairs using String Values:")
objStringValues.Add("1001", "Henry Ford")
lstData.Items.Add(objStringValues.Key(0) & " = " & _
    objStringValues.Value(0))
```

Again you add another blank line to the list box and then add a key/value pair that uses an `Integer` data type for the `value` parameter to the `objIntegerValues` object. Then you add that key/value pair to the list box:

```
'Add an empty string to the ListBox
lstData.Items.Add(String.Empty)

'Demonstrates the use of Generics
lstData.Items.Add("Generics Class Key/Value Pairs using Integer Values:")
objIntegerValues.Add("Henry Ford", 1001)
lstData.Items.Add(objIntegerValues.Key(0) & " = " & _
    objIntegerValues.Value(0))
```

After you add another blank line to the list box, you use a Using . . . End Using block to create a new object of the Computer class, add the free memory and total memory of your computer to the list box, and then dispose of the Computer class.

When you use a class, you typically instantiate it using the New keyword as you did with your Generics class, use the class, and then dispose of the class by calling its Dispose method if it implements one. The problem with that scenario is that when an exception occurs, the resource may or may not be disposed of. Even if you implement the code using structure error handling, a topic I'll discuss later in this chapter, you are not always guaranteed to be able to dispose of the class.

The Using statement is an efficient means of acquiring a resource, using it, and then disposing of it, regardless of whether an exception occurs. There is one caveat to this: the class that you use in a Using . . . End Using block must implement the IDisposable interface. This is why you added this interface to your Computer class.

In the following code, the object name, objMemory, has not been defined anywhere except in the Using statement. The Using statement takes care of declaring this object for you and sets it to a new instance of the class that you specify, which in this case is the Computer class. Keep in mind that the object, objMemory, is local to the Using . . . End Using block and you can only reference it within this block.

When the End Using statement is reached, the Common Language Runtime (CLR) automatically calls the Dispose method on the Computer class, thereby releasing its reference to it, and the Computer class executes any cleanup code that has been implemented in the Dispose method:

```
'Add an empty string to the ListBox
lstData.Items.Add(String.Empty)

'Demonstrates the use of the Using statement
'Allows acquisition, usage and disposal of the resource
lstData.Items.Add("Computer Class Properties:")
Using objMemory As New Computer
    lstData.Items.Add("FreeMemory = " & objMemory.FreeMemory)
    lstData.Items.Add("TotalMemory = " & objMemory.TotalMemory)
End Using
```

Once again you add another blank line to the list box, and then you get to the final bit of code in this procedure. In this section of code we wanted to demonstrate the use of the Continue statement. The Continue statement is an efficient means of immediately transferring control to the next iteration of a loop. Instead of coding a lot of If . . . Then statements in a loop, you can merely test to see whether a condition is what you want and if it is not, you can call the Continue statement to pass control to the next iteration of a Do, For, or While loop.

Take a look at the code that you have here. First you declare a couple of variables and set their values. The first variable, strPassword, is declared and set to a password that contains upper- and lowercase letters. The second variable, strLowerCaseLetters, is declared and set to an empty string so that the variable is initialized.

Next, you set up a For . . . Next loop to check each character in the strPassword variable. The If . . . Then statement uses the Like operator to compare a character in the password variable to a pattern of letters. If a match is found, the Like operator returns a value of True. However, you are using a negative comparison here, because you have included the Not keyword in the If . . . Then statement, so if the character in the password variable is not like one of the letters in the pattern, [a-z], you'll execute the next statement, which is the Continue statement.

If the character in the password variable is a lowercase letter, you concatenate the character to the strLowerCaseLetters variable, which is why you needed to initialize this variable to an empty string when you declared it.

Finally, after all lowercase letters have been extracted from the password variable, you display the results of the strLowerCaseLetters variable in the list box on your form:

```
'Add an empty string to the ListBox
lstData.Items.Add(String.Empty)

'Demonstrates the use of the Continue statement
Dim strPassword As String = "POpPassword"
Dim strLowerCaseLetters As String = String.Empty
'Extract lowercase characters from string
For intIndex As Integer = 0 To strPassword.Length - 1
    'Demonstrates the use of the Continue statement
    'If no uppercase character is found, continue the loop
    If Not strPassword.Substring(intIndex, 1) Like "[a-z]" Then
        'No uppercase character found, continue loop
        Continue For
    End If
    'Lowercase character found, save it
    strLowerCaseLetters &= strPassword.Substring(intIndex, 1)
Next

'Display lowercase characters
lstData.Items.Add("Password lower case characters:")
lstData.Items.Add(strLowerCaseLetters)
End Sub
```

At this point, you are probably pretty eager to run your project and test your code. In this next Try It Out, you examine the Exception Assistant in Visual Studio 2008. This useful assistant provides help when an unhandled exception occurs in your code.

Try It Out   Exception Assistant

1. Start your project by clicking the Start button on the toolbar or by clicking the Debug menu and choosing the Start menu item.

2. When your form is displayed, click the Start button on your form to have your code in the Click event handler for the Start button executed. You'll immediately see the Exception Assistant shown in Figure 10-8.

   Note that the Exception Assistant dialog box displays the type of exception that occurred in the title bar of the dialog box. It also provides links to some basic troubleshooting tips and also a link at the bottom that provides the details of the exception.

Figure 10-8

3. Click the View Detail link in Exception Assistant dialog box to view the View Detail dialog box shown in Figure 10-9. You are mainly interested in the exception message, and, as you can see, it informs you that the object reference has not been set to an instance of an object. Basically, you have not initialized the variable strData.

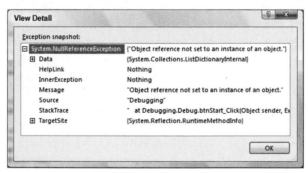

Figure 10-9

4. Click the OK button to close the View Detail dialog box and then click the Close button (×) in the upper right-hand corner of the Exception Assistant dialog box to close it.

5. Now click the Stop Debugging button on the toolbar or click the Debug menu and select the Stop Debugging menu item.

6. Locate the following section of code at the beginning of the btnStart_Click procedure:

```
If strData.Length > 0 Then
    lstData.Items.Add(strData)
End If
```

7. Modify that code as shown here:

```
If strData IsNot Nothing Then
    If strData.Length > 0 Then
        lstData.Items.Add(strData)
    End If
Else
    strData = "String now initialized"
    lstData.Items.Add(strData)
End If
```

8. Now run your project and click the Start button on your form once it is displayed. All of your code should have executed, and the list box should be populated with the various results of the processing that took place in the btnStart_Click procedure.

How It Works

When an unhandled error occurs in your code while debugging, the Exception Assistant dialog box is displayed and provides troubleshooting tips for the exception as well as a link to view the details of the exception as was shown in Figure 10-8. Figure 10-9 displayed the View Detail dialog box, which provides the detailed information about the exception which can also be an invaluable tool for determining the exact cause of the exception.

You modified the code that caused the error as shown here. Because the string variable strData was declared but never initialized, the variable is Nothing. This means that it has not been set to an instance of the String class and therefore the properties and methods of the variable cannot be referenced without causing a NullReferenceException as shown in Figure 10-8.

To rectify this problem, you first test the strData variable to see if it is not equal to Nothing by using the IsNot operator as shown in the first line of code here. If the variable has been initialized, then you can execute the code in the If statement. Otherwise, processing falls through to the Else statement and here you set the variable to a string constant and then display the contents of the variable in the list box:

```
If strData IsNot Nothing Then
    If strData.Length > 0 Then
        lstData.Items.Add(strData)
    End If
Else
    strData = "String now initialized"
    lstData.Items.Add(strData)
End If
```

An alternative to the previous code example would be to use a Try . . . Catch block to handle the exception. This technique is demonstrated later in this chapter.

Setting Breakpoints

When trying to debug a large program, you may find that you want to debug only a section of code; that is, you want your code to run up to a certain point and then stop. This is where breakpoints come in handy; they cause execution of your code to stop anywhere a breakpoint is set. You can set breakpoints anywhere in your code and your code runs up to that point and stops.

Note that execution of the code stops before the line on which the breakpoint is set.

You can set breakpoints when you write your code, and you can also set them at run time by switching to your code and setting the breakpoint at the desired location. You cannot set a breakpoint while your program is actually executing a section of code such as the code in a loop, but you can when the program is idle and waiting for user input.

When the development environment encounters a breakpoint, execution of your code halts, and your program is considered to be in break mode. While your program is in break mode, a lot of debugging features are available. In fact, a lot of debugging features are available to you only while your program is in break mode.

You can set breakpoints by clicking the gray margin next to the line of code on which you want to set the breakpoint. When the breakpoint is set, you see a solid red circle in the gray margin and the line is highlighted in red. When you are done with a particular breakpoint you can remove it by clicking the solid red circle. You see more of this in the Try It Out exercise in this section.

Sometimes you'll want to debug code in a loop, such as one that reads data from a file. You know that the first *x* number of records are good, and it is time-consuming to step through all the code repetitively until you get to what you suspect is the bad record. A breakpoint can be set inside the loop and you can set a hit counter on it. The code inside the loop executes the number of times that you specified in the hit counter and then stops and places you in break mode. This can be a real time saver, and you will be taking a look at breakpoint hit counts later in this section. You can also set a condition on a breakpoint, such as when a variable contains a certain value or when the value of a variable changes. You also take a look at this later in this section.

Try It Out   Working with Breakpoints

1. The first thing that you want to do is to set a breakpoint in your code. Using Figure 10-10 as a guide, set the breakpoint in your code by clicking the gray margin to the left of the line of code shown.

```
Start Page  Debug.vb  Computer.vb  Generics.vb  Customer.vb  Debug.vb [Design]
btnStart                                          Click
    Private Sub btnStart_Click(ByVal sender As Object, _
        ByVal e As System.EventArgs) Handles btnStart.Click

        'Declare variables
        Dim strData As String

        lstData.Items.Add("String variable data:")
        If strData IsNot Nothing Then
            If strData.Length > 0 Then
                lstData.Items.Add(strData)
            End If
        Else
            strData = "String now initialized"
            lstData.Items.Add(strData)
        End If
```

Figure 10-10

2. Run the project.

3. To get to the code where the breakpoint is set, click the Start button on your form. The code executes up to the breakpoint, and the development environment window receives focus, making it the topmost window. The entire line should be highlighted in yellow and the breakpoint circle in the margin should now contain a yellow arrow in it pointing to the line of code where execution has been paused, which is the End If statement that was shown in Figure 10-10.

Also note that there are a few new windows at the bottom of the development environment. What you see will vary depending on which windows you have specified to be shown — you can choose different ones using the tabs at the bottom.

Take a pause in the Try It Out to learn about some of the features of the IDE in debug mode.

The Breakpoints Window

You can display the Breakpoints window, if the tab is not shown, in the bottom-right of the IDE by clicking the Breakpoints icon on the Debug toolbar or by selecting Debug ⇨ Windows ⇨ Breakpoints. The Breakpoints window shows what line of code the current breakpoint is at, any conditions it has, and the hit count if applicable, as shown in Figure 10-11.

Figure 10-11

The Breakpoints window shows all the breakpoints you have set in your code. When a breakpoint is encountered, it is highlighted in the code and also highlighted in the Breakpoint window, as shown in Figure 10-11. In this window, you can set new breakpoints, delete existing breakpoints, and change the properties of the breakpoints. You will see more of this later in the chapter.

Useful Icons on the Toolbar

In this Try It Out, you want to step through your code line by line. On the Standard toolbar in the IDE there are three icons of particular interest to you as shown in Figure 10-12.

❑ The first icon is the Step Into icon. When you click this icon, you can step through your code line by line. This includes stepping into any function or procedure that the code calls and working through it line by line.

❑ The second icon is the Step Over icon. This works in a similar way to Step Into, but you pass straight over the procedures and functions — they still execute, but all in one go. You then move straight on to the next line in the block of code that called the procedure.

❑   Last is the Step Out icon. This icon allows you to jump to the end of the procedure or function that you are currently in and to move to the line of code *after* the line that called the procedure or function. This is handy when you step into a long procedure and want to get out of it. The rest of the code in the procedure still gets executed, but you do not step through it.

Figure 10-12

There is one more really useful button worth adding to the toolbar: Run To Cursor. The Run To Cursor icon enables you to place your cursor anywhere in the code following the current breakpoint where execution has been paused and then click this icon. The code between the current breakpoint and where the cursor is positioned is executed, and execution stops on the line of code where the cursor is located.

To add this button, you right-click any empty area of the toolbar and choose Customize from the context menu. In the Customize dialog box, click the Commands tab, and then select Debug in the Categories list. In the Commands list, select Run To Cursor. After you select Run To Cursor, you drag its icon from the Commands list onto the debug toolbar, to form a group of icons as shown in Figure 10-13, and then click the Close button to close the Customize dialog box.

Figure 10-13

You are now ready to continue working through the Try It Out.

<hr>

Try It Out   **Working with Breakpoints (cont.)**

1.   You ended the last step of the Try It Out at the breakpoint. Before continuing, you want to examine the contents of the string variable, strData. Hover your mouse over the variable to view a Data Tip, as shown in Figure 10-14. Notice that the variable name is listed along with its contents, a magnifying glass, and a down arrow.

Clicking the contents of the variable in the Data Tip puts you in edit mode for the variable, and you can actually change the contents of that variable. Clicking the magnifying glass will cause the contents of the variable to be displayed automatically in the Text Visualizer dialog box, which is a useful tool for displaying the data for string variables that contain a significant amount of data. Clicking the down arrow provides you a drop-down list of options for viewing the contents of the variable and contains an option for Text Visualizer, XML Visualizer, and HTML Visualizer.

Figure 10-14

2.   At this point, you'll want to test the debugging icons on the toolbar, starting with the Run To Cursor icon first. Place your cursor on the line of code that calls the ListCustomer procedure as shown in Figure 10-15.

Click the Run To Cursor icon on the toolbar. The code between the breakpoint at the `End If` statement shown in Figure 10-14 and the line of code that calls the `ListCustomer` procedure, shown in Figure 10-15, is executed. Your project stops execution on the line of code on which you have your cursor.

```
objCustomerList.Add(New Customer(1001, "Henry For"))
objCustomerList.Add(New Customer(1002, "Orville Wright"))
For Each objCustomer As Customer In objCustomerList
    ListCustomer(objCustomer)
Next
```

Figure 10-15

3. Click the Step Into icon next, and you should now be at the beginning of the `ListCustomer` procedure. Data Tips can be displayed for objects that contain multiple values as well as variables that contain only a single value.

Hover your mouse over the `customerToList` parameter for this procedure to display the Data Tip for this object. You'll see a plus sign next to the object name in the Data Tip. Click the plus sign, or simply hover your mouse over it, and the contents of the object are displayed as shown in Figure 10-16.

Note that this Data Tip not only displays the properties in the `Customer` class, the class that the `customerToList` object is derived from, but also the private variables in that class. You also have the same options for viewing the contents of string variables, which is indicated by the presence of the magnifying glass and down arrow icons.

Since the text, which is supposed to read "`Henry Ford`", is misspelled, you'll want to correct it in the Data Tip. This can be done by editing the `strName` variable in the Data Tip. Click the text "`Henry For`" in the Data Tip to put it into edit mode. Correct the text by adding the letter d at the end of the text and then click the name or variable name in the Data Tip. Note that the text for both the property and variable has been updated with your corrections.

It should be noted that you can change the contents of `Integer` data types in the Data Tip as well.

Figure 10-16

4. Click the Step Into icon once more and you should be at the first line of code in the `ListCustomer` procedure.

5. Since you do not want to see any of this code at this time, you are going to step out of this procedure. This places you back at the line of code that called this procedure. Click the Step Out icon. Note that you are taken out of the `ListCustomer` procedure and back to where the call originated.

6. Now click the Step Into icon twice more so that you are back at the call to the `ListCustomer` procedure once again.

7. The final icon to be tested is the Step Over icon. Click this icon now and note that you have totally stepped over the execution of the `ListCustomer` procedure. The procedure was actually executed. However, since you chose to step over it, the debugger does not show you that the procedure was executed.

8. Continue processing as normal and have the rest of the code execute without interruption. If you hover your mouse over the Start icon on the toolbar, you will notice that the tooltip has been changed from Start to Continue. Click this icon to let the rest of the code run. You should now see your completed form as shown in Figure 10-17.

Figure 10-17

In the following Try It Out, you examine the Breakpoint Hit Count dialog box. The Breakpoint Hit Count dialog box allows you to define the number of executions of a loop should be performed before the IDE stops execution of your code and puts it into break mode. As previously described, this is useful for processing loops, because you can specify how many iterations the loop should make before you encounter a breakpoint.

Try It Out   **Using the Breakpoint's Hit Count**

1. Stop your project and set a breakpoint in the For loop as shown in Figure 10-18. Remember that to set a breakpoint, you need to click in the gray margin on the line of code where the breakpoint should be.

Start your project again by clicking the Start icon on the toolbar.

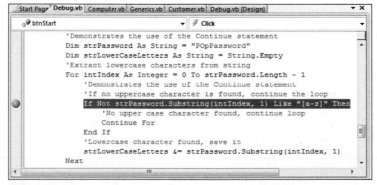

Figure 10-18

2. In the Breakpoints window, right-click the second breakpoint and choose Hit Count from the context menu to invoke the Breakpoint Hit Count dialog box.

3. The breakpoint that you currently have set halts execution every time it is encountered. Change it to break only when the loop enters its third execution. You do this by selecting the option break when the hit count is equal to in the drop-down list and then entering the number 3 in the text box displayed next to it, as shown in Figure 10-19.

Figure 10-19

Click the OK button to close this dialog box. Notice the Hit Count column in the Breakpoints window in the IDE. The second breakpoint now displays the Hit Count condition that you just defined.

4. At this point, click the Start button on the form. By clicking the Start button you are again stopped at your first breakpoint.

5. This breakpoint is highlighted in the Breakpoints window. You no longer need this breakpoint, so click it and then click the Delete icon in the Breakpoints window; the breakpoint will be deleted. Your code is still paused at this point, so click the Continue button on the Debug toolbar.

6. You are now stopped at your breakpoint in the For loop as it enters its third execution. Notice that the Breakpoints window shows the hit count criteria that you selected and also the current hit count.

As you can see, this is a handy way to have a loop execute a definite number of iterations before breaking at a defined breakpoint.

7. Now let your code continue executing by clicking the Continue button on the Debug toolbar.

8. Stop your project once the form has been displayed.

In the following Try It Out, you modify the properties of the only breakpoint that you have left.

Try It Out   **Changing Breakpoint Properties**

1. In the previous Try It Out, you modified the breakpoint while the project was running. This time you modify the breakpoint while the project is stopped. To view the Breakpoints window, click the Debug menu, choose Windows, and then choose the Breakpoints sub menu item.

2. In the Breakpoints window right-click the breakpoint, and choose Hit Count from the context menu to display the Breakpoint Hit Count dialog box. Notice the Reset button. When you click this button, you reset the hit counter for the next execution, but this is not what you'll do at this point.

3. Here you'll change the hit count back to its original setting. Select break always in the drop-down box and then click the OK button to close this dialog box.

4. To set a specific condition for this breakpoint, right-click the breakpoint and choose Condition from the context menu to invoke Breakpoint Condition dialog box. Enter the condition as shown in Figure 10-20. This causes this breakpoint to break only when the variable `intIndex` is equal to 3. Note that you could also specify that the breakpoint would be activated when the value of a variable changes. Click the OK button to close the dialog box and then start your project.

Figure 10-20

5. Click the Start button on your form. Once the `intIndex` variable is equal to 3, the breakpoint is activated, and the execution of the code is paused at the line where the breakpoint is specified. This is actually your fourth time into the loop, as the `For ... Next` loop specifies a starting index of 0 for the variable `intIndex`.

6. Finally, go ahead and let your code finish executing by clicking the Continue button on the Debug toolbar. Once your form is displayed, go ahead and stop your project.

Debugging Using the Watch Window

The Watch window provides a method for you to watch variables and expressions easily while the code is executing — this can be invaluable when you are trying to debug unwanted results in a variable. You can even change the values of variables in the Watch window. You can also add as many variables and expressions as needed to debug your program. This provides a mechanism that allows you to watch the values of your variables change without any intervention on your part.

You can add and delete a variable or expression to the QuickWatch dialog box only when your program is in break mode. Therefore, before you run your program, you need to set a breakpoint before the variable or expression that you want to watch. When the breakpoint has been reached, you can add as many Watch variables or expressions as needed.

In the following Try It Out, you add the `intIndex` variable to the Watch window and also add an expression using the `intIndex` variable. This enables you to observe this variable and expression as you step through your code.

Try It Out   Using QuickWatch

1. Start your program again. When your form displays, switch to the IDE and clear the current breakpoint by deleting it in the Breakpoints window or by clicking it in the gray margin where it is set. Then set a new breakpoint as shown in Figure 10-21.

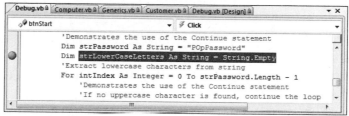

Figure 10-21

2. You can add a QuickWatch variable or expression only while your program is paused. Click the Start button on the form so the breakpoint will be encountered and your program paused.

3. When the breakpoint has been encountered, right-click the variable, `intIndex`, in the `For...Next` loop and choose QuickWatch from the context menu to invoke the QuickWatch dialog box. Note that this variable has not only been added to the Expression drop-down box but has also been placed in the Current value grid in the dialog, as shown in Figure 10-22. Click the Add Watch button to add this variable to the Watch window.

Since the variable is declared in the `For...Next` *loop, you see an error here. You can safely ignore this error, because once the loop has started processing, the variable will be declared.*

Figure 10-22

4. While you have the QuickWatch dialog box open, set an expression to be evaluated. Add the expression **intIndex = 1** in the Expression drop-down box. Then click the Add Watch button to have this expression added to the Watch window. Now close the QuickWatch dialog box by clicking the Close button.

5. If you do not see the Watch window at the bottom of the IDE, select Debug ⇨ Windows ⇨ Watch ⇨ Watch 1. You should see a variable and an expression in the Watch window, as shown in Figure 10-23.

The second watch expression that you added here returns a value of `True` when the `intIndex` variable equals 1, so Visual Studio 2008 sets the type to `Boolean` once you enter the `For...Next` loop.

Figure 10-23

6. Step through your code line by line so that you can watch the value of the variable and expression change. Click the Step Into icon on the Debug toolbar to step to the next line of code. Keep clicking the Step Into icon to see the values of the variable and expression in the Watch window change.

As you step through the loop in your code, you continue to see the value for the `intIndex` variable change in the Watch window. When the value of the variable in the Watch window turns the color red, as shown in Figure 10-24, the value has just been changed. You can manually change the value anytime by entering a new value in the Value column in the Watch window.

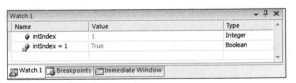

Figure 10-24

7. When you are done, click the Continue icon on the Debug toolbar to let your code finish executing. Then stop your project once the form has been displayed.

Debugging with the Locals Window

The Locals window is similar to the Watch window, except that it shows all variables and objects for the current function or procedure. The Locals window also lets you change the value of a variable or object, and the same rules that apply to the Watch window apply here (that is, the program must be paused before a value can be changed). The text for a value that has just changed also turns red, making it easy to spot the variable or object that has just changed.

The Locals window is great if you want a quick glance at everything that is going on in a function or procedure, but it is not very useful for watching the values of one or two variables or expressions. The reason for this is that the Locals window contains all variables and objects in a procedure or function. Therefore, if you have a lot of variables and objects, you have to scroll through the window constantly to view the various variables and objects. This is where the Watch window comes in handy; it lets you watch just the variables that you need. In this Try It Out, you examine the contents of the Locals window in two different procedures. This demonstrates how the contents of the Locals window change from one procedure to the next.

Try It Out   Using the Locals Window

1. To prepare for this exercise, you need to have the current breakpoint set and set a new breakpoint in the `ListCustomer` procedure. Locate the `ListCustomer` procedure and set a breakpoint on the one line of code in that procedure:

    ```
    lstData.Items.Add(customerToList.CustomerID & _
        " - " & customerToList.CustomerName)
    ```

2. Now start your program.

3. If you do not see the Locals window at the bottom of the IDE, select Debug ⇨ Windows ⇨ Locals. Notice that at this point the Locals window contains no variables or objects. This is because you have not entered a procedure or function. Click the Start button on the form, and your breakpoint in the `ListCustomer` procedure is encountered first and execution is paused.

4. Notice the various objects and their types listed in the Locals window. The first item in the list is Me, which is the form itself. If you expand this item, you see all the objects and controls associated with your form. If you expand the `customerToList` object, you'll see the properties and variables defined in the `Customer` class from which this object is derived as shown in Figure 10-25.

Figure 10-25

5. Now click the Continue icon on the Debug toolbar until you encounter your second breakpoint.

6. Now take a look at the Locals window, and you see a different set of objects and variables. The one constant item in both procedures is Me, which is associated with the form.

7. If you step through a couple of lines of code in the loop where the breakpoint has paused your program, you see the values in the Locals window change. You can continue to step through your code, or you can click the Continue icon on the Debug toolbar to let your program run to completion.

    After you change your build configuration from Debug to Release, debugging is no longer available; even if you have breakpoints set in your code, they will not be encountered.

8. To clear all breakpoints in your code, you can delete each breakpoint in the Breakpoints window, or you can click the Debug menu and choose Delete All Breakpoints. When you are done, stop your project.

Error Handling

Error handling is an essential part of any good code. In Visual Basic 2008 the error mechanism is based on the concept of *exceptions* that can be *thrown* to raise an error and *caught* when the error is handled. If you do not provide any type of error handling and an error occurs, your user receives a message about an unhandled exception, which is provided by the CLR, and then the program may terminate, depending on the type of error encountered. This is not a user-friendly message and does not inform the user about the true nature of the error or how to resolve it. The unhandled error could also cause users to lose the data that they were working with or leave the user and the data in an unknown state.

Visual Studio 2008 provides *structured error-handling* statements that are common across all languages. Structured error handling is a way to organize blocks of code in a structure that handles errors. In this section you examine structured error handling and how it can be incorporated into your programs with very little effort.

Structured error handling in Visual Studio 2008 is incorporated with the `Try...Catch...Finally` block. You execute the code that might throw an exception in the `Try` block, and you handle anticipated errors in the `Catch` block. The `Finally` block, which is optional, is always executed, if present, and allows you to place any cleanup code there regardless of whether an error has occurred. If an error occurs that was not handled in the `Catch` block, the CLR displays its standard error message and terminates your program. Therefore, it is important to try to anticipate all possible errors for the code that is contained in the `Try` block.

Take a look at the syntax for the `Try...Catch...Finally` statement:

```
Try
    [try statements]
    [Exit Try]
Catch exceptionvariable As exceptiontype
    [catch statements]
    [Exit Try]
  [Additional Catch blocks]
Finally
    [finally statements]
End Try
```

❑ The try statements are the statements to be executed that may cause an error.

❑ The *exceptionvariable* can be any variable name. It will be set to contain the value of the error that is thrown.

❑ The *exceptiontype* specifies the exception class type that the exception belongs to. If this type is not supplied, your Catch block handles any exception defined in the System.Exception class. This argument allows you to specify the type of exception that you maybe looking for. An example of a specific exception is IOException, which is used when performing any type of IO (input/output) against a file.

❑ The catch statements handle and process the error that has occurred.

❑ The finally statements are executed after all other processing has occurred.

❑ The optional Exit Try statement allows you to completely break out of a Try ... Catch ... Finally block and resume execution of code immediately following the Try ... Catch ... Finally block.

You can have multiple Catch blocks, meaning that you can test for multiple errors with different exception types within the same Try block. When an error occurs among the try statements, control is passed to the appropriate Catch block for processing.

When you define a Catch block, you can specify a variable name for the exception and define the type of exception you want to catch, as shown in the following code fragment. This code defines an exception variable with a name of IOExceptionErr, and the type of exception is an IOException. This example traps any type of IO exception that may occur when processing files and stores the error information in an object named IOExceptionErr:

```
Catch IOExceptionErr As IOException
    ...
    code to handle the exception goes here
    ...
```

When dealing with mathematical expressions, you can define and catch the various errors that you may encounter such as a divide-by-zero exception. You can also catch errors such as overflow errors, which may occur when multiplying two numbers and trying to place the result in a variable that is too small for the result. However, in cases such as these, it may be better to check for problems in advance — you should use exceptions only in exceptional circumstances.

Using Structured Error Handling

In the following Try It Out you add some structured error handling to the sample program with which you have been working. When you first ran the Debugging project you received the NullReferenceException that was shown in Figure 10-8, because you tried to access the properties of the strData string variable before it had been set. This code is a prime candidate for structured error handling. You temporarily bypassed the problem at that point by using an If ... Then ... Else statement to first see whether the variable had been initialized. A cleaner way to handle such a case is in a Try ... Catch block.

Try It Out   Structured Error Handling

1. Modify the code for the `strData` variable in the `btnStart_Click` procedure as shown:

```
lstData.Items.Add("String variable data:")
Try
    If strData.Length > 0 Then
        lstData.Items.Add(strData)
    End If
Catch NullReferenceExceptionErr As NullReferenceException
    strData = "String now initialized"
    lstData.Items.Add(strData)
End Try
```

How It Works

The code you entered contains a `Try` block and a `Catch` block. You opted not to use the `Finally` block in this error-handling routine because the `Catch` block performs the necessary code to set the `strData` variable and have the contents of that variable added to the list box on your form:

```
Try
    If strData.Length > 0 Then
        lstData.Items.Add(strData)
    End If
Catch NullReferenceExceptionErr As NullReferenceException
    strData = "String now initialized"
    lstData.Items.Add(strData)
End Try
```

When you try to access the `Length` property of the `strData` variable in the `Try` block, a `NullReferenceException` exception is thrown because the variable has been declared but not set.

The error that you want to trap is a `NullReferenceException`, and that exception is specified in the `Catch` block. You defined the variable `NullReferenceExceptionErr` for the exception variable argument; the standard practice among most developers is to use the exception name along with a suffix of `Err`. You then defined the type of exception that you want to test for and trap.

You place your error-handling code within the `Catch` block, as you have done here. When a `NullReferenceException` occurs, you set the `strData` variable to a string constant and then add the contents of that variable to the list box on your form.

Try It Out   Testing Your Error Handler

1. Set a breakpoint on the `Try` statement and then run your project. Once the form is displayed, click the Start button.

2. Once the breakpoint is encountered, right-click the variable `strData` and choose Add Watch from the context menu. Click the Watch 1 window so that you can view the contents of the variable.

3.   At this point, the `strData` variable has a value of `Nothing`. Click the Step Into icon on the toolbar, and you'll be taken to the first line of code in the `Try` block.

4.   Click the Step Into icon again. A `NullReferenceException` is thrown, and you are taken to the `Catch` block.

5.   Note the value of the variable in the Watch 1 window, click the Step Into icon once more, and note the value of the variable in the Watch 1 window, as shown in Figure 10-26.

Figure 10-26

6.   Click the Continue icon on the toolbar to allow the rest of your code to run.

As you become more familiar with the types of errors that can occur, you will be able to write more sophisticated structured error handlers. This comes only with experience and testing. You will discover more errors and will be able to handle them only by thoroughly testing your code. The online documentation for most methods that you use in Visual Studio 2008 will have Exceptions sections that list and explain the possible exceptions that could occur by using the method.

Summary

This chapter covered some useful debugging tools that are built into the Visual Studio 2008 development environment. You saw how easy it is to debug your programs as you stepped through the various Try It Out sections.

In our discussion of breakpoints, we showed you how to stop the execution of your program at any given point. As useful as this is, setting breakpoints with a hit counter in a loop is even more useful, because you are able to execute a loop several times before encountering a breakpoint in the loop.

You also examined some of the various windows available while debugging your program, such as the Locals window and the Watch window. These windows provide you with valuable information about the variables and expressions in your program. You are able to watch the values change and are able to change the values to control the execution of your code.

You should know what types of major errors you may encounter while developing and debugging your code. You should be able to recognize syntax and execution errors and possibly correct them. Although debugging a program for logic errors may be difficult at first, it does become easier with time and experience.

This chapter also covered structured error handling, and you should incorporate this knowledge into your programs at every opportunity. Structured error handling provides you with the opportunity to handle and correct errors at runtime.

In summary, you should know the following:

❑   How to recognize and correct major types of errors

❑   How to use breakpoints successfully to debug your program

❑   How to use the Locals and Watch windows to see and change variables and expressions

❑   How to use structured error handling

Exercises

1.   Using your Debugging project, add a Try . . . Catch block to the ListCustomer procedure to handle an Exception error. In the Catch block, add code to display a message box with the error message.

2.   The Try . . . Catch block that you added in Exercise 1 should never throw an error. However, you can throw your own error so that you can test your code in the Catch block. Add a Throw statement as the first line of code in the Try block. Consult the online help for the syntax of the Throw statement.

Building Objects

You may have heard the term *object oriented* a lot since you first started using computers. You may also have heard that it is a scary and tricky subject to understand. In its early years it was, but today's modern tools and languages make object orientation (OO) a wonderfully easy-to-understand concept that brings massive benefits to software developers. This is mainly because languages such as Visual Basic, C++, and, of course, Visual Basic 2008 and C# have matured to a point where they make creating objects and the programs that use them very easy indeed. With these development tools, you will have no problem understanding even the most advanced object-oriented concepts and will be able to use them to build exciting object-based applications.

You have been using objects and classes throughout this book, but in this chapter you look at object orientation in detail and build on the foundations of the previous chapters to start producing some cool applications using Visual Basic 2008.

In this chapter, you will:

❑   Build a reusable object with methods and properties

❑   Inherit the object that you build in another object

❑   Override methods and properties in your base object

❑   Create your own namespace

Understanding Objects

An object is almost anything you can think of. We work with physical objects all the time: televisions, cars, customers, reports, light bulbs — anything. In computer terms, an object is a representation of a thing that we want to manipulate in our application. Sometimes, the two definitions map exactly onto each other. So, if you have a physical car object sitting in your driveway and want to describe it in software terms, you build a software car object that sits in your computer.

Likewise, if you need to write a piece of software that generates a bill for a customer, you may well have a Bill object and a Customer object. The Customer object represents the customer and may be capable of having a name, address, and also have the capability to generate the bill. The Bill object would represent an instance of a bill for a customer and would be able to impart the details of the bill and may also have the capability to print itself.

What is important here is the concept that the object has the intelligence to produce actions related to it — the Customer object can generate the bill. In effect, if you have a Customer object representing a customer, you can simply say to it: "Produce a bill for me." The Customer object would then go away and do all the hard work related to creating the bill. Likewise, when you have a Bill object, you can say to it: "Print yourself." What you have here are two examples of object behavior.

Objects are unbelievably useful because they turn software engineering into something conceptually similar to wooden building blocks. You arrange the blocks (the objects) to build something greater than the sum of the parts. The power of objects comes from the fact that, as someone using objects, you don't need to understand how they work behind the scenes. You're familiar with this with real-world objects too. When you use a mobile phone, you don't need to understand how it works inside. Even if you do understand how a mobile phone works inside — even if you made it yourself — it's still much easier to use the mobile phone's simple interface. The interface can also prevent you from accidentally doing something that breaks the phone. The same is true with computer objects. Even if you build all the objects yourself, having the complicated workings hidden behind a simple interface can make your life much easier and safer.

Object orientation is perhaps best explained by using a television metaphor. Look at the television in your home. There are several things you know how to do with it:

❏   Watch the image on the screen

❏   Change channel

❏   Change volume

❏   Switch it on or off

What you don't have to do is understand how everything works to allow you to carry out these activities. If asked, most people couldn't put together the components needed to make a modern television. We could, with a little research and patience, come up with something fairly basic, but nothing as complex as the one sitting in my home. However, we do understand how to use a television. We know how to change the channel, change the volume, switch it on and off, and so on.

Objects in software engineering work in basically the same way. When you have an object, you can use it and ask it do things without having to understand how the internals of it actually work. This is phenomenally powerful, as you'll see soon.

Software objects typically have the following characteristics:

❏   **Identity** — *User:* "What are you?" *TV:* "I'm a TV."

❏   **State** — *User:* "What channel am I watching?" *TV:* "You're watching Channel 4."

❏   **Behavior** — *User:* "Please turn up the volume to 50%." Then, we can use the State again. *User:* "How loud is the volume?" *TV:* "50%."

Encapsulation

The core concept behind object-orientation is *encapsulation*. This is a big word, but it's very simple to understand. What this means is that the functionality is wrapped up in a self-contained manner and that you don't need to understand what it's actually doing when you ask it to do something.

If you remember in Chapter 3, you built a function that calculated the area of a circle. In that function, you encapsulated the logic of calculating the area in such a way that anyone using the function could find the area without having to know how to perform the operation. This is the same concept but taken to the next level.

> *Objects are often referred to as black boxes. If you imagine software objects as small plastic boxes with buttons on the top and connectors on the side, with a basic understanding of what the box does, together with a general understanding of how boxes generally plug together, you can build up a complex system with them without ever having to have the capability of building a box independently.*

Methods and Properties

You interact with objects through methods and properties. These can be defined as:

❑ *Methods* are ways of instructing an object to do something.

❑ *Properties* are things that describe features of an object.

A method was defined previously as a self-contained block of code that does something. This is true, but it is a rather simplistic definition. In fact the strict definition of a method applies only to OO and is a way to manipulate an object — a way to instruct it to perform certain behaviors. In previous chapters you created methods that instructed an object — in most cases a form — to do something. When you create a form in Visual Basic 2008, you are actually defining a new type of Form object.

So, if you need to turn on the TV, you need to find a method that does this, because a method is something you get the object to do. When you invoke the method, the object itself is supposed to understand what to do to satisfy the request. To drive the point home, you don't care what it actually does; you just say, "Switch on." It's up to the TV to switch on relays to deliver power, boot up the circuitry, warm up the electron gun, and all the other things that you don't need to understand!

> *Invoke means the same as call, but is more OO-friendly. It reminds us that we are invoking a method on something, rather than just calling a chunk of code.*

On the other hand, if you need to change the channel, you might set the channel property. If you want to tune into Channel 10, you set the channel property to the value 10. Again, the object is responsible for reacting to the request, and you don't care about the technical hoops it has to go through to do that.

Events

In Visual Basic 2008 you listen for events to determine when something has happened to a control on a form. You can consider an event as something that an object does. In effect, someone using an object can listen to events, like a Click event on a button or a PowerOn event on a TV. When the event is received, the developer can take some action. In OO terms, there is the SwitchOn method that gets invoked on the

TV object; when the TV has warmed up (some old TVs take ages to warm up), it raises a `PowerOn` event. You could then respond to this event by adjusting the volume to the required level.

An event might also be used when the performer of an action is not the only entity interested in the action taking place. For example, when you have the TV on, you might go and get a drink during a commercial break. However, while you're in the kitchen, you keep your ears open for when the program starts again. Effectively you are listening for a `ProgramResume` event. You do not cause the program to resume, but you do want to know when it does.

Visibility

To build decent objects you have to make them easy for other developers to use. For example, internally it might be really important for your TV object to know what frequency the tuner needs, but does the person using the TV care? More importantly, do you actually want the developer to be able to change this frequency directly? What you're trying to do is make the object more *abstract*.

Some parts of your object will be private, whereas other parts will be public. The public interface is available for others to use. The private parts are what you expect the object itself to use internally. The logic for the object exists in the private parts and may include methods and properties that are important but won't get called from outside the object. For example, a TV object might have methods for `ConnectPower`, `WarmUp`, and so on. These would be private and would all be called from the public `SwitchOn` method. Similarly, while there is a public `Channel` property there will probably be a private `Frequency` property. The TV could not work without knowing the signal frequency it was receiving, but the users are only interested in the channel.

Now that you understand the basics of object orientation, take look at how you can use objects within an application.

You'll notice that some of the code samples you in previous chapters included a line that looked similar to this:

```
lstData.Items.Add(strData)
```

That's a classic example of object orientation! `lstData` is, in fact, an object. `Items` is a property of the `lstData` object. The `Items` property is an object in its own right and has an `Add` method. The period (`.`) tells Visual Basic 2008 that the word to the right is a *member* of the word to the left. So, `Items` is a member of `lstData` and `Add` is a member of `Items`. Members are either properties or methods of an object.

`lstData` is an instance of a class called `System.Windows.Forms.ListBox` (or just `ListBox`). This class is part of the .NET Framework you learned about in Chapter 2.

The `ListBox` class can display a list of items on the form and let a user choose a particular one. Again, here's the concept of encapsulation. You as a user of `ListBox` don't need to know anything about technologies involved in displaying the list or listening for input. You may not have even heard of GDI+, stdin, keyboard drivers, display drivers, or anything else that goes into the complex action of displaying a list on a form, yet you still have the capability to do it.

The `ListBox` is an example of an object that you can see. Users can look at a program running and know that there is a `ListBox` involved. Most objects in OO programming are invisible and represent something in memory.

What Is a Class?

A *class* is the definition of a particular kind of object. The class is made up of the software code needed to store and retrieve the values of the properties, carry out the methods, and undergo the events pertaining to that kind of object. This is effectively the circuitry inside the black box. If you want to build a software object, you have to understand how the internals work. You express those internals with Visual Basic 2008 code. So, when the software developer using your object says, "Turn up the volume," you have to know how to instruct the amplifier to increase the output. (As a side note, remember that the amplifier is just another object. You don't necessarily need to know how it works inside. In OO programming, you will often find that one object is made up of other objects with some code to link them — just as a TV is made of standard components and a bit of custom circuitry.)

Each object belonging to a class is an *instance* of the class. So, if you have 50 TV objects, you have 50 instances of the TV class. The action of creating an instance is called *instantiation*. From now on, we will say that you *create classes* but *instantiate objects*. The difference is used to reduce ambiguity. Creating a class is done at design time when you're building your software and involves writing the actual code. Instantiating an object is done at run time, when your program is being used.

A classic analogy is the cookie cutter. You can go out to your workshop and shape a piece of metal in the shape of a Christmas tree. You do this once and put the cutter in a drawer in your kitchen. Whenever you need to create Christmas tree cookies, you roll some dough (the computer's memory) and stamp out however many you need. In effect you're instantiating cookies. You can reuse the cutter later to create more cookies, each the same shape as the ones before.

When you've instantiated the objects, you can manipulate each object's properties defined for the class, and you can invoke the methods defined for the class on the object. For example, suppose you build a class once at design time that represents a television. You can instantiate the class twice to make two objects from that class — say, one to represent the TV in the living room and one to represent the TV in the bedroom. Because both instances of the object share the same class, both instances have the same properties and methods. To turn on either TV you invoke the `SwitchOn` method on it. To change the channel you set its `Channel` property, and so on.

Building Classes

You have already started building classes, particularly in Chapters 5 and 10. In general, when you design an algorithm, you will discover certain objects described. You need to abstract these real-world objects into a software representation. Here's an example:

1. Select a list of 10 customers from the database.
2. Go through each customer and prepare a bill for each.
3. When each bill has been prepared, print it.

For a pure object-oriented application (and with .NET you end up using objects to represent everything) every real-world object need a software object. For example:

❑ **Customer:** An object that represents a customer

❑ **Bill:** An object that represents a bill that is produced

❑ **Printer:** An object that represents a hardware printer that can be used to print the bill

When you write software in Visual Basic 2008, you are given a vast set of classes called the Microsoft .NET Framework Classes. These classes describe virtually everything about the computing environment that you're trying to write software for. Writing object-oriented software for .NET is simply an issue of using objects that fit your needs and creating new objects if required. Typically, while building an application, some of the classes you need are included in the .NET Framework, whereas you have to build others yourself.

For example, some objects in the .NET Framework provide printing functionality and database access functionality. As your algorithm calls for both kinds of functionality, you don't need to write your own. If you need to print something, you create an object that understands how to print, tell it what you want to print, and then tell it to print it. Again, this is encapsulation — you don't care how to turn your document into PostScript commands and send it down the wire to the printer; the object knows how to do this for itself. In this example, there are classes that deal with printing that you can use to print bills, although there's no specific `Printer` object.

In some cases, objects that you need to represent do not exist in the .NET Framework. In this example, you need a `Customer` object and a `Bill` object.

Reusability

Perhaps the hardest aspect of object-oriented programming is to understand how to divide responsibility for the work. One of the most beautiful aspects of object orientation is *code reuse*. Imagine that your company needs several different applications: one to display customer bills, one to register a new customer, and one to track customer complaints. In each of those applications, you need to have a `Customer` object.

To simplify the issue, those three projects are not going to be undertaken simultaneously. You start by doing the first; when finished, you move on to the second; when you've finished that, you move on to the third. Do you want to build a new `Customer` class for each project, or do you want to build the class once and reuse it in each of the other two projects?

Reuse is typically regarded as something that's universally good, although there is a tradeoff. Ideally, if you build a `Customer` class for one project, and another project you're working on calls for another `Customer` class, you should use the same one. However, it may well be that you can't just plug the class into another project for some reason. We say "for some reason" because there are no hard and fast rules when it comes to class design and reuse. It may also be easier or more cost-effective to build simple classes for each project rather than try to create one complex object that does everything. This might sound like it requires a degree in clairvoyance, but luckily it comes with experience! As you develop more and more applications, you'll gain a better understanding of how to design great, reusable objects.

Each object should be responsible for activities involving itself and no more. We've discussed only two objects — Bill and Customer — so you'll look only at those.

The activity of printing a bill (say, for telephone charges) follows this algorithm:

❑   For a given customer, find the call details for the last period.

❑   Go through each call and calculate the price of each one.

❑   Aggregate the cost of each call into a total.

❑   Apply tax charges.

❑   Print out the bill, with the customer's name, address, and bill summary on the first page and then the bill details on subsequent pages.

You have only two places where you can code this algorithm: the Bill object or the Customer object. Which one do you choose?

The calls made are really a property of the Customer. Basically, you are using these details to create a bill. Most of the functionality would be placed in the Bill object. A Customer is responsible for representing a customer, not representing a bill. When you create a Bill object, you would associate it with a particular customer by using a Cust property, like this:

```
myBill.Cust = myCustomer
```

The Bill object would then know that it was a bill for a given customer (represented by the myCustomer object) and could use the customer's details when creating a bill. You might want to change some other properties of the Bill, such as where it will be mailed to, whether it should contain a warning because it is overdue, and so on. Finally, the Bill would have a Print method:

```
myBill.Print()
```

The Bill object would then *use* a Printer object in order to print the bill. The Bill object would be said to be the user or *consumer* of the Printer object. It would even be said to consume the Printer object, even though (at least you hope) the printer is not used up or destroyed in printing the bill.

Designing an Object

Contrary to what we've said so far, in this first project you're not going to define an algorithm and then build objects to support it. For this rather academic example, we're going to walk you through some of the features of a typical object — in this case, a car.

There are certain facts you might want to know about the object:

❑   *What it looks like:* A car includes things like make, model, color, number of doors, and so on. These aspects of the car rarely change during the object's lifetime.

❑   *Its capabilities:* Horsepower, engine size, cylinder configuration, and so on.

❏ *What it's doing:* Whether it's stationary, moving forward or backwards, and its speed and direction.

❏ *Where it is:* The Global Positioning System (GPS) coordinates of its current position. This is effectively its position relative to another object (the planet Earth). Likewise, controls on forms have coordinates that describe their location relative to the form (say, in pixels to the right of and below the top left corner).

You might also want to be able to control the object, for example:

❏ Tell it to accelerate.

❏ Tell it to decelerate.

❏ Tell it to turn left.

❏ Tell it to turn right.

❏ Tell it to straighten out of a turn.

❏ Tell it to do a three-point-turn.

❏ Tell it to stop completely.

There are three concepts of an object that you need to be aware of: identity, state, and behavior. We'll assume that the identity aspect is covered because you know what the class is, so the state and behavior are of interest here.

State

State describes facts about the object now. For example, a car's location and speed are part of its state. When designing objects, you need to think about what aspects of state you need to handle. It might not be useful to know a customer's speed, for example, but you might well want to know that customer's current address.

State tends to be implemented as values inside an object. Some of these values are publicly available through properties, and some are private. Also, some aspects of state might be publicly readable but not changeable. For example, cars have a speedometer that is readable to anybody using the car. But you can't change the car's speed by playing with the speedometer — you need to alter the car's behavior by using the brake or accelerator.

Behavior

While a car might have a read-only Speed property, it would have methods to accelerate and decelerate. When you invoke an object's method, you are telling your object to do something — so behavior is usually associated with methods. Properties can also be associated with behavior. When you set a property to a particular value (such as by changing the setting of a control), you can trigger behavior.

Behavior is implemented as a set of Visual Basic 2008 statements that do something. This will usually involve one or both of the following:

❑ *Changing its own state:* When you invoke the `accelerate` method on a car, it should get faster if it is capable of doing so.

❑ *Somehow affecting the world outside the object:* This could be manipulating other objects in the application, displaying something to the user, saving something to a disk, or printing a document.

In this chapter, you won't build all of the properties and methods discussed. Instead, you'll build a handful of the more interesting ones. You begin in the following Try It Out by creating your new project and the `Car` class.

Try It Out   **Creating a New Project and the Car Class**

1.   Start Visual Basic 2008 and select File ⇨ New Project from the menu.

2.   When the New Project dialog box appears, select the Console Application template and enter the name of the project as **Objects**. Click OK to create the project.

3.   You now need to create a new class. This is done through the Solution Explorer, so right-click the Objects project and select Add ⇨ Class. This prompts you for a new class name, so enter **Car.vb** as the class name and click Add. The new class has been added to the Solution Explorer and the editor now shows the code listing for it, albeit empty.

Storing State

State describes what the object understands about itself, so if you give a car object some state, for example, "You are blue," you're giving the car object a fact: "The car I represent is blue."

How do you actually manage state in your classes? State is typically held in variables, and you define those variables within the class. You see how to do this in a moment.

Usually, the methods and properties you build will either affect or use the state in some way. Imagine you've built a property that changes the color of the car. When you set that property, the variable that's responsible for storing the state is changed to reflect the new value that it has been given. When you retrieve (*get*) that property, the variable responsible for storing the state is read, and the current value is returned to the caller.

In a way, then, properties *are* behaviors. Under the hood, a public property has two methods: a `Get` method and a `Set` method (defined by `Get ... End Get` and `Set ... End Set` blocks of code, as you have already encountered in Chapter 5). A simple `Get` method for the `Color` property contains code to tell the caller what color the car is. A simple `Set` method for the `Color` property sets a value that represents the car's color. In a real application, though, `Color` would probably mean something more than just remembering a value. In a driving game, for example, the `Set` method of the `Color` property would need to make the screen display change the color in which the car is shown on the screen.

When a property has no behavior at all, you can cheat. In the next Try It Out, you create a `Color` property by declaring a `Color` variable and making it public. When a property is implemented like this, it is also called a *field*. Although this can be a useful and very fast technique for adding properties, declaring a field instead of the `Property`, `Get`, and `Set` blocks is not actually recommended, but for this small example it is just fine.

Try It Out   Creating an Object and Adding a Color Property

1. In the `Car` class, add this code:

```
Public Color As String
```

2. That's it! However, you do need a way of consuming the class so that you can see it working. Open `Module1.vb` and add this code:

```
Sub Main()
        'Create a new car object
        Dim objCar As New Car

        'Set the Color property to Red
        objCar.Color = "Red"

        'Show what the value of the property is
        Console.WriteLine("My car is this color:")
        Console.WriteLine(objCar.Color)

        'Wait for input from the user
        Console.ReadLine()
End Sub
```

3. Save your project by clicking the Save All button on the toolbar.

4. Now run the project. A new window similar to Figure 11-1 appears.

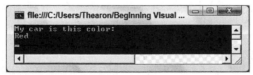

Figure 11-1

5. Press Enter to end the program.

How It Works

Defining the field is easy. The following line of code:

```
Public Color As String
```

tells the class that you want to create a variable called `Color` and you want the field to hold a string of text characters. The use of the `Public` keyword when you declare the `Color` variable tells the class that the variable is accessible to developers using the `Car` class, not only from within the class itself.

> *Variables defined in the location between the `Public Class` and `End Class` lines, but outside of any functions, are known as* member variables *in the class itself and as* fields *to consumers of the class.*

Using the object is simple, and you do this from within `Module1.vb`. This process actually takes two steps. First, you have to declare a variable to refer to an object for the class; second, you instantiate the object. The following line of code creates an object variable called `objCar` and tells it that it's going to hold exclusively any objects created using the `Car` class:

```
Dim objCar As Car
```

When you define the variable, it doesn't yet have an object instance associated with it; you are simply identifying the type of object. It's a bit like telling the computer to give you a hook that you can hang a `Car` object on, and call the hook `objCar`. You haven't hung anything on it yet — to do that you have to create an instance of the class. This is done using the `New` keyword:

```
Set objCar = New Car
```

But Visual Basic 2008 allows you to combine both steps into one line of code:

```
'Create a new car object
Dim objCar As New Car
```

So, what you're saying here is: "let `objCar` refer to a newly created object instantiated from the class `Car`." In other words, "create a new car and hang it on the hook called `objCar`." You now have a `Car` object and can refer to it with the name `objCar`.

> *Note that in OO programming, the same object can be hanging on several different hooks at the same time and, therefore, have several different names. This might seem confusing, but in most cases it is a really intuitive way to work. Imagine how cool it would be if your keys could be on several hooks at the same time — they'd be so much easier to find!*

After you have an object instance, you can set its properties and call its methods. Here is how you set the `Color` property:

```
'Set the Color property to Red
objCar.Color = "Red"
```

After the property has been set, it can be retrieved as many times as you want or its value changed at a later point. Here, retrieval is illustrated by passing the `Color` property to the `WriteLine` method on the `Console` class:

```
'Show what the value of the property is
Console.WriteLine("My car is this color:")
Console.WriteLine(objCar.Color)
```

The `Console.ReadLine` line means that the program does not continue until you press Enter. Basically the console window is waiting for input from you.

```
'Wait for input from the user
Console.ReadLine()
```

Console applications are a good way to test in-memory objects because you don't need to worry about setting up a user interface. You can just display lines of text whenever you want. The objects you build work just as well in a Windows application, though.

Even though this is not really a property from the point of view of a developer using the class, it works just like one. In fact, real properties are methods that look like variables to users of the class. Whether you use a method or a property really depends on what the users of your class find easier. You'll start to see this in the next section.

Real Properties

Now that you've seen how to cheat, let's see how to do things properly. The property you saw can be set to pretty much anything. As long as it's a string, it will be accepted. Also, setting the property doesn't do anything except change the object's internal state. Often you want to control what values a property can be set to; for example, you might have a list of valid colors that a car can be. You might also want to associate a change to a property with a particular action. For example, when you change a channel on the TV, you want it to do a bit more than just change its mind about what channel it's displaying. You want the TV to show a different picture! Just changing the value of a variable won't help here.

Another reason to use real properties is that you want to prevent the user of the class from directly changing the value. This is called a *read-only property*. The car's speed is a good example of how a class that models a real-world object should behave like that real-world object. If you are going 60 mph, you cannot simply change the speed to a value you prefer. You can read the speed of a car from the speedometer, but you cannot change (write) the speed of the car by physically moving the needle around the dial with your finger. You have to control the car in another fashion, which you do by stepping on the gas pedal to accelerate or on the brake pedal to decelerate. To model this feature in the `Car` class, you use methods (`Accelerate`, `Decelerate`) that affect the speed and keep a read-only property around called `Speed` that will report on the current speed of the vehicle.

You'll still need to keep the speed around in a member variable, but what you need is a member variable that can be seen or manipulated only by the class itself. You accomplish this by using the `Private` keyword:

```
Private intSpeed As Integer
```

The `intSpeed` variable is marked as `Private` and can, therefore, be accessed only by functions defined inside the class itself. Users of `Car` will not even be aware of its presence.

Now you'll see how you can build a property that will give the user of the object read-only access to the car's speed.

Try It Out   Adding a Speed Property

1. To define a private variable, use the `Private` instead of the `Public` keyword. Add this statement to the `Car` class:

```
Public Color As String
Private intSpeed As Integer
```

2. To report the speed, you need to build a read-only property. Add this code to your `Car` class:

```
'Speed - read-only property to return the speed
Public ReadOnly Property Speed() As Integer
    Get
        Return intSpeed
    End Get
End Property
```

3. Now, you build a method called `Accelerate` that adjusts the speed of the car by however many miles-per-hour you give it. Add this code after the `Speed` property:

```
'Accelerate - add mph to the speed
Public Sub Accelerate(ByVal accelerateBy As Integer)
    'Adjust the speed
    intSpeed += accelerateBy
End Sub
```

4. To test the object, you need to make some changes to the `Main` procedure in Module1. Open the file and modify the code as shown:

```
Sub Main()
    'Create a new car object
    Dim objCar As New Car

    'Report the speed
    Console.WriteLine("The car's speed is:")
    Console.WriteLine(objCar.Speed)

    'Accelerate
    objCar.Accelerate(5)

    'Report the new speed
    Console.WriteLine("The car's speed is now:")
    Console.WriteLine(objCar.Speed)

    'Wait for input from the user
    Console.ReadLine()
End Sub
```

5. Now run the project. A new window similar to Figure 11-2 appears.

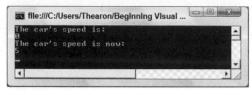

Figure 11-2

How It Works

The first thing you do is define a private member variable called `intSpeed` in the `Car` class:

```
Private intSpeed As Integer
```

By default, when the object is created, `intSpeed` has a value of zero because this is the default value for the `Integer` data type.

You then define a read-only property that returns the current speed:

```
'Speed - readonly property to return the speed
Public ReadOnly Property Speed() As Integer
    Get
        Return intSpeed
    End Get
End Property
```

When you define properties, you can set them to be read-only (through the `ReadOnly` keyword), write-only (through the `WriteOnly` keyword), or both readable and writable by using neither. Reading a property is known as *getting* the value, whereas writing to a property is known as *setting* the value. The code between `Get` and `End Get` is executed when the property is read. In this case, the only thing you're doing is returning the value currently stored in `intSpeed`.

You also created a method called `Accelerate`. This method doesn't have to return a value, so you use the `Sub` keyword:

```
'Accelerate - add mph to the speed
Public Sub Accelerate(ByVal accelerateBy As Integer)
    'Adjust the speed
    intSpeed += accelerateBy
End Sub
```

The method takes a single parameter called `accelerateBy`, which you use to tell the method how much to increase the speed by. The only action of the method is to adjust the internal member `intSpeed`. In real life, the pressure on the accelerator pedal, along with factors such as wind speed and road surface, affect the speed. The speed is an outcome of several factors — not something you can just change. You need some complex code to simulate this. Here you are just keeping things simple and incrementing the `intSpeed` variable with the value passed to the method.

Accelerating a car is another example of encapsulation. To accelerate the car in a real-world implementation you need an actuator of some kind to open the throttle further until the required speed is reached. As consumers of the object, you don't care how this is done. All you care about is how to tell the car to accelerate.

Consuming this new functionality is simple. First, you create the variable and instantiate the object as you did in the previous exercise:

```
'Create a new car object
Dim objCar As New Car
```

Next, you write the current speed:

```
'Report the speed
Console.WriteLine("The car's speed is:")
Console.WriteLine(objCar.Speed)
```

Notice how you're using the read-only Speed property to get the current speed of the car. When the object is first created, the internal _speed member will be set at 0.

Now you call Accelerate and use it to increase the speed of the car:

```
'Accelerate
objCar.Accelerate(5)
```

Finally, you write out the new speed:

```
'Report the new speed
Console.WriteLine("The car's speed is now:")
Console.WriteLine(objCar.Speed)
```

Read/Write Properties

Why would you need to use the Property keyword to define properties that are both readable and writable if you can achieve the same effect with a line like this?

```
Public Color As String
```

If you build the property manually using the Property keyword, you can write code that is executed whenever the property is set or gotten. This is extremely powerful!

For example, the Property keyword allows you to provide validation for new values. Imagine you had a property called NumberOfDoors. You wouldn't want this to be set to nonsense values like 0 or 23453. Rather, you would have some possible range. For modern cars this is going to range from 2 to 5.

> This is an important consideration for developers building objects. It's imperative that you make life as easy as possible for a developer to consume your object. Dealing with problems like making sure a car can't have 10 million doors is an important aspect of object design.

Likewise, you might not have the information to return to the consumer of your object when you are asked to return the property; you might have to retrieve the value from somewhere, or otherwise calculate it. You might have a property that describes the total number of orders a customer has ever made or the total number of chew toys a dog has destroyed in his life. If you build this as a property, you can intercept the instruction to get the value and find the actual value you require on demand from some other data store, such as a database or a web service. You'll see this in later chapters.

For now, let's deal with the number-of-doors problem.

Try It Out   Adding a NumberOfDoors Property

1. The first thing you need to do is build a private member that will hold the number of doors. You're going to define this member as having a default of 5. Add this code in the Car class as highlighted here:

```
Public Color As String
Private intSpeed As Integer
Private intNumberOfDoors As Integer = 5
```

2. Now you can build a property that gets and sets the number of doors, provided the number of doors is always between 2 and 5. Add this code to your Car class directly beneath the Accelerate method:

```
'NumberOfDoors - get/set the number of doors
Public Property NumberOfDoors() As Integer
    'Called when the property is read
    Get
        Return intNumberOfDoors
    End Get
    'Called when the property is set
    Set(ByVal value As Integer)
        'Is the new value between two and five
        If value >= 2 And value <= 5 Then
            intNumberOfDoors = value
        End If
    End Set
End Property
```

In this chapter, you're going to ignore the problem of telling the developer if the user has provided an invalid value for a property. Ideally, whenever this happens, you need to throw an exception. The developer will be able to detect this exception and behave accordingly. (For example, if the user typed the number of doors as 9999 into a text box, the program could display a message box telling the user that they have provided an invalid value for the number of doors, since no car has that many doors.) You learned about exception handling in Chapter 10.

3. To test the property, you need to change the Main procedure in Module1 by modifying the code as indicated here:

```
Sub Main()
    'Create a new car object
    Dim objCar As New Car

    'Report the number of doors
    Console.WriteLine("The number of doors is:")
```

```
        Console.WriteLine(objCar.NumberOfDoors)

        'Try changing the number of doors to 1000
        objCar.NumberOfDoors = 1000

        'Report the number of doors
        Console.WriteLine("The number of doors is:")
        Console.WriteLine(objCar.NumberOfDoors)

        'Now try changing the number of doors to 2
        objCar.NumberOfDoors = 2

        'Report the number of doors
        Console.WriteLine("The number of doors is:")
        Console.WriteLine(objCar.NumberOfDoors)

        'Wait for input from the user
        Console.ReadLine()
    End Sub
```

Try running the project. You should see a screen like the one in Figure 11-3.

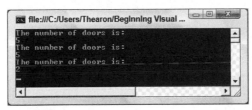

Figure 11-3

How It Works

First you define a private member variable called intNumberOfDoors. You also assign the default value of 5 to this variable.

```
Private intNumberOfDoors As Integer = 5
```

The motivation behind setting a value at this point is simple: You want intNumberOfDoors to always be between 2 and 5. When the object is created, the intNumberOfDoors will be assigned a value of 5. Without this assignment, intNumberOfDoors would have a default value of 0. This would be inconsistent with the understanding that the number of doors must always be between 2 and 5, so you guard against it.

Next comes the property itself. The Get portion is simple — just return the value held in intNumberOfDoors — but the Set portion involves a check to ensure that the new value is valid. The new value is passed in through a parameter called value:

```
        'NumberOfDoors - get/set the number of doors
        Public Property NumberOfDoors() As Integer
            'Called when the property is read
            Get
                Return intNumberOfDoors
            End Get
```

```
            'Called when the property is set
            Set(ByVal value As Integer)
                'Is the new value between two and five
                If value >= 2 And value <= 5 Then
                    intNumberOfDoors = value
                End If
            End Set
        End Property
```

The test code you add to Module1 is not very complex. You simply display the initial value of intNumberOfDoors and then try to change it to 1000. The validation code in the NumberOfDoors property won't change the intNumberOfDoors member variable if an inconsistent number is used, so when you report the number of doors again, you find it hasn't changed from 5. Lastly, you try setting it to 2, which is a valid value, and this time, when you report the number of doors, you get an output of 2.

Even though read–write properties and public variables seem to work the same way, they are very different. When your Visual Basic 2008 code is compiled, the compiled code treats property calls as a call to a method. Always using properties instead of public variables makes your objects more flexible and extendable. Of course, using public variables is easier and quicker. You need to decide what is most important in each case.

The IsMoving Method

When building objects you should always have the following question in the back of your mind. "How can I make this object easier to use?" For example, if the consumer needs to know whether the car is moving, what would be the easiest way to determine this?

One way would be to look at the Speed property. If this is zero, it can be assumed that the car has stopped. (On most cars the speed is not reported when the car is moving in reverse. So assume, for now, that you have only forward gears!) However, relying on the developers using the object to understand this relies on their having an understanding of whatever is being modeled. Common sense tells us that an object with a speed of "zero mph" is stationary, but should you assume anyone consuming the object shares your idea of common sense?

Instead, it's good practice to create methods that deal with these eventualities. One way you can solve this problem is by creating an IsMoving method.

Try It Out   **Adding an IsMoving Method**

1.   All the IsMoving method needs in order to work is a simple test to look at the speed of the car and make a True or False determination as to whether it's moving. Add this code to the Car class after the NumberOfDoors property:

```
    'IsMoving - is the car moving?
    Public Function IsMoving() As Boolean
        'Is the car's speed zero?
        If Speed = 0 Then
            Return False
```

```
        Else
            Return True
        End If
    End Function
```

2. To test this method, make these changes to the `Main` procedure in Module1 with this new code as indicated:

```
Sub Main()
    'Create a new car object
    Dim objCar As New Car

    'Accelerate the car to 25mph
    objCar.Accelerate(25)

    'Report whether or not the car is moving
    If objCar.IsMoving = True Then
        Console.WriteLine("The car is moving.")
    Else
        Console.WriteLine("The car is stopped.")
    End If

    'Wait for input from the user
    Console.ReadLine()
End Sub
```

3. Now try running the project. A new window similar to Figure 11-4 appears.

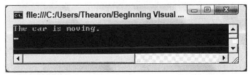

Figure 11-4

How It Works

You created a simple method that examines the value of the Speed property and returns True if the speed is not zero, False if it is.

```
'IsMoving - is the car moving?
Public Function IsMoving() As Boolean
    'Is the car's speed zero?
    If Speed = 0 Then
        Return False
    Else
        Return True
    End If
End Function
```

Although this method is simple, it removes the conceptual leap required on the part of the consumer to understand whether the object is moving. There's no confusion as to whether the car is moving based on interpreting the value of one or more properties; one simple method returns a definitive answer.

Of course, before you go off building hundreds of methods for every eventuality, remember that ironically, the more methods and properties an object has, the harder it is to understand. Take care while designing the object and try to strike the right balance between too few and too many methods and properties.

You may be wondering why you used a method here when this is actually a property. All you are doing is reporting the object's state without affecting its behavior. There is no reason for not using a property here. However, using a method does remind users of the object that this value is calculated and is not a simple report of an internal variable. It also adds a bit of variety to your examples and reminds you how easy it is to add a method!

Constructors

One of the most important aspects of object design is the concept of a *constructor*. As mentioned in Chapter 10, this is a piece of initialization code that runs whenever an object is instantiated. It's extremely useful when you need the object to be set up in a particular way before you use it. For example, it can be used to set up default values, just as you did for the number of doors earlier.

In this Try It Out, you take a look at a simple constructor.

Try It Out   Creating a Constructor

1. For the sake of this discussion, you're going to remove the default value of 5 from the intNumberOfDoors member. Make this change to the Car class:

```
Public Color As String
Private intSpeed As Integer
Private intNumberOfDoors As Integer
```

2. Add this method, which forms the constructor. Any code within this method is executed whenever an object is created from the Car class:

```
'Constructor
Public Sub New()
    'Set the default values
    Color = "White"
    intSpeed = 0
    intNumberOfDoors = 5
End Sub
```

Setting the intSpeed to 0 here is actually redundant, as it will have that value already (since all Integer variables are set to 0 when they are declared), but it's included to make the example complete.

3. To test the action of the constructor, you create a separate procedure that displays the car's details. Add the `DisplayCarDetails` procedure in Module1:

```
'DisplayCarDetails - procedure that displays a car's details
Sub DisplayCarDetails(ByVal theCar As Car)
    'Display the details of the car
    Console.WriteLine("Color: " & theCar.Color)
    Console.WriteLine("Number of doors: " & theCar.NumberOfDoors)
    Console.WriteLine("Current speed: " & theCar.Speed)
End Sub
```

4. Modify the `Main` procedure in Module1 to call the `DisplayCarDetails` procedure:

```
Sub Main()
    'Create a new car object
    Dim objCar As New Car

    'Display the details of the car
    DisplayCarDetails(objCar)

    'Wait for input from the user
    Console.ReadLine()
End Sub
```

5. Try running the project, and you should see output similar to Figure 11-5.

Figure 11-5

How It Works

The code in the constructor is called whenever an object is created. This is where you take an opportunity to set the values for the members:

```
'Constructor
Public Sub New()
    'Set the default values
    Color = "White"
    intSpeed = 0
    intNumberOfDoors = 5
End Sub
```

You see the results of the changes made to the properties when you run the project and see the details of the car displayed in the window. A constructor must always be a subroutine (defined with the `Sub` keyword) and must always be called `New`. This provides consistency in the .NET Framework for all class constructors and the framework will always execute this procedure when a class is instantiated.

When you test the object, you use a separate function called `DisplayCarDetails` in Module1. This is useful when you need to see the details of more than one `Car` object or want to see the details of the `Car` object multiple times in your code.

Inheritance

Although the subject of *inheritance* is quite an advanced object-oriented programming topic, it is really useful. In fact, the .NET Framework itself makes heavy use of it, and you have already created classes that inherit from another class — every Windows form that you write is a new class inherited from a simple blank form (the starting point when you create a form).

Inheritance is used to create objects that have everything another object has, but also some of their own bits and pieces. It's used to extend the functionality of objects, but it doesn't require you to have an understanding of how the internals of the object work. This is in line with your quest of building and using objects without having to understand how the original programmers put them together.

Inheritance enables you to, in effect, take another class and bolt on your own functionality, either by adding new methods and properties or by replacing existing methods and properties. For example, you can move from a general car class to more specific variations — for example, sports car, SUV, van, and so on.

So, if you wanted to model a sports car, it is likely that you would want to have a default number of doors as 2 instead of 5, and you might also like to have properties and methods that help you understand the performance of the car, such as `Weight` and `PowerToWeightRatio`, as shown in Figure 11-6.

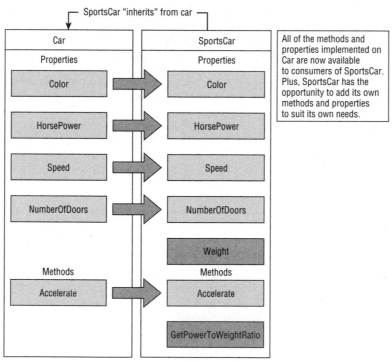

Figure 11-6

One thing that you need to understand about inheritance is the way that access to public and private members is controlled. Any public member, such as Color, is accessible to inheriting classes. However, private members such as intSpeed are not. This means that if SportsCar has to change the speed of the car, it has to do so through the properties and methods provided in the Car class itself.

In other commonly encountered terminology, the inheriting class is called a derived class, *and the class it inherits from is its* base class. Car *is the base class from which* SportsCar *is derived. The terms* subclass *and* superclass *are also used.* SportsCar *is a subclass of* Car; Car *is the superclass of* SportsCar. *The sub and super prefixes mean the same as they do in speaking of subsets and supersets in mathematics.*

Adding New Methods and Properties

To illustrate inheritance, in the next Try It Out you create a new class called SportsCar, which inherits from Car and enables you to see the power-to-weight ratio of your sports car.

Try It Out   Inheriting from Car

1. For this demonstration, you need to add an additional public variable to the Car class that represents the horsepower of the car. Of course, if you want to make it really robust, you would use a property and ensure a sensible range of values. But here, simplicity and speed win out. Open the Car class and add this line of code as indicated:

```
Public Color As String
Public HorsePower As Integer

Private intSpeed As Integer
Private intNumberOfDoors As Integer
```

2. Create a new class in the usual way by right-clicking the Objects project in the Solution Explorer and selecting Add ⇨ Class. Enter the name of the class as **SportsCar.vb** and click Add.

3. To tell SportsCar that it inherits from Car, you need to use the Inherits keyword. Add this code to SportsCar:

```
Public Class SportsCar
    Inherits Car
End Class
```

4. At this point, SportsCar has all the methods and properties that Car has. What you want to do now is add a new public variable called Weight to the SportsCar class:

```
Public Weight As Integer
```

5. To test the new class you need to add a new procedure to Module1. Add the following procedure:

```
'DisplaySportsCarDetails - procedure that displays a sports car's details
Sub DisplaySportsCarDetails(ByVal theCar As SportsCar)
    'Display the details of the sports car
    Console.WriteLine()
    Console.WriteLine("Sports Car Horsepower: " & theCar.HorsePower)
    Console.WriteLine("Sports Car Weight: " & theCar.Weight)
End Sub
```

6. Modify the `Main` procedure in Module1. Pay close attention to the fact that you need to create a `SportsCar` object, not a `Car` object, in order to get at the `Weight` property. Add the new code as indicated:

```
Sub Main()
    'Create a new sports car object
    Dim objCar As New SportsCar

    'Modify the number of doors
    objCar.NumberOfDoors = 2

    'Set the horsepower and weight(kg)
    objCar.HorsePower = 240
    objCar.Weight = 1085

    'Display the details of the car
    DisplayCarDetails(objCar)
    DisplaySportsCarDetails(objCar)

    'Wait for input from the user
    Console.ReadLine()
End Sub
```

7. Try running the project and you'll see an output similar to that shown in Figure 11-7.

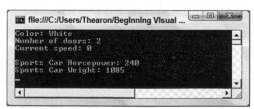

Figure 11-7

How It Works

The directive to make `SportsCar` inherit from `Car` is done with the `Inherits` keyword:

```
Public Class SportsCar
    Inherits Car
```

At this point, the new SportsCar class contains all the methods and properties in the Car class, but it cannot see or modify the private member variables. When you add your new property:

```
Public Weight As Integer
```

you have a new property that's available only when you create instances of SportsCar and not available to you if you are creating plain instances of Car. This is an important point to realize — if you don't create an instance of SportsCar, you'll get a compile error if you try to access the Weight property. Weight isn't, and never has been, a property of Car (see Figure 11-6 for a clarification of this situation).

The new DisplaySportsCarDetails procedure displays the Horsepower property from the Car class and the Weight property from the SportsCar class. Remember that, since the SportsCar class inherits from the Car class, it contains all of the methods and properties in the Car class:

```
'DisplaySportsCarDetails - procedure that displays a sports car's details
Sub DisplaySportsCarDetails(ByVal theCar As SportsCar)
    'Display the details of the sports car
    Console.WriteLine()
    Console.WriteLine("Sports Car Horsepower: " & theCar.HorsePower)
    Console.WriteLine("Sports Car Weight: " & theCar.Weight)
End Sub
```

You instantiate a new SportsCar object in your Main procedure, and this allows you to get and set the value for the Weight property:

```
'Create a new sports car object
Dim objCar As New SportsCar
```

You are able to call the DisplayCarDetails procedure and pass it a SportsCar object, because SportsCar is a subclass of Car — that is, every SportsCar is also a Car. The DisplayCarDetails procedure does not access any of the properties of the SportsCar class, so call this procedure passing it the SportsCar object that you created. You then call the DisplaySportsCarDetails procedure to display the properties of both the Car class and the SportsCar class:

```
'Display the details of the car
DisplayCarDetails(objCar)
DisplaySportsCarDetails(objCar)
```

Adding a GetPowerToWeightRatio Method

A GetPowerToWeightRatio method could be implemented as a read-only property (in which case you would probably call it PowerToWeightRatio instead), but for this discussion you'll add it as a method in the next Try It Out.

Try It Out   **Adding a GetPowerToWeightRatio Method**

1. For this method, all you need to do is divide the horsepower by the weight. Add this code to the `SportsCar` class:

```
'GetPowerToWeightRatio - work out the power to weight
Public Function GetPowerToWeightRatio() As Double
    'Calculate the horsepower
    Return CType(HorsePower, Double) / CType(Weight, Double)
End Function
```

2. To see the results, add the highlighted code to the `DisplaySportsCarDetails` procedure in Module1:

```
'DisplaySportsCarDetails - procedure that displays a sports car's details
Sub DisplaySportsCarDetails(ByVal theCar As SportsCar)
    'Display the details of the sports car
    Console.WriteLine()
    Console.WriteLine("Sports Car Horsepower: " & theCar.HorsePower)
    Console.WriteLine("Sports Car Weight: " & theCar.Weight)
    Console.WriteLine("Power to Weight Ratio: " & theCar.GetPowerToWeightRatio)
End Sub
```

Run the project and you'll see something similar to Figure 11-8.

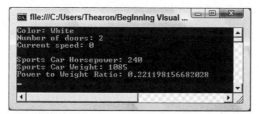

Figure 11-8

How It Works

Again, all you've done is add a new method to the new class called `GetPowerToWeightRatio`. This method then becomes available to anyone working with an instance of `SportsCar` as shown in Figure 11-9.

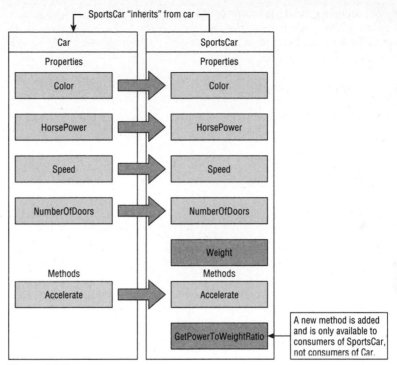

Figure 11-9

The only thing you have to be careful of is that if you divide an integer by an integer you get an integer result, but what you actually want here is a floating-point number. You have to convert the integer `HorsePower` and `Weight` properties to `Double` values in order to see the results:

```
'Calculate the horsepower
Return CType(HorsePower, Double) / CType(Weight, Double)
```

Changing Defaults

In addition to adding new properties and methods, you might want to change the way an existing method or property works from that of the base class. To do this, you need to create your own implementation of the method or property.

Think back to the discussion on constructors. These are methods that are called whenever the object is created and let you get the object into a state where it can be used by a developer. In this constructor you set the default `_numberOfDoors` value to be 5. However, in a sports car, this number should ideally be 2, which is what you set using the `NumberOfDoors` property. But wouldn't it be nice to have this automatically done in the constructor of the `SportsCar` class?

If you are creating a derived class want to replace a method or property existing in the base class with your own, the process is called *overriding*. In this next Try It Out, you learn how to override the base class's constructor.

Try It Out   Overriding a Constructor

1. To override the constructor in the base class, all you have to do is create your own constructor in the SportsCar class. Add this code to SportsCar:

```
'Constructor
Public Sub New()
    'Change the default values
    Color = "Green"
    NumberOfDoors = 2
End Sub
```

2. Remove the following code from the Main procedure in Module1.

```
'Modify the number of doors
objCar.NumberOfDoors = 2
```

3. Run your project to test your constructor in the SportsCar class. You should see output similar to Figure 11-10.

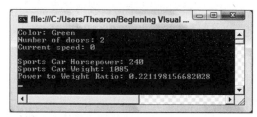

Figure 11-10

How It Works

The new constructor that you added to SportsCar runs after the existing one in Car. The .NET Framework knows that it's supposed to run the code in the constructor of the base class before running the new constructor in the class that inherits from it, so in effect it runs this code first:

```
'Constructor
Public Sub New()
    'Set the default values
    Color = "White"
    intSpeed = 0
    intNumberOfDoors = 5
End Sub
```

And then it runs this code:

```
'Constructor
Public Sub New()
    'Change the default values
    Color = "Green"
    NumberOfDoors = 2
End Sub
```

To summarize what happens:

1. The constructor on the base class `Car` is called.

2. `Color` is set to `White`.

3. `intSpeed` is set to `0`.

4. `intNumberOfDoors` is set to `5`.

5. The constructor on the new class `SportsCar` is called.

6. `Color` is set to `Green`.

7. `NumberOfDoors` is set to `2`.

Because you defined `intNumberOfDoors` as a private member in `Car`, you cannot directly access it from inherited classes, just as you wouldn't be able to access it directly from a consumer of the class. Instead, you rely on being able to set an appropriate value through the `NumberOfDoors` property.

Polymorphism: Scary Word, Simple Concept

Another very common word mentioned when talking about object-oriented programming is *polymorphism*. This is, perhaps the scariest term, but one of the easiest to understand! In fact, you have already done it in the previous example.

Look again at the code for `DisplayCarDetails`:

```
'DisplayCarDetails - procedure that displays a car's details
Sub DisplayCarDetails(ByVal theCar As Car)
    'Display the details of the car
    Console.WriteLine("Color: " & theCar.Color)
    Console.WriteLine("Number of doors: " & theCar.NumberOfDoors)
    Console.WriteLine("Current speed: " & theCar.Speed)
End Sub
```

The first line says that the parameter you want to accept is a `Car` object. But when you call the object, you're actually passing it a `SportsCar` object.

Look at how you create the object and call `DisplayCarDetails`:

```
'Create a new sportscar object
Dim objCar As New SportsCar

'Display the details of the car
DisplayCarDetails(objCar)
```

How can it be that if the function takes a `Car` object, you're allowed to pass it as a `SportsCar` object?

Well, *polymorphism* (which comes from the Greek for *many forms*) means that an object can be treated as if it were a different kind of object, provided common sense prevails. In this case, you can treat a `SportsCar` object like a `Car` object because `SportsCar` inherits from `Car`. This act of inheritance dictates that what a `SportsCar` object can do must include everything that a `Car` object can do; therefore, you can treat the two objects in the same way. If you need to call a method on `Car`, `SportsCar` must also implement the method.

This does not hold true the other way round. Your `DisplaySportsCarDetails` function, defined like this:

```
Sub DisplaySportsCarDetails(ByVal theCar As SportsCar)
```

cannot accept a `Car` object. `Car` is not guaranteed to be able to do everything a `SportsCar` can do, because the extra methods and properties you add to `SportsCar` won't exist on `Car`. `SportsCar` is a more specific type of `Car`.

To summarize, when people talk about polymorphism, this is the action they are referring to — the principle that an object can behave as if it were another object without the developer having to go through too many hoops to make it happen.

Overriding More Methods

Although you've overridden `Car`'s constructor, for completeness you should look at how to override a normal method.

To override a method you need to have the method in the base `Car` class. Because `Accelerate` shouldn't change depending on whether you have a sports car or a normal car, and `IsMoving` was added for ease of use — and hence doesn't really count in this instance as it isn't a behavior of the object — you need to add a new method called `CalculateAccelerationRate`. Assume that on a normal car this is a constant, and on a sports car you change it so that it takes the power-to-weight ratio into consideration. In the following Try It Out, you add another method to override.

Try It Out   **Adding and Overriding Another Method**

1.   Add this method to the Car class:

```
'CalculateAccelerationRate - assume a constant for a normal car
Public Function CalculateAccelerationRate() As Double
    'If we assume a normal car goes from 0-60 in 14 seconds,
    'that's an average rate of 4.2 mph/s
    Return 4.2
End Function
```

2.   To test the method, change the DisplayCarDetails procedure in Module1 to read like this:

```
'DisplayCarDetails - procedure that displays a car's details
Sub DisplayCarDetails(ByVal theCar As Car)
    'Display the details of the car
    Console.WriteLine("Color: " & theCar.Color)
    Console.WriteLine("Number of doors: " & theCar.NumberOfDoors)
    Console.WriteLine("Current speed: " & theCar.Speed)
    Console.WriteLine("Acceleration rate: " & _
        theCar.CalculateAccelerationRate)
End Sub
```

3.   Run the project and you get an output similar to Figure 11-11.

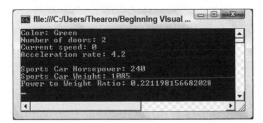

Figure 11-11

You've built a method on Car as normal. This method always returns a value of 4.2 mph/s for the acceleration rate.

Of course, our acceleration calculation algorithm is pure fantasy — no car is going to accelerate at the same rate irrespective of the gear, environment, current speed, and so on.

4.   To override the method, you just have to provide a new implementation in SportsCar. However, there's one thing you need to do first. To override a method you have to mark it as Overridable. To do this, open the Car class again and add the Overridable keyword to the method:

```
Public Overridable Function CalculateAccelerationRate() As Double
```

5. Now, you can create a method with the same name in the `SportsCar` class. To override the method in the base class, you must add the `Overrides` keyword before the method type (`Function` or `Procedure`):

```
'CalculateAccelerationRate - take the power/weight into consideration
Public Overrides Function CalculateAccelerationRate() As Double
    'You'll assume the same 4.2 value, but you'll multiply it
    'by the power/weight ratio
    Return 4.2 * GetPowerToWeightRatio()
End Function
```

You didn't add the `Overrides` *keyword when you overrode the constructor; you didn't need to! Visual Basic 2008 handled this for you.*

6. Run the project; you get an adjusted acceleration rate as shown in Figure 11-12.

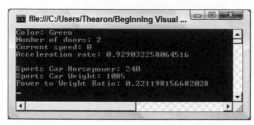

Figure 11-12

How It Works

Overriding the method lets you create your own implementation of an existing method on the object. Again, coming back to this concept of encapsulation, the object consumers don't have to know that anything is different about the object — they just call the method in the same way as they would for a normal `Car` object. This time, however, they get a result rather different than the constant value they always got on the normal `Car` object.

When you override a method, it's quite different from overriding a constructor. When you override a constructor, the original constructor still gets called first. When you override a method, the original method gets called only if you specifically call it from inside the new overriding method using `MyBase.MethodName`. *For example, you could invoke* `MyBase.CalculateAccelerationRate` *from* `SportsCar` *to return a value of* `4.2`.

Inheriting from the Object Class

The final thing to look at, with respect to inheritance, is that if you create a class without using the `Inherits` clause, the class automatically inherits from a class called `Object`. This object provides you with a few methods that you can guarantee are supported by every object you'll ever have. Most of these methods are beyond the scope of this book. However, the two most useful methods at this level are:

❑   `ToString`: This method returns a string representation of the object. You can override this to provide a helpful string value for any object; for example, you might want a person object to return that person's name. If you do not override it, it will return the name of the class.

❑   `GetType`: This method returns a `Type` object that represents the data type of the object.

Remember, you do not have to inherit explicitly from `Object`. This happens automatically.

Objects and Structures

You created a structure in Chapter 5. Like a class, a structure provides a way to group several pieces of information together that all refer to one thing. A structure can even have methods and properties as well as member variables, just as a class can. Here are some of the differences between structures and classes.

In terms of semantics, structures are known as *value types* and classes are known as *reference types*. That is, a variable representing a structure means the actual chunk of computer memory that stores the contents of the structure itself, whereas a variable representing a class instance is actually, as you have seen, a "hook" on which the object hangs.

This explains the difference in instantiation — you don't need to use the New keyword to instantiate a structure before you use it, because it is a value type, just like an integer. You do have to use the New keyword with a form or other complex object because it is a class instance — a reference type.

You have seen that two different object variable hooks can be used to hang up the same object. If you set a property in the object using one of the hooks, its value will be as you set it if you get it using the other hook.

```
Dim objMyCar As New Car     'objMyCar.Color is "White"
Set objThisCar = objMyCar   'same object, different hooks
objThisCar.Color = "Beige"  'now objMyCar.Color is also "Beige"
```

Two different structure variables, on the other hand, always refer to different groups of pieces of information.

```
Dim structMyCustomer As Customer, structThisCustomer As Customer
structMyCustomer.FirstName = "Victor"
structThisCustomer = structMyCustomer   'different structures
structThisCustomer.FirstName = "Victoria"
'structMyCustomer.FirstName is still "Victor"
```

Also, you cannot inherit from a structure — another important consideration when choosing whether to use a class or a structure.

The Framework Classes

Although Chapter 2 included a general discussion of the .NET Framework in general, a more in-depth look at some aspects of the .NET Framework's construction can help you when building objects. In particular, you want to take a look at namespaces and how you can create your own namespaces for use within your objects.

Namespaces

The .NET Framework is actually a vast collection of classes. There are over 4,000 classes in the .NET Framework all told, so how are you as a developer supposed to find the ones that you want?

The .NET Framework is divided into a broad set of namespaces that group similar classes together. This limits the number of classes that you have to hunt through if you're looking for a specific piece of functionality.

These namespaces are also hierarchical in nature, meaning that a namespace can contain other namespaces that further group classes together. Each class must belong to exactly one namespace — it can't belong to multiple namespaces.

Most of the .NET Framework classes are lumped together in a namespace called System, or namespaces that are also contained within System. For example:

❑   System.Data contains classes related to accessing data stored in a database.

❑   System.Xml contains classes used to read and write XML documents.

❑   System.Windows.Forms contains classes for drawing windows on the screen.

❑   System.Net contains classes for communicating over a network.

The fact that namespaces exist means that all of the objects you've been using actually have longer names than the ones used in your software code. Until this point, you've been using a shorthand notation to refer to classes.

In fact, earlier when we said that everything has to be derived from Object, we were stretching it a bit. Because Object is contained within the System namespace, its full name is System.Object. Likewise, Console is actually shorthand for System.Console, meaning that this line:

```
Console.ReadLine()
```

is actually the same as this line:

```
System.Console.ReadLine()
```

This can get a little silly, especially when you end up with object names like System.Web.Services.Description.ServiceDescription.

.NET automatically creates a shorthand version of all the classes within System, so you don't have to type System all the time. Later, you'll see how you can add shorthand references to other namespaces.

There is also the My namespace, which you've already seen in use in some of the earlier chapters. This namespace provides access to the common classes that you're most likely to need in your everyday programming tasks.

Like the System namespace, the My namespace contains a collection of other classes, which in turn contain classes of their own. At the top level, there is the My.Application class, which provides a wealth of information related to the currently executing application such as the application's assembly name, the current path to the application's executable file, and so on. There is also the My.Computer class, which provides detailed information about the computer the application is executing on, such as the amount of free space on the hard drive and the amount of available memory.

The My.Forms class provides access to the various forms in the application and allows you to manipulate those forms easily; for example, you can show, hide, and close them. There is also the My.Resources class, which provides quick and easy access to an application's resource files if it contains them. You can place localized text strings and images in a resource file and use the My.Resources class to gain access to these resources for use in your application.

The My.Settings class provides access to an application's configuration file if it has one and allows you to quickly read the settings needed by your application such as startup settings or database connection information. It also allows you to create, persist, and save user settings for your application. Finally, there is the My.User class, which provides a wealth of information related to the current user of your application, such as login name and the domain name that the user is logged into.

Every class must be in exactly one namespace, but what about the classes we've made so far? Well, this project has a default namespace, and your new classes are placed into this namespace. In the next Try It Out, you discover a current namespace.

Try It Out   Finding the Name of the Current Namespace

1. To see the namespace that you're using, double-click My Project in the Solution Explorer.

2. The Root Namespace entry in the Objects Property Pages window gives the name of the namespace that will be used for new classes, as shown in Figure 11-13.

Figure 11-13

What this means is that your classes have the text `Objects` prefixed to them, like this:

- ❏ The `Car` class is actually called `Objects.Car`.
- ❏ The `SportsCar` class is actually called `Objects.SportsCar`.

As you may have guessed, .NET automatically creates a shorthand version of your classes too, so you can refer to SportsCar instead of having to type Objects.SportsCar.

The motivation behind using namespaces is to make life easier for developers using your classes. Imagine that you give this project to another developer for use and they have already built their own class called `Car`. How do they tell the difference between their class and your class?

Yours will actually be called `Objects.Car`, whereas theirs will have a name like `MyOwnProject.Car` or `YaddaYadda.Car`. Namespaces remove the ambiguity of class names. (Of course, we didn't choose a very good namespace, because it doesn't really describe the classes that the namespace contains — we just chose a namespace that illustrates the purpose of the chapter.)

The Imports Statement

Now you know you don't need to prefix your classes with `Car` or `System` because .NET automatically creates a shorthand version, but how do you do this yourself? The answer is the `Imports` statement!

If you go back to Chapter 10, you might remember this code from the top of the Debug form:

```
Imports System.Collections.Generic

Public Class Debug
```

You may recall this code as well:

```
'Using the List<T> class
Private objCustomerList As New List(Of Customer)
```

You used the `Imports` statement to import the `System.Collections.Generic` namespace into your project. You needed to do this to access to the `List<T>` class. The full name of this class is `System.Collections.Generic.List(Of T)`, but because you added a namespace import declaration, you could just write `List(Of Customer)` instead, substituting the `Customer` class in place of the `T` parameter.

All `Imports` statements must be written at the top of the code file you want to use them in, before any other code including the `Class` declaration.

However, if you import two namespaces that have an identically named class or child namespace, Visual Basic 2008 cannot tell what you are after (like `Car.Car` and `MyOwnProject.Car`). If this happens, Visual Basic 2008 informs you that the name is ambiguous — in which case the quickest and easiest thing to do is to specify the full name that you're after.

Creating Your Own Namespace

Namespaces are defined by wrapping the `Class ... End Class` definition in a `Namespace ... End Namespace` definition. By default, classes created in Visual Basic 2008 are automatically assigned to a root namespace. Visual Studio 2008 automatically names this root namespace based on the project name. In the next Try It Out, you learn to create a namespace.

Try It Out   **Creating a Namespace**

1. Using the Solution Explorer, double-click My Project. The Root Namespace field tells you the name. In this case, the root namespace name is `Objects`.

2. It's often recommended that you build your namespaces such that the full names of the classes you develop are prefixed with the name of your company. For example, if your company were called MyCodeWidgets, ideally you would want the `Car` class called `MyCodeWidgets.Car`. To do this, change the Root Namespace field from Objects to **MyCodeWidgets** (see Figure 11-14). Then click the Save button on the toolbar to have this change applied to your project.

Figure 11-14

3. The Visual Studio 2008 Object Browser is a useful tool that allows you to see what classes you have available in your project. You can find it by selecting View ⇨ Object Browser from the menu bar. When the Object Browser is displayed, the first item is usually All Components. You can click My Solution in the Browse combo box and then navigate to find your `Car` class (see Figure 11-15).

Figure 11-15

4. Note that you can also see the methods, properties, and member variables listed for the class. Pertinent to this discussion, however, is the namespace. This is immediately above the class and is indicated by the icon containing the open and closed brace symbols ({}).

   That's fine, but imagine now that you have two projects both containing a class called `Car`. You need to use namespaces to separate the `Car` class in one project from the `Car` class in another. Open the Code Editor for `Car` and add `Namespace CarPerformance` before the class definition and `End Namespace` after it. (I've omitted the code for brevity.)

```
Namespace CarPerformance
    Public Class Car
    ...
    End Class
End Namespace
```

5. Open the Object Browser again and you'll see a screen like the one in Figure 11-16.

Figure 11-16

6. Since you added the `CarPerformance` namespace to the `Car` class, any code that references the `Car` class needs to import that namespace to be able to access the shorthand methods of the `Car` class.

If you take a look at the `SportsCar` class, you'll notice that Visual Studio 2008 is reporting an error on the `Inherits` statement for `Car`. Hover your mouse over `Car` in your code and then move your mouse into the gray box and then click it.

You can see in Figure 11-17 that you have two options: Import the namespace, or prefix `Car` in the `Inherits` statement with the namespace. You want to choose the first option so click Import MyCodeWidget.CarPerformance. This causes the `Imports` statement to be added to the top of the `SportsCar` class.

Figure 11-17

7. If you click the Error List tab at the bottom of the IDE, you'll notice that it is reporting one remaining error. Double-click the error in the Error List, and the IDE takes you to the line of code in error.

8. You should now be at the `DisplayCarDetails` procedure in Module1 and see that the error is on the `Car` class in the parameter to the procedure. Hover your mouse over `Car` in your code, move your mouse into the gray box, and then click it.

This time you have three options for correcting the error. Choose the second option, Change Car to CarPerformance.Car.

How It Works

What you've done is put `Car` inside a namespace called `CarPerformance`. Because this namespace is contained within `MyCodeWidgets`, the full name of the class becomes `MyCodeWidgets` `.CarPerformance.Car`. If you put the classes of the other (imaginary) project into `CarDiagnostics`, it would be called `MyCodeWidgets.CarDiagnostics.Car`. Note that Module1 still appears directly inside `MyCodeWidgets`. That's because you haven't wrapped the definition for Module1 in a namespace as you did with `Car`. Running your project at this point will produce the same results as before.

Inheritance in the .NET Framework

Inheritance is an advanced object-oriented topic. However, it's really important to include this here because the .NET Framework makes heavy use of inheritance.

One thing to understand about inheritance in .NET is that no class can inherit directly from more than one class. As everything must inherit from `System.Object`, if a class does not specifically state that it inherits from another class, it inherits directly from `System.Object`. The upshot of this is that everything must inherit directly from exactly one class (everything, that is, except `System.Object` itself).

When we say that each class must inherit directly from exactly one class, we mean that each class can mention only one class in its `Inherits` statement. The class that it's inheriting from can also inherit from another class. So, for example, you could create a class called `Porsche` that is inherited from `SportsCar`. You could then say that it *indirectly* inherits from `Car`, but it *directly* inherits from only one class — `SportsCar`. In fact, many classes indirectly inherit from lots of classes — but there is always a direct ancestry, where each class has exactly one parent.

You may want to have some functionality in different classes that are not related to each other by inheritance. You can solve the problem by putting that functionality in an interface that both classes implement, like the `IDisposable` interface you encountered in Chapter 10.

Summary

In this chapter, you looked at how to start building your own objects. You kicked off by learning how to design an object in terms of the properties and methods that it should support and then built a class that represented a car. You then started adding properties and methods to that class and used it from within your application.

Before moving on to the subject of inheritance, you looked at how an object can be given a constructor — a block of code that's executed whenever an object is created. The discussion of inheritance demonstrated a number of key aspects of object-oriented design, including polymorphism and overriding.

To summarize, you should know how to:

❑   Create properties and methods in a class

❑   Provide a constructor for your class to initialize the state of your class

❑   Inherit another class

❑   Override properties and methods in the inheriting class

❑   Create your own namespace for a class

Exercises

1.   Modify your `Car` class to implement the `IDisposable` interface. In the `Main` procedure in Module1, add code to dispose of the `objCar` object after calling the `DisplaySportsCarDetails` procedure.

2.   Modify the code in the `Main` procedure in Module1 to encapsulate the declaration and usage of the `SportsCar` class in a `Using ... End Using` statement. Remember that the `Using ... End Using` statement automatically handles disposal of objects that implement the `IDisposable` interface.

Advanced Object-Oriented Techniques

In Chapter 11, you looked at how you can build your own objects. Prior to that, you had been mostly using objects that already existed in the .NET Framework to build your applications. In this chapter, you'll take a look at some more object-oriented software development techniques.

In the first half of this chapter, you create your own classes. You will create a single-tier application like the others we have discussed so far in this book. The idea of creating two-tier applications, as opposed to single-tier applications, will be introduced in Chapter 14. You then learn about creating your own shared properties and methods. These are very useful when you want a method or property to apply to a class as a whole rather than a specific instance of that class. Finally, you look at memory management in Visual Studio 2008 and what you can do to clean up your objects properly.

In this chapter, you will:

❑   Create classes that can be used by multiple applications

❑   Learn about shared properties and methods

❑   Learn about memory management in the .NET Framework

Building a Favorites Viewer

In the first half of this chapter, you're going to build a simple application that displays all your Internet Explorer favorites and provides a button that you can click to open the URL in Internet Explorer. This application illustrates a key point regarding code reuse and some of the reasons why building code in an object-oriented fashion is so powerful.

Internet Shortcuts and Favorites

You're most likely familiar with the concepts of favorites in Internet Explorer. What you may not know is how Internet Explorer stores those favorites. In fact, the Favorites list is available to all other applications — provided you know where to look.

Windows applications have the option of storing data in separate user folders within a main folder. On earlier Windows systems such as Windows XP this folder is called `C:\Documents and Settings`. On Windows Vista this folder is called `C:\Users`. In Figure 12-1 you can see that my computer has two user folders: `Admin` and `Thearon`.

> *Admin is the default user that was specified on this computer when Windows Vista was set up. This will most likely be different for you. For users who are using Windows XP, Administrator is the default administrator on your computer and a folder called Administrator will be displayed. The Default folder is a special folder that Windows uses whenever a new user logs onto the computer for the first time. The Public folder is where public documents, downloads, music, videos, and pictures are stored that are accessible to all users of that computer.*

Figure 12-1

Depending on how the security of your computer is configured, you may not be able to access the `C:\Users` folder. If you can, open the folder whose name matches the name that you supply when you log on. In the screenshots throughout this chapter, I've used `Thearon`. (If you cannot consistently open the folder, ask your system administrator to help you log in as a different user or give you the appropriate permissions.) If you open this folder, you'll find another group of folders. You'll see something like Figure 12-2 (though it may look different depending upon how your login is configured).

Figure 12-2

You'll notice that in Figure 12-1 some of these folder icons appear as faint icons, whereas others appear as normal folder icons. The computer is configured to show all folders, so you may find that on your machine the faint folders do not appear because these are normally hidden. This doesn't matter, because the one you're specifically looking for — Favorites — will appear whatever your system settings are.

This folder (Thearon on this computer) is where Windows stores a lot of folders that are related to the operation of your computer for your login account, for example:

❑   AppData stores application data related to the applications that you use.

❑   Contacts stores the Windows contacts similar to the contacts stored in Microsoft Outlook.

❑   Desktop stores the folders and links that appear on your desktop.

❑   Documents stores any folders or documents that you create.

❑   Downloads stores any downloaded files from the Web.

❑   Favorites stores a list of Internet Explorer favorites.

It's the Favorites folder that you're interested in here, so open it. You'll see something like Figure 12-3 (obviously, this list will be different on your computer, because you'll have different favorites).

Figure 12-3

You'll notice that the links inside this folder relate to the links that appear in the Favorites menu in your browser. If you double-click one of those links, you'll see that Internet Explorer opens and navigates to the URL that the favorite points to.

You can be fairly confident at this stage that, if you have a folder of links that appear to be favorites, you can create an application that opens this folder and can do something with the links — namely, iterate through all of them, add each of them to a list, find out what URL it belongs to, and provide a way to open that URL from your application. In the example that follows, you're going to ignore the folders and just deal with the favorites that appear in the root Favorites folder.

Your final application will look like Figure 12-4.

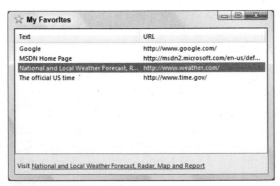

Figure 12-4

Using Classes

So far in this book, you've built basic applications that do something, but most functionality that they provide has been coded into the applications' forms. Here, you're about to build some functionality that can load a list of favorites from a user's computer and provide a way to open Internet Explorer to show the URL. However, you do it in a way that means you can use the *list of favorites* functionality elsewhere.

The best way to build this application is to create a set that includes the following classes:

❑ `WebFavorite`, which represents a single favorite and has member variables such as `Name` and `Url`

❑ `Favorites`, which can scan the favorites list on the user's computer, creating a new `WebFavorite` object for each favorite

❑ `WebFavoriteCollection`, which contains a collection of `WebFavorite` objects

These three classes provide the *back-end* functionality of the application — in other words, all classes that do something but do not present the user with an interface. This isolates the code in the classes and allows you to reuse the code from different parts of the application — *code reuse*. You also need a *front end* to this application, which, in this case, will be a Windows form with a couple of controls on it.

In the following sections, you build your classes and Windows application and come up with the application shown in Figure 12-4. You start by building the Windows Application project in the following Try It Out.

Try It Out   **Creating Favorites Viewer**

1. Open Visual Studio 2008 and create a new Windows Forms Application project called **Favorites Viewer**.

2. Rename Form1.vb in the Solution Explorer to **Viewer.vb** and then modify the form properties as follows:

❑ Set `Font` to **Segoe UI, Regular, 8pt.**

❑ Set `Icon` to `C:\Program Files\Microsoft Visual Studio 9.0\Common7\VS2008 ImageLibrary\1033\VS2008ImageLibrary\Objects\ico_format\WinVista\ Favorites.ico.`

❑ Set `Size` to **470, 300.**

❑ Set `StartPosition` to **CenterScreen.**

❑ Set `Text` to **My Favorites.**

3. Add a ListView control to the form and size it to look similar to Figure 12-5 and set these properties:

❑ Set `Name` to **lvwFavorites.**

❑ Set `Anchor` to **Top, Bottom, Left, Right.**

❏   Set `FullRowSelect` to **True**.

❏   Set `View` to **Details**.

4.   Select the Columns property in the Properties window for the lstFavorites control. Click the ellipsis dots (...) button to display the ColumnHeader Collection Editor dialog box.

5.   Click the Add button. Set these properties on the new column header:

❏   Set `Name` to **hdrName**.

❏   Set `Text` to **Name**.

❏   Set `Width` to **220**.

6.   Click the Add button again to add a second column. Set these properties on the new column header:

❏   Set `Name` to **hdrUrl**.

❏   Set `Text` to **URL**.

❏   Set `Width` to **220**.

7.   Click OK to close the editor.

8.   Add a LinkLabel control to the bottom of the form and set these properties:

❏   Set `Name` to **lnkUrl**.

❏   Set `Anchor` to **Bottom, Left, Right**.

❏   Set `TextAlign` to **MiddleLeft**.

9.   Your completed form should now look similar to the one shown in Figure 12-5.

Figure 12-5

10.   Save your project by clicking the Save All button on the toolbar.

How It Works

All that you've done here is to build the basic shell of the application, the form that will display the results of the processing. You started by modifying some basic properties of the form and then added two controls: a list view and a link label. The ListView control will be used to display the name and URL of each favorite in your Favorites folder. The LinkLabel control will be used to launch a browser with the selected favorite URL in the list.

That's the basics of the form put together. In the next Try It Out, you look at how you can add the back-end classes. In previous chapters, you learned how to add classes to a Visual Studio 2008 project, so you will use this knowledge to create the back end of your application.

Try It Out   **Building WebFavorite**

1. Using the Solution Explorer, right-click Favorites Viewer. Select Add ⇨ Class from the menu to display the Add New Item – Favorites Viewer dialog box. Enter a name of **WebFavorite.vb** and then click the Add button.

2. Add this namespace import declaration to the top of the code listing:

```
Imports System.IO

Public Class WebFavorite
```

3. This class will need to implement the IDisposable interface, so add this Implements statement. When you press Enter, Visual Studio 2008 inserts the members and methods associated with the IDisposable interface:

```
Public Class WebFavorite
    Implements IDisposable
```

4. Now add these two members after the IDisposable interface code inserted by Visual Studio 2008:

```
#End Region

    'Public Members
    Public Name As String
    Public Url As String
```

5. Now add the Load method, which will load the member variables in this class:

```
    Public Sub Load(ByVal fileName As String)
        'Declare variables
        Dim strData As String
        Dim strLines() As String
        Dim strLine As String
        Dim objFileInfo As New FileInfo(fileName)
```

```
    'Set the Name member to the file name minus the extension
    Name = objFileInfo.Name.Substring(0, _
        objFileInfo.Name.Length - objFileInfo.Extension.Length)

    Try
        'Read the entire contents of the file
        strData = My.Computer.FileSystem.ReadAllText(fileName)

        'Split the lines of data in the file
        strLines = strData.Split(New String() {ControlChars.CrLf}, _
            StringSplitOptions.RemoveEmptyEntries)

        'Process each line looking for the URL
        For Each strLine In strLines
            'Does the line of data start with URL=
            If strLine.StartsWith("URL=") Then
                'Yes, set the Url member to the actual URL
                Url = strLine.Substring(4)
                'Exit the For...Next loop
                Exit For
            End If
        Next
    Catch IOExceptionErr As IOException
        'Return the exception to the caller
        Throw New Exception(IOExceptionErr.Message)
    End Try
End Sub
```

How It Works

It will be useful to examine how the WebFavorite class populates itself when the Load method is invoked.

The first thing you do is declare the variables needed by this method. The strData variable is used to receive the entire contents of the favorite's shortcut file. The strLines() variable is used to create an array containing each individual line of data from the strData variable, and the strLine variable is used to iterate through the array of lines. Finally, the objFileInfo object gets the file information from the full path and file name passed to this method.

```
    Public Sub Load(ByVal fileName As String)
        'Declare variables
        Dim strData As String
        Dim strLines() As String
        Dim strLine As String
        Dim objFileInfo As New FileInfo(fileName)
```

Next, the Name member is set to just the file name of the favorite's shortcut file; for example Google. This is the name of the favorite that shows up on the Favorites list in the browser. The fileName parameter passed to this method will contain the complete path to the file, the filename, and the file extension (for example, C:\Users\Thearon\Favorites\Google.url). What you have to do is extract only the file name from the complete path.

You do this by using the `objFileInfo` object, which has been initialized to an instance of the `FileInfo` class with the `fileName` variable passed to it. The `FileInfo` class provides several methods that return the various parts of the complete file path and name, such as only the file name and only the file extension.

You use the `Name` property of the `objFileInfo` object to get just the filename and extension of the file without the path, and you use the `Substring` method of the `Name` property to extract the filename minus the file extension. To supply the parameters to the `Substring` method, you also use the `Length` property of the `Name` property in the `objFileInfo` object to determine how long the file name is and the `Length` property of the `Extension` property to determine how long the file extension is.

So basically what you're saying here is, "Take a substring, starting at the first character, and continue for the complete length of the string minus the length of the `Extension` property." This, in effect, removes the `.url` from the end. Remember that the array of characters that make up a string is zero-based; thus you specify a starting position of 0 for the `SubString` method.

```
'Set the Name member to the file name minus the extension
Name = objFileInfo.Name.Substring(0, _
        objFileInfo.Name.Length - objFileInfo.Extension.Length)
```

You read the entire contents of the file next into the `strData`. Because you are reading from a file, you'll want to encapsulate the logic in a `Try . . . Catch` block to handle any IO exceptions that might occur.

The first thing that you do in this `Try . . . Catch` block is read the entire contents of the file into the `strData` variable. This is done using the `My.Computer` namespace and the `ReadAllText` method of the `FileSystem` class. This method handles all the details of opening the file, reading the entire contents, closing the file, and releasing the resources used to perform these operations.

```
Try
    'Read the entire contents of the file
    strData = My.Computer.FileSystem.ReadAllText(fileName)
```

After the contents of the file have been read, the `strData` variable will contain something similar to the data shown here. This is the data from the `C:\Users\Thearon\Favorites\Google.url` shortcut file.

```
[DEFAULT]
BASEURL=http://www.google.com/
[InternetShortcut]
URL=http://www.google.com/
IDList=
IconFile=http://www.google.com/favicon.ico
IconIndex=1
[{000214A0-0000-0000-c120-000000000046}]
Prop3=19,2
```

Now that you have the entire contents of the favorite's shortcut file in a single string variable, you split the contents of the `strData` variable into separate lines. This is done using the `Split` method of the `String` class, from which the `strData` variable is derived. The `Split` method is an overloaded method, and the version that you are using here accepts an array of strings as the first parameter and the split options as the second parameter.

The data in the strData variable is separated with a carriage return and line feed character combination, and thus you provide a string array containing only one entry, ControlChars.CrLf, as the first parameter of the Split method. The split options parameter of the Split method is a value in the StringSplitOptions enumeration that lets you specify how empty elements are handled. Here you specify the RemoveEmptyEntries constant of that enumeration, to remove any empty entries in the array that are returned.

```
'Split the lines of data in the file
strLines = strData.Split(New String() {ControlChars.CrLf}, _
    StringSplitOptions.RemoveEmptyEntries)
```

Next you need to process each line of data in the strLines array using a For . . . Next loop. You are looking for the line of data that begins with "URL=". Using an If . . . Then statement, you check the strLine variable to see whether it begins with the specified text. The StartsWith method of the String class, the class from which the strLine variable is derived, returns a Boolean value of True if the string that is being tested contains the string that is passed to this method and a value of False if it does not.

If the line of data being tested starts with the text "URL=", then it is the actual URL that you want to save in the Url member of the class. To do so, you use the SubString method to get the URL in the strLine variable minus the beginning text. In order to do this, you pass a starting position of 4 to the SubString method, telling it to start extracting data at position 4, because positions 0 – 3 contain the text "URL=". Once you find the data that you are looking for and set the Url member there's no need to process the rest of the strLines array, so you exit the For . . . Next loop.

```
'Process each line looking for the URL
For Each strLine In strLines
    'Does the line of data start with URL=
    If strLine.StartsWith("URL=") Then
        'Yes, set the Url member to the actual URL
        Url = strLine.Substring(4)
        'Exit the For...Next loop
        Exit For
    End If
Next
```

The Catch block handles any IO exception that might be thrown. Here you want to return the exception to the caller of this method, so you throw a new Exception and pass it the Message property of the IOExceptionErr variable. This gracefully handles any IO exceptions in this class and returns the message of the exception to the caller.

```
    Catch IOExceptionErr As IOException
        'Return the exception to the caller
        Throw New Exception(IOExceptionErr.Message)
    End Try
End Sub
```

Scanning Favorites

So that you can scan the favorites, in the next Try It Out you add a couple of new classes to the project. The first, `WebFavoriteCollection`, holds a collection of `WebFavorite` objects. The second, `Favorites`, physically scans the Favorites folder on the computer, creates new `WebFavorite` objects, and adds them to the collection.

Try It Out   **Scanning Favorites**

1. Using the Solution Explorer, create a new class called **WebFavoriteCollection**. This class will be instantiated to an object that can hold a number of `WebFavorite` objects.

2. Add the highlighted code in your class:

```
Public Class WebFavoriteCollection
    Inherits CollectionBase

    Public Sub Add(ByVal Favorite As WebFavorite)
        'Add item to the collection
        List.Add(Favorite)
    End Sub

    Public Sub Remove(ByVal Index As Integer)
        'Remove item from collection
        If Index >= 0 And Index < Count Then
            List.Remove(Index)
        End If
    End Sub

    Public ReadOnly Property Item(ByVal Index As Integer) As WebFavorite
        Get
            'Get an item from the collection by its index
            Return CType(List.Item(Index), WebFavorite)
        End Get
    End Property
End Class
```

3. Create another new class called **Favorites**. This will be used to scan the Favorites folder and return a `WebFavoriteCollection` containing a `WebFavorite` object for each favorite in the folder. Like the `WebFavorite` class, this class implements the `IDisposable` interface. Enter the following highlighted code and press Enter to add the properties and methods of the `IDisposable` interface to your class:

```
Public Class Favorites
    Implements IDisposable
```

4. Next, add this member below the code for the `IDisposable` interface:

```
'Public member
Public FavoritesCollection As WebFavoriteCollection
```

5. You need a read-only property that can return the path to the user's Favorites folder. Add the following code to the Favorites class:

```
Public ReadOnly Property FavoritesFolder() As String
    Get
        'Return the path to the user's Favorites folder
        Return Environment.GetFolderPath( _
            Environment.SpecialFolder.Favorites)
    End Get
End Property
```

6. Finally, you need a method that's capable of scanning through the Favorites folder looking for files. When it finds one, it creates a WebFavorite object and adds it to the Favorites collection. You provide two versions of this method — one that automatically determines the path of the favorites by using the FavoritesFolder property and one that scans through a given folder. To create this overloaded method, add the following code to the Favorites class:

```
Public Sub ScanFavorites()
    'Scan the Favorites folder
    ScanFavorites(FavoritesFolder)
End Sub

Public Sub ScanFavorites(ByVal folderName As String)
    'If the FavoritesCollection member has not been instantiated
    'then instaniate it
    If FavoritesCollection Is Nothing Then
        FavoritesCollection = New WebFavoriteCollection
    End If

    'Process each file in the Favorites folder
    For Each strFile As String In _
        My.Computer.FileSystem.GetFiles(folderName)

        'If the file has a url extension...
        If strFile.EndsWith(".url", True, Nothing) Then

            Try
                'Create and use a new instance of the
                'WebFavorite class
                Using objWebFavorite As New WebFavorite
                    'Load the file information
                    objWebFavorite.Load(strFile)

                    'Add the object to the collection
                    FavoritesCollection.Add(objWebFavorite)
                End Using
            Catch ExceptionErr As Exception
                'Return the exception to the caller
                Throw New Exception(ExceptionErr.Message)
            End Try

        End If

    Next
End Sub
```

To make all of this work, you need to have the Favorites Viewer project create an instance of a `Favorites` object, scan the favorites, and add each one it finds to the list. You do this in the next Try It Out.

How It Works

There's a lot to take in there, but a good starting point is the `WebFavoriteCollection` class. This illustrates an important best practice when working with lists of objects. As you saw in Chapter 5, you can hold lists of objects in one of two ways: in an array or in a collection.

When building classes that work with lists, the best practice is to use a collection. You should build collections that are also tied into using whatever types you're working with, so in this example you built a `WebFavoriteCollection` class that exclusively holds a collection of `WebFavorite` objects.

You derived `WebFavoriteCollection` from `CollectionBase`. This provides the basic list that the collection will use:

```
Public Class WebFavoriteCollection
    Inherits CollectionBase
```

To fit in with the .NET Framework's way of doing things, you need to define three methods on a collection that you build. The `Add` method adds an item to the collection:

```
Public Sub Add(ByVal Favorite As WebFavorite)
    'Add item to the collection
    List.Add(Favorite)
End Sub
```

The `List` property is a protected member of `CollectionBase` that only code within classes inheriting from `CollectionBase` can access. You access this property to add, remove, and find items in the list. You can see from the `Add` method here that you specified that the item must be a `WebFavorite` object. This is why you're supposed to build collections using this technique — because you can add objects only of type `WebFavorite`; anyone who has hold of a `WebFavoriteCollection` object knows that it will contain objects only of type `WebFavorite`. This makes life much easier for users, because they will not get nasty surprises when they discover it contains something else, and therefore it reduces the chance of errors. The `Remove` method that you built removes an item from the list:

```
Public Sub Remove(ByVal Index As Integer)
    'Remove item from collection
    If Index >= 0 And Index < Count Then
        List.Remove(Index)
    End If
End Sub
```

The `Item` method lets you get an item from the list when given a specific index:

```
Public ReadOnly Property Item(ByVal Index As Integer) As WebFavorite
    Get
        'Get an item from the collection by its index
        Return CType(List.Item(Index), WebFavorite)
    End Get
End Property
```

So how do you populate this collection? Well, in the `Favorites` class you built an overloaded method called `ScanFavorites`. The second version of this method takes a folder and examines it for files that end in `.url`. But before you look at that, you need to look at the `FavoritesFolder` property.

Since the location of the Favorites folder can change depending on the currently logged-in user, you have to ask Windows where this folder actually is. To do this, you use the shared `GetFolderPath` method of the `System.Environment` class:

```
Public ReadOnly Property FavoritesFolder() As String
    Get
        'Return the path to the user's Favorites folder
        Return Environment.GetFolderPath( _
            Environment.SpecialFolder.Favorites)
    End Get
End Property
```

The `GetFolderPath` method uses one of the constants from the `Environment.SpecialFolder` enumeration. This enumeration provides constants for many different special folders that you are likely to need access to when writing applications.

When the application asks this class to load in the favorites from the Favorites folder, it calls `ScanFavorites`. The first version of this method accepts no parameters. It looks up the location of the user's Favorites folder and passes that to the second version of this overloaded method:

```
Public Sub ScanFavorites()
    'Scan the Favorites folder
    ScanFavorites(FavoritesFolder)
End Sub
```

The first thing that the second version of this overloaded method does is check to ensure that the `FavoritesCollection` member has been instantiated using the `WebFavoriteCollection` class. If it hasn't, it instantiates this member using that class:

```
Public Sub ScanFavorites(ByVal folderName As String)
    'If the FavoritesCollection member has not been instantiated
    'then instaniate it
    If FavoritesCollection Is Nothing Then
        FavoritesCollection = New WebFavoriteCollection
    End If
```

Next, you want to get a list of files in the Favorites folder and process them. You do this by calling the `GetFiles` method in the `FileSystem` class and passing it the path and name of the Favorites folder. This class exists in the `My.Computer` namespace as indicated by the following code.

The `GetFiles` method returns an array of filenames, and you process this array using a `For Each...Next` loop. You declare the variable, `strFile`, inline in the `For Each` loop, as indicated in the following code, and this variable will be set to a file name in the Favorites folder for each iteration of the loop.

```
'Process each file in the Favorites folder
For Each strFile As String In _
    My.Computer.FileSystem.GetFiles(folderName)
```

Within the loop, you first test the file name to see whether it is a Favorites file by checking to see whether it contains a `.url` file extension. The `strFile` variable is derived from the `String` class; thus you can use the `EndsWith` method to determine whether the file name ends with the `.url` file extension.

The `EndsWith` method is an overloaded method, and the version that you are using here accepts three parameters. The first parameter accepts the value to be compared to the end of the string, and here you supply the text `.url`. The next parameter accepts a `Boolean` value indicating whether the `EndsWith` method should ignore the case of the text when making the comparison. You do want to ignore the case when making the comparison, so you pass a value of `True` for this parameter. The final parameter accepts the culture information that will be used when making the comparison. Passing a value of `Nothing` here indicates that you want to use the current culture information defined on the user's computer:

```
'If the file has a url extension...
If strFile.EndsWith(".url", True, Nothing) Then
```

If the file name being processed does contain the `.url` file extension, then you want to load the file information and have it added to the Favorites collection. Since you are using the `WebFavorite` class and this class reads the file, the potential for an exception exists. Therefore, you need to encapsulate the next block of code in a `Try . . . Catch` block to handle any exceptions that might be thrown by the `WebFavorite` class.

The first thing that you do in the `Try` block is use a `Using . . . End Using` block to declare, instantiate, use, and destroy the `WebFavorite` class. Remember that you can use the `Using` statement only with a class that implements the `IDisposable` interface, which is why you added that interface to the `WebFavorite` class.

The first thing that you do in the `Using . . . End Using` block is call the `Load` method on the `objWebFavorite` object, passing it the file name of the favorite's shortcut file. Then you add the `objWebFavorite` to the Favorites collection.

```
Try
    'Create and use a new instanace of the
    'WebFavorite class
    Using objWebFavorite As New WebFavorite
        'Load the file information
        objWebFavorite.Load(strFile)

        'Add the object to the collection
        FavoritesCollection.Add(objWebFavorite)
    End Using
```

The `Catch` block contains the necessary code to handle an exception that might be thrown by the `WebFavorite` class and to return that exception to the caller of this method. This is done by throwing a new `Exception`, passing it the message received in the `ExceptionErr` variable.

```
                    Catch ExceptionErr As Exception
                        'Return the exception to the caller
                        Throw New Exception(ExceptionErr.Message)
                    End Try

                End If

            Next
        End Sub
```

In the following Try It Out, you implement the functionality in your form to use the `Favorites` class to gather all of your Internet Favorites and the `WebFavorite` class to load those shortcuts in the ListView control on your form.

Try It Out   **Creating an Instance of a Favorites Object**

1.   View the code for the Viewer form and select (Viewer Events) in the Class Name combo box and select Load in the Method Name combo box. Add the highlighted code:

```
Private Sub Viewer_Load(ByVal sender As Object, _
    ByVal e As System.EventArgs) Handles Me.Load

        Try
            'Create and use a new instanace of the Favorites class
            Using objFavorites As New Favorites

                'Scan the Favorites folder
                objFavorites.ScanFavorites()

                'Process each objWebFavorite object in the
                'favorites collection
                For Each objWebFavorite As WebFavorite In _
                    objFavorites.FavoritesCollection

                    'Declare a ListViewItem object
                    Dim objListViewItem As New ListViewItem

                    'Set the properties of the ListViewItem object
                    objListViewItem.Text = objWebFavorite.Name
                    objListViewItem.SubItems.Add(objWebFavorite.Url)

                    'Add the ListViewItem object to the ListView
                    lvwFavorites.Items.Add(objListViewItem)
                Next

            End Using
        Catch ExceptionErr As Exception
            'Display the error
            MessageBox.Show(ExceptionErr.Message, "Favorites Viewer", _
                MessageBoxButtons.OK, MessageBoxIcon.Warning)
        End Try
    End Sub
```

2. Run the project and you should see something similar to Figure 12-6.

Figure 12-6

How It Works

Since both the `Favorites` and `WebFavorite` classes can throw an exception, you must handle any exceptions that might be thrown. Therefore, all your code is encapsulated in a `Try . . . Catch` block. You use a `Using . . . End Using` statement to declare, instantiate, and destroy the object created with the `Favorites` class. Regardless of whether this class throws an exception, the `Using` statement destroys the `objFavorites` object that it declares.

```
Private Sub Viewer_Load(ByVal sender As Object, _
    ByVal e As System.EventArgs) Handles Me.Load

    Try
        'Create and use a new instanace of the Favorites class
        Using objFavorites As New Favorites
```

Inside the `Using . . . End Using` block the `objFavorites` object scans the users Favorites folder by calling the `ScanFavorites` method. The effect here is that a new `WebFavoritesCollection` object is created and filled and will be accessible through the `FavoritesCollection` property.

```
        'Scan the Favorites folder
        objFavorites.ScanFavorites()
```

After the `ScanFavorites` method finishes, you take each `WebFavorite` in the `FavoritesCollection` and add it to the ListView control on your form. You do this by first declaring a `ListViewItem` and then setting the `Text` property to the Favorite name. Then you add the URL of the favorite to the `SubItems` collection, and finally you add the `objListViewItem` to the `Items` collection of the ListView control.

```
            'Process each objWebFavorite object in the
            'favorites collection
            For Each objWebFavorite As WebFavorite In _
                objFavorites.FavoritesCollection

                'Declare a ListViewItem object
                Dim objListViewItem As New ListViewItem
```

```
                                'Set the properties of the ListViewItem object
                                objListViewItem.Text = objWebFavorite.Name
                                objListViewItem.SubItems.Add(objWebFavorite.Url)

                                'Add the ListViewItem object to the ListView
                                lvwFavorites.Items.Add(objListViewItem)
                        Next

                End Using
```

You wrap up this code with the Catch block, which handles any exceptions thrown and displays the exception message in a message dialog box.

```
                Catch ExceptionErr As Exception
                        'Display the error
                        MessageBox.Show(ExceptionErr.Message, "Favorites Viewer", _
                                MessageBoxButtons.OK, MessageBoxIcon.Warning)
                End Try
        End Sub
```

That's it! Now you can display a list of the favorites installed on the user's machine. However, you can't actually view favorites, so let's look at that now.

Viewing Favorites

Now that all of your code is in place to retrieve and display a list of favorites, in the next Try It Out you add some code to display the selected favorite in the LinkLabel control on your form and then add some code to the control to process the selected link in Internet Explorer.

Try It Out   Viewing Favorites

1. In the Code Editor for Viewer, click lvwFavorites in the Class Name combo box and the Click event in the Method Name combo box. Add the following highlighted code to the Click event handler:

```
        Private Sub lvwFavorites_Click(ByVal sender As Object, _
            ByVal e As System.EventArgs) Handles lvwFavorites.Click

                'Update the link label control Text property
                lnkUrl.Text = "Visit " & lvwFavorites.SelectedItems.Item(0).Text

                'Clear the default hyperlink
                lnkUrl.Links.Clear()

                'Add the selected hyperlink to the LinkCollection
                lnkUrl.Links.Add(6, lvwFavorites.SelectedItems.Item(0).Text.Length, _
                        lvwFavorites.SelectedItems.Item(0).SubItems(1).Text)

        End Sub
```

2. Next, click lnkUrl in the Class Name combo box and select the `LinkClicked` event in the Method Name combo box. Add the following highlighted code to the `LinkClicked` event:

```
Private Sub lnkUrl_LinkClicked(ByVal sender As Object, _
    ByVal e As System.Windows.Forms.LinkLabelLinkClickedEventArgs) _
    Handles lnkUrl.LinkClicked

    'Process the selected link
    Process.Start(e.Link.LinkData)

End Sub
```

3. Run the project. You should now see that when a URL is selected from the list, the LinkLabel control changes to reflect the name of the selected item (refer to Figure 12-4). When you click the link, Internet Explorer opens the URL in the LinkLabel control's LinkCollection.

How It Works

When you click an item in the list view control, the `Click` event is fired for that control. You add code to the `Click` event to load the LinkLabel control with the selected link. You start by first setting the `Text` property of the LinkLabel control. This is the text that will be displayed on the form as shown in Figure 12-4.

You set the `Text` property using the static text *Visit* followed by the actual favorite name. The Favorite name is retrieved from the list view control's `Item` collection. Each row in the list view control is called an item and the first column contains the text of the item. Each column past the first column in a row is a subitem of the item (the text in the first column). The text that gets displayed in the link label is taken from the `Text` property of the `Item` collection.

```
Private Sub lvwFavorites_Click(ByVal sender As Object, _
    ByVal e As System.EventArgs) Handles lvwFavorites.Click

    'Update the link label control Text property
    lnkUrl.Text = "Visit " & lvwFavorites.SelectedItems.Item(0).Text
```

The `Links` property of the LinkLabel control contains a `LinkCollection` that contains a default hyperlink consisting of the text that is displayed in the LinkLabel control. You clear this collection and set it using the correct hyperlink for the selected Favorite. You do this by calling the `Clear` method on the `Links` property.

```
    'Clear the default hyperlink
    lnkUrl.Links.Clear()
```

Finally, you add your hyperlink using the subitem of the selected item in the ListView control. The `Add` method of the `Links` property is an overloaded method, and the method that you are using here expects three parameters: `start`, `length`, and `linkdata`. The `start` parameter specifies the starting position of the text in the `Text` property that you want as the hyperlink, and the `length` parameter specifies how long the hyperlink should be.

You do not want the word *Visit* to be part of the hyperlink, so you specify the starting position to be 6, which takes into account the space after the word *Visit*. Then you specify the `length` parameter using the `Length` property of the `Text` property of the selected item in the list view control. Finally, you specify the linkdata parameter by specifying the selected subitem from the list view control. This subitem contains the actual URL for the favorite.

```
        'Add the selected hyperlink to the LinkCollection
        lnkUrl.Links.Add(6, lvwFavorites.SelectedItems.Item(0).Text.Length, _
            lvwFavorites.SelectedItems.Item(0).SubItems(1).Text)
    End Sub
```

When a hyperlink on the LinkLabel control is clicked, it fires the LinkClicked event, and this is where you place your code to process the hyperlink of the favorite being displayed in this control. The LinkLabelLinkClickedEventArgs class contains information about the link label and, in particular, the actual hyperlink in the LinkCollection.

To retrieve the hyperlink, you access the LinkData property of the Link property. Then you pass this data to the Start method of the Process class, which causes a browser to be open and display the selected hyperlink:

```
    Private Sub lnkUrl_LinkClicked(ByVal sender As Object, _
        ByVal e As System.Windows.Forms.LinkLabelLinkClickedEventArgs) _
        Handles lnkUrl.LinkClicked

        'Process the selected link
        Process.Start(e.Link.LinkData)
    End Sub
```

An Alternative Favorite Viewer

You know that building separate classes promotes code reuse, but let's prove that. If code reuse is such a hot idea, without having to rewrite or change any of the code you should be able to build another application that can use the functionality in the classes to find and open favorites.

In this case, you might have given a colleague the Favorites, WebFavorite, and WebFavoriteCollection classes, and that colleague should be able to build a new application that uses this functionality without having to understand the internals of how Internet shortcuts work or how Windows stores the user's favorites.

Building a Favorites Tray

In this section, you build an application that displays a small icon on the system tray. Clicking this icon opens a list of the user's favorites as a menu, as shown in Figure 12-7. Clicking a favorite automatically opens Internet Explorer to the URL.

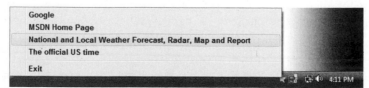

Figure 12-7

To demonstrate this principle of code reuse, you need to create a new Visual Basic 2008 project.

Try It Out · Building a Favorites Tray

1. Using Visual Studio 2008, select File ⇨ Add ⇨ New Project from the menu and create a new Visual Basic 2008 Windows Forms Application project called **Favorites Tray**.

2. When the Designer for Form1 appears, click the form in the Forms Designer and then change the `WindowState` property to **Minimized** and change the `ShowInTaskbar` property to **False**. This, effectively, prevents the form from being displayed.

3. Using the Toolbox, drag a NotifyIcon control onto the form. Set the `Name` property of the new control to **icnNotify** and set the `Text` property to **Right-click me to view Favorites** and set the `Icon` property to `C:\Program Files\Microsoft Visual Studio 9.0\Common7\VS2008ImageLibrary\1033\VS2008ImageLibrary\Objects\ico_format\WinVista\Favorites.ico`.

4. Next, open the Code Editor for Form1. In the Class Name combo box at the top of the Code Editor, select (Form1 Events), and in the Method Name combo box select VisibleChanged. Add this highlighted code to the event handler:

    ```
    Private Sub Form1_VisibleChanged(ByVal sender As Object, _
        ByVal e As System.EventArgs) Handles Me.VisibleChanged

        'If the user can see us, hide us
        If Me.Visible = True Then Me.Visible = False

    End Sub
    ```

5. Right-click the Favorites Tray project in the Solution Explorer and select Set As Startup Project. Now try running the project. You should discover that the tray icon is added to your system tray as shown in Figure 12-8, but no form window will appear. If you hover your mouse over the icon, you'll see the message that you set in the `Text` property of the Notify Icon control.

Figure 12-8

6. Also, you'll notice that there appears to be no way to stop the program! Flip back to Visual Studio 2008 and select Debug ⇨ Stop Debugging from the menu.

7. When you do this, although the program stops, the icon remains in the tray. To get rid of it, hover the mouse over it and it should disappear.

Windows redraws the icons in the system tray only when necessary (for example, when the mouse is passed over an icon).

How It Works

Setting a form to appear minimized (WindowState = Minimized) and telling it not to appear in the taskbar (ShowInTaskbar = False) has the effect of creating a window that's hidden. You need a form to support the tray icon, but you don't need the form for any other reason. However, this is only half the battle, because the form could appear in the Alt+ Tab application switching list, unless you add the following code, which you already did:

```
Private Sub Form1_VisibleChanged(ByVal sender As Object, _
    ByVal e As System.EventArgs) Handles Me.VisibleChanged

    'If the user can see us, hide us
    If Me.Visible = True Then Me.Visible = False
End Sub
```

This event handler has a brute force approach that says, "If the user can see me, hide me."

Displaying Favorites

In the next Try It Out, you look at how to display the favorites. The first thing you need to do is include the classes built in Favorites Viewer in this Favorites Tray solution. You can then use the Favorites object to get a list of favorites back and build a menu.

Try It Out   Displaying Favorites

1.   To display favorites, you need to get hold of the classes defined in the Favorites Viewer project. To do this you add the Favorites, WebFavorite, and WebFavoriteCollection classes to this project.

Using the Solution Explorer, right-click the Favorites Tray project and select Add ⇨ Existing Item. Browse to the classes in your Favorites Viewer project and find the Favorites class. After clicking Add, the class appears in the Solution Explorer for this project. You can select multiple files at once by holding down the Ctrl key.

2.   Repeat this for the WebFavorite and WebFavoriteCollection classes.

3.   Create a new class in Favorites Tray by clicking the project once more and selecting Add ⇨ Class. Call the new class **WebFavoriteMenuItem.vb** and then click the Add button to add this class to the project.

4.   Set the new class to inherit from System.Windows.Forms.MenuItem by adding this code:

```
Public Class WebFavoriteMenuItem
    Inherits MenuItem
```

5. Add this member and method to the class:

```
'Public member
Public Favorite As WebFavorite

'Constructor
Public Sub New(ByVal newFavorite As WebFavorite)
    'Set the property
    Favorite = newFavorite

    'Update the text
    Text = Favorite.Name
End Sub
```

6. Unlike `ListViewItem`, `MenuItem` objects can react to themselves being clicked by overloading the `Click` method. In the Class Name combo box at the top of the Code Editor, select (`WebFavoriteMenuItem` Events) and then select the `Click` event in the Method Name combo box. Add the following highlighted code to the `Click` event handler:

```
Private Sub WebFavoriteMenuItem_Click(ByVal sender As Object, _
    ByVal e As System.EventArgs) Handles Me.Click

    'Open the favorite
    If Not Favorite Is Nothing Then
        Process.Start(Favorite.Url)
    End If

End Sub
```

7. You need to do a similar trick to add an Exit option to your pop-up menu. Using the Solution Explorer create a new class called **ExitMenuItem.vb** in the Favorites Tray project. Add the following highlighted code to this class:

```
Public Class ExitMenuItem
    Inherits MenuItem

    'Constructor
    Public Sub New()
        Text = "Exit"
    End Sub

    Private Sub ExitMenuItem_Click(ByVal sender As Object, _
        ByVal e As System.EventArgs) Handles Me.Click

        Application.Exit()
    End Sub
End Class
```

8. Finally, you're in a position where you can load the favorites and create a menu for use with the tray icon. Add these members to Form1:

```
Public Class Form1
    'Public member
    Public Favorites As New Favorites()

    'Private member
    Private blnLoadCalled As Boolean = False
```

9. In the Class Name combo select (Form1 Events) and, in the Method Name combo box, select the Load event. Then add the following highlighted code to this event handler:

```
Private Sub Form1_Load(ByVal sender As Object, _
    ByVal e As System.EventArgs) Handles Me.Load

    'Load the favorites
    Favorites.ScanFavorites()

    'Create a new context menu
    Dim objMenu As New ContextMenu()

    'Process each favorite
    For Each objWebFavorite As WebFavorite In Favorites.FavoritesCollection
        'Create a menu item
        Dim objItem As New WebFavoriteMenuItem(objWebFavorite)
        'Add it to the menu
        objMenu.MenuItems.Add(objItem)
    Next

    'Add a separator menu item
    objMenu.MenuItems.Add("-")

    'Now add the Exit menu item
    objMenu.MenuItems.Add(New ExitMenuItem())

    'Finally, tell the tray icon to use this menu
    icnNotify.ContextMenu = objMenu

    'Set the load flag and hide ourselves
    blnLoadCalled = True
    Me.Hide()

End Sub
```

10. Modify the Form1_VisibleChanged procedure as follows:

```
Private Sub Form1_VisibleChanged(ByVal sender As Object, _
    ByVal e As System.EventArgs) Handles Me.VisibleChanged

    'Don't set the Visible property until the Load event has
    'been processed
    If blnLoadCalled = False Then
        Return
```

```
        End If

        'If the user can see us, hide us
        If Me.Visible = True Then Me.Visible = False

    End Sub
```

11. Run the project, and the icon will appear on the system tray. Right-click the icon, and you'll see a list of favorites as was shown in Figure 12-7. Clicking one opens Internet Explorer; clicking Exit closes the application.

How It Works

One thing to note is that, because of the order of events that are fired for your form, you have to create a variable in Form1 called blnLoadCalled. This variable makes sure that your favorites get loaded in the form's Load event.

The WebFavoriteMenuItem class accepts a WebFavorite object in its constructor, and it configures itself as a menu item using the class. However, this class provides a Click method that you can overload. So, when the user selects the item from the menu, you can immediately open the URL:

```
    Private Sub WebFavoriteMenuItem_Click(ByVal sender As Object, _
        ByVal e As System.EventArgs) Handles Me.Click

        'Open the favorite
        If Not Favorite Is Nothing Then
            Process.Start(Favorite.Url)
        End If
    End Sub
```

The ExitMenuItem class does a similar thing. When this item is clicked, you call the shared Application.Exit method to quit the program:

```
    Private Sub ExitMenuItem_Click(ByVal sender As Object, _
        ByVal e As System.EventArgs) Handles Me.Click

        Application.Exit()
    End Sub
```

The important thing here is not the construction of the application itself but rather the fact that you can reuse the functionality you built in a different project. This underlines the fundamental motive for reuse; it means you don't have to reinvent the wheel every time you want to do something.

The method of reuse described here was to add the existing classes to your new project, hence making a second copy of them. This isn't efficient, because it takes double the amount of storage needed for the classes; however, the classes are small, so the cost of memory is minimal. It did save you from having to create the classes from scratch, allowing you to reuse the existing code, and it was very easy to do.

An alternative way of reusing classes is to create them in a class library. This class library is a separate project that can be referenced by a number of different applications so that only one copy of the code is required. This is discussed in Chapter 13.

Using Shared Properties and Methods

On occasion, you might find it useful to access methods and properties that are not tied to an instance of an object but are still associated with a class.

Imagine you have a class that stores the user name and password of a user for a computer program. You might have something that looks like this:

```
Public Class User
    'Public members
    Public Username As String

    'Private members
    Private strPassword As String
End Class
```

Now imagine that the password for a user has to be of a minimum length. You create a separate member to store the length and implement a property like this:

```
Public Class User
    'Public members
    Public Username As String
    Public MinPasswordLength As Integer = 6

    'Private members
    Private strPassword As String

    'Password property
    Public Property Password() As String
        Get
            Return strPassword
        End Get
        Set(ByVal value As String)
            If value.Length >= MinPasswordLength Then
                strPassword = value
            End If
        End Set
    End Property
End Class
```

That seems fairly straightforward. But now imagine that you have five thousand user objects in memory. Each `MinPasswordLength` variable takes up 4 bytes of memory, meaning that 20 KB of memory is being used to store the same value. Although 20 KB of memory isn't a lot for modern computer systems, it's extremely inefficient, and there is a better way.

Using Shared Procedures

Ideally, you want to store the value for the minimum password length in memory against a specific class once and share that memory between all of the objects created from that class, as you'll do in the following Try It Out.

Try It Out   Using Shared Properties

1. Close the existing solution if it is still open and create a new Windows Forms Application project called **Shared Demo**.

2. When the Designer for Form1 appears, change the Text property of the form to **Shared Demo** and then drag a ListBox, a Label, and a NumericUpDown control from the Toolbox onto the form and arrange them as shown in Figure 12-9.

Figure 12-9

3. Set the Name property of the ListBox control to **lstUsers**.

4. Set the Name property of the NumericUpDown control to **nudMinPasswordLength,** set the Maximum property to **10**, and set the Value property to **6**.

5. Using the Solution Explorer, create a new class named **User**. Add the highlighted code to the class:

```
Public Class User
    'Public members
    Public Username As String
    Public Shared MinPasswordLength As Integer = 6

    'Private members
    Private strPassword As String

    'Password property
    Public Property Password() As String
        Get
            Return strPassword
        End Get
        Set(ByVal value As String)
            If value.Length >= MinPasswordLength Then
                strPassword = value
            End If
        End Set
    End Property

End Class
```

6. View the code for Form1 and add this highlighted member:

```
Public Class Form1
    'Private member
    Private arrUserList As New ArrayList()
```

7. Add this method to the `Form1` class:

```
Private Sub UpdateDisplay()
    'Clear the list
    lstUsers.Items.Clear()

    'Add the users to the list box
    For Each objUser As User In arrUserList
        lstUsers.Items.Add(objUser.Username & ", " & objUser.Password & _
            " (" & User.MinPasswordLength & ")")
    Next
End Sub
```

8. Select (Form1 Events) in the Class Name combo box at the top of the Code Editor and the `Load` event in the Method Name combo box. Add the highlighted code to the `Load` event:

```
Private Sub Form1_Load(ByVal sender As Object, _
    ByVal e As System.EventArgs) Handles Me.Load

    'Load 100 users
    For intIndex As Integer = 1 To 100
        'Create a new user
        Dim objUser As New User
        objUser.Username = "Stephanie" & intIndex
        objUser.Password = "password15"

        'Add the user to the array list
        arrUserList.Add(objUser)
    Next

    'Update the display
    UpdateDisplay()

End Sub
```

9. Select `nudMinPasswordLength` in the Class Name combo box at the top of the Code Editor and the `ValueChanged` event in the Method Name combo box. Add the highlighted code to the `ValueChanged` event:

```
Private Sub nudMinPasswordLength_ValueChanged(ByVal sender As Object, _
    ByVal e As System.EventArgs) Handles nudMinPasswordLength.ValueChanged

    'Set the minimum password length
    User.MinPasswordLength = nudMinPasswordLength.Value
    'Update the display
    UpdateDisplay()

End Sub
```

10. Save your project by clicking the Save All button on the toolbar.

11. Run the project. You should see a screen like the one shown in Figure 12-10.

Figure 12-10

12. Scroll the NumericUpDown control up or down, and the list updates and the number in parentheses changes to correspond to the number shown in the NumericUpDown control.

How It Works

To create a member variable, property, or method on an object that is shared, you use the `Shared` keyword.

```
Public Shared MinPasswordLength As Integer = 6
```

This tells Visual Basic 2008 that the item should be available to all instances of the class.

Shared members can be accessed from within nonshared properties and methods as well as from shared properties and methods. For example, here's the `Password` property, which can access the shared `MinPasswordLength` member:

```
'Password property
Public Property Password() As String
    Get
        Return strPassword
    End Get
    Set(ByVal value As String)
        If value.Length >= MinPasswordLength Then
            strPassword = value
        End If
    End Set
End Property
```

What's important to realize here is that although the `Password` property and `strPassword` member belong to the particular instance of the `User` class, `MinPasswordLength` does not; therefore, if it is changed the effect is felt throughout all the object instances built from the class in question.

In the form, `UpdateDisplay` is used to populate the list. You can gain access to `MinPasswordLength` as if it were a normal, nonshared public member of the `User` object:

```
Private Sub UpdateDisplay()
    'Clear the list
    lstUsers.Items.Clear()

    'Add the users to the list box
    For Each objUser As User In arrUserList
        lstUsers.Items.Add(objUser.Username & ", " & objUser.Password & _
            " (" & User.MinPasswordLength & ")")
    Next
End Sub
```

At this point, you have a listing of users that shows that the `MinPasswordLength` value of each is set to 6 (refer to Figure 12-10).

Things start to get interesting when you scroll the NumericUpDown control and change `MinPasswordLength`. As this is a shared member, you don't specifically *need* an instance of the class. Instead, you can set the property just by using the *class* name:

```
Private Sub nudMinPasswordLength_ValueChanged(ByVal sender As Object, _
    ByVal e As System.EventArgs) Handles nudMinPasswordLength.ValueChanged

    'Set the minimum password length
    User.MinPasswordLength = nudMinPasswordLength.Value

    'Update the display
    UpdateDisplay()
End Sub
```

When building this method, you may notice that after you type `User.`, Visual Studio 2008's IntelliSense pops up a list of members, including the `MinPasswordLength` property, as shown in Figure 12-11.

Figure 12-11

Shared members, properties, and methods can all be accessed through the class directly — you don't specifically need an instance of the class.

When you change this member with code in the `ValueChanged` event handler, you update the display, and this time you can see that the perceived value of `MinPasswordLength` has seemingly been changed for *all* instances of `User`, even though you changed it in only one place.

Using Shared Methods

Although you've seen how to make a public member variable shared, you haven't seen how to do this with a method. In the following Try It Out, you look at an example of how to build a shared method that can create new instances of User. The main limitation with a shared method is that you can access other shared methods and shared properties only in the class in which it is defined.

This is a hypothetical example of using a shared method, as you could do the same job here with a customized constructor.

Try It Out   Using a Shared Method

1. Open the Code Editor for User. Add the following code to the User class:

```
Public Shared Function CreateUser(ByVal userName As String, _
    ByVal password As String) As User

    'Delcare a new User object
    Dim objUser As New User()

    'Set the User properties
    objUser.Username = userName
    objUser.Password = password

    'Return the new user
    Return objUser
End Function
```

2. Open the Code Editor for Form1 and locate the Load event handler. Change the code so that it looks like this. You'll notice that as you type in the code, as soon as you type User., IntelliSense offers CreateUser as an option:

```
Private Sub Form1_Load(ByVal sender As Object, _
    ByVal e As System.EventArgs) Handles Me.Load

    'Load 100 users
    For intIndex As Integer = 1 To 100
        'Create a new user
        Dim objUser As New User

        objUser = User.CreateUser("Stephanie" & intIndex, "password15")

        'Add the user to the array list
        arrUserList.Add(objUser)
    Next

    'Update the display
    UpdateDisplay()
End Sub
```

3. If you run the project, you get the same results as the previous example.

How It Works

The important thing to look at here is the fact that `CreateUser` appears in the IntelliSense list after you type the class name. This is because it is shared and you do not need a specific instance of a class to access it. You create the method as a shared method by using the `Shared` keyword:

```
Public Shared Function CreateUser(ByVal userName As String, _
        ByVal password As String) As User
```

One thing to consider with shared methods is that you can access only members of the class that are also shared. You cannot access nonshared methods, simply because you don't know what instance of the class you're actually running on. Likewise, you cannot access `Me` from within a shared method for the same reason.

Understanding Object-Oriented Programming and Memory Management

Object orientation has an impact on how memory is used in an operating system. .NET is heavily object oriented, so it makes sense that .NET would have to optimize the way it uses memory to best suit the way objects are used.

Whenever you create an object, you're using memory. Most of the objects you use have *state*, which describes what an object knows. The methods and properties that an object has will either affect or work with that state. For example, an object that describes a file on disk will have state that describes its name, size, folder, and so on. Some of the state will be publicly accessible through properties. For example, a property called `Size` returns the size of the file. Some state is private to the object and is used to keep track of what the object has done or what it needs to do.

Objects use memory in two ways. First, something needs to keep track of the objects that exist on the system in memory. This is usually a task shared between you as an application developer and .NET's Common Language Runtime (CLR). If you create an object, you'll have to hold a reference to it in your program's memory so that you know where it is when you need to use its methods and properties. The CLR also needs to keep track of the object to determine when you no longer need it. Secondly, the CLR needs to allocate memory to the object so that the object can store its state. The more state an object has, the more memory it will need to use it.

The most expensive resource on a computer is the memory. *Expense* here means in terms of what you get for your money. For about $100, you can buy a 120 GB hard drive, but for the same amount of money you can't buy 1 GB of memory. Retrieving data from memory is thousands of times faster than retrieving it from disk so there's a tradeoff — if you need fast access, you have to store it in memory, but there isn't as much memory available as there is hard disk space.

When building an application, you want to use as little memory as possible, so there's an implication that you want to have as few objects as possible and that those objects should have as little state as possible. The upside is that, today, computers have a lot more memory than they used to have, so your programs can use more memory than their predecessors of 10 years ago. However, you still need to be cognizant of your application's memory usage.

The CLR manages memory in several distinct ways. First, it's responsible for creating objects at the request of the application. With a heavily object-oriented programming platform like .NET, this is going to happen all the time, so Microsoft has spent an enormous amount of time making sure that the CLR creates objects in the most efficient way. The CLR, for example, can create objects far faster than its Component Object Model (COM) predecessor could. Secondly, the CLR is responsible for cleaning up memory when it's no longer needed. In the developer community, the manner in which the CLR cleans up objects is one of the most controversial.

Imagine you're writing a routine that opens a file from disk and displays the contents on the screen. Well, with .NET you could use perhaps two .NET Framework objects to open the file and read its contents — namely `System.IO.FileStream` and `System.IO.StreamReader`. However, after the contents have been read, do you need these objects anymore? Probably not, so you remove your references to the objects and make the memory the objects were using available for creating more objects.

Imagine now that you don't remove your references to the objects. In this situation, the memory that the objects were using can't be used by anyone else. Now imagine that happening several thousand times. The amount of memory that's being wasted keeps growing. In extreme circumstances, the computer runs out of memory, meaning that other applications wouldn't ever be able to create any objects. This is a pretty catastrophic state of affairs.

We describe an object that is no longer needed but that holds onto memory as a *leak*. Memory leaks are one of the biggest causes of reliability problems on Windows, because when a program is no longer able to obtain memory, it will crash.

With .NET this *should* never happen, or, at the very least, to leak memory you would have to go to some pretty extreme steps. This is because of a feature called *garbage collection*. When an object is no longer being used, the *Garbage Collector* automatically removes the object from memory and makes the memory it was using available to other programs.

Garbage Collection

The Garbage Collector (GC) works by keeping track of how many parts of a program have a reference to an object. If it gets to the point where there are no open references to the object, it is deleted.

To understand this, think back to the discussion of scope in Chapter 3. Imagine you create a method and at the top of that method you define a variable with local scope. That variable is used to store an object (it doesn't matter what kind of object is used for this discussion). At this point, one part of the program knows about the object's existence — that is, the variable is holding a reference to the object. When you return from the method, the variable goes out of scope, and therefore the variable forgets about the object's existence; in other words, the only reference to the object is lost. At this point, no one knows about the object, and so it can be safely deleted.

For an example, look at the following code:

```
Dim objObject As New MyObject
Console.WriteLine(objObject.GetType().FullName)
objObject = Nothing
```

This code snippet creates a new object from class MyObject, invokes a method on it, and then removes the reference to the object. In this case, when you create the object, the objObject variable is the only thing that holds a reference to it. In the last line, objObject is set to Nothing, hence removing the only reference to the object. The GC is then free to remove the reference to the object.

The GC does not run constantly. Instead, it runs periodically based on a complex algorithm that measures the amount of work the computer is doing and how many objects might need to be deleted. When the GC runs, it looks through the master list of all the objects the program has ever created for any that can be deleted at this point.

In old-school programming, programmers were responsible for deleting their own objects and had the freedom to say to an object, "You, now, clean yourself up and get out of memory." With .NET this ability is gone. Rather, an object will be deleted at some *indeterminate* time in the future.

Exactly when this happens is nondeterministic — in other words, as a developer you don't know when the GC is going to run. This means that there is no immediate connection between the removal of the last reference to an object and the physical removal of that object from memory. This is known as *nondeterministic finalization*.

Releasing Resources

In some cases, objects that you build may need access to certain system and network resources, such as files and database connections. Using these resources requires a certain discipline to ensure that you don't inadvertently cause problems.

Here's an example — if you create a new file, write some data to it, but forget to close it, no one else will be able to read data from that file. This is because you have an *exclusive lock* on the file; it doesn't make sense for someone to be able to read from a file when it's still being written to. You must take care to release system resources should you open them.

When an object has access to scarce system or network resources like this, it's important that the caller tell the object that it can release those resources as soon as they're no longer needed. For example, here's some code that creates a file:

```
'Open a file
Dim objFileStream As New FileStream("c:\myfile.txt", FileMode.Create)
'Do something with the file
...
'Close the file
objFileStream.Close()
'Release your reference to the object
objFileStream = Nothing
```

As soon as you finish working with the file, you call Close. This tells .NET that the consumer is finished with the file and Windows can make it available for other applications to use. This is known as *releasing the lock*. When you release the object reference in the next line by setting objFileStream = Nothing, this is an entirely separate action from calling Close.

The FileStream object releases the lock on the file when its Finalize method is called. However, as you've just learned, the time period between the instance of the FileStream object becoming a candidate for garbage collection (which happens when `objFileStream = Nothing`) and `Finalize` being called is nondeterministic. So, if you had not called `Close`, the file would have remained open for a period of time, which would have caused problems for anyone else who needed to use the file.

Another way to release resources within objects is to implement the `IDisposable` interface, which you did with the `WebFavorite` and `Favorites` classes. This interface provides a `Dispose` method for your objects, in which you can put code to clean up the resources used in that class.

Ideally, the consumer of these objects would call the `Dispose` methods on these objects when they are done using them, but if they do not, the `Finalize` method in these objects will when the GC runs.

Defragmentation and Compaction

As the last item in its bag of tricks, the GC is able to defragment and compact memory. In much the same way that your computer's hard disk needs periodic defragmentation to make it run more efficiently, so does memory. Imagine you create 10 small objects in memory, each about 1 KB in size. Imagine that .NET allocates them all on top of each other, so you end up taking up one 10 KB piece of memory. (In reality, you don't usually care where objects exist in memory, so this discussion is a bit academic.)

Next, imagine you want to create another object and this object is of medium size, say about 3 KB. .NET has to create this object at the end of the 10 KB block. This means that you'll have allocated 13 KB in total.

Then imagine that you delete every other small object, so now your 10 KB block of memory has holes in it. Not much of a problem, but imagine you want to create another 3 KB object. Although there's 5 KB of space in the original block, you can't put it there because no gap is big enough. Instead, it has to go on the end, meaning your application is now taking up 16 KB of memory.

What the GC can do is defragment memory, which means that it removes the gaps when objects have been removed, as shown in Figure 12-12. The upshot of this is that your application uses memory more efficiently, so applications take up less memory.

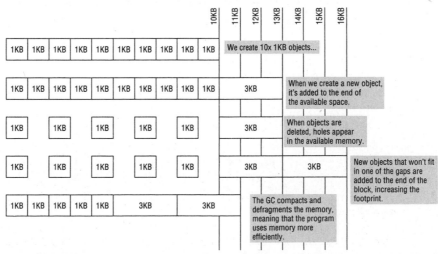

Figure 12-12

Although this may not seem like a big deal on a PC with 1 GB of memory available, consider that .NET could potentially be running on much smaller devices where memory usage is a big deal, for example, a mobile device with 32 MB of memory in total. Besides, imagine making three thousand 5 KB savings in this example; then you've have saved over 15 MB of memory! Chapter 25 introduces you to writing applications for mobile devices and to topics that you need to be aware of when coding for these devices.

Summary

In this chapter, you took a look at some more valuable techniques that you are able to use to assist the building of object-oriented software. Initially, you examined the idea of reuse. Specifically, you looked at classes that allow you to examine the Internet Explorer Favorites stored on the user's computer. You consumed these classes from two applications — one standard desktop application and also a mini-application that exists on the system tray.

You then examined the idea of shared members, properties, and methods. Sharing these kinds of items is a powerful way to make common functionality available to all classes in an application.

Finally, you examined how consumers of objects should ensure that scarce systems resources are freed whenever an object is deleted by the Garbage Collector using the `Dispose` and `Finalize` methods.

To summarize, you should know how to:

- ❏ Build a class that inherits from the `System.Collections.CollectionBase` namespace, add methods that allow you to add and remove objects from the collection, and provide a property that allows an application to query for the number of items in the collection

- ❏ Use the collection class in your own application to create objects and add them to the collection

- ❏ Use shared properties and methods in a class that can be shared among all instantiated instances of the class

- ❏ Properly dispose of resources to make efficient use of the Garbage Collector

Exercise

1. Modify the Favorites Viewer project to select the first favorite in the ListView control automatically after it has been loaded so that the LinkLabel control displays the first item when the form is displayed.

    You also need to modify the `Load` event in Form1, and ensure that the ListView control contains one or more items before proceeding. You do this by querying the `Count` property of the `Items` property of the ListView control. Then you select the first item in the ListView control using the `lstFavorites.Items(0).Selected` property and call the `Click` event for the ListBox control to update the LinkLabel control.

Building Class Libraries

In this chapter, you're going to look at building libraries of classes, a process that gathers many of the concepts covered in this book, so let's have a quick review. So far, you've learned a lot about developing Windows applications by dragging controls onto forms, editing their properties, and adding code. When you edit a form in the Form Designer, you are actually designing a new class that inherits from the `System.Windows.Forms.Form` class.

When you make changes to the form in the designer, the designer works out what code needs to be added to the class. You can view this code by clicking the Show All Files icon in the Solution Explorer and then opening the designer-generated code for your form. When you run the program, an instance of this class is created — an object. Like most objects, the form has state and behavior — you can have variables and controls on the form (state) and you can perform actions when, for example, the user clicks a button on the form (behavior). In theory, you could write your forms without using the designer at all; very few programmers work this way while creating Windows forms.

Right from the start you've been creating classes. You've also looked at creating your own classes from scratch. Recall what you studied about building objects in Chapter 11, where you created a project called Objects, which contained the classes `Car` and `SportsCar`. These classes were used in a console application because it made the objects easier to test, but they would have worked just as well in a Windows application. You could even have used them in a web application or web service. In fact, one of the key benefits of using classes is that once you've designed a good one, you can use it over and over again in different applications.

In this chapter, you will:

- ❏ Create your own class libraries and learn how to get information about existing libraries that are not part of the .NET Framework.

- ❏ Learn to assign strong-name assemblies (compiled files) to ensure that all assemblies have a unique identity.

- ❏ Register assemblies in a repository called the Global Assembly Cache (GAC) so that they can be shared between applications on the same computer.

Understanding Class Libraries

In Chapter 12 you used the same classes in two different applications. You built a favorites viewer in your application and a task bar application using the same underlying classes. You did this by creating the class in one application and then adding a copy of that code to the second. This was a quick and easy way of reusing code, but there were some problems with it:

❑   To use the class you needed to have access to the source code file. One of the advantages of classes and objects is that they can be a black box. Developers should not need to know what goes on inside the classes they use. It is often a good thing if they don't. Also, if you've developed a class, you might want to keep your source code secret. You might be happy to let people use it, but not let them copy the way it works or improve it, or even claim it as their own work.

❑   Every time the program that uses the class is compiled, the class needs to be compiled too. This is not really a problem if the application uses a few simple classes, but if it's using a lot of complex classes, it will make compilation slower. It will also make the resulting program very big because one .exe file will include all of the classes.

❑   If you realize that there is a bug in the class or that there is a way to make it faster or more efficient, you need to make the change in lots of different places — in every application that uses the class.

The solution is class libraries. A *class library* is a collection of classes that compile to a file: a Windows Dynamic Link Library (DLL, or .dll file). You cannot run a class library by itself, but you can use the classes in it from your applications. You can use a class library without the source code; it does not need to be recompiled when the application is compiled, and if the library changes, the applications using it will automatically get the advantage of the improved code.

Creating a Class Library

These are instructions for creating a class library in Visual Studio.

Try It Out   **Creating a Class Library**

1.   In Visual Studio 2008 select File ⇨ New Project.

2.   Select Visual Basic from the Project Types list and then choose the Class Library icon from the Templates list as shown in Figure 13-1. Enter the name **Internet Favorites**.

3.   Click OK. A new Class Library project will be created with a default class called Class1.vb. Right-click Class1.vb in the Solution Explorer and choose Delete.

Figure 13-1

How It Works

That was really easy. Let's just think about what Visual Studio 2008 is doing during these two steps. First, you choose a Class Library project. The template that you choose controls how Visual Studio 2008 sets up the project and what type of file it compiles to. The most obvious difference is that when you start a Windows Forms application you get a blank form in the Forms Designer. The blank form is called `Form1.vb`. When you start a class library, you get no designer and a blank class called `Class1.vb`.

There are also more subtle differences. When you create a Windows Forms application, Visual Studio 2008 knows that you will be compiling it into a program that can run. When you choose a Class Library, Visual Studio 2008 knows that the resulting library will not be run on its own — so the choices you make here affect what Visual Studio 2008 does when you build the project. Selecting a Class Library means that Visual Studio 2008 will build the project into a `.dll` (Dynamic Link Library) file instead of an `.exe` (Executable) file.

After clicking OK, you delete the blank class that Visual Studio 2008 generates. Having classes with the name `Class1` is not very helpful — it's much better to start from scratch with meaningful file and class names.

In the previous chapter you created classes and used the same class in two projects: Favorites Viewer and Favorites Tray. In the following sections you see how to convert these applications so that both of them use a copy of the same compiled class library. Of course, this is a somewhat unrealistic situation. Usually, you would build a class library and application rather than create an application and then split it into a smaller application and a class library. However, this will give you a good idea of how you would create a class library from scratch, and it will be much faster. First of all, open the Favorites Viewer project using another instance of Visual Studio 2008. Remember that this project consists of the following files:

- ❑ `Favorites.vb` contains the `Favorites` class.

- ❑ `WebFavorite.vb` contains the `WebFavorite` class.

- ❑ `WebFavoriteCollection.vb` contains the `WebFavoriteCollection` class.

- ❑ `Form1.vb` contains the `Form1` class, which represents the application's main form.

Of these, the first three listed are also used in the Favorites Tray. The remaining file is specific to this particular application. You want to build a class library that contains `Favorites`, `WebFavorite`, and `WebFavoriteCollection`.

Building a Class Library for Favorites Viewer

When you're writing Visual Basic 2008 applications, a solution can contain multiple projects. At the moment you have two projects in the solution: the Favorites Viewer application and the Favorites Tray application. In the next Try It Out, you add a Class Library project to this solution and then move the classes from the Windows Forms Application project to the Class Library project.

Try It Out   Adding a Class Library Project to an Existing Solution

1. Switch to the instance of Visual Studio 2008 containing the Internet Favorites project.

2. Save the project and then close Visual Studio 2008.

3. Switch to the instance of Visual Studio 2008 containing the Favorites Viewer project.

4. Click the File menu and select Add ⇨ Existing Project.

5. Navigate to the where you saved your Internet Favorites project and then select the `Internet Favorites.vbproj` file. Click Open to add this project to the solution.

6. Right-click the Favorites Viewer project in the Solution Explorer and select Set As StartUp Project.

7. Now right-click the Favorites Tray project in the Solution Explorer and select Remove.

How It Works

Now you have two projects within your solution. You have a Windows Forms application and a class library. Currently, the class library is empty; all the classes that you want to add to it are in the Favorites Viewer project.

You have already seen how to add a new class to a Windows Forms application, and you can add new classes to a class library in exactly the same way. You just right-click the Internet Favorites project and select Add ⇨ Class. You don't want to do that, though, because the classes already exist. The quickest way to move a class between two projects in the same solution is to drag and drop them, which is what you do in the next Try It Out.

Try It Out   **Moving Classes Between Projects**

1. Select the `Favorites.vb` file in the Solution Explorer, as shown in Figure 13-2, and drag it onto the Internet Favorites project. This causes a copy of the `Favorites` class to be added to the Internet Favorites project.

Figure 13-2

2. Follow the same procedure for `WebFavorite.vb` and `WebFavoriteCollection.vb`.

3. Right-click the `Favorites.vb` file in the Favorites Viewer project and select Delete from the context menu to delete the file from that project.

4. Follow the same procedure for `WebFavorite.vb` and `WebFavoriteCollection.vb`.

You now have a Class Library project and a Windows Forms Application project. However, even though they are both contained in the same solution, they cannot see each other. If you try running the application now, you will see an error that type `Favorites` is not defined.

These errors occur because the code in `Form1.vb` cannot see the classes in the class library. There are two stages to solving this problem:

❑ Add a reference to the Class Library project, so that the Windows Forms application knows to look for the compiled `Internet Favorites.dll` file that contains the classes. Previously, all code was compiled into one file, so you didn't need to do this.

❑ Add an `Imports` statement to Form1, so that it can see the classes in the `Internet_Favorites` namespace without giving a fully qualified name (that is, including the namespace as well as the class name). Previously, all classes were in the same namespace, so you didn't need to do this. As discussed in Chapter 4, classes are by default given their project name as their namespace. When a project contains a space in the name, Visual Studio 2008 replaces the blank space in the name with an underscore (_) character.

If this doesn't seem very clear — don't worry! Both of these things are easy to do.

Adding a Reference and Imports Statement

1. Right-click the Favorites Viewer project in the Solution Explorer and select Add Reference.

2. Select the Projects tab in the Add Reference dialog box and you'll see that the Internet Favorites project is already populated in the list, as shown in Figure 13-3. Click OK to have this reference added to your Favorites Viewer project.

Figure 13-3

3. Right-click `Viewer.vb` in the Solution Explorer and select View Code. Add the following line right at the very top of the code file:

```
Imports Internet_Favorites
```

How It Works

By adding a reference in steps 1 and 2, you tell Visual Studio 2008 that the `Favorites Viewer.exe` file will require the `Internet Favorites.dll` file to run. Visual Studio 2008 can use the classes exposed from Internet Favorites to check the syntax of the code, so the automatic underlining of errors and so on will work correctly.

> *Whenever you want to use a class library you must add a reference to it. You can add references to projects within the solution or to compiled DLLs.*

However, if you try to run the application before you perform step 3, you still get errors, because the classes in the Favorites Viewer application would be trying to use classes in the `Internet Favorites` class library without giving a fully qualified name. Unless you specify otherwise, classes are given the name of the project they are in as their namespace name. This means that the classes you moved from Favorites Viewer to Internet Favorites changed namespace too.

The easiest way to cope with this problem is to add an `Imports` statement to the top of the classes that rely on this class library. This is what you did in Step 3, but remember that you have two other choices:

❑   You can use fully qualified names every time you want to access a class in the class library from a class in the application. This requires quite a few changes.

❑   You can change the namespace of either the classes in the application or the classes in the class library. If the namespace was the same for both projects, you do not need to use fully qualified names or have an `Imports` statement. However, because the two projects are quite different, it would not really be sensible to give both of them the same namespace.

The `Imports` statement means that any time there is a reference to a class that is not qualified with a namespace, the Visual Basic 2008 compiler will check the `Internet_Favorites` namespace to see whether a matching class exists there. Therefore, the compiler will be able to resolve the class name when you insert the `Imports` statement.

That's it! You have converted your Windows Forms application into a small client application and a class library. Run the application and it will work perfectly, and you'll see the same results you saw in the previous chapter; the application displays a list of your Internet Favorites shortcuts.

Note that when you run this application, Visual Studio 2008 compiles the class library to a DLL, then compiles the application to an EXE, and then runs the EXE. It needs to compile the DLL first because the compiler depends upon it while compiling the EXE.

A Multitiered Application

In the previous demonstration, you split your application into two *tiers* or layers. The class library is a tier that handles the concept of a favorite and obtains a list of the user's favorites from their computer. The other tier presents the favorites to the user and enables the user to perform actions on them. Class libraries are a powerful tool for creating tiered applications, because they enable you to completely separate the code that exists in different tiers. You may often hear the term *n-tier design*. What this means is that an application has at least three separate tiers. Usually, these three tiers are:

❑   A *data tier* is concerned with obtaining raw data from a data source such as a database, text file, or, in this case, your Favorites folder and then writing data back. It generally is not concerned with what the data means. It just enables data read and write operations.

❑   A *business tier* is concerned with applying certain business rules to the data retrieved from the data source or ensuring that data that is being written to the data source obeys these rules. In this case, there may certain sites that you would not want to list in your Favorites viewer, or you may want to ensure that URLs are valid before displaying them. The business tier may also contain code for manipulating or working with data — for example, the code needed to open a particular favorite.

❑   A *presentation tier* displays the data to the users and lets them interact with it in some way. In this case, you have a Windows Form that displays a list of favorites and a link button that lets users view them.

Your application is so small that there's no practical need to separate the data tier and the business tier. However, in a big application it can make the project far more manageable, even if it does mean spending a bit more time on design before the coding starts.

One of the great things about tiers is that you can mix and match them quite easily. For example, if a new browser becomes popular, then you could change the data tier to read a different data format but still use the same presentation tier and business tier. This would be much easier if the data tier and business tier were separate.

Soon, you are going to use your class library, which is really a combination of the business and data tiers, in conjunction with a different presentation tier, namely the Favorites Tray application.

In this chapter, you are working with existing projects so that you can concentrate specifically on class libraries rather than on writing code. In most cases you would develop the class library first and then develop applications to use that library. Of course, as you are building the application, you might decide to modify the library slightly. Using Visual Studio 2008 you can do this very easily. When working in Visual Studio 2008 you can make any changes you like to the code in the library, and the change will instantly be available in the application.

Using Strong Names

Your complete solution now compiles to two files: a DLL and an EXE. You have written both files. Nobody else is writing applications that rely on the DLL, and nobody else is going to change the DLL. In real life, this is often not the case. Often you use off-the-shelf DLLs, or two separate developers are working on the DLL and the EXE.

For example, imagine that Matt is working on `Internet Favorites.dll` and Robbin is working on `Favorites Viewer.exe`. Matt decides that `ScanFavorites` is not a very good name for a method and changes it to `LoadFavorites`. Then he recompiles the DLL. Later, Robbin runs `Favorites Viewer.exe`. `Favorites Viewer.exe` tries to call `ScanFavorites` in the DLL, but the method no longer exists. This generates an error and the program doesn't work.

Of course, Matt shouldn't really have made the change to the DLL. He should have known that applications existed that required the `ScanFavorites` method. All too often, however, developers of libraries don't realize this. They make changes to DLLs that render existing software unusable.

Another possible scenario is that Jay is working on a system to manage favorites, and he creates a file called `Internet Favorites` that is different from the one that Matt developed. There is a danger that the two different DLLs will be confused, and once again Favorites Viewer will stop working.

These DLL management problems have been a nightmare for Windows developers, and it spawned the expression "DLL Hell." However, Visual Basic 2008 goes a long way toward solving the problem. The problem is connected with two things:

❑ There can be several versions of a DLL, and these can all work in different ways. It is not possible to tell the version from the file name alone.

❑ Different people can write DLLs with the same file name.

Strongly named assemblies store information about their version and their author within the assembly itself. Because of this, it would be possible to tell the difference between the DLL used (when Favorites Viewer compiled) and the changed version. It would also be possible to tell the difference between Matt's `Internet Favorites.dll` and Jay's `Internet Favorites.dll`. Strong naming can also store information about other properties that helps uniquely identify an assembly (for example, the culture for which it was written), but you concentrate on version and author.

Signing Assemblies

One way to certify who wrote an assembly is to sign it. To do this, you generate a key pair and sign the assembly with it. A key-pair is unique and, therefore, can identify the person or company who wrote an assembly. The principles behind assembly signing are quite advanced, but the actual practice is quite simple.

A strongly named assembly cannot reference a simply named assembly, because it would lose the versioning control that it enjoys.

Two steps are involved in creating a strongly named or signed assembly:

❏   Create a key pair that you can use to sign your assembly, as you do in the next Try It Out.

❏   Apply this key pair to your assembly, so that it will be used to sign the assembly at the time of compilation.

Try It Out   **Creating a Key Pair**

1.   First, you create a new key pair. From the Windows Start menu select All Programs ⇨ Microsoft Visual Studio 2008 ⇨ Visual Studio Tools ⇨ Visual Studio 2008 Command Prompt.

If you are running on Windows Vista, you will most likely need to run the command prompt with administrator privileges. To do this, instead of left-clicking the Visual Studio 2008 Command Prompt, right-click it and choose Run as administrator from the context menu.

2.   Type the following into the command prompt that appears:

```
sn -k InternetFavoriteskey.snk
```

This generates a key pair in the folder where the command is run (in this case, `C:\Program Files\Microsoft Visual Studio 9.0\VC`).

How It Works

Running the Visual Studio 2008 command prompt opens a DOS-style command window with the environment set up so that you can use the .NET command-line tools. You use this environment to run the Visual Studio 2008 strong naming command, `sn`. The k switch means that the command generates a new key pair and writes it to the specified file.

Now you have a key pair in the file `C:\Program Files\Microsoft Visual Studio 9.0\VC\InternetFavoriteskey.snk`. If you want, you can move this to a more convenient location, such as your project folder for the Internet Favorites project. After this, in the next Try It Out, you use it to sign your assembly.

Try It Out   Signing the FavoritesLib Assembly

1. In the Solution Explorer, double-click the My Project file in the Internet Favorites project.

2. Now click the Signing tab along the left side of the project file, as shown in Figure 13-4.

3. Select the Sign the assembly check box.

4. In the Choose a strong name key file combo box, select <Browse . . .> and then browse to the location of your key file and select it.

5. Build your project, and the DLL will then be strongly named.

Figure 13-4

How It Works

When you compile an assembly with a key file, it adds a copy of your public key to the assembly. It also adds a hash of the whole assembly, encrypted using the private key.

With public–private key cryptography, a message encrypted with one key can be decrypted only with the other key. You can't use the same key to encrypt and decrypt. You can give a public key to a lot of people and they can encrypt messages with it. If you keep the private key secret, nobody else will be able to read the encrypted messages — even if they have a copy of the public key.

You can also make this work the other way around. If you encrypt a message with the private key, people can use the public key to decrypt it. If the decryption works and you haven't let somebody else get their hands on your private key, it proves that you wrote the message.

Part of the purpose of signing an assembly is to prove who wrote it and to prove that it has not been tampered with. This could be done by encrypting the whole assembly using the private key and then decrypting the whole assembly using the public key when it needs to be used. However, this would be very slow. Instead, the Visual Basic 2008 compiler takes a hash of the assembly and encrypts that using the private key. If anybody tries to tamper with the assembly, the hash will cease to be valid.

Assembly Versions

Visual Basic 2008 automatically keeps track of versions for you. When you build an assembly, a number signifying the version is automatically updated. There are four elements of this number: major version, minor version, build, and revision. If you click the Application tab of the project file and then click the Assembly Information button, you see the assembly version near the bottom of the Assembly Information dialog box.

This means that when you compile this assembly, the major version will be 1, the minor version will be 0, and the build and revision number will be generated by Visual Studio 2008. Every time you recompile the assembly, Visual Basic 2008 will adjust these numbers to ensure that every compilation has a unique version number. You could choose to replace the build and revision numbers with your own hard-coded numbers and increment them yourself, but if you're happy with Visual Basic 2008's decision, then you can just leave it. If you are changing an assembly significantly, you may want to change the major or minor version — and, of course, you are free to do that.

It is recommended that you set the entire version number manually, especially when you are releasing the assembly formally, so that you have complete control. It will then be easier to manage different versions and bring in fewer unfortunate deployment problems.

Registering Assemblies

You've seen how an assembly can contain information to prove who wrote it (in the sense that a unique identifier is unique per publisher) and information to prove its own version. This is really useful, because it means that executables using these assemblies know what assembly author and version to look for in place of just a file name. However, this doesn't prevent Matt from overwriting an existing DLL with a new version — it just means that applications using the DLL will be able to tell that it's changed.

This is where the Global Assembly Cache (GAC) comes in. The GAC can ensure that several versions of the same assembly are always available. If your application requires the InternetFavorites assembly version 1 and Matt's application requires the assembly version 2, both can go in the GAC and both can be available. Moreover, assemblies with the same name but written by different people can go in the GAC. You can guarantee that your applications will use the same assembly while running as they did when they were compiled, provided the required assembly is in the GAC.

To register an assembly into the GAC, you simply need to drag the relevant .dll file into the GAC (located in the c:\windows\assembly folder on Windows XP and Windows Vista).

Gacutil Utility

Gacutil.exe is a utility provided with the .NET Framework for installing/uninstalling assemblies into the GAC via a command line.

From the Windows Start menu, select Programs ➪ Microsoft Visual Studio 2008 ➪ Visual Studio Tools ➪ Visual Studio 2008 Command Prompt. Navigate to the bin folder for your Internet Favorites project and then enter the following command to install your assembly into the GAC:

```
Gacutil -i "internet favorites.dll"
```

In the console window, you can use the i and u options to install and uninstall, respectively.

```
Gacutil -u "internet favorites"
```

Why Is My Assembly Not Visible in the References Dialog Box?

It is important to understand that the GAC is not shown in the References dialog box within Visual Studio. For this reason, after you add your assembly to the GAC, you will not see it in the References dialog box and must browse for it.

Visual Studio does, however, look for assemblies to load into the References dialog box by checking keys in the Registry that map to physical paths on your drive. In the next Try It Out, you list your assembly in the References dialog box.

Try It Out   Getting Your Assembly Listed in the References Dialog Box

1. Click Start and Select Run.

2. Type **regedit** and press Enter.

3. In the Registry Editor locate the key HKEY_LOCAL_MACHINE\SOFTWARE\Microsoft\ .NETFramework\AssemblyFolders.

4. Right-click AssemblyFolders and select New ➪ Key.

5. Create the key with any name that you wish. We named ours **Developer Assemblies**.

6. Double-click (Default) value key in the pane and enter a path. We added **C:\Developer Assemblies**. (See Figure 13-5.)

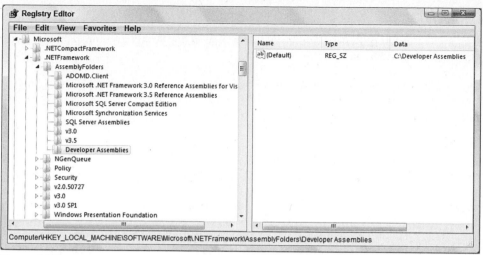

Figure 13-5

7. Open Windows Explorer and create the new directory that you specified in the previous step, if it doesn't exist, and then copy the `InternetFavorites.dll` into this directory

8. You may have to stop and start Visual Studio 2008 for this to take effect, but when you do, you will see the assembly listed in this directory from within the References Dialog Box as shown in Figure 13-6.

Figure 13-6

Designing Class Libraries

By now, you should be aware of how useful class libraries are and have an understanding of the nature of classes, objects, and class libraries.

When designing an application, it is best to understand what you are dealing with. Much like an architect designing a house, you need to understand how things work (the rules, the regulations, and the recommendations) in order to know how to draw the best plan.

When software architects plan, draw out, and generate template code for components and applications, they may use a drawing tool such as Microsoft Visio, which integrates with Visual Studio 2008. Visio contains various types of symbol libraries that can be used for creating schematics, flowcharts, and other diagrams. A very well-known set of descriptive symbols and diagram types is Unified Modeling Language (UML), which has its own symbols and rules for drawing software and architecture models. UML has various types of symbol libraries containing symbols that have different meaning and functions. These symbols have been derived from previous modeling symbols to form something of a fusion of styles. UML also has many types of diagrams. These diagrams range from deployment-type diagrams to component definition diagrams.

If you want to learn more about UML, take a look at the UML Bible *(Wiley, ISBN: 0-7645-2604-9)*

If the questions "How many parameters and methods should an object expose?" and "Should an object have properties rather than methods?" are not answered correctly, your object would not be rendered completely useless, although it may be ineffective. There are, however, some things to consider.

Imagine a class library that contains over 40 methods and properties on each of its 20 or so classes. Also imagine that each class's methods contain at least 15 parameters. This component might be a little daunting — in fact, a component should never be designed this way.

Instead, when designing your objects, try to follow the golden rule: simplicity. Simplicity is probably the most crucial element that you can have in your classes. While creating an extremely large class library is not necessarily a bad thing, using a small number of related classes, aided by a few other class libraries, is by far a better solution.

When you're dealing with a large, complex set of business rules for a large system, the code within the library can be extremely complicated, often leading to debugging and maintenance nightmares. In many situations, getting around the fact that many objects need to be created is a difficult task, but the point that needs to come across is that many situations lend themselves to reuse. The more reusable the classes are, the smaller the end-product will be and the easier it will be to create new applications that need the same functionality provided by the components.

Every developer who uses your class library should be able to do so successfully, without any major effort or a tremendous amount of reading. You can achieve this in the following ways:

❑ Try to keep your methods to five or six parameters *maximum*, unless completely necessary. This will make coding easier.

❑ Make sure that all of those parameters and your methods have meaningful names. Try to spell out the function rather than keeping it short. As an example, it is not easy to identify the meaning of `StdNo` as it is to identify the meaning of `StudentNumber`.

❏ Do not overexert yourself by adding every conceivable method and functional enhancement that an object can have; rather think ahead but code later. You can easily complicate matters for your developers by granting them too many choices, and, at the same time, you may be adding functionality that will never be used.

❏ Try to keep classes within your library to a minimum, because better reuse comes from keeping your libraries smaller.

❏ Properties are extremely useful in a class, and they enable it to be used more easily.

Using Third-Party Class Libraries

A class library compiles to a `.dll` file. To use the class library you need only the DLL, you don't need the source code. This means that you can give your DLL to other people to use and you can use other people's DLLs in your own applications. To demonstrate how to use a DLL, you're going to use the `Internet Favorites.dll` file that you created in the next Try It Out.

You've already seen how to create references to other projects in a solution. This is a really good way to develop and test class libraries and applications at the same time. In this example you're going to pretend that you didn't create `Internet Favorites.dll`. You're going to modify the Favorites Tray application so that it uses `Internet Favorites.dll`. This is a very quick way to demonstrate the use of DLLs, but remember that in real life you would add a reference to the DLL early on in developing the application and then write code to use the DLL.

Try It Out   **Using Internet Favorites.dll in the Favorites Tray Application**

1. Open the Favorites Tray project.

2. Delete the following files from the project: `Favorites.vb`, `WebFavorite.vb`, and `WebFavoriteCollection.vb`.

3. Now you need to add a reference to `Internet Favorites.dll`. Right-click the Favorites Tray project and select Add Reference. Scroll down the list of components in the .NET tab until you find Internet Favorites. Select it and then click the OK button to close the Add Reference dialog box.

4. Remember that the classes in the class library are in the `Internet_Favorites` namespace, so you need to tell your code to look in that namespace for class names you use. Add the following Imports statement to the top of `Form1.vb` and `WebFavoriteMenuItem.vb`:

```
Imports Internet_Favorites
```

You do not need to add it to `ExitMenuItem.vb` because this class does not use any of the classes in the library.

5. Run the program. It will work as normal, but will be using the class library now instead of classes within the application's `.exe` file.

How It Works

This process works more easily than adding a reference to another project does. You still use the classes in the class library in exactly the same way regardless of whether you reference the Class Library project or the compiled DLL. The main difference is that you cannot see or edit the class library's source code.

However, the Visual Studio 2008 environment can still tell a lot about the classes even without the source code. For example, IntelliSense still works. This is because Visual Studio 2008 can tell from the DLL itself what methods and properties are available on each class. You can investigate a class without using IntelliSense but using the Object Browser.

Viewing Classes with the Object Browser

To view classes that can be used within Visual Basic 2008, you can use a quick and easy tool known as the Object Browser. You can also use the Object Browser to view class names and method names on objects. The Object Browser window can be viewed inside Visual Studio 2008 by pressing F2. It is also available by clicking the View ⇨ Object Browser menu or by clicking the Object Browser icon on the toolbar.

The Object Browser is basically used for a quick reference to the classes you need to see. The Object Browser will show all assemblies that are used in the current Solution, including Visual Basic Projects and compiled DLLs.

The browser shows all members including methods, enumerations, and constants. Each member type is shown with a different icon. Figure 13-7 shows the `Internet_Favorites.Favorites` class. You select this class by choosing the `Internet_Favorites` assembly and then within that the `Internet_Favorites` namespace and then within that the `Favorites` class.

Figure 13-7

Remember that an assembly can contain several namespaces and that the same namespace can be spread across several assemblies. It just happens that in Visual Basic 2008 you normally have a single namespace inside a single assembly of the same name.

The MSDN Library documentation that gets installed with Visual Studio 2008 contains plenty of information about classes in the .NET Framework, so you don't often need to use the Object Browser when you're using only .NET Framework classes. It is really useful, however, when you are using a DLL from a third party that does not come with documentation. Often the method and property names can give you a clue about what's happening. Of course, this underlines why it is necessary to choose good names for your classes and their members.

On other occasions, the DLL will provide short descriptions of each of its classes and members. This is done using attributes, which is a subject outside the scope of this text.

Summary

Class libraries are an integral part of Visual Basic 2008; they are important to all of the languages in the .NET Framework. They encompass what you use and what you need to know in terms of the common language runtime and within your development projects.

In this chapter, you have considered the nature of class libraries and how to view the properties and methods contained within them using the Object Browser. You have also seen how the .NET Framework allows developers to avoid DLL Hell through the use of keys and signatures, and you looked at some of the broad issues regarding designing your own components.

In Chapter 14, you learn how to create Windows Forms controls that are components with a user interface, as opposed to class library projects, which are purely code-based. There too, you will see the importance of reusable and stable code.

Exercise

1. Modify the Favorites Viewer project to use the compiled `InternetFavorites.dll` instead of the Internet Favorites project.

Creating Windows Forms User Controls

In this book, you have used many of the controls that come with the .NET Framework, from the Button and the TextBox controls to the ListBox control. You may even have tried to use some of the more advanced controls such as the DataGrid and the TreeView controls. Although at first some of them may be hard to use, they offer a lot of functionality. These controls make it easy to create a user interface in your applications. Once you get to know how to use all their features, you will find that creating user interfaces also becomes a faster experience. Another important aspect that makes controls so useful is that they are reusable. You can drag and drop a Button control onto any form in any new Windows project and it *works* as a button should. The reuse factor is an important reason why Visual Basic, in general, became one of the most popular and is one of the most powerful development languages in use today. Did you know that you owe much of what you experience today in Visual Studio 2008, like Windows Forms Controls, to Visual Basic? The history of Windows Forms Controls has roots in something known as controls Visual Basic Extension (VBX). This later became more widely known as ActiveX, and today, revitalized and reborn into the .NET Framework, it is known as Windows Forms Controls.

In this chapter, you will:

- ❑ Learn what a Windows Forms Control is and how it works
- ❑ Create and use a Windows Forms Control
- ❑ Learn to add methods and events to your control
- ❑ Learn to code for design time and runtime

These controls are best suited for Windows Forms rather than web applications. To learn about Web Forms User Controls you should turn to Chapter 20. This chapter concentrates on the Windows Forms version.

Additionally, you will need Microsoft Visual Basic 2008 Professional Edition or above in order to complete the Try It Out exercises in this chapter.

Windows Forms Controls

Today, there are several good reasons for wanting to create Windows Forms Controls:

❏ You can use the same control throughout an application or in lot of different applications, thus saving on code (reuse).

❏ You can keep code relating to a control within the control's class, making the code cleaner and easier to understand. For example, you could write a button that handles its own click event — meaning you don't need to handle the event in your form's code.

There are two main ways to reuse controls between applications. The first is to add the control's source file to every project in which you need the control. Then, when you build the application, the control is compiled into the main executable. This is the approach you take in this chapter, because it is simpler and allows you to concentrate on how it works.

The second way is to build a control library. Control libraries are similar to the class libraries that you examined in the previous chapter. In fact, they *are* class libraries that happen to contain UI-driven classes. Like any other class library, a control library will compile to its own assembly, which you can use in your applications. This method is attractive, because it means you can distribute the assembly to other developers without giving away your source code. You can also make changes to the assembly, and these will be reflected in the applications that use it — even without the applications being recompiled. The techniques for building the controls are the same regardless of whether you are using a control library or using a control only within your application project.

Creating and Testing a User Control

You might find in the applications that you build, that you have a common need for a control that goes to a database to retrieve certain information, such as login information. If you want to build a robust control, you need to make it as useful as possible to developers using it down the line, while requiring the minimum amount of labor to get it working. You will probably want to encapsulate the functionality of connecting to the database, querying the results, and populating the control with information, so that subsequent developers using your control do not have to know how to do this. This is a key principle of encapsulation — to make life easier for the next developer. In this way, you can also benefit from the more tangible advantage of reducing costs through quality application development and code reuse.

Creating a user control from scratch is not difficult. From one perspective, it is similar to building the Windows forms. In this section, you create a Windows application that uses User Controls. In the first Try It Out, you create a simple control that has three basic Button controls inside of it.

When you create your own custom control that uses (hosts) existing controls inside of it, the control is known as an aggregate control.

A different message is displayed when each button is clicked. You then see how this control can be used in a standard Windows Forms application.

Try It Out   **Building Your First Control**

1. Open Visual Studio 2008 and, on the File menu, select New Project. In the New Project dialog box, select Visual Basic in the Project Types list and Windows Forms Control Library in the Templates list. Enter **MyNamespaceControl** in the Name field and then click OK.

2. Right-click UserControl1.vb in the Solution Explorer and choose Rename from the context menu and change the name to **MyNamespace.vb**. You will have something that looks very much like a form's designer without the title bar or borders. Usually, when building a control, you drag on other controls and define a way in which those controls interact. This extra behavior defines a control's purpose and makes it useful.

3. Drag three Button controls from the Toolbox and drop them on the form and set their Text properties using Figure 14-1 as a guide. Also resize the control so that it also looks similar to Figure 14-1.

Figure 14-1

4. Set the Name properties of the Button controls to **btnApplicationCopyright**, **btnScreenBounds**, and **btnScreenWorkingArea**, respectively.

5. At the moment, this control won't do anything when the buttons are clicked — you need to wire up the event code behind the Click event for each button in order for it to work. Double-click the ApplicationCopyright button and add the highlighted code:

```
Private Sub btnApplicationCopyright_Click(ByVal sender As System.Object, _
    ByVal e As System.EventArgs) Handles btnApplicationCopyright.Click

    MessageBox.Show(My.Application.Info.Copyright)
End Sub
```

6. Select btnScreenBounds in the Class Name combo box at the top of the Code Editor and select the Click event in the Method Name combo box. Add the following highlighted code to the Click event handler:

```
Private Sub btnScreenBounds_Click(ByVal sender As Object, _
    ByVal e As System.EventArgs) Handles btnScreenBounds.Click

    MessageBox.Show(My.Computer.Screen.Bounds.ToString)
End Sub
```

7. Finally, select btnScreenWorkingArea in the Class Name combo box and select the `Click` event in the Method Name combo box. Add this code to the `Click` event handler:

```
Private Sub btnScreenWorkingArea_Click(ByVal sender As Object, _
    ByVal e As System.EventArgs) Handles btnScreenWorkingArea.Click

    MessageBox.Show(My.Computer.Screen.WorkingArea.ToString)
End Sub
```

8. Save your project by clicking the Save All button on the toolbar.

9. Now run your project. The user control will be displayed in a TestContainer dialog box as shown in Figure 14-2. From here, you can test your control by clicking each of the buttons and the appropriate information will be displayed in a message box. When you are done, click the Close button.

Figure 14-2

How It Works

Building the UI for the control is not at all different from building the UI for a Windows application. You simply drag the necessary controls from the Toolbox and drop them on the control designer. Then you wire up the events for the code using the same techniques that you've used all along when building Windows applications.

The code that you added for the btnApplicationCopyright button displays the copyright information for your application. This is done by using the `My.Application` namespace and retrieving the copyright information with the `Copyright` property of the `Info` class.

```
Private Sub btnApplicationCopyright_Click(ByVal sender As System.Object, _
    ByVal e As System.EventArgs) Handles btnApplicationCopyright.Click

    MessageBox.Show(My.Application.Info.Copyright)
End Sub
```

The code that you added for the btnScreenBounds button will display the current boundaries of the computer screen, which is determined from the screen resolution settings. This is done by using the My.Computer namespace and retrieving the screen boundary information with the Bounds property of the Screen class.

```
Private Sub btnScreenBounds_Click(ByVal sender As Object, _
    ByVal e As System.EventArgs) Handles btnScreenBounds.Click

    MessageBox.Show(My.Computer.Screen.Bounds.ToString)
End Sub
```

The code that you added for the btnScreenWorkingArea button will display the current working area of the screen. This is the area of the screen that is available to your application's forms. This is done by using the My.Computer namespace and retrieving the screen working area information with the WorkingArea property of the Screen class.

```
Private Sub btnScreenWorkingArea_Click(ByVal sender As Object, _
    ByVal e As System.EventArgs) Handles btnScreenWorkingArea.Click

    MessageBox.Show(My.Computer.Screen.WorkingArea.ToString)
End Sub
```

When you built the solution, the control was automatically added to the Toolbox in the MyNamespaceControl Components tab. This will not become evident, however, until you add a Windows application to this solution. This will allow you to use your user control in your application just as you would with any other control in the toolbox.

To test the control, you can't just run the project. Instead, you have to put the control onto a form, which will be covered in the following Try It Out.

Try It Out   **Adding Your New User Control to a Form**

1.   Click the File menu and choose Add ⇨ New Project.

2.   In the Add New Project dialog box, ensure that Windows Forms Application is selected in the Templates pane, enter a project name of **Controls**, and then click OK.

3.   Click the MyNamespaceControl Components tab of the Toolbox and drag the MyNamespace control onto Form1.

4. Right-click the Controls project in the Solution Explorer and choose Set as Startup Project from the context menu.

5. Run your project. The control appears on the form, and clicking the buttons has the same effects as you tested the control in the TestContainer dialog box.

How It Works

A custom-built control works the same as any other control that you've used up until this point. You simply drag the control from the Toolbox, drop it on your form, and run your project. You didn't need to wire up any code for the Click events of the buttons, because that functionality is part of the control itself.

Exposing Properties from User Controls

A user control is implemented as a class. Therefore, anything that you can do with a class, you can also do with a user control. This means that you can add properties, methods, and events to the user control that can be manipulated by whoever is consuming it. First, take a look at adding a new property to your control.

Your control can have two sorts of properties: those that can be manipulated from the Properties window at design time and those that have to be programmatically manipulated at runtime. For example, at design time you might want to change properties pertaining to the color or the font used to draw the control. But at runtime you might want to change properties that depend on the contents of a file that the user selected, and so on. Usually, if the property is a fairly simple type such as String, Integer, or Boolean and doesn't have parameters, it can be manipulated at design time. If the property is a complex object, such as a database or file connection, or if it has parameters, you'll have to manipulate the property at runtime.

Adding Properties

In the following Try It Out, you take a look at adding a property to your control. The property you're going to add is called ApplicationName. This property will contain the name of your application. When this property is changed, you'll want to display the text in the title bar of the message boxes on the control.

Try It Out   Adding a New Property to the MyNamespace Control

1. To add a new property you need a member variable that will store the value. Switch to the Code Editor for MyNamespace and add the following highlighted code:

```
Public Class MyNamespace

    'Private members
    Private strApplicationName As String = String.Empty
```

2. When this property is set, you need to set the text in the private member that you just defined. Add this code directly after the lines you added in step 1:

```
Public Property ApplicationName() As String
    Get
        Return strApplicationName
    End Get
    Set(ByVal value As String)
        strApplicationName = value
    End Set
End Property
```

3. To have the message boxes display the application name in the title bar, you need to set the caption parameter of the Show method of the MessageBox class. Modify the Click events for each of the buttons as shown:

```
Private Sub btnApplicationCopyright_Click(ByVal sender As System.Object, _
    ByVal e As System.EventArgs) Handles btnApplicationCopyright.Click

    MessageBox.Show(My.Application.Info.Copyright, _
        strApplicationName)
End Sub

Private Sub btnScreenBounds_Click(ByVal sender As Object, _
    ByVal e As System.EventArgs) Handles btnScreenBounds.Click

    MessageBox.Show(My.Computer.Screen.Bounds.ToString, _
        strApplicationName)
End Sub

Private Sub btnScreenWorkingArea_Click(ByVal sender As Object, _
    ByVal e As System.EventArgs) Handles btnScreenWorkingArea.Click

    MessageBox.Show(My.Computer.Screen.WorkingArea.ToString, _
        strApplicationName)
End Sub
```

4. To expose the new property for this control to Form1, you need to build the project. Right-click the MyNamespaceControl project in the Solution Explorer and select Build from the context menu. The new property will now be exposed.

5. Switch to the Form Designer for Form1 and select the MyNamespace1 control and delete it. Then drag a new MyNamespace control from the Toolbox and drop it on your form. In the Properties window the new ApplicationName property will appear under the Misc category (or in the usual place if you have the properties arranged alphabetically).

6. Set the ApplicationName property to **My Windows Application**.

7. Run your project and click any of the buttons on the form. Each message box will display the text My Windows Application in the title bar of the message box.

How It Works

You'll notice that the default value of an empty string for the ApplicationName property has passed through to the designer. If you change the property in the Properties window, the text displayed in the title bar of the message boxes of the control will change.

When the designer needs to update the Properties window, it calls into the object and requests the ApplicatioName property. Likewise, when you change the value, it calls into the object and sets the property. This also happens when the form is loaded from disk when you start up the designer.

Exposing Methods from User Controls

As you've probably guessed, if you can expose new properties for your control, you can also expose new methods. All that you need to do to make this happen is to add a public function or procedure to the control, and then you'll be able to call it from the form that's hosting the control, which you do in the next Try It Out.

Try It Out   Adding a Method to the MyNamespace Control

1. Switch to the Code Editor for MyNamespace.vb and add this function:

```
Public Function TaskBarHeight() As Integer
    Return My.Computer.Screen.Bounds.Height - _
        My.Computer.Screen.WorkingArea.Height
End Function
```

2. Switch to the Forms Designer for Form1. Drag a Button control from the Toolbox and drop it on your form. Set the Name property to **btnTaskbarHeight** and the Text property to **Taskbar Height**.

3. Double-click the button and add the following highlighted code to its Click event handler:

```
Private Sub btnTaskbarHeight_Click(ByVal sender As System.Object, _
    ByVal e As System.EventArgs) Handles btnTaskbarHeight.Click

    MessageBox.Show("Taskbar Height = " & _
        MyNamespace1.TaskBarHeight & " pixels", "Form1")
End Sub
```

4. Run your project and click the Taskbar Height button on Form1. You'll see a message box with the calculated height of the taskbar.

How It Works

Exposing a function or procedure from a user control is no different from exposing a function or procedure from a class. You just need to mark the function or procedure as Public so that it is exposed to the user of the class.

The `TaskBarHeight` function calculates the height of the taskbar by subtracting the working area height from the screen bounds height and returning the calculated value.

```
Public Function TaskBarHeight() As Integer
    Return My.Computer.Screen.Bounds.Height - _
        My.Computer.Screen.WorkingArea.Height
End Function
```

When you call the `TaskBarHeight` function from your code in Form1, you specify the control name of `MyNamespace1` and then choose the `TaskBarHeight` function from the drop-down list in IntelliSense.

```
Private Sub btnTaskbarHeight_Click(ByVal sender As System.Object, _
    ByVal e As System.EventArgs) Handles btnTaskbarHeight.Click

    MessageBox.Show("Taskbar Height = " & _
        MyNamespace1.TaskBarHeight & " pixels", "Form1")
End Sub
```

There was no need to recompile the MyNamespaceControl control to expose this new function to Form1, as it did not affect the control's user interface or properties.

Exposing Events from User Controls

Now that you've seen how to expose your own properties and methods from your control, you need to take a look at how to expose your own events from the control. When you add events to one of your own controls, people who use your control can take action in their code when the event is raised.

In the next Try It Out, you add three events that return the data that is displayed in the message boxes that get displayed when the buttons are clicked.

Try It Out   Defining and Raising Events

1. Defining an event is as simple as adding an `Event` statement, the event name, and the parameters that the event will return. Add the following highlighted code to the `MyNamespace.vb` file:

```
'Private members
Private strApplicationName As String = String.Empty

'Public Events
Public Event ApplicationCopyrightChanged(ByVal text As String)
Public Event ScreenBoundsChanged(ByVal bounds As Rectangle)
Public Event ScreenWorkingAreaChanged(ByVal bounds As Rectangle)
```

2. To raise an event you need to specify the `RaiseEvent` statement, passing it the event name as well as the parameters for the event being raised. Modify the code in `MyNamespace.vb` as follows:

```
Private Sub btnApplicationCopyright_Click(ByVal sender As System.Object, _
    ByVal e As System.EventArgs) Handles btnApplicationCopyright.Click

    RaiseEvent ApplicationCopyrightChanged( _
        My.Application.Info.Copyright)
    MessageBox.Show(My.Application.Info.Copyright, _
        strApplicationName)
End Sub

Private Sub btnScreenBounds_Click(ByVal sender As Object, _
    ByVal e As System.EventArgs) Handles btnScreenBounds.Click

    RaiseEvent ScreenBoundsChanged(My.Computer.Screen.Bounds)
    MessageBox.Show(My.Computer.Screen.Bounds.ToString, _
        strApplicationName)
End Sub

Private Sub btnScreenWorkingArea_Click(ByVal sender As Object, _
    ByVal e As System.EventArgs) Handles btnScreenWorkingArea.Click

    RaiseEvent ScreenWorkingAreaChanged(My.Computer.Screen.WorkingArea)
    MessageBox.Show(My.Computer.Screen.WorkingArea.ToString, _
        strApplicationName)
End Sub
```

How It Works

As mentioned earlier, to define an event, you specify the `Event` statement, the event name, and the parameters that the event will return. Most events for controls are going to be Click or Changed; thus you have specified the different button names suffixed with the word `Changed`.

The Application Copyright button returns the application copyright as a string; thus, the parameter for the `ApplicationCopyrightChanged` event is specified as a `String` data type. The Screen Bounds and Screen Working Area buttons return the screen information in a `Rectangle` structure; thus you specified the `Rectangle` structure as the data type for these events.

```
'Public Events
Public Event ApplicationCopyrightChanged(ByVal text As String)
Public Event ScreenBoundsChanged(ByVal bounds As Rectangle)
Public Event ScreenWorkingAreaChanged(ByVal bounds As Rectangle)
```

To raise an event, you have to use the `RaiseEvent` statement. This looks after the tricky aspect of actually telling the control's owner what event has been raised and passes it the appropriate parameters.

You'll have noticed that when you typed the word `RaiseEvent`, Visual Studio 2008 IntelliSense kicked in and provided a drop-down list of the events that you defined. This is just another example of how the IDE makes your life as a developer much easier.

In each instance of raising the events, you simply pass the event being raised; the data that will be displayed in the message box when the appropriate button is clicked.

```
Private Sub btnApplicationCopyright_Click(ByVal sender As System.Object, _
    ByVal e As System.EventArgs) Handles btnApplicationCopyright.Click

    RaiseEvent ApplicationCopyrightChanged( _
        My.Application.Info.Copyright)
    MessageBox.Show(My.Application.Info.Copyright, _
        strApplicationName)
End Sub

Private Sub btnScreenBounds_Click(ByVal sender As Object, _
    ByVal e As System.EventArgs) Handles btnScreenBounds.Click

    RaiseEvent ScreenBoundsChanged(My.Computer.Screen.Bounds)
    MessageBox.Show(My.Computer.Screen.Bounds.ToString, _
        strApplicationName)
End Sub

Private Sub btnScreenWorkingArea_Click(ByVal sender As Object, _
    ByVal e As System.EventArgs) Handles btnScreenWorkingArea.Click

    RaiseEvent ScreenWorkingAreaChanged(My.Computer.Screen.WorkingArea)
    MessageBox.Show(My.Computer.Screen.WorkingArea.ToString, _
        strApplicationName)
End Sub
```

All that remains now is to detect when the event has fired and do something. This is known as *consuming* an event. When a control fires an event, you can hook into the event handler. By doing this, you receive notification that the event has fired and can do something with the data that the event exposes. This is one of the core concepts of the control/event methodology that you have been using throughout this book.

Try It Out   **Consuming Events**

1. Switch to the Forms Designer for Form1 and add three TextBox controls as shown in Figure 14-3. Set the Name properties to **txtApplicationCopyright**, **txtScreenBounds**, and **txtScreenWorkingArea**, respectively.

Figure 14-3

2. Switch to the Code Editor for Form1 and select MyNamespace1 in the Class Name combo box at the top of the Code Editor. Click in the Method Name combo box, and you'll see your `ApplicationCopyrightChanged` event in the Method Name combo box as shown in Figure 14-4. Remember, although you specifically defined three events for this control, you still get all of the other events that were defined on the various base classes that your control class inherits from:

Figure 14-4

3. Of course, if you select the control and an event, you are automatically given a handler stub into which you can add your event-handling code, just as you have been doing with the other controls that you've used all along. Select the `ApplicationCopyrightChanged` event in the Method Name combo box. Now add the following highlighted code to the `ApplicationCopyrightChanged` event handler:

```
Private Sub MyNamespace1_ApplicationCopyrightChanged(ByVal text As String) _
    Handles MyNamespace1.ApplicationCopyrightChanged

    txtApplicationCopyright.Text = text
End Sub
```

4. Select MyNamespace1 in the Class Name combo box and the `ScreenBoundsChanged` event in the Method Name combo box. Add the following highlighted code:

```
Private Sub MyNamespace1_ScreenBoundsChanged(ByVal bounds As _
    System.Drawing.Rectangle) Handles MyNamespace1.ScreenBoundsChanged

    txtScreenBounds.Text = bounds.ToString
End Sub
```

5. Finally, select MyNamespace1 in the Class Name combo box and the `ScreenWorkingAreaChanged` event in the Method Name combo box. Add the following highlighted code to the `ScreenWorkingAreaChanged` event handler:

```
Private Sub MyNamespace1_ScreenWorkingAreaChanged(ByVal bounds As _
    System.Drawing.Rectangle) Handles MyNamespace1.ScreenWorkingAreaChanged

    txtScreenWorkingArea.Text = bounds.ToString
End Sub
```

6.   Run your project. When you click each of the buttons, the corresponding text box will be populated with the data returned by the event, and then the message box will be displayed.

How It Works

Consuming control events in your application is very straightforward and something that you've been doing all along with Button and TextBox controls. You merely select the control name in the Class Name combo box in the Code Editor and the appropriate event in the Method Name combo box and then write the appropriate code to consume, or handle, the event that has been raised by the control. In the case of the MyNamespace control, you are consuming three different events: ApplicationCopyrightChanged, ScreenBoundsChanged, and ScreenWorkingAreaChanged.

For the ApplicationCopyrightChanged event, you simply take the text returned from the event and set it in the Text property of your text box.

```
Private Sub MyNamespace1_ApplicationCopyrightChanged(ByVal text As String) _
    Handles MyNamespace1.ApplicationCopyrightChanged

    txtApplicationCopyright.Text = text
End Sub
```

The ScreenBoundsChanged event is a little different. This event returns data in a Rectangle structure, which you must convert to a String data type in order to set it in the Text property of your text box. This is done using the ToString method of the Rectangle structure.

```
Private Sub MyNamespace1_ScreenBoundsChanged(ByVal bounds As _
    System.Drawing.Rectangle) Handles MyNamespace1.ScreenBoundsChanged

    txtScreenBounds.Text = bounds.ToString
End Sub
```

The ScreenWorkingAreaChanged event is like the ScreenBoundsChanged event. This event also returns data in a Rectangle structure, which must be converted to a String data type before it can be set in the Text property of your text box.

```
Private Sub MyNamespace1_ScreenWorkingAreaChanged(ByVal bounds As _
    System.Drawing.Rectangle) Handles MyNamespace1.ScreenWorkingAreaChanged

    txtScreenWorkingArea.Text = bounds.ToString
End Sub
```

Design Time or Runtime

In certain circumstances, it's useful to know whether your control is in design mode or run mode. The control is in design mode when a form is being designed and the properties of the control are being set; it is in run mode when the form is being run and the control is able to expose methods and events.

As an example, imagine that you have a control that establishes a database connection when a certain property is set. It might not be appropriate for that control to establish the connection when the form is being designed, but you will want it to when the application is being run.

Usually, a control itself has a Boolean property called `DesignMode`, which returns `True` if the control is in design mode and `False` if it isn't.

In this next Try It Out, you're going to modify the MyNamespace control by adding a Label and Timer control to it. The `Text` property of the label will be updated with the text *Design Mode* when your MyNamespace control is in design mode and updated with the current time when the control is in run mode.

Try It Out   Creating a Control That Understands Design Mode

1. Switch to the Control Designer for the MyNamespace control. Expand the height of the control so that you can place a Label control underneath the last button.

2. Drag a Label control from the Toolbox and center it underneath the last button control. Set the Name property to **lblTime**.

3. Drag and drop a Timer control from the Components tab of the Toolbox onto the Control Designer. The timer will be added to the bottom of the IDE. Accept the default properties for this control and ensure that the Enabled property is set to **False** and that Interval is set to **100**.

4. Switch to the Code Editor for your MyNamespace control. You can detect when your control has been added to a form through the `InitLayout` method, which is defined on `System .Windows.Forms.Control`. This happens both at design time and at runtime. This is the best point to determine which mode you're in and, if appropriate, to start the timer. Add the following code:

```
Protected Overrides Sub InitLayout()
    MyBase.InitLayout()

    'Are we in design mode?
    If DesignMode Then
        lblTime.Text = "Design Mode"
    Else
        Timer1.Enabled = True
    End If
End Sub
```

5. The last thing to do is to add code to the `Tick` event of the timer. Select Timer1 in the Class Name combo box at the top of the Code Editor and the `Tick` event in the Method Name combo box. Add the highlighted code to the `Tick` event handler:

```
Private Sub Timer1_Tick(ByVal sender As Object, _
    ByVal e As System.EventArgs) Handles Timer1.Tick

        'Display the time
        lblTime.Text = Now.ToLongTimeString

    End Sub
```

6. You'll need to build the project before the changes to the control can be picked up by your Controls application. Build the project by right-clicking the MyNamespaceControl project in the Solution Explorer and choosing Build from the context menu.

7. Open the Forms Designer for Form1 in the Controls project. Delete the current MyNamespace control from the form and drag a new one from the Toolbox and drop it on your form. You'll see the text `Design Mode` as shown in Figure 14-5.

Figure 14-5

8. Run the project. You will see that the `Design Mode` text is replaced by the current time.

How It Works

The `InitLayout` method is fired when the control is initialized, both at design time and at runtime. The `DesignMode` property of your control returns a `Boolean` value of `True` when the control is in design mode and a value of `False` when the control is in run mode.

If your control is in design mode, you simply want to display the text `Design Mode` on your label control. When the control is in run mode, you want to enable the Timer control, and the Timer control will update the label with the current time.

```
Protected Overrides Sub InitLayout()
    MyBase.InitLayout()

    'Are we in design mode?
    If DesignMode Then
        lblTime.Text = "Design Mode"
    Else
        Timer1.Enabled = True
    End If
End Sub
```

Of course, there are many other occasions when you might want your code to behave differently at runtime than at design time. An example could be that validation rules for a property will be different. In these cases, you would check the control's DesignMode property in exactly the same way.

The Tick event of the Timer control gets called at the specified interval of the Timer control, which in this case is every 100 milliseconds. When the Tick event is fired, you want to update the Text property of the label control with the current time. This is done by retrieving the current long time from the ToLongTimeString property of the Now object.

```
Private Sub Timer1_Tick(ByVal sender As Object, _
    ByVal e As System.EventArgs) Handles Timer1.Tick

    'Display the time
    lblTime.Text = Now.ToLongTimeString
End Sub
```

Because you made changes to the actual UI of the control, you had to rebuild the control and then delete the current control from Form1 and get a new instance of it from the Toolbox. You don't have to do this when simply making code changes to the control, because those changes are automatically picked up.

Creating a Command Link Control

Windows Vista introduced a lot of new controls in the operating system such as the Command Link control shown in Figure 14-6. Unfortunately, some of these controls are not available in the Visual Studio 2008 toolbox and are not available in the .NET Framework. To use those controls in your applications, you need to create a Windows Forms Control that inherits the base control and then sets the appropriate properties and parameters needed to create the control desired.

In this next section, you create a Command Link control that can be used in your own applications. Since this is a new control in the Windows Vista operating system, it is not available in previous Windows operating systems. If you are not running Windows Vista, you can skip this section of the chapter.

Figure 14-6

Building the Command Link Control

In this Try It Out, you build the Command Link control. The Command Link control is actually just a Button control with a different style and additional properties. Since your control will inherit from the `Windows.Forms.Button` class, it may be worthwhile to review the section on Inheritance in Chapter 11.

Try It Out **Creating the Command Link Control**

1. In Visual Studio 2008, click the File menu and select New Project. In the New Project dialog box, select Visual Basic in the Project Types list and Windows Forms Control Library in the Templates list. Enter **ButtonExtended** in the Name field and then click OK.

2. Right-click UserControl1.vb in the Solution Explorer and select Delete from the context menu.

3. Right-click the ButtonExtended project in the Solution Explorer and select Add ⇨ Class from the context menu. In the Add New Item – ButtonExtended dialog box, enter **CommandLink.vb** and click Add.

4. Add the following `Imports` statements at the top of the class:

```
Imports System.Windows.Forms
Imports System.Runtime.InteropServices
Imports System.ComponentModel

Public Class CommandLink
```

5. Since this control inherits from the `Windows.Forms.Button` class, it should have the standard Button icon in the Toolbox. Add the following code above the `Class` statement:

```
<ToolboxBitmap(GetType(System.Windows.Forms.Button))> _
Public Class CommandLink
```

6. Add the following `Inherits` statement so that this control will inherit the base properties and methods in the `Button` class:

```
Public Class CommandLink
    Inherits Button
```

7. Add the following variables, objects, and constants:

```
'Private variables and objects
Private blnUACShield As Boolean = False
Private strSupplementalExplanation As String = String.Empty
Private objBitmap As Bitmap

'Private constants
Private Const BS_COMMANDLINK As Integer = 14
Private Const BCM_SETNOTE As Integer = 5641
Private Const BCM_SETSHIELD As Integer = 5644
Private Const BM_SETIMAGE As Integer = 247
```

8. You'll need to call some unmanaged code from your Visual Basic 2008 code to so add the following shared functions:

```
'SendMessage API
<DllImport("user32.dll", CharSet:=CharSet.Unicode)> _
Private Shared Function SendMessage(ByVal hWnd As IntPtr, _
    ByVal msg As Integer, ByVal wParam As Integer, _
    ByVal lParam As String) As Integer
End Function

<DllImport("user32.dll")> _
Private Shared Function SendMessage(ByVal hWnd As IntPtr, _
    ByVal msg As Integer, ByVal wParam As Integer, _
    ByVal lParam As Boolean) As Integer
End Function

<DllImport("user32.dll")> _
Public Shared Function SendMessage(ByVal hWnd As IntPtr, _
    ByVal msg As Integer, ByVal wParam As Integer, _
    ByVal lParam As Integer) As Integer
End Function
```

9. You need a constructor for your control to override the default Button style. Add this code to your class:

```
Public Sub New()
    'Set the FlatStyle property
    Me.FlatStyle = FlatStyle.System
End Sub
```

10. A Command Link button is larger than a standard Button control so you need to override the default size of the Button control when a developer adds the control to their form. Add this code:

```
Protected Overrides ReadOnly Property DefaultSize() _
    As System.Drawing.Size
    Get
        'Set the new default size of the control
        'when placed on a form
        Return New Size(270, 60)
    End Get
End Property
```

11. The CreateParams property initializes the style of the button so add this code:

```
Protected Overrides ReadOnly Property CreateParams() _
    As System.Windows.Forms.CreateParams
    Get
        'Set the style of the Button to CommandLink
        Dim objCreateParams As CreateParams = MyBase.CreateParams
        objCreateParams.Style = objCreateParams.Style Or BS_COMMANDLINK
        Return objCreateParams
    End Get
End Property
```

12. After initializing the style of the `Button` class to create a Command Link button, the default image on the button is a green arrow. You need to create a property to override the default image and to display the User Access Control (UAC) shield image to indicate that elevated user privileges will be needed to perform the actions associated with the Command Link button. Add the following code to create the `UACShield` property:

```
<Category("Appearance"), _
Description("Indicates if the UAC shield icon will be displayed " & _
"on the control."), _
DefaultValue(False)> _
Public Property UACShield() As Boolean
    Get
        Return blnUACShield
    End Get
    Set(ByVal value As Boolean)
        blnUACShield = value
        'Add the shield icon to the control
        SendMessage(Me.Handle, BCM_SETSHIELD, 0, blnUACShield)
    End Set
End Property
```

13. A supplemental explanation is used when a Command Link is not self-explanatory. Add the following code to create the `SupplementalExplanation` property:

```
<Category("Appearance"), _
Description("The optional supplemental explanation for the control."), _
DefaultValue("")> _
Public Property SupplementalExplanation() As String
    Get
        Return strSupplementalExplanation
    End Get
    Set(ByVal value As String)
        strSupplementalExplanation = value
        'Add the supplemental explanation to the control
        SendMessage(Me.Handle, BCM_SETNOTE, 0, value)
    End Set
End Property
```

14. The final bit of code needed will override the default `Image` property of the `Button` class to allow you to display an image other than the default green arrow or UAC shield:

```
<Category("Appearance"), _
Description("The image that will be displayed on the control."), _
DefaultValue(GetType(Nullable))> _
Public Shadows Property Image() As Bitmap
    Get
        Return objBitmap
    End Get
    Set(ByVal value As Bitmap)
        objBitmap = value
        UACShield = False
        If value IsNot Nothing Then
            'Add the image to the control instead of using the default image
```

```
                SendMessage(Me.Handle, BM_SETIMAGE, 1, objBitmap.GetHicon.ToInt32)
        End If
    End Set
End Property
```

15. Double-click My Project in the Solution Explorer. The property page for the project will open to the Application tab.

16. Click the Assembly Information button. In the Assembly Information dialog box, enter a description in the Description field, a company name in the Company Name field and copyright information in the Copyright field. Click OK to save your changes and close the dialog box.

17. Save your project by clicking the Save All button on the toolbar.

18. Right-click the ButtonExtended project in the Solution Explorer and choose Build from the context menu.

19. In the Solution Explorer, double-click the `CommandLink.vb` file to open the Components Designer. Hover your mouse over the Toolbox to open it and then right-click in the Common Controls tab and select Choose Items from the context menu.

20. In the Choose Toolbox Items dialog box, click the Browse button on the .NET Framework Components tab and browse to the `bin\Release` folder for this project. In the Open dialog box, select `ButtonExtended.dll` and then click Open. Then click OK in the Choose Toolbox Items dialog box to close it.

21. Your CommandLink control is now listed in the Toolbox at the bottom of the Common Controls tab. You can move the control up in the list by dragging it to a new location.

22. Close Visual Studio 2008.

How It Works

This code starts with three `Imports` statements. The `Button` class exists in three different namespaces and you need your control to differentiate which namespace it belongs to which is why you include the `System.Windows.Forms` namespace. The `System.Runtime.InteropServices` namespace is needed to call unmanaged code from your Visual Basic 2008 managed code. The `System .ComponentModel` namespace is needed to provide the attributes for the control properties that you define:

```
Imports System.Windows.Forms
Imports System.Runtime.InteropServices
Imports System.ComponentModel
```

Each control in the Toolbox has an associated icon. Since this control inherits and extends the Button control, it only makes sense to use the Button controls icon in the Toolbox. The `ToolboxBitmapAttribute` class is used to specify the icon from the Button control. Note that although you are using the `ToolboxBitmapAttribute` class, you specify only `ToolboxBitmap` in the code. This is true for all types of attributes as you'll discover later when we discuss the attributes used on the properties that you defined. The constructor for the `ToolboxBitmapAttribute` class in this code uses an object with an embedded image to be used for the icon. You use the GetType operator to return an object of the Button class:

```
<ToolboxBitmap(GetType(System.Windows.Forms.Button))> _
Public Class CommandLink
```

Since the Button class is the base class for this control, you inherit the Button class through the use of the Inherits statement:

```
Public Class CommandLink
    Inherits Button
```

Next, you declare the variables, objects, and constants that will be used throughout the code. The blnUACShield variable is used to keep track of the UACShield property to determine if the UAC Shield should be displayed or not. The strSupplementalExplanation variable is used to hold the supplemental explanation text when set. The objBitmap object is used to hold the image set in the Image property.

The following constants are used to set the Button style to Command Link, to set the supplemental explanation text, set the UAC Shield icon, and to set an image that overrides the default green arrow icon and UAC Shield icon:

```
'Private variables and objects
Private blnUACShield As Boolean = False
Private strSupplementalExplanation As String = String.Empty
Private objBitmap As Bitmap

'Private constants
Private Const BS_COMMANDLINK As Integer = 14
Private Const BCM_SETNOTE As Integer = 5641
Private Const BCM_SETSHIELD As Integer = 5644
Private Const BM_SETIMAGE As Integer = 247
```

The three functions that follow are calls to the SendMessage API in unmanaged code in the user32.dll. The SendMessage API sends a message to a window and in this project the form hosting the control. Notice that these are overloaded functions differing only in their last parameter. The DllImportAttribute class is used to specify that the method defined is exposed through unmanaged code. You pass the DLL name of the unmanaged code to the constructor of the DllImport attribute. The first function also specifies the CharSet field to indicate to the compiler how to marshal string parameters to the unmanaged code. Here you specify that strings should be sent as Unicode:

```
'SendMessage API
<DllImport("user32.dll", CharSet:=CharSet.Unicode)> _
Private Shared Function SendMessage(ByVal hWnd As IntPtr, _
    ByVal msg As Integer, ByVal wParam As Integer, _
    ByVal lParam As String) As Integer
End Function

<DllImport("user32.dll")> _
Private Shared Function SendMessage(ByVal hWnd As IntPtr, _
    ByVal msg As Integer, ByVal wParam As Integer, _
    ByVal lParam As Boolean) As Integer
End Function
```

```
<DllImport("user32.dll")> _
Public Shared Function SendMessage(ByVal hWnd As IntPtr, _
    ByVal msg As Integer, ByVal wParam As Integer, _
    ByVal lParam As Integer) As Integer
End Function
```

Now you get to the constructor for your class. You have seen the default style for a button in the numerous projects that you have built. You want to override the default style of the button so you set the FlatStyle property to the System constant from the FlatStyle enumeration. This indicates that the operating system will determine the style to be used:

> When setting the FlatStyle property to System for a Button control, the Background, ImageAlign, Image, ImageIndex, ImageList and TextAlign properties will be ignored. You have added code to override the Image property to allow an image to be set in the Command Link.

```
Public Sub New()
    'Set the FlatStyle property
    Me.FlatStyle = FlatStyle.System
End Sub
```

The DefaultSize property is used to set the control's initial size when it is created on a form. The DefaultSize property is defined as Overridable which allows you to specify the Overrides keyword to override the default behavior of this property. Here you define a new default size for the control when it is created on a form:

```
Protected Overrides ReadOnly Property DefaultSize() _
    As System.Drawing.Size
    Get
        'Set the new default size of the control
        'when placed on a form
        Return New Size(270, 60)
    End Get
End Property
```

The CreateParams class is used to specify information about the initial state and appearance of a control when it is created. You can also override the CreateParams property as shown in the following code. However, it is important that you create a CreateParams object and set it to the base class's CreateParams object, which is what you have done in the first line of code. This ensures that your control will use the CreateParams class defined for the base class that you are inheriting and that your control will work the way it was initially intended in the base class and then allows you to override the necessary properties to get the look and feel desired.

After you create a CreateParams object that is set from the base class's CreateParams property, you can then proceed to override the properties of the CreateParams class. In the second line of code, you set the Style property in the CreateParams class using a bitwise combination of the current style plus the style defined in the BS_COMMANDLINK constant. This causes your normal button to appear as a Command Link button. Since this is a read-only property, you return the CreateParams object that you created here:

```
Protected Overrides ReadOnly Property CreateParams() _
    As System.Windows.Forms.CreateParams
    Get
        'Set the style of the Button to CommandLink
        Dim objCreateParams As CreateParams = MyBase.CreateParams
        objCreateParams.Style = objCreateParams.Style Or BS_COMMANDLINK
        Return objCreateParams
    End Get
End Property
```

Next, you want to add some additional properties for the new Command Link control that you are creating. The green arrow shown in the first Command Link in Figure 14-6 is the default icon that is displayed for a Command Link control. To display the user access control (UAC) shield icon (the icon shown in the second Command Link in Figure 14-6) in the Command Link control, you need to create a property to override the default icon. The UACShield property does just that.

This property starts out by defining the CategoryAttribute class that specifies the category in the Properties window that this property will be displayed under when the properties are sorted by category. The DescriptionAttribute class provides the description for this property that gets displayed at the bottom of the Properties window when this property is selected. Finally the DefaultValueAttribute class provides a default value for this property when the control is created. Since this property gets and sets a Boolean data type, the DefaultValue has been specified as False, indicating that no UAC Shield should be displayed by default when the control is created.

The Get portion of this property returns the value contained in the blnUACShield variable. The Set portion of this property first stores the Boolean value set in this property in the blnUACShield variable and then calls the SendMessage API passing it a number of parameters.

The first parameter is the handle to this control and the second parameter is the BCM_SETSHIELD constant indicating that the SendMessage API should set or remove a UAC Shield from the Command Link control. The third parameter is not used so a value of 0 is passed. The final parameter is a Boolean value indicating whether to set the UAC Shield icon or to remove it. Here you pass the value contained in the blnUACShield variable:

```
<Category("Appearance"), _
Description("Indicates if the UAC shield icon will be displayed " & _
"on the control."), _
DefaultValue(False)> _
Public Property UACShield() As Boolean
    Get
        Return blnUACShield
    End Get
    Set(ByVal value As Boolean)
        blnUACShield = value
        'Add the shield icon to the control
        SendMessage(Me.Handle, BCM_SETSHIELD, 0, blnUACShield)
    End Set
End Property
```

The next property that you create is the SupplementalExplanation property. This property gets or sets the supplemental explanation text that is displayed beneath the main text of the control. A supplemental explanation is optional and thus the DefaultValueAttribute class is specified with an empty string so that this control is initialized with no text set in the SupplementalExplanation property.

The Get portion of this property returns the text contained in the strSupplementalExplanation variable. The Set portion of this property sets the text passed to it in the strSupplementalExplanation variable and then calls the SendMessage API to set the supplemental explanation for this control.

Again, the handle to this control is passed as the first parameter to the SendMessage API and then the BCM_SETNOTE constant is passed as the second parameter. The third parameter is not used and a value of 0 is passed for that parameter. The final parameter contains the supplemental text in the value variable.

```
<Category("Appearance"), _
Description("The optional supplemental explanation for the control."), _
DefaultValue("")> _
Public Property SupplementalExplanation() As String
    Get
        Return strSupplementalExplanation
    End Get
    Set(ByVal value As String)
        strSupplementalExplanation = value
        'Add the supplemental explanation to the control
        SendMessage(Me.Handle, BCM_SETNOTE, 0, value)
    End Set
End Property
```

The final property is the Image property and the code here shadows the Image property in the base class. This means that this code redeclares that property and only this code will be executed. The CategoryAttribute and DescriptionAttribute class provide the category and description of this property in the Properties window. Notice that the DefaultValueAttribute class for this property has been set to the Nullable class. The Nullable class supports setting a value to nothing. Since this property gets and sets a Bitmap object, you must set the Bitmap returned from this property to nothing, hence the Nullable class. The GetType operator returns a Type object of the specified type that is passed to it. Since you pass the Nullable class to the GetType operator, it returns a value of Nothing.

The Get portion of this property returns the image stored in the objBitmap object. The Set portion of this property is a little more involved. First, you set the image contained in the value parameter in the objBitmap object. Then you call the UACShield property passing it a value of False to turn off the UAC Shield icon if it is currently displayed.

Finally, you make sure the value parameter is not Nothing, which indicates that the Image property is being cleared. If the value parameter is not Nothing, then you call the SendMessage API passing it the handle to this control and the BM_SETIMAGE constant. You pass a value of 1 for the wParam parameter and the integer handle to the image.

You get the handle to the image by calling the GetHicon method on the objBitmap object, which returns the handle to the image as a IntPtr structure. Since the lParam parameter of the SendMessage API expects an Integer data type, you call the ToInt32 method of the IntPtr structure to convert the handle to an Integer data type.

After the `SendMessage` API is called, it sets the image in the Command Link control overriding the default green arrow with the image specified.

```
<Category("Appearance"), _
Description("The image that will be displayed on the control."), _
DefaultValue(GetType(Nullable))> _
Public Shadows Property Image() As Bitmap
    Get
        Return objBitmap
    End Get
    Set(ByVal value As Bitmap)
        objBitmap = value
        UACShield = False
        If value IsNot Nothing Then
            'Add the image to the control instead of using the default image
            SendMessage(Me.Handle, BM_SETIMAGE, 1, objBitmap.GetHicon.ToInt32)
        End If
    End Set
End Property
```

In Step 20 of the Try It Out, you add the new Command Link control to the Common Components tab of the Toolbox. This makes this control always available in the Toolbox to other applications, as you'll see in the next Try It Out exercise.

Using the Command Link Control

In this Try It Out, you build a simple application that uses the new Command Link control and exercises all of the properties that you added.

Try It Out   **Using the Command Link Control**

1. In Visual Studio 2008, click the File menu and select New Project. In the New Project dialog box, select Visual Basic in the Project Types list and Windows Forms Application in the Templates list. Enter **Command Link Control Demo** in the Name field and then click OK.

2. Click Form1 in the Forms Designer and then set the form properties as follows:

    ❑   Set `BackColor` to **White**.

    ❑   Set `ControlBox` to **False**.

    ❑   Set `Font` to **Segoe UI, Regular, 8pt**.

    ❑   Set `Size` to **395, 300**.

    ❑   Set `Text` to **Program Error**.

3. Add a Label control to your form and align it to the upper-left corner of your form. Set the following properties of the Label control:

- ❑ Set `Font` to **Segoe UI, Regular, 12pt**.
- ❑ Set `ForeColor` to **Navy**.
- ❑ Set `Text` to **This program has discovered a problem with the installed device.dll file**.
- ❑ Set `AutoSize` to **False**.
- ❑ Set `Size` to **350, 50**.

4. In the Toolbox under the Common Controls tab, drag a CommanLink control and position it beneath the Label control on your form. Set the following properties of this control:

- ❑ Set `Size` to **343, 45**.
- ❑ Set `Text` to **Send a Report to Wrox**.

5. Drag another CommandLink control from the Toolbox and position it beneath the first one. Set its properties as follows:

- ❑ Set `Size` to **343, 65**.
- ❑ Set `SupplementalExplanation` to **You can reinstall the program to fix a corrupt installation file**.
- ❑ Set `Text` to **Reinstall the Program**.
- ❑ Set `UACShield` to **True**.

6. Drag a third CommandLink control from the Toolbox and position it beneath the last one. Set its properties as follows:

- ❑ Set `Size` to **343, 60**.
- ❑ Set `SupplementalExplanation` to **Search the Internet for a solution to this problem**.
- ❑ Set `Text` to **Search for a Solution Online**.

7. Click the ellipse button in the Image property to invoke the Select Resource dialog box. Click the Import button to invoke the Open dialog box and browse to `C:\Program Files\ Microsoft Visual Studio 9.0\Common7\VS2008ImageLibrary\1033\ VS2008ImageLibrary\Objects\png_format\WinVista` and select the `mynet.png` file. Click Open in the Open dialog box and then click OK in the Select Resource dialog box.

8. Double-click the CommandLink1 button and add the following code to the event handler:

```
Private Sub CommandLink1_Click(ByVal sender As System.Object, _
    ByVal e As System.EventArgs) Handles CommandLink1.Click

    MessageBox.Show("Sending a report to Wrox.", _
        My.Application.Info.Title, MessageBoxButtons.OK)
End Sub
```

9. In the Class Name combo box, select CommandLink2 and in the Method Name combo box, select the Click event. Add the following code to the event handler:

```
Private Sub CommandLink2_Click(ByVal sender As Object, _
        ByVal e As System.EventArgs) Handles CommandLink2.Click

    MessageBox.Show("Reinstalling the program.", _
            My.Application.Info.Title, MessageBoxButtons.OK)

End Sub
```

10. Select CommandLink3 in the Class Name combo box and select the Click event in the Method Name combo box. Add the highlighted code to the event handler:

```
Private Sub CommandLink3_Click(ByVal sender As Object, _
        ByVal e As System.EventArgs) Handles CommandLink3.Click

    MessageBox.Show("Searching the Internet.", _
            My.Application.Info.Title, MessageBoxButtons.OK)
    Me.Close()

End Sub
```

11. Save your project by clicking the Save All button on the toolbar.

12. Run your project. When your form displays it should look similar to the one shown in Figure 14-7. The Command Link with the blue line around it is the default button. Simply pressing the Enter key will invoke the Click event handler for it. Also note that as you hover your mouse over each Command Link that the Command Link getting the focus fades in with a gray background and the Command Link losing focus fades out from a gray background back to a white background.

    Clicking the third Command Link displays the message dialog box and then closes the form.

Figure 14-7

How It Works

The CommandLink control works the same way as any other control in the Toolbox. You drag the control onto your form, resize it if necessary, and then set the properties of the control. You then wire up the appropriate event handler for the control to perform the actions needed.

You'll notice that when you drag a CommandLink control from the Toolbox onto your form that the green arrow is the default icon displayed. To change the default green arrow to the UAC Shield, you set the UACShield property to **True**. To provide your own image, as shown in the third Command Link in Figure 14-7, you set the Image property to the image desired.

Changing the Text property of the control changes the main label of the control providing a one-line explanation of the controls function. Supplemental explanation text is not displayed since the SupplementalExplanation property has an empty string as its default value. If a supplemental explanation is required for the control, you set the SupplementalExplanation property to provide more details.

The default event handler for the Command Link is the Click event just as it is for the Button control. This is because this control inherits the Button class so it inherits all of its properties, events, and methods. You merely change the style of the control through your implementation of this class and provided additional properties to enhance the controls appearance.

For design concepts, usage patterns, and guidelines for the Command Link, refer to the MSDN Command Links article at http://msdn2.microsoft.com/en-us/library/aa511455.aspx.

Summary

This chapter showed two ways of creating Windows Forms controls with some encapsulated functionality. You looked at building a user control that aggregated a number of existing controls usefully. You extended the new control with properties, methods, and events. This control, once compiled, was shown in the Toolbox under its own tab.

You also took a look at how to create a control that inherits the base class of an existing control changing it appearance and adding additional properties to enhance its appearance. This CommandLink control was added to the Toolbox under the Common Controls tab making it available to all applications that you create.

To summarize, you should know:

- ❑ What a Windows Forms control is and how it works
- ❑ How to create a Windows Forms control
- ❑ How to add methods and events to your control
- ❑ How to code for design time and runtime
- ❑ How to create a create a control that inherits from an existing control

Exercise

1. Add a property to the MyNamespace control called SuppressMsgBox, which contains a Boolean value. Add code to the Click event handlers for each of the buttons on this control to show the message box when the SuppressMsgBox property is False and to suppress the message box when this property is True.

Programming Custom Graphics

So far, you have built user interfaces entirely from existing controls or controls that you created based on other controls. When you are writing programs with Visual Basic 2008, you also have the freedom to draw your own user interface. This gives you absolute freedom over the look and feel of your programs, and makes certain programming tasks possible.

In this chapter, you look at the graphics and drawing functionality available in Visual Basic 2008. You will be introduced to the concepts by building a fairly complex drawing program, just to illustrate how simple drawing your own user interface actually is. Toward the end of the chapter, you will examine some of the multimedia features of Visual Basic 2008 and learn how you can display common Internet file formats such as `.gif`, `.jpg`, and `.png`.

In this chapter, you will:

❑ Learn about the `System.Drawing` namespace

❑ Use pens and brushes

❑ Learn how to select and use colors

❑ Size and stretch images

❑ Create your own Paint program

Building a Simple Paint Program

In this section, you create a simple Paint program by creating a new Windows application project and building some user controls that you will wire up to provide functionality for the application.

Creating a Project with User Controls

Your motivation for building user controls for this application is simple: its good practice to break the application down into components. By following this technique, if you want to pull your paint functionality out of this application and into another, you can do it relatively easily.

What you are doing here with your controls is taking over the responsibility for painting them. Whenever you do this, you are creating owner drawings. Therefore, the controls you build are known as owner-drawn user controls.

Try It Out   **Creating the Project**

1. Create a new Visual Basic Windows Forms Application project. Call it **Wrox Paint**.

2. In the Solution Explorer, right-click the WroxPaint project and select Add ⇨ User Control. Set the name to **PaintCanvas.vb** and click Add.

3. Make sure the Form Designer for PaintCanvas is showing. Click the background of the control, and from the Properties window, change the BackColor property to White. (To do this, use the BackColor property's drop-down list, change to the Custom tab, and click the white box in the top-left corner.)

4. Save your project by clicking the Save All button on the toolbar.

5. Before you can use the control you need to build the project. From the menu select Build ⇨ Build WroxPaint. This will create the new PaintCanvas control and let you use it.

6. Now, go back to the Forms Designer for Form1. Click the Toolbox, and then click the Wrox Paint Components tab and select the new PaintCanvas control and drag it onto your form. Set the Dock property of the PaintCanvas control to **Fill**.

7. For the sake of neatness change the Text property of the form to **Wrox Paint**.

How Drawing Programs Work

Your computer screen is made up of pixels — hundreds of thousands of them. They are very small, but when working together they make a display on the screen. Since pixels on any given display are always of a uniform size, they are the common unit of measurement used in computer graphics.

To find out how big your desktop is, minimize all your windows and right-click your Windows desktop. Vista users should select Personalize from the context menu while everyone else should select Properties. Vista users should then select Display Settings and all other users select the Settings tab in the Display Properties dialog box. The slider in the bottom-left corner controls the size of your desktop — or, rather, it controls the number of pixels on your display. In Figure 15-1, you can see that the screen is set to 1,280 pixels across and 768 pixels down.

Figure 15-1

There are two very common computer graphics techniques: raster and vector. It is very useful to understand the difference between the two.

Raster Graphics

Raster graphics work a little like a physical canvas: You have a space, and you fill it up with color using various tools like brushes and pens. In a raster graphics program, the space is divided up into pixels. Each pixel has a color, and it's the drawing program's responsibility to set the color of each one depending on what kind of drawing tool you're using and the position and movement of the mouse.

The graphics program stores the image that you've drawn as a bitmap, this being a description of the pixels that make up the image and the color of each. A bitmap is basically a two-dimensional array of pixels. Each element in the array, accessed through a pair of (x, y) coordinates, stores a color value.

> *The name* bitmap *comes from the days when computer displays were monochrome, so each pixel could be only black or white and therefore could be stored in a single bit.*

If you draw a rectangle in a raster graphics package, that rectangle is abstracted to a set of pixels on the bitmap. After it's been drawn, you can't change the rectangle at all, other than using other tools to draw over it or draw another one.

> *.jpg, .gif, and .png images use a variation of the bitmap format to save images. However, they are compressed in particular ways to save space and download time when used in web pages.*

Vector Graphics

Vector graphics packages work in a different way. When you draw a rectangle onto the canvas, they physically record the fact that a rectangle exists at a given location. Vector graphics packages store a blueprint of how to draw the image, rather than storing the image that's been drawn. They do not abstract the rectangle down to a set of pixels. What this means is that you can pick it up again and move it, or change its shape or color later on, because the package has an understanding of what it is.

A number of modern graphics packages, such as Abode Photoshop, offer a hybrid approach to this, combining raster graphics with vector graphics.

Even in a vector graphics program, the screen itself works in pixels and is a raster format. Therefore, for the program to be able to display the drawing, the picture recorded by the package has to be converted into a raster format for the display. This process is known as *rendering*.

Your paint package is going to be a vector-based drawing package, for no other reason than it makes it easier to understand how drawing works in the .NET Framework. You're going to build a set of objects that represent certain shapes — namely, circles and squares — and hold them in a list.

The GraphicsItem Class

In your application, you're going to have two basic drawing types: circle and square. Each drawing type will need to have an understanding of where it appears on the canvas (and ultimately, the screen), what its color is, and whether it is filled. You'll build a base class called `GraphicsItem`, from which you'll derive `GraphicsCircle`.

Try It Out   **Building GraphicsItem and GraphicsCircle**

1.   Create a new class by right-clicking Wrox Paint in the Solution Explorer and selecting Add ⇨ Class. Name the class **GraphicsItem.vb** and click Add.

2.   Add this code to `GraphicsItem`. Remember to add the `MustInherit` keyword to the first line (that's why we highlighted it). The `MustInherit` keyword tells Visual Basic 2008 that you cannot create instances of `GraphicsItem` directly. Instead, you have to create classes that inherit from it.

```
Public MustInherit Class GraphicsItem
'Public members
Public Color As Color
Public IsFilled As Boolean
Public Rectangle As Rectangle

'Public methods
Public MustOverride Sub Draw(ByVal graphics As Graphics)

'Add an item at the given point
Public Sub SetPoint(ByVal x As Integer, ByVal y As Integer, _
    ByVal graphicSize As Integer, ByVal graphicColor As Color, _
    ByVal graphicIsFilled As Boolean)

    'Set the rectangle depending on the graphic and the size
    Rectangle = New Rectangle(x - (graphicSize / 2), y - (graphicSize / 2), _
        graphicSize, graphicSize)
```

```
            'Set the Color and IsFilled members
            Color = graphicColor
            IsFilled = graphicIsFilled
        End Sub
End Class
```

3. Create another class named **GraphicsCircle.vb**. Add the following highlighted code. After you type `Inherits GraphicsItem` and press Enter, an empty `Draw` procedure will be added to your class, and you can add the code shown here to it.

```
    Public Class GraphicsCircle
        Inherits GraphicsItem

        Public Overrides Sub Draw(ByVal graphics As System.Drawing.Graphics)
            'Create a new pen
            Dim objSolidBrush As New SolidBrush(Me.Color)

            'Draw the circle
            graphics.FillEllipse(objSolidBrush, Me.Rectangle)
        End Sub
    End Class
```

How It Works

When you created the `GraphicsItem` class, you added the `MustInherit` keyword to the `Class` declaration. This instructs Visual Basic 2008 not to let developers create instances of this class but to force them to inherit this class.

When you created the `Draw` method in this class, you used the `MustOverride` keyword. This has a similar meaning to `MustInherit` — you use it to force derived classes to add their own implementation for a particular method without providing any implementation in the base class. The `MustOverride` keyword can be used only in `MustInherit` classes.

The `SetPoint` method is used to populate an object depending on the position of the mouse and the current graphic size and color. The first thing you need to do in this method is to set up the rectangle.

When you want to draw a circle, you provide the center point, whereas .NET expects the position of the top-left corner of the rectangle that encloses the circle. Therefore, the top-left corner of the rectangle must be adjusted up and left depending on the size provided through `graphicSize` parameter. You pass the top-left corner through as the first and second parameters to the rectangle's constructor. The third parameter supplied is the width, and the fourth provides the height.

After you have the parameter, you need to store the color and also a flag that indicates whether the circle is filled.

```
Public MustInherit Class GraphicsItem
    'Public members
    Public Color As Color
    Public IsFilled As Boolean
    Public Rectangle As Rectangle

    'Public methods
    Public MustOverride Sub Draw(ByVal graphics As Graphics)
```

```
      'Add an item at the given point
      Public Sub SetPoint(ByVal x As Integer, ByVal y As Integer, _
          ByVal graphicSize As Integer, ByVal graphicColor As Color, _
          ByVal graphicIsFilled As Boolean)

          'Set the rectangle depending on the graphic and the size
          Rectangle = New Rectangle(x - (graphicSize / 2), y - (graphicSize / 2), _
              graphicSize, graphicSize)

          'Set the Color and IsFilled members
          Color = graphicColor
          IsFilled = graphicIsFilled
      End Sub
  End Class
```

When you created the GraphicsCircle class, you inherited the GraphicsItem class. Once you typed the Inherits GraphicsItem statement and pressed Enter, Visual Studio 2008 automatically added an empty Draw method, and all you had to do was add your own code to this method.

Painting is usually a matter of calling some simple methods on the Graphics object. This method draws and fills an ellipse (or circle, depending on which parameters you provide). Note that there's a similar method called DrawEllipse, which doesn't fill in the ellipse after it's drawn.

You'll also notice that at the top of the method you created a new SolidBrush object. You then pass this brush through to the FillEllipse method. This SolidBrush object, as you have probably guessed, describes the kind of brush you want to use.

```
  Public Class GraphicsCircle
      Inherits GraphicsItem

      Public Overrides Sub Draw(ByVal graphics As System.Drawing.Graphics)
          'Create a new pen
          Dim objSolidBrush As New SolidBrush(Me.Color)

          'Draw the circle
          graphics.FillEllipse(objSolidBrush, Me.Rectangle)
      End Sub
  End Class
```

Screen and Client Coordinates

When you get into the world of building your own painting code for your user interface, you usually have to work a lot with the mouse. We have already mentioned that in Windows and the .NET Framework, the base currency of drawing is the pixel. This means that when you ask the mouse for its position (for example, when verifying that the user has moved the mouse across your control or clicked one of the buttons), you get back a set of coordinates given in pixels. If the user clicks the mouse in the very top-left pixel, you'll get back coordinates of (0, 0). If you're using a 1280 × 768 display and the user clicks in the very bottom-right pixel, you'll get back coordinates of (1280, 768).

Although this seems straightforward, there is a wrinkle. When you click inside a window, the coordinates are adjusted depending on where the window itself is on the screen.

In Figure 15-2, the WroxPaint program is shown towards the bottom-right corner of the screen. This display is configured at 1280 pixels across and 786 pixels down, which means that the top-left corner of WroxPaint itself is at approximately (600, 400), according to the screen.

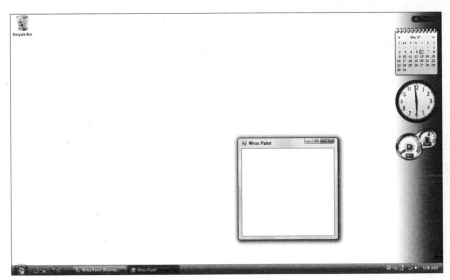

Figure 15-2

However, every window has a *client area*, which is the area the programmer can use to report the program's output. This client area is exclusive of the window border, the caption, menu, scrollbars, and the toolbar. When you are drawing onto the control or form, you are always dealing with this client area. The coordinates you use when drawing are adjusted so that the position of the window itself on the screen becomes irrelevant. These coordinates are known as *client coordinates*.

If you click the top-left corner of the WroxPaint paint area (the white part), there are actually two different coordinates that you can get:

❑   The first one will be around (610, 435), a little in and down from the top-left corner of the window. These are the *screen coordinates*, also known as the *absolute position*.

❑   The second pair will be around (0, 0), and these are the adjusted client coordinates. If you click the same graphic in the client, you will get (0, 0) irrespective of where the window is positioned on the screen. This is sometimes known as the *relative position*.

Listening to the Mouse and Drawing GraphicsCircle Objects

For your graphics application to work, you'll monitor what the user is doing with the mouse, create new objects derived from GraphicsItem, and store them in a big list. When it is time for you to draw, you'll go through this list and ask each GraphicsItem in turn to render itself on the screen. You try drawing in the next Try It Out.

Try It Out   **Drawing**

1. In the Solution Explorer, right-click the PaintCanvas control and select View Code. Add these enumerations to the class as highlighted. The first will be used to store the current graphics mode/tool, while the second stores the size of the pen used for drawing:

```
Public Class PaintCanvas
    'Public enumerations
    Public Enum GraphicTools As Integer
        CirclePen = 0
    End Enum

    Public Enum GraphicSizes As Integer
        Small = 4
        Medium = 10
        Large = 20
    End Enum
End Class
```

2. Next, add these members to this class:

```
'Public members
Public GraphicsItems As New ArrayList()
Public GraphicTool As GraphicTools = GraphicTools.CirclePen
Public GraphicSize As GraphicSizes = GraphicSizes.Medium
Public GraphicColor As Color = Color.Black
```

Here is what each member will do. Notice that you define a default value for these members to make initialization of the application easier:

- ❑ GraphicItems will hold a list of the GraphicsItem objects that make up the drawing.

- ❑ GraphicsTool will keep track of which graphic tool is currently being used.

- ❑ GraphicsSize will keep track of how big you want each graphic to be.

- ❑ GraphicsColor will keep track of the color of the item that you want to draw.

3. Drawing the items on the page is a two-phase process. When the user moves the mouse around on the control, you want to create new GraphicsCircle objects and add them to the GraphicsItems list. At some point, Windows will ask you to paint the control, so you'll need to go through the GraphicsItems list and draw each one in turn. Add this method to PaintCanvas:

```
Private Sub DoMousePaint(ByVal e As MouseEventArgs)
    'Store the new item somewhere
    Dim objGraphicsItem As GraphicsItem

    'What tool are you using?
    Select Case GraphicTool

        'CirclePen
        Case GraphicTools.CirclePen
```

```
        'Create a new graphics circle
        Dim objGraphicsCircle As New GraphicsCircle()

        'Set the point for drawing
        objGraphicsCircle.SetPoint(e.X, e.Y, GraphicSize, _
            GraphicColor, True)

        'Store this for addition
        objGraphicsItem = objGraphicsCircle

End Select

'Were you given an item?
If objGraphicsItem IsNot Nothing Then

    'Add it to the list
    GraphicsItems.Add(objGraphicsItem)

    'Invalidate the control
    Me.Invalidate()

End If
End Sub
```

4. In the Class Name combo at the top of the Code Editor, select (PaintCanvas Events) and in the Method Name combo box select the MouseDown event. Add the following highlighted code to the new event handler:

```
Private Sub PaintCanvas_MouseDown(ByVal sender As Object, _
    ByVal e As System.Windows.Forms.MouseEventArgs) Handles Me.MouseDown

        'Is the left mouse button down?
        If e.Button = MouseButtons.Left Then
            DoMousePaint(e)
        End If
End Sub
```

5. Select (PaintCanvas Events) in the Class Name combo box and the MouseMove event in the Method Name combo box. Add the following highlighted code to the MouseMove event handler:

```
Private Sub PaintCanvas_MouseMove(ByVal sender As Object, _
    ByVal e As System.Windows.Forms.MouseEventArgs) Handles Me.MouseMove

        'Is the left mouse button down?
        If e.Button = MouseButtons.Left Then
            DoMousePaint(e)
        End If
End Sub
```

6. Finally, select (PaintCanvas Events) in the Class Name combo box and the Paint event in the Method Name combo box. Add the following highlighted code:

```
Private Sub PaintCanvas_Paint(ByVal sender As Object, _
    ByVal e As System.Windows.Forms.PaintEventArgs) Handles Me.Paint

    'Go through the list
    For Each objGraphicsItem As GraphicsItem In GraphicsItems
        'Ask each item to draw itself
        objGraphicsItem.Draw(e.Graphics)
    Next
End Sub
```

7. Run the project and draw on the control by holding down the left mouse button and dragging the mouse over the surface.

You now have a working paint program, but you'll notice that the more you paint the more it flickers. This illustrates an important aspect of drawing, as you'll see when you fix it. For now, look at what you've done.

How It Works

When the user moves the mouse over the control, an event called MouseMove is fired. You have hooked into this event by adding the event handler for the MouseMove event. When this event handler is fired, you check to see whether the left mouse button is down, and if it is, you pass the System.Windows.Forms.MouseEventArgs object that you were given over to your private DoMousePaint method.

```
Private Sub PaintCanvas_MouseMove(ByVal sender As Object, _
    ByVal e As System.Windows.Forms.MouseEventArgs) Handles Me.MouseMove

    'Is the left mouse button down?
    If e.Button = MouseButtons.Left Then
        DoMousePaint(e)
    End If
End Sub
```

DoMousePaint is the method that you'll use to handle the drawing process. In this case, whenever the MouseMove event is received, you want to create a new GraphicsCircle item and add it to the list of vectors that make up your image.

As DoMousePaint will ultimately do more than add circles to the vector list, you need to do things in a (seemingly) counterintuitive order. The first thing you need is to declare an object to hold the new GraphicsItem class that will be created — so declare objGraphicsItem:

```
Private Sub DoMousePaint(ByVal e As MouseEventArgs)
    'Store the new item somewhere
    Dim objGraphicsItem As GraphicsItem
```

Then you look at your `GraphicTool` property to determine what you're supposed to be drawing. At this point, because you only have one tool defined, this will always be a circle:

```
'What tool are you using?
Select Case GraphicTool

    'CirclePen
    Case GraphicTools.CirclePen

        'Create a new graphics circle
        Dim objGraphicsCircle As New GraphicsCircle()
```

After you have the `GraphicsCircle`, you call the `SetPoint` method, which, if you recall, was defined on `GraphicsItem`. This method is responsible for determining the point on the canvas where the item should appear. You give `SetPoint` the current drawing size and color, and tell it to draw a filled shape.

```
        'Set the point for drawing
        objGraphicsCircle.SetPoint(e.X, e.Y, GraphicSize, _
            GraphicColor, True)
```

After you have called `SetPoint`, you store the `GraphicsCircle` in `objGraphicsItem` and close the `Select ... End Select` statement.

```
        'Store this for addition
        objGraphicsItem = objGraphicsCircle

End Select
```

When a new `GraphicsItem` is stored in `objGraphicsItem`, you have to add it to the list.

```
'Were you given an item?
If objGraphicsItem IsNot Nothing Then

    'Add it to the list

    GraphicsItems.Add(objGraphicsItem)
```

Finally, you have to *invalidate* the control. You have to do this to tell Windows that something about the appearance of the control has changed. The program will not tell the control to paint itself unless something has told Windows that the control needs painting. Calling `Me.Invalidate` in this way tells Windows that the appearance of the control is invalid and therefore needs updating.

```
    'Invalidate the control
    Me.Invalidate()

End If
```

Although you can invalidate the control with the `Invalidate` method, the control will be invalidated whenever Windows detects it needs redrawing. This may happen when the window is restored after being minimized, another window obscures an area that's been made visible, and so on.

That covers everything from the user dragging the mouse over the control to adding a new GraphicsCircle item to the list. Now what?

With the control marked as requiring painting, it's up to Windows to choose a time for the window to be painted. To increase the performance of the windowing subsystem, windows are drawn only when the system has enough spare time to do it. Painting is not considered to be a crucial task to the operating system. You cannot rely on painting being done immediately, or within a given time-span of your marking something as invalid. At some point, the control will be asked to paint itself. You may have noticed this effect when your computer is being used heavily — an image on the screen will appear to freeze for a period before the display is updated.

Do not try to force Windows to paint when it doesn't want to. There are thousands of lines of optimization code in the Windows operating system to make sure that things are painted at absolutely the best time. Invalidate your control when you need to flag something as needing to be redrawn, and let nature take its course.

When it is ready, the Paint event will be called. You tap into this event by adding an event handler for the Paint event. All that you have to do is loop through the entire array of GraphicsItem objects that you've collected in GraphicsItems and ask each one to draw itself.

```
Private Sub PaintCanvas_Paint(ByVal sender As Object, _
    ByVal e As System.Windows.Forms.PaintEventArgs) Handles Me.Paint

    'Go through the list
    For Each objGraphicsItem As GraphicsItem In GraphicsItems
        'Ask each item to draw itself
        objGraphicsItem.Draw(e.Graphics)
    Next
End Sub
```

The Paint event passes through its parameters as a PaintEventArgs object. This object, among other things, contains a property called Graphics. This property returns a System.Drawing.Graphics object.

When you have hold of a graphics object, you are able to draw to the control, the form, the printer, or whatever it is that's given you as an object. This object contains a bundle of methods and properties that are actually used for painting. To keep in line with the principle of only painting when needed, in typical day-to-day work you shouldn't try to create or otherwise obtain one of these objects. If you're given one, then it's time to paint!

Now that you know how the painting works, let's see whether you can get rid of the flickering!

Invalidation

The example you have been working on is designed to flicker and slow down to illustrate an important consideration that you need to bear in mind when drawing controls: Do the least amount of work possible! Drawing to the screen is slow. The less you draw, the faster the performance of your application should be and the better it should look on the screen.

The control flickers because painting is a two-stage process. Before you're asked to paint, Windows automatically erases the region behind the area that needs to be painted. This means the whole control flashes white as everything is erased and then you fill in the details.

What you want to do is to invalidate only the area that contains the new `GraphicsItem`. When you invalidate the control, you don't have to invalidate the whole thing. If you want, you can just invalidate a small area, as you do in the next Try It Out.

Try It Out   Invalidating a Small Area

1. In the `PaintCanvas` class, find the `DoMousePaint` method. Modify the `Me.Invalidate` method at the end to include this parameter to invalidate just a `Rectangle`:

```
'Invalidate the Control
Me.Invalidate(objGraphicsItem.Rectangle)
```

2. Run the project. You'll notice now that when you paint it doesn't flicker.

How It Works

After you call `SetPoint` on the new `GraphicsCircle` object, the `Rectangle` property is updated to contain the bounding rectangle of the circle.

This time, when you call the `Me.Invalidate` method, you pass this rectangle in. In this way, only a tiny area of the control is invalidated, therefore, only that tiny area is erased. After it is erased, you get the opportunity to draw your circle.

Optimized Drawing

You'll notice that if you draw a lot on the control, after a while the edge of the line starts to become almost jagged. What you're experiencing here is that as the `GraphicsItems` list grows, more calls to `FillEllipse` are made. Because drawing on the screen is slow, the more you have to do this, the longer the drawing process takes to aggregate. This lengthened drawing process prevents all of the `MouseMove` events from being fired, and so the line appears to stutter. In the following Try It Out section you see how you can avoid this problem.

Try It Out   Optimized Drawing

1. Find the `PaintCanvas_Paint` method on the `PaintCanvas` class. Add this code as highlighted:

```
Private Sub PaintCanvas_Paint(ByVal sender As Object, _
    ByVal e As System.Windows.Forms.PaintEventArgs) Handles Me.Paint

    'Go through the list
    For Each objGraphicsItem As GraphicsItem In GraphicsItems
        'Do we need to be drawn?
        If e.ClipRectangle.IntersectsWith(objGraphicsItem.Rectangle) Then
```

```
                    'Ask each item to draw itself
                    objGraphicsItem.Draw(e.Graphics)
            End If
        Next
    End Sub
```

2. Run the project. You should now find that the drawing process is smoother.

How It Works

The `PaintEventArgs` object contains another property called `ClipRectangle`. This rectangle describes the area of the control that has been invalidated and is known as the *clipping rectangle*. The `Rectangle` class contains a method called `IntersectsWith` that can tell whether two given rectangles overlap and returns a `Boolean` value indicating whether they intersect.

As you know, a rectangle describes the bounds of each of your `GraphicsItem` objects, so you can use this rectangle with `IntersectsWith`. If the `GraphicsItem` overlaps, it needs drawing; otherwise, you move on to the next control.

The two techniques you've seen here — invalidating only what changes and drawing only what falls into the invalidated region — are by far the two most important techniques you'll come across when painting. If you skip either of these, your control has a good chance of being sluggish and flickering.

Choosing Colors

Now that you can do some basic painting, you'll build a control that lets you choose the color that you're painting in. Like a lot of graphics programs, you'll build this so that you have a palette of different colors and you're able to choose two at a time — one for the left mouse button and one for the right.

There are a number of different ways to build this control, and perhaps the most logical is to create a control that contains a bundle of Button controls, each configured so that it displays the color that it represents. However, this example shows you how to build a control completely from scratch. The techniques that you'll learn here will be really useful if you want to roll your own controls that display a picture of something and have hot regions on them. *Hot regions* are regions that fire an event when you click them. What you're doing might seem a little obscure, but it's a great example!

Creating the ColorPalette Control and Sizing the Control

To create the color palette control in the next Try It Out, you're going to need two classes. One, named `ColorPalette`, is derived from `UserControl` and will provide the user interface (UI) for the palette itself. The other, named `ColorPaletteButton`, will be used to display the actual color box on the palette.

Since you are handling the layout of the buttons on the control, you need to respond to the `Resize` event. This event is fired whenever the user changes the size of the control. You can hook into this event by adding an event handler for the `Resize` event.

When `Resize` is fired, you need to alter the position of each of the buttons, starting in the top-left corner and continuing in strips across the whole width of the control. When you've filled up one row, you need to start a new row.

Try It Out   **Creating the ColorPalette Control**

1. In the Solution Explorer, add a new class to the Wrox Paint project named **ColorPaletteButton**
    .vb and add the following highlighted code to it:

```
Public Class ColorPaletteButton
    'Public members
    Public Color As Color = System.Drawing.Color.Black
    Public Rectangle As Rectangle

    'Constructor
    Public Sub New(ByVal newColor As Color)
        Color = newColor
    End Sub

    'Move the button to the given position
    Public Sub SetPosition(ByVal x As Integer, ByVal y As Integer, _
                    ByVal buttonSize As Integer)

        'Update the members
        Rectangle = New Rectangle(x, y, buttonSize, buttonSize)
    End Sub

    'Draw the button
    Public Sub Draw(ByVal graphics As Graphics)
        'Draw the color block
        Dim objSolidBrush As New SolidBrush(Color)
        graphics.FillRectangle(objSolidBrush, Rectangle)

        'Draw an edge around the control
        Dim objPen As New Pen(System.Drawing.Color.Black)
        graphics.DrawRectangle(objPen, Rectangle)
    End Sub
End Class
```

2. Now add a user control to the Wrox Paint project named **ColorPalette**. Right-click the control
    and choose View Code from the context menu. Add these members to the top of the class
    definition:

```
Public Class ColorPalette
    'Public members
    Public Buttons As New ArrayList()
    Public ButtonSize As Integer = 15
    Public ButtonSpacing As Integer = 5
    Public LeftColor As Color = Color.Black
    Public RightColor As Color = Color.White
```

Here is what the members will do:

❑   Buttons holds a list of the buttons on the palette.

❑   ButtonSize defines the size of each of the buttons on the palette.

❑   ButtonSpacing defines the gap between each button.

❑   `LeftColor` holds the current color that is assigned to the left mouse button.

❑   `RightColor` holds the current color that is assigned to the right mouse button.

3.   Next, add this method to the class:

```
'Add a new color button to the control
Public Sub AddColor(ByVal newColor As Color)
    'Create the button
    Dim objColorPaletteButton As New ColorPaletteButton(newColor)

    'Add it to the list
    Buttons.Add(objColorPaletteButton)
End Sub
```

4.   When you create the control, you want a set of basic colors to be always available. Add this code for the constructor to the class. This will create 10 basic colors. After you type **Public Sub New** and press Enter, the unhighlighted code that follows will automatically be added to the constructor. Add the following highlighted code to your constructor:

```
Public Sub New()

    ' This call is required by the Windows Form Designer.
    InitializeComponent()

    ' Add any initialization after the InitializeComponent() call.

    'Add the colors
    AddColor(Color.Black)
    AddColor(Color.White)
    AddColor(Color.Red)
    AddColor(Color.Blue)
    AddColor(Color.Green)
    AddColor(Color.Gray)
    AddColor(Color.DarkRed)
    AddColor(Color.DarkBlue)
    AddColor(Color.DarkGreen)
    AddColor(Color.DarkGray)
End Sub
```

5.   In the Code Editor for the `ColorPalette` class, select (ColorPalette Events) in the Class Name combo box and the `Resize` event in the Method Name combo box. Add this highlighted code to the `Resize` event handler:

```
Private Sub ColorPalette_Resize(ByVal sender As Object, _
    ByVal e As System.EventArgs) Handles Me.Resize

    'Declare variables to hold the position
    Dim intX As Integer
    Dim intY As Integer

    'Go through the array and position the buttons
    For Each objColorPaletteButton As ColorPaletteButton In Buttons
```

```
                        'Position the button
                        objColorPaletteButton.SetPosition(intX, intY, ButtonSize)

                        'Move to the next one
                        intX += (ButtonSize + ButtonSpacing)

                        'Do we need to go down to the next row
                        If intX + ButtonSize > Width Then

                            'Move y
                            intY += (ButtonSize + ButtonSpacing)

                            'Reset x
                            intX = 0

                        End If

                    Next

                    'Redraw
                    Me.Invalidate()
                End Sub
```

6. You still need to paint the control. Select (ColorPalette Events) in the Class Name combo box
    and the Paint event in the Method Name combo box. Add this highlighted code:

    ```
    Private Sub ColorPalette_Paint(ByVal sender As Object, _
            ByVal e As System.Windows.Forms.PaintEventArgs) Handles Me.Paint

        'Loop through the buttons
        For Each objColorPaletteButton As ColorPaletteButton In Buttons

            'Do we need to draw?
            If e.ClipRectangle.IntersectsWith(objColorPaletteButton.Rectangle) Then
                objColorPaletteButton.Draw(e.Graphics)
            End If

        Next
    End Sub
    ```

7. Before you can draw the control onto Form1, you need to build the project. Select
    Build ⇨ Build Wrox Paint from the menu.

8. After the project has been built, open the Designer for Form1. Click the PaintCanvas control
    on Form1 and, in the Properties window, set the Dock property to **None**. Now resize the form
    to add a little space at the bottom and make the form wider if so desired.

9. In the ToolBox under the Wrox Paint Components tab, drag a ColorPalette control to the bottom of
    you form and set its Name property to **paletteColor**. Now set its Dock property to **Bottom**.

10. Now click the PaintCanvus control, resize it if necessary, and set its Anchor property to **Top,
    Bottom, Left, Right.** Your form should now look similar to Figure 15-3.

Figure 15-3

11. If you now try to rearrange the form a little, you should see that your sizing code has proven successful.

How It Works

Hopefully, the behavior of `ColorPaletteButton` shouldn't be too much of a mystery. You have members on the class that hold the color and a rectangle, and you also provide a constructor that automatically populates the color:

```
Public Class ColorPaletteButton
    'Public members
    Public Color As Color = System.Drawing.Color.Black
    Public Rectangle As Rectangle

    'Constructor
    Public Sub New(ByVal newColor As Color)
        Color = newColor
    End Sub
```

When the button is asked to paint itself, all you do is draw one filled rectangle of the color specified in the `Color` property using the `FillRectangle` method, and for neatness you surround it with a black border using the `DrawRectangle` method:

```
    'Draw the button
    Public Sub Draw(ByVal graphics As Graphics)
        'Draw the color block
        Dim objSolidBrush As New SolidBrush(Color)
        graphics.FillRectangle(objSolidBrush, Rectangle)

        'Draw an edge around the control
        Dim objPen As New Pen(System.Drawing.Color.Black)
        graphics.DrawRectangle(objPen, Rectangle)
    End Sub
```

When you resize the form (a subject you'll deal with soon), you pass the top-left corner of the button through to SetPosition. All this method does is update the Rectangle property:

```
'Move the button to the given position
Public Sub SetPosition(ByVal x As Integer, ByVal y As Integer, _
                       ByVal buttonSize As Integer)

    'Update the members
    Rectangle = New Rectangle(x, y, buttonSize, buttonSize)
End Sub
```

The ColorPalette_Resize method is perhaps the most interesting method here. This is a common algorithm used whenever you need to manage the position of controls or other graphic objects. You know the size of each object (in your case it's a combination of ButtonSize and ButtonSpacing) and you know the bounds of the control. All you do is start in the top left and keep moving right until you have no more space, in which case you flip down to the next row. Here is how you start — you set up a loop that iterates through all of the buttons:

```
Private Sub ColorPalette_Resize(ByVal sender As Object, _
    ByVal e As System.EventArgs) Handles Me.Resize

    'Declare variables to hold the position
    Dim intX As Integer
    Dim intY As Integer

    'Go through the array and position the buttons
    For Each objColorPaletteButton As ColorPaletteButton In Buttons
```

Throughout the loop, intX and intY hold the current coordinates of the top-left corner of the control. When you start, this is (0, 0) or, rather, the very top left of the client area of the control. For each button, you call SetPosition, passing in the current coordinates together with the size of the button:

```
        'Position the button
        objColorPaletteButton.SetPosition(intX, intY, ButtonSize)
```

After each button, you move intX to the right. In addition to adjusting by the size of the button, you also add a small gap to make the control more esthetically pleasing:

```
        'Move to the next one
        intX += (ButtonSize + ButtonSpacing)
```

If you detect that you don't have enough space to fit the next control completely on the current row, you adjust intY down to the next row and reset intX back to the beginning:

```
        'Do we need to go down to the next row
        If intX + ButtonSize > Width Then

            'Move y
            intY += (ButtonSize + ButtonSpacing)
```

```
                    'Reset x
                    intX = 0

            End If

        Next
```

Finally, after you've moved all of the buttons, you invalidate the control so that you can see the changes.

```
        'Redraw
        Me.Invalidate()
    End Sub
```

Responding to Clicks

Your control is going to fire an event whenever the left or right mouse button is clicked on a color button. To that end, in the next Try It Out you add some events to your ColorPalette control that the control will raise. The application using this control will be able to add the event handlers and take action when the event has been raised by this control.

Try It Out   **Responding to Clicks**

1.   Go back to the Code Editor for `ColorPalette`. Add these events to the top of the class after your public members:

```
'Public events
Public Event LeftClick(ByVal sender As Object, ByVal e As EventArgs)
Public Event RightClick(ByVal sender As Object, ByVal e As EventArgs)
```

2.   You need a general-purpose method that will return the button that's positioned directly beneath the mouse. Add this method:

```
Public Function GetButtonAt(ByVal x As Integer, ByVal y As Integer) _
    As ColorPaletteButton

    'Set the default return value
    GetButtonAt = Nothing

    'Go through each button in the collection
    For Each objColorPaletteButton As ColorPaletteButton In Buttons
        'Is this button in the rectangle?
        If objColorPaletteButton.Rectangle.Contains(x, y) Then
            Return objColorPaletteButton
        End If
    Next
End Function
```

3. Now, select (ColorPalette Events) in the Class Name combo box and then select the `MouseUp` event in the Method Name combo box. Your motivation for using `MouseUp` rather than `MouseDown` will become apparent soon. Add this highlighted code to the event handler:

```
Private Sub ColorPalette_MouseUp(ByVal sender As Object, _
    ByVal e As System.Windows.Forms.MouseEventArgs) Handles Me.MouseUp

        'Find the button that we clicked
        Dim objColorPaletteButton As ColorPaletteButton = GetButtonAt(e.X, e.Y)

        If Not objColorPaletteButton Is Nothing Then

            'Was the left button clicked
            If e.Button = MouseButtons.Left Then

                'Set the color
                LeftColor = objColorPaletteButton.Color

                'Raise the event
                RaiseEvent LeftClick(Me, New EventArgs())

            ElseIf e.Button = MouseButtons.Right Then

                'Set the color
                RightColor = objColorPaletteButton.Color

                'Raise the event
                RaiseEvent RightClick(Me, New EventArgs())

            End If

        End If
    End Sub
```

4. To test the new method, open the Forms Designer for Form1. Select the PaintCanvas control and set its `Name` property to **Canvas**.

5. Open up the Code Editor for Form1. Select `paletteColor` in the Class Name combo box, and select the `LeftClick` event in the Method Name combo box. Add this highlighted code to the event handler:

```
    Private Sub paletteColor_LeftClick(ByVal sender As Object, _
        ByVal e As System.EventArgs) Handles paletteColor.LeftClick

        Canvas.GraphicColor = paletteColor.LeftColor
    End Sub
```

6. Run your project. You should be able to use the color palette to change the color laid down by the left mouse button.

How It Works

Although you've called your buttons `ColorPaletteButton`, they don't behave in the way you're used to seeing buttons behave. Button controls, like the ones you have been using until now, have the intelligence to detect when they've been clicked and fire an event to tell you what happened. Your color palette buttons, on the other hand, have until now been areas on the control painted in a pretty color. Now you actually need to write the logic to determine when a button is clicked.

The key to this is the `GetButtonAt` method. This method takes a set of client coordinates and returns the `ColorPaletteButton` object that contains the point you asked for. In this case, you use the `Contains` method of the `Rectangle` object to see whether the coordinates are contained within the rectangle.

```
Public Function GetButtonAt(ByVal x As Integer, ByVal y As Integer) _
    As ColorPaletteButton

    'Set the default return value
    GetButtonAt = Nothing

    'Go through each button in the collection
    For Each objColorPaletteButton As ColorPaletteButton In Buttons
        'Is this button in the rectangle?
        If objColorPaletteButton.Rectangle.Contains(x, y) Then
            Return objColorPaletteButton
        End If
    Next
End Function
```

Of course, it could be the case that there is no button under the coordinates if the user clicks the mouse on a blank area of the control. If this is the case, `GetButtonAt` will return `Nothing`:

As you know, the `Button` property of `MouseEventArgs` tells you which button was used, or in this case, released. If it's the left button, you update `LeftColor` and raise the `LeftClick` event:

```
Private Sub ColorPalette_MouseUp(ByVal sender As Object, _
    ByVal e As System.Windows.Forms.MouseEventArgs) Handles Me.MouseUp

    'Find the button that we clicked
    Dim objColorPaletteButton As ColorPaletteButton = GetButtonAt(e.X, e.Y)

    If Not objColorPaletteButton Is Nothing Then

        'Was the left button clicked
        If e.Button = MouseButtons.Left Then

            'Set the color
            LeftColor = objColorPaletteButton.Color

            'Raise the event
            RaiseEvent LeftClick(Me, New EventArgs())
```

Alternatively, it could be the right mouse button:

```
        ElseIf e.Button = MouseButtons.Right Then

            'Set the color
```

```
                    RightColor = objColorPaletteButton.Color

                    'Raise the event
                    RaiseEvent RightClick(Me, New EventArgs())

            End If

        End If
    End Sub
```

At the moment, `PaintCanvas` can deal with only one color, which is why you've only hooked up the `LeftClick` event. When you receive this event, you set the appropriate property on `Canvas`, and this new color will be used when creating new `GraphicsCircle` objects:

```
    Private Sub paletteColor_LeftClick(ByVal sender As Object, _
        ByVal e As System.EventArgs) Handles paletteColor.LeftClick

        Canvas.GraphicColor = paletteColor.LeftColor
    End Sub
```

Dealing with Two Colors

In the next Try It Out you extend `PaintCanvas` so that it can deal with two colors. You'll do this by adding two public members that will track the color chosen for the left mouse button and the right mouse button. You'll also be modifying your existing code to determine whether the left mouse button was clicked or whether the right mouse button was clicked.

Try It Out   **Dealing with Two Colors**

1. You need an additional property in `PaintCanvas` that will let you store the alternative color. For the sake of clarity, you'll also change the name of the existing `GraphicColor` property to `GraphicLeftColor`. Open the Code Editor for the `PaintCanvas` class and make the highlighted changes:

```
'Public members
Public GraphicsItems As New ArrayList()
Public GraphicTool As GraphicTools = GraphicTools.CirclePen
Public GraphicSize As GraphicSizes = GraphicSizes.Medium

Public GraphicLeftColor As Color = Color.Black
Public GraphicRightColor As Color = Color.White
```

2. In the DoMousePaint method you need to examine the Button property of MouseEventArgs to determine which color you want to use. Make these two changes to DoMousePaint as highlighted:

```
Private Sub DoMousePaint(ByVal e As MouseEventArgs)
    'Store the new item somewhere
    Dim objGraphicsItem As GraphicsItem

    'What color do we want to use?
    Dim objColor As Color = GraphicLeftColor

    If e.Button = MouseButtons.Right Then
        objColor = GraphicRightColor
    End If

    'What tool are you using?
    Select Case GraphicTool

        'Circlepen
        Case GraphicTools.CirclePen

            'Create a new graphics circle
            Dim objGraphicsCircle As New GraphicsCircle()

            'Set the point for drawing
            objGraphicsCircle.SetPoint(e.X, e.Y, GraphicSize, _
                objColor, True)

            'Store this for addition
            objGraphicsItem = objGraphicsCircle

    End Select

    'Were you given an item?
    If objGraphicsItem IsNot Nothing Then

        'Add it to the list
        GraphicsItems.Add(objGraphicsItem)

        'Invalidate the Control
        Me.Invalidate(objGraphicsItem.Rectangle)

    End If
End Sub
```

3. At the moment, MouseDown and MouseMove events will call DoMousePaint only if the left button is pressed. You need to change this so that it will accept either the left or right button. Make the following highlighted changes:

```
Private Sub PaintCanvas_MouseDown(ByVal sender As Object, _
    ByVal e As System.Windows.Forms.MouseEventArgs) Handles Me.MouseDown

        'Is the left or right mouse button down?
        If e.Button = MouseButtons.Left Or e.Button = MouseButtons.Right Then
            DoMousePaint(e)
        End If
End Sub

Private Sub PaintCanvas_MouseMove(ByVal sender As Object, _
    ByVal e As System.Windows.Forms.MouseEventArgs) Handles Me.MouseMove

        'Is the left or right mouse button down?
        If e.Button = MouseButtons.Left Or e.Button = MouseButtons.Right Then
            DoMousePaint(e)
        End If
End Sub
```

4. Next, you need to change the event handler in Form1 to set the `GraphicLeftColor` property rather than the `GraphicColor` property. Open the Code Editor for Form1 and make this change as highlighted:

```
Private Sub paletteColor_LeftClick(ByVal sender As Object, _
    ByVal e As System.EventArgs) Handles paletteColor.LeftClick

        Canvas.GraphicLeftColor = paletteColor.LeftColor
End Sub
```

5. Finally, you need to add an event handler for the `RightClick` event. Select `paletteColor` in the Class Name combo box and the `RightClick` event in the Method Name combo box. Add this highlighted code:

```
Private Sub paletteColor_RightClick(ByVal sender As Object, _
    ByVal e As System.EventArgs) Handles paletteColor.RightClick

        Canvas.GraphicRightColor = paletteColor.RightColor
End Sub
```

When you run the project, you should be able to assign different colors to the left and right mouse buttons and use both of the buttons to paint on the form.

Indicating the Assigned Buttons

You've no doubt noticed that, at this point, using WroxPaint is a little confusing. There's no indication as to which color is assigned to which button. You need to resolve this issue, so in the next Try It Out you'll display the letter L on the color assigned to the left button and the letter R on the color assigned to the right button.

Try It Out   **Indicating the Assigned Buttons**

1.   First, you'll make the `ColorPaletteButton` objects aware of which button they're assigned to, if any. Open the Code Editor for the `ColorPaletteButton` class and add this enumeration to the top of the class:

```
Public Class ColorPaletteButton
    'Public enumerations
    Public Enum ButtonAssignments As Integer
        None = 0
        LeftButton = 1
        RightButton = 2
    End Enum
```

2.   Next, add this new member (highlighted), which will keep track of the button's assignment:

```
    'Public members
    Public Color As Color = System.Drawing.Color.Black
    Public Rectangle As Rectangle
    Public ButtonAssignment As ButtonAssignments = ButtonAssignments.None
```

3.   After the button has a way of storing what it's assigned to, you can change the `Draw` method to draw the L or R as appropriate. Add the following highlighted code to `Draw`:

```
    'Draw the button
    Public Sub Draw(ByVal graphics As Graphics)
        'Draw the color block
        Dim objSolidBrush As New SolidBrush(Color)
        graphics.FillRectangle(objSolidBrush, Rectangle)

        'Draw an edge around the control
        Dim objPen As New Pen(System.Drawing.Color.Black)
        graphics.DrawRectangle(objPen, Rectangle)

        'Are you selected?
        If ButtonAssignment <> ButtonAssignments.None Then

            'Create a font
            Dim objFont As New Font("Segoe UI", 8, FontStyle.Bold)

            'Set the default button assignment
            Dim strButtonText As String = "L"

            'Update the button assignment if necessary
            If ButtonAssignment = ButtonAssignments.RightButton Then
                strButtonText = "R"
            End If

            'What brush do you want?
            If Color.R < 100 Or Color.B < 100 Or Color.G < 100 Then
                objSolidBrush = New SolidBrush(System.Drawing.Color.White)
            Else
                objSolidBrush = New SolidBrush(System.Drawing.Color.Black)
            End If
```

```
                        'Draw the text 'L' or 'R'
                        graphics.DrawString(strButtonText, objFont, objSolidBrush, _
                            Rectangle.Left, Rectangle.Top)
                End If
        End Sub
```

4. To keep track of which button is selected, you need to add some private members to the ColorPalette class. Open the Code Editor for this class and add this code:

```
    'Private members
    Private LeftButton As ColorPaletteButton
    Private RightButton As ColorPaletteButton
```

5. The next wrinkle you have to fix is quite verbose but relatively straightforward. Basically, you have to make sure that a button cannot be assigned to both the left and right buttons — for no other reason than that you just don't have a way of reporting that information to the user. Also, you have to muddle with the invalidation code. You'll detail that once you have the example working. Make these changes to ColorPalette_MouseUp as highlighted:

```
Private Sub ColorPalette_MouseUp(ByVal sender As Object, _
    ByVal e As System.Windows.Forms.MouseEventArgs) Handles Me.MouseUp

        'Find the button that we clicked
        Dim objColorPaletteButton As ColorPaletteButton = GetButtonAt(e.X, e.Y)

        If Not objColorPaletteButton Is Nothing Then

                'Was the left button clicked
                If e.Button = MouseButtons.Left Then

                        'Make sure that this button is not the current right button
                        If objColorPaletteButton IsNot RightButton Then

                                'Set the color
                                LeftColor = objColorPaletteButton.Color

                                'Clear the existing selection.
                                If LeftButton IsNot Nothing Then

                                        LeftButton.ButtonAssignment = _
                                            ColorPaletteButton.ButtonAssignments.None

                                        Me.Invalidate(LeftButton.Rectangle)

                                End If

                                'Mark the button
                                objColorPaletteButton.ButtonAssignment = _
                        ColorPaletteButton.ButtonAssignments.LeftButton

                                Me.Invalidate(objColorPaletteButton.Rectangle)

                                LeftButton = objColorPaletteButton
```

```
                              'Raise the event
                              RaiseEvent LeftClick(Me, New EventArgs())

            End If

        ElseIf e.Button = MouseButtons.Right Then

            'Make sure this button is not the current left button
            If objColorPaletteButton IsNot LeftButton Then

                'Set the color
                RightColor = objColorPaletteButton.Color

                'Clear the existing selection
                If RightButton IsNot Nothing Then

                    RightButton.ButtonAssignment = _
                        ColorPaletteButton.ButtonAssignments.None

                    Me.Invalidate(RightButton.Rectangle)

                End If

                'Mark the button
                objColorPaletteButton.ButtonAssignment = _
            ColorPaletteButton.ButtonAssignments.RightButton

                Me.Invalidate(objColorPaletteButton.Rectangle)

                RightButton = objColorPaletteButton

                'Raise the event
                RaiseEvent RightClick(Me, New EventArgs())

            End If

        End If

    End If
End Sub
```

6. Finally, you have to set up the first two colors added to the control as being the selected buttons when the control is started. This involves updating your `leftButton` and `rightButton` members as well as setting the `ButtonAssignment` property on the button itself. Add the highlighted code to `AddColor`:

```
'Add a new color button to the control
Public Sub AddColor(ByVal newColor As Color)
    'Create the button
    Dim objColorPaletteButton As New ColorPaletteButton(newColor)

    'Add it to the list
    Buttons.Add(objColorPaletteButton)
```

```
              'Do we have a button assigned to the left button yet?
              If LeftButton Is Nothing Then

                  objColorPaletteButton.ButtonAssignment = _
                      ColorPaletteButton.ButtonAssignments.LeftButton

                  LeftButton = objColorPaletteButton

              ElseIf RightButton Is Nothing Then 'How about the right button?

                  objColorPaletteButton.ButtonAssignment = _
                      ColorPaletteButton.ButtonAssignments.RightButton

                  RightButton = objColorPaletteButton

              End If
        End Sub
```

7. Run the project now, and you should see that when you change the color selection, an L and R appear on the buttons, as shown in Figure 15-4.

Figure 15-4

How It Works

The first thing you did was add an enumeration to the ControlPaletteButton class that could be used to set the state of the button:

```
'Public enumerations
Public Enum ButtonAssignments As Integer
    None = 0
    LeftButton = 1
    RightButton = 2
End Enum
```

As you can see from the enumeration, a palette button can either be assigned to no mouse buttons, the left mouse button, or the right mouse button. You also added members to the ControlPalette class to keep track of which button was selected. This makes your life a little easier when it comes to changing the selection. When you select a new palette button, you have to set the ButtonAssignment property of the old button to ButtonAssignments.None. Just being able to look in the LeftButton or RightButton member, as appropriate, saves you from having to look through the entire list of buttons to find the one you need to change. The `ColorPalette_MouseUp` method starts to look a little more complex when you add this new functionality. When you want to assign the left mouse button to a palette button, you have to make sure that the palette button is not already assigned to the right mouse button:

```
Private Sub ColorPalette_MouseUp(ByVal sender As Object, _
    ByVal e As System.Windows.Forms.MouseEventArgs) Handles Me.MouseUp

    'Find the button that we clicked
    Dim objColorPaletteButton As ColorPaletteButton = GetButtonAt(e.X, e.Y)

    If Not objColorPaletteButton Is Nothing Then

        'Was the left button clicked
        If e.Button = MouseButtons.Left Then

            'Make sure that this button is not the current right button
            If objColorPaletteButton IsNot RightButton Then
```

If you can set the color, you update the `LeftColor` property as you did before:

```
                'Set the color
                LeftColor = objColorPaletteButton.Color
```

If another button is already assigned to the left mouse button, you need to set its `ButtonAssignment` property back to `None`. You also have to invalidate this button so that the button is redrawn and the L is removed:

```
                'Clear the existing selection.
                If LeftButton IsNot Nothing Then

                    LeftButton.ButtonAssignment = _
                        ColorPaletteButton.ButtonAssignments.None

                    Me.Invalidate(LeftButton.Rectangle)

                End If
```

Next, you set the new button's `ButtonAssignment` property to `Left`. You also invalidate the button (so that you can draw the L on this one instead) and update the `LeftButton` property to point at the new button:

```
                'Mark the button
                objColorPaletteButton.ButtonAssignment = _
            ColorPaletteButton.ButtonAssignments.LeftButton

                Me.Invalidate(objColorPaletteButton.Rectangle)

                LeftButton = objColorPaletteButton
```

Finally, you fire the `LeftClick` event as you did before:

```
                'Raise the event
                RaiseEvent LeftClick(Me, New EventArgs())
```

The remainder of `ColorPalette_MouseUp` is the same as this but is obviously reversed to deal with the right-hand button.

When it's time to draw the button, you can check to see whether a button assignment is set. If it is, you draw some text. (You've only fleetingly covered drawing text here, but you'll deal with it in more detail later in this chapter.) To draw the text, you need to create a new `System.Drawing.Font` object. Here you're creating a new object for 8-point Segoe UI in bold:

```
Public Sub Draw(ByVal graphics As Graphics)
    'Draw the color block
    Dim objSolidBrush As New SolidBrush(Color)
    graphics.FillRectangle(objSolidBrush, Rectangle)

    'Draw an edge around the control
    Dim objPen As New Pen(System.Drawing.Color.Black)
    graphics.DrawRectangle(objPen, Rectangle)

    'Are you selected?
    If ButtonAssignment <> ButtonAssignments.None Then

        'Create a font
        Dim objFont As New Font("Segoe UI", 8, FontStyle.Bold)
```

Next, you choose the text to draw:

```
        'Set the default button assignment
        Dim strButtonText As String = "L"

        'Update the button assignment if necessary
        If ButtonAssignment = ButtonAssignments.RightButton Then
            strButtonText = "R"
        End If
```

Choosing the brush you want is quite tricky. You can't just choose a color, because there's a chance it won't show up on the color that you're drawing. Instead, you have to examine the color to see whether it is a light color or a dark color. If it's dark, you choose to draw the letter in white; otherwise, you draw it in black:

```
        'What brush do you want?
        If Color.R < 100 Or Color.B < 100 Or Color.G < 100 Then
            objSolidBrush = New SolidBrush(System.Drawing.Color.White)
        Else
            objSolidBrush = New SolidBrush(System.Drawing.Color.Black)
        End If
```

Finally, you actually draw the text:

```
        'Draw the text 'L' or 'R'
        graphics.DrawString(strButtonText, objFont, objSolidBrush, _
            Rectangle.Left, Rectangle.Top)
    End If
End Sub
```

Using Advanced Colors

So far, the only colors you've used are the ones defined by the .NET Framework, such as `Color.Black` and `Color.Blue`. The list of colors available to you on the `Color` structure is considerable, but you can define your own colors if you want to.

> *To find a list of predefined colors use the MSDN documentation to display "all members" of the "Color structure." Alternatively, you can use IntelliSense from within the code editor to display a list of possibilities.*

Windows defines a color as a 24-bit number, with the three bytes of the 24 bits representing a red value, a green value, and a blue value — this is commonly known as RGB. In effect, each component represents one of a possible 256 shades of red, green, or blue. By combining these shades you can get any color from a possible set of 16.7 million. For example, setting red to 255 and setting blue and green to 0 would result in bright red. Setting all components to 255 would give white. Setting all to 0 would give black, and so on.

> *If you're used to mixing paints, these color combinations may seem strange. This is because you are working with colored lights instead of colored paints — they combine in different ways.*

In the following Try It Out section, you see how you can choose a color and then manually add that color as a button to the control palette.

Try It Out   **Creating Custom Colors**

1. Open the Form Designer for the `ColorPalette` control. In the Properties window find the `BackColor` property.

2. Drop down the list and change to the Custom tab. Right-click in one of the 16 blank squares at the bottom. This will bring up the Color dialog box.

3. Use the two controls at the top to find a color you like. In the bottom-right corner, you'll see three text boxes marked Red, Green, and Blue, as shown in Figure 15-5. Write down the values in these boxes.

Figure 15-5

4. Close the Define Color dialog box.

5. Open up the Code Editor for `ColorPalette` to access the constructor. In the constructor, define a new button as in the following highlighted code, but replace the three values I've used here with three values you noted. (Do this in order — the first value is the red component, the second is green, and the third is blue.)

```
Public Sub New()

    ' This call is required by the Windows Form Designer.
    InitializeComponent()

    ' Add any initialization after the InitializeComponent() call.
    'Add the colors
    AddColor(Color.Black)
    AddColor(Color.White)
    AddColor(Color.Red)
    AddColor(Color.Blue)
    AddColor(Color.Green)
    AddColor(Color.Gray)
    AddColor(Color.DarkRed)
    AddColor(Color.DarkBlue)
    AddColor(Color.DarkGreen)
    AddColor(Color.DarkGray)
    AddColor(Color.FromArgb(208, 112, 222))
End Sub
```

6. Now run the project; the color you selected should appear in the palette.

The `FromArgb` method is a shared method on the `Color` class. You can use this to define any color that you like, so long as you follow the "red, green, blue" convention Windows itself uses.

Using the Color Dialog Box

In this Try It Out, you use the Color dialog box that's built into Windows to let the user add colors to the palette.

Try It Out   Using the Color Dialog Box

1. Open the Form Designer for ColorPalette. From the toolbar, select a ColorDialog control and drag it onto the form; the control will be positioned at the bottom of the IDE. Change the name of the control to **dlgColor**.

2. Now, open the Code Editor for ColorPalette. Find the `ColorPalette_MouseUp` method. Whenever the user clicks the background of the control (in other words, doesn't click a button), you want to display the dialog box. Go to the bottom of the method and add an `Else` clause along with this code. (I've omitted most of the existing code for brevity.)

```
Private Sub ColorPalette_MouseUp(ByVal sender As Object, _
    ByVal e As System.Windows.Forms.MouseEventArgs) Handles Me.MouseUp

    'Find the button that we clicked
    Dim objColorPaletteButton As ColorPaletteButton = GetButtonAt(e.X, e.Y)

    If Not objColorPaletteButton Is Nothing Then
        . . .
            RaiseEvent RightClick(Me, New EventArgs())

        End If

    End If

    Else
        'Display the color dialog
        If dlgColor.ShowDialog = DialogResult.OK Then

            'Add the new color
            AddColor(dlgColor.Color)

            'Resize the palette to show the dialog
            OnResize(New EventArgs())

        End If

    End If
End Sub
```

3. Run the project. When you click the background to the palette, you should have the
   opportunity to add your own colors (see Figure 15-6).

Figure 15-6

Using System Colors

Now you know that you can choose colors from a list of possibilities as well as define your own. The final thing you need to learn about colors is the idea of system colors.

When using Windows, the user has the ability to define all of the colors that are used for things like buttons, menus, captions, and so on. If you're building the UI for your own controls, it's reasonable to assume that from time to time you'll need to know what these colors are so that your controls have the same look and feel as the existing controls in the system.

System colors are exposed through the `System.Drawing.SystemColors` class. If you want to find a list of all the system colors, look in the MSDN documentation under `System.Drawing.SystemColors` class. Alternatively, use IntelliSense when in the Code Editor or the Object Browser.

In this Try It Out, you'll add a button to the control palette that is the same as the menu bar.

Try It Out   Adding System Colors

1. Open the Code Editor for `ColorPalette.Designer.vb`. Find the constructor and add the following highlighted code:

    ```
    Public Sub New()

        ' This call is required by the Windows Form Designer.
        InitializeComponent()

        ' Add any initialization after the InitializeComponent() call.
        'Add the colors
        AddColor(Color.Black)
        AddColor(Color.White)
        AddColor(Color.Red)
        AddColor(Color.Blue)
        AddColor(Color.Green)
        AddColor(Color.Gray)
        AddColor(Color.DarkRed)
        AddColor(Color.DarkBlue)
        AddColor(Color.DarkGreen)
        AddColor(Color.DarkGray)
        AddColor(Color.FromArgb(208, 112, 222))
        AddColor(Drawing.SystemColors.MenuBar)
    End Sub
    ```

2. Run the project. You should see a new color that matches the menu bar color.

Using Different Tools

Now that you have successfully cracked the nut of drawing filled circles on the page, turn your attention to building the other tools that you can use to put your applications together. In the next Try It Out, you add a menu that lets you select the tool you want.

If you need a refresher on how to use the Visual Basic 2008 Menu Designer, refer to Chapter 9.

Try It Out   Adding a Tools Menu

1. Open the Forms Designer for Form1 and change the Anchor property for Canvas to Bottom, Right, Left.

2. Click the title bar of the form and then resize the form so that there is enough room for a MenuStrip control at the top.

3. Drag a MenuStrip control onto the top of the form; then right-click MenuStrip1 and choose Insert Standard Items from the context menu to have the standard menus inserted.

4. Resize the form if necessary so that the Canvas control is just under the menu. Then click the Canvas control and change the Anchor property to Top, Bottom, Right, Left.

5. Click the Tools menu on the MenuStrip and then click in the white Type Here box that appears at the bottom of the Tools menu and enter **Ci&rcle**. Using the Properties window set the Checked property to **True** and the CheckOnClick property to **True**.

6. In the new Type Here box at the bottom, enter **&Hollow Circle**, and in the Properties window, set the CheckOnClick property to **True**. You can see the results of these steps in Figure 15-7.

Figure 15-7

Implementing Hollow Circle

Up until now, you have used a solid circle as the graphics pen to perform the drawing on your form. In this Try It Out, you'll be implementing the functionality to use the hollow circle graphics pen. You'll also be adding the necessary code that will allow you to select which pen you want to use from the Tools menu.

Try It Out **Implementing Hollow Circle**

1. The first thing you need to do is change the `GraphicTools` enumeration defined in the `PaintCanvas` class to include the hollow circle tool. Open the Code Editor for `PaintCanvas` and add the following highlighted code to the enumeration:

```
Public Class PaintCanvas
    'Public enumerations
    Public Enum GraphicTools As Integer
        CirclePen = 0
        HollowCirclePen = 1
    End Enum
```

2. Switch to the Code Editor for Form1. In the Class Name combo box, select `CircleToolStripMenuItem`, and then select the `Click` event in the Method Name combo box. Add the following highlighted code to the `Click` event handler:

```
Private Sub CircleToolStripMenuItem_Click(ByVal sender As Object, _
    ByVal e As System.EventArgs) Handles CircleToolStripMenuItem.Click

        'Set the tool
        Canvas.GraphicTool = PaintCanvas.GraphicTools.CirclePen

        'Uncheck the Hollow Circle menu item
        HollowCircleToolStripMenuItem.Checked = False
    End Sub
```

3. Select `HollowCircleToolStripMenuItem` in the Class Name combo box and the `Click` event in the Method Name combo box. Add the following highlighted code:

```
Private Sub HollowCircleToolStripMenuItem_Click(ByVal sender As Object, _
    ByVal e As System.EventArgs) Handles HollowCircleToolStripMenuItem.Click

        'Set the tool
        Canvas.GraphicTool = PaintCanvas.GraphicTools.HollowCirclePen

        'Uncheck the Circle menu item
        CircleToolStripMenuItem.Checked = False
    End Sub
```

4.   It only makes sense that, since you've implemented a menu, you should add code to the Exit menu item. Select exitToolStripMenuItem in the Class Name combo box and the Click event in the Method Name combo. Then add the following highlighted code to the Click event handler:

```
Private Sub exitToolStripMenuItem_Click(ByVal sender As Object, _
    ByVal e As System.EventArgs) Handles exitToolStripMenuItem.Click

        'Close the application
        Me.Close()
End Sub
```

5.   Open the Code Editor for PaintCanvas again and modify the Select Case GraphicTool statement in the DoMousePaint method as follows:

```
        'What tool are you using?
        Select Case GraphicTool

            'CirclePen
            Case GraphicTools.CirclePen

                'Create a new graphics circle
                Dim objGraphicsCircle As New GraphicsCircle()

                'Set the point for drawing
                objGraphicsCircle.SetPoint(e.X, e.Y, GraphicSize, _
                    objColor, True)

                'Store this for addition
                objGraphicsItem = objGraphicsCircle

            'HollowCirclePen
            Case GraphicTools.HollowCirclePen

                'Create a new graphics circle
                Dim objGraphicsCircle As New GraphicsCircle()

                'Set the point for drawing
                objGraphicsCircle.SetPoint(e.X, e.Y, GraphicSize, _
                    objColor, False)

                'Store this for addition
                objGraphicsItem = objGraphicsCircle

        End Select
```

6. Next, you need to change the `GraphicsCircle` class itself so that it knows when to draw a filled circle and when to draw a hollow circle. Open the Code Editor for `GraphicsCircle` and add the following highlighted code to the `Draw` method:

```
Public Overrides Sub Draw(ByVal graphics As System.Drawing.Graphics)
    If IsFilled = True Then

        'Create a new pen
        Dim objSolidBrush As New SolidBrush(Me.Color)

        'Draw the circle
        graphics.FillEllipse(objSolidBrush, Me.Rectangle)

    Else

        'Create a pen
        Dim pen As New Pen(Me.Color)

        'Use DrawEllipse instead
        Dim objRectangle As Rectangle = Me.Rectangle
        objRectangle.Inflate(-1, -1)
        graphics.DrawEllipse(pen, objRectangle)

    End If
End Sub
```

7. Finally, run the program. You should be able to select a new graphic tool from the menu and draw both filled and hollow circles, as shown in Figure 15-8.

Figure 15-8

How It Works

When the menu options are selected, `Click` events get fired. You can respond to these messages and set the `GraphicsTool` property on the `PaintCanvas` control to a new mode. When you change the mode, you also need to change the check mark on the menu. The currently selected menu item will be automatically checked, but you need to uncheck the menu item that isn't selected. You do this by setting the `Checked` property of the opposite menu item to **False**.

```
Private Sub HollowCircleToolStripMenuItem_Click(ByVal sender As Object, _
    ByVal e As System.EventArgs) Handles HollowCircleToolStripMenuItem.Click

    'Set the tool
    Canvas.GraphicTool = PaintCanvas.GraphicTools.HollowCirclePen

    'Uncheck the Circle menu item
    CircleToolStripMenuItem.Checked = False
End Sub
```

Irrespective of the mode used, `PaintCanvas.DoMousePaint` still gets called whenever the mouse draws on the control. However, you do need to accommodate the new tool by changing the `Select Case GraphicTool` statement to look for `HollowCirclePen` as well as `CirclePen`. Depending on which is selected, you pass `True` (filled) or `False` (not filled) through to `SetPoint`:

```
'What tool are you using?
Select Case GraphicTool

    'CirclePen
    Case GraphicTools.CirclePen

        'Create a new graphics circle
        Dim objGraphicsCircle As New GraphicsCircle()

        'Set the point for drawing
        objGraphicsCircle.SetPoint(e.X, e.Y, GraphicSize, _
            objColor, True)

        'Store this for addition
        objGraphicsItem = objGraphicsCircle

    'HollowCirclePen
    Case GraphicTools.HollowCirclePen

        'Create a new graphics circle
        Dim objGraphicsCircle As New GraphicsCircle()

        'Set the point for drawing
        objGraphicsCircle.SetPoint(e.X, e.Y, GraphicSize, _
            objColor, False)

        'Store this for addition
        objGraphicsItem = objGraphicsCircle

End Select
```

In `GraphicsCircle` itself, choosing whether to use the `FillEllipse` method to draw a filled circle or use the `DrawEllipse` method for a hollow one is a simple determination. The only wrinkle you have to contend with is `DrawEllipse`; the width and height of the bounding rectangle have to be one pixel smaller than those used for `FillEllipse`. This is due to an idiosyncrasy in the way the Windows graphics subsystem works. You'll often find when working with graphics features that you have to experiment a little!

```
Public Overrides Sub Draw(ByVal graphics As System.Drawing.Graphics)
    If IsFilled = True Then

        'Create a new pen
        Dim objSolidBrush As New SolidBrush(Me.Color)

        'Draw the circle
        graphics.FillEllipse(objSolidBrush, Me.Rectangle)

    Else

        'Create a pen
        Dim pen As New Pen(Me.Color)

        'Use DrawEllipse instead
        Dim objRectangle As Rectangle = Me.Rectangle
        objRectangle.Inflate(-1, -1)
        graphics.DrawEllipse(pen, objRectangle)

    End If
End Sub
```

Now that you've learned the basics of building user controls that support their own user interface, take a look at the image-handling capabilities in Visual Basic 2008.

Working with Images

The .NET Framework has very good support for loading and saving common image formats. In particular, you're able to load images of these types:

❑   .bmp: The standard Windows bitmap format

❑   .gif: The standard lossless common Internet file format for graphic files and small images

❑   .jpeg or .jpg: The standard lossy common Internet file format for photo-quality images

❑   .png: The competitor to .gif that doesn't have the tricky licensing implications

❑   .tiff: The standard file format for storing and manipulated scanned documents

❑   .wmf / .emf: The standard file formats for saving Windows Metafiles

❑   .ico: The standard file format for program icons

❑   .exif: The preferred file format for storage used internally with digital cameras

Prior to .NET, developers wanting to work with the most common Internet file formats (namely, .gif and .jpeg) had to buy third-party libraries. Now, support is built directly into the .NET Framework, so from day one you can start building applications that can handle these formats. What's more surprising is that the .NET Framework also supports saving these files. This allows you to load a .gif file and save it as, say, a .bmp or .png file. There are two ways in which you can use images with Visual Basic 2008. First, you can use the PictureBox control that you can find in the Visual Studio 2008 Toolbox. This is a control that you place on a form, set a reference to an image, either at design time or runtime and it deals with painting itself. This is a quick way of getting a fixed image on a form. The second way in which you can use images is inside your owner-draw controls. In the following exercise, you'll see how you can tweak WroxPaint so that, rather than drawing on a dull, white background, you're actually drawing on an image you load.

Drawing Images

The property on the control takes a System.Drawing.Image object. In addition to using the Image class with PictureBox and a few other controls in the .NET Framework, you can also use it with your own owner-draw controls.

In the next Try It Out, you start by providing a way for your owner-drawn controls to display an image loaded from one of the supported image formats.

Try It Out   Setting the BackgroundImage

1. Open the Designer for Form1. Using the Toolbox drag an OpenFileDialog control onto the form. Set the Name property of the control to **dlgFileOpenBackground**.

2. Switch to the Code Editor for Form1. You are going to wire up the Open menu item under the File menu to show the Open File dialog box. Select openToolStripMenuItem in the Class Name combo box and then select the Click event in the Method Name combo box. Add the following highlighted code to the Click event handler:

```
Private Sub openToolStripMenuItem_Click(ByVal sender As Object, _
    ByVal e As System.EventArgs) Handles openToolStripMenuItem.Click
```

```
        'Set the open file dialog properties
        With dlgFileOpenBackground
            .Filter = "Image files (*.gif,*.jpg,*.jpeg,*.bmp,*.wmf,*.png)" & _
                "|*.gif;*.jpg;*.jpeg;*.bmp;*.wmf;*.png|All files (*.*)|*.*"
            .FilterIndex = 1
            .Title = "Open Picture Files"
        End With


        'Show the dialog
        If dlgFileOpenBackground.ShowDialog() = DialogResult.OK Then

            'Create a new image that references the file
            Dim backgroundImage As Image = _
             Image.FromFile(dlgFileOpenBackground.FileName)

            'Set the background of the canvas
            Canvas.BackgroundImage = backgroundImage

        End If
    End Sub
```

3. Run the project. Select File ➪ Open from the menu and find a .bmp, .jpg, .jpeg, or .gif file somewhere on your computer. (If you try to open a file from the network, you may get a security exception.) The image will be displayed as shown in Figure 15-9.

Figure 15-9

How It Works

If you said, "But I didn't do anything!" you're quite right — you didn't have to write any code to support the background image. By default, the Control class from which UserControl is ultimately derived already supports a BackgroundImage property, and you've set this to the image you loaded. Therefore, the base class is dealing with drawing the image.

The loading is actually done with the shared FromFile method on the Image class. This method is the easiest way of loading a file from a disk:

```
'Show the dialog
If dlgFileOpenBackground.ShowDialog() = DialogResult.OK Then

    'Create a new image that references the file
    Dim backgroundImage As Image = _
     Image.FromFile(dlgFileOpenBackground.FileName)

    'Set the background of the canvas
    Canvas.BackgroundImage = backgroundImage

End If
```

Finally, when you're actually drawing on the image, you may find the paint process sluggish. This is because the control is spending a lot of time drawing the image onto the control, and this slows everything down. Try using a smaller image, or consider this Try It Out an illustration of how to manipulate images rather than a neat paint package!

Scaling Images

If you resize the form, you'll notice that the image is actually tiled. More importantly, if you make the control too small to accommodate the whole image, the sides of the image are clipped. What you want is for the image to be scaled so that it fits the control exactly. Therefore, in the next Try It Out, you take over control of drawing the background image from the base Control class and provide a new implementation of the BackgroundImage property.

Try It Out   Drawing the Image Yourself

1.   Open the Code Editor for PaintCanvas.

2.   Rather than adding your code to draw the image to the Paint method, you're going to work with a different event called OnPaintBackground. This method is called before the Paint method. Add the following code:

```
Protected Overrides Sub OnPaintBackground( _
    ByVal e As System.Windows.Forms.PaintEventArgs)

    'Paint the invalid region with the background brush
    Dim backgroundBrush As New SolidBrush(BackColor)
    e.Graphics.FillRectangle(backgroundBrush, e.ClipRectangle)

    'Paint the image
    If Not BackgroundImage Is Nothing Then

        'Find our client rectangle
        Dim clientRectangle As New Rectangle(0, 0, Width, Height)

        'Draw the image
        e.Graphics.DrawImage(BackgroundImage, clientRectangle)

    End If
End Sub
```

3.   Now select (PaintCanvas Events) in the Class Name combo box and the Resize event in the Method Name combo box. Add the following highlighted code to the Resize event handler:

```
Private Sub PaintCanvas_Resize(ByVal sender As Object, _
    ByVal e As System.EventArgs) Handles Me.Resize

    'Invalidate the control
    Me.Invalidate()
End Sub
```

4. Now run the project again. This time, when you open the image it will appear stretched or shrunken to fit the whole screen and will adjust itself as you resize the form as shown in Figure 15-10.

Figure 15-10

How It Works

All you're trying to do is take over the action of drawing the background image. As mentioned before, painting is a two-phase process: First, the background is erased (the PaintBackground event), and second, the control is given the opportunity to paint its user interface (the Paint event).

With the BackgroundImage property set, when the base class needs to draw the background, it will automatically draw the image. You should stop it from doing this; otherwise you'll effectively be drawing the image twice — in other words, it'll draw the image and then you'll draw your own image on top of it.

However, you do need to mimic the functionality that erases the background; otherwise things will not work properly. To do this, you create a new SolidBrush that uses the current background color (BackColor) and paint it on the area that's marked as invalid (ClipRectangle):

```
Protected Overrides Sub OnPaintBackground( _
    ByVal e As System.Windows.Forms.PaintEventArgs)

    'Paint the invalid region with the background brush
    Dim backgroundBrush As New SolidBrush(BackColor)
    e.Graphics.FillRectangle(backgroundBrush, e.ClipRectangle)
```

After you have painted the background, you then need to draw the image. You can do this easily by using the DrawImage method of the Graphics object. But to stretch the image you need to provide a rectangle that describes the bounds of the image. When you have that, you give DrawImage both the image and the rectangle, and the image is drawn.

```
                    'Paint the image
                    If Not BackgroundImage Is Nothing Then

                        'Find our client rectangle
                        Dim clientRectangle As New Rectangle(0, 0, Width, Height)

                        'Draw the image
                        e.Graphics.DrawImage(BackgroundImage, clientRectangle)

                    End If
                End Sub
```

Preserving the Aspect Ratio

The problem you have now is that the image is stretched out of shape. Ideally, you want to make the image bigger or smaller while preserving the *aspect ratio*, which is the ratio between the width and the height, of the image. The aspect ratio describes the ratio between the width and height of the image.

The .NET Framework does not have any support for preserving the aspect ratio when it stretches an image. However, with a little work, you can do this yourself.

Try It Out   **Preserving the Aspect Ratio**

1. Open the Code Editor for PaintCanvas again. Add the following highlighted code to OnPaintBackground.

```
Protected Overrides Sub OnPaintBackground( _
        ByVal e As System.Windows.Forms.PaintEventArgs)

        'Paint the invalid region with the background brush
        Dim backgroundBrush As New SolidBrush(BackColor)
        e.Graphics.FillRectangle(backgroundBrush, e.ClipRectangle)

        'Paint the image
        If Not BackgroundImage Is Nothing Then

            'Find our client rectangle
            Dim clientRectangle As New Rectangle(0, 0, Width, Height)

            'How big is the image?
            Dim intImageWidth As Integer = BackgroundImage.Width
            Dim intImageHeight As Integer = BackgroundImage.Height

            'What's the aspect ratio?
            Dim ratio As Double = _
                CType(intImageHeight, Double) / CType(intImageWidth, Double)
```

```
                'Scale the image
                If intImageWidth > clientRectangle.Width Then
                    intImageWidth = clientRectangle.Width
                    intImageHeight = _
                        CType(CType(intImageWidth, Double) * ratio, Integer)
                End If

                If intImageHeight > clientRectangle.Height Then
                    intImageHeight = clientRectangle.Height
                    intImageWidth = _
                        CType(CType(intImageHeight, Double) / ratio, Integer)
                End If

                'You need to center the image
                Dim pntImageLocation As New Point( _
                    (clientRectangle.Width / 2) - (intImageWidth / 2), _
                    (clientRectangle.Height / 2) - (intImageHeight / 2))
                Dim sizImageSize As New Size(intImageWidth, intImageHeight)
                Dim recImageRectangle As New Rectangle(pntImageLocation, sizImageSize)

                'Draw the image
                e.Graphics.DrawImage(BackgroundImage, recImageRectangle)

        End If
    End Sub
```

2. Run the project. Now if you load an image, it will scale and preserve the aspect ratio.

How It Works

Preserving the aspect ratio is a bit of rudimentary math coupled with throwing a few rectangles together. First, you need to know how big the area that you have to fit the image into actually is. You call this `clientRectangle`.

```
        Protected Overrides Sub OnPaintBackground( _
            ByVal e As System.Windows.Forms.PaintEventArgs)

            'Paint the invalid region with the background brush
            Dim backgroundBrush As New SolidBrush(BackColor)
            e.Graphics.FillRectangle(backgroundBrush, e.ClipRectangle)

            'Paint the image
            If Not BackgroundImage Is Nothing Then

                'Find our client rectangle
                Dim clientRectangle As New Rectangle(0, 0, Width, Height)
```

Next, you need to look at the image itself to see how big it is. You then need to know the aspect ratio. If, for example, you had an aspect ratio of 2:1 (width:height), and you had an image that was 200 pixels wide, you would know that the height had to be 100 pixels. Alternatively, if it were 25 pixels tall, it would be 50 pixels wide.

```
'How big is the image?
Dim intImageWidth As Integer = BackgroundImage.Width
Dim intImageHeight As Integer = BackgroundImage.Height

'What's the aspect ratio?
Dim ratio As Double = _
    CType(intImageHeight, Double) / CType(intImageWidth, Double)
```

When you calculate the aspect ratio, you want a floating-point number, so you have to convert the `Integer` width and height values to `Double`.

Next, you look at the shape of the client area compared to the shape of the image. If the native width of the image (in other words the size before its scaled) is wider than the width of the window, you fix the width of the image as being equal to the width of the client area. After you've done that, you use the aspect ratio to work out how tall the image should be. (Again, you've used conversions to `Double`s to make sure that the calculations work properly.)

```
'Scale the image
If intImageWidth > clientRectangle.Width Then
    intImageWidth = clientRectangle.Width
    intImageHeight = _
        CType(CType(intImageWidth, Double) * ratio, Integer)
End If
```

Alternatively, if the height of the client area is taller than the height of the image, you need to do the opposite — in other words, fix the height of the image and then work out the width:

```
If intImageHeight > clientRectangle.Height Then
    intImageHeight = clientRectangle.Height
    intImageWidth = _
        CType(CType(intImageHeight, Double) / ratio, Integer)
End If
```

At this point you have an adjusted width and height of the image. When you have that, to start drawing, you need to work out the upper-left corner. To do this, you divide the width of the client area by two to get the exact middle and subtract half of the width of the image from it. This gives you the x coordinate at which drawing should start. Then, you do the same for the height:

```
'You need to center the image
Dim pntImageLocation As New Point( _
    (clientRectangle.Width / 2) - (intImageWidth / 2), _
    (clientRectangle.Height / 2) - (intImageHeight / 2))
```

When you have the location, you build a rectangle using the adjusted width and height:

```
Dim sizImageSize As New Size(intImageWidth, intImageHeight)
Dim recImageRectangle As New Rectangle(pntImageLocation, sizImageSize)
```

Finally, you use DrawImage to actually draw the image on the screen:

```
'Draw the image
e.Graphics.DrawImage(BackgroundImage, recImageRectangle)

    End If
End Sub
```

More Graphics Methods

In this chapter, you have used a few of the graphics features available with the .NET Framework. There are some commonly used methods on the Graphics object that we haven't touched.

Whenever you have a Graphics object, either when you're building owner-draw controls or forms, try using these methods:

❑   DrawLine draws a single line between two points.

❑   DrawCurve and DrawClosedCurve draw a curve between a set of points.

❑   DrawArc draws a portion of a circle.

❑   DrawBezier draws a cubic Bezier curve defined by four points.

❑   DrawPie draws a slice of a circle (like a pie chart).

❑   DrawPolygon draws regular and irregular polygons from an array of points.

❑   DrawIcon draws Windows icons.

All of these methods use the Brush, Pen, Point, and Rectangle objects that you've seen used throughout this chapter. Each of these methods has an associated Fill method that fills in the shape after it's drawn it.

Summary

In this chapter, you looked at how you could build your own user interface on your controls and forms. Previously, you have been able to build your user interface only by plugging other people's controls together. Here you focused on building controls derived from System.Windows.Forms.UserControl, because you're interested in building component-based software.

After a discussion of the difference between vector and raster graphics, you proceeded to build a simple application that allowed the user to draw dots on the screen using the mouse. You then looked at building a separate control that provided the user with a set of colors that they could choose from when drawing. You saw how to use the Color dialog box to add new colors and how to create new colors using the Windows RGB (red, green, blue) color scheme.

Finally, you took a look at the Image class and saw how this could load a variety of file formats, including Windows bitmap, .jpeg, and .gif. You also saw how to scale images and preserve their aspect ratio.

To summarize, you should know how to:

❑ Use the mouse events to capture the current x, y coordinates of the mouse on the screen.

❑ Invalidate only the rectangle that you are working in to prevent screen flicker.

❑ Add and use named system colors as well as custom defined colors using their RGB values.

❑ Use the different graphics tools such as circle and hollow circle.

❑ Load, resize, and preserve the aspect ratio of images.

Accessing Databases

Most applications manipulate data in some way. Visual Basic 2008 applications often manipulate data that come from relational databases. To do this, your application needs to interface with relational database software such as Microsoft Access, Microsoft SQL Server, Oracle, or Sybase.

Visual Studio 2008 provides the data access tools and wizards to connect to these databases and retrieve and update their data. In this chapter, you will look at some of these tools and wizards and use them to retrieve data from a database.

In Chapter 17, you will concentrate more on writing code directly, which gives you more flexibility and control than relying on Visual Studio 2008 to create it for you. With practice, writing code will also take less time than working through a wizard.

In this chapter, you will:

- ❑ Learn what a database really is
- ❑ Examine the SQL SELECT statement
- ❑ Examine data access components
- ❑ Examine data binding in Windows Forms
- ❑ Use the data access wizards in Visual Studio 2008

Note that in order to work through the exercises in this chapter, you will need Microsoft Access 2000 or later.

What Is a Database?

A database consists of one or more large, complex files that store data in a structured format. The database engine, in your case Microsoft Access, manages the file or files and the data within those files.

Microsoft Access Objects

A Microsoft Access database file, which has the extension *mdb*, contains tables, queries, forms, reports, pages, macros, and modules, which are referred to as database objects. That's a lot of information in one large file, but Microsoft Access manages this data quite nicely. Forms, reports, pages, macros, and modules are generally concerned with letting users work with and display data. You will be writing Visual Basic 2008 applications to do this, so the only database objects you're really concerned about at the moment are tables and queries.

Tables

A table contains a collection of data, which is represented by one or more columns and one or more rows of data. Columns are typically referred to as fields in Microsoft Access, and the rows are referred to as records. Each field in a table represents an attribute of the data stored in that table. For example, a field named First Name would represent the first name of an employee or customer. This field is an attribute of an employee or customer. A record in a table contains a collection of fields that form a complete set of attributes of one instance of the data stored in that table. For example, suppose a table contains two fields: First Name and Last Name. These two fields in a single record describe the name of that one person. This is illustrated in Figure 16-1.

Figure 16-1

Queries

A query in a database is a group of Structured Query Language (SQL) statements that allow you to retrieve and update data in your tables. Queries can be used to select or update all of the data in one or more tables or to select or update specific data in one or more tables.

Query objects in Microsoft Access are a hybrid of two types of objects in SQL Server: views and stored procedures. Using database query objects can make your Visual Basic 2008 code simpler, because you have fewer complex SQL queries included in your code. They can also make your programs faster, because database engines can compile queries when you create them, whereas the SQL code in a Visual Basic 2008 program needs to be reinterpreted every time it's used.

To really understand the implications of queries, you need to learn some SQL. Fortunately, compared to other programming languages, basic SQL is really simple.

The SQL SELECT Statement

The American National Standards Institute (ANSI) defines the standards for ANSI SQL. Most database engines implement ANSI SQL to some extent and often add some features specific to the given database engine.

The benefit of ANSI SQL is that, once you learn the basic syntax for SQL, you have a solid grounding from which you can code the SQL language in almost any database. All you need to learn is a new interface for the database that you are working in. Many database vendors extended SQL to use advanced features or optimizations for their particular database. It is best to stick with ANSI standard SQL in your coding whenever possible, in case you want to change databases at some point.

The SQL SELECT statement selects data from one or more fields in one or more records and from one or more tables in your database. Note that the SELECT statement only selects data — it does not modify the data in any way.

The simplest allowable SELECT statement is like this:

```
SELECT * FROM Employees;
```

This means "retrieve every field for every record in the Employees table." The * indicates "every field." Employees indicates the table name. Officially, SQL statements in Microsoft Access should end in a semicolon. It usually doesn't matter if you forget the semicolons, as Access will add them automatically.

If you wanted to retrieve only first and last names, you can give a list of field names instead of a *:

```
SELECT [First Name], [Last Name] FROM Employees;
```

You need to enclose these field names in square brackets because these field names contain spaces. The square brackets indicate to the SQL interpreter that, even though there is a space in the name, it should treat First Name as one object name and Last Name as another object name. Otherwise, the interpreter would be unable to follow the syntax.

SQL is a lot like plain English — even a nonprogrammer could probably understand what it means. Now say you wanted to retrieve only the employees whose last names begin with D. To do this, you add a WHERE clause to your SELECT statement:

```
SELECT [First Name], [Last Name] FROM Employees WHERE [Last Name] LIKE 'D*';
```

A WHERE clause limits the selection of data to only those records that match the criteria in the WHERE clause. The preceding SELECT statement would cause the database to look at the Last Name column and only select those records where the employee's last name begins with the letter D.

Last, if you want to retrieve these items in a particular order, you can, for example, order the results by first name. You just need to add an ORDER BY clause to the end:

```
SELECT [First Name], [Last Name] FROM Employees
            WHERE [Last Name] LIKE 'D*' ORDER BY [First Name];
```

This means that if you have employees called Angela Dunn, Zebedee Dean, and David Dunstan, you will get the following result:

```
Angela    Dunn
David     Dunstan
Zebedee   Dean
```

You're specifying a specific command here, but the syntax is pretty simple — and very similar to how you would describe what you want to an English speaker. Usually, when ordering by a name, you want to order in an ascending order so that A comes first and Z comes last. If you were ordering by a number, though, you might want to have the bigger number at the top — for example, so that a product with the highest price appears first. Doing this is really simple — just add DESC (short for descending) to the ORDER BY clause, which causes the results to be ordered in descending order:

```
SELECT [First Name], [Last Name] FROM Employees
            WHERE [Last Name] LIKE 'D*' ORDER BY [First Name] DESC;
```

The D* means "begins with a D followed by anything." If you had said *D* it would mean "anything followed by D followed by anything," basically, "contains D." The preceding command would return the following:

```
Zebedee   Dean
David     Dunstan
Angela    Dunn
```

If you want to make it clear that you want the results in an ascending order, you can add ASC to the ORDER BY clause instead of DESC. But you don't really need to, since this is the default sort order.

You can summarize this syntax in the following way:

```
SELECT select-list
    FROM table-name
    [WHERE search-condition]
    [ORDER BY order-by-expression [ASC | DESC]]
```

This means that you must provide a list of fields to include or use a * to select them all. You must provide a table-name. You can choose to provide a search-condition. You can choose to provide an order-by-expression, and if you do, you can make it either ascending or descending.

SQL gets considerably more complicated when you start working with several tables in the same query. But, for various reasons, you don't need to do this all that much when working with Visual Basic 2008.

Anyway, the best way to get SQL into your head is to practice. Before moving on, please try to answer these questions in your head:

❑ How would you write a query to retrieve the Name, Description, and Price fields from a table called Product?

❑ What would you add to the query to retrieve only items with DVD in their description?

❑ How would you order the results so that the most expensive item comes first?

Queries in Access

SQL is really a basic programming language, and if you are a programmer who needs to access databases, you will need to use it. However, Microsoft Access provides wizards and visual tools that enable novice programmers to write queries without knowing SQL. Even for SQL programmers, these can sometimes prove useful. These tools, demonstrated in this section, end up producing SQL statements that you can view and modify if you wish, so they can be a good way to learn more about SQL.

Creating a Customer Query

In this Try It Out, you use Access to create a simple query that will select customer information from the Customer table in the Northwind.mdb database. You'll need to ensure that the sample databases were installed when you installed Microsoft Access or Microsoft Office. You'll create this query and then view the SQL SELECT statement that gets generated by Access.

Try It Out   Creating a Customer Query

1. For Access 2000: Open Microsoft Access and click the Open icon on the toolbar. In the Open dialog box, navigate to C:\Program Files\Microsoft Office\Office11\Samples\ and open Northwind.mdb. Then click the OK button.

    For Access 2003: Open Microsoft Access and click the Help menu. Next, choose Sample Databases and then choose Northwind Sample Database. If the samples are not installed, you will be prompted to install them. They are stored in the same location as the Access 2000 database based on the Office installation directory.

    The path to Microsoft Office will vary depending on the version you have installed and the installation path chosen at setup.

2. When the database opens, you will see two sections in the navigation bar on the left: Objects and Groups. The Objects section lists all of your database object types, which were discussed in the section on databases. You can also use Groups to gather related objects of any type, in any way you want (see Figure 16-2).

Figure 16-2

3. Since you want to take a look at how an SQL `SELECT` statement is built by Access, click the Queries icon under the Objects tab.

4. You are going to build a new query, so double-click Create query in Design view in the results window (see Figure 16-3).

Figure 16-3

5. The Show Table dialog box appears and allows you to select one or more tables to be in your query. You only want to select one table: Customers. Click the Customers table and then click the Add button to have this table added to the Query Designer. Then click the Close button to close the Show Table dialog box.

6. The Customers table is displayed with all available fields plus an asterisk. You can select the fields that you want to be added to your query, or you can select the asterisk, which will select all fields from the table. For this exercise just select a few fields for your query. Double-click

CompanyName in the Customers table to add it to the first column in the grid below the table. The Field and Table cells are automatically filled in. You also want to sort the data by this field, so click in the Sort cell and choose Ascending to have the results of your query sorted by this field. Your screen should now look like Figure 16-4. Notice that the primary key for the table is in bold: **CustomerID**.

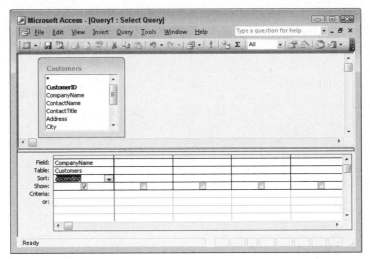

Figure 16-4

7. You now need to add the ContactName field to your grid. Double-click this field in the Customers table and it will be automatically added to the next available column in the grid. Then add ContactTitle in the same way. Your completed query should now look like the one in Figure 16-5.

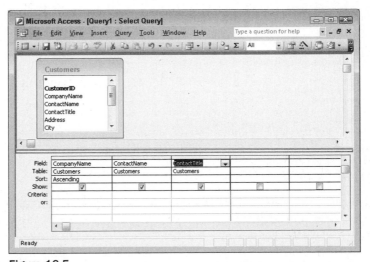

Figure 16-5

8. Click the Save icon on the toolbar, enter the name **CustomerQuery** in the Save As dialog box, and then click OK.

9. On the toolbar click the run icon, indicated by an exclamation point (!), and you will see results similar to the ones shown in Figure 16-6. Notice that the results are sorted on the CompanyName field in ascending order.

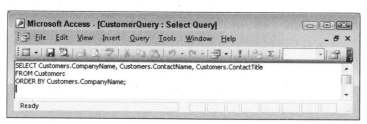

Figure 16-6

How It Works

From the choices you made, Access generates an SQL statement. To look at it, click the View menu and select the SQL View menu item. This will display the SQL statements as shown in Figure 16-7.

Notice that you have the basic SQL SELECT statement followed by the field names. Access has prefixed each field name with the table name. Remember that brackets are required only when the field names contain spaces. The table name prefix is actually required only when selecting data from multiple tables where both tables have a field with the same name. However, to reduce the chance of errors, Access has prefixed all fields with the table name.

Figure 16-7

The FROM clause in your SELECT statement specifies the table that data is being selected from (in this case, the Customers table).

The ORDER BY clause specifies which fields should be used to sort the data, and in this case the CompanyName field has been specified.

How does this SQL statement actually get built? When you first started creating this query you added a table name. Before any fields were added to the grid, Access generated the following SQL statement:

```
SELECT
FROM Customers;
```

Of course, this on its own is not a valid SQL statement. When you added the first field and set the sort order for that field, the following SQL statement was generated — which is valid:

```
SELECT Customer.CompanyName
FROM Customers
ORDER BY Customers.CompanyName;
```

As you continued to add fields, the rest of the field names were added to the SQL statement until the complete SQL statement shown in Figure 16-7 was generated.

The next section discusses the basic data access components that are needed in Windows Forms to display data. Since you have been using Microsoft Access in your examples here, the focus is on the data access components provided in Visual Studio 2008 that assist you in accessing the data in an Access database.

Data Access Components

There are three main data access components in Visual Basic 2008 that you need for retrieving and viewing data from the database: BindingSource, TableAdapter, and DataSet. The BindingSource and DataSet components are located in the Toolbox under the Data tab, as shown in Figure 16-8. The TableAdapter can be automatically generated depending on the path you take when adding data access components, as you'll soon discover. Take a brief look at each one of these components in turn.

Figure 16-8

These components are known as data components and are simply classes, like everything else in the .NET Framework. In this chapter, you will simply see how to use some of them in a Windows application. Data components will be discussed as a whole in the next chapter.

DataSet

The DataSet component is a cache of data that is stored in memory. It's a lot like a mini database engine, but its data exists in memory. You can use it to store data in tables, and using the DataView component (covered in Chapter 17), you can query the data in various ways.

The DataSet is very powerful. In addition to storing data in tables, it stores a rich amount of metadata, or "data about the data." This includes things like table and column names, data types, and the information needed to manage and undo changes to the data. All of this data is represented in memory in Extensible Markup Language (XML). A DataSet can be saved to an XML file and then loaded back into memory very easily. It can also be passed in XML format over networks, including the Internet.

Since the DataSet component stores all of the data in memory, you can scroll through the data both forward and backward, and can also make updates to the data in memory. The DataSet component is very powerful, and you will be exploring this component in more detail in the next chapter. In this chapter, you will simply be using it to store data and bind it to a control on your form.

DataGridView

The DataGridView component is a container that allows you to bind data from your data source and have it displayed in a spreadsheet-like format, displaying the columns of data horizontally and the rows of data vertically.

The DataGridView component also provides many properties that allow you to customize the appearance of the component itself, as well as properties that allow you to customize the column headers and the display of data.

More important, though, are the quick links at the bottom of the Properties window for the DataGridView component, which allow you to customize the appearance of the DataGridView itself through several predefined format styles. You'll see this later in this chapter.

BindingSource

The BindingSource component acts like a bridge between your data source (DataSet) and your data-bound controls (that is, controls that are bound to data components). Any interaction with the data from your controls goes through the BindingSource component, which in turn communicates with your data source.

For example, your DataGridView control will be initially filled with data. When you request that a column be sorted, the DataGridView control will communicate that intention to the BindingSource, which in turn communicates that intention to the data source.

The BindingSource component is the component that you will bind to the DataSource property of your controls, as you'll see later in this chapter.

BindingNavigator

The BindingNavigator component provides a standard UI component that allows you to navigate through the records that are in your data source. It looks very similar to the record navigator shown at the bottom of Figure 16-6.

The BindingNavigator component is bound to your BindingSource component much as the DataGridView component is. When you click the Next button in the BindingNavigator component, it in turn sends a request to the BindingSource component for the next record, and the BindingSource component in turn sends the request to the data source.

TableAdapter

There's one last component to talk about: the TableAdapter. This component does not reside in the ToolBox but can be automatically generated for you depending on how you add your data access components to your project.

The TableAdapter contains the query that is used to select data from your database as well as connection information for connecting to your database. It also contains methods that will fill the DataSet in your project with data from the database. You can also choose to have the TableAdapter generate INSERT, UPDATE, and DELETE statements based on the query that is used to select data.

The TableAdapter is covered in more detail in Chapter 17.

Data Binding

Data binding means taking data referenced by your BindingSource and binding it to a control. In other words, the control will receive its data from your data access components, and the data will be automatically displayed in the control for the user to see and manipulate. In Visual Basic 2008, most controls support some level of data binding. Some are specifically designed for it, such as the DataGridView and TextBox. In your next Try It Out, you will be binding data from a BindingSource component to a DataGridView control, so this is where you want to focus your attention. Later in this chapter you'll bind data to a TextBox control.

In this Try It Out, you will be using the data access wizards in Visual Studio 2008 to create the data components necessary to bind data to a DataGridView control. You will be using the `Northwind.mdb` sample database again as your data source.

Try It Out   Binding Data to a DataGridView Control

1. Create a new Windows Forms Application project called **Northwind Customers DataGridView**.

2. Click the Data tab in the toolbox and then drag a DataGridView control from the toolbox and drop it on your form. The DataGridView control will display the Tasks dialog box as shown in Figure 16-9.

Figure 16-9

3. Click the drop-down arrow in the Choose Data Source combo box and then click the Add Project Data Source link at the bottom of the list that is displayed. This displays the Data Source Configuration Wizard.

4. The Choose a Data Source Type screen allows you to choose the data source for your data. As you can see from this screen, shown in Figure 16-10, you have several options for a data source. You can click the Database icon for connecting to various databases such as SQL Server, Oracle, and Access; the Web Service icon for connecting to a web service; or the Object icon for connecting to your business logic components.

    Click the Database icon and click the Next button.

Figure 16-10

5. In the Choose Your Data Connection screen, click the New Connection button.

6. In the Choose Data Source dialog box, select Microsoft Access Database File in the Data Source list and then click the Continue button.

7. In the Add Connection dialog box, click the Browse button and navigate to the samples folder for Microsoft office. By default, this will be in the folder `C:\Program Files\Microsoft Office\Office11\Samples\` for a default installation of Microsoft Office 2003 (11 is the version and will change based on your version of Office).

   Select the `Northwind.mdb` database in the Select Microsoft Access Database File dialog box and click the Open button to have the path and file name added to the text field on the Add Connection dialog box. You can click the Test Connection button to verify your choices. Click the OK button when you are done to close the Add Connection dialog box and then click the Next button on the Choose Your Data Connection screen.

   You will be prompted with a dialog box that informs you that the data file is not part of your project and asks if you want to add it. Click the Yes button in this dialog box.

8. Click the Next button on the Save the Connection String to the Application Configuration File screen.

9. The Choose Your Database Objects screen allows you to select the data that your application needs. Here you have the option to select data directly from the tables in your database, data generated from the execution of various views and stored procedures, or data generated from the execution of functions.

   You'll be using the query that you created in the last Try It Out exercise, so expand the Views node in the Database objects list and then select the check box for CustomerQuery as shown in Figure 16-11. If you expand CustomerQuery, you'll see the columns that are returned from this query. Click the Finish button when you are done.

At this point, the wizard will generate a DataSet object named `NorthwindDataSet`, a BindingSource object named `CustomerQueryBindingSource`, and a TableAdapter object named `CustomerQueryTableAdapter`.

Figure 16-11

10. Since you will not be adding, editing, or deleting records from this table, uncheck the check box next to these options in the Tasks dialog box. You will, however, want to implement sorting in your DataGridView component, so check the check box next to Enable Column Reordering. When you are done, click the title bar of the form to hide the Actions dialog.

11. Click the DataGridView control and, in the Properties window, set the Dock property to **Fill.**

12. At this point you can run your project to see the results. Click the Start button on the toolbar, and your form will be displayed with the DataGridView control populated with data.

You can click the column headers to have the data in the DataGridView sorted in ascending order. Clicking the same column header again will sort the data in descending order. Each sort order will be indicated with an arrow pointing up for ascending and down for descending.

At this point you have not written a single line of code to achieve these results, which just goes to prove how powerful the data wizards in Visual Basic 2008 are.

How It Works

The preceding approach is the easiest and most straightforward approach. You start by adding a DataGridView control to your form, which prompts you with the Tasks dialog box for the DataGridView.

This dialog box allowes you to create a new Data Source via the Data Source Configuration Wizard, which walks you through a series of steps. First, you identify the type of data source that you wanted to use. Then you specify the type of database object that you want to use to retrieve your data; in this step you merely chose to use a specific table in your database and select specific columns from that table.

When you click the Finish button, several components are automatically generated and added to your project. These include the TableAdapter, DataSet, and BindingSource. The BindingSource is the component that is bound to the DataSource property of the DataGridView control.

Remember that the BindingSource's job is to communicate the data needs of the control to the data source, which in this case is the DataSet containing all of the data. The DataSet is populated with data by the TableAdapter when your form is loaded.

The most important point of this exercise is to show the ease with which you are able to create a data-bound application and the simple fact that you do not have to write a single line of code to achieve the end results.

In this next Try It Out exercise, you'll be using several TextBox controls on your form and will bind each text box to a certain field in your BindingSource. You'll then be using a BindingNavigator control to navigate through the records in your DataSet.

Try It Out   Binding Data to TextBox Controls

1. Create a new Windows Forms Application project called **Northwind Customers BindingNavigator**.

2. Add three Label controls and three TextBox controls to your form. Arrange the controls so that your form looks similar to Figure 16-12, and set the Text properties of the Label controls.

Figure 16-12

3. Click the first text box on your form and then expand the (DataBindings) property in the Properties window by clicking the plus sign next to it. Then click the Text property under the DataBindings property. Now click the drop-down arrow for the Text property.

At this point you'll see the Data Source window shown in Figure 16-13. Click the Add Project Data Source link to invoke the Data Source Configuration Wizard, which you saw in the previous Try It Out exercise.

Figure 16-13

4. Select the Database icon in the Choose a Data Source Type screen and click the Next button.

5. In the Choose Your Data Connection screen, click the New Connection button.

6. In the Add Connection dialog box, click the Browse button and navigate to the samples folder for Microsoft office. By default, this will be in the folder `C:\Program Files\Microsoft Office\Office11\Samples\` for a default installation of Microsoft Office 2003 (11 is the version and will change based on your version of Office).

   Select the `Northwind.mdb` database in the Select Microsoft Access Database File dialog box and click the Open button to have the path and file name added to the text field on the Add Connection dialog box. Click the OK button when you are done to close the Add Connection dialog box and then click the Next button on the Choose Your Data Connection screen.

   You will be prompted with a dialog box that informs you that the data file is not part of your project and asks if you want to add it. Click the Yes button in this dialog box.

7. Click the Next button on the Save the Connection String to the Application Configuration File screen.

8. In the Choose Your Database Objects screen, expand the Tables node in the Database objects list and then expand the Customers table. Select the check box for CompanyName, ContactName, and ContactTitle. Click Finish.

9. Click the drop-down arrow next to the Text property in the Properties Window. At this point, you'll see the Data Source window shown in Figure 16-14. Expand the Other Data Sources node, the Project Data Sources node, the NorthwindDataSet node, and finally the Customers node.

Now click the CompanyName field. The window will close, and the Text field under the DataBindings property will be bound to the CompanyName field in your DataSet.

If you look at the bottom of the IDE, you'll notice that a NorthwindDataSet component, CustomersBindingSource component, and CustomersTableAdapter component have been automatically generated.

Figure 16-14

10. Click the second text box on your form, and then click the Text property under the DataBindings property in the Properties window. Now click the drop-down arrow for the Text property; then expand the CustomersBindingSource node in the Data Source window, and then click the ContactName field.

11. Click the third text box on your form, and then click the Text property under the DataBindings property in the Properties window. Click the drop-down arrow for the Text property, expand the CustomersBindingSource node in the Data Source window, and then click the ContactTitle field.

12. Return to the toolbox, drag a BindingNavigator control from the Data tab, and drop it on your form. The BindingNavigator control will be automatically docked to the top of the form.

13. In the Properties window, locate the BindingSource property, and then click that field. Now click the drop-down arrow for the BindingSource property and choose CustomersBindingSource from the list.

14. Finally, click the Start button on the toolbar to run your project. Your form that is displayed should look similar to the one shown in Figure 16-15. You'll be able to navigate through the records in your data source, navigating backward and forward as well as being able to go the first and last record.

Clicking the Delete button will delete records from your DataSet but will not delete records from the database. Likewise, clicking the Add button will add an empty record to your DataSet but not to the database. You would need to write some code to actually have the database updated with the changes from your DataSet.

The beauty of using the DataNavigator control is that you've quickly built a form that will navigate through the records of your database without you having to write a single line of code.

Figure 16-15

How It Works

First you add three Label and TextBox controls to your form. You then set the DataBindings properties of the text boxes. When you set the Text DataBinding property of the first text box, you are prompted to add a new data source, which again invokes the Data Source Configuration Wizard.

You use the Data Source Configuration Wizard in this exercise in the same manner as you did in the previous exercise. When you complete the Data Source Configuration Wizard, it automatically generates TableAdapter, DataSet, and BindingSource components. You are then able to choose which field in the DataSet to bind to the DataBinding Text property.

When you add the BindingNavigator control to your form, setting it up is a matter of simply choosing the BindingSource that is generated by the Data Source Configuration Wizard in the BindingSource property in the Properties window.

Again, this exercise has demonstrated the simplicity with which you can create data-bound applications without the need to write any code.

Summary

You started this chapter by exploring what a database actually is and then looked at the SQL SELECT statement. You put this knowledge to use by creating a query in the `Northwind.mdb` database to see the SQL statements that Access generated for you.

You then took a look at the basics of binding data to controls on a form, specifically the DataGridView control and TextBox controls. You have examined the necessary basic data access components required to retrieve data from an Access database and bind that data to your controls. You used the components provided in the Data tab of the Toolbox for your data access, and used the wizards to generate the necessary code to connect to the database and retrieve the data.

After working through this chapter, you should know:

❑ What a database is and the basic objects that make up a database

❑ How to use the SQL SELECT statement to select data from a database

❑ How to use the Data Source Configuration Wizard to create the data access components needed to perform data binding

❑ How to bind data to a DataGridView control

❑ How to bind data to TextBox controls and use the BindingNavigator control

You have seen that the wizards provided in Visual Studio 2008 make it simple to bind data quickly to the controls on a form. Sometimes, however, you need more control on how you interact with the data in a database and how you bind the data to the controls on a form. Chapter 17 takes a different approach to data binding by programmatically binding data to controls on a form. You will also be exploring the data access components in more detail and will learn how to set their properties and to execute their methods from your code.

Exercises

1. Create a new query in your Northwind database to select FirstName, LastName, and Title from the Employees table. Order the results by the LastName column and save your query as EmployeeQuery. Then create a Windows application with a DataGridView control that uses the EmployeeQuery.

2. Using the query created in Exercise 1, create a new Windows application that uses the BindingNavigator control and bind the fields from your query to text boxes on your form.

Database Programming with SQL Server and ADO.NET

Chapter 16 introduced database programming. You obtained data from a single table in an Access database and displayed it on a grid. You managed to give the user some cool features while writing virtually no code.

You used wizards that wrote most of the code for you — including setting up the connection, configuring the data adapter, and generating a typed dataset. This works great for simple database access using one or two tables, but writing the code yourself can give you a lot more control.

This chapter dives much deeper into the topic of database access. The database access technologies you used in the previous chapter, including components for retrieving data, storing data in memory, and binding data to controls, are collectively called *ADO.NET*. You will explore how you can use the built-in capabilities of ADO.NET to retrieve and update data from databases. You will also learn to manipulate, filter, and edit data held in memory by the DataSet.

The data you extract will be bound to controls on your form, so you will also need to explore binding more thoroughly. You will see how you can use controls to view one record at a time (for example, using text boxes) and how to navigate between records, using the CurrencyManager object.

In this chapter, you will:

❑   Learn about ADO.NET objects

❑   Bind data to controls

❑   Search for and sort in-memory data using ADO.NET DataView objects

❑   Select, insert, update, and delete data in a database using ADO.NET

❑   Learn how to use Language-Integrated Query (LINQ) to write VB code and select data from different data sources and update a database

You will also learn how to access SQL Server databases using the `SqlClient` data provider. As mentioned in the previous chapter, `SqlClient` is significantly faster than `OleDb`, but it works only with SQL Server databases. To complete the exercises in this chapter, you need to have access to a version of MSDE, SQL Server 2000, or SQL Server 2005, as well as full access to the Pubs database. If you do not have a copy of the Pubs database, you can lookup where to find the Pubs database for your version on your favorite search engine. Also, you may use the links in the list that follows to find a script to create the database. When this chapter uses the term *SQL Server*, the term includes SQL Server 2000, as well as MSDE and SQL Server 2005. The database can reside in SQL Server on your local machine or in SQL Server on a network.

Need help locating a copy of the SQL Server? You can download SQL Server 2005 Express for free. The version used for this chapter is SQL Server Express with Advanced Services. You can get it from `www.microsoft.com/sql` and choose editions from the menu. The direct url is `http://msdn2`
`.microsoft.com/en-us/express/bb410792.aspx`. This site also has links for downloading sample 2005 databases (not Pubs) and Books Online (SQL Help files).

Need help locating a copy of the Pubs database? Go to the following resources:

❑　SQL Server 2000 scripts and instructions can be downloaded from `www.microsoft.com/`
`downloads/details.aspx?FamilyID=06616212-0356-46A0-8DA2-EEBC53A68034&`
`displaylang=en`. This script will work with 2005 versions. This is the easiest place to get the database.

❑　If the links are hard to type, just go to `www.microsoft.com/downloads` and search for SQL Server Sample Databases. The search results will contain the preceding link.

❑　The msi package you download and install will install to `C:\SQL Server 2000 Sample`
`Databases` (drive may change based on your configuration). You can then open the file `instpubs.sql` into SQL Management Studio and execute the code and the Pubs database will be created and loaded with data.

Here are some notes for installing SQL 2005 Express with Advanced Services:

❑　On the Feature Selection Screen, be sure to install all of the Client Components. This installs Microsoft SQL Server Management Studio Express, which is a terrific tool for writing SQL and managing your databases outside of Visual Studio.

❑　For Chapter 17, you may install a named instance of WROX to avoid having to customize the code.

❑　Chapter 17 uses mixed mode authentication to allow a user name and password to be passed into SQL Server. The chapter uses the `sa` login with a password of `wrox`, which has system administrator rights. This is not normally how you would login your application to SQL Server. For production, create a login that has a few rights as possible to use or use windows authentication where you can give rights to users or groups.

ADO.NET

ADO.NET is designed to provide a *disconnected architecture*. This means that applications connect to the database to retrieve a load of data and store it in memory. They then disconnect from the database and manipulate the in-memory copy of the data. If the database needs to be updated with changes made to the in-memory copy, a new connection is made and the database is updated. The main in-memory data store is the `DataSet`, which contains other in-memory data stores, such as `DataTable` objects. You can filter and sort data in a `DataSet` using `DataView` objects, as you will see later in the chapter.

Using a disconnected architecture provides many benefits, of which the most important to you is that it allows your application to *scale up*. This means that your database will perform just as well supporting hundreds of users as it does supporting ten users. This is possible because the application connects to the database only long enough to retrieve or update data, thereby freeing available database connections for other instances of your application or other applications using the same database.

ADO.NET Data Namespaces

The core ADO.NET classes exist in the `System.Data` namespace. This namespace, in turn, contains some child namespaces. The most important of these are `System.Data.SqlClient` and `System.Data.OleDb`. These provide classes for accessing SQL Server databases and OLE (Object Linking and Embedding) DB-compliant databases, respectively. You've already used classes from the `System.Data.OleDb` namespace in the previous chapter, where you used `OleDbConnection` and `OleDbDataAdapter`. In this chapter, you use `System.Data.SqlClient` with its equivalent classes, including `SqlConnection` and `SqlDataAdapter`.

Another child namespace also exists in the `System.Data` namespace: `System.Data.Odbc`. The `System.Data.Odbc` namespace provides access to older Open Database Connectivity (ODBC) data sources that do not support the `OleDb` technology.

The `System.Data.SqlClient`, `System.Data.OleDb`, and `System.Data.Odbc` namespaces are known as *data providers* in ADO.NET. There are other data providers available; in this book, you concentrate on only the first two.

In this chapter, you access SQL Server databases using the `SqlClient` namespace. However, in ADO.NET, the different data providers work in a very similar way. So the techniques you use here can be easily transferred to the `OleDb` classes. Also, the techniques you learned in the previous chapter using `OleDb` apply to `SqlClient` classes. With ADO.NET, you use the data provider that best fits your data source — you do not need to learn a whole new interface, because all data providers work in a very similar way.

As you start working with ADO.NET, you will soon learn how the pieces fit together, and this chapter helps you in that reaching that goal.

Since the space here is limited, you focus on the specific classes that are relevant to the example programs in this chapter. The following list contains the ADO.NET classes that you will be using:

- ❑ `SqlConnection`
- ❑ `SqlDataAdapter`
- ❑ `SqlCommand`
- ❑ `SqlParameter`

Remember that these are specifically `SqlClient` classes, but that the `OleDb` namespace has very close equivalents. Whenever you want to use these classes, you must add a reference to the `System.Data` namespace. You can use the `Imports` keyword, so you do not have to fully qualify members of the `SqlClient` namespace in your code, as shown in the following code fragment:

```
Imports System.Data.SqlClient
```

If you want to use the core ADO.NET classes, such as `DataSet` and `DataView` without typing the full name, you must import the `System.Data` namespace, as shown in the next code fragment:

```
Imports System.Data
```

You should already be familiar with importing different namespaces in your project. However, to be thorough, you also cover this when you go through the hands-on exercises.

Next, we'll take a look at the main classes that exist in the `System.Data.SqlClient` namespace.

The SqlConnection Class

The `SqlConnection` class is at the heart of the classes discussed in this section, because it provides a connection to an SQL Server database. When you construct an `SqlConnection` object, you can choose to specify a *connection string* as a parameter. The connection string contains all the information required to open a connection to your database. If you don't specify one in the constructor, you can set it using the `SqlConnection.ConnectionString` property. In the previous chapter, Visual Studio .NET built a connection string for you from the details you specified in the Data Link Properties dialog box. However, it is often more useful or quicker to write a connection string manually — so let's take a look at how connection strings work.

Working with the Connection String Parameters

The way that the connection string is constructed depends on what data provider you are using. When accessing SQL Server, you usually provide a `Server` and a `Database` parameter, as shown in the following table.

Parameter	Description
Server	The name of the SQL Server that you want to access. This is usually the name of the computer that is running SQL Server. You can use `(local)` or `localhost` if SQL Server is on the same machine as the one running the application. If you are using named instances of SQL Server, then this parameter would contain the computer name followed by a backslash followed by the named instance of SQL Server.
Database	The name of the database that you want to connect to.

You also need some form of authentication information, which you can provide in two ways: by using a user name and password in the connection string or by connecting to SQL Server using the NT account under which the application is running. If you want to connect to the server by specifying a user name and password, you need to include additional parameters in your connection string, as shown in the following table.

Parameter	Description
User ID	The user name for connecting to the database. An account with this user ID needs to exist in SQL Server and have permission to access the specified database.
Password	The password for the specified user.

However, SQL Server can be set up to use the Windows NT account of the user who is running the program to open the connection. In this case, you don't need to specify a user name and password. You just need to specify that you are using *integrated security*. (The method is called integrated security because SQL Server is integrating with Windows NT's security system and provides the most secure connection because the User ID and Password parameters need not be specified in the code.) You do this using the Integrated Security parameter, which you set to True when you want the application to connect to SQL Server using the current user's NT account.

Of course, for this to work, the user of the application must have permission to use the SQL Server database. This is granted using the SQL Server Enterprise Manager.

To see how these parameters function in a connection string to initialize a connection object, look at the following code fragment. It uses the SqlConnection class to initialize a connection object that uses a specific user ID and password in the connection string:

```
Dim objConnection As SqlConnection = New _
    SqlConnection("Server=localhost\wrox;Database=pubs;" & _
    "User ID=sa;Password=wrox;")
```

This connection string connects to an SQL Server database. The Server parameter specifies that the database resides on the local machine. The Database parameter specifies the database that you want to access — in this case it is the pubs database. Finally, the User ID and Password parameters specify the User ID and password of the user defined in the database. As you can see, each parameter has a value assigned to it using =, and each parameter-value pair is separated by a semicolon.

Opening and Closing the Connection

After you initialize a connection object with a connection string, as shown previously, you can invoke the methods of the SqlConnection object such as Open and Close, which actually open and close a connection to the database specified in the connection string. An example of this is shown in the following code fragment:

```
' Open the database connection...
objConnection.Open()
' ... Use the connection
' Close the database connection...
objConnection.Close()
```

Although many more properties and methods are available in the SqlConnection class, the ones mentioned so far are all you are really interested in to complete the hands-on exercises, and they should be enough to get you started.

SqlCommand

The `SqlCommand` class represents an SQL command to execute against a data store. The command is usually a select, insert, update, or delete query, and can be an SQL string or a call to a stored procedure. The query being executed may contain parameters or it may not.

In the example in Chapter 16, the Data Adapter Configuration Wizard generated a command object for you (although in that case it was an `OleDbCommand`). In that case, a data adapter used the command to fill a dataset. You look at how to write code to do this later in the chapter. For the moment, look at command objects alone. You learn how they relate to data adapters in the next section.

The constructor for the `SqlCommand` class has several variations, but the simplest method is to initialize an `SqlCommand` object with no parameters. Then, after the object has been initialized, you can set the properties you need to perform the task at hand. The following code fragment shows how to initialize an `SqlCommand` object:

```
Dim objCommand As SqlCommand = New SqlCommand()
```

When using data adapters and datasets, there isn't much call for using command objects on their own. They will mainly be used for executing a particular select, delete, insert, or update, so that is what you do in this chapter. You can also use command objects with a data reader. A *data reader* is an alternative to a `DataSet` that uses fewer system resources but provides far less flexibility. In this book, you will concentrate on using the `DataSet`, because it is the more common and useful of the two.

The Connection Property

Certain properties must be set on the `SqlCommand` object before you can execute the query. The first of these properties is the `Connection` property. This property is set to an `SqlConnection` object, as shown in the next code fragment.

```
objCommand.Connection = objConnection
```

For the command to execute successfully, the connection must be open at the time of execution.

The CommandText Property

The next property that must be set is the `CommandText` property. This property specifies the SQL string or stored procedure to be executed. Most databases require that you place all *string* values in single quote marks, as shown here:

```
Dim objConnection As SqlConnection = New _
            SqlConnection("server=(local);database=pubs;user id=sa;password=")
Dim objCommand As SqlCommand = New SqlCommand()
objCommand.Connection = objConnection
objCommand.CommandText = "INSERT INTO authors " & _
                    "(au_id, au_lname, au_fname, contract) " & _
                    "VALUES('123-45-6789', 'Barnes', 'David', 1)"
```

The `INSERT` statement is a very simple one that means, "Insert a new row into the `authors` table. In the `au_id` column put `'123-45-6789'`, in the `au_lname` column put `'Barnes'`, in the `au_fname` column put `'David'`, and in the contract column put `'1'`."

This is the basic way that INSERT statements work in SQL. You have INSERT INTO followed by a table name. You then have a series of column names, in parentheses. You then have the VALUES keyword followed by a set of values, to be inserted into the columns that you've just named and in the same order.

This assumes that you know the values to insert when you are writing the program, which is unlikely in most cases. Fortunately, you can create commands with parameters and then set the values of these parameters separately. Let's have a look at how to use parameters.

The Parameters Collection

Placeholders are variables prefixed with an at (@) sign in the SQL statement; they get filled in by parameters. So if you wanted to update the authors table as discussed in the previous section, but didn't know the values at design time, you would do this:

```
Dim objConnection As SqlConnection = New _
                SqlConnection("server=(local);database=pubs;user id=sa;password=")
Dim objCommand As SqlCommand = New SqlCommand()
objCommand.Connection = objConnection
objCommand.CommandText = "INSERT INTO authors " & _
                    "(au_id, au_lname, au_fname, contract) " & _
                    "VALUES(@au_id,@au_lname,@au_fname,@au_contract)"
```

Here, instead of providing values, you provide placeholders. Placeholders, as mentioned, always start with an @ symbol. They do not need to be named after the database column that they represent, but it is often easier if they are, and it helps to self-document your code.

Next, you need to create parameters that will be used to insert the values into the placeholders when the SQL statement is executed. You need to create and add parameters to the Parameters collection of the SqlCommand object. The term *parameters* here refers to the parameters required to provide data to your SQL statement or stored procedure, *not* to the parameters that are required to be passed to a Visual Basic 2008 method.

You can access the Parameters collection of the SqlCommand object by specifying the Parameters property. After you access the Parameters collection, you can use its properties and methods to create one or more parameters in the collection. The easiest way to add a parameter to a command is demonstrated in the following example:

```
Dim objConnection As SqlConnection = New _
                SqlConnection("server=(local);database=pubs;user id=sa;password=")
Dim objCommand As SqlCommand = New SqlCommand()
objCommand.Connection = objConnection
objCommand.CommandText = "INSERT INTO authors " & _
                    "(au_id, au_lname, au_fname, contract) " & _
                    "VALUES(@au_id,@au_lname,@au_fname,@au_contract)"
objCommand.Parameters.AddWithValue ("@au_id", txtAuId.Text)
objCommand.Parameters.AddWithValue ("@au_lname", txtLastName.Text)
objCommand.Parameters.AddWithValue ("@au_fname", txtFirstName.Text)
objCommand.Parameters.AddWithValue ("@au_contract", chkContract.Checked)
```

The `AddWithValue` method here accepts the name of the parameter and the object that you want to add. In this case, you are using the `Text` property of various `Text` box objects on a (fictitious) form for most of the columns. For the `Contract` column you use the `Checked` property of a check box on the same form. In previous versions of ADO.NET, you could use the `add` method to add a parameter with a value. That overload is now obsolete.

The ExecuteNonQuery Method

Finally, you can execute the command. To do this, the connection needs to be opened. You can invoke the `ExecuteNonQuery` method of the `SqlCommand` object. This method executes the SQL statement and causes the data to be inserted into the database. It then returns the number of rows that were affected by the query, which can be a useful way to check that the command worked as expected. To complete your code fragment, you need to open the connection, execute the query, and close the connection again:

```
Dim objConnection As SqlConnection = New _
                    SqlConnection("server=(local);database=pubs;user id=sa;password=")
Dim objCommand As SqlCommand = New SqlCommand()
objCommand.Connection = objConnection
objCommand.CommandText = "INSERT INTO authors " & _
                "(au_id, au_lname, au_fname, contract) " & _
                "VALUES(@au_id,@au_lname,@au_fname,@au_contract)"
objCommand.Parameters.AddWithValue("@au_id", txtAuId.Text)
objCommand.Parameters.AddWithValue("@au_lname", txtLastName.Text)
objCommand.Parameters.AddWithValue("@au_fname", txtFirstName.Text)
objCommand.Parameters.AddWithValue("@au_contract ", chkContract.Checked)
objConnection.Open()
objCommand.ExecuteNonQuery()
objConnection.Close()
```

SqlDataAdapter

The `SqlDataAdapter` class is similar to the `OleDbDataAdapter` that you configured with wizards in the previous chapter. The main difference is that the `OleDbDataAdapter` can access any data source that supports OLE DB, while the `SqlDataAdapter` supports only SQL Server databases. You can use them in a similar way though; you can configure an `SqlDataAdapter` using wizards, just as you configured an `OleDbDataAdapter` in the previous chapter (provided you are accessing an SQL Server data source). In this chapter, you look at how to configure and use an `SqlDataAdapter` in code, but these guidelines also apply to the `OleDbDataAdapter`.

Data adapters act as bridges between your data source and in-memory data objects such as the `DataSet`. To access the data source, they use the command objects you've just looked at. These command objects are associated with connections, so the data adapter relies on command and connection objects to access and manipulate the data source.

The `SqlDataAdapter` class's `SelectCommand` property is used to hold an `SqlCommand` that retrieves data from the data source. The data adapter then places the result of the query into a `DataSet` or `DataTable`. The `SqlDataAdapter` also has `UpdateCommand`, `DeleteCommand`, and `InsertCommand` properties. These are also `SqlCommand` objects, used to write changes made to a `DataSet` or `DataTable` back to the data source. This may all seem complicated, but in fact the tools are really easy to use. You learned enough SQL in the previous chapter to write a `SelectCommand`, and there are tools called *command builders* that you can use to automatically create the other commands based on this.

Take a look at the `SelectCommand` property, and then look at how you can create commands for updating, deleting, and inserting records.

The SelectCommand Property

The `SqlDataAdapter` class's `SelectCommand` property is used to fill a `DataSet` with data from an SQL Server database, as shown in Figure 17-1:

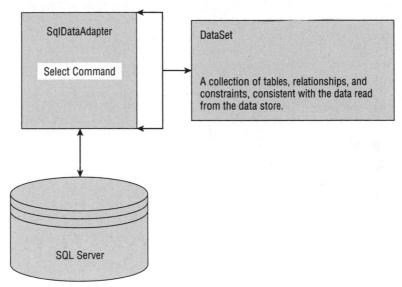

Figure 17-1

When you want to read data from the data store, you must set the `SelectCommand` property of the `SqlDataAdapter` class first. This property is an `SqlCommand` object and is used to specify what data to select and how to select that data. Therefore the `SelectCommand` property has properties of its own, and you need to set them just as you would set properties on a normal command. You've already seen the following properties of the `SqlCommand` object:

❑   `Connection`: Sets the `SqlConnection` object to be used to access the data store.

❑   `CommandText`: Sets the SQL statements or stored procedure name to be used to select the data.

In the previous examples of `SqlCommand` objects, you used straight SQL statements. If you want to use stored procedures, you need to be aware of an additional property, `CommandType`, which sets a value that determines how the `CommandText` property is interpreted.

In this chapter, you are going to concentrate on SQL statements, but stored procedures are often useful too, particularly if they already exist in the database. If you want to use one, set the `CommandText` property to the name of the stored procedure (remember to enclose it in quote marks because the compiler treats this as a string), and set the `CommandType` property to `CommandType.StoredProcedure`.

Setting SelectCommand to SQL Text

Take a look at how you set these properties in code. The code fragment that follows shows the typical settings for these properties when executing SQL text:

```
' Declare SqlDataAdapter object...
Dim objDataAdapter As New SqlDataAdapter()

' Assign a new SqlCommand to the SelectCommand property
objDataAdapter.SelectCommand = New SqlCommand()

' Set the SelectCommand properties...
objDataAdapter.SelectCommand.Connection = objConnection
objDataAdapter.SelectCommand.CommandText = _
    "SELECT au_lname, au_fname FROM authors " & _
    "ORDER BY au_lname, au_fname"
```

The first thing that this code fragment does is declare the `SqlDataAdapter` object. This object has a `SelectCommand` property set to a new `SqlCommand`; you just need to set that command's properties. You set the properties by first setting the `Connection` property to a valid connection object, one that will already have been created before the code that you see here. Next, you set the `CommandText` property to your SQL SELECT statement.

Setting SelectCommand to a Stored Procedure

This next code fragment shows how you could set these properties when you want to execute a *stored procedure*. A stored procedure is a group of SQL statements that are stored in the database under a unique name and are executed as a unit. The stored procedure in this example (`usp_select_author_titles`) uses the same SQL statement that you used in the previous code fragment:

```
' Declare SqlDataAdapter object...
Dim objDataAdapter As New SqlDataAdapter()

' Assign a new SqlCommand to the SelectCommand property
objDataAdapter.SelectCommand = New SqlCommand()

' Set the SelectCommand properties...
objDataAdapter.SelectCommand.Connection = objConnection
objDataAdapter.SelectCommand.CommandText = "usp_select_author_titles"
objDataAdapter.SelectCommand.CommandType = CommandType.StoredProcedure
```

The `CommandText` property now specifies the name of the stored procedure that you want to execute instead of the SQL string that was specified in the previous example. Also notice the `CommandType` property. In the first example, you did not change this property, because its default value is `CommandType.Text`, which is what you need to execute SQL statements. In this example, it is set to a value of `CommandType.StoredProcedure`, which indicates that the `CommandText` property contains the name of a stored procedure to be executed.

Using Command Builders to Create the Other Commands

The `SelectCommand` is all you need to transfer data from the database into your `DataSet`. After you let your users make changes to the `DataSet`, though, you will want to write the changes back to the database. You can do this by setting up command objects with the SQL for inserting, deleting, and updating. Alternatively, you can use stored procedures. Both of these solutions require knowledge of SQL outside the scope of this book. Fortunately, there is an easier way; you can use *command builders* to create these commands. It takes only one more line:

```
' Declare SqlDataAdapter object...
Dim objDataAdapter As New SqlDataAdapter()

' Assign a new SqlCommand to the SelectCommand property
objDataAdapter.SelectCommand = New SqlCommand()

' Set the SelectCommand properties...
objDataAdapter.SelectCommand.Connection = objConnection
objDataAdapter.SelectCommand.CommandText = "usp_select_author_titles"
objDataAdapter.SelectCommand.CommandType = CommandType.StoredProcedure
' automatically create update/delete/insert commands
Dim objCommandBuilder As SqlCommandBuilder = New SqlCommandBuilder
(objDataAdapter)
```

Now you can use this `SqlDataAdapter` to write changes back to a database. You look more at this later in the chapter. For know, look at the method that gets data from the database to the `DataSet` in the first place: the `Fill` method.

The Fill Method

You use the `Fill` method to populate a `DataSet` object with the data that the `SqlDataAdapter` object retrieves from the data store using its `SelectCommand`. However, before you do this you must first initialize a `DataSet` object. To use the `DataSet` object in your project, you must add a reference to `System.Xml`.

```
' Declare SqlDataAdapter object...
Dim objDataAdapter As New SqlDataAdapter()

' Assign a new SqlCommand to the SelectCommand property
objDataAdapter.SelectCommand = New SqlCommand()

' Set the SelectCommand properties...
objDataAdapter.SelectCommand.Connection = objConnection
objDataAdapter.SelectCommand.CommandText = "usp_select_author_titles"
objDataAdapter.SelectCommand.CommandType = CommandType.StoredProcedure
Dim objDataSet as DataSet = New DataSet()
```

Now that you have a `DataSet` and `SqlDataAdapter`, you can fill your `DataSet` with data. The `Fill` method has several overloaded versions, but you will be discussing the one most commonly used. The syntax for the `Fill` method is shown here:

```
SqlDataAdapter.Fill(DataSet, string)
```

The *DataSet* argument specifies a valid `DataSet` object that will be populated with data. The *string* argument gives the name you want the table to have in the `DataSet`. Remember that one `DataSet` can contain many tables. You can use any name you like, but usually it's best to use the name of the table from which the data in the database has come. This helps you self-document your code and makes the code easier to maintain.

The following code fragment shows how you invoke the `Fill` method. The string `"authors"` is specified as the *string* argument. This is the name you want to use when manipulating the in-memory version of the table; it is also the name of the table in the data source.

```
' Declare SqlDataAdapter object...
Dim objDataAdapter As New SqlDataAdapter()

'Create an instance of a new select command object
objDataAdapter.SelectCommand = New SqlCommand

' Set the SelectCommand properties...
objDataAdapter.SelectCommand.Connection = objConnection
objDataAdapter.SelectCommand.CommandText = "usp_select_author_titles"
objDataAdapter.SelectCommand.CommandType = CommandType.StoredProcedure
Dim objDataSet as DataSet = New DataSet()
' Fill the DataSet object with data...
objDataAdapter.Fill(objDataSet, "authors")
```

The `Fill` method uses the `SelectCommand.Connection` property to connect to the database. If the connection is already open, the data adapter will use it to execute the `SelectCommand` and leave it open after it's finished. If the connection is closed, then the data adapter will open it, execute the `SelectCommand`, and then close it again.

You now have data in memory and can start manipulating it independently of the data source. Notice that the `DataSet` class does not have `Sql` at the start of its class name. This is because `DataSet` is not in the `System.Data.SqlClient` namespace; it is in the parent `System.Data` namespace. The classes in this namespace are primarily concerned with manipulating data in memory, rather than obtaining data from any particular data source. Once you have the data loaded into a `DataSet`, it no longer matters what data source it came from (unless you need to write it back). Let's have a look at two of the classes in this namespace: the `DataSet` and the `DataView`.

The DataSet Class

The `DataSet` class is used to store data retrieved from a data store and stores that data in memory on the client. The `DataSet` object contains a collection of tables, relationships, and constraints that are consistent with the data read from the data store. It acts as a lightweight database engine all by itself, enabling you to store tables, edit data, and run queries against it using a `DataView` object.

The data in a `DataSet` is disconnected from the data store, and you can operate on the data independently from the data store. You can manipulate the data in a `DataSet` object by adding, updating, and deleting the records. You can apply these changes back to the original data store afterwards using a data adapter.

The data in a `DataSet` object is maintained in Extensible Markup Language (XML, which is discussed in detail in Chapter 18), meaning that you can save a `DataSet` as a file or easily pass it over a network. The XML is shielded from you as a developer, and you should never need to edit the XML directly. All editing of the XML is done through the properties and methods of the `DataSet` class. Many developers like using XML and will sometimes choose to manipulate the XML representation of a `DataSet` directly, but this is not essential.

Like any XML document, a DataSet can have a *schema* (a file that describes the structure of the data in one or more XML files). When you generated a typed DataSet in the previous chapter, an XML Schema Definition (XSD) file was added to the Solution Explorer, as shown in Figure 17-2.

Figure 17-2

This file is an XML schema for the data that the CustomerDataSet would hold. From this, Visual Studio .NET was able to create a class that inherited from the DataSet and that used this particular schema. A DataSet schema contains information about the tables, relationships, and constraints stored in the DataSet. Again, this is shielded from you, and you do not need to know XML to work with a DataSet.

Since the DataSet contains the actual data retrieved from a data store, you can bind the DataSet to a control or controls to have them display (and allow editing of) the data in the DataSet. You did this a bit in Chapter 16, and you will see more later in this chapter.

DataView

The DataView class is typically used for sorting, filtering, searching, editing, and navigating the data from a DataSet. A DataView is *bindable*, meaning that it can be bound to controls in the same way that the DataSet can be bound to controls. Again, you learn more about data binding in code later in this chapter.

A DataSet can contain a number of DataTable objects; when you use the SqlDataAdapter class's Fill method to add data to a DataSet, you are actually creating a DataTable object inside the DataSet. The DataView provides a custom view of a DataTable; you can sort or filter the rows, for example, as you can in an SQL query.

You can create a DataView from the data contained in a DataTable that contains only the data that you want to display. For example, if the data in a DataTable contains all authors sorted by last name and first name, you can create a DataView that contains all authors sorted by first name and then last name. Or, if you wanted, you could create a DataView that contained only last names or certain names.

Although you can view the data in a DataView in ways different from the underlying DataTable, it is still the same data. Changes made to a DataView affect the underlying DataTable automatically, and changes made to the underlying DataTable automatically affect any DataView objects that are viewing that DataTable.

The constructor for the `DataView` class initializes a new instance of the `DataView` class and accepts the `DataTable` as an argument. The following code fragment declares a `DataView` object and initializes it using the `authors` table from the `DataSet` named `objDataSet`. Notice that the code accesses the `Tables` collection of the `DataSet` object, by specifying the `Tables` property and the table name:

```
' Set the DataView object to the DataSet object...
Dim objDataView = New DataView(objDataSet.Tables("authors"))
```

The Sort Property

Once a `DataView` has been initialized and is displaying data, you can alter the view of that data. For example, suppose you want to sort the data in a different order than in the `DataSet`. To sort the data in a `DataView`, you set the `Sort` property and specify the column or columns that you want sorted. The following code fragment sorts the data in a `DataView` by author's first name and then last name:

```
objDataView.Sort = "au_fname, au_lname"
```

Note that this is the same syntax as the ORDER BY clause in an SQL SELECT statement. As in the SQL ORDER BY clause, sorting operations on a `DataView` are always performed in an ascending order by default. If you wanted to perform the sort in descending order, you would need to specify the DESC keyword, as shown in the next code fragment:

```
objDataView.Sort = "au_fname, au_lname DESC"
```

The RowFilter Property

When you have an initialized `DataView`, you can filter the rows of data that it will contain. This is similar to specifying a WHERE clause in an SQL SELECT statement; only rows that match the criteria will remain in the view. The underlying data is not affected, though. The `RowFilter` property specifies the criteria that should be applied on the `DataView`. The syntax is similar to the SQL WHERE clause. It contains at least a column name followed by an operator and the value. If the value is a string, it must be enclosed in single quote marks as shown in the following code fragment, which retrieves only the authors whose last names are `Green`:

```
' Set the DataView object to the DataSet object...
objDataView = New DataView(objDataSet.Tables("authors"))
objDataView.RowFilter = "au_lname = 'Green'"
```

If you want to retrieve all rows of authors except those with the last name of `Green`, you would specify the not equal to operator as shown in this example:

```
' Set the DataView object to the DataSet object...
objDataView = New DataView(objDataSet.Tables("authors"))
objDataView.RowFilter = "au_lname <> 'Green'"
```

You can also specify more complex filters, as you could in SQL. For example, you can combine several criteria using an AND operator:

```
objDataView.RowFilter = "au_lname <> 'Green' AND au_fname LIKE 'D*'"
```

This returns authors whose last names are not `Green` and whose first names begin with `D`.

The Find Method

If you want to search for a specific row of data in a DataView, you invoke the Find method. The Find method searches for data in the sort key column of the DataView. Therefore, before invoking the Find method, you first need to sort the DataView on the column that contains the data that you want to find. The column that the DataView is sorted on becomes the sort key column in a DataView object.

For example, suppose you want to find the author who has a first name of Ann. You would need to sort the DataView by first name to set this column as the sort key column in the DataView, and then invoke the Find method, as shown in the following code fragment:

```
Dim intPosition as Integer
objDataView.Sort = "au_fname"
intPosition = objDataView.Find("Ann")
```

If it finds a match, the Find method returns the position of the record within the DataView. Otherwise, the DataView returns a null value, indicating that no match was found. If the Find method finds a match, it stops looking and returns only the position of the first match. If you know there is more than one match in your data store, you could filter the data in the DataView, which is a subject that is covered shortly.

The Find method is not case sensitive, meaning that to find the author who has a first name of Ann, you could enter either the text Ann or the text ann.

The Find method looks for an exact case-insensitive match, so this means that you must enter the whole word or words of the text that you are looking for. For example, suppose you are looking for the author who has the first name of Ann. You cannot enter An and expect to find a match; you must enter all the characters or words that make up the author's name. Notice that the following example specifies all lowercase letters, which is perfectly fine:

```
Dim intPosition as Integer
objDataView.Sort = "au_fname"
intPosition = objDataView.Find("ann")
```

You have seen that a DataView can be sorted on more than one column at a time. If you want to sort on more than one column, you need to supply an array of values to the Find method instead of just a single value. For example, you may want to find where Simon Watts appears in the DataView, if at all:

```
Dim intPosition As Integer
Dim arrValues(1) As Object
objDataView.Sort = "au_fname, au_lname"

' Find the author named "Simon Watts".
arrValues(0)= "Simon"
arrValues(1) = "Watts"
intPosition = objDataView.Find(arrValues)
```

The ADO.NET Classes in Action

You've now looked at the basics of the ADO.NET classes and how they allow you to retrieve and insert data into SQL Server. No doubt your head is spinning from information overload at this point, so the best way to ensure that you understand how to use all of the objects, methods, and properties that you have been looking at is to actually use them. In the next two Try It Outs, you'll see how to exploit the power of the `DataSet` object to expose data to your users. You may find that you'll want to come back and reread the previous section after you've completed the Try It Outs; this will help to clarify ADO.NET in your mind.

The first Try It Out implements the `SqlConnection`, `SqlDataAdapter`, and `DataSet` classes. You will see firsthand how to use these classes in a simple example in which you need to retrieve read-only data and display that data in a data grid. In fact, what you do here will be very similar to the example in the previous chapter, but you will be doing it in code instead of using wizards.

> *When writing your programs, you may often use a combination of wizards and coding to create powerful programs quickly and easily. The components created in the previous chapter by drag and drop can be manipulated in code in exactly the same way as objects created in code. In the previous chapter, you used wizards almost all the time. In this chapter you concentrate on code.*

Examining a DataSet Example

Before you dive into the details of creating the program, take a look at the data and the relationships of the data that you want to display. The data that you want comes from the Pubs database in SQL Server. If you are using SQL Server 2000, SQL Server 2005 or MSDE, you should be seeing the exact same data. Some versions SQL Server 2005 may not come with the Pubs database. The link to get the database is at the beginning of the chapter.

You want to display a list of authors, their book titles, and the price of their books. Figure 17-3 shows the tables that this data resides in and also the relationship of the tables:

Figure 17-3

You want to display the author's first and last names, which reside in the `authors` table, and the title and price of the book, which reside in the `titles` table. Because an author can have one or more books and a book can have one or more authors, the `titles` table is joined to the `authors` table via a *relationship table* called `titleauthor`. This table contains the many-to-many relationship of authors to books.

Having looked at the relationship of the tables and knowing what data you want, take a look at the SQL `SELECT` statement that you need to create to get this data:

```
SELECT au_lname, au_fname, title, price
FROM authors
JOIN titleauthor ON authors.au_id = titleauthor.au_id
JOIN titles ON titleauthor.title_id = titles.title_id
ORDER BY au_lname, au_fname
```

The first line of the `SELECT` statement shows the columns that you want to select. The second line shows the main table that you are selecting data from, which is `authors`.

The third line *joins* the `titleauthor` table to the `authors` table using the `au_id` column. Therefore, when you select a row of data from the `authors` table, you also get every row in the `titleauthor` table that matches the `au_id` in the selected row of the `authors` table. This join returns only authors who have a record in the `titleauthor` table.

The fourth line joins the `titles` table to the `titleauthor` table using the `title_id` column. Hence, for every row of data that is selected from the `titleauthor` table, you select the corresponding row of data (having the same `title_id` value) from the `titles` table. The last line of the `SELECT` statement sorts the data by the author's last name and first name using the `ORDER BY` clause. Now, create the project in the next Try It Out.

Try It Out   DataSet Example

1. Create a new Windows Forms application called **DatasetExample**.

2. Set the following properties of the form:

    ❑   Set `Size` to **600, 230**.

    ❑   Set `StartPosition` to **CenterScreen**.

    ❑   Set `Text` to **Bound DataSet**.

3. From the Toolbox, locate the DataGridView control under the Windows Forms tab and drag it onto your form. Set the properties of the DataGridView as follows:

    ❑   Set `Name` to **grdAuthorTitles**.

    ❑   Set `Anchor` to **Top, Bottom, Left, Right**.

    ❑   Set `Location` to **0, 0**.

    ❑   Set `Size` to **592, 203**.

4. First, you add the Imports statements for the namespaces you will use. Open the code window for your form and add these namespaces as highlighted at the very top of your code:

```
' Import Data and SqlClient namespaces...
Imports System.Data
Imports System.Data.SqlClient

Public Class Form1

End Class
```

5. Next, you need to declare the objects necessary to retrieve the data from the database, so add the following highlighted code. Ensure that you use a user ID and password that have been defined in your installation of SQL Server:

```
Public Class Form1
    Dim objConnection As New SqlConnection _
        ("server=localhost\wrox;database=pubs;user id=sa;password=wrox")

    Dim objDataAdapter As New SqlDataAdapter()
    Dim objDataSet As New DataSet()
End Class
```

Notice your connection string in the constructor for this object. You need to change the server *parameter to point to the machine where SQL Server is running if it is not running on your local machine. You also need to change the* user id *and* password *parameters to use a valid login that has been provided or that you set up yourself. If the* user id *that you use has no password assigned, then specify the* password *argument but do not enter anything for the actual password. For example,* password=;.

6. To add a handler for the form's Load event, select (Form1 Events) in first combo box the (General) and then select Load in the second combo box (Declarations). Insert the following highlighted code:

```
Private Sub Form1_Load(ByVal sender As Object, ByVal e As System.EventArgs) _
        Handles Me.Load
    ' Set the SelectCommand properties...
    objDataAdapter.SelectCommand = New SqlCommand()
    objDataAdapter.SelectCommand.Connection = objConnection
    objDataAdapter.SelectCommand.CommandText = _
        "SELECT au_lname, au_fname, title, price " & _
        "FROM authors " & _
        "JOIN titleauthor ON authors.au_id = titleauthor.au_id " & _
        "JOIN titles ON titleauthor.title_id = titles.title_id " & _
        "ORDER BY au_lname, au_fname"
    objDataAdapter.SelectCommand.CommandType = CommandType.Text

    ' Open the database connection...
    objConnection.Open()

    ' Fill the DataSet object with data...
    objDataAdapter.Fill(objDataSet, "authors")
```

```
' Close the database connection...
objConnection.Close()

' Set the DataGridView properties to bind it to our data...
grdAuthorTitles.AutoGenerateColumns = True
grdAuthorTitles.DataSource = objDataSet
grdAuthorTitles.DataMember = "authors"

    ' Clean up
    objDataAdapter = Nothing
    objConnection = Nothing
End Sub
```

7. Run the project to see what you get. You should see results similar to Figure 17-4:

Figure 17-4

8. Note that the `DataGridView` control has built-in sorting capabilities. If you click a column header, the data in the grid will be sorted by that column in ascending order. If you click the same column again, the data will be sorted in descending order.

Note that error handling has been omitted from the exercise, to preserve space. You should always add the appropriate error handling to your code. Review Chapter 10 for error-handling techniques.

How It Works

To begin with, you imported the following namespaces:

```
' Import Data and SqlClient namespaces...
Imports System.Data
Imports System.Data.SqlClient
```

Remember that the `System.Data` namespace is required for the `DataSet` and `DataView` classes, and that the `System.Data.SqlClient` namespace is required for the `SqlConnection`, `SqlDataAdapter`, `SqlCommand`, and `SqlParameter` classes. You will be using only a subset of the classes just mentioned in this example, but you do require both namespaces.

Then you declared the objects that were necessary to retrieve the data from the database. These objects were declared with class-level scope, so you placed those declarations just inside the class:

```
Public Class Form1
    Inherits System.Windows.Forms.Form

    Dim objConnection As New SqlConnection _
        ("server=localhost\wrox;database=pubs;user id=sa;password=wrox")

    Dim objDataAdapter As New SqlDataAdapter()
    Dim objDataSet As DataSet = New DataSet()
```

The first object that you declared was an SqlConnection object. Remember that this object establishes a connection to your data store, which in this case is SQL Server.

The next object that you declared was an SqlDataAdapter object. This object is used to read data from the database and populate the DataSet object.

The last object in your declarations was the DataSet object, which serves as the container for your data. Remember that this object stores all data in memory and is not connected to the data store.

In this particular example, there was no need to give these objects class-level scope. You use them in only one method, and they could have been declared there. However, if your application enabled users to write changes back to the database, you would want to use the same connection and data adapter objects for reading and writing to the database. In that case, having class-level scope would be really useful.

With your objects defined, you placed some code to populate the DataSet object in the initialization section of the form. Your SqlDataAdapter object is responsible for retrieving the data from the database. Therefore, you set the SelectCommand property of this object. This property is an SqlCommand object, so the SelectCommand has all the properties of an independent SqlCommand object:

```
' Set the SelectCommand properties...
objDataAdapter.SelectCommand = New SqlCommand()
objDataAdapter.SelectCommand.Connection = objConnection
objDataAdapter.SelectCommand.CommandText = _
    "SELECT au_lname, au_fname, title, price " & _
    "FROM authors " & _
    "JOIN titleauthor ON authors.au_id = titleauthor.au_id " & _
    "JOIN titles ON titleauthor.title_id = titles.title_id " & _
    "ORDER BY au_lname, au_fname"
```

First, you initialize the SelectCommand by initializing an instance of the SqlCommand class and assigning it to the SelectCommand property.

Then you set the Connection property to your connection object. This property sets the connection to be used to communicate with your data store.

The CommandText property is then set to the SQL string that you wanted to execute. This property contains the SQL string or stored procedure to be executed to retrieve your data. In this case you used an SQL string, which was explained in detail in the SQLDataAdapter section earlier.

After all of the properties are set, you open your connection, fill the dataset, and then close the connection again. You open the connection by executing the Open method of your SqlConnection object:

```
' Open the database connection...
objConnection.Open()
```

You then invoke the Fill method of the SqlDataAdapter object to retrieve the data and fill your DataSet object. In the parameters for the Fill method, you specify the DataSet object to use and the table name. You set the table name to authors, even though you are actually retrieving data from several tables in the data store:

```
' Fill the DataSet object with data...
objDataAdapter.Fill(objDataSet, "authors")
```

After you fill your DataSet object with data, you need to close the database connection. You do that by invoking the Close method of the SqlConnection object:

```
' Close the database connection...
objConnection.Close()
```

As you learned earlier, you do not have to open and close the connection explicitly. The Fill method of the SqlDataAdapter executes the SelectCommand and leaves the connection in the same state as when the method was invoked. In this case, the Fill method left the connection open. If you did not explicitly write code to open and close the connection, the SqlDataAdapter.Fill method would open and close the connection for you.

Then you set some properties of the DataGridView to bind your data to it. The first of these properties is the AutoGenerateColumns property. Here you let the control create all of the columns you needed by setting the AutoGenerateColumns property to True. The next property is the DataSource property, which tells the DataGridView where to get its data:

```
' Set the DataGridView properties to bind it to our data...
grdAuthorTitles.AutoGenerateColumns = True
grdAuthorTitles.DataSource = objDataSet
grdAuthorTitles.DataMember = "authors"
```

The DataMember property selects the table in the data source, and here you set it to authors, which is the table used in your DataSet object.

Then, to free memory, you clean up the objects that are no longer being used.

```
' Clean up
objDataAdapter = Nothing
objConnection = Nothing
```

When you ran the example, the DataGridView control read the schema information from the DataSet object (which the DataSet object created when it was filled) and created the correct number of columns for your data in the DataGridView control. It has also used the column names in the schema as the column names for the grid, and each column had the same default width. The DataGridView also read the entire DataSet object and placed the contents into the grid.

In the next Try It Out, you take a look at some of the DataGridView properties that you can use to make this a more user-friendly display of data.

Changing the DataGridView Properties

1.   Here are some changes you can make to make your `DataGridView` more user-friendly:

   ❑   Add your own column header names.

   ❑   Adjust the width of the column that contains the book titles so that you can easily see the full title.

   ❑   Change the color of every other row so that the data in each one stands out.

   ❑   Make the last column in the grid (which contains the price of the books) right-aligned.

You can do all this by making the following highlighted modifications to your code in the `Form1_Load` method:

```
' Set the DataGridView properties to bind it to our data...
grdAuthorTitles.DataSource = objDataSet
grdAuthorTitles.DataMember = "authors"

' Declare and set the currency header alignment property...
Dim objAlignRightCellStyle As New DataGridViewCellStyle
objAlignRightCellStyle.Alignment = DataGridViewContentAlignment.MiddleRight

' Declare and set the alternating rows style...
Dim objAlternatingCellStyle As New DataGridViewCellStyle()
objAlternatingCellStyle.BackColor = Color.WhiteSmoke
grdAuthorTitles.AlternatingRowsDefaultCellStyle = objAlternatingCellStyle

' Declare and set the style for currency cells ...
Dim objCurrencyCellStyle As New DataGridViewCellStyle()
objCurrencyCellStyle.Format = "c"
objCurrencyCellStyle.Alignment = DataGridViewContentAlignment.MiddleRight

' Change column names and styles using the column index
grdAuthorTitles.Columns(0).HeaderText = "Last Name"
grdAuthorTitles.Columns(1).HeaderText = "First Name"
grdAuthorTitles.Columns(2).HeaderText = "Book Title"
grdAuthorTitles.Columns(2).Width = 225

' Change column names and styles using the column name
grdAuthorTitles.Columns("price").HeaderCell.Value = "Retail Price"
grdAuthorTitles.Columns("price").HeaderCell.Style = objAlignRightCellStyle
grdAuthorTitles.Columns("price").DefaultCellStyle = objCurrencyCellStyle
```

```
' Clean up
objDataAdapter = Nothing
objConnection = Nothing

objCurrencyCellStyle = Nothing
objAlternatingCellStyle = Nothing
objAlignRightCellStyle = Nothing
```

End Sub

2. Run your project again. You should now see results similar to Figure 17-5. You can compare this figure to Figure 17-4 and see a world of difference. It's amazing what setting a few properties will do to create a more user-friendly display.

	Last Name	First Name	Book Title	Retail Price
▶	Bennet	Abraham	The Busy Executive's Database Guide	$19.99
	Blotchet-Halls	Reginald	Fifty Years in Buckingham Palace Kitchens	$11.95
	Carson	Cheryl	But Is It User Friendly?	$22.95
	DeFrance	Michel	The Gourmet Microwave	$2.99
	del Castillo	Innes	Silicon Valley Gastronomic Treats	$19.99
	Dull	Ann	Secrets of Silicon Valley	$20.00
	Green	Marjorie	The Busy Executive's Database Guide	$19.99

Figure 17-5

How It Works

The DataGridView uses inherited styles to format the output table the users see. Style inheritance allows you to apply default styles that cascade to all cells, rows, columns, or headers under the parent style. Then, you can change only individual items that do not match the default styles. The architecture of styles is very powerful. You can set individual style properties or create your own DataGridViewCellStyle objects to set multiple style properties and reuse them.

To start, you declare a DataGridViewCellStyle object. Then you change the alignment to middle right. (This allows you to align the price column later.)

```
' Declare and set the currency header alignment property...
Dim objAlignRightCellStyle As New DataGridViewCellStyle
objAlignRightCellStyle.Alignment = DataGridViewContentAlignment.MiddleRight
```

The first thing that you do here is alternate the background color of each row of data. This helps each row of data stand out and makes it easier to see the data in each column for a single row. The Color structure provides a large list of color constants, as well as a few methods that can be called to generate colors:

```
' Declare and set the alternating rows style...
Dim objAlternatingCellStyle As New DataGridViewCellStyle()
objAlternatingCellStyle.BackColor = Color.WhiteSmoke
grdAuthorTitles.AlternatingRowsDefaultCellStyle = objAlternatingCellStyle
```

Next, changes to the currency cells for Retail Price are set up. You change the format to currency and right-align the column.

```
' Declare and set the style for currency cells ...
Dim objCurrencyCellStyle As New DataGridViewCellStyle()
objCurrencyCellStyle.Format = "c"
objCurrencyCellStyle.Alignment = DataGridViewContentAlignment.MiddleRight
```

Some changes to the format of the DataGridView are easy to make at the property level. Column titles can simply be changed by accessing the column and setting HeaderText or HeaderCell.Value properties. You set both properties in the code that follows.

You changed the book title column width to 225 to display the title in a more readable format. Next, you set the styles on the price column based on the style objects above. What is great about using style objects is you can apply the same styles to multiple objects. For example, if you have three columns that hold dollar amounts, you would set up one style object and reuse this style on all three columns.

```
' Change column names and styles using the column index
grdAuthorTitles.Columns(0).HeaderText = "Last Name"
grdAuthorTitles.Columns(1).HeaderText = "First Name"
grdAuthorTitles.Columns(2).HeaderText = "Book Title"
grdAuthorTitles.Columns(2).Width = 225

' Change column names and styles using the column name
grdAuthorTitles.Columns("price").HeaderCell.Value = "Retail Price"
grdAuthorTitles.Columns("price").HeaderCell.Style = objAlignRightCellStyle
grdAuthorTitles.Columns("price").DefaultCellStyle = objCurrencyCellStyle
```

You have now seen how to bind the DataSet object to a control, in this case a DataGridView control. In the next Try It Out, you expand on this knowledge by binding several controls to a DataView object and by using the CurrencyManager object to navigate the data in the DataView object. However, before you get to that point, read about data binding and how you can bind data to simple controls, such as the TextBox control, and how to navigate the records.

Data Binding

The DataGridView control is a great tool for displaying all your data at one time. You can also use it for editing, deleting, and inserting rows, provided you have the logic to write changes back to the data source. However, you often want to use a control to display a single column value from one record at a time. In cases like these, you need to bind individual pieces of data to simple controls, such as a TextBox, and display only a single row of data at a time. This type of data binding gives you more control over the data, but it also increases the complexity of your programs, because you must write the code to bind the data to the controls and also write the code to navigate between records. This section takes a look at what is involved in binding data to simple controls and also how to manage the data bindings.

In this discussion, the term *simple controls* refers to controls that can display only one item of data at a time, such as TextBox, a Button, a CheckBox, or a RadioCheck. Controls such as ComboBox, ListBox, and

`DataGridView` can contain more than one item of data and are not considered simple controls when it comes to data binding. Generally speaking, nonsimple controls have particular properties intended for binding to a data object such as a `DataTable` or `Array`. When binding to simple controls, you are actually binding a particular item of data to a particular property. This is usually the `Text` property, but it does not need to be.

BindingContext and CurrencyManager

Each form has a built-in `BindingContext` object that manages the bindings of the controls on the form. Since the `BindingContext` object is already built into each form, you don't need to do anything to set it up.

The `BindingContext` object manages a collection of `CurrencyManager` objects. The `CurrencyManager` is responsible for keeping the data-bound controls in sync with their data source and with other data-bound controls that use the same data source. This ensures that all controls on the form are showing data from the same record. The `CurrencyManager` manages data from a variety of objects such as `DataSet`, `DataView`, `DataTable`, and `DataSetView`. Whenever you add a data source to a form, a new `CurrencyManager` is automatically created. This makes working with data-bound controls very convenient and simple.

> *The* `CurrencyManager` *gets its name because it keeps the controls current with respect to the data in the data source. The controls do not represent currency (monetary amounts).*

If you have multiple data sources in your form, you can declare a `CurrencyManager` variable and set it to refer to the appropriate `CurrencyManager` object for a given data source in the collection managed by the `BindingContext` object. You then have the capability to manage the data in the data-bound controls explicitly.

The following code fragment, using the `DataSet` object that you have been using in the previous example, defines and sets a reference to the `CurrencyManager` that manages the data source that contains the local `authors` table. First, the code declares a variable using the `CurrencyManager` class. Then it sets this `CurrencyManager` variable to the currency manager for the `DataSet` object (`objDataSet`) contained in the `BindingContext` object. The `CType` function is used to return an object that is explicitly converted. The `CType` function accepts two arguments: the expression to be converted and the type to which the expression is to be converted. Since the expression is to evaluate to a `CurrencyManager` object, `CurrencyManager` is specified for the type argument:

```
Dim objCurrencyManager As CurrencyManager
objCurrencyManager = _
    CType(Me.BindingContext(objDataSet), CurrencyManager)
```

After you have a reference to the data source object, you can manage the position of the records using the `Position` property, as shown in the following example. This example advances the current record position in the `objDataSet` object by one record:

```
objCurrencyManager.Position += 1
```

If you wanted to move backward one record, you would use the following code:

```
objCurrencyManager.Position -= 1
```

To move to the first record contained in the DataSet object, you would use the following code:

```
objCurrencyManager.Position = 0
```

The Count property of the CurrencyManager contains the number of records in the DataSet object managed by the CurrencyManager. Therefore, to move to the very last record, you would use the following code:

```
objCurrencyManager.Position = objCurrencyManager.Count - 1
```

Note that this code specified the Count value minus one. Since the Count property contains the actual number of records and the DataSet object has a base index of zero, you must subtract one from the Count value to get the index to the last record.

Binding Controls

When you want to bind a data source to a control, you set the DataBindings property for that control. This property accesses the ControlBindingsCollection class. This class manages the bindings for each control, and it has many properties and methods. The method of interest here is Add.

The Add method creates a binding for the control and adds it to the ControlBindingsCollection. The Add method has three arguments, and its syntax is shown here:

```
object.DataBindings.Add(propertyname, datasource, datamember)
```

In this syntax, note the following:

- ❑   *object* represents a valid control on your form.
- ❑   The *propertyname* argument represents the property of the control to be bound.
- ❑   The *datasource* argument represents the data source to be bound and can be any valid object, such as a DataSet, DataView, or DataTable, that contains data.
- ❑   The *datamember* argument represents the data field in the data source to be bound to this control.

An example of how the Add method works is shown in the following code. This example binds the column name au_fname in the objDataView object to the Text property of a text box named txtFirstName:

```
txtFirstName.DataBindings.Add("Text", objDataView, "au_fname")
```

Sometimes, after a control has been bound, you may want to change the bindings for that control. To do this, you can use the Clear method of the ControlBindingsCollection. The Clear method clears the collection of all bindings for this control. Then you can make the change you need. An example of this method is shown in the following code fragment:

```
txtFirstName.DataBindings.Clear()
```

Now that you have had a look at the BindingContext, CurrencyManager, and ControlBindingsCollection objects, learn how all of these pieces fit and work together in a practical hands-on exercise.

Binding Example

The following Try It Out demonstrates not only how to use the `BindingContext`, `CurrencyManager`, and `ControlBindingsCollection` objects but also how to use the `DataView`, `SqlCommand`, and `SqlParameter` classes.

You will be using the query from the previous example as the base for your new query and will display all authors' first and last names, as well as their book titles and the prices of their books. However, this example differs from the last one in that it displays only one record at a time.

You use the `CurrencyManager` object to navigate the records in the `DataView` object and provide the functionality to move forward and backward as well as to the first and last records.

Try It Out   **Binding Simple Controls**

1.   Create a new Windows Forms application project called `BindingExample`. Set the various form properties as follows:

❑   Set `FormBorderStyle` to **FixedDialog**.

❑   Set `MaximizeBox` to **False**.

❑   Set `MinimizeBox` to **False**.

❑   Set `Size` to **430, 360**.

❑   Set `StartPosition` to **CenterScreen**.

❑   Set `Text` to **Binding Controls**.

2.   Drag a ToolTip control from the toolbox and drop it on your form to add it to the designer.

3.   You are going to add objects to the form, so that the form ends up looking like Figure 17-6.

Figure 17-6

The steps that follow provide property settings to produce an exact replica of this form. However, the cosmetic properties are not as important; if you wish, you can approximate the layout visually. It is crucial, however, to use the same control names as those used here in your own application.

4. Add a GroupBox control to the form. You can find the GroupBox controls under the Containers node in the toolbox. Set the GroupBox1 properties according to the following list:

❑ Set Location to **8, 8**.

❑ Set Size to **408, 128**.

❑ Set Text to **Authors && Titles**.

Note that to have an ampersand (&) displayed in the GroupBox *title you have to write* **&&**; *because a single & causes the character following it to be underlined.*

5. Using this list, add the required controls to GroupBox1 and set their properties:

❑ Add a Label control. Name it **Label1** and set its Location to **8, 26**; Text to **Last Name**.

❑ Add a Label control. Name it **Label2** and set Location to **8, 50**; Text to **First Name**.

❑ Add a Label contol. Name it **Label3** and set Location to **8, 74**; Text to **Book Title**.

❑ Add a Label control. Name it **Label4** and set Location to **8, 98**; Text to **Price**.

❑ Add a TextBox control. Name it **txtLastName** and set Location to **72, 24**; Size to **88, 20**; ReadOnly to **True**.

❑ Add a TextBox control. Name it **txtFirstName** and set Location to **72, 48**; Size to **88, 20**; ReadOnly to **True**.

❑ Add a TextBox control. Name it **txtBookTitle** and set Location to **72, 72**; Size to **328, 20**.

❑ Add a TextBox control. Name it **txtPrice** and set Location to **72, 96**; Size to **48, 20**.

6. Now add a second GroupBox and set its properties according to this list:

❑ Set Location to **8, 144**.

❑ Set Size to **408, 168**.

❑ Set Text to **Navigation**.

7. In GroupBox2, add the following controls:

❑ Add a Label control. Name it **Label5** and set Location to **8, 23**; Text to **Field**.

❑ Add a Label control. Name it **Label6** and set Location to **8, 48**; Text to **Search Criteria**.

❑ Add a ComboBox control. Name it **cboField** and set Location to **88, 21**; Size to **88, 21**; DropDownStyle to **DropDownList**.

❑ Add a TextBox control. Name it **txtSearchCriteria** and set `Location` to **88, 48**; Size to **200, 20**.

❑ Add a TextBox control. Name it **txtRecordPosition** and set `Location` to **152, 130**; Size to **85, 20**; TabStop to **False**; TextAlign to **Center**.

❑ Add a Button control. Name it **btnPerformSort** and set `Location` to **304, 16**; Size to **96, 24**; Text to **Perform Sort**.

❑ Add a Button control. Name it **btnPerformSearch** and set `Location` to **304, 48**; Size to **96, 24**; Text to **Perform Search**.

❑ Add a Button control. Name it **btnNew** and set `Location` to **40, 88**; Size to **72, 24**; Text to **New**.

❑ Add a Button control. Name it **btnAdd** and set `Location` to **120, 88**; Size to **72, 24**; Text to **Add**.

❑ Add a Button control. Name it **btnUpdate** and set `Location` to **200, 88**; Size to **72, 24**; Text to **Update**.

❑ Add a Button control. Name it **btnDelete** and set `Location` to **280, 88**; Size to **72, 24**; Text to **Delete**.

❑ Add a Button control. Name it **btnMoveFirst** and set `Location` to **88, 128**; Size to **29, 24**; Text to **I<**; ToolTip on ToolTip1 to **Move First**.

❑ Add a Button control. Name it **btnMovePrevious** and set `Location` to **120, 128**; Size to **29, 24**; Text to **<**; ToolTip on ToolTip1 to **Move Previous**.

❑ Add a Button control. Name it **btnMoveNext** and set `Location` to **240, 128**; Size to **29, 24**; Text to **>**; ToolTip on ToolTip1 to **Move Next**.

❑ Add a Button control. Name it **btnMoveLast** and set `Location` to **272, 128**; Size to **29, 24**; Text to **>I**; ToolTip on ToolTip1 to **Move Last**.

8. Finally, add a StatusStrip control. Leave its name as the default StatusStrip1, and its default location and size. Click the new StatusStrip1 control on the form, and you have an option to add a StatusLabel control in the menu. Select StatusLabel from the menu and leave the default settings.

9. When you are done, your completed form should look like the one shown in Figure 17-6.

10. Again, you need to add imports to the namespaces needed. To do this, switch to Code Editor view and then insert the following lines of code at the very top:

```
' Import Data and SqlClient namespaces...
Imports System.Data
Imports System.Data.SqlClient
```

11. Next you need to declare the objects that are global in scope to this form, so add the following highlighted code:

```
Public Class Form1
    ' Declare objects...
    Dim objConnection As New SqlConnection _
        ("server=localhost\wrox;database=pubs;user id=sa;password=wrox;")
    Dim objDataAdapter As New SqlDataAdapter( _
        "SELECT authors.au_id, au_lname, au_fname, " & _
        "titles.title_id, title, price " & _
        "FROM authors " & _
        "JOIN titleauthor ON authors.au_id = titleauthor.au_id " & _
        "JOIN titles ON titleauthor.title_id = titles.title_id " & _
        "ORDER BY au_lname, au_fname", objConnection)
    Dim objDataSet As DataSet
    Dim objDataView As DataView
    Dim objCurrencyManager As CurrencyManager
```

Be sure to update the connection string to match your settings for the user id *and* password, *and also set the* Server *to the machine where SQL Server is running if it is not your local machine.*

12. The first procedure you need to create is the `FillDataSetAndView` procedure. This procedure, along with the following ones, is called in your initialization code. Add the following code to the form's class, just below your object declarations:

```
Private Sub FillDataSetAndView()
    ' Initialize a new instance of the DataSet object...
    objDataSet = New DataSet()

    ' Fill the DataSet object with data...
    objDataAdapter.Fill(objDataSet, "authors")

    ' Set the DataView object to the DataSet object...
    objDataView = New DataView(objDataSet.Tables("authors"))

    ' Set our CurrencyManager object to the DataView object...
    objCurrencyManager = CType(Me.BindingContext(objDataView), CurrencyManager)
End Sub
```

13. The next procedure you need to create actually binds the controls on your form to your `DataView` object:

```
Private Sub BindFields()
    ' Clear any previous bindings...
    txtLastName.DataBindings.Clear()
    txtFirstName.DataBindings.Clear()
    txtBookTitle.DataBindings.Clear()
```

```
        txtPrice.DataBindings.Clear()

        ' Add new bindings to the DataView object...
        txtLastName.DataBindings.Add("Text", objDataView, "au_lname")
        txtFirstName.DataBindings.Add("Text", objDataView, "au_fname")
        txtBookTitle.DataBindings.Add("Text", objDataView, "title")
        txtPrice.DataBindings.Add("Text", objDataView, "price")

        ' Display a ready status...
        ToolStripStatusLabel1.Text = "Ready"
    End Sub
```

14. Now you need a procedure that displays the current record position on your form:

```
Private Sub ShowPosition()
    'Always format the number in the txtPrice field to include cents
    Try
        txtPrice.Text = Format(CType(txtPrice.Text, Decimal), "##0.00")
      Catch e As System.Exception
          txtPrice.Text = "0"
        txtPrice.Text = Format(CType(txtPrice.Text, Decimal), "##0.00")
    End Try
    ' Display the current position and the number of records
    txtRecordPosition.Text = objCurrencyManager.Position + 1 & _
    " of " & objCurrencyManager.Count()
End Sub
```

15. You've added some powerful procedures to your form. But at the moment, there is no code to call them. You want these procedures, as well as some other code, to execute every time the form loads. So return to the Form Designer, double-click the Form Designer, and add the following highlighted code to the Form Load method. (Note that you must click an area outside of the GroupBox controls.)

```
Private Sub Form1_Load(ByVal sender As System.Object, _
                       ByVal e As System.EventArgs) Handles MyBase.Load
    ' Add items to the combo box...
    cboField.Items.Add("Last Name")
    cboField.Items.Add("First Name")
    cboField.Items.Add("Book Title")
    cboField.Items.Add("Price")

    ' Make the first item selected...
    cboField.SelectedIndex = 0

    ' Fill the DataSet and bind the fields...
    FillDataSetAndView()
    BindFields()

    ' Show the current record position...
    ShowPosition()
End Sub
```

16. Next, you add the code for your navigation buttons. You need to switch back and forth between the Design and Code views, double-clicking each button and then adding the code, or you can select the buttons in the Class Name combo box and then select the Click event in the Method Name combo box. Add the code as highlighted to the procedure for the btnMoveFirst button first:

```
Private Sub btnMoveFirst_Click(ByVal sender As Object, _
            ByVal e As System.EventArgs) Handles btnMoveFirst.Click
    ' Set the record position to the first record...
    objCurrencyManager.Position = 0

    ' Show the current record position...
    ShowPosition()
End Sub
```

17. Add code as highlighted to the btnMovePrevious button next:

```
Private Sub btnMovePrevious_Click(ByVal sender As Object, _
            ByVal e As System.EventArgs) Handles btnMovePrevious.Click
    ' Move to the previous record...
    objCurrencyManager.Position -= 1

    ' Show the current record position...
    ShowPosition()
End Sub
```

18. The next procedure you want to add code to is the btnMoveNext procedure:

```
Private Sub btnMoveNext_Click(ByVal sender As Object, _
            ByVal e As System.EventArgs) Handles btnMoveNext.Click
    ' Move to the next record...
    objCurrencyManager.Position += 1

    ' Show the current record position...
    ShowPosition()
End Sub
```

19. The final navigation procedure that you need to code is the btnMoveLast procedure:

```
Private Sub btnMoveLast_Click(ByVal sender As Object, _
            ByVal e As System.EventArgs) Handles btnMoveLast.Click
    ' Set the record position to the last record...
    objCurrencyManager.Position = objCurrencyManager.Count - 1

    ' Show the current record position...
    ShowPosition()
End Sub
```

20. At this point, you have entered a lot of code and are probably anxious to see the results of your work. Run the project to see how your DataView object gets bound to the controls on the form and to see the CurrencyManager object at work as you navigate through the records.

After your form displays, you should see results similar to Figure 17-7. The only buttons that work are the navigation buttons, which change the current record position. Test your form by navigating to the next and previous records and by moving to the last record and the first record. Each time you move to a new record, the text box between the navigation buttons will be updated to display the current record.

While you are on the first record, you can try to move to the previous record, but nothing will happen, because you are already on the first record. Likewise, you can move to the last record and try to navigate to the next record, and nothing will happen, because you are already on the last record.

If you hover your mouse pointer over the navigation buttons, you will see a ToolTip indicating what each button is for. This just provides a nicer interface for your users.

Figure 17-7

Note that error handling has been omitted from the exercise to preserve space. You should always add the appropriate error handling to your code. Please review Chapter 10 for error-handling techniques.

How It Works: Namespaces and Object Declaration

As usual, you import the `System.Data` and `System.Data.SqlClient` namespaces. Next, you declare the objects on your form. The first three objects should be familiar to you, because you used them in your last project.

Take a closer look at the initialization of the `SqlDataAdapter` object. You use a constructor that initializes this object with a string value for the `SelectCommand` property and an object that represents a connection to the database. This constructor saves you from writing code to manipulate the `SqlDataAdapter` properties; it's already set up.

The `SELECT` statement that you use here is basically the same as in the previous project, except that you add a couple more columns in the *select list* (the list of columns directly following the word `SELECT`).

The `au_id` column in the select list is prefixed with the table name `authors`, because this column also exists in the `titleauthor` table. Therefore, you must tell the database which table to get the data from for this column. This is the same for the `title_id` column, except that this column exists in the `titles` and `titleauthor` tables:

```
Dim objConnection As New SqlConnection _
    ("server=bnewsome;database=pubs;user id=sa;password=!p@ssw0rd!;")
Dim objDataAdapter As New SqlDataAdapter( _
    "SELECT authors.au_id, au_lname, au_fname, " & _
    "titles.title_id, title, price " & _
    "FROM authors " & _
    "JOIN titleauthor ON authors.au_id = titleauthor.au_id " & _
    "JOIN titles ON titleauthor.title_id = titles.title_id " & _
    "ORDER BY au_lname, au_fname", objConnection)
Dim objDataSet As DataSet
Dim objDataView As DataView
Dim objCurrencyManager As CurrencyManager
```

The last two objects are new but were discussed in the section on binding. You use the `DataView` to customize your view of the records returned from the database, and stored in the `dataset`. The `CurrencyManager` object controls the movement of your bound data, as you saw in the previous section.

How It Works: FillDataSetAndView

The first procedure you create is the `FillDataSetAndView` procedure. This procedure will be called several times throughout your code and will get the latest data from the database and populate your `DataView` object.

First, you need to initialize a new instance of the `DataSet` object. You do this here because this procedure might be called more than once during the lifetime of the form. If it is, you do not want to add new records to the records already in the `dataset`; you always want to start afresh:

```
Private Sub FillDataSetAndView()
    ' Initialize a new instance of the DataSet object...
    objDataSet = New DataSet()
```

Next, you invoke the `Fill` method on `objDataAdapter` to populate the `objDataSet` object. Then you specify that your `DataView` object will be viewing data from the `authors` table in the `DataSet` object. Remember that the `DataView` object allows you to sort, search, and navigate through the records in the `dataset`:

```
    ' Fill the DataSet object with data...
    objDataAdapter.Fill(objDataSet, "authors")

    ' Set the DataView object to the DataSet object...
    objDataView = New DataView(objDataSet.Tables("authors"))
```

After you initialize your `DataView` object, you want to initialize the `CurrencyManager` object. Remember that the `BindingContext` object is built into every Windows form and contains a collection of `CurrencyManagers`. The collection contains the available data sources, and you choose the `DataView` object:

```
    ' Set our CurrencyManager object to the DataView object...
    objCurrencyManager = _
        CType(Me.BindingContext(objDataView), CurrencyManager)
```

How It Works: BindFields

The next procedure that you create (`BindFields`) binds the controls on your form to your `DataView` object. This procedure first clears any previous bindings for the controls and then sets them to your `DataView` object.

> *It is important to clear the bindings first because, after you modify the `DataView` object by adding, updating, or deleting a row of data, the `DataView` object will show only the changed data. Therefore, after you update the database with your changes, you must repopulate our `DataView` object and rebind your controls. If you didn't do this, the data that would actually be in the database and the data in the `DataView` may not be the same.*

Using the `DataBindings` property of the controls on you form, you execute the `Clear` method of the `ControlBindingsCollection` class to remove the bindings from them. Notice that the controls that you bound are all the text boxes on your form that will contain data from the `DataView` object:

```
Private Sub BindFields()
    ' Clear any previous bindings to the DataView object...
    txtLastName.DataBindings.Clear()
    txtFirstName.DataBindings.Clear()
    txtBookTitle.DataBindings.Clear()
    txtPrice.DataBindings.Clear()
```

After you clear the previous bindings, you can set the new bindings back to the same data source, our `DataView` object. You do this by executing the `Add` method of the `ControlBindingsCollection` object returned by the `DataBindings` property. As described earlier, the `Add` method has three arguments, which are shown in the code that follows:

❑ The first argument is *propertyname* and specifies the property of the control to be bound. Since you want to bind your data to the `Text` property of the text boxes, you have specified `"Text"` for this argument.

❑ The next argument is the *datasource* argument and specifies the data source to be bound. Remember that this can be any valid object, such as a `DataSet`, `DataView`, or `DataTable`, that contains data. In this case, you are using a `DataView` object.

❑ The last argument specifies the *datamember*. This is the data field in the data source that contains the data to be bound to this control. Note that you have specified the various column names from your `SELECT` statement that you executed in the previous procedure.

```
    ' Add new bindings to the DataView object...
    txtLastName.DataBindings.Add("Text", objDataView, "au_lname")
    txtFirstName.DataBindings.Add("Text", objDataView, "au_fname")
    txtBookTitle.DataBindings.Add("Text", objDataView, "title")
    txtPrice.DataBindings.Add("Text", objDataView, "price")
```

The last thing you do in this procedure is set a message in the status bar using the `Text` property of `ToolStripStatusLabel1`:

```
    ' Display a ready status...
    ToolStripStatusLabel1.Text = "Ready"
End Sub
```

How It Works: ShowPosition

The `CurrencyManager` object keeps track of the current record position within the `DataView` object.

The `price` column in the `titles` table in `Pubs` is defined as a `Currency` data type. Therefore, if a book is priced at 40.00 dollars, the number that you get is `40`; the decimal portion is dropped. The `ShowPosition` procedure seems like a good place to format the data in the `txtPrice` text box, because this procedure is called whenever you move to a new record:

```
Private Sub ShowPosition()
    'Always format the number in the txtPrice field to include cents
    Try
        txtPrice.Text = Format(CType(txtPrice.Text, Decimal), "##0.00")
    Catch e As System.Exception
        txtPrice.Text = "0"
        txtPrice.Text = Format(CType(txtPrice.Text, Decimal), "##0.00")
    End Try

    ' Display the current position and the number of records
    txtRecordPosition.Text = objCurrencyManager.Position + 1 & _
                                " of " & objCurrencyManager.Count()
End Sub
```

This part of the function is enclosed in a `Try...Catch` block in case the `txtPrice` is empty. If `txtPrice` is empty, the `Format` function throws a handled exception, and the exception handler defaults the price to `0`. The second line of code in this procedure uses the `Format` function to format the price in the `txtPrice` text box. This function accepts the numeric data to be formatted as the first argument and a format string as the second argument. For the format function to work correctly, you need to convert the string value in the `txtPrice` field to a `decimal` value using the `CType` function.

The last line of code displays the current record position and the total number of records that you have. Using the `Position` property of the `CurrencyManager` object, you can determine which record you are on. The `Position` property uses a zero-based index, so the first record is always `0`. Therefore, you specified the `Position` property plus 1 to display the true number.

The `CurrencyManager` class's `Count` property returns the actual number of items in the list, and you are using this property to display the total number of records in the `DataView` object.

How It Works: Form_Load

Now that you've looked at the code for the main procedures, you need to go back and look at your initialization code.

You have a combo box on your form that will be used when sorting or searching for data. This combo box needs be populated with data representing the columns in the `DataView` object. You specify the `Add` method of the `Items` property of the combo box to add items to it. Here you are specifying text that represents the columns in the `DataView` object in the same order that they appear in the `DataView` object:

```
'Add any initialization after the InitializeComponent() call

' Add items to the combo box...
cboField.Items.Add("Last Name")
cboField.Items.Add("First Name")
cboField.Items.Add("Book Title")
cboField.Items.Add("Price")
```

After you have loaded all of the items into your combo box, you want to select the first item. You do this by setting the `SelectedIndex` property to 0. The `SelectedIndex` property is zero-based, so the first item in the list is item 0.

```
' Make the first item selected...
cboField.SelectedIndex = 0
```

Next, you call the `FillDataSetAndView` procedure to retrieve the data, and then call the `BindFields` procedure to bind the controls on your form to your `DataView` object. Finally, you call the `ShowPosition` procedure to display the current record position and the total number of records contained in your `DataView` object:

```
' Fill the DataSet and bind the fields...
FillDataSetAndView()
BindFields()

' Show the current record position...
ShowPosition()
```

How It Works: Navigation Buttons

The procedure for the `btnMoveFirst` button causes the first record in the `DataView` object to be displayed. This is accomplished using the `Position` property of the `CurrencyManager` object. Here you set the `Position` property to 0, indicating that the `CurrencyManager` should move to the first record:

```
' Set the record position to the first record...
objCurrencyManager.Position = 0
```

Because your controls are bound to the `DataView` object, they always stay in sync with the current record in the `DataView` object and display the appropriate data.

After you reposition the current record, you need to call the `ShowPosition` procedure to update the display of the current record on your form:

```
' Show the current record position...
ShowPosition()
```

Next, you add the code for the `btnMovePrevious` button. You move to the prior record by subtracting 1 from the `Position` property. The `CurrencyManager` object automatically detects and handles the beginning position of the `DataView` object. It will not let you move to a position prior to the first record; it just quietly keeps its position at 0:

```
' Move to the previous record...
objCurrencyManager.Position -= 1
```

Again, after you have repositioned the current record being displayed, you need to call the `ShowPosition` procedure to display the current position on the form.

In the btnMoveNext procedure, you want to increment the Position property by 1. Again, the CurrencyManager automatically detects the last record in the DataView object and will not let you move past it:

```
' Move to the next record...
   objCurrencyManager.Position += 1
```

You call the ShowPosition procedure to display the current record position.

When the btnMoveLast procedure is called, you want to move to the last record in the DataView object. You do accomplish this by setting the Position property equal to the Count property minus one. Then you call the ShowPosition procedure to display the current record:

```
' Set the record position to the last record...
objCurrencyManager.Position = objCurrencyManager.Count - 1

' Show the current record position...
ShowPosition()
```

Now that you have built the navigation, you move on to add sorting functionality to this project in the next Try It Out.

Try It Out   Including Sorting Functionality

1. Double-click the Perform Sort button on the form in design mode to have the empty procedure added to the form class, or select the button in the Class Name combo box and then select the Click event in the Method Name combo box. Insert the following highlighted code in the btnPerformSort_Click event procedure:

```
Private Sub btnPerformSort_Click(ByVal sender As Object, _
       ByVal e As System.EventArgs) Handles btnPerformSort.Click
    ' Determine the appropriate item selected and set the
    ' Sort property of the DataView object...
    Select Case cboField.SelectedIndex
        Case 0 'Last Name
            objDataView.Sort = "au_lname"
        Case 1 'First Name
            objDataView.Sort = "au_fname"
        Case 2 'Book Title
            objDataView.Sort = "title"
        Case 3 'Price
            objDataView.Sort = "price"
    End Select

    ' Call the click event for the MoveFirst button...
    btnMoveFirst_Click(Nothing, Nothing)

    ' Display a message that the records have been sorted...
    ToolStripStatusLabel1.Text = "Records Sorted"
End Sub
```

2. Test the new functionality by running it; click the Start button to compile and run it. Select a column to sort and then click the Perform Sort button. You should see the data sorted by the column that you have chosen. Figure 17-8 shows the data sorted by book price:

Figure 17-8

How It Works

First, you determine which field you should sort on. This information is contained in the cboField combo box.

```
' Determine the appropriate item selected and set the
' Sort property of the DataView object...
Select Case cboField.SelectedIndex
    Case 0 'Last Name
        objDataView.Sort = "au_lname"
    Case 1 'First Name
        objDataView.Sort = "au_fname"
    Case 2 'Book Title
        objDataView.Sort = "title"
    Case 3 'Price
        objDataView.Sort = "price"
End Select
```

Using a Select Case statement to examine the SelectedIndex property of the combo box, you can determine which field the user has chosen. After you have determined the correct entry in the combo box, you can set the Sort property of the DataView object using the column name of the column that you want sorted. After the Sort property has been set, the data is sorted.

After the data has been sorted, you want to move to the first record, and there are a couple of ways you can do this. You could set the Position property of the CurrencyManager object and then call the ShowPosition procedure, or you can simply call the btnMoveFirst_Click procedure, passing it Nothing for both arguments. This is the procedure that would be executed had you actually clicked the Move First button on the form.

The `btnMoveFirst_Click` procedure has two arguments: `ByVal sender As Object` and `ByVal e As System.EventArgs`. Since these arguments are required (even though they're not actually used in the procedure), you need to pass something to them, so you pass the `Nothing` keyword. The `Nothing` keyword is used to disassociate an object variable from an object. Thus by using the `Nothing` keyword, you satisfy the requirement of passing an argument to the procedure, but have not passed any actual value:

```
' Call the click event for the MoveFirst button...
btnMoveFirst_Click(Nothing, Nothing)
```

After the first record has been displayed, you want to display a message in the status bar indicating that the records have been sorted. You did this by setting the `Text` property of the status bar as you have done before.

Note that another way to accomplish this is to have a procedure called `MoveFirst`, and to call that from here *and* from the `btnMoveFirst_Click` procedure. Some developers would opt for this method instead of passing `Nothing` to a procedure.

In the next Try It Out, you take a look at what's involved in searching for a record.

Try It Out   Including Searching Functionality

1. Double-click the Perform Search button or select the button in the `Class Name` combo box and then select the `Click` event in the `Method Name` combo box, and add the following highlighted code to the `btnPerformSearch_Click` event procedure:

```
Private Sub btnPerformSearch_Click(ByVal sender As Object, _
        ByVal e As System.EventArgs) Handles btnPerformSearch.Click
    ' Declare local variables...
    Dim intPosition As Integer

    ' Determine the appropriate item selected and set the
    ' Sort property of the DataView object...
    Select Case cboField.SelectedIndex
        Case 0 'Last Name
            objDataView.Sort = "au_lname"
        Case 1 'First Name
            objDataView.Sort = "au_fname"
        Case 2 'Book Title
            objDataView.Sort = "title"
        Case 3 'Price
            objDataView.Sort = "price"
    End Select

    ' If the search field is not price then...
    If cboField.SelectedIndex < 3 Then
        ' Find the last name, first name, or title...
        intPosition = objDataView.Find(txtSearchCriteria.Text)
    Else
```

```
              ' otherwise find the price...
              intPosition = objDataView.Find(CType(txtSearchCriteria.Text, Decimal))
          End If
          If intPosition = -1 Then
              ' Display a message that the record was not found...
              ToolStripStatusLabel1.Text = "Record Not Found"
          Else
              ' Otherwise display a message that the record was
              ' found and reposition the CurrencyManager to that
              ' record...
              ToolStripStatusLabel1.Text = "Record Found"
              objCurrencyManager.Position = intPosition
          End If

          ' Show the current record position...
          ShowPosition()
      End Sub
```

2. Test the searching functionality that you added. Run the project and select a field in the Field combo box that you want to search on, and then enter the search criteria in the Search Criteria text box. Finally, click the Perform Search button.

If a match is found, you see the first matched record displayed, along with a message in the status bar indicating that the record was found, as shown in Figure 17-9. If no record was found, you see a message in the status bar indicating the record was not found.

Figure 17-9

How It Works

This is a little more involved than previous Try It Outs, because there are multiple conditions that you must test for and handle, such as a record that was not found. The first thing that you do in this procedure is declare a variable that will receive the record position of the record that has been found or not found.

```
          ' Declare local variables...
          Dim intPosition As Integer
```

Next, you sort the data based on the column used in the search. The Find method searches for data in the sort key. Therefore, by setting the Sort property, the column that is sorted on becomes the sort key in the DataView object. You use a Select Case statement, just as you did in the previous procedure:

```
' Determine the appropriate item selected and set the
' Sort property of the DataView object...
Select Case cboField.SelectedIndex
    Case 0 'Last Name
        objDataView.Sort = "au_lname"
    Case 1 'First Name
        objDataView.Sort = "au_fname"
    Case 2 'Book Title
        objDataView.Sort = "title"
    Case 3 'Price
        objDataView.Sort = "price"
End Select
```

The columns for the authors' first and last names, as well as the column for the book titles, all contain text data. However, the column for the book price contains data that is in a currency format. Therefore, you need to determine which column you are searching on, and if that column is the price column, you need to format the data in the txtSearchCriteria text box to a decimal value.

Again, you use the SelectedIndex property of the cboField combo box to determine which item has been selected. If the SelectedIndex property is less than 3, you know that you want to search on a column that contains text data.

You then set the intPosition variable to the results returned by the Find method of the DataView object. The Find method accepts the data to search for as the only argument. Here you pass it the data contained in the Text property of the txtSearchCriteria text box.

If the SelectedIndex equals 3, you are searching for a book with a specific price, and this requires you to convert the value contained in the txtSearchCriteria text box to a decimal value. The CType function accepts an expression and the data type that you want to convert that expression to and returns a value, in this case a decimal value. This value is then used as the search criterion by the Find method.

```
' If the search field is not price then...
If cboField.SelectedIndex < 3 Then
    ' Find the last name, first name or title...
    intPosition = objDataView.Find(txtSearchCriteria.Text)
Else
    ' otherwise find the price...
    intPosition = objDataView.Find(CType(txtSearchCriteria.Text, Decimal))
End If
```

After you execute the Find method of the DataView object, you need to check the value contained in the intPosition variable. If this variable contains a value of –1, no match was found. Any value other than –1 points to the record position of the record that contains the data. So, if the value in this variable is –1, you want to display a message in the status bar that says that no record was found.

If the value is greater than –1, you want to display a message that the record was found and position the `DataView` object to that record using the `Position` property of the `CurrencyManager` object:

```
ToolStripStatusLabel1.Text = "Record Found"
objCurrencyManager.Position = intPosition
```

It is worth noting that the `Find` *method of the* `DataView` *object performs a search looking for an exact match of characters. There is no wildcard search method here, so you must enter the entire text string that you want to search for. The case, however, does not matter, so the name* `Ann` *is the same as* `ann`, *and you do not need to be concerned with entering proper case when you enter your search criteria.*

Last, you want to show the current record position, which you do by calling the `ShowPosition` procedure.

Now all that is left is to add the functionality to add, update, and delete records. Take a look at what is required to add a record first.

Try It Out   Adding Records

1. Add just two lines of code to the `btnNew_Click` procedure:

```
Private Sub btnNew_Click(ByVal sender As Object, _
            ByVal e As System.EventArgs) Handles btnNew.Click
    ' Clear the book title and price fields...
    txtBookTitle.Text = ""
    txtPrice.Text = ""
End Sub
```

2. Add code to the `btnAdd_Click` procedure. This procedure is responsible for adding a new record. This procedure has the largest amount of code by far of any of the procedures you have coded or will code in this project. The reason for this is the relationship of book titles to authors and the primary key used for book titles:

```
Private Sub btnAdd_Click(ByVal sender As Object, _
            ByVal e As System.EventArgs) Handles btnAdd.Click
    ' Declare local variables and objects...
    Dim intPosition As Integer, intMaxID As Integer
    Dim strID As String
    Dim objCommand As SqlCommand = New SqlCommand()

    ' Save the current record position...
    intPosition = objCurrencyManager.Position
    ' Create a new SqlCommand object...
    Dim maxIdCommand As SqlCommand = New SqlCommand _
        ("SELECT MAX(title_id) AS MaxID " & _
        "FROM titles WHERE title_id LIKE 'DM%'", objConnection)

    ' Open the connection, execute the command
    objConnection.Open()
```

```vb
Dim maxId As Object = maxIdCommand.ExecuteScalar()

' If the MaxID column is null...
If maxId Is DBNull.Value Then
    ' Set a default value of 1000...
    intMaxID = 1000
Else
    ' otherwise set the strID variable to the value in MaxID...
    strID = CType(maxId, String)
    ' Get the integer part of the string...
    intMaxID = CType(strID.Remove(0, 2), Integer)
    ' Increment the value...
    intMaxID += 1
End If

' Finally, set the new ID...
strID = "DM" & intMaxID.ToString

' Set the SqlCommand object properties...
objCommand.Connection = objConnection
objCommand.CommandText = "INSERT INTO titles " & _
    "(title_id, title, type, price, pubdate) " & _
    "VALUES(@title_id,@title,@type,@price,@pubdate);" & _
    "INSERT INTO titleauthor (au_id, title_id) VALUES(@au_id,@title_id)"

' Add parameters for the placeholders in the SQL in the
' CommandText property...

' Parameter for the title_id column...
objCommand.Parameters.AddWithValue ("@title_id", strID)

' Parameter for the title column...
objCommand.Parameters.AddWithValue ("@title", txtBookTitle.Text)

' Parameter for the type column
objCommand.Parameters.AddWithValue ("@type", "Demo")
' Parameter for the price column...
objCommand.Parameters.AddWithValue ("@price", txtPrice.Text).DbType _
                                = DbType.Currency

' Parameter for the pubdate column
objCommand.Parameters.AddWithValue ("@pubdate", Date.Now)

' Parameter for the au_id column...
objCommand.Parameters.AddWithValue _
            ("@au_id", BindingContext(objDataView).Current("au_id"))

' Execute the SqlCommand object to insert the new data...
Try
    objCommand.ExecuteNonQuery()
Catch SqlExceptionErr As SqlException
```

```
            MessageBox.Show(SqlExceptionErr.Message)
        End Try

        ' Close the connection...
        objConnection.Close()

        ' Fill the dataset and bind the fields...
        FillDataSetAndView()
        BindFields()

        ' Set the record position to the one that you saved...
        objCurrencyManager.Position = intPosition

        ' Show the current record position...
        ShowPosition()

        ' Display a message that the record was added...
        ToolStripStatusLabel1.Text = "Record Added"
    End Sub
```

3. Run your project. Find an author that you want to add a new title for and then click the New button. The Book Title and Price fields will be cleared, and you are ready to enter new data to be added as shown in Figure 17-10. Take note of the number of records in the `DataView` (25 in Figure 17-10).

Figure 17-10

4. Enter a title and price for the new book and click the Add button. You will see a message in the status bar indicating that the record has been added, and you will also see that the number of records has changed (to 26) as shown in Figure 17-11:

Figure 17-11

Now that you have added a record, examine what you actually did.

How It Works

Remember that the only data that you can add is a new book title and its price. So instead of selecting the data in each of these fields, deleting it, and then entering the new data, you want to be able to simply click the New button. The job of the New button is to clear the book title and price fields for you. All you need to do is set the Text properties of these text boxes to an empty string as shown here:

```
' Clear the book title and price fields...
txtBookTitle.Text = ""
txtPrice.Text = ""
```

When you click the New button, the fields are cleared. If you are updating or editing a record, those changes are lost. You would normally put logic into your application to prevent that problem, but for this example that type of validation was left out.

The primary key used in the `titles` table is not the database's `Identity` column. `Identity` columns use a sequential number and automatically increment the number for you when a new row is inserted. Instead of an `Identity` column, the primary key is made up of a category prefix and a sequential number. This means that you must first determine the maximum number used in a category and then increment that number by 1 and use the new number and category prefix for the new key.

The first thing that you want to do in the `btnAdd_Click` event procedure is declare your local variables and objects that will be used here. The `intPosition` variable will be used to save the current record position, and the `intMaxID` variable will be used to set and increment the maximum sequential number for a category. The `strID` will be used to store the primary key from the `authors` table and to set the new key for the `authors` table. Finally, the `objCommand` object will be used to build a query to insert a new record into the `titleauthor` and `titles` tables.

Before you do anything, you want to save the position of the current record that you are on. This enables you to go back to this record once you reload the `DataView` object, which will contain the new record that you add in this procedure:

```
intPosition = objCurrencyManager.Position
```

You need to execute a command on the database to work out what ID to give your new title. You use an SqlCommand object to do this. You pass in an SQL string and the connection that you use throughout your program. This SQL string selects the maximum value in the title_id column, where the title_id value begins with the prefix of DM.

There is no category for demo, so you add all of the test records under this category and use the category prefix of DM, enabling you to identify quickly the records that you have inserted just in case you want to get rid of them manually later.

Because the MAX function you use is an *aggregate function* (meaning that it is a function that works on groups of data), the data is returned without a column name. Therefore, you use the AS keyword in the SELECT statement and tell SQL Server to assign a column name to the value, in this case MaxID. You use a LIKE clause in the SELECT statement to tell SQL Server to search for all values that begin with DM:

```
Dim maxIdCommand As SqlCommand = New SqlCommand( _
    "SELECT MAX(title_id) AS MaxID " & _
    "FROM titles WHERE title_id LIKE 'DM%'", objConnection)
```

This sets up your command object but doesn't execute it. To execute it, you need to open the connection and then call one of the SqlCommand execute methods. In this case you use ExecuteScalar:

```
' Open the connection, execute the command
objConnection.Open()
Dim maxId As Object = maxIdCommand.ExecuteScalar()
```

ExecuteScalar is a useful method when you have a database command that returns a single value. Other commands you've used so far have returned a whole table of values (you have used these as the SelectCommand of a data adapter), or no values at all (you have executed these with ExecuteNonQuery). In this case, you are interested in only one number, so you can use ExecuteScalar. This returns the first column of the first row in the result set. In this case, there is only one column and one row, so that is what you get.

You want to check for a Null value returned from the command, so you compare the resulting Object against the Value property of the DBNull class:

```
' If the MaxID column is null...
If maxId Is DBNull.Value Then
```

If the expression evaluates to True, you have no primary key in the titles table that begins with DM, so you set the initial value of the intMaxID variable to a value of 1000. You choose 1000 because all of the other primary keys contain a numeric value of less than 1000:

```
' Set a default value of 1000...
intMaxID = 1000
```

If the column value evaluates to `False`, then you have at least one primary key in the `titles` table that begins with DM. In this case, you need to obtain the integer portion of this ID to work out which integer to use for your ID. To do this, you must convert your `maxId` object to a `String`:

```
Else
    ' otherwise set the strID variable to the value in MaxID...
    strID = CType(maxId, String)
```

Then you can extract the integer portion of the key by using the `Remove` method of the string variable, `strID`. The `Remove` method removes the specified number of characters from a string. You specify the offset at which to begin removing characters and the number of characters to be removed. This method returns a new string with the removed characters. In this line of code, you are removing the prefix of DM from the string so that all you end up with is the integer portion of the string. You then use the `CType` function to convert the string value, which contains a number, to an `Integer` value, which you place in the `intMaxID` variable. Finally, you increment it by one to get the integer portion of the ID that you will use:

```
    ' Get the integer part of the string...
    intMaxID = CType(strID.Remove(0, 2), Integer)
    ' Increment the value...
    intMaxID += 1
End If
```

After you get the integer part, you build a new primary key in the `strID` variable by concatenating the numeric value contained in the `intMaxID` variable with the prefix DM:

```
    ' Finally, set the new ID...
    strID = "DM" & intMaxID.ToString
```

Next, you build the SQL statements to insert a new row of data into the `titles` and `titleauthor` tables. If you look closely, there are two separate INSERT statements in the `CommandText` property of your `objCommand` object. The two INSERT statements are separated by a semicolon, which enables you to concatenate multiple SQL statements. The SQL statements that you build use placeholders that get filled in by the `SqlParameter` objects.

> Note that because of the relationship between the `titles` table and the `authors` table, you must first insert a new title for an author into the `titles` table and then insert the relationship between the title and the author in the `titleauthor` table. You'll notice that your INSERT statements are specifying the columns that you want to insert data into and then the values that are to be inserted, some of which are represented by placeholders.

You have seen the properties of the `SqlCommand` object before. This time, however, you are using properties rather than the constructor. You set the `Connection` property to an `SqlConnection` object and then set the `CommandText` property to the SQL string that you want executed, in this case, the two separate INSERT statements:

```
objCommand.Connection = objConnection
objCommand.CommandText = "INSERT INTO titles " & _
    "(title_id, title, type, price, pubdate) " & _
    "VALUES(@title_id,@title,@type,@price,@pubdate);" & _
    "INSERT INTO titleauthor (au_id, title_id) VALUES(@au_id,@title_id)"
```

You then add entries to the `Parameters` collection property for each of your placeholders in the preceding SQL statements. Where the same parameter name is used twice in the `CommandText` property — as `title_id` is here — you need only one `SqlParameter` object:

```
' Add parameters for the placeholders in the SQL in the
' CommandText property...

' Parameter for the title_id column...
objCommand.Parameters.AddWithValue ("@title_id", strID)

' Parameter for the title column...
objCommand.Parameters.AddWithValue ("@title", txtBookTitle.Text)

' Parameter for the type column
objCommand.Parameters.AddWithValue ("@type", "Demo")

' Parameter for the price column...
objCommand.Parameters.AddWithValue _
                    ("@price", txtPrice.Text).DbType = DbType.Currency

' Parameter for the pubdate column
objCommand.Parameters.AddWithValue ("@pubdate", Date.Now)

' Parameter for the au_id column...
objCommand.Parameters.AddWithValue ("@au_id", BindingContext _
        (objDataView).Current("au id"))
```

For the `@title_id` parameter, you use the `strID` variable that you created and set earlier in this method. For the `@title` parameter, you use the text in the Book Title text box entered by the user. For the `@price` parameter, you use the text in the Price text box. However, the `Text` property is a `String`. SQL Server cannot automatically convert between a `String` and a `Currency` data type, so you specify that the parameter is of the `DbType.Currency` data type.

For `@au_id` you need to use the ID of the currently selected author. There are no bound controls for the `au_id` column, so you need to use some code to obtain the value. Take a close look at that particular statement:

```
BindingContext(objDataView).Current("au_id")
```

Here you are getting the form's `BindingContext` for the `objDataView` data source, which is the one you're using for all of your bound controls. When you're accessing a `DataView` through `BindingContext`, the `Current` property returns a `DataRowView` object. This object represents the view of the particular row that the user is currently looking at. You are then able to select a particular column from that row, thus giving you a specific value. Here, of course, you are obtaining the `au_id` column.

The remaining parameters mark that the new record is a `Demo` record and timestamp the record with the current date and time:

```
' Parameter for the type column
objCommand.Parameters.AddWithValue ("@type", "Demo")

' Parameter for the pubdate column
objCommand.Parameters.AddWithValue ("@pubdate", Date.Now)
```

After you add all your parameters, you execute the command using the ExecuteNonQuery method. This causes your SQL statements to be executed and the data inserted. After your new data is inserted, you close the database connection.

This is the one spot in your code that is really subject to failure, so very basic error handling is included here. You execute your INSERT statement inside the Try block of your error handler, and if an error is encountered, the code in the Catch block will be executed. The code there simply displays a message box that shows the error encountered:

```
' Execute the SqlCommand object to insert the new data...
Try
    objCommand.ExecuteNonQuery()
Catch SqlExceptionErr As SqlException
    MessageBox.Show(SqlExceptionErr.Message)
Finally
    ' Close the connection...
    objConnection.Close()
End Try
```

Then the FillDataSetAndView and BindFields procedures are called to reload the DataView object and to clear and rebind your controls. This ensures that you get all new data added, updated, or deleted in the tables in SQL Server.

You then reposition the DataView object back to the record that was being displayed by setting the Position property of the CurrencyManager using the intPosition variable. This variable was set using the current record position at the beginning of this procedure.

The position that you set here is only approximate. It does not take into account any records that have been inserted or deleted by someone else or you. It is possible that the title you just inserted for a specific author could be returned prior to the title that was displayed before. If you need more detailed control over the actual record position, you need to add more code to handle finding and displaying the exact record that was displayed; however, this is beyond the scope of this book.

After you reposition the record that is being displayed, you call the ShowPosition procedure to show the current record position.

Finally, you display a message in the status bar indicating that the record has been added.

In the next Try It Out, you code the btnUpdate_Click procedure. This procedure is a little simpler because all you need to do is update existing records in the titles table. You do not have to add any new records, so you do not have to select any data to build a primary key.

Updating Records

1. To the `btnUpdate_Click` event procedure, add the following highlighted code:

```
Private Sub btnUpdate_Click(ByVal sender As Object, _
            ByVal e As System.EventArgs) Handles btnUpdate.Click
    ' Declare local variables and objects...
    Dim intPosition As Integer
    Dim objCommand As SqlCommand = New SqlCommand()

    ' Save the current record position...
    intPosition = objCurrencyManager.Position

    ' Set the SqlCommand object properties...
    objCommand.Connection = objConnection
    objCommand.CommandText = "UPDATE titles " & _
            "SET title = @title, price = @price WHERE title_id = @title_id"
    objCommand.CommandType = CommandType.Text

    ' Add parameters for the placeholders in the SQL in the
    ' CommandText property...

    ' Parameter for the title field...
    objCommand.Parameters.AddWithValue ("@title", txtBookTitle.Text)

    ' Parameter for the price field...
    objCommand.Parameters.AddWithValue ("@price", txtPrice.Text).DbType _
                                = DbType.Currency

    ' Parameter for the title_id field...
    objCommand.Parameters.AddWithValue _
                ("@title_id", BindingContext(objDataView).Current("title_id"))

    ' Open the connection...
    objConnection.Open()

    ' Execute the SqlCommand object to update the data...
    objCommand.ExecuteNonQuery()

    ' Close the connection...
    objConnection.Close()

    ' Fill the DataSet and bind the fields...
    FillDataSetAndView()
    BindFields()
    ' Set the record position to the one that you saved...
    objCurrencyManager.Position = intPosition

    ' Show the current record position...
    ShowPosition()

    ' Display a message that the record was updated...
    ToolStripStatusLabel1.Text = "Record Updated"
End Sub
```

2. Run your project. You can update the price of the book that you have just added, or you can update the price of another book. Choose a book, change the price in the Price field, and then click the Update button.

When the record has been updated, you see the appropriate message in the status bar and the record will still be the current record, as shown in Figure 17-12:

Figure 17-12

How It Works

As always, the first thing that you want to do is declare your variables and objects. You need one variable to save the current record position and one object for the `SqlCommand object`. Next, you save the current record position just as you did in the last procedure.

By adding the following code, you set the `Connection` property of the `SqlCommand` object using your `objConnection` object. Then you set the `CommandText` property using an SQL string. The SQL string here contains an `UPDATE` statement to update the `title` and `price` columns in the `titles` table. Note that there are three placeholders in this `UPDATE` statement. Two placeholders are for the `title` and `price`, and one is for the `title_id` in the `WHERE` clause:

```
' Set the SqlCommand object properties...
objCommand.Connection = objConnection
    objCommand.CommandText = "UPDATE titles " & _
            "SET title = @title, price = @price WHERE title_id = @title_id"
objCommand.CommandType = CommandType.Text
```

Again, after you set the `CommandText` property, you set the `CommandType` property to indicate that this is an SQL string.

You need to add the appropriate parameters to the `Parameters` collection. The first parameter that you add is for the `title` column in your `UPDATE` statement. The title of the book is coming from the `Text` property of the `txtBookTitle` text box on your form.

The second parameter is for the price in your UPDATE statement. This parameter is used to update the price of a book, and the data is coming from the txtPrice text box on your form. Once again, you need to set the DbType explicitly for this parameter.

This last parameter was for your WHERE clause in the UPDATE statement. The data for the Value property comes directly from the form's BindingContext, as the au_id did in the Adding Records example.

The rest of the procedure is similar to the btnAdd_Click event procedure.

You code the final procedure, btnDelete_Click, in the next Try It Out.

Try It Out   Deleting Records

1. To include delete functionality in your project, add the following highlighted code to the btnDelete_Click event procedure:

```
Private Sub btnDelete_Click(ByVal sender As Object, _
        ByVal e As System.EventArgs) Handles btnDelete.Click
    ' Declare local variables and objects...
    Dim intPosition As Integer
    Dim objCommand As SqlCommand = New SqlCommand()

    ' Save the current record position - 1 for the one to be
    ' deleted...
    intPosition = Me.BindingContext(objDataView).Position - 1

    ' If the position is less than 0 set it to 0...
    If intPosition < 0 Then
        intPosition = 0
    End If

    ' Set the Command object properties...
    objCommand.Connection = objConnection
    objCommand.CommandText = "DELETE FROM titleauthor " & _
            "WHERE title_id = @title_id;" & _
            "DELETE FROM titles WHERE title_id = @title_id"
    ' Parameter for the title_id field...
    objCommand.Parameters.AddWithValue _
                ("@title_id", BindingContext(objDataView).Current("title_id"))

    ' Open the database connection...
    objConnection.Open()

    ' Execute the SqlCommand object to update the data...
    objCommand.ExecuteNonQuery()

    ' Close the connection...
    objConnection.Close()

    ' Fill the DataSet and bind the fields...
```

```
        FillDataSetAndView()
        BindFields()

        ' Set the record position to the one that you saved...
        Me.BindingContext(objDataView).Position = intPosition

        ' Show the current record position...
        ShowPosition()

        ' Display a message that the record was deleted...
        ToolStripStatusLabel1.Text = "Record Deleted"
    End Sub
```

2. To test this functionality, run your project, choose any book that you want to delete, and then click the Delete button. Keep in mind, however, that the Pubs database is a sample database for everyone to use, and it's probably a good idea to delete a book that you have added. Before you delete a book, however, take note of the record count that is displayed on the form (see Figure 17-13). You may see an error because of a constraint in the database. This is because there is sales data for this book. Find the book you added and it will not have sales data associated with it.

Figure 17-13

After the delete has been performed, you will see one less record in the record count on the form.

How It Works

This procedure is a little more involved than the `btnUpdate_Click` procedure, because of the relationship of `titles` to `authors`. Remember that there is a relationship table to join `authors` and `titles`. You must delete the row in the `titleauthor` relationship table before you can delete the row of data in the `titles` table. Therefore, you need two DELETE statements in your SQL string.

Note that this time after you declare your variables, you specify the `Position` property minus 1. This allows the user to be on the last record and delete it. You also allowed the user to be on the first record as you check the value of the `intPosition` variable. If it is less than 0, you know that the user was on the first record, so you set it to 0; this means that when you restore the record position later, it is once again on the first record.

Note also that you did not use the CurrencyManager object this time. Instead, you used the BindingContext object and specified the objDataView object as the object to be manipulated. Remember that the BindingContext object is automatically part of the form, and there is nothing you need to do to add it. The reason for using the BindingContext object here is to demonstrate how to use it and so that you know that you do not have to use the CurrencyManager object to navigate the records contained in the objDataView:

```
' Declare local variables and objects...
Dim intPosition As Integer
Dim objCommand As SqlCommand = New SqlCommand()

' Save the current record position - 1 for the one to be
' deleted...
intPosition = Me.BindingContext(objDataView).Position - 1

' If the position is less than 0 set it to 0...
If intPosition < 0 Then
    intPosition = 0
End If
```

When you set the properties of your SqlCommand object, the SQL string specified in the CommandText property contains two DELETE statements separated by a semicolon. The first DELETE statement deletes the relationship between the titles and authors tables for the book being deleted. The second DELETE statement deletes the book from the titles table:

```
' Set the Command object properties...
objCommand.Connection = objConnection
objCommand.CommandText = "DELETE FROM titleauthor " & _
    "WHERE title_id = @title_id;" & _
    "DELETE FROM titles WHERE title_id = @title_id"
```

Again, you use placeholders for the primary keys in WHERE clauses of your DELETE statements.

This statement uses only one parameter. The next line sets it up in the normal way:

```
' Parameter for the title_id field...
 objCommand.Parameters.AddWithValue ("@title_id", _
BindingContext(objDataView).Current("title_id"))
```

The rest of the code is the same as the code for the previous two methods, and should be familiar by now. That wraps up this project. Hopefully you will walk away with some valuable knowledge about data binding and how to perform inserts, updates, and deletes using SQL to access a database.

Remember that error handling is a major part of any project. Except for one place in your code, it was omitted to conserve space. You also omitted data validation, so trying to insert a new record with no values could cause unexpected results and errors. Now, let's take a look at a terrific new feature, LINQ to SQL.

LINQ to SQL

One of the new features in Visual Studio 2008 is Language-Integrated Query (LINQ). At its heart, LINQ is a simple Object Relational Mapping (ORM) implantation. LINQ allows you, the programmer, to quickly design objects that are mapped to your SQL relational data and program against them in your favorite .NET language. You get the benefits of full IntelliSense and a structure similar to one you are used to when dealing with objects. With LINQ to SQL, you can query, update, insert, and delete your data. Also, you can call stored procedures. As you will see in just a bit, this is amazing.

LINQ can be used to query more than databases. In fact, LINQ can be used to integrate any object that supports the IEnumerable<T> interface. This means any array, collection, dictionary, and so on can be queried by LINQ. LINQ to SQL includes the designer for mapping tables, views and other database objects to .NET classes called Entity classes. When you instantiate an Entity class in your code it is called an Entity.

This book just brushes the surface of what LINQ can do. With no SQL at all, you populate a DataGridView with data from the Pubs database. Let's get to it.

Try It Out **Query a database with LINQ**

1. Create a new Windows Forms application called **LinqToSQL**.

2. Next, add a new LINQ to SQL Classes item to the project. Name it **Pubs.dbml.** To add this, right-click the project in Solution Explorer, choose Add New Item, and select LINQ to SQL Classes under Common Items.

3. Use the Object Relational Designer to create the Entity classes you need. To do this, open Server Explorer and click the icon to Connect to a Database and complete the Add Connection Wizard shown in Figure 17-14.

If you move this to another server, you will need to change the Connection String of the DataContext Object the wizard creates. To do this, double-click the dbml file the wizard creates and select the PubsDataContext object. In the Connection, you can change the server to point to the new server and make other adjustments such as user name and password.

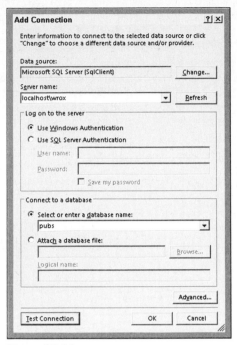

Figure 17-14

4. Change the Data Source to Microsoft SQL Server (SqlClient). Put in your server name. Choose the type of authentication and user information to login to your database server. For database name, enter **pubs**. Click the Test Connection button to verify your choices. When you get a valid connection, click OK.

5. Now, expand the new Data Connection in Server Explorer and view the tables as shown in Figure 17-15. Drag the `authors` table and the `titleauthor` table on to the designer. You will not use the `titleauthor` table in this Try It Out, but notice the relationship created for you by the Designer.

Figure 17-15

6. Save the project.

7. On the form add a DataGridView with the default properties. Increase the width of the form and DataGridView so you can display more fields on the form.

8. Go to the code behind next. In the form1 load sub, add the following code.

```
Dim PubsDB As New PubsDataContext
Dim authors = From author In PubsDB.authors _
              Where author.state = "CA"
DataGridView1.DataSource = authors
```

9. Run the application to see all authors in California. You should see a form like Figure 17-16.

Figure 17-16

10. Add the following code to form load. Here you are selecting a single row from the database. Run the application and notice the new form title as shown in Figure 17-17.

```
Dim author1 = PubsDB.authors.SingleOrDefault(Function(au) au.au_id = "172-32-1176")
Me.Text = author1.au_fname + " " + author1.au_lname
```

Figure 17-17

11. Add the following code to form load between the last two lines you added. Here you are selecting a single row from the database and then changing it. Run the application and note the new form title and the updated grid last name as shown in Figure 17-18.

```
Dim author1 = PubsDB.authors.SingleOrDefault(Function(au) au.au_id = "172-32-1176")

author1.au_lname = "Test"
PubsDB.SubmitChanges()

Me.Text = author1.au_fname + " " + author1.au_lname
```

Figure 17-18

How It Works

This application shows just how amazing LINQ is to developers. By writing one simple VB query and binding to a DataGridView, you were able to filter records from an object. In this case, it was an Entity class representing a database table. First, you declare a new instance of the PubsDataContext as PubsDB. PubsDB is now considered an entity.

```
Dim PubsDB As New PubsDataContext
```

Next, you declare an object named authors to hold the results of the query against the authors table. The query is a simple where clause for all authors in the state "CA".

```
Dim authors = From author In PubsDB.authors _
              Where author.state = "CA"
```

The third line simply binds the result of the LINQ query to the DataGridView.

```
DataGridView1.DataSource = authors
```

The last four lines were added to allow data updates. First, you selected a single row using the `SingleOrDefault` method. If the database might return nothing, you need to use this method otherwise you can use the method `Single`. Once you get an instance of a single author, you can update any column. You updated the last name to `"Test"`. To push the changes to the database, just call `SubmitChanges()`. Finally, you put the new value in the title of the form:

```
Dim author1 = PubsDB.authors.SingleOrDefault(Function(au) au.au_id = "172-32-1176")
author1.au_lname = "Test"
PubsDB.SubmitChanges()
Me.Text = author1.au_fname + " " + author1.
```

Now, that was what you call easy. You should use the IntelliSense to view the objects, properties, and methods available to you with LINQ. It is a simple way to work with your data. In the chapter exercises, you get to research LINQ to Objects and write a query against a dictionary object.

Summary

This chapter covers a few very important ADO.NET classes, particularly the `SqlConnection`, `SqlDataAdapter`, `SqlCommand`, and `SqlParameter` classes. You saw firsthand how valuable these classes can be when selecting, inserting, updating, and deleting data. These particular classes are specifically for accessing SQL Server, but similar principles apply to the OLE DB counterparts.

You also saw the `DataSet` and `DataView` classes from the `System.Data` namespace put to use, and you used both of these classes to create objects that were bound to the controls on your forms. Of particular interest to this discussion is the `DataView` object, as it provides the functionality to perform sorting and searching of data. The `DataView` class provides the most flexibility between the two classes, because you can also present a subset of data from the `DataSet` in the `DataView`.

You saw how easy it is to bind the controls on your form to the data contained in either the `DataSet` or the `DataView`. You also saw how to manage the navigation of the data in these objects with the `CurrencyManager` class. This class provides quick and easy control over the navigation.

This chapter has demonstrated using manual control over the navigation of data on the form and manual control over the insertion, update, and deletion of data in a data store. You should use the techniques that you learned in this chapter when you need finer control of the data, especially when dealing with complex table relationships such as you have dealt with here.

You also got a taste of LINQ. LINQ is a topic that deserves an entire book, but you saw how powerful it is. In a few lines of code (no SQL), you were able to write a query to filter a group of objects like you can in SQL.

To summarize, after reading this chapter you should:

❑   Feel comfortable using the ADO.NET classes discussed in this chapter

❑   Know when to use the `DataSet` class and when to use the `DataView` class

❑   Know how to bind controls on your form manually to either a `DataSet` or a `DataView` object

❑   Know how to use the `CurrencyManager` class to navigate the data in a `DataSet` or `DataView` object

❑   Know how to sort and search for data in a `DataView` object

❑   Be familiar with the Object Relational Desiner in Visual Studio

❑   Know how to use LINQ to query an Entity Class

Exercises

1.   Create a Windows Forms application that will display data to the user from the Authors table in the Pubs database. Use a DataGridView object to display the data. Use the simple select statement here to get the data:

```
Select * From Authors
```

2.   Looking at the DataGridView, it is not very user-friendly. Update the column headings to make more sense. If you know SQL, you can give each column an alias. The current column header names are au_id, au_lname, au_fname, phone, address, city, state, zip, and contract. The solution to this exercise will give each column an alias in SQL.

3.   Create a Windows Forms application. On form1, add a ListBox named ListBox1. On form load, create a dictionary object with key/value pairs of names and states of your friends. Now, write a query to return all of your friends in a certain state. Take your result and bind it to the ListBox using a for each loop. You may need to add a reference to System.Data.Linq.

ASP.NET

As we look to the future, the Internet is sure to increase its presence in business. Developers need to gain knowledge of building robust, dynamic web sites. In this chapter, you will learn about building Web Forms applications. You will focus on the basics for web site development and move to database-driven applications. With Visual Studio 2008, you will be building data-driven sites in no time.

Visual Studio 2008 is the best tool for creating ASP.NET sites on the market today. It provides you with the best Intellisense, debugging, and control library to create web sites written in Visual Basic. You can build ASP.NET web sites (sometimes referred to as Web Forms applications), web services and even sites targeted for mobile devices in VS 2008. Also, you do not need IIS or any web server to host your site with VS 2008; ASP.NET Development Server is a built-in web server you can use to host your sites while developing them.

In this chapter, you will:

❑ Look at a basic overview of web applications (thin-client applications)

❑ See the advantages of Web Forms versus Windows Forms

❑ Understand the control toolbox

❑ Explore client and server processing

❑ Assess the possible locations for web sites in VS 2008 (IIS and ASP.NET Development Server)

Error handling has been omitted from all of the Try It Outs *in this chapter to save space. You should always add the appropriate error handling to your code. Review Chapter 10 for error-handling techniques.*

Before you get your first look at the code, you will have a short lesson on the building blocks developers use to create web applications.

Thin-Client Architecture

In previous chapters, you have seen thick-client applications in the type of Windows Forms applications. Most of the processing is completed by the client application you built earlier, and many of the applications stood on their own and needed no other applications or servers. In web development, on the other hand, most of the processing is completed on the server and then the result is sent to the browser.

When you develop Web Forms applications, you do not have to distribute anything to the user. Any user who can access your web server and has a web browser can be a user. You must be careful with the amount of processing you place on the client. When you design a thin-client system, you must be aware that your users or customers will use different clients to access your application. If you try to use too much processing on the client, it may cause problems for some users. This is one of the major differences between Windows and Web Forms applications. You will learn about the major difference between these two types of Visual Studio 2008 applications later in this chapter.

When dealing with a Windows Forms application, you have a compiled program that must be distributed to the user's desktop before they can use it. Depending upon the application, there may also be one or more supporting DLLs or other executables that also need to be distributed along with the application.

In thin-client architecture, there is typically no program or DLL to be distributed. Users merely need to start their browsers and enter the URL of the application web site. The server hosting the web site is responsible for allocating all resources the web application requires. The client is a navigation tool that displays the results the server returns.

All code required in a thin-client application stays in one central location: the server hosting the web site. Any updates to the code are immediately available the next time a user requests a web page.

Thin-client architecture provides several key benefits. First and foremost is the cost of initial distribution of the application — there is none. In traditional client/server architecture, the program would have to be distributed to every client who wanted to use it, which could be quite a time-consuming task if the application is used in offices throughout the world.

Another major benefit is the cost of distributing updates to the application — again, there is none. All updates to the web site and its components are distributed to the web server. Once an update is made, it is immediately available to all users the next time they access the updated web page. In traditional client/server architecture, the updated program would have to be distributed to every client, and the updates could take days or weeks to roll out. Thin-client architecture allows a new version of an application to be distributed instantly to all the users without having to touch a single desktop.

Another major benefit is that you can make changes to the back-end architecture and not have to worry about the client. Suppose, for example, that you want to change the location of the database from a low-end server to a new high-end server. The new server would typically have a new machine name. In a traditional client/server application, the machine name of the database server is stored in the code or Registry setting. You would need to modify either the code or the Registry setting for every person who uses the application. In thin-client architecture, you simply need to update the setting of the web server to point to the new database server and you are in business, and so are all of the clients.

You can see that in a thin-client architecture model, any client with a browser can access your web site and immediately have access to updates. In fact, if your changes were transparent to the user, the client wouldn't even know that changes had been made.

Now that you have a basic understanding of thin-client architecture, look at how Web Forms work.

Web Forms versus Windows Forms

In this section, you will get an overview of the advantages of both Windows Forms and Web Forms. This will give you an idea of when you build each type of application to solve a customer's problem. You will almost always have to choose between these two types of architecture when building solutions. It is important to understand some of the advantages of both.

Windows Forms Advantages

Windows Forms applications have advantages in some types of systems. Typically, applications that require a responsive interface, such as a point-of-sale system at a retail store, are Windows Forms applications. Also, in most cases, processor-intensive applications such as games or graphics programs are better suited to a Windows Forms program.

A major advantage for Windows Forms is trust. When a user installs the application, it is given trust in the current zone. With this high-enough level of trust, you can store data and state about the current session on the local computer. The user can run the application and it can interact with the local file system or Registry seamlessly. Trust is very limited, however, for an Internet application.

Another advantage is having control over the client application. This allows you to build a very powerful, rich, user interface. You will see that there are numerous controls not available to a Web Form (although this is becoming less of a difference) that permit the developer to create user-friendly applications. Windows Forms allow for a more ample user interface.

Also, application responsiveness is an advantage with Windows Forms. With most or all of the processing being done on the client, the need to send data over the wire can be reduced. Any amount of data sent to servers can cause latency. For an application running locally on a computer, the normal events are handled more quickly. Also, the speed of data transmission over a local network is much faster than the typical Internet connection. This speed will allow data to move across the wire faster and create less of a bottleneck for the user.

Web Forms Advantages

The advantages of Web Forms may seem to be greater than the advantages of Windows Forms. Do not permit this to transform you into a full-time web developer for every project. There will always be times when Windows Forms are a better solution.

The greatest advantage for a web application is distribution. To distribute a Web Forms application, just install it on the web server. That is it. No need to create an installation for every version of Windows and ship CDs. When you make a change, just publish the change to the web server, and the next time a customer comes to the site, he or she will use the latest application.

Version control, or change control, is another advantage. With all of your application code at the same location, making changes is a breeze. You never have to worry about one user on version 8 and another on version 10; all users access the same application. As soon as you publish the change, all users see the update with no user intervention necessary.

Have you heard the term *platform independence*? Web applications have it. It doesn't matter what type of computer the user has — as long as there is a browser and a connection to your web server, the user can access your application. There is no need to build application versions for different operating systems.

These advantages can add up to millions of dollars of savings over a Windows application. Being able to make quick changes and maintain one code base are great advantages. Still, there are times when a web application will not provide an adequate user experience. Make sure you evaluate both options for every project. Now, let's look more closely at Web Forms development.

Web Applications: The Basic Pieces

In its simplest form, a web application is just a number of web pages. For the user to access the web pages, there must be a web server and browser. A request is made by the browser for the page on the server. The server then processes the web page and returns the output to the browser. The user sees the page inside the browser window. The pages that the users see may contain HyperText Markup Language (HTML), cascading style sheets (CSS), and client-side script. Finally, the page displays in the browser for the user.

In this section, you will receive a basic overview of each piece of the system.

Web Servers

There are many web servers on the market today. The most well known web servers in use today are Microsoft Internet Information Services (IIS) and Apache. For this book, you will focus exclusively on IIS.

Browsers

Every user of a Web Forms application must have a browser. The four most popular browsers are Microsoft Internet Explorer (IE), Mozilla Firefox, Netscape, and Opera. When you develop public web sites, you must be aware that the site may render differently in each browser. You will find that IE is the most lenient when it comes to valid HTML. We will focus on IE 7 for this book.

HyperText Markup Language

Also known as HTML, this is the presentation or design layout of the web page. HTML is a tag-based language that allows you to change the presentation of information. For example, to make text bold in HTML, just place the <b> tag around the text. The following text is an example of HTML.

```
This is <b>bold</b> in HTML.
```

If the previous text is then rendered by a browser, it would be displayed like this:

```
This is bold in HTML.
```

Browsers will interpret HTML and should conform to the standards from the World Wide Web Consortium (W3C). The W3C was created to develop common protocols for the Web in the 1990s. You can read more about the W3C at their web site, at www.w3.org/.

Although VS 2008 allows you to design ASP.NET web sites without firsthand knowledge of HTML, you gain have hands-on exercises creating web pages with HTML later in the chapter.

VBScript and JavaScript

A major part of web development is client-side script. If you are creating an application for the public that uses client-side script, you will need to use JavaScript for support in all browsers. VBScript is a Microsoft-centric language that is more like Visual Basic syntax, so when developing an intranet site where you can control which version of IE the user uses, you can use VBScript.

Client-side scripting is typically used for data validation and dynamic HTML (DHTML). Validation scripts enforce rules that may require the user to complete a field on the screen before continuing. DHTML scripts allow the page to change programmatically after it is in memory on the browser. Expanding menus is an example of DHTML. Currently, IE supports more DHTML than is required by the W3C. This may cause you to have to create DHTML for each target browser.

One of the great features of Visual Studio 2008 is the validation and navigation controls. You can drag these controls onto your web page without writing any client-side script. In most instances, these controls will manage, but for others, you will need to be self-sufficient in the creation of client-side script. For this reason, you will write some of your own scripts later in this chapter.

Cascading Style Sheets

Cascading style sheets (CSS) allows for the separation of layout and style from the content of a web page. You can use CSS to change fonts, colors, alignment, and many other aspects of web page presentation. The best part of CSS is it can be applied to entire site. By using a master CSS page, you can easily maintain and quickly change the look and feel of the entire web site by changing one page. You will learn more about CSS in this chapter.

Active Server Pages

With Visual Studio 2008, a new version of Active Server Pages is here: ASP.NET. This new version makes it even easier to create dynamic, data-driven web sites. This section will explain the features and benefits of ASPX or Web Forms.

Benefits of ASP.NET Web Pages

When you create web applications, you could use many solutions. The most common types of pages are Active Server Pages (.asp and .aspx), JavaServer Pages (.jsp), Cold Fusion Pages (.cfm) and basic HTML (.htm or .html). In this book, you will mainly focus on ASPX, but you will see some HTML also.

Execution time is one benefit in which ASP.NET stands out above the rest. When an ASP.NET page is requested the first time, a compiled copy is placed into memory on the server for the next request. This provides for great performance gains over interpreted languages.

Using Visual Studio 2008 to design your applications also makes a big difference in productivity. The .NET Framework supplies thousands of namespaces, objects, and controls for use developing Web Forms applications. Also, ASP.NET also supports all .NET-compatible languages. By default, Visual Basic 2008, C#, and JScript.NET are all available in Visual Studio 2008.

Special Web Site Files

When you work with ASP.NET, you will see many special files. These files are very important and each could have an entire chapter written about it. The two files discussed here, global.asax and web.config, enable you to make sitewide changes from one location. There is much more to learn about these, and you can do research at http://msdn2.microsoft.com/.

Global.asax

The global.asax file allows you to add code to certain application-level events. The most common events are Application_Start, Application_End, Session_Start, Session_End, and Application_Error. Application start and end events fire when the actual web application inside of IIS changes state. This event will fire with the first request to a web site after the server or IIS is restarted. The session events fire on a per user/browser session on the web server. When you save data to the user's session, you must be careful. This data will be saved for every user/browser that is browsing the application. This can create an extra load on the server. The final event is Application_Error. You can use this to log all unhandled events in one common place. Make sure to redirect users to a friendly error page after logging the error.

Web.config

Web.config is exactly what it appears to be — a configuration file for the web application; it is an XML document. You can update many application settings for security, errors, and much, much more. In most production apps, you will store your connection string to the database here.

Development

As you build Web Forms applications in Visual Studio 2008, you will work in the IDE you are familiar with from Windows Forms applications. As you work with web pages, you will have the option of using what is known as a *code-behind* page. This will allow you to keep your application logic separate from the presentation code. You will have three views to work from: Design, Source, and Code view, the common ways to build applications. Design and Source view are for the .aspx page that contains the user interface and data validation. The Code view is the .vb file that is the code-behind page. Visual Studio 2008 makes creating web applications an easy task.

Controls: The Toolbox

The default controls you will use to build web applications are all in the Toolbox. If you do not see the Toolbox, press Ctrl+Alt+X to view it. The controls are organized by category. The categories along with some controls are shown in Figure 18-1. At left, the Toolbox is shown with just the categories; at center, the Standard controls tab is expanded to show the list of controls; at right, the Data tab has been expanded.

Figure 18-1

The Toolbox is fully customizable. You can add, remove, or rearrange any tab or control by right-clicking the Toolbox and using the context menu options. Also, you can copy common code snippets to the Toolbox as a shortcut. To copy code to the Toolbox, highlight the text and drag it onto the tab where you want to add the shortcut. Next, right-click the shortcut and rename it so that it makes sense. To insert code onto a page, just drag the shortcut to the location where you want the code. In this chapter, you will gain hands-on experience working with controls on many tabs.

Building Web Applications

In this section, you will create a small web application demonstrating different aspects of web development. In accomplishing this, you will see how the basics of Web Forms applications work.

Creating a Web Form for Client- and Server-Side Processing

The Web Form in this Try It Out will contain HTML and server controls. The HTML controls will have client-side processing, and the server controls will process the code on the server.

Try It Out   Server and Client-Side Processing

1.   Start this project by choosing File ➪ New Web Site. Make sure Visual Basic is the language, and select ASP.NET web site on the Templates pane. For the Location, change the drop-down box to File System and enter *[The default path for VS 2008]*\Client_ServerProcessing. A default path for Vista will look like **C:\Users\Bryan\Documents\Visual Studio 2008\WebSites\ Client_ServerProcessing**. Click OK to create a file system site that will use the built-in development web server for testing. The New Web Site dialog box will look like Figure 18-2.

Figure 18-2

2.   Visual Studio will create the default folders and files for the web site. Take a look at the Solution Explorer window, shown in Figure 18-3. The Default.aspx page will be open in the IDE.

Figure 18-3

3.   Add the following standard controls to Default.aspx while in Design mode. (To get to Design mode, while viewing the .aspx page click the Design option on the lower left of the pane, or simply press Shift+F7.) Do not worry about the position of the controls for now, but make sure you use controls from the Standard and HTML tabs on the toolbox.

The area at the bottom of the `Default.aspx` page that has Design, Split, Source, and other HTML tags to the right is known as the *tag navigator*.

First, add the controls to the form. You can arrange them in any order for now.

❑   From the Standard controls tab, add one Button and two Label controls.

❑   From the HTML controls tab, add one Input (Button) control.

4.   Now, change the properties of the controls. Refer to Figure 18-4 as a guide.

❑   Set the ID of the Standard:Button to **btnServer** and the Text to **Server**.

❑   Set the ID of the HTML:Input (Button) to **btnClient** and the Value to **Client**.

❑   Set the ID of the upper Standard:Label to **lblServer** and the Text to **Server**.

❑   Set the ID of the lower Standard:Label to **lblClient** and the Text to **Client**.

5.   You will have to enter line breaks and spaces on the page to move the controls around. This is called *relative positioning*; each control is placed relative to the previous control. You can also use *absolute positioning*, which is like what you are used to in Windows Forms applications. Arrange the controls so they resemble Figure 18-4. When you finish, press Ctrl+F5 to run the project without debugging and see the page in the browser.

Figure 18-4

6.   Close the browser and go back to Visual Studio 2008. Double-click the btnServer to jump to the `btnServer_Click` event handler. Depending on your settings, you will be either on the code-behind page or working in the source of the `.aspx` page. Add the following highlighted code to the event:

```
Sub btnServer_Click(ByVal sender As Object, ByVal e As System.EventArgs)
    lblServer.Text = "Changed"
End Sub
```

Run the program again by pressing Ctrl+F5 and test the button's Click event. The label will display Changed after you click the Server button.

7. Create an event handler for the HTML Input (Button) and add a title to the page. (Make sure you have the Default.aspx page open in the IDE and the Properties Window has DOCUMENT selected.) To add a title, find the Title property and set it to **My First Page**. On the tag navigator, click Source to change to HTML view. In the Client Object & Events combo box, choose btnClient. Next, select onclick in the event combo box and add this highlighted code to the event VS 2008 creates. Note: JavaScript is case sensitive.

```
function btnClient_onclick() {
    document.getElementById("lblclient").innerText = "Changed";
    document.getElementById("lblServer").innerText = "Server";
}
```

8. Run the project again by pressing Ctrl+F5. Test both buttons.

How It Works

Now you can see that Web Forms development is very similar to Windows Forms development. This is one of the benefits of .NET development and Visual Studio 2008. Microsoft has made it easy for any developer to switch from device to web to Windows development with only a small learning curve.

First, look at the HTML source. The first line of code is the Page directive:

```
<%@ Page Language="VB" AutoEventWireup="false" CodeFile="Default.aspx.vb"
Inherits="_Default" %>
```

Depending on the mode you develop in, you may see different default attributes set by Visual Studio 2008. If you work with code in the .aspx page, only the Language attribute is set by Visual Studio 2008.

The Page directive has over 30 attributes that can be set. I will discuss only the default attributes. If you want to explore the rest, search for @Page in the help files for VS 2008 or on http://msdn2 .microsoft.com/.

Take a look at the default attributes in the Default.aspx page. First, you see the Language attribute. This is set to the language that all server code will compile into. AutoEventWireup is the second attribute. Visual Studio 2008 sets this attribute to false. If you leave this attribute out of the Page directive, the default value is true, and certain events can be executed twice. Microsoft recommends always setting the AutoEventWireup attribute to false. Next, you have the CodeFile attribute. This is the page that contains the code when using a separate code file or the code-behind page. Finally, there is the Inherits attribute. This is simply the class name the page will inherit from.

The next line in the source code is the !DOCTYPE element. This tells IE 6 and later that the document conforms to the XHTML 1.0 Document Type Definition (DTD) specified by the W3C for English:

```
<!DOCTYPE html PUBLIC "-//W3C//DTD XHTML 1.0 Transitional//EN"
"http://www.w3.org/TR/xhtml1/DTD/xhtml1-transitional.dtd">
```

The actual HTML root element is next. You will see this element with no attributes set in many instances. Here VS has specified that the namespace for custom tags will be http://www.w3.org/1999/xhtml. If you browse to this site, you will see that this is the XHTML namespace defined by the W3C.

```
<html xmlns="http://www.w3.org/1999/xhtml" >
```

After the root HTML element is the HEAD element. Children of this element are items that are not rendered, but may affect how the page displays. You will place SCRIPT, META, TITLE, LINK, STYLE, and other elements here to define the page's look and feel. LINK and STYLE elements are both used for CSS.

The first element is TITLE. This is the title the browser displays for the page. Next, there is a META object that defines the client scripting language as VBScript. After the META object is the client script you created.

The root script tags define the section of the page that is available to add procedures. The only event is the onclick event of the btnClient control. When you click the client button, this procedure executes. The first line of the subroutine uses the getElementById function to find the object in the document that has an ID of lblclient. Once it is found, the innerText is set to Changed. The same function is used to find the lblServer object on the next line. The innerText is then changed to Server. This is added to reset the Server button's label.

```
<head runat="server">
    <title>My First Page</title>

<script language="javascript" type="text/javascript">
// <!CDATA[

function btnClient_onclick() {
  document.getElementById("lblclient").innerText = "Changed";
  document.getElementById("lblServer").innerText = "Server";
}

// ]]>
</script>
</head>
```

What you may not notice is the difference in the way each button performs event handling. It is hard to notice running locally, but go back to the web page and watch the status bar of the browser while you click each button. When you click the Server button, the page actually calls the web server to process the event. The Client button did not call back to the server; the browser handled the event itself.

Now, you are at the BODY tag. This is where Visual Studio adds the controls. All objects inside the FORM tag are sent back to the server for processing.

```
<body>
    <form id="form1" runat="server">
```

When you click the Server button, the form is actually submitted to the server. Here are two lines of HTML that are sent to the browser from the ASP.NET DLL.

```
<form name="form1" method="post" action="Default.aspx" id="form1">
<input type="submit" name="btnServer" value="Server" id="btnServer" />
```

You can look at the HTML source set to the browser by choosing View ⇨ Source from the IE menu.

The browser knows that `btnServer` is a submit button. The function of a submit button is to pass form data back to a web server. In this case, the action is set to `Default.aspx`. The form uses the `post` method to send data to `Default.aspx`. For most pages you will create, you can stay in design mode and never look at the HTML if you are not comfortable with it.

The final portion of the code displayed on the `Default.aspx` page was the markup for the controls. These are the controls you placed onto the design area of the form.

```
        <div>
        <asp:Button ID="btnServer" runat="server" Text="Server" />
                 
        <asp:Label ID="lblServer" runat="server"
Text="Server"></asp:Label>
        <br />
        <br />
        <input id="btnClient" type="button" value="Client" onclick="return
btnClient_onclick()" />[{[SPACE]}]    
        <asp:Label ID="lblClient" runat="server"
Text="Client"></asp:Label>
        <br />
        </div>
        </form>
</body>
</html>
```

Finally, look at the `Default.aspx.vb` page. In the code for the `OnClick` event of the `btnServer` control, you set the text of the label to `Changed`.

```
Partial Class _Default
    Inherits System.Web.UI.Page

    Protected Sub btnServer_Click(ByVal sender As Object,
ByVal e As System.EventArgs) Handles btnServer.Click
        lblServer.Text = "Changed"
    End Sub
End Class
```

─────────────────

You have completed your first ASP.NET page. In this exercise, you saw a few basic controls and learned that client and server code are handled differently. In the next section, you will learn where you can host web sites with Visual Studio 2008.

Web Site Locations with VS 2008

When you create a new site, you will have a choice of locations for the site. The example in this chapter uses the File System location for the web site, as shown in Figure 18-5. One advantage of this location is that the web server is not accessible to external users.

Always make sure you test your site on the actual version of IIS running on the production server before going live.

Figure 18-5

There are three other ways to work with web site projects, as you can see in left panel of the Choose Location window. The first is using local IIS (see Figure 18-6).

Figure 18-6

If you have a local web server, you can host your application there. This allows others to see the site and test it. The second option is to use an FTP site. In this case, you are most likely using a hosting company. All you have to do is add the location and authentication information, and you can code your application on the production server. You can see the setup screen for an FTP site in Figure 18-7.

Figure 18-7

The final option is a Remote Site. Again, this also may be used when you use a hosting company. If your hosting company supports FrontPage Extensions, you can use this option as shown in Figure 18-8.

Figure 18-8

Performing Data Entry and Validation

One of the basic functions of almost every web site is to gather some kind of information from the user. You probably have seen screens that have links such as Contact us or Create an account. Any place you see a text box on a web page, data entry and validation are probably taking place. In this Try It Out, you will learn the basics of using built in validation controls and accessing the data the user enters into the web page.

Try It Out   **Data Entry and Validation**

1.   Create a new web site and name it **DataEntry** by choosing File ⇨ New Web Site from the menu.

2.   Add four labels, three text boxes, and one button to the `Default.aspx` page. Make sure you use server controls from the Standard tab of the Toolbox. Using the format menu, set each control's positioning to **absolute**. Finally, align the controls to resemble Figure 18-9.

Figure 18-9

3.   Set the properties of the eight controls and the document.

❑   Set the `Title` of the Document to **Data Entry and Validation**.

❑   Set the `ID` of the Button to **btnComplete** and the `Text` to **Complete**.

❑   Set the `ID` of the upper-left TextBox to **txtFirstName**.

❑   Set the `ID` of the upper-right TextBox to **txtLastName**.

❑   Set the `ID` of the lower TextBox to **txtEmail**.

❑   Set the `ID` of the upper-left Label to **lblFirstName** and the `Text` to **First Name**.

❑   Set the `ID` of the upper-right Label to **lblLastName** and the `Text` to **Last Name**.

❑   Set the `ID` of the middle Label to **lblEmail** and the `Text` to **Email**.

❑   Set the `ID` of the lower Label to **lblWelcome** and `Text` to **Welcome**.

4. Test the page by pressing Ctrl+F5. When the page opens, you will test three items. First, enter your name and e-mail and then click the Complete button. The page will post back to the server, and the HTML returned will still have your data in the textboxes. This is default behavior known as *view state*. Second, type the text **<SCRIPT>alert "Hi"</SCRIPT>** into the First Name text box and click Complete. You will see the error message shown in Figure 18-10. ASP.NET 3.5 has a feature called *request validation* that will check for any dangerous input from the user unless you explicitly turn it off. Finally, test the tab order. You can control the tab order by the order the controls appear in the HTML source or by the `TabIndex` property on each control. Change the tab order if it is not correct.

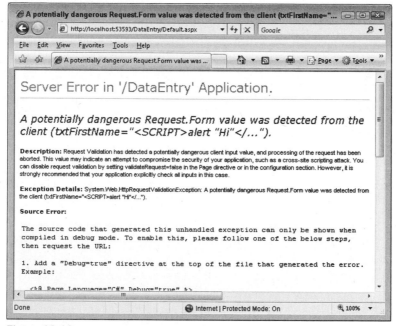

Figure 18-10

5. It is time to do something with the data the user enters. First, you need to open the code-behind page. The easiest way to do this is press F7. Next, add an event handler for page load. To do this, select `_Default Events` from the Objects combo box on the left and `Load` from the Events combo box. Add the following highlighted code to update `lblWelcome` with the data input.

```
Protected Sub _Default_Load(ByVal sender As Object, _
        ByVal e As System.EventArgs) Handles Me.Load
    If Page.IsPostBack Then
        'If this is a postback and not the initial page load
        'Display the data to the user
        Me.lblWelcome.Text = "Hello " + Me.txtFirstName.Text + " " + _
        Me.txtLastName.Text + "<BR>" + "Your email address is " + _
        Me.txtEmail.Text
    End If
End Sub
```

6. Add validation to the input. Visual Studio has built-in controls just for this. To see the controls, switch to Design mode by clicking the View Designer icon on the Solution Explorer. Go to the Toolbox and find the Validation tab, which includes prebuilt controls to assist with data validation. Add two RequiredFieldValidator controls and one ValidationSummary control to the form. Use the layout menu to set each control's positioning to absolute.

Set the following properties for RequiredFieldValidator:

- ❑ Set `ID` to **rfvFirstName.**
- ❑ Set `Display` to **None.**
- ❑ Set `ControlToValidate` to **txtFirstName.**
- ❑ Set `ErrorMessage` to **First name is required.**

Set the following properties for RequiredFieldValidator:

- ❑ Set `ID` to **rfvEmail.**
- ❑ Set `Display` to **None.**
- ❑ Set `ControlToValidate` to **txtEmail.**
- ❑ Set `ErrorMessage` to **Email is required**.

Set ValidationSummary's `ID` to **ValidationSummary**. Your page should look like Figure 18-11 when you finish.

Figure 18-11

7. Run your project and try to submit blank entries for first name and e-mail. You will see two error messages similar to those displayed in Figure 18-12.

Figure 18-12

This quick example explains how easy data validation is in ASP 3.5. Other controls are available for enforcing data validation. The CompareValidator control tests a control to make sure it matches a value. This value can be a constant, another control, or even a value from a data store. RangeValidator tests that a value is within a specified range. For example, you can test to make sure a person is between 18 and 35 years old.

How It Works

Without writing any code, you are able to require that data entry fields are completed on a web page. You take advantage of controls already created for quick and hearty data validation.

You use the RequiredFieldValidator control to make sure the user entered data. You set a couple of properties on the control. You set the ErrorMessage to a string that displays in the ValidationSummary control. Setting Display="None" causes the error message not to be shown inside of the RequiredFieldValidator control. The required property, ControlToValidate, is set to the ID of the control that was required.

```
<asp:RequiredFieldValidator ID="rfvFirstName" runat="server"
ErrorMessage="First  name is required" Display="None"
ControlToValidate="txtFirstName" style="z-index: 1;left: 272px;
top: 325px;position: absolute">
</asp:RequiredFieldValidator>
```

The style attribute is added by Visual Studio when using absolute positioning. With absolute positioning, you can drag and drop controls basically where you want them.

You use the ValidationSummary control as a central location for displaying all error messages. If you decide not to use a summary object, you could set the `display` property of the individual validation controls to `true`. Then, the error messages are displayed within the validation control. No property changes are needed to use the ValidationSummary control. You just add it to the form at the location you wanted to display validation messages.

```
<asp:ValidationSummary ID="ValidationSummary1" runat="server"
style="z-index: 1;
left: 9px;top: 313px;position: absolute;height: 38px;width: 882px" />
```

The only code you write is added to the Page_Load event named _Default_Load. Here, you tested for a postback using the IsPostBack property of the Page object. If it was a postback, you display the name and e-mail entered by the user. You can still use the Page_Load event in VS 2008. To insert the event automatically, go into design view on the aspx page and double-click on the page (not on any controls). The event will be generated and you will be brought to the new event in the code behind.

```
If Page.IsPostBack Then
    'If this is a post back and not the initial page load
    'Display the data to the user
    Me.lblWelcome.Text = "Hello " + Me.txtFirstName.Text + " " + _
    Me.txtLastName.Text + "<BR>" + "Your email address is " + _
    Me.txtEmail.Text
End If
```

Designing the Site's Look and Feel

In the past, a major drawback of web development was maintaining a consistent look and feel across an entire site in a manageable way. Developers created user controls and inserted server-side includes in every page to try and accomplish this. For the most part, this worked. The hard part was making sure the opening tags that were in certain include files were closed in the pages that included them. Another cause of frustration for the designer was making sure all user controls or include files displayed in the same location. This took time, and with every changed page, someone had to make sure the entire site looked OK. Today, Visual Studio 2008 has the tools that can be used to maintain a consistent look and feel.

Themes, navigation controls, and master pages are the tools to accomplish a consistent look and feel. You will learn about all three in the next Try It Out.

Try It Out   Building Your First Web Site

1.   Create a new site and name the project **SiteLookAndFeel**.

2.   To start the project, you add many files and folders. First, add a master page by right-clicking the project name in Solution Explorer and selecting Add New Item from the context menu. In the dialog box that opens, choose Master Page and click Add.

3.   Change the page directive on the `Default.aspx` page to reference the new master page:

```
<%@ Page Language="VB" AutoEventWireup="false"
CodeFile="Default.aspx.vb"
Inherits="_Default" MasterPageFile="~/MasterPage.master" %>
```

4.   Add the following new files and folders.

   ❑   Add a new Theme Folder under the root and name it **Red**. To do this, right-click the solution in Solution Explorer and choose Add ASP.Net Folder ➪ Theme. This creates a main folder named App_Themes and a subfolder. Name the subfolder **Red**. Under App_Themes, add another ASP.Net folder named **Brown**. Next, add a new skin file (**Brown.skin**) to the Brown subfolder. Also, add a new style sheet to the Brown folder and name it **Brown.css**. To the Red subfolder, add three new text files. Name them **Button. Skin**, **TextBox.Skin**, and **Red.Skin**.

   ❑   Under the root directory for the site, add five new Web Forms: **News.aspx**, **NewsYesterday .aspx**, **NewsToday.aspx**, **Events.aspx**, and **Contact.aspx**. Make sure you select the check box to choose a master page for each new Web Form. Place code in a separate file. After you click Add, you will see a dialog box for choosing a master page with one option; `MasterPage.master`. Select `MasterPage.master` and continue for each new page. If you forget to add the master page, you can add to the page declarations in Source view.

   ❑   Finally, add a new site map. Right-click the project in Solution Explorer and add a new item. In the dialog box, select Site Map and click Add. You can leave the default name of `Web.sitemap`. When you finish, the Solution Explorer window will look like Figure 18-13.

Figure 18-13

5. Open the `Web.sitemap` file and update the code to match this code as highlighted:

```xml
<?xml version="1.0" encoding="utf-8" ?>
<siteMap xmlns="http://schemas.microsoft.com/AspNet/SiteMap-File-1.0" >
    <siteMapNode url="Default.aspx" title="Home"
    description="Back to the main page" roles="" >
        <siteMapNode url="News.aspx" title="News"
        description="Your front page news." roles="">
            <siteMapNode url="NewsToday.aspx" title="Today's News"
            description="Today's top stories" roles="" />
            <siteMapNode url="NewsYesterday.aspx" title="Yesterday's News"
            description="Yesterday's top stories" roles="" />
        </siteMapNode>
        <siteMapNode url="Events.aspx" title="Upcoming Events"
        description="Today's top stories" roles="" />
        <siteMapNode url="Contact.aspx" title="Contact Us"
        description="Today's top stories" roles="" />
    </siteMapNode>
</siteMap>
```

6. Double-click the `Brown.css` style sheet in Solution Explorer to open the file. By default, it has a blank definition for the BODY element in the file. To add a definition, you can hand-code it after you learn the syntax, but for now use the built-in designer. Right-click anywhere on the page and select Add Style Rule from the context menu. The Add Style Rule dialog box opens as shown in Figure 18-14. Select the HR element and add it to the style rule hierarchy by clicking the right arrow button. When you click OK, an empty element with no style definitions is added to the page.

Figure 18-14

To add the style definitions you want to modify, you can use the Designer again or use IntelliSense. To use the Designer, right-click inside of the element definition start and end tags and select Build Style from the context menu. Open the Designer. The designer looks like Figure 18-15. To use IntelliSense, start typing inside any element and you will see all styles for that element.

Now, close the designer and add the following highlighted code to the HR definition by typing the code, and you will see the IntelliSense feature:

```
HR
{
        color:#cc1800;
        height:12px;
}
```

Figure 18-15

7. Define the master page layout. Double-click the MasterPage.master file in the root directory to open the file. While in Source view, update the HTML code for the master page as highlighted:

```
<%@ Master Language="VB" CodeFile="MasterPage.master.vb"
    Inherits="MasterPage" %>

<!DOCTYPE html PUBLIC "-//W3C//DTD XHTML 1.1//EN"
"http://www.w3.org/TR/xhtml11/DTD/xhtml11.dtd">

<html xmlns="http://www.w3.org/1999/xhtml" >
<head runat="server">
    <title>Untitled Page</title>
    <Style>
    .TableLayout {width: 700px; background-color:#ffcc66;}
    .border{border-style:solid; border-color:black;
            border-width:thin;}
    </Style>
</head>
<body bgcolor="#cc0000">
  <form id="form1" runat="server">
    <div>
```

```
<table id="tblMasterLayoutHeader" class="TableLayout"
cellpadding="0" cellspacing="0" align="center"
height="450">
 <tr>
  <td style="width: 100px" rowspan=2 class="border">
  <!-- Add the menu to the page -->
   <asp:Menu ID="Menu1" Runat="server" >
    <Items>
     <asp:MenuItem Value="Home" Text="Home"
      NavigateUrl="Default.aspx"> </asp:MenuItem>
     <asp:MenuItem Value="News" Text="News"
      NavigateUrl="News.aspx">
      <asp:MenuItem Value="Today" Text="Today"
       NavigateUrl="NewsToday.aspx"></asp:MenuItem>
      <asp:MenuItem Value="Yesterday" Text =
       "Yesterday" NavigateUrl="NewsYesterday.aspx">
       </asp:MenuItem>
     </asp:MenuItem>
     <asp:MenuItem Value="Events" Text="Events"
      NavigateUrl="Events.aspx"> </asp:MenuItem>
     <asp:MenuItem Value="Contact Us" Text="Contact Us"
      NavigateUrl="Contact.aspx"> </asp:MenuItem>
    </Items>
   </asp:Menu>
  </td>
  <td bgcolor="#000000" class="border" >
  <!-- Main title -->
   <asp:Label ID="Label1" Runat="server" Text="Beginning Visual
    Basic 2008" Font-Names="Arial" Font Bold="true"
    ForeColor="#ffcc33" Font-Size="28pt" />
  </td>
 </tr>
 <tr>
  <td class="border">
  <!-- Site map path under Title -->
   <asp:SiteMapPath ID="smpMain" Runat="server">
   </asp:SiteMapPath>
  </td>
 </tr>
 <tr>
  <td class="border" colspan="2" height="100%" valign="top"
   align="center">
  <!-- All site content will go here -->
   <asp:contentplaceholder id="ContentPlaceHolder1"
    runat="server">
   </asp:contentplaceholder><br />
  </td>
 </tr>
 <tr>
  <td class="border" align="center" colspan="2">
  <!-- Footer -->
   <asp:Label ID="Label2" Runat="server" Text="©2008, All rights
    reserved." Font-Names="Arial" Font-Bold="true"
    ForeColor="black" Font-Size="10pt" ></asp:Label>
```

```
            </td>
          </tr>
        </table>
    </div>
  </form>
</body>
</html>
```

8. Open the `Default.aspx` page. Make sure the Page declarations match these and add the following.

```
<%@ Page Language="VB" MasterPageFile="~/MasterPage.master"
    AutoEventWireup="false"
ClassName="Default_aspx" title="Untitled Page" Theme="Red"%>
<asp:Content ContentPlaceHolderID="ContentPlaceHolder1" Runat="Server">
    <asp:TextBox ID="txtTest" Runat="server">Just some text</asp:TextBox>
    <hr /><br />
    <asp:Button ID="btnTest" Runat="server" Text="Button" />
</asp:Content>
```

9. Change the `News.aspx` page to match the code here.

```
<%@ Page Language="VB" MasterPageFile="~/MasterPage.master"
    AutoEventWireup="false"
ClassName="News_aspx" title="Untitled Page" theme="Brown"%>
<asp:Content ID="Content1" ContentPlaceHolderID="ContentPlaceHolder1"
Runat="Server">
    <asp:TextBox ID="txtTest" Runat="server">Just some text</asp:TextBox>
    <asp:Button ID="btnTest" Runat="server" Text="Button" />
</asp:Content>
```

10. Here is the code listing for the `Button.Skin` page under the Red theme. Open this page and add the code listed here.

```
<asp:Button runat="server" ForeColor="Red" Font-Name="Arial"
  Font-Size="28px" Font-Weight="Bold" />
```

11. Open `TextBox.Skin` under the Red theme folder and add the code listed here.

```
<asp:TextBox runat="server" ForeColor="Red" Font-Name="Arial"
  Font-Size="28px" Font-Weight="Bold" />
```

12. Open `Brown.Skin` under the Brown theme folder and add the code listed here.

```
<asp:Button runat="server" ForeColor="Brown" Font-Name="Arial"
  Font-Size="28px" Font-Weight="Bold" />
<asp:TextBox runat="server" ForeColor="Brown" Font-Name="Arial"
  Font-Size="28px" Font-Weight="Bold" />
```

13. On the other Web Forms, you may need to change the ContentPlaceHolderID to ContentPlaceHolder1. This is because you changed the master page after adding these forms.

So the second line of code for Contact.aspx, Events.aspx, NewsToday.aspx, and NewsYesterday will be changed to the listing here:

```
<asp:Content ID="Content1" ContentPlaceHolderID="ContentPlaceHolder1"
Runat="Server"></asp:Content>
```

14. Run the application and test the navigation and layout. Play around; the site has a lot of functionality. Pay close attention to the navigation controls. Your site will resemble Figure 18-16.

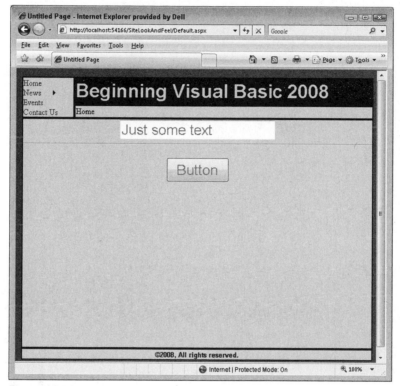

Figure 18-16

How It Works

You are able to take advantage of some of the newest controls to ASP.NET 2.0 in this Try It Out. The combination of these controls allows you to create a simple, yet powerful example of proper site design and layout. The master page maintains the same page layout across the entire site. You add the HTML used to lay out the look and feel of the site. All of the navigation for the entire site is located in this one page. If you ever need to change the menu or site map, you could change one page and that change would cascade across the entire site.

`ContentPlaceHolder` offers a mistake-free way to add logic to each additional page. If you work in a team, a designer would create the site layout and the master page.

Another element you add is the reusable styles. You use styles to apply a class name to objects that you want to modify. Styles are very powerful and play a huge role in web site design.

The final item used for the layout of the master page is the Menu control. You use XML format to build a hierarchy of parent/child menu items that render the site navigation main menu. Here is the full code listing for `MasterPage.master`.

```
<%@ Master Language="VB" CodeFile="MasterPage.master.vb"
    Inherits="MasterPage" %>

<!DOCTYPE html PUBLIC "-//W3C//DTD XHTML 1.1//EN"
"http://www.w3.org/TR/xhtml11/DTD/xhtml11.dtd">

<html xmlns="http://www.w3.org/1999/xhtml" >
<head runat="server">
    <title>Untitled Page</title>
    <Style>
    .TableLayout {width: 700px; background-color:#ffcc66;}
    .border{border-style:solid; border-color:black;
            border-width:thin;}
    </Style>
</head>
<body bgcolor="#cc0000">
 <form id="form1" runat="server">
  <div>
     <table id="tblMasterLayoutHeader" class="TableLayout"
     cellpadding="0" cellspacing="0" align="center"
     height="450">
      <tr>
       <td style="width: 100px" rowspan=2 class="border">
       <!-- Add the menu to the page -->
         <asp:Menu ID="Menu1" Runat="server" >
          <Items>
            <asp:MenuItem Value="Home" Text="Home"
             NavigateUrl="Default.aspx"> </asp:MenuItem>
            <asp:MenuItem Value="News" Text="News"
              NavigateUrl="News.aspx">
             <asp:MenuItem Value="Today" Text="Today"
              NavigateUrl="NewsToday.aspx"></asp:MenuItem>
             <asp:MenuItem Value="Yesterday" Text =
              "Yesterday" NavigateUrl="NewsYesterday.aspx">
             </asp:MenuItem>
            </asp:MenuItem>
            <asp:MenuItem Value="Events" Text="Events"
             NavigateUrl="Events.aspx"> </asp:MenuItem>
            <asp:MenuItem Value="Contact Us" Text="Contact Us"
             NavigateUrl="Contact.aspx"> </asp:MenuItem>
          </Items>
         </asp:Menu>
       </td>
       <td bgcolor="#000000" class="border" >
       <!-- Main title -->
```

```
             <asp:Label ID="Label1" Runat="server" Text="Beginning Visual
               Basic 2008" Font-Names="Arial" Font-Bold="true"
               ForeColor="#ffcc33" Font-Size="28pt" />
           </td>
         </tr>
         <tr>
          <td class="border">
          <!-- Site map path under Title -->
           <asp:SiteMapPath ID="smpMain" Runat="server">
           </asp:SiteMapPath>
          </td>
         </tr>
         <tr>
          <td class="border" colspan="2" height="100%" valign="top"
           align="center">
          <!-- All site content will go here -->
           <asp:contentplaceholder id="ContentPlaceHolder1"
           runat="server">
           </asp:contentplaceholder><br />
          </td>
         </tr>
         <tr>
          <td class="border" align="center" colspan="2">
          <!-- Footer -->
           <asp:Label ID="Label2" Runat="server" Text="©2008, All rights
             reserved." Font-Names="Arial" Font-Bold="true"
             ForeColor="black" Font-Size="10pt" ></asp:Label>
          </td>
         </tr>
       </table>
    </div>
   </form>
 </body>
 </html>
```

The Menu control is very customizable. Instead of hard-coding the menu, you could bind the menu to a dataset. You could also change the orientation. The menu displays vertically for the site, but you could use a horizontal format by changing the `Orientation` property. The other items you could change are the styles of the menu items. You could change the look of the menu using styles or themes.

You leave the Red.Skin page blank. You will change this later in the chapter.

The Button.Skin page defines the styles for a Button control when the Red theme was applied.

```
<asp:Button runat="server" ForeColor="Red" Font-Name="Arial"
  Font-Size="28px" Font-Weight="Bold" />
```

This TextBox.skin page defines the styles for a TextBox control when the Red theme is applied.

```
<asp:TextBox runat="server" ForeColor="Red" Font-Name="Arial"
  Font-Size="28px" Font-Weight="Bold" />
```

For the `Default.aspx` page, you add a reference to the master page and set the theme to `Red` in the `Page` directive. Then, inside the Content control, you add a text box, horizontal rule, line break, and button. When you see the page, the text is red, bold, and large just as the theme (see Figure 18-16).

```
<%@ Page Language="VB" AutoEventWireup="false"
   CodeFile="Default.aspx.vb" Inherits="_Default"
   MasterPageFile="~/MasterPage.master" Theme="Red" %>

<asp:Content ID="Content1" ContentPlaceHolderID="ContentPlaceHolder1"
 runat="server">
 <asp:TextBox ID="txtTest" Runat="server">Just some text</asp:TextBox>
 <hr /><br />
 <asp:Button ID="btnTest" Runat="server" Text="Button" />
</asp:Content>
```

You apply the `Brown.css` style sheet to the theme. The only element you modify in the style sheet was the horizontal rule. You change the color (red) and height. You can update any object using the style sheet. Your output should display the updated styles shown in Figure 18-17.

```
body {}
HR
{
     color:#cc1800;
     height:12px;
}
```

The `Brown.skin` page defines the styles for Button and TextBox controls when the Brown theme is applied.

```
<asp:Button runat="server" ForeColor="Brown" Font-Name="Arial"
   Font-Size="28px" Font-Weight="Bold" />
<asp:TextBox runat="server" ForeColor="Brown" Font-Name="Arial"
   Font-Size="28px" Font-Weight="Bold" />
```

On `News.aspx` you add a reference to the master page and set the theme to `Brown` in the `Page` directive. Then, inside the Content control, you add a textbox, horizontal rule, line break, and button. When you see the page, the text is red, bold, and large just as the theme defined. You should see a page like Figure 18-17 in your browser.

```
<%@ Page Language="VB" MasterPageFile="~/MasterPage.master" AutoEventWireup=
    "false" ClassName="News_aspx" title="Untitled Page" theme="Brown"%>
<asp:Content ID="Content1" ContentPlaceHolderID=cphPageContent Runat=Server>
    <asp:TextBox ID="txtTest" Runat="server">Just some text</asp:TextBox>
    <hr /><br />
    <asp:Button ID="btnTest" Runat="server" Text="Button" />
</asp:Content>
```

Figure 18-17

The sitemap file is used by the SiteMap control. This control allows you to see what level you are on at the site. You could easily navigate up one level at a time or all the way to the home page. The control gives you an easy interface for navigating through the site. The outermost level of the SiteMap control is displayed on the Today's News page as shown in Figure 18-18

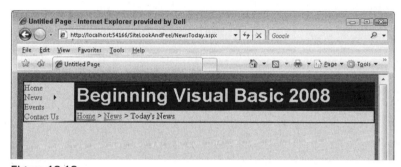

Figure 18-18

Using the GridView to Build a Data-Driven Web Form

The data controls in ASP.NET 2.0 add the ability to program *declaratively*. This no-code architecture allows you to look at the source of the Web Form and see your layout and design along with attributes that allow for data access and data manipulation. If you have any experience with HTML or ASP.NET 1.1, you will find this new method of data access compact and astoundingly simple.

In this Try It Out, you will see two of the best controls in ASP.NET 3.5. The first is the SqlDataSource control, and the second is the GridView control. You will set properties and attributes of these controls and also the child elements of them. Without writing any server-side or client-side code, you will create a web application to display data in the pubs database and update it.

The following Try It Out requires access to SQL Server with the pubs *database installed.*

Try It Out   **No-Code Data Viewing and Updating**

1.   Create a new web site and name it **DataGridView**.

2.   Use the Source view and add the changes highlighted here to the Default.aspx page. Make sure to change the values of the ConnectionString to match your development environment.

```
<%@ Page Language="VB" AutoEventWireup="false"
  CodeFile="Default.aspx.vb" Inherits="_Default" %>

<!DOCTYPE html PUBLIC "-//W3C//DTD XHTML 1.0 Transitional//EN"
"http://www.w3.org/TR/xhtml1/DTD/xhtml1-transitional.dtd">
<html xmlns="http://www.w3.org/1999/xhtml">
<head runat="server">
    <title>Grid View</title>
</head>
<body>
<form id="form1" runat="server">
<div>
    <asp:SqlDataSource ID="sdsAuthors" Runat="server"
                       ProviderName = "System.Data.SqlClient"
                       ConnectionString = "Server=bnewsome; User ID=sa;
                       Password=!p@ssw0rd!;Database=pubs; "
                       SelectCommand = "SELECT au_id, au_lname,
                       au_fname, phone,
                       address, city, state, zip FROM authors"
                       UpdateCommand = "UPDATE authors
                       SET au_lname = @au_lname,
                       au_fname = @au_fname, phone = @phone,
                       address = @address,
                       city = @city, state = @state, zip = @zip
                       WHERE au_id = @original_au_id" >
    <UpdateParameters>
        <asp:Parameter Type="String" Name="au_lname"></asp:Parameter>
        <asp:Parameter Type="String" Name="au_fname"></asp:Parameter>
        <asp:Parameter Type="String" Name="phone"></asp:Parameter>
        <asp:Parameter Type="String" Name="address"></asp:Parameter>
        <asp:Parameter Type="String" Name="city"></asp:Parameter>
        <asp:Parameter Type="String" Name="state"></asp:Parameter>
        <asp:Parameter Type="String" Name="zip"></asp:Parameter>
        <asp:Parameter Type="String" Name="au_id"></asp:Parameter>
    </UpdateParameters>
    </asp:SqlDataSource>

    <asp:GridView ID="gdvAuthors" Runat="server"
     DataSourceID="sdsAuthors" AllowPaging="True" AllowSorting="True"
     AutoGenerateColumns=False DataKeyNames="au_id" >
        <PagerStyle BackColor="Gray" ForeColor="White"
         HorizontalAlign="Center" />
```

```
      <HeaderStyle BackColor="Black" ForeColor="White" />
      <AlternatingRowStyle BackColor="LightGray" />
      <Columns>
        <asp:CommandField ButtonType="Button" ShowEditButton="true" />
        <asp:BoundField Visible="false" HeaderText="au_id"
                        DataField="au_id" SortExpression="au_id">
                        </asp:BoundField>
        <asp:BoundField HeaderText="Last Name" DataField="au_lname"
                        SortExpression="au_lname"></asp:BoundField>
        <asp:BoundField HeaderText="First Name" DataField="au_fname"
                        SortExpression="au_fname"></asp:BoundField>
        <asp:BoundField HeaderText="Phone" DataField="phone"
                        SortExpression="phone"></asp:BoundField>
        <asp:BoundField HeaderText="Address" DataField="address"
                        SortExpression="address"></asp:BoundField>
        <asp:BoundField HeaderText="City" DataField="city"
                        SortExpression="city"></asp:BoundField>
        <asp:BoundField HeaderText="State" DataField="state"
                        SortExpression="state"></asp:BoundField>
        <asp:BoundField HeaderText="Zip Code" DataField="zip"
                        SortExpression="zip"></asp:BoundField>
      </Columns>
    </asp:GridView>
  </div>
  </form>
  </body>
  </html>
```

3. Run the application without debugging by pressing Ctrl+F5. You will see the data grid display similar to Figure 18-19.

Figure 18-19

Test the functions of the grid. At the bottom, you can move to any page of the data. Also, sorting is available by clicking any of the column headers. After trying both of these, update a row. To edit an author's data, click the Edit button on the left of the author's row. The screen refreshes, and you will see a new grid that looks like Figure 18-20.

Figure 18-20

Change any field and click the update button to make the change permanent. You can cancel a change by clicking any link or button other than the Update button.

How It Works

Now that was easy. By adding two controls, you created a fairly robust data access page. We'll explain how this happened.

First, you create the SqlDataSource control. The following table explains each attribute you add or change for the SqlDataSource control. The code follows.

Attribute or Element	Description
ID	The control's identifier.
Runat	Defines that the code for the control is run at the server before the page is sent to the browser.
ProviderName	Used to set the provider to access the data store. In this case, it is SQLClient, the managed provider for SQL Server.
ConnectionString	This string value is used to gain access to the database resource, pubs.

Attribute or Element	Description
SelectCommand	The SQL statement passed to the database to retrieve the data that is displayed in the grid. This could be a stored procedure name.
UpdateCommand	The SQL statement that is used to update the data. You could use a stored procedure name in place of the SQL statement in this case.
UpdateParameters and Parameter objects	The update parameters object is a collection of parameters the application uses to fill in the blanks in the update statement. For example, the parameter @city in the update statement passes a value to the database so that the Author's record is updated. This parameter, @city, is replaced with the actual value you enter into the city text box. In the future, when you use parameters, the database will determine the syntax. Some databases will just use a question mark for each parameter name. Also, in some cases the order of the parameter object matters. For this application, the names are the only part that makes a difference, not the order. Another common property not used here is DefaultValue. The DefaultValue property would replace a null value with the value set in the property itself.
Parameter: Type	This is the string for every parameter. This value is determined based on the data type on each column in the database.
Parameter: Name	The name property is the actual name used by the UpdateCommand for each parameter.

```
<asp:SqlDataSource ID="sdsAuthors" Runat="server"
                   ProviderName = "System.Data.SqlClient"
                   ConnectionString = "Server=bnewsome; User ID=sa;
                   Password=!p@ssw0rd!;Database=pubs; "
                   SelectCommand = "SELECT au_id, au_lname,
                   au_fname, phone,
                   address, city, state, zip FROM authors"
                   UpdateCommand = "UPDATE authors
                   SET au_lname = @au_lname,
                   au_fname = @au_fname, phone = @phone,
                   address = @address,
                   city = @city, state = @state, zip = @zip
                   WHERE au_id = @original_au_id" >
    <UpdateParameters>
       <asp:Parameter Type="String" Name="au_lname"></asp:Parameter>
       <asp:Parameter Type="String" Name="au_fname"></asp:Parameter>
       <asp:Parameter Type="String" Name="phone"></asp:Parameter>
       <asp:Parameter Type="String" Name="address"></asp:Parameter>
       <asp:Parameter Type="String" Name="city"></asp:Parameter>
       <asp:Parameter Type="String" Name="state"></asp:Parameter>
       <asp:Parameter Type="String" Name="zip"></asp:Parameter>
       <asp:Parameter Type="String" Name="au_id"></asp:Parameter>
    </UpdateParameters>
</asp:SqlDataSource>
```

The second control you add to the form is the GridView. Its attributes are described in the following table.

Attribute or Element	Description
ID	The control's identifier.
Runat	Defines that the code for the control is run at the server before the page is sent to the browser.
DataSourceID	The ID of the SqlDataSource object is used here.
AllowPaging	Can be set to TRUE or FALSE. Turns on sorting features of the grid.
AllowSorting	Can be set to TRUE or FALSE. Turns on sorting features of the grid.
AutoGenerateColumns	Can be set to TRUE or FALSE. Turns on sorting features of the grid.
DataKeyNames	The primary key used by the database table.
PagerStyle	This element defines the style of the paging area of the grid.
HeaderStyle	This element defines the style of the header row area of the grid.
AlternatingRowStyle	This element defines the style of the every other row of the grid.
Columns	A collection of column objects.
CommandField	Two properties of this object are used. The first is ButtonType. This is set to a type of button. You can insert a button, image, or link as a value. If left blank, the default is link.
BoundField	This element allows for the binding of the data to the grid. For a better user interface, you use the Visible property to hide the primary key column. Also, you set the SortExpression of each column. This converts every column header to a link. When clicked, the data is sorted by that column. Next, you change the column headers with the HeaderText property. If this is blank, the column names are used as headers. Finally, the field to bind to is set using the DataField property.

```
<asp:GridView ID="gdvAuthors" Runat="server"
DataSourceID="sdsAuthors"
              AllowPaging="True" AllowSorting="True"
AutoGenerateColumns=False
              DataKeyNames="au_id" >
    <PagerStyle BackColor="Gray" ForeColor="White"
HorizontalAlign="Center" />
    <HeaderStyle BackColor="Black" ForeColor="White" />
    <AlternatingRowStyle BackColor="LightGray" />
    <Columns>
      <asp:CommandField ButtonType="Button" ShowEditButton="true" />
      <asp:BoundField Visible="false" HeaderText="au_id"
                    DataField="au_id" SortExpression="au_id">
                    </asp:BoundField>
```

```
                  <asp:BoundField HeaderText="Last Name" DataField="au_lname"
                                  SortExpression="au_lname"></asp:BoundField>
                  <asp:BoundField HeaderText="First Name" DataField="au_fname"
                                  SortExpression="au_fname"></asp:BoundField>
                  <asp:BoundField HeaderText="Phone" DataField="phone"
                                  SortExpression="phone"></asp:BoundField>
                  <asp:BoundField HeaderText="Address" DataField="address"
                                  SortExpression="address"></asp:BoundField>
                  <asp:BoundField HeaderText="City" DataField="city"
                                  SortExpression="city"></asp:BoundField>
                  <asp:BoundField HeaderText="State" DataField="state"
                                  SortExpression="state"></asp:BoundField>
                  <asp:BoundField HeaderText="Zip Code" DataField="zip"
                                  SortExpression="zip"></asp:BoundField>
              </Columns>
          </asp:GridView>
```

Summary

In this chapter, you learned what thin-client development is. You saw the advantages of Web Forms and Windows Forms and why you would choose one type of application over the other. Maybe the low distribution cost of web applications is a major factor in your decision to create a web application over a Windows application. Also, you read about the basic pieces that constitute a typical web application. From layout and formatting to database integration, you gained knowledge of the best features of ASP.NET and how they are implemented. Finally, you designed a code-free page that updated data in a database.

If you like web development, there is much more than can be explained in this chapter. To continue learning, we recommend navigating to Wrox.com and clicking on the ASP.NET link to find more resources to take you to the next level of web development.

You should know how to:

❑ Choose between Web Forms and Windows Forms applications to suit your purpose

❑ Use the toolbox for ASP.NET

❑ Create a web site project in Visual Studio 2008

❑ Choose between the possible locations for web sites in Visual Studio 2008

Exercises

1. Create a new web site, name it **ExerciseOne**, and create it as a local site using the file system and ASP.NET Development Server. Run the web site to make sure it is running in ASP.NET Development Server.

2. Create a new web site, name it **ExerciseTwo**, and create it as a local IIS. Run the web site to make sure it is *not* running in ASP.NET Development Server. (You will need IIS on your local machine to complete this exercise.) Note that Vista requires you to run Visual Studio as an administrator for this to work.

Web Projects

In Chapter 18, you learned how to implement many pieces of the puzzle that is web development. Now, you put it all together to build the foundation for a secure public web site. You create a skeleton web site in this chapter, with security that is ready for content. Although you won't be writing any Visual Basic code, you end up with a consistent look and feel and role-based forms authentication. You will be amazed at the ease of creation and the flexibility built into ASP.NET.

In this chapter, you will:

❑   Have an overview of the two most popular methods of web site security

❑   Learn about the Web Site Administration Tool

❑   Implement web site security using forms authentication

❑   Add rules and roles to a security scheme

❑   Create a secure web site with little or no code written

Error handling has been omitted from all of the Try It Outs in this chapter to save space. You should always add the appropriate error handling to your code. Review Chapter 9 for error-handling techniques.

Web Site Authentication

As you design web applications, you need to consider security at an early point in the project. Always understand who will have access to your site and who will not. In many cases, parts of the site will be open to the public and parts will be secure and for members only. This may require multiple methods of security. There are two standard types of web authentication strategies: windows and forms authentication.

Windows Authentication

The simplest type of authentication is windows authentication. This type of authentication is perfect for intranet sites. It is actually implemented by IIS and keeps the authentication mechanisms separate from the tasks of developing the actual intranet site. What happens is that IIS requires the user either to be logged into the server's domain or to log in with a valid domain account. If the user is already authenticated with a valid domain account, access to the site is seamless with no interruption to the user experience. When the user is not logged into the server's domain, a valid login is required. This method of authentication is set up via the IIS Management Console.

Forms Authentication

For a public web site, forms authentication is an easy solution to implement. Users who try to visit the site must provide credentials to gain access to the site. When an unauthorized user requests a web page, the user is redirected to the login page. From here, a current user can log in, or new users can click a link to create an account. Without a valid user name or password, the visitor cannot browse secured areas of the site. With ASP.NET 2.0, built-in controls make forms authentication quick and easy to implement as a security model.

Web Site Administration Tool (WAT)

ASP.NET is driven by `web.config` files. In the past, developers had to hand-code the XML configuration files to set up functionality such as debugging, security, or tracing. Now, there is an interface to set up these configuration files for web applications: the Web Site Administration Tool (WAT).

When you use the WAT, you will see five tabs (Home, Security, Profile, Application, and Provider). You will set site security using the Security tab in this chapter, and we give you a brief summary of the others. The first tab is Home. Home is the main tab and displays info on your other options. Next is the Profile tab. You use this tab to collect and store data on your site's visitors. Application is another tab, enabling application configuration. Here you can set up site attributes such as counters, tracing, and Simple Mail Transfer Protocol (SMTP). The final tab is Provider. Use this tab to change the default data provider for the site. The default provider is AspNetAccessProvider for Microsoft Access. You use the WAT to set up the web site in the next Try It Out.

In this Try It Out, you set up the files for a new web site and use the WAT to implement forms authentication.

Try It Out   Forms Authentication Configuration

In this exercise, you start the web site that you will work on during this chapter. First, you add the file structure to the new site. Then you set up the forms authentication security model.

1. Create a new web site project named **TheClub**. Be sure to use the file system for the site location.

2. Make the following changes to the site using Solution Explorer. To add items to a site using Solution Explorer, right-click the root folder or project and choose Add new item. In the dialog box, select the type of item (Web Form, text file, and so on) and supply the name. When you finish with step 2, your site will look like Figure 19-1. For all of the pages you add, clear the check box to place code in a separate file.

Add a master page and name it **Main.master.** Set all Web Forms you add to use this master page. You have an option to select a master page when you add the forms by selecting a box to Select Master Page.

Add the following regular folders to the site:

❑   Admin

❑   Members

Add the following theme folder to the site: You should right-click the project name in Solution Explorer and then choose Add ASP.NET Folder ➪ Theme Folder. The folder you add will be placed under a new App_Themes directory.

❑   MainTheme

Add the following Web Forms to the site's root folder (and remember to check the box to select a master page):

❑   Login.aspx

❑   ChangePassword.aspx

❑   CreateNewUser.aspx

Set the Login.aspx page to the start page.

Right-click the page in Solution Explorer and choose Set As Start Page.

Add the following Web Forms to the Admin folder (and remember to check the box to select a master page):

❑   Default.aspx

❑   ViewUsers.aspx

Add the following Web Forms to the Members folder (and remember to select the box to select a master page):

❑   Default.aspx

❑   ViewAuthors.aspx

❑   ViewTitles.aspx

Add the following text file to the MainTheme folder:

❑   Main.skin

Figure 19-1

3. Next, choose Website ⇨ ASP.NET Configuration under the Main menu to use the WAT. The menu is shown in Figure 19-2.

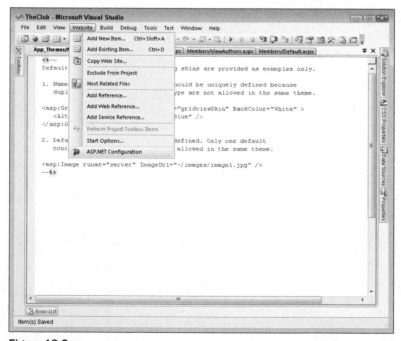

Figure 19-2

The Visual Web Developer Web Server starts and opens the Web Site Administration Tool. Figure 19-3 shows the default page for the tool. You use this tool to set up security for the site.

Figure 19-3

4. Now, click the Security link to set up the site security.

5. We walk you through the wizard. Know that you can make any changes using the wizard from the main security page. Click the link on the security home page to use the Security Setup Wizard.

6. The Security Setup Wizard has seven steps. The first is the Welcome screen, which gives you an overview of the entire process. At the lower right of each step, you see options to navigate through the wizard. On the Welcome screen, move to step 2 by clicking Next.

7. Step 2 allows you to select the access method. You have two options here, as shown in Figure 19-4. The first option is From the internet. If you choose this option, the wizard sets up the site for forms authentication. This method uses a data source to store user account information and allow the public to access the site. The second option is From a local area network, and it sets the site to use windows authentication. You can use this option for an intranet application within a private network. For TheClub web site, choose From the internet and click Next to move to step 3.

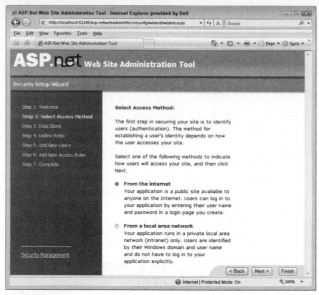

Figure 19-4

8. The third step is for data store information. You will see the default data provider for the site. To change this, you have to quit the wizard and make the change on the Provider tab. Just click Next to keep the default and move to step 4. The default data store uses Microsoft Access behind the scenes.

9. You can enable roles-based security on step 4. With roles-based security, you can manage site access for many users in a role quickly. Select the box to enable roles, and then click Next to add a new role. Figure 19-5 shows the Create New Role screen. Type the role name **Admin** into the text box and click Add Role. On the next screen, you can edit or add roles. For this site, you will have just one role, Admin. Click Next.

Figure 19-5

10. Step 5 allows you to create new users. You do not have to create users here, but it is an easy interface if you have a few to create. For this project, add the Admin user as shown in Figure 19-6. Set the User Name to **Admin.** You can set the rest of the fields to any values you can remember. When you finish, click the Create User button. You see a successful creation note on the next screen. Since you are only adding one user, click Next.

Figure 19-6

11. The last step prior to completing the wizard is step 6, Add New Access Rules. This is where you set up the users who will have access to areas of the site. You add three rules. You need to remember that rules are applied to web folders. Always make sure the correct folder is highlighted when you add a rule.

As shown in Figure 19-7, the default rule is to allow anonymous users to access the site. Now, add a new rule. Make sure the Admin directory is highlighted, and click the Role radio button. Select the Admin role and then, under the Permission heading, turn on the radio button for Allow and click Add This Rule. You add the two other rules after completing the wizard. To finish the wizard, click Next to move to the final confirmation and then click Finish. You are taken back to the main security page, where you will complete the rest of the rules.

Figure 19-7

12. From the main security page, click the Manage Access Rules link. On the next screen, click the Admin folder to see the new rule. Now click the Add New Access Rule link. You add a rule to deny all-user access to this folder. Move the rules up or down so that they match Figure 19-8.

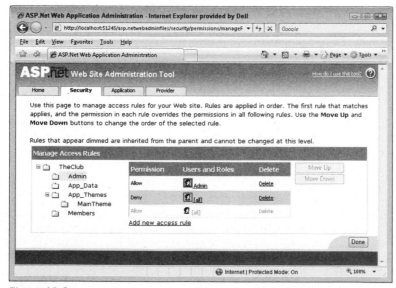

Figure 19-8

13. Next, click the Members directory and add a rule to deny anonymous users. The rules for the Members folder look like Figure 19-9.

Figure 19-9

14. Now, you test the security settings. Do not worry that the Web Forms are blank. This test is just for the security settings.

Run the web site and you are taken to the home page of the root directory. The URL is `http://localhost:(port#)/TheClub/Login.aspx`. You are prompted to enable debugging. Select Modify the Web.Config file to enable debugging and then click OK to run the site. You may be prompted that script debugging is disabled. Just continue through this if you see the message box. *Note:* You should turn on script debugging while developing. So if you see the prompt, go back and follow the instructions to turn on script debugging later). Now, close the browser or stop debugging.

In Solution Explorer, right-click the ViewAuthors.aspx under the folder Members and chose View in Browser. The security should return you to the `Login.asp` page. The URL should look like `http://localhost:51220/TheClub/login.aspx?ReturnUrl=% 2fTheClub%2fMembers%2fViewAuthors.aspx`.

15. Test the Admin directory and you will see the same result.

How It Works

So what did the wizard do? Take a look at the project's Solution Explorer. Make sure you refresh the view. It resembles Figure 19-10. Look closely and you will see new `web.config` files and an Access database. These new additions manage the security options you set using the wizard.

Figure 19-10

A site can be changed with settings in a `web.config` file. When you step through the wizard, settings are configured in `web.config` files per folder. If you opened one of the config files, you would see the settings that are added. Also, an Access database is created to manage the users and roles. That's it. To manage the security of the site, you do not need to know how to manipulate the `web.config` files manually.

Take a closer look at this URL, which sent you to the login page while testing (`http://localhost:51220/TheClub/login.aspx?ReturnUrl=%2fTheClub%2fadmin%2fdefault.aspx`) and you will see a question mark. The question mark represents the beginning of the query string. The query string is one way to pass data between the browser and server to maintain state. In this case, a variable (`ReturnUrl`) has a value from the web server. The value has some encoded characters that may seem confusing. The forward slash is encoded in the query string and represented by `%2f`. So if you replace the characters `%2f` with a forward slash, then the value of `ReturnUrl` is `/TheClub/admin/default.aspx`. When your login is successful, the sever uses the `ReturnUrl` to send you back to the place you were trying to visit — in this case, theAdminfolder.

Okay, so now you have a secure site. Next, take a look at the built-in login controls available in ASP.NET 3.5.

Login Controls

The Microsoft ASP team has encapsulated the most common functionality for authentication into a group of login controls that make your job as a developer easier. You can take the default behavior of these controls or customize almost every aspect of their functionality and design. The following table lists the available login controls. You are not required to use these controls. If you prefer, you can hand-code your own logic to use the same membership APIs to enforce forms authentication.

Control Name	Description
Login	Contains all of the elements necessary to provide a login area for a web site.
LoginView	Allows for templates to display the correct information to a user based on authentication and roles.
LoginStatus	Displays a link to log in or log out based on the user's status.
LoginName	Displays the current user's name.
ChangePassword	Allows users to change their password.
CreateUserWizard	Creates an area for new users to create a new account on the web site.
PasswordRecovery	Sends a user's forgotten or new password via e-mail. *Note:* E-mail is not a secure means of data transmission. The security risks of this control should be considered before it is implemented on your web site.

In the next Try It Out, you use most of the login controls to implement a membership strategy.

Try It Out   Layout and Login Controls

Now that you have security set up, you need to add the layout and functionality to allow visitors to log in. In this Try It Out, you gain knowledge about most of the Login controls in ASP.NET 3.5.

To complete this exercise, make the following changes to the pages of the site. As you make these changes, type the HTML markup into the pages as highlighted. You get firsthand experience working with the IntelliSense for ASP.NET 3.5. As you type, you will be able to set properties and attributes quickly. You may find it faster than dragging controls from the Toolbox onto the form.

1. Start by opening `Main.master` and adding the highlighted code:

```
<%@ Master Language="VB" %>
<!DOCTYPE html PUBLIC "-//W3C//DTD XHTML 1.0 Transitional//EN"
"http://www.w3.org/TR/xhtml1/DTD/xhtml1-transitional.dtd">

<script runat="server">
</script>

<html xmlns="http://www.w3.org/1999/xhtml">
<head runat="server">
    <title>Untitled Page</title>
</head>
<body bgcolor="black">
    <form id="form1" runat="server">
    <div>
    <table cellpadding="5" cellspacing="0" width="600" height="400"
```

```
         bgcolor="white" border="1" bordercolor="black">
      <tr>
         <td width="150" valign="top">
         <!-- Menu Column -->
            <asp:Menu ID="Menu1" Runat="server">
               <Items>
                  <asp:MenuItem NavigateUrl="~/Default.aspx"
Text="Home"></asp:MenuItem>
                  <asp:MenuItem Text="Members">
                     <asp:MenuItem NavigateUrl="Members/ViewAuthors.aspx"
Text="View Authors"></asp:MenuItem>
                     <asp:MenuItem NavigateUrl="Members/ViewTitles.aspx"
Text="View Titles"></asp:MenuItem>
                  </asp:MenuItem>
                  <asp:MenuItem Text="Admin">
                     <asp:MenuItem NavigateUrl="Admin/ViewUsers.aspx"
Text="View Users"></asp:MenuItem>
                  </asp:MenuItem>
               </Items>
            </asp:Menu>
            <br /><br /><br />
            <asp:LoginView ID="LoginView1" Runat="server">
               <AnonymousTemplate>
                  <asp:Menu ID="Menu2" Runat="server">
                     <Items>
                        <asp:MenuItem NavigateUrl="~/CreateNewUser.aspx"
Text="Create Account"></asp:MenuItem>
                     </Items>
                  </asp:Menu>
               </AnonymousTemplate>
               <LoggedInTemplate>
                  <asp:Menu ID="Menu3" Runat="server">
                     <Items>
                        <asp:MenuItem NavigateUrl="~/ChangePassword.aspx"
Text="Change Password"></asp:MenuItem>
                     </Items>
                  </asp:Menu>
               </LoggedInTemplate>
            </asp:LoginView>
         </td>
         <td valign="top">
            <table cellpadding="0" cellspacing="0" width="100%" border="0">
               <tr>
                  <td width="85%">
                     <asp:Label ID="Label1" Runat="server" Text="My First
Company Site" Font-Bold="true" Font-Size="24px"></asp:Label>
                  </td>
                  <td width="15%">
                     <!-- Login Status Area -->
                     <asp:LoginStatus ID="LoginStatus1" Runat="server" />
                  </td>
               </tr>
               <tr>
```

```
                        <td colspan="2">
                            <hr color="black" size="2" />
                        </td>
                    </tr>
                    <tr>
                        <td colspan="2">
                            User:
                            <asp:LoginView ID="LoginView2" Runat="server">
                                <AnonymousTemplate>Guest, Please log in</
AnonymousTemplate>
                                <LoggedInTemplate><asp:LoginName ID="LoginName1"
Runat="server" /></LoggedInTemplate>
                            </asp:LoginView>
                        </td>
                    </tr>
                    <tr>
                        <td colspan="2">
                            <hr color="black" size="2" />
                        </td>
                    </tr>
                    <tr>
                        <td colspan="2" valign="top" height="100%">
                            <asp:contentplaceholder id="ContentPlaceHolder1"
runat="server">
                            </asp:contentplaceholder>
                        </td>
                    </tr>
                </table>
            </td>
        </tr>
    </table>
    </div>
    </form>
</body>
</html>
```

2. In `Default.aspx` (under the root folder), delete the default code and insert the following code (see Figure 19-11):

```
<%@ Page Language="VB" AutoEventWireup="false" CodeFile="Default.aspx.vb"
Inherits="_Default" MasterPageFile="~/Main.master" Title="Home" %>
```

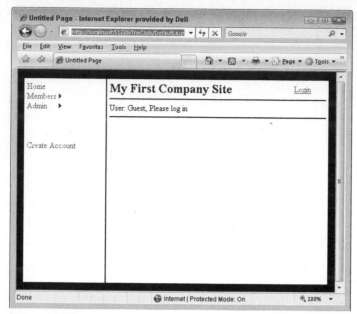

Figure 19-11

3. In `Login.aspx` (see Figure 19-12), delete the default code and add the following code:

```
<%@ Page Language="VB" MasterPageFile="~/Main.master" Title="Login" %>
<asp:content ContentPlaceHolderID="ContentPlaceHolder1" Runat="server">
  <asp:Login ID="Login1" runat="server">
  </asp:Login>
</asp:content>
```

Figure 19-12

4. In `ChangePassword.aspx` (see Figure 19-13), delete the default code and add the following code:

```
<%@ Page Language="VB" MasterPageFile="~/Main.master" Title="Change Password" %>
<asp:Content ID="Content2" ContentPlaceHolderID="ContentPlaceHolder1"
Runat="Server">
    <asp:ChangePassword ID="ChangePassword1" Runat="server">
    </asp:ChangePassword>
</asp:Content>
```

Figure 19-13

5. In `CreateNewUser.aspx` (see Figure 19-14), delete the default code and add the following code:

```
<%@ Page Language="VB" MasterPageFile="~/Main.master" Title="Create New
Account" %>
<asp:Content ID="Content2" ContentPlaceHolderID="ContentPlaceHolder1"
Runat="Server">
<asp:CreateUserWizard ID="CreateUserWizard1" Runat="server">
    </asp:CreateUserWizard>
</asp:Content>
```

Figure 19-14

6. In `ViewAuthors.aspx`, delete the default code and add the following:

```
<%@ Page Language-"VB" MasterPageFile="~/Main.master" Title="View Authors" %>
<asp:Content ID="Cnt1" ContentPlaceHolderID="ContentPlaceHolder1"
Runat="server">
    <asp:Label ID="Label1" Runat="server" Text="Add Code to View Author Info
Later"></asp:Label>
</asp:Content>
```

7. In `ViewTitles.aspx`, delete the default code and add the following:

```
<%@ Page Language="VB" MasterPageFile="~/Main.master" Title="View Titles" %>
<asp:Content ID="Cnt1" ContentPlaceHolderID="ContentPlaceHolder1"
Runat="server">
    <asp:Label ID="Label1" Runat="server" Text="Add Code to View Title Info
Later"></asp:Label>
</asp:Content>
```

8. In `ViewUsers.aspx`, delete the default code and add the following:

```
<%@ Page Language="VB" MasterPageFile="~/Main.master" Title="View Users" %>
<asp:Content ID-"Cnt1" ContentPlaceHolderID="ContentPlaceHolder1"
Runat="server">
    <asp:Label ID="Label1" Runat="server" Text="Add Code to View User Info
Later"></asp:Label>
</asp:Content>
```

9. Now test the site. You can add a new account and then log in. Test the new pages to make sure they all work correctly. All of the authentication functionality will work. As you test the site using IIS and work with the configuration tool, you may see errors where the Access database is locked by another process. You can shut down the web servers to free the lock.

How It Works

As you play with the new site, you should be amazed. In older technologies, that level of functionality would have taken days to complete.

All your work on the site layout is on the master page. The first change sets the background color for the page to black:

```
<body bgcolor="black">
```

The next change involves the table layout for the page. Tables are a common layout tool in web development. To set up the table layout, you add rows and cells and, in some cases, nested tables inside of cells. Table layout is an art you will learn with experience. First, take a look at the tags used to format a table in the following table.

Tag	Description
<table>	The root tag for a table.
<tr>	A row in a table.
<td>	A cell in a row in a table.

When you set up the table layout, the cells by default are spaced apart. Setting the `cellpadding` and `cellspacing` properties makes it easier to lay out the page the way you want it. The `colspan` attribute of the cell tag allows the cell to span 2 columns. Basically, both columns were merged into one in that row.

The main table is set to a size of 600 by 400 with a white background. This allows for the table to maintain a standard size even when no content is present. The main table contains one row and two columns. The first column is used for the menu. The second column has a nested table with five rows that contain one or two columns each. This table is set to a width of 100% to force the table to fill up the second column. This allows the HR controls to span the entire length of the parent column. The second table is for the site title, user name, and content placeholder.

```
<table cellpadding="5" cellspacing="0" width="600" height="400"
bgcolor="white" border="1" bordercolor="black">
  <tr>
    <td width="150" valign="top">
    </td>
    <td valign="top">
      <table cellpadding="0" cellspacing="0" width="100%" border="0">
        <tr>
          <td width="85%">
          </td>
          <td width="15%">
          </td>
        </tr>
```

```
            <tr>
               <td colspan="2">
                  <hr color="black" size="2" />
               </td>
            </tr>
            <tr>
               <td colspan="2">
               </td>
            </tr>
            <tr>
               <td colspan="2">
                  <hr color="black" size="2" />
               </td>
            </tr>
            <tr>
               <td colspan="2" valign="top" height="100%">
               </td>
            </tr>
         </table>
      </td>
   </tr>
</table>
```

The next part of the master page is the menu. Just as in Chapter 18, you add the menu control for site navigation. The difference is that you add multiple menu controls based on the login status. The `LoginView` control templates you work with allow the user to see a validate menu based on the authentication status of the user.

```
<asp:Menu ID="Menu1" Runat="server">
   <Items>
      <asp:MenuItem NavigateUrl="~/Default.aspx" Text="Home"></asp:MenuItem>
      <asp:MenuItem Text="Members">
         <asp:MenuItem NavigateUrl="Members/ViewAuthors.aspx" Text="View
Authors" />
         <asp:MenuItem NavigateUrl="Members/ViewTitles.aspx" Text="View Titles">
      </asp:MenuItem>
      <asp:MenuItem Text="Admin">
         <asp:MenuItem NavigateUrl="Admin/ViewUser.aspx" Text="View Users" />
      </asp:MenuItem>
   </Items>
</asp:Menu>
<br /><br /><br />
<asp:LoginView ID="LoginView1" Runat="server">
   <AnonymousTemplate>
      <asp:Menu ID="Menu2" Runat="server">
         <Items>
            <asp:MenuItem NavigateUrl="~/CreateNewUser.aspx" Text="Create
Account" />
         </Items>
      </asp:Menu>
   </AnonymousTemplate>
   <LoggedInTemplate>
      <asp:Menu ID="Menu3" Runat="server">
         <Items>
            <asp:MenuItem NavigateUrl="~/ChangePassword.aspx" Text="Change
Password" />
```

```
        </Items>
      </asp:Menu>
    </LoggedInTemplate>
</asp:LoginView>
```

The web site title is added with a Label control:

```
<asp:Label ID="Label1" Runat="server" Text="My First Company Site"
      Font-Bold="true" Font-Size="24px"></asp:Label>
```

Under the title, you add a section to display the user name. Again, you use the LoginView control and display the name when the user is logged in. For anonymous users, you display: Guest, Please log in.

```
<!-- Login Status Area -->
<asp:LoginStatus ID="LoginStatus1" Runat="server" />
User:
<asp:LoginView ID="LoginView2" Runat="server">
  <AnonymousTemplate>Guest, Please log in</AnonymousTemplate>
  <LoggedInTemplate>
    <asp:LoginName ID="LoginName1" Runat="server" />
  </LoggedInTemplate>
</asp:LoginView>
```

Finally, to validate the site layout, you add a contentplaceholder control. This control is where the actual content will appear on other pages.

```
<asp:contentplaceholder id="ContentPlaceHolder1"
runat="server"></asp:contentplaceholder>
```

The change you make to the default page is to add the hookup to the master page and change the title to Home.

```
<%@ Page Language="VB" AutoEventWireup="false" CodeFile="Default.aspx.vb"
Inherits="_Default" MasterPageFile="~/Main.master" Title="Home" %>
```

For the Login page, you change the title, add the Content control, and hook it up with the contentplaceholder you add on the master page. This is where you allow content to be added throughout the site.

Inside the Content control, you place a Login control, and it is displayed in the appropriate location on the page. The Login control has all of the logic you need built in.

```
<%@ Page Language="VB" MasterPageFile="~/Main.master" Title="Change Password" %>

<asp:Content ID="Content2" ContentPlaceHolderID="ContentPlaceHolder1"
Runat="Server">
    <asp:ChangePassword ID="ChangePassword1" Runat="server">
    </asp:ChangePassword>
</asp:Content>
```

For the Change Password page, you change the title, add the Content control, and hook it up with the contentplaceholder you add on the master page.

Inside the Content control, you place the ChangePassword control, and it is displayed in the appropriate location on the page. The ChangePassword control has all of the logic you need built in.

```
<%@ Page Language="VB" MasterPageFile="~/Main.master" Title="Change Password"
%>
<asp:Content ID="Content2" ContentPlaceHolderID="ContentPlaceHolder1"
Runat="Server">
    <asp:ChangePassword ID="ChangePassword1" Runat="server">
    </asp:ChangePassword>
</asp:Content>
```

For the Create New User page, you change the title, add the `Content` control, and hook it up with the `contentplaceholder` you add on the master page.

Inside the `Content` control, you place the `CreateUserWizard` control, and it is displayed in the appropriate location on the page. The `CreateUserWizard` control has all of the logic you need built in.

```
<%@ Page Language="VB" MasterPageFile="~/Main.master" Title="Create New
Account" %>

<asp:Content ID="Content2" ContentPlaceHolderID="ContentPlaceHolder1"
Runat="Server">
    <asp:CreateUserWizard ID="CreateUserWizard1" Runat="server">
    </asp:CreateUserWizard>
</asp:Content>
```

For the View Authors page, you change the title, add the `Content` control, and hook it up with the `contentplaceholder` you add on the master page.

Inside the `Content` control you place the `Label` control, and it is displayed in the appropriate location on the page. This page is left without functionality for this project.

```
<%@ Page Language="VB" MasterPageFile="~/Main.master" Title="View Authors" %>
<asp:Content ID="Cnt1" ContentPlaceHolderID="ContentPlaceHolder1"
Runat="server">
    <asp:Label ID="Label1" Runat="server" Text="Add Code to View Author Info
Later"></asp:Label>
</asp:Content>
```

For the View Titles page, you change the title, add the `Content` control, and hook it up with the `contentplaceholder` you add on the master page.

You place the `Label` control inside of the `Content` control, and it is displayed in the appropriate location on the page. This page is left without functionality for this project.

```
<%@ Page Language="VB" MasterPageFile="~/Main.master" Title="View Titles" %>
<asp:Content ID="Cnt1" ContentPlaceHolderID="ContentPlaceHolder1"
Runat="server">
    <asp:Label ID="Label1" Runat="server" Text="Add Code to View Title Info
Later"></asp:Label>
</asp:Content>
```

For the View Users page, you change the title, add the `Content` control, and hook it up with the `contentplaceholder` you add on the master page.

Inside the `Content` control, you place the `Label` control, and it is displayed in the appropriate location on the page. This page is left without functionality for this project.

```
<%@ Page Language="VB" MasterPageFile="~/Main.master" Title="View Users" %>
<asp:Content ID="Cnt1" ContentPlaceHolderID="ContentPlaceHolder1"
Runat="server">
    <asp:Label ID="Label1" Runat="server" Text="Add Code to View User Info
Later"></asp:Label>
</asp:Content>
```

You cannot access the View Users page yet. When you try, you are sent to the Login.aspx page, because you are not a member of the Admin role. You add the Admin user to the Admin role in the next Try It Out.

Try It Out **Managing Roles**

The Web Site Administration Tool has an interface to manage roles.

1. To open the tool, click Website ⇨ ASP.NET Configuration. From the home page, choose the Security tab. On the bottom half of the screen, you will see a table of options for Roles. Click the link to Create or Manage Roles (see Figure 19-15).

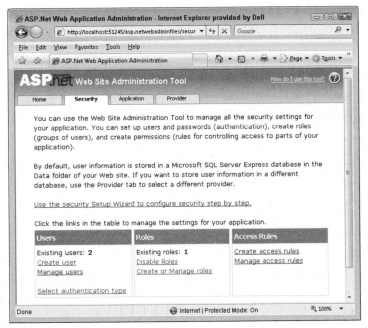

Figure 19-15

2. On the next screen, you will see a list of roles for the web site. The only role will be Admin. Click Manage for the Admin role, as shown in Figure 19-16.

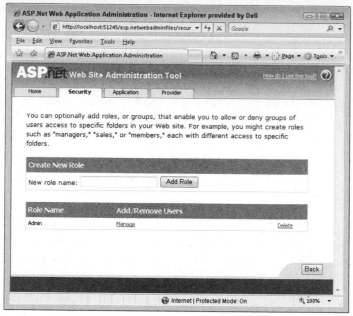

Figure 19-16

3. Click the link for user names starting with the letter *A*. All of the users that match your criteria will be available to add to the Admin role. Select the check box User Is In Role to add the Admin user to the role, as shown in Figure 19-17. Clicking the box adds the user to the role. After you click the check box, close the browser and see whether you can access the View Users page. You should be able to access the page now.

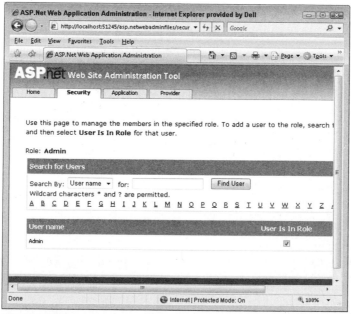

Figure 19-17

How It Works

When you make the change to the Admin folder, which contains the View Users page, only users that are part of the Admin role are allowed access. The tool allows you to add the Admin user to the Admin role. When this is done, the Admin user can access the Admin folder and therefore the View Users page.

Summary

In this chapter, you built the skeleton for a functional web site with security. You used built-in controls and what you learned in Chapter 17 to complete a site with no Visual Basic code. The controls were self-contained, and the default values worked well.

You were able to set up security using the WAT. You saw how easy it was to enforce forms authentication in ASP.NET. After you completed the work in this chapter, you should have been flabbergasted. The amount of code required to implement these features in ASP.NET was reduced to almost nothing. You saw the future of web development in this chapter.

To summarize, you should know how to:

❑   Use the Web Site Administration Tool

❑   Define site layout using master pages

❑   Implement site security using forms authentication

❑   Apply role management to site security

❑   Work with the built-in Login controls

Exercises

1.   Change the font to appear red for an asp:label control using the Main.skin page (created in TheClub site already) for every page under the Members directory. To do this, you can change the theme attribute on every page or change the web.config file for the directory. For this exercise, change the web.config file. You have not seen the web.config file syntax for this, so I will show it to you. Add the change to the web.config file that will apply the theme to the Web Forms under the Members folder. Use the code snippet here as a guide:

```
<configuration>
    <system.web>
        <pages theme="MainTheme" />
        <authorization>
            <deny users="?" />
        </authorization>
    </system.web>
</configuration>
```

2. The Login controls you used in this chapter are fully customizable. In this exercise, you will make some a change to the look of the login control on the Login.aspx page. Change the font color of the Login control to red by adding the tag and font color properties to the Main.skin file. Point the web.config file under the root folder to use the MainTheme. (You did this in Exercise 1 under a different directory.)

Visual Basic 2008 and XML

Put simply, Extensible Markup Language (XML) is used for exchanging data between applications. Although it has been around for some time, XML has established itself as the de facto data exchange standard for Internet applications. Today, XML is used not only on the Internet but to exchange data between many different platforms and applications.

In this chapter, you are not going to get bogged down in the details regarding XML such as its validation and well-formedness. Instead, you get a general introduction to XML, and then you look at its role with Visual Basic 2008. After that, you focus on using XML inside an application.

In this chapter, you:

- ❑ Gain a deeper understanding of XML and what it looks like
- ❑ Learn how to read and write XML files
- ❑ Learn how to serialize and deserialize XML data
- ❑ Learn how to navigate through an XML document
- ❑ Learn how to change existing XML data and add new data to an XML document

Understanding XML

The need for XML is simple: In commercial environments, applications need to exchange information in order to integrate. This integration is more applicable to the line-of-business software that a company may have rather than to desktop productivity applications such as Microsoft Office. For example, a company may have invested in a piece of software that allows it to track the stock in its warehouse — that piece of software would be an example of line-of-business software.

Integration has traditionally been very difficult to do, and XML, together with web services are technologies designed to reduce the difficulty and cost involved in software integration. In reducing the difficulty of software integration, there is a knock-on benefit in terms of the ease with which more general data/information exchange can occur.

For example, imagine you are a coffee retailer who wants to place an order with a supplier. The old-school technique of doing this is to phone or fax your order. However, this introduces a human element into the equation. It is likely that your own line-of-business applications (telling you what products you have sold) are suggesting that you buy more of a certain machine or certain blend of coffee. From that suggestion, you formulate an order and transmit it to your supplier. In the case of phone or fax orders, a human being at the supplier then has to transcribe the order into his or her own line-of-business system for processing.

An alternative way of carrying out this order would be to get the suggestion that has been raised by your line-of-business system to create an order automatically in the remote system of your supplier. This makes life easier and more efficient for both you and the management of your chosen supplier. However, getting to a point where the two systems are integrated in this way requires a lot of negotiation, coordination, and cost. Thus, it is relevant only for people doing a lot of business with each other.

Before the Internet, for two companies to integrate in this way, specific negotiations had to be undertaken to set up some sort of proprietary connection between the two companies. With the connection in place, data is exchanged not only in order to place the order with the supplier, but also for the supplier to report the status of the order back to the customer. With the Internet, this proprietary connection is no longer required. As long as both parties are on the Internet, data exchange can take place.

However, without a common language for this data exchange to be based on, the problem is only half solved. XML is this common language. As the customer, you can create an XML document that contains the details of the order. You can use the Internet to transmit that order written in XML to the supplier, either over the Web, through e-mail, or by using web services. The supplier receives the XML document, decodes it, and raises the order in their system. Likewise, if the supplier needs to report anything back to the customer, they can construct a different document (again using XML), and use the Internet to transmit it back again.

The actual structure of the data contained within the XML document is up to the customer and supplier to decide. (Usually it's for the supplier to decide upon and the customer to adhere to.) This is where the *extensible* in XML comes in. Any two parties who wish to exchange data using XML are completely free to decide exactly what the documents should look like.

This does not sound amazing, because companies in the past and even today still use comma-separated files. These files had a format and worked similarly. So what does XML have that the previous formats did not?

XML is a lot more descriptive, and it can be validated against a schema. A schema defines what the XML document or fragment should look like. Even without a schema, XML can potentially describe itself well enough for others to ascertain what the data is. In line with the benefits of previous file formats, XML is also a text-based format. This means that XML can be moved between platforms using Internet technologies such as e-mail, the Web, FTP, and other file copy techniques. Traditional software integration was difficult when binary data had to be moved between platforms such as Windows, Unix, Macintosh, AS/400, or OS/390, so the fact that XML is text-based makes it easier to send data across platforms.

What Does XML Look Like?

If you have any experience with HTML, XML is going to look familiar to you. In fact, both have a common ancestor in Standard Generalized Markup Language (SGML). In many ways, XML is not a language, as the name suggests, but is rather a set of rules for *defining your own* markup languages that allow the exchange of data. XML is not a stand-alone technology either; in fact, a whole lot of different related specifications dictate what you can and cannot do with XML. Such specifications include the following (not the best late-night reading, at least if you want to be an alert and attentive reader):

- ❑ URI (Uniform Resource Identifiers): `www.ietf.org/rfc/rfc2396.txt`
- ❑ UTF-8 (Unicode Transformation Format): `www.utf-8.com/`
- ❑ XML (Extensible Markup Language): `www.w3.org/TR/REC-xml`
- ❑ XML Schema: `www.w3.org/XML/Schema`
- ❑ XML Information Set: `www.w3.org/TR/xml-infoset/`

Although the specifications may not beat a book such as this in terms of format, layout, and ease of understanding, they have a whole lot to offer the XML fan. If you feel up to it, you can read more about XML after this introduction.

XML is tag based, meaning that the document is made up of *tags* that contain data. Here is how you might choose to describe this book in XML:

```
<Book>
    <Title>Beginning VB 2008</Title>
    <ISBN>xxxx191347</ISBN>
    <Publisher>Wrox</Publisher>
</Book>
```

In XML, you delimit tags using the < and > symbols. There are two sorts of tags: start tags such as `<Title>` and end tags such as `</Title>`. Together, the tags and the content between them are known as an *element*. In the previous example, the `Title` element is written like this:

```
<Title>Beginning VB 2008 </Title>
```

The `ISBN` element looks like this:

```
<ISBN>xxxx191347</ISBN>
```

And the `Publisher` element looks like this:

```
<Publisher>Wrox</Publisher>
```

Note that elements can contain other elements. In this case, for example, the `Book` element contains three subelements:

```
<Book>
    <Title>Beginning VB 2008</Title>
    <ISBN>xxxx191347</ISBN>
    <Publisher>Wrox</Publisher>
</Book>
```

The structure formed by elements nested inside other elements can also be represented as a tree with, for example, `Title`, `ISBN`, *and* `Publisher` *as branches from the root Book. Therefore, many use terms such as* node, parent, *and* child *instead of* element.

If you were given this XML document, you would need to have an understanding of its structure. Usually, the company that designed the structure of the document will tell you what it looks like. In this case, someone might tell you that if you first look for the Book element and then the Title element, you will determine the title of the book. The value between the `<Title>` start tag and the `</Title>` end tag is the title (in this case, Beginning VB 2008.)

As in HTML, XML can also use what are known as attributes. An *attribute* is a named piece of information descriptive to the node (element) wherein it is located. When you use attributes, you must enclose them in quotes. Here is the same XML fragment as the previous one, but this time using attributes:

```
<Book>
    <Title ISBN="xxxx191347">Beginning VB 2008</Title>
<Publisher>Wrox</Publisher>
</Book>
```

XML is largely common sense, which is one of the things that make it so simple. For example, you can probably guess what this document represents, even though you may have only just started thinking about XML:

```
<Books>
    <Book>
        <Title>Beginning VB 2008 </Title>
        <ISBN>xxxx191347</ISBN>
        <Publisher>Wrox</Publisher>
    </Book>
    <Book>
        <Title>Professional Visual Basic.Net</Title>
        <ISBN>1861005555</ISBN>
        <Publisher>Wrox</Publisher>
    </Book>
</Books>
```

XML for Visual Basic Newcomers

As a newcomer to programming and Visual Basic, it is unlikely that you will be undertaking projects that involve complex integration work. If XML is so popular because it makes systems integration so much easier, how is it relevant to a newcomer?

The answer to this question is that, in addition to being a great tool for integration, XML is also a great tool for storage and general data organization. Before XML, the two ways that an application could store its data were by using a separate database or by having its own proprietary file format with code that could save into and read from it.

In many cases, a database is absolutely the right tool for the job, because you need the fast access, shared storage, and advanced searching facilities that a database such as Access or SQL Server gives you. In other cases, such as with a graphics package or word processor, building your own proprietary format is the right way to go. The reasons for this may be you want the application to be light and do not want to have the hassle of showing the user how to set up and maintain a database, or simply do not want to deal with the licensing implications of needing a separate application to support yours.

XML gives you a new way of storing application data, although it is still based on the concept of defining your own proprietary application storage format. The key difference, in contrast to formats such as .doc files for Word documents, however, is that the XML storage format is a universal standard.

The Address Book Project

You're going to build a demonstration application that allows you to create an XML file format for an address book. You'll be able to create a list of new addresses and save the whole lot as an XML file on your local disk. You'll also be able to load the XML file and walk through the addresses one by one.

Creating the Project

As always, the first thing you have to do is to create a new project.

Try It Out   **Creating the Project**

1. Open Visual Studio 2008 and select File ⇨ New Project from the menu. Create a new Visual Basic .NET Windows Forms Application project and name it **Address Book**.

2. The Form Designer for Form1 will open. Change its Text property to **Address Book**. Now add 10 text boxes, 12 labels, and a button to the form so that it looks like Figure 20-1. Note that you have grid alignment bars to help align the controls on the form. Another option for aligning controls is to use the Format menu.

Figure 20-1

3. The text boxes should be named as follows:

   1. **txtFirstName**

   2. **txtLastName**

   3. **txtCompanyName**

   4. **txtAddress1**

   5. **txtAddress2**

   6. **txtCity**

   7. **txtRegion**

   8. **txtPostalCode**

   9. **txtCountry**

   10. **txtEmail**

4. Set the text properties of the labels and button to match Figure 20-1.

5. The button should be named **btnSave**. Finally, the Label control marked (number) should be called **lblAddressNumber**.

That's all you need to do with respect to form design. Let's move on and write some code to save the data as an XML file.

The SerializableData Class

Your application is going to have two classes: Address and AddressBook. Address will be used to store a single instance of a contact in the address book. AddressBook will store your entire list of addresses and provide ways for you to navigate through the book.

Both of these classes will be inherited from another class called SerializableData. This base class will contain the logic needed for saving the addresses to disk and loading them back again. In XML parlance, the saving process is known as *serialization* and the loading process is known as *deserialization*. In this next Try It Out, you're going to build the SerializableData and Address classes so that you can demonstrate saving a new address record to disk.

Try It Out   **Building SerializableData**

1. The first class you need to build is the base SerializableData class. Using the Solution Explorer, right-click the Address Book project and select Add ➪ Class. Call the new class **SerializableData** and click Add.

2. Right-click the project in Solution Explorer and choose Add Reference. Click the .NET tab and then select System.XML.dll. Next, add these namespace import directives at the top of the class definition:

```
Imports System.IO
Imports System.Xml.Serialization
Public Class SerializableData
End Class
```

3. Next, add these two methods to the class:

```
' Save - serialize the object to disk...
Public Sub Save(ByVal filename As String)
    ' make a temporary filename...
    Dim tempFilename As String
    tempFilename = filename & ".tmp"
    ' does the file exist?
    Dim tempFileInfo As New FileInfo(tempFilename)
    If tempFileInfo.Exists = True Then tempFileInfo.Delete()
    ' open the file...
    Dim stream As New FileStream(tempFilename, FileMode.Create)
    ' save the object...
    Save(stream)
    ' close the file...
    stream.Close()
    ' remove the existing data file and
    ' rename the temp file...
    tempFileInfo.CopyTo(filename, True)
    tempFileInfo.Delete()
End Sub
' Save - actually perform the serialization...
Public Sub Save(ByVal stream As Stream)
    ' create a serializer...
    Dim serializer As New XmlSerializer(Me.GetType)
    ' save the file...
    serializer.Serialize(stream, Me)
End Sub
```

4. Add a new class called **Address**. Set the class to derive from SerializableData, like this:

```
Public Class Address
    Inherits SerializableData
End Class
```

5. Next, add the members to the class that will be used to store the address details:

```
Public Class Address
    Inherits SerializableData

    ' members...
    Public FirstName As String
    Public LastName As String
```

```
        Public CompanyName As String
        Public Address1 As String
        Public Address2 As String
        Public City As String
        Public Region As String
        Public PostalCode As String
        Public Country As String
        Public Email As String
End Class
```

6. Go back to the Form Designer for Form1 and double-click the Save button to have the `Click` event handler created. Add this highlighted code to it:

```
Private Sub btnSave_Click(ByVal sender As System.Object, _
    ByVal e As System.EventArgs) Handles btnSave.Click
    ' create a new address object...
    Dim address As New Address()
    ' copy the values from the form into the address...
    PopulateAddressFromForm(address)
    ' save the address...
    Dim filename As String = DataFilename
    address.Save(filename)
    ' tell the user...
    MsgBox("The address was saved to " & filename)
End Sub
```

7. Visual Studio highlights the fact that you haven't defined the `DataFilename` property or the `PopulateAddressFromForm` method by underlining these respective names. To remove these underlines, first add the `DataFileName` property to the Form1 code:

```
' DataFilename - where should we store our data?
Public ReadOnly Property DataFilename() As String
    Get
        ' get our working folder...
        Dim folder As String
        folder = Environment.CurrentDirectory
        ' return the folder with the name "Addressbook.xml"...
        Return folder & "\AddressBook.xml"
    End Get
End Property
```

8. Now you need to add the `PopulateAddressFromForm` method to your Form1 code:

```
' PopulateAddressFromForm - populates Address from the form fields...
Public Sub PopulateAddressFromForm(ByVal address As Address)
    ' copy the values...
    address.FirstName = txtFirstName.Text
    address.LastName = txtLastName.Text
    address.CompanyName = txtCompanyName.Text
    address.Address1 = txtAddress1.Text
```

```
        address.Address2 = txtAddress2.Text
        address.City = txtCity.Text
        address.Region = txtRegion.Text
        address.PostalCode = txtPostalCode.Text
        address.Country = txtCountry.Text
        address.Email = txtEmail.Text
    End Sub
```

9.   Run the project and fill in an address.

10.   Click the Save button. A message box lets you know where the file has been saved.

11.   Use Windows Explorer to navigate to the folder that this XML file has been saved into. Double-click it, and Internet Explorer should open and list the contents. What you see should be similar to the contents listed here:

```
<?xml version="1.0" encoding="utf-8"?>
<Address xmlns:xsi="http://www.w3.org/2001/XMLSchema-instance"
    xmlns:xsd="http://www.w3.org/2001/XMLSchema">
  <FirstName>Bryan</FirstName>
  <LastName>Newsome</LastName>
  <CompanyName>Wiley Publishing</CompanyName>
  <Address1>11 First Avenue</Address1>
  <Address2 />
  <City>No where</City>
  <Region>South East</Region>
  <PostalCode>28222</PostalCode>
  <Country>USA</Country>
  <Email>Bryan@email.com</Email>
</Address>
```

How It Works

Look at the XML that's been returned. For this discussion, you can ignore the first line, starting `<?xml`, because all that's doing is saying, "Here is an XML version 1.0 document." You can also ignore the `xmlns` attributes on the first and second lines, because all they are doing is providing some extra information about the file, which at this level is something that you can let .NET worry about and don't need to get involved with. With those two parts removed, this is what you get:

```
<Address>
  <FirstName>Bryan</FirstName>
  <LastName>Newsome</LastName>
  <CompanyName>Wiley Publishing</CompanyName>
  <Address1>11 First Avenue</Address1>
  <Address2 />
  <City>No where</City>
  <Region>South East</Region>
  <PostalCode>28222</PostalCode>
  <Country>USA</Country>
  <Email>Bryan@email.com</Email>
</Address>
```

You can see how this is pretty similar to the code described previously in this chapter — you have start tags and end tags, and when taken together these tags form an element. Each element contains data, and it's pretty obvious that, for example, the CompanyName element contains Bryan's company name.

You'll notice as well that there are Address start and end tags at the top and at the bottom of the document. All of the other elements are enclosed by these tags, and this means that each of the elements in the middle belongs to the Address element. The Address element is the first element in the document and is therefore known as the *top-level element* or *root element*.

> It's worth noting that an XML document can only have one root element; all other elements in the document are child elements of this root.

Look at the <Address2 /> line. By placing the slash at the end of the tag, what you're saying is that the element is empty. You could have written this as <Address2></Address2>, but this would have used more storage space in the file. The XmlSerializer class itself chooses the naming of the tags, which is discussed later in this chapter.

So now you know what was created; but how did you get there? Follow the path of the application from the clicking of the Save button.

The first thing this method did was create a new Address object and call the PopulateAddressFromForm method. (This method just reads the Text property for every text box on the form and populates the matching property on the Address object.)

```
Private Sub btnSave_Click(ByVal sender As System.Object, _
    ByVal e As System.EventArgs) Handles btnSave.Click
    ' create a new address object...
    Dim address As New Address()
    ' copy the values from the form into the address...
    PopulateAddressFromForm(address)
```

Then, you ask the DataFilename property (which you wrote in step 7 of this Try It Out) to give you the name of a file that you can save the data to. You do this by using the Environment.CurrentDirectory property to return the folder that the address book is executing in and then tacking "\AddressBook.xml" to the end of this directory pathway. This is going to be the convention you use when saving and loading files with your application — you won't bother with giving the user the opportunity to save a specific file. Rather, you'll just assume that the file you want always has the same name and is always in the same place:

```
    ' save the address...
    Dim filename As String = DataFilename
```

You then call the Save method on the Address object. This method is inherited from SerializableData, and in a moment you'll take a look at what this method actually does. After you've saved the file, you tell the user where it is:

```
    address.Save(filename)
    ' tell the user...
    MsgBox ("The address was saved to " & filename)
End Sub
```

It's the two Save methods on SerializableData that are the really interesting part of this project. The first version of the method takes a file name and opens the file. The second version of the method actually saves the data using the `System.Xml.Serialization.XmlSerializer` class, as you'll soon see.

When you save the file, you want to be careful. You have to save over the top of an existing file, but you also want to make sure that, if the file save fails for any reason, you don't end up trashing the only good copy of the data the user has. This is a fairly common problem with a fairly common solution: You save the file to a different file, wait until you know that everything has been saved properly, and then replace the existing file with the new one.

To get the name of the new file, you just tack `.tmp` onto the end. So, if you had the file name given as `C:\MyPrograms\AddressBook\AddressBook.xml`, you'd actually try and save to `C:\MyPrograms\AddressBook\AddressBook.xml.tmp`. If this file exists, you delete it by calling the `Delete` method:

```
' Save - serialize the object to disk...
Public Sub Save(ByVal filename As String)
    ' make a temporary filename...
    Dim tempFilename As String
    tempFilename = filename & ".tmp"
    ' does the file exist?
    Dim tempFileInfo As New FileInfo(tempFilename)
    If tempFileInfo.Exists = True Then tempFileInfo.Delete()
```

When the existing `.tmp` file is gone, you can create a new file. This returns a `System.IO.FileStream` object:

```
    ' open the file...
    Dim stream As New FileStream(tempFilename, FileMode.Create)
```

You then pass this stream to another overloaded `Save` method. You'll go through this method in a moment, but for now all you need to know is that this method does the actual serialization of the data.

Then, you close the file:

```
    ' close the file...
    stream.Close()
```

Finally, you replace the existing file with the new file. You have to do this with `CopyTo` (the `True` parameter you pass to this method means: overwrite any existing file) and finally delete the temporary file:

```
    ' remove the existing data file and
    ' rename the temp file...
    tempFileInfo.CopyTo(filename, True)
    tempFileInfo.Delete()
End Sub
```

The other version of `Save` takes a `Stream` argument instead of a `String` and looks like this:

```
' Save - actually perform the serialization...
Public Sub Save(ByVal stream As Stream)
    ' create a serializer...
    Dim serializer As New XmlSerializer(Me.GetType)
    ' save the file...
    serializer.Serialize(stream, Me)
End Sub
```

The `System.Xml.Serialization.XmlSerializer` class is what you use to actually serialize the object to the stream that you specify. In this case, you're using a stream that points to a file, but later in this chapter you'll use a different kind of file.

`XmlSerializer` needs to know ahead of time what type of object it's saving. You use the `GetType` method to return a `System.Type` object that references the class that you actually are saving, which in this case is `Address`. The reason `XmlSerializer` needs to know the type is because it works by iterating through all of the properties on the object, looking for ones that are both readable and writable (in other words, ones that are not flagged as read-only or write-only). Every time it finds such a property, `XmlSerializer` writes the property to the stream, which in this case means that the property subsequently gets written to the `AddressBook.xml` file.

`XmlSerializer` bases the name of the element in the XML document on the name of the matching property. For example, the `FirstName` element in the document matches the `FirstName` property on `Address`. In addition, the top-level element of `Address` matches the name of the `Address` class; in other words, the root element name matches the class name. `XmlSerializer` is a great way of using XML in your programs because you don't need to mess around creating and manually reading XML documents — it does all the work for you.

Loading the XML File

Now you can load the address back from the XML file on the disk. In this next Try It Out, you'll be adding the methods necessary to deserialize the XML back into data that you can work with in your application.

Try It Out   **Loading the XML File**

1. Using the Solution Explorer, open the code editor for `SerializableData`. Add these two methods:

```
' Load - deserialize from disk...
Public Shared Function Load(ByVal filename As String, _
                ByVal newType As Type) As Object
    ' does the file exist?
    Dim fileInfo As New FileInfo(filename)
    If fileInfo.Exists = False Then
        ' create a blank version of the object and return that...
        Return System.Activator.CreateInstance(newType)
    End If
    ' open the file...
    Dim stream As New FileStream(filename, FileMode.Open)
    ' load the object from the stream...
    Dim newObject As Object = Load(stream, newType)
    ' close the stream...
    stream.Close()
    ' return the object...
```

```
        Return newObject
    End Function
    Public Shared Function Load(ByVal stream As Stream, _
                    ByVal newType As Type) As Object
        ' create a serializer and load the object....
        Dim serializer As New XmlSerializer(newType)
        Dim newObject As Object = serializer.Deserialize(stream)
        ' return the new object...
        Return newobject
    End Function
```

2. Go back to the Form Designer for Form1. Add a new button. Set the Text property of the new button to **&Load** and the Name to **btnLoad**.

3. Double-click the Load button and add the following highlighted code to the event handler:

```
Private Sub btnLoad_Click(ByVal sender As System.Object, _
        ByVal e As System.EventArgs) Handles btnLoad.Click
    ' load the address using a shared method on SerializableData...
    Dim newAddress As Address = _
     SerializableData.Load(DataFilename, GetType(Address))
    ' update the display...
    PopulateFormFromAddress(newAddress)
End Sub
```

4. You'll also need to add this method to Form1:

```
' PopulateFormFromAddress - populates the form from an
' address object...
Public Sub PopulateFormFromAddress(ByVal address As Address)
    ' copy the values...
    txtFirstName.Text = address.FirstName
    txtLastName.Text = address.LastName
    txtCompanyName.Text = address.CompanyName
    txtAddress1.Text = address.Address1
    txtAddress2.Text = address.Address2
    txtCity.Text = address.City
    txtRegion.Text = address.Region
    txtPostalCode.Text = address.PostalCode
    txtCountry.Text = address.Country
    txtEmail.Text = address.Email
End Sub
```

5. Run the project and click the Load button or press Alt + L. The address should be loaded from the XML file and displayed on the screen. After clicking the Load button, you should see what you typed and saved previously as shown in Figure 20-2.

Figure 20-2

How It Works

Deserialization is the opposite of serialization. It can be used to load the XML data from the file, whereas before you saved the XML data to the file. (Note that here I'm using the word file for simplification. In fact, you can serialize to and deserialize from any kind of stream.)

Whenever you ask XmlSerializer to deserialize an object for you, it creates a new object. You can use this functionality to get XmlSerializer to create a new object for you rather than having to create one yourself. This is a good candidate for an overloaded method on the SerializableData object. You create an overloaded method called Load, the first version of which takes a file name and also a System.Type object. This Type object represents the type of object you ultimately want to end up with. Specifically, you'll need to pass in a Type object that tells XmlSerializer where to find a list of properties that exist on your Address object.

Since XmlSerializer doesn't save .NET class namespaces or assembly information into the XML file, it relies on an explicit statement saying which class the file contains; otherwise things get ambiguous. (Imagine you had a hundred assemblies on your machine, each containing a class called Address. How could XmlSerializer know which one you mean?)

Obviously, when the method is called, the first thing you do is check to see whether the file exists. If it doesn't, you'll return a blank version of the object that you asked for.

```
' Load - deserialize from disk...
Public Shared Function Load(ByVal filename As String, _
                ByVal newType As Type) As Object
    ' does the file exist?
    Dim fileInfo As New FileInfo(filename)
    If fileInfo.Exists = False Then
        ' create a blank version of the object and return that...
        Return System.Activator.CreateInstance(newType)
    End If
```

If the file does exist, you open it and pass it to the other version of Load, which you'll see in a moment. You then close the file and return the new object to the caller:

```
' open the file...
Dim stream As New FileStream(filename, FileMode.Open)
' load the object from the stream...
Dim newObject As Object = Load(stream, newType)
' close the stream...
stream.Close()
' return the object...
Return newObject
End Function
```

The other version of Load uses the XmlSerializer again and, as you can see, it's no more complicated than when you used it last time. Except, of course, that the Deserialize method returns a new object to you:

```
Public Shared Function Load(ByVal stream As Stream, _
                ByVal newType As Type) As Object
    ' create a serializer and load the object....
    Dim serializer As New XmlSerializer(newType)
    Dim newObject As Object = serializer.Deserialize(stream)
    ' return the new object...
    Return newobject
End Function
```

When it's deserializing, XmlSerializer goes through each of the properties on the new object that it has created, again looking for ones that are both readable and writable. When it finds one, it takes the value stored against it in the XML document and sets the property. The result: You are given a new object, fully populated with the data from the XML document.

Once you've called Load and have gotten a new Address object back, you pass the new object to PopulateFormFromAddress:

```
Private Sub btnLoad_Click(ByVal sender As System.Object, _
        ByVal e As System.EventArgs) Handles btnLoad.Click
    ' load the address using a shared method on SerializableData...
    Dim newAddress As Address = _
      SerializableData.Load(DataFilename, GetType(Address))
    ' update the display...
    PopulateFormFromAddress(newAddress)
End Sub
```

Changing the Data

To prove that nothing funny is going on, in the next Try It Out you'll change the XML file using Notepad and try clicking the Load button again.

Changing the Data

1. Open Windows Notepad and load the XML file into it. Inside the `FirstName` element, change the name that you entered to something else. Then save the file and exit Notepad.

2. Go back to the Address Book program. Click the Load button again. The new name that you entered will be loaded.

How It Works

What you've done here is proven that `XmlSerializer` does indeed use the `AddressBook.xml` file as the source of its data. You changed the data, and when you loaded the `Address` object again, the `FirstName` property had indeed been changed to the new name that you entered.

Sending E-mail

For the following Try It Out, you'll see how you can integrate this application with an e-mail client such as Outlook or Outlook Express using the e-mail data from your addresses. You'll be using the Process class to start the e-mail client associated with the `mailto` protocol, as you will see in a few moments.

Sending E-mail from the Client

1. Go back to the Form1 designer and, using the Toolbox, draw a LinkLabel control underneath the Email label. Set its `Text` property to **Send Email** and change its `Name` property to **lnkSendEmail** as shown in Figure 20-3.

Figure 20-3

Note that this will work with a normal Button control, too.

2. Double-click the LinkLabel control. This creates an event handler for the `LinkClicked` event. Add this code:

```
Private Sub lnkSendEmail_LinkClicked(ByVal sender As System.Object, _
   ByVal e As System.Windows.Forms.LinkLabelLinkClickedEventArgs) _
   Handles lnkSendEmail.LinkClicked
      ' start the e-mail client...
      System.Diagnostics.Process.Start("mailto:" & txtEmail.Text)
End Sub
```

3. Run the project and click the Load button. Ensure you have an e-mail address entered in the Email field and then click the Send Email link. Your e-mail client should display a new mail message with the To: field filled in with your e-mail address.

How It Works

Windows has a built-in capability to decode Internet addresses and fire up the programs that are associated with them.

When an e-mail client such as Outlook or Outlook Express is installed, it registers a protocol called `mailto` with Windows, just as, when a web browser such as Internet Explorer is installed, it registers the protocol HTTP, familiar to anyone who browses the Web.

If you were to close the mail message, click the Start button from the Windows task bar, select Run, enter mailto: followed by the e-mail address from your program, and then click OK, the same mail message would appear.

In your code, you take the current value of the txtEmail field and put `mailto:` at the beginning. This turns the e-mail address into a URL. You then call the shared `Start` method on the `System.Diagnostics.Process` class, passing it this URL:

```
Private Sub lnkSendEmail_LinkClicked(ByVal sender As System.Object, _
   ByVal e As System.Windows.Forms.LinkLabelLinkClickedEventArgs) _
   Handles lnkSendEmail.LinkClicked
      ' start the e-mail client...
      System.Diagnostics.Process.Start("mailto:" & txtEmail.Text)
End Sub
```

The `Start` method behaves in exactly the same way as the Run dialog box does. Both tap into Windows' built-in URL-decoding functionality. In this case, you've used this functionality to integrate your application with Outlook. However, if you'd specified a protocol of `http:` rather than `mailto:`, your application could have opened a web page. Likewise, if you had supplied a path to a Word document, or Excel spreadsheet, the application could open those too. Note that when you're working with a file, you don't need to supply a protocol — for example, you only need to do this:

```
c:\My Files\My Budget.xls
```

Creating a List of Addresses

The purpose of this Try It Out is to build an application that allows you to store a list of addresses in XML. At the moment you can successfully load just one address, so now you have to turn your attention to managing a list of addresses.

The class you're going to build to do this is called AddressBook. This class will inherit from SerializableData because ultimately you want to get to a point where you can tell the AddressBook object to load and save itself to the XML file without you having to do anything.

Try It Out   **Creating AddressBook**

1. Using Solution Explorer, create a new class called AddressBook.

2. Add this namespace declaration:

```
Imports System.Xml.Serialization
Public Class AddressBook
End Class
```

3. Set the class to inherit from SerializableData as shown in the highlighted code:

```
Imports System.Xml.Serialization
Public Class AddressBook
    Inherits SerializableData
End Class
```

4. To store the addresses, you're going to use a System.Collections.ArrayList object. You also need a method that you can use to create new addresses in the list. Add the following highlighted member and method to the class:

```
Imports System.Xml.Serialization
Public Class AddressBook
    Inherits SerializableData
    ' members...
    Public Items As New ArrayList()
    ' AddAddress - add a new address to the book...
    Public Function AddAddress() As Address
        ' create one...
        Dim newAddress As New Address()
        ' add it to the list...
        Items.Add(newAddress)
        ' return the address...
        Return newAddress
    End Function
End Class
```

5. Open the Code Editor for Form1. Add these members to the top of the class:

```
Public Class Form1
    ' members...
    Public AddressBook As AddressBook
    Private _currentAddressIndex As Integer
```

6. Next, add this property to Form1:

```
' CurrentAddress - property for the current address...
ReadOnly Property CurrentAddress() As Address
    Get
        Return AddressBook.Items(CurrentAddressIndex - 1)
    End Get
End Property
```

7. Then add this property to Form1:

```
' CurrentAddressIndex - property for the current address...
Property CurrentAddressIndex() As Integer
    Get
        Return _currentAddressIndex
    End Get
    Set(ByVal Value As Integer)
        ' set the address...
        _currentAddressIndex = Value
        ' update the display...
        PopulateFormFromAddress(CurrentAddress)
        ' set the label...
        lblAddressNumber.Text = _
        _currentAddressIndex & " of " & AddressBook.Items.Count
    End Set
End Property
```

8. Double-click the form to create the Load event for Form1 and add this highlighted code to the handler:

```
Private Sub Form1_Load(ByVal sender As System.Object, _
        ByVal e As System.EventArgs) Handles MyBase.Load
    ' load the address book...
    AddressBook = _
      SerializableData.Load(DataFilename, GetType(AddressBook))
    ' if the address book only contains one item, add a new one...
    If AddressBook.Items.Count = 0 Then AddressBook.AddAddress()
    ' select the first item in the list...
    CurrentAddressIndex = 1
End Sub
```

9. Now that you can load the address book, you need to be able to save the changes. From the left drop-down list, select (Form1 Events). From the right list, select FormClosed. Add the highlighted code to the event handler, and also add the SaveChanges and UpdateCurrentAddress methods:

```
Private Sub Form1_FormClosed(ByVal sender As Object, ByVal e As _
    System.Windows.Forms.FormClosedEventArgs) Handles Me.FormClosed
    ' save the changes...
    UpdateCurrentAddress()
    SaveChanges()
End Sub
```

```
' SaveChanges - save the address book to an XML file...
Public Sub SaveChanges()
    ' tell the address book to save itself...
    AddressBook.Save(DataFilename)
End Sub
' UpdateCurrentAddress - make sure the book has the current
' values currently entered into the form...
Private Sub UpdateCurrentAddress()
    PopulateAddressFromForm(CurrentAddress)
End Sub
```

Before you run the project, it's very important that you delete the existing AddressBook.xml *file. If you don't,* XmlSerializer *will try to load an* AddressBook *object from a file containing an* Address *object, and an exception will be thrown.*

10. Run the project. Don't bother entering any information into the form, because the save routine won't work — we've deliberately introduced a bug to illustrate an issue with XmlSerializer. Close the form, and you should see the exception thrown as shown in Figure 20-4:

Figure 20-4

How It Works (or Why It Doesn't!)

When the form is loaded, the first thing you do is ask SerializableData to create a new AddressBook object from the AddressBook.xml file. Because you deleted this before you ran the project, this file won't exist, and, as you recall, you rigged the Load method so that if the file didn't exist it would just create an instance of whatever class you asked for. In this case, you get an `AddressBook`:

```
Private Sub Form1_Load(ByVal sender As System.Object, _
        ByVal e As System.EventArgs) Handles MyBase.Load
    ' load the address book...
    AddressBook = _
        SerializableData.Load(DataFilename, GetType(AddressBook))
```

However, the new address book won't have any addresses in it. You ask `AddressBook` to create a new address if the list is empty:

```
    ' if the address book only contains one item, add a new one...
    If AddressBook.Items.Count = 0 Then AddressBook.AddAddress()
```

At this point, either you'll have an `AddressBook` object that's been loaded from the file and therefore contains a set of `Address` objects, or you'll have a new `AddressBook` object that contains one, blank address. You set the `CurrentAddressIndex` property to 1, meaning the first item in the list:

```
    ' select the first item in the list...
    CurrentAddressIndex = 1
End Sub
```

The setter for the `CurrentAddressIndex` property does a number of things. First, it updates the private `_currentAddressIndex` member:

```
' CurrentAddressIndex - property for the current address...
Property CurrentAddressIndex() As Integer
    Get
        Return _currentAddressIndex
    End Get
    Set(ByVal Value As Integer)
        ' set the address...
        _currentAddressIndex = Value
```

Then the setter uses the `CurrentAddress` property to get the `Address` object that corresponds to whatever `_currentAddressIndex` is set to. This `Address` object is passed to `PopulateFormFromAddress`, whose job it is to update the display:

```
        ' update the display...
        PopulateFormFromAddress(CurrentAddress)
```

Finally, it changes the `lblAddressNumber` control so that it displays the current record number:

```
        ' set the label...
        lblAddressNumber.Text = _
            _currentAddressIndex & " of " & AddressBook.Items.Count
    End Set
End Property
```

You'll just quickly look at `CurrentAddress`. This property's job is to turn an integer index into the corresponding `Address` object stored in `AddressBook`. However, because `AddressBook` works on the basis of an `ArrayList` object that numbers items from `0`, and your application starts numbering items at `1`, you have to decrement your index value by 1 to get the matching value from `AddressBook`:

```
' CurrentAddress - property for the current address...
ReadOnly Property CurrentAddress() As Address
    Get
        Return AddressBook.Items(CurrentAddressIndex - 1)
    End Get
End Property
```

All good so far, but why is `XmlSerializer` throwing an exception? Well the problems occur when you close the application. This fires the `FormClosed` method, which ultimately calls the `Save` method of `AddressBook`.

As you know, to save an object to disk, `XmlSerializer` walks through each of the properties looking for ones that are readable and writable. So far, you've used `XmlSerializer` only with `System.String`, but when the object comes across a property that uses a complex type, such as `Address`, it uses the same principle — in other words, it looks through all of the properties that the complex type has. If properties on that that object return complex types, it will drill down again. What it's doing is looking for simple types that it knows how to turn into text and write to the XML document.

However, some types cannot be turned into text, and at this point `XmlSerializer` chokes. The `ArrayList` object that you're using to store a list of addresses had some properties that cannot be converted to text, which is the reason the exception is being thrown. What you need to do is provide an alternative property that `XmlSerializer` can hook into in order to get a list of addresses and tell it not to bother trying to serialize the `ArrayList`.

Ignoring Members

Although `XmlSerializer` cannot cope with certain data types, it has no problems with arrays. You've also seen that `XmlSerializer` has no problems with your `Address` class, simply because this object doesn't have any properties of a type that `XmlSerializer` cannot support. In the next Try It Out, you'll provide an alternative property that returns an array of `Address` objects and tells `XmlSerializer` to keep away from the `Items` property because `XmlSerializer` cannot deal with `ArrayList` objects.

Try It Out   Ignoring Members

1. Open the Code Editor for `AddressBook`. Find the `Items` property and prefix it with the `System.Xml.Serialization.XmlIgnore` attribute:

```
Public Class AddressBook
    Inherits SerializableData
    <XmlIgnore()>Public Items As New ArrayList
```

2. Now, add this new property to the `AddressBook` class:

```
' Addresses - property that works with the items
' collection as an array...
Public Property Addresses() As Address()
    Get
        ' create a new array...
        Dim addressArray(Items.Count - 1) As Address
        Items.CopyTo(addressArray)
        Return addressArray
    End Get
    Set(ByVal Value As Address())
        ' reset the arraylist...
        Items.Clear()
        ' did you get anything?
        If Not Value Is Nothing Then
            ' go through the array and populate items...
            Dim address As Address
            For Each address In Value
                Items.Add(address)
            Next
        End If
    End Set
End Property
```

3. Run the project and then close the application; this time everything functions correctly. Run the project again, and then enter some data into the address fields. Close the application and you should find that `AddressBook.xml` does contain data. (We've removed the `xmlns` and `?xml` values for clarity here.)

```
<AddressBook>
  <Addresses>
    <Address>
      <FirstName>Bryan</FirstName>
      <LastName>Newsome</LastName>
      <CompanyName>Wiley</CompanyName>
      <Address1>123 Main St</Address1>
      <Address2 />
      <City>Big City</City>
      <Region>SE</Region>
      <PostalCode>28222</PostalCode>
      <Country>USA</Country>
      <Email>Bryan@email.com</Email>
    </Address>
  </Addresses>
</AddressBook>
```

How It Works

The XML that got saved into your file proves that your approach works, but why?

At this point, your AddressBook object has two properties: Items and Addresses. Both are read/write properties, so both are going to be examined as candidates for serialization by XmlSerializer. As you know, Items returns an ArrayList object, and Addresses returns an array of Address objects.

However, you have now marked Items with the XmlIgnore attribute. This means, not surprisingly, that XmlSerializer ignores the property, despite the fact that it is readable and writable. Instead, the serializer moves on to the Addresses property.

The Get portion of the Addresses property is what interests you. All you do is create a new array of Address objects and use the CopyTo method on the ArrayList to populate it:

```
' Addresses - property that works with the items
' collection as an array...
Public Property Addresses() As Address()
    Get
        ' create a new array...
        Dim addressArray(Items.Count - 1) As Address
        Items.CopyTo(addressArray)
        Return addressArray
    End Get
    Set(ByVal Value As Address())
        ...
    End Set
End Property
```

When XmlSerializer gets an array of objects that it can deal with, all it does is iterate through the array, serializing each of these contained objects in turn. You can see this in the XML that you received: The structure of the XML contained within the Addresses element exactly matches the structure of the XML you saw when you tested the process and wrote a single Address object to the file:

```
<AddressBook>
  <Addresses>
    <Address>
      <FirstName>Bryan</FirstName>
      <LastName>Newsome</LastName>
      <CompanyName>Wiley</CompanyName>
      <Address1>123 Main St</Address1>
      <Address2 />
      <City>Big City</City>
      <Region>SE</Region>
      <PostalCode>28222</PostalCode>
      <Country>USA</Country>
      <Email>Bryan@email.com</Email>
    </Address>
  </Addresses>
</AddressBook>
```

Loading Addresses

If you're lucky, loading addresses should just work! Close the program and run the project again. You will see a record as shown in Figure 20-5: The Load button does not work at this point. Don't worry, you don't need it anymore.

Figure 20-5

You already set up the project to load the address book the first time you ran the project after creating the `AddressBook` class itself. This time, however, `AddressBook.Load` can find a file on the disk, and so, rather than creating a blank object, it's getting `XmlSerializer` to deserialize the lot. As `XmlSerializer` has no problems writing arrays, you can assume that it has no problem reading them.

It's the `Set` portion of the `Addresses` property that does the magic this time. When working with this property, be careful if you are passed a blank array (in other words, `Nothing`); you want to prevent exceptions being thrown:

```
' Addresses - property that works with the items
' collection as an array...
Public Property Addresses() As Address()
    Get
        ...
    End Get
    Set(ByVal Value As Address())
        ' reset the arraylist...
        Items.Clear()
        ' did you get anything?
        If Not Value Is Nothing Then
```

```
            ' go through the array and populate items...
            Dim address As Address
            For Each address In Value
                Items.Add(address)
            Next
        End If
        End Set
    End Property
```

For each of the values in the array, all you have to do is take each one in turn and add it to the list.

Adding New Addresses

Next, you'll look at how you can add new addresses to the list. In this Try It Out, you'll be adding four new buttons to your form. Two buttons allow you to navigate through the list of addresses, and two buttons allow you to add and delete addresses.

Try It Out   **Adding New Addresses**

1. Open the Form Designer for `Form1` and disable the Load and Save buttons before adding the four new buttons shown in Figure 20-6.

Figure 20-6

2. Name the buttons in turn **btnPrevious**, **btnNext**, **btnNew**, and **btnDelete** and set their `Text` properties to **Previous**, **Next**, **New**, and **Delete**, respectively.

3. Double-click the New button to create a `Click` handler. Add the highlighted line to the event handler, and also add the `AddNewAddress` method:

```
Private Sub btnNew_Click(ByVal sender As System.Object, _
        ByVal e As System.EventArgs) Handles btnNew.Click
    AddNewAddress()
End Sub
Public Function AddNewAddress() As Address
    ' save the current address...
    UpdateCurrentAddress()

    ' create a new address...
    Dim newAddress As Address = AddressBook.AddAddress
    ' update the display...
    CurrentAddressIndex = AddressBook.Items.Count
    ' return the new address...
    Return newAddress
End Function
```

4. Run the project. Click New and a new address record is created. Enter a new address:

5. Close the program and the changes will be saved. Open up `AddressBook.xml`, and you should see the new address.

How It Works

This time you have a new `Address` object added to the XML document. It is contained within the `Addresses` element, so you know that it is part of the same array.

The implementation was very simple — all you had to do was ask `AddressBook` to create a new address, and then you updated the `CurrentAddressIndex` property so that it equaled the number of items in the `AddressBook`. This had the effect of changing the display so that it went to record 2 of 2, ready for editing.

However, it is important that, before you actually do this, you save any changes that the user might have made. With this application, you are ensuring that any changes the user makes will always be persisted into the XML file. Whenever the user closes the application, creates a new record, or moves backward or forward in the list, you want to call `UpdateCurrentAddress` so that any changes are saved:

```
Public Function AddNewAddress() As Address
    ' save the current address...
    UpdateCurrentAddress()
```

After you've saved any changes, it is safe to create the new record and show the new record to the user:

```
    ' create a new address...
    Dim newAddress As Address = AddressBook.AddAddress
    ' update the display...
    CurrentAddressIndex = AddressBook.Items.Count
    ' return the new address...
    Return newAddress
End Function
```

Navigating Addresses

Now that you can add new addresses to the address book, you need to wire up the Next and Previous buttons so that you can move through the list. In this Try It Out, you'll be adding the code that reads the next or previous address from the array of addresses maintained by the AddressBook class. Before reading the next or previous address, however, you'll also want to ensure that any changes made to the current address are updated, and you'll be calling the appropriate procedures to update the current address before navigating to a new address.

Try It Out   **Navigating Addresses**

1. Open the Form Designer for Form1. Double-click the Next button to create a new Click handler. Add this code and the associated MoveNext method:

```
Private Sub btnNext_Click(ByVal sender As System.Object, _
    ByVal e As System.EventArgs) Handles btnNext.Click

    MoveNext()

End Sub

Public Sub MoveNext()
    ' get the next index...
    Dim newIndex As Integer = CurrentAddressIndex + 1
    If newIndex > AddressBook.Items.Count Then
        newIndex = 1
    End If
    ' save any changes...
    UpdateCurrentAddress()
    ' move the record...
    CurrentAddressIndex = newIndex
End Sub
```

2. Next, flip back to the Form Designer and double-click the Previous button. Add the highlighted code:

```
Private Sub btnPrevious_Click(ByVal sender As System.Object, _
    ByVal e As System.EventArgs) Handles btnPrevious.Click

    MovePrevious()

End Sub

Public Sub MovePrevious()
    ' get the previous index...
    Dim newIndex As Integer = CurrentAddressIndex - 1
    If newIndex = 0 Then
        newIndex = AddressBook.Items.Count
    End If
    ' save changes...
    UpdateCurrentAddress()
    ' move the record...
    CurrentAddressIndex = newIndex
End Sub
```

3. Run the project. You should now be able to move between addresses.

How It Works

All you've done here is wire up the buttons so that each one changes the current index. By incrementing the current index, you move forward in the list. By decrementing it, you move backward.

However, it's very important that you don't move outside the bounds of the list (in other words, try to move to a position before the first record or to a position after the last record), which is why you check the value and adjust it as appropriate. When you move forward (MoveNext), you flip to the beginning of the list if you go off the end. When you move backward (MovePrevious), you flip to the end if you go off the start.

In both cases, you make sure that before you actually change the CurrentAddressIndex property, you call UpdateCurrentAddress to save any changes:

```
Public Sub MoveNext()
    ' get the next index...
    Dim newIndex As Integer = CurrentAddressIndex + 1
    If newIndex > AddressBook.Items.Count Then
        newIndex = 1
    End If
    ' save any changes...
    UpdateCurrentAddress()
    ' move the record...
    CurrentAddressIndex = newIndex
End Sub
```

Deleting Addresses

To finish the functionality of your address book, you'll deal with deleting items. When deleting items, you must take into account that the item you are deleting is the last remaining item. In this case, you have to provide the appropriate code to add a new blank address. This Try It Out provides this and all necessary functionality to delete an address properly.

Try It Out   Deleting Addresses

1. Go back to the Form Designer for Form1 and double-click the Delete button. Add this code to the event handler, and also add the DeleteAddress method:

```
Private Sub btnDelete_Click(ByVal sender As System.Object, _
        ByVal e As System.EventArgs) Handles btnDelete.Click
    ' ask the user if they are ok with this?
    If MsgBox ("Are you sure you want to delete this address?", _
        MsgBoxStyle.Question Or MsgBoxStyle.YesNo) = _
        MsgBoxResult.Yes Then
        DeleteAddress(CurrentAddressIndex)
    End If
End Sub
```

```
' DeleteAddress - delete an address from the list...
Public Sub DeleteAddress(ByVal index As Integer)
    ' delete the item from the list...
    AddressBook.Items.RemoveAt(index - 1)
    ' was that the last address?
    If AddressBook.Items.Count = 0 Then
        ' add a new address?
        AddressBook.AddAddress()
    Else
        ' make sure you have something to show...
        If index > AddressBook.Items.Count Then
            index = AddressBook.Items.Count
        End If
    End If
    ' display the record...
    CurrentAddressIndex = index
End Sub
```

2. Run the project. You should be able to delete records from the address book. Note that if you delete the last record, a new record is automatically created.

How It Works

The algorithm you've used here to delete the records is an example of how to solve another classic programming problem.

Your application is set up so that it always has to display a record. That's why, when the program is first run and there is no `AddressBook.xml`, you automatically create a new record. Likewise, when an item is deleted from the address book, you have to find something to present to the user.

To physically delete an address from the disk, you use the `RemoveAt` method on the `ArrayList` that holds the `Address` objects.

```
' DeleteAddress - delete an address from the list...
Public Sub DeleteAddress(ByVal index As Integer)
    ' delete the item from the list...
    AddressBook.Items.RemoveAt(index - 1)
```

Again, notice here that, because you're working with a zero-based array, when you ask to delete the address with an index of 3, you actually have to delete the address at position 2 in the array.

The problems start after you've done that. It could be that you've deleted the one remaining address in the book. In this case, because you always have to display an address, you create a new one:

```
' was that the last address?
If AddressBook.Items.Count = 0 Then
    ' add a new address?
    AddressBook.AddAddress()
```

Alternatively, if there are items in the address book, you have to change the display. In some cases, the value that's currently stored in `CurrentAddressIndex` will be valid. For example, if you had five records and are looking at the third one, `_currentAddressIndex` will be 3. If you delete that record, you have four records, but the third one as reported by `_currentAddressIndex` is still 3 and is still valid. However, as 4 has now shuffled into 3's place, you need to update the display.

It could be the case that you've deleted the last item in the list. When this happens, the index isn't valid, because the index would be positioned over the end of the list. (Suppose you have four items in the list; delete the fourth one, and you only have three, but _currentAddressIndex would be 4, which isn't valid.) So, when the last item is deleted, the index will be over the end of the list, so you set it to be the last item in the list:

```
Else
    ' make sure you have something to show...
    If index > AddressBook.Items.Count Then
        index = AddressBook.Items.Count
    End If
End If
```

Whatever actually happens, you still need to update the display. As you know, the CurrentAddressIndex property can do this for you:

```
    ' display the record...
    CurrentAddressIndex = index
End Sub
```

Testing at the Edges

This brings us to a programming technique that can greatly help you test your applications. When writing software, things usually go wrong at the edge. For example, you have a function that takes an integer value, but in order for the method to work properly, the value supplied must lie between 0 and 99.

When your algorithm works properly when you give it a valid value, test some values at the boundaries of the valid data. For example: -1, 0, 99, and 100. In most cases, if your method works properly for one or two of the possible valid values, it works properly for the entire set of valid values. Testing a few values at the edge shows you where potential problems with the method lie.

A classic example of this is with your MoveNext and MovePrevious methods. If you had a hundred addresses in your address book and tested only that MoveNext and MovePrevious worked between numbers 10 and 20, it most likely would have worked between 1 and 100. However, the moment you move past 100 (in other words "go over the edge"), problems can occur. If you hadn't handled this case properly by flipping back to 1, your program would have crashed.

Integrating with the Address Book Application

So far, you've built an application that is able to save and load its data as an XML document. You've also taken a look at the document as it's been changing over the course of the chapter, so by now you should have a pretty good idea of what an XML document looks like and how it works.

The beginning of this chapter pitched XML as a technology for integrating software applications. It then went on to say that for newcomers to Visual Basic, using XML for integration is unlikely to be something that you would do on a day-to-day basis, and so you've been using XML to store data. In the rest of this chapter, we're going to demonstrate why XML is such a good technology for integration. What you'll do is build a separate application that, with very little work, is able to read in and understand the proprietary data format that you've used in AddressBook.xml.

Using XML is an advanced topic, so, if you would like to learn more about the technology and its application, try the following books:

- *Beginning XML, 2nd Edition* (ISBN 1-86100-559-8)
- *Visual Basic .NET and XML: Harness the Power of XML in VB.NET Applications* (ISBN 0-471-26509-8)

Demonstrating the Principle of Integration

Before you build the application that can integrate with your address book application, you should try to understand the principles involved. Basically, XML documents are good for integration because they can be easily read, understood, and changed by other people. Old-school file formats require detailed documentation to understand and often don't evolve well — that is, when new versions of the format are released, software that worked with the old formats often breaks.

XML documents are typically easily understood. Imagine you'd never seen or heard of your address book before, and look at this XML document:

```
<Addresses>
    <Address>
        <FirstName>Bryan</FirstName>
        <LastName>Newsome</LastName>
        <CompanyName>Wiley</CompanyName>
        <Address1>123 Main St</Address1>
        <Address2 />
        <City>Big City</City>
        <Region>SE</Region>
        <PostalCode>28222</PostalCode>
        <Country>USA</Country>
        <Email>Bryan@email.com</Email>
    </Address>
</Addresses>
```

Common sense tells you what this document represents. You can also perceive how the program that generated it uses it. In addition, you can use the various tools in .NET to load, manipulate, and work with this document. To an extent, you still need to work with the people that designed the structure of the document, especially when more esoteric elements come into play, but you can use this document to some meaningful effect without too much stress.

Provided that you know what structure the document takes, you can build your own document or add new things to it. For example, if you know that the Addresses element contains a list of Address elements, and that each Address element contains a bunch of elements that describe the address, you can add your own Address element using your own application.

To see this happening, you can open the `AddressBook.xml` file in Notepad. You need to copy the last `Address` element (complete with the contents) to the bottom of the document, but make sure it remains inside the `Addresses` element. Change the address data to something else. Here's mine:

```
<?xml version="1.0" encoding="utf-8"?>
<AddressBook xmlns:xsi="http://www.w3.org/2001/XMLSchema-instance"
xmlns:xsd="http://www.w3.org/2001/XMLSchema">
  <Addresses>
    <Address>
      <FirstName>Bryan</FirstName>
      <LastName>Newsome</LastName>
      <CompanyName>Wiley</CompanyName>
      <Address1>123 Main St</Address1>
      <Address2 />
      <City>Big City</City>
      <Region>SE</Region>
      <PostalCode>28222</PostalCode>
      <Country>USA</Country>
      <Email>Bryan@email.com</Email>
    </Address>
    <Address>
      <FirstName>Jennifer</FirstName>
      <LastName>Newsome</LastName>
      <CompanyName />
      <Address1>123 Main St</Address1>
      <Address2 />
      <City>Big City</City>
      <Region>SE</Region>
      <PostalCode>28222</PostalCode>
      <Country>USA</Country>
      <Email />
    </Address>
  </Addresses>
</AddressBook>
```

Finally, if you save the file and run the address book application, you should find that you have two addresses and that the last one is the new one that you added. What this shows is that you can manipulate the document and gain some level of integration.

Reading the Address Book from Another Application

To further the illustration, what you do in the next Try It Out is build a completely separate application from Address Book that's able to load in the XML file that Address Book uses and do something useful with it. Specifically, you'll extract all of the addresses in the file and display a list of names with their matching e-mail addresses.

Reading Address Book Data

1. Create a new Windows Forms Application project. Call it **Address List**.

2. On Form1, draw a ListBox control. Change its `IntegralHeight` property to **False,** its `Dock` property to **Fill,** and its `Name` to **lstEmails**, as shown in Figure 20-7.

Figure 20-7

3. Double-click the form's title bar. Add this code to the `Load` event handler. Remember to add a reference to `System.Xml.dll` this namespace declaration:

```
Imports System.Xml
Public Class Form1
Private Sub Form1_Load(ByVal sender As System.Object, _
        ByVal e As System.EventArgs) Handles MyBase.Load
    ' where do we want to get the XML from...
    Dim filename As String = _
        "C:\Users\Bryan\Documents\Visual Studio 2008\Projects\Address _
Book\bin\Debug\AddressBook.xml"
    ' open the document...
    Dim reader As New XmlTextReader(filename)
    ' move to the start of the document...
    reader.MoveToContent()
    ' start working through the document...

    Dim addressData As Collection = Nothing
    Dim elementName As String = Nothing
    Do While reader.Read
        ' what kind of node to we have?
        Select Case reader.NodeType
            ' is it the start of an element?
            Case XmlNodeType.Element
                ' if it's an element start, is it "Address"?
                If reader.Name = "Address" Then
                    ' if so, create a new collection...
                    addressData = New Collection()
                Else
                    ' if not, record the name of the element...
                    elementName = reader.Name
```

```
                            End If
                    ' if we have some text, try storing it in the
                    ' collection...
                    Case XmlNodeType.Text
                        ' do we have an address?
                        If Not addressData Is Nothing Then
                            addressData.Add(reader.Value, elementName)
                        End If
                    ' is it the end of an element?
                    Case XmlNodeType.EndElement
                        ' if it is, we should have an entire address stored...
                        If reader.Name = "Address" Then
                            ' try to create a new listview item...
                            Dim item As String = Nothing
                            Try
                                item = addressData("firstname") & _
                                    " " & addressData("lastname")
                                item &= " (" & addressData("email") & ")"
                            Catch
                            End Try
                            ' add the item to the list...
                            lstEmails.Items.Add(item)
                            ' reset...
                            addressData = Nothing
                        End If
                End Select
        Loop
    End Sub
End Class
```

We've assumed in this code listing that your AddressBook.xml *will be in* C:\Users\Bryan\ Documents\Visual Studio 2008\Projects\Address Book\bin\Debug. *If yours isn't, change the file name value specified at the top of the code.*

4. Run the project; you should see something like what is shown in Figure 20-8. Notice that addresses that don't have an e-mail address display without problems, as the Email element in your XML file contains an empty string value instead of a null value as is typically found in databases.

Figure 20-8

How It Works

To fully appreciate the benefit of this exercise (and therefore the benefit of XML), imagine that before writing the application you'd never seen the XML format used by the Address Book application. Since XML is a text-based format, you're able to open it in a normal text editor, read it, and make assumptions about how it works. You know that you want to get a list of names and e-mail addresses, and you understand that you have an array of Address elements, each one containing the three elements you need: FirstName, LastName, and Email. All that remains is to extract and present the information.

Since announcing .NET, Microsoft has a made a big deal about how it is built on XML. This shows in the .NET Framework support for XML — there is a dazzling array of classes for reading and writing XML documents. The XmlSerializer object that you've been using up until now is by far the easiest one to use, but it relies on your having classes that match the document structure exactly. Therefore, if you are given a document from a business partner, you won't have a set of classes that matches the document. As a result, you need some other way to read the document and fit it into whatever classes you do have.

In your Address List project, you don't have applicable AddressBook or Address classes, so you had to use some classes to step through a file. The one you're using is System.Xml.XmlTextReader. This class provides a pointer that starts at the top of the document and, on command, moves to the next part of the document. (Each of these parts is called a *node*.) The pointer will stop at anything, and this includes start tags, end tags, data values, and whitespace.

So, when you start, the first thing XmlTextReader tells you about is this node:

```
<?xml version="1.0" encoding="utf-8"?>
```

When you ask it to move on, it tells you about this node:

```
<AddressBook xmlns:xsi="http://www.w3.org/2001/XMLSchema-instance"
xmlns:xsd="http://www.w3.org/2001/XMLSchema">
```

Then, when you ask it to move on again, it tells you about this node:

```
<Addresses>
```

Then it tells you about <Address>, <FirstName>, -Bryan, </FirstName>, and <LastName>, and so on until it gets to the end of the document. In between each one of these, you may or may not get told about whitespace nodes. By and large, you can ignore these.

What your algorithm has to do, then, is get hold of an XmlTextReader and start moving through the document one piece at a time. When you first start, the pointer is set ahead of the first node in the document. Each call to Read moves the pointer along one node, so the first call to Read that you see at the start of the Do . . . While loop actually sets the pointer to the first node:

```
Private Sub Form1_Load(ByVal sender As System.Object, _
            ByVal e As System.EventArgs) Handles MyBase.Load
    ' where do you want to get the XML from...
    Dim filename As String = _
"C:\Documents and Settings\Administrator\My Documents\" & _
"Visual Studio\Projects\Address Book\Address Book\bin\Debug\" & _
```

```
"AddressBook.xml"

        ' open the document...
        Dim reader As New XmlTextReader(filename)
        ' move to the start of the document...
        reader.MoveToContent()
        ' start working through the document...
        Dim addressData As Collection, elementName As String
        Do While reader.Read
```

You can use the `NodeType` property of `XmlTextReader` to find out what kind of node you're looking at. If you have an `Element` node, this maps directly onto a start tag in the document. You can use the `Name` property to get the name of the tag. When you find the `<Address>` start tag, you create a new collection called `addressData`. If the start tag that you're looking at isn't the `<Address>` tag, you store the name in `elementName` for later use:

```
        ' what kind of node to we have?
        Select Case reader.NodeType
            ' is it the start of an element?
            Case XmlNodeType.Element
                ' if it's an element start, is it "Address"?
                If reader.Name = "Address" Then
                    ' if so, create a new collection...
                    addressData = New Collection()
                Else
                    ' if not, record the name of the element...
                    elementName = reader.Name
                End If
```

Alternatively, the node you get might be a lump of text. If this is the case, you check to see whether `addressData` points to a `Collection` object. If it does, you know that you are inside an `Address` element. Remember, you've also stored the name of the element that you are looking at inside `elementName`. This means that if `elementName` is set to `FirstName`, you know you're in the `FirstName` element, and therefore the text element you're looking at must be the first name in the address. You then add this element name and the value into the collection for later use:

```
        ' if we have some text, try storing it in the
        ' collection...
        Case XmlNodeType.Text
            ' do we have an address?
            If Not addressData Is Nothing Then
                addressData.Add(reader.Value, elementName)
            End If
```

As you work through the file, you'll get to this point for each of the elements stored in the `Address` element. Effectively, by the time you reach `</Address>`, `addressData` will contain entries for each value stored against the address in the document.

To detect when you get to the `</Address>` tag, you need to look for `EndElement` nodes:

```
        ' is it the end of an element?
        Case XmlNodeType.EndElement
```

When you get one of these, if Name is equal to Address, you know that you have reached </Address>, and this means that addressData should be fully populated. You form a string and add it to the list:

```
' if it is, you should have an entire address stored...
If reader.Name = "Address" Then
    ' try to create a new listview item...
    Dim item As String
    Try
        item = addressData("firstname") & _
                " " & addressData("lastname")
        item &= " (" & addressData("email") & ")"
    Catch
    End Try
    ' add the item to the list...
    lstEmails.Items.Add(item)
    ' reset...
    addressData = Nothing
End If
```

You'll notice that in your Try . . . Catch you won't do anything if an exception does occur. To keep this example simple, you're going to ignore any problems that do occur. Specifically, you'll run into problems if the Address element you're looking through has subelements missing — for example, you might not always have an e-mail address for each address, as was shown in Figure 20-8.

You then continue the loop. On each iteration of the loop, XmlTextReader.Read is called, which advances the pointer to the next node. If there are no more nodes in the document, Read returns False, and the loop stops:

```
        End Select
    Loop
End Sub
```

I hope that this example has illustrated the power of XML from a software integration perspective. With very little work, you've managed to integrate the Address Book and Address List applications together.

If you want to experiment with this a little, try adding and deleting addresses from the Address Book. You'll need to close the program to save the changes to AddressBook.xml, but each time you start Address List, you should see the changes you made.

Summary

This chapter introduced the concept of XML. XML is a language based on open standards and can be used as a tool for software integration. Within a single organization, XML can be used to transport data across platforms easily. It also allows two organizations to define a common format for data exchange and, because XML is text-based, it can easily be moved around using Internet technologies such as e-mail, the Web, and FTP. XML is based on building up a document constructed of tags and data.

XML is primarily used for integration work to make the tasks of data transportation and exchange easier, and you, as a newcomer to Visual Basic and programming in general, are unlikely to do integration work (as it's typically done by developers with lots of experience). Nevertheless, this chapter helped you get an idea of what this is all about by focusing on using the `System.Xml.Serialization.XmlSerializer` class to save entire objects to disk (known as *serialization*). This same object was used to load objects from disk (known as *deserialization*). You built a fully functional address book application that was able to use an XML file stored on the local computer as its primary source of data.

To round off the chapter and to demonstrate that XML is great for software integration work, you wrote a separate application that was able to load and make sense of the XML document used by the Address Book application.

You should:

❑   Have a better understanding of XML and know what it looks like

❑   Be able to serialize and deserialize XML data into objects

❑   Be able to manipulate XML data in your applications

❑   Be able to use the `XMLTextReader` class to walk through an XML document

Exercises

1.   Create an XML document that describes a table lamp. You can describe the lamp using a number of different attributes. You should describe items such as shade, bulbs and base. You can validate your XML at a site such as `www.w3schools.com/dom/dom_validate.asp` that offers a free validator.

2.   Expand on what you learned in the chapter by investigating how to place comments in an XML file. As a beginner, one of the most important tasks you can learn is how to research and find answers to questions. For this exercise, search the Web using your favorite search engine and try to find the syntax for inserting comments in XML. When you find the answer, test the comment in the same XML validator you used to test Exercise 1.

Distributed Computing with Windows Communication Foundation

With the release of the .NET Framework 3.0, came Windows Communication Foundation (WCF). WCF was the integration of distributed technologies like web services, MSMQ, and .NET Remoting into the same framework. WCF creates a baseline so all of your distributing programming is similar. Now, developers can use all of these technologies without having to completely learn each of them as new. This chapter focuses on the Web.

In this chapter, you will:

❑ Get an overview of SOAP, the method used to exchange data with web services

❑ Build a web service

❑ Get an overview of WCF

❑ Learn how to build WCF services and learn how to consume them

What Is a Web Service?

When you use the Internet, the two things you most likely use it for are sending (and receiving) e-mail and surfing the Web. These two applications are, by far, the most popular uses of the Internet.

However, from time to time as Internet usage grows, new technologies and applications that have the potential to change forever the way you use the Internet are released. In recent times, Napster was a commercial product that grew from nothing to ridiculously huge in a very short space of time. (In fact, the rate of growth of Napster, until the various court decisions that clipped its wings took hold, was far in excess of the rate of growth of the Web itself!) Naturally, its fall from grace was just as fast.

Building upon the success of the World Wide Web as you know it today, web services have the potential to be the next big thing. The Web is a great way to share information. However, the problem with the Web as it is today is that to use it you have to be a human. Web sites are built to be read with human eyes and interpreted with the human mind. Web services, on the other hand, are built to be read and interpreted by computer programs, not by humans. Web services are, in effect, web sites for computers to use. These web sites tend to be dynamic in nature, so they don't contain static unchanging content but can react and adapt to choices and selections. For example, you might want to use a web service that accepts a quantity in U.S. dollars and returns the number of equivalent euros.

Why is this a good thing? When building computer systems in a commercial information technology environment, the most costly factor is integrating disparate computer systems. Imagine you have two pieces of software: one used to keep track of stock in your warehouse, the other used to capture customer orders. These two pieces of software were developed by different companies and bought at different times. However, when an order is placed using the second piece of software, that software should be able to tell the warehousing software that a quantity of a particular product has been sold. This may trigger some autonomous action in the warehousing software, such as placing an order to replenish the stock or asking someone to go and pick it off the shelf.

When two pieces of software work together, you call it *integration*. Integration is rarely easy, and on large installations it often involves hiring teams of consultants and spending thousands of dollars on custom-written integration software.

Without going into too much detail, web services make integration far, far easier. By making something that much easier, you inevitably make it far, far cheaper, and that's why it's predicted to be the next big thing. Not only will companies who are already integrating have a more cost-effective option than before, but companies will also be able to integrate their computer systems in previously unseen ways. Web services will also provide opportunities for new businesses wanting to introduce specialized services with relative ease.

The commercial pros and cons of web services, together with a discussion of the movers and shakers in this particular space, are beyond the scope of this book. However, if you would like to learn more, take a look at http://msdn.microsoft.com/webservices.

How Does a Web Service Work?

First of all, web services are based upon completely open standards that are not tied to any particular platform or any particular company. Part of their attraction is that it doesn't matter whether you deploy your web service on Solaris, Unix, Macintosh, or Windows; anyone will be able to connect to and use your web service. This is the same with normal web sites; you do not care what platform the web sites you visit every day actually run on, as long as they work.

Second, the .NET implementation of web services is entirely based on a programming paradigm with which developers have been falling in love for years: object orientation. If you're used to using objects (and by Chapter 21 of this book, you should be!), you'll have absolutely no problems with web services.

The principle behind a web service is that you build a class that has methods. However, the traditional system of deployment and instantiation does not apply. Here is what happens traditionally:

1. A developer builds a class.

2. That class is installed (copied onto a computer).

3. A piece of software running on that *same* computer creates an instance of the class (the object).

4. The piece of software calls a method on the object.

5. The object does something and returns a value.

6. The piece of software receives the value and does something with it.

Here is what happens with a web service:

1. A developer builds a class.

2. That class is copied onto a server computer running a web server such as Microsoft IIS.

3. A piece of software running on a *different, remote* computer (usually located somewhere on the Internet) asks the web server to run a particular method on the class.

4. The server creates an instance of the class and calls the method.

5. The server returns the results of the method to the calling computer.

6. The piece of software on the remote computer receives the value and does something with it.

You can see that the technique is very similar, but there's a disconnection between the server that the object is actually installed on and the computer that wants to use the object. In fact, with a web service, there is a huge process gulf (namely, the Internet) between the client of the object and the object itself. A solution to handle this disconnection is provided by the standards used by and specifically developed for web services.

SOAP

As web services are, in effect, web sites for computers to use, they've been built on the same technology that made the World Wide Web so popular — specifically, the Hypertext Transfer Protocol (HTTP) standard that powers all web servers.

When you're dealing with web sites for people to read, the client (browser) and server usually exchange a mixture of documents. HTML documents, and their extension technologies like Dynamic HTML and JavaScript, describe the page layout and text on the page, and common image formats like GIF and JPEG are used to exchange images.

However, when you're dealing with web sites for computers to use, you exchange only one kind of document. These are known as SOAP documents.

> SOAP was originally an acronym for Simple Object Access Protocol, but the current standard at W3C has removed this terminology.

When a client application wants to ask the web service for some information, such as the current stock level for a product or the status of an order, or to get the computer at the end of the connection to do something such as convert currencies or place an order, the application constructs a SOAP request document. Using HTTP, this document is sent over the Internet to the web server that powers the web service. This document contains all the information that the web service needs to determine what has been asked for. As web services work on the common object/method paradigm, the request document includes such things the name of the method and any data that should be passed through to the method as parameters.

At the server end, the web service receives the SOAP request, deserializes it, and runs the appropriate piece of software. (You're going to build some of these appropriate pieces of software in this chapter.) During the call, the method generates a SOAP response document that contains the information to be passed back to the caller. Like the request document, this new document is transferred using HTTP through the web server.

SOAP documents are constructed with XML. This means that if you read a SOAP document, it'll look very similar to the sort of document that you saw in Chapter 20. However, at the level of Visual Basic, you don't need to look too hard at the SOAP documents. As you work through the chapter, you'll see some of the SOAP response documents that come back from the server, but you won't be seeing any of the request documents.

You know that web service technology is not tied to a specific platform, so from a developer's perspective the value of choosing one platform over another is determined by how transparent this SOAP document construction and transfer work actually is or what is available at the site where development will take place. .NET is very good for building and using web services; you don't have to go within a hundred yards of a SOAP document. (This is why in this chapter you're not going to dwell on SOAP too much, even though without SOAP you wouldn't be able to do anything you can do in this chapter.) On some other platforms that are equally good for building web services, you need to jump through a few more hoops to create powerful web services.

Obviously, this chapter is concerned with how web services work with .NET. But first, have a close look at Figure 21-1, as it provides a simple form of the architecture behind web services.

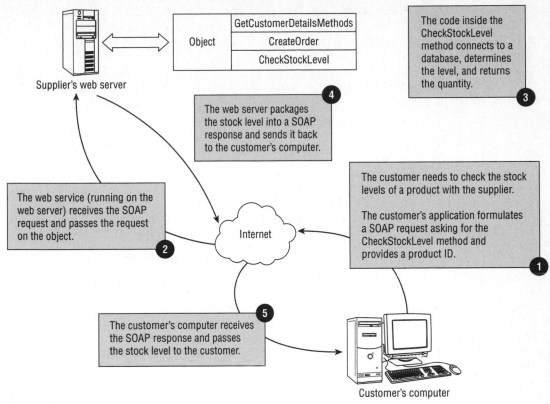

	GetCustomerDetailsMethods
Object	CreateOrder
	CheckStockLevel

The code inside the CheckStockLevel method connects to a database, determines the level, and returns the quantity.

3

Supplier's web server

The web server packages the stock level into a SOAP response and sends it back to the customer's computer.

4

The web service (running on the web server) receives the SOAP request and passes the request on the object.

2

Internet

The customer needs to check the stock levels of a product with the supplier.

The customer's application formulates a SOAP request asking for the CheckStockLevel method and provides a product ID.

1

The customer's computer receives the SOAP response and passes the stock level to the customer.

5

Customer's computer

Figure 21-1

Building a Web Service

Building web services with Visual Studio 2008 is a breeze. In this section, you build a simple web service and are introduced to some of the concepts involved. Specifically, you see how to include the appropriate attributes to expose a method as a web service method. You also learn how to test your web methods using the test harness built into web services.

A Web Services Demonstration

A web service is basically a class that sits on the server. Some of the methods on that class are marked in a special way, and it's by looking for these special marks that .NET knows which methods to publish on the service. You'll see how this works as you go through the first Try It Out. Anyone wishing to use the web service can then call these methods on the remote web service, as if the method existed in a class installed on their local computer. You'll also see a method that allows you to test the web service from within Internet Explorer.

Try It Out   A Demonstration Web Service

1. Open Visual Studio and select File ➪ New Web Site from the menu.

2. Make sure Visual Basic is selected in the Language box, and File System in the Location box, and select ASP.NET Web Service from the upper list. Enter the name as **DemoService** and click OK (see Figure 21-2).

Figure 21-2

Web services are based on ASP.NET technology, so the project is created in the same way as the web applications you worked with in Chapter 18. If you have problems creating the project, refer to that chapter for troubleshooting information.

Visual Studio 2008 creates a new virtual directory and create a new page called `Service.asmx`, where `.asmx` stands for Active Server Methods. (The extra x comes from the original name of ASP.NET: ASP+. The x is the plus sign turned through 45 degrees.) This page represents one service, and a web service project (or site) can contain many different services.

3. If the `service.vb` page is not open, use the Solution Explorer to open it. It is located in the `App_Code` folder. When Visual Studio 2008 created the page, it put an example method on the service called `HelloWorld`. The code looks like the code shown here:

```
<WebMethod()> _
Public Function HelloWorld() As String
    Return "Hello World"
End Function
```

Run the project by selecting Debug ➪ Start Debugging from the menu. You will be asked to either run the project without debugging or add a config file to enable debugging. Choose to create a config file with debugging enabled, and continue. For security reasons, you would turn off debugging before releasing an application into production. The project is compiled and the ASP.NET Development Server starts. You may be shown a warning about script debugging. You can continue or follow the instructions to allow script debugging if it is turned off in your Internet Explorer settings.

In the task bar, right-click the icon for the ASP.NET Development Server and choose Open In Web Browser. Internet Explorer opens and displays the pages in the site. Click the link for the `Service.asmx` page. This is the test interface. On this initial page, all of the methods supported by the service appear in a bulleted list at the top of the page.

You use the `web.config` file to make numerous changes to your site configuration in the real world. For the purposes of this example, we will not go into detail on this file, but know that you can make sitewide changes to security, caching, custom settings, and more. You can learn more about using the `web.config` file by searching for `web.config` at `http://msdn2.microsoft.com`.

4. Click the HelloWorld link. This opens another page that lets you run the method. This page contains the web method name, a button to invoke the web method for testing, and the protocols supported for this web method. Note that two protocols are listed: SOAP and HTTP POST.

5. Click the Invoke button. This opens another browser window. This window contains the SOAP response from the server, as shown in the following code:

```
<?xml version="1.0" encoding="utf-8" ?>
<string xmlns="http://tempuri.org/">Hello World</string>
```

How It Works

Just as Web Forms have a class behind the `.aspx` page, web services have a class behind each `.asmx` page. This class is the one that you enabled the `HelloWorld` method on. If you look at the definition for the class, you'll see that it's inherited from `System.Web.Services.WebService`:

```
Public Class Service
    Inherits System.Web.Services.WebService
```

The `WebService` class is responsible for presenting the pages that you clicked through in Internet Explorer to invoke the `HelloWorld` method. (You can use another browser to test the service, but Visual Studio 2008 chooses Internet Explorer by default.) These pages are known as the *test interface*. Methods on the class that you want exposed to the web service must be marked with the `WebMethod` attribute. You can see this attribute defined at the beginning of the method (note that it must be encased in a fashion similar to HTML tags):

```
<WebMethod()> __
Public Function HelloWorld() As String
    Return "Hello World"
End Function
```

Before the test page opens, you are asked to add a config file to enable debugging or continue without debugging. If you plan to test the web service, choose to add a config file. A new file, named `web.config`, is added to the project. Remember always to disable debugging before releasing your web service to a production environment. When the test interface starts, it displays the methods flagged to be exposed on the server. When you click through to the page tied to a specific method, the test interface presents a form that you can use to invoke it.

When the method is invoked, to the method it is just like a normal call — in other words, there's nothing special about writing web services, and everything that you've learned so far still applies.

You already know that web services are powered by SOAP. When you click the Invoke button, the SOAP message that's returned to the caller (in this case, your Internet Explorer) contains the response. You can see that this is indeed the value you returned from the method buried within a block of XML:

```
<?xml version="1.0" encoding="utf-8" ?>
<string xmlns="http://tempuri.org/">Hello World</string>
```

The structure of the XML that makes up the SOAP message, by and large, is not important. However, when you're working through more examples, we'll point out where the actual results can be found.

Adding More Methods

Now you build some methods that illustrate your web service actually doing something. In this next Try It Out exercise, you add a web method that calculates the square root of the number that you pass into it. You'll be adding the web method and writing the code to calculate the square root, as well as testing this new web method.

Try It Out   Adding a SquareRoot Method

1. Open the Code Editor for `Service.vb`. Add this new method to the `Service` class below the existing `HelloWorld` method:

```
Public Function GetSquareRoot(ByVal number As Double) As Double
    Return Math.Sqrt(number)
End Function
```

   If you can't type into the code window, it means that the instance of Internet Explorer that Visual Studio 2008 opened is still running. Close down the test interface windows and any extra windows displaying the SOAP responses, and the project should stop running. Alternatively, select Debug ⇨ Stop Debugging from the menu.

2. Run the project. You'll notice that the new method does not appear in the list at the top of the page. In fact, you will see the same screen that was shown previously. This is due to the fact that you didn't mark the method with the `WebMethod` attribute. I did this to show you that a class can contain methods that, although public, are not exposed on the web service. Close the browser and add the `WebMethod` attribute:

```
<WebMethod()> _
Public Function GetSquareRoot(ByVal number As Double) As Double
    Return Math.Sqrt(number)
End Function
```

3. Run the project again and you should see the new method at the top of the page. Next, you are going to cause an error to see what error messages look like.

4. To see the correct error message for this example, you may have to change a setting in your browser. Make sure you uncheck Show friendly HTTP error messages under the Advanced tab from the Tools ⇨ Internet Options menu in Internet Explorer.

5. Click the GetSquareRoot link. This time, the Invoke form should offer a way to enter a number because of the `WebMethod` parameter. Without entering a number, click Invoke.

6. When the new browser appears, you won't see a SOAP response; instead you'll see something that looks like this:

```
System.ArgumentException: Cannot convert  to System.Double.
Parameter name: type ---> System.FormatException: Input string was not in a
   correct format.
```

You'll see this kind of message whenever you enter invalid information into the Invoke form. In this case, it's telling you that it cannot convert to `System.Double`, which should be a big giveaway that it can't convert an empty string to a floating-point value.

7. Close the browser window and enter **2** into the number field. Click Invoke and you'll get this response:

```
<?xml version="1.0" encoding="utf-8" ?>
<double xmlns="http://tempuri.org/">1.4142135623730952</double>
```

How It Works

If you look in the SOAP message that was returned, you'll find a `double` value that's as close as you can get to the square root of 2.

```
<?xml version="1.0" encoding="utf-8" ?>
<double xmlns="http://tempuri.org/">1.4142135623730952</double>
```

So you know that the method works. You should have also seen by now that building simple web services is not hard. This is Microsoft's intent with the web services support in .NET — the plumbing to build a service is remarkably easy. Everything you've learned about creating classes, building methods with parameters, and returning values is paying dividends here, because there's virtually no learning curve. You can concentrate on building the logic behind the web service, which, after all, is the bit you get paid to do!

Understanding WCF Services

One of the goals of WCF is to create a platform where developers can choose between different types of distributed services without having to make a single choice between the main technologies: Web Services, Microsoft Message Queue, .NET Remoting, and Enterprise Services. This means you can now build applications with any one or any mix of these distributed applications that work together seamlessly in the framework. To make this happen, WCF services have common attributes.

The following list defines some of the common parts of WCF.

- ❑ **Service Contract:** This attribute tells the CLR that the interface or class needs to maintain WCF metadata. You can work with this programmatically, as you will see in the next Try It Out, and the CLR handles all the behind-the-scenes stuff for you.

- ❑ **Operation Contract:** This attribute specifies which methods are available via WCF. Only methods explicitly marked will be available.

- ❑ **End Point:** The end point contains all the required information on the address, bindings, and contract that the client needs to communicate with the service.

- ❑ **Address:** This is where the end point is expressed as a Uri.

- ❑ **Binding:** How to communicate with the service. Soap and HTTP Get are possible binding types you will see in the next try it out.

- ❑ **Service Host:** The service host is used to expose a WCF service to a client application.

- ❑ **Messages:** WCF communicates by exchanging messages.

When designing applications in a service oriented or distributed environment you should look to WCF for your platform. To implement the technology, you can build in security and transactions and pass messages via many technologies with similar code. As a developer, it will be easy to write code to host a message queue and then write code to host a web service in the application. Typically, that application would have specialists to handle each type of communication.

WCF is a very broad topic and this chapter demonstrates only a couple of common uses for it. To learn more, you can visit the main web site for WCF at http://wcf.netfx3.com. Now, let's build an application to take advantage of WCF.

WCF Services

The previous example showed how simple a web service can be to create. Now, let's look at another way to create the same GetSquareRoot Web Service from inside a console application. Using features of the WCF, this is also pretty easy.

Try It Out   **Creating Services in a Console Application**

1.   To start, create a new console application named **GetSquareRoot**. See Figure 21-3 for the correct settings.

Figure 21-3

2.   Next, add references to `System.ServiceModel` and `System.ServiceModel.Web`. See Figure 21-4.

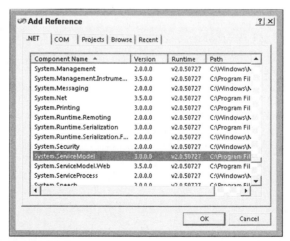

Figure 21-4

3. Now, to the code. Open the page module1.vb. At the top of the module1.vb page, add three imports.

```
Imports System.ServiceModel
Imports System.ServiceModel.Description
Imports System.ServiceModel.Web
```

4. Add the service contract, ISquareRoot.

```
<ServiceContract()> _
Public Interface ISquareRoot
    <OperationContract()> _
    <WebGet()> _
    Function GetSquareRoot(ByVal dblNumber As Double) As Double
End Interface
```

5. Add a class to implement it. Add the SquareRoot class as follows:

```
Public Class SquareRoot
    Implements ISquareRoot
    Public Function GetSquareRoot(ByVal dblNumber As Double) As Double Implements _
ISquareRoot.GetSquareRoot
        Return Math.Sqrt(dblNumber)
    End Function
End Class
```

6. Inside of module1 add the procedure for using HTTP to communicate between the console application and the service. In this example, you add error handling so the services can be closed properly in case of an error.

```
Module Module1

    Public Sub HttpChannel()
        Dim dblNumber As Double
        Dim dblInput As Double
        Try
            Dim wcfSquareRootHTTP As New WebChannelFactory(Of ISquareRoot) _
(New Uri("http://localhost/SquareRoot/Web"))
            Dim channelHTTP As ISquareRoot = wcfSquareRootHTTP.CreateChannel()

            Console.WriteLine("Enter a number to get the square root via http? ")
            dblInput = Console.ReadLine()
            Console.WriteLine("Calling GetSquareRoot over http:")
            dblNumber = channelHTTP.GetSquareRoot(dblInput)
            Console.WriteLine("The square root of " + dblInput.ToString + " is " _
+ dblNumber.ToString)

            Console.WriteLine("Press enter to continue and close the HTTP channel")
            Console.ReadLine()

            wcfSquareRootHTTP.Close()
```

```
        Catch ex As Exception
            Throw ex
        End Try
    End Sub
```

7. Add the procedure for SOAP communication.

```
Public Sub SoapChannel()
    Dim dblNumber As Double
    Dim dblInput As Double
    Try

        Dim wcfSquareRootSoap As New ChannelFactory(Of ISquareRoot) _
(New BasicHttpBinding(), "http://localhost/SquareRoot/Soap")
        Dim channelSoap As ISquareRoot = wcfSquareRootSoap.CreateChannel()

        Console.WriteLine("Enter a number to get the square root via soap? ")
        dblInput = Console.ReadLine()
        Console.WriteLine("Calling GetSquareRoot over soap:")
        dblNumber = channelSoap.GetSquareRoot(dblInput)
        Console.WriteLine("The square root of " + dblInput.ToString + " is " + _
            dblNumber.ToString)
        Console.WriteLine("Press enter to continue and close the SOAP channel")
        Console.ReadLine()
        Console.WriteLine("")

        wcfSquareRootSoap.Close()
    Catch ex As Exception
        Throw ex
    End Try

End Sub
```

8. Finally, add the code to the main subroutine

```
Sub Main()
        Dim shSquareRoot As New ServiceHost(GetType(SquareRoot), _
New Uri("http://localhost/SquareRoot"))

        Dim epSquareRoot As ServiceEndpoint
        epSquareRoot = shSquareRoot.AddServiceEndpoint(GetType(ISquareRoot), _
New WebHttpBinding(), "Web")
        epSquareRoot.Behaviors.Add(New WebHttpBehavior())

        shSquareRoot.AddServiceEndpoint(GetType(ISquareRoot), _
New BasicHttpBinding(), "Soap")

        Try
            shSquareRoot.Open()

            SoapChannel()
            HttpChannel()

            Console.WriteLine("Done.  Press any key to exit and close the host")
```

```
            Console.ReadLine()
            shSquareRoot.Close()

    Catch ex As Exception
            Console.WriteLine("Application Error: " + ex.Message)
            Console.ReadLine()
            shSquareRoot.Abort()
    End Try

    End Sub
End Module
```

9. Run the project. Enter some values and test the application. You see output as shown in Figures 21-5 and 21-6.

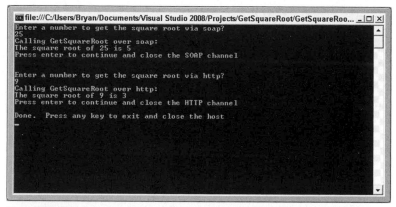

Figure 21-5

Figure 21-6

How It Works

This time, you create an application to communicate with a service via different communication channels. The service SquareRoot provides the same functionality as it did in the previous Try It Out but you don't create a Web Service project. Within the code, you create a WCF service that can accept communication via SOAP and HTTP. This is how the code breaks down.

To start, you add references to System.ServiceModel and System.ServiceModel.Web. These namespaces contain core functionality for WCF. Then, you add imports to three namespaces you used to save a few keystrokes.

```
Imports System.ServiceModel
Imports System.ServiceModel.Description
Imports System.ServiceModel.Web
```

Next, you define the service contract. To do this, you create an interface that will later be implemented in the SquareRoot class. Creating a separate interface was not a requirement, but it is the recommended model for creating contracts programmatically. Another way to create a contract is by using svcutil.exe, but why not just add the attribute labels and let the framework handle all of the behind the scenes items?

To the interface, you add the <ServiceContract()>, <OperationContract()> and <WebGet()> attributes. This tells .NET that the interface marked with <ServiceContract()> carries a WCF contract and public methods were marked with the <OperationContract()> attribute. The <WebGet()> attribute tells the Framework that the method would be made available via HTTP Get:

```
<ServiceContract()> _
Public Interface ISquareRoot
    <OperationContract()> _
    <WebGet()> _
    Function GetSquareRoot(ByVal dblNumber As Double) As Double
End Interface
```

After you create the interface, you need to implement it. To do that, you create a new class named SquareRoot. The class implements the ISquareRoot interface and is available for use as a WCF service. The simple class has one method. The GetSquareRoot method accepts a number, performs the operation to calculate the square root and then returns the answer to the caller:

```
Public Class SquareRoot
    Implements ISquareRoot
    Public Function GetSquareRoot(ByVal dblNumber As Double) As Double Implements _
ISquareRoot.GetSquareRoot
        Return Math.Sqrt(dblNumber)
    End Function
End Class
```

Next, you write the code to do all of the work. The first subroutine you add is HttpChannel. This procedure sets up the service to be called over HTTP, hooks the client up and makes the communication work. To start, you declare a couple of storage variables dblNumber and dblInput for use later. Then, you start a try/catch. This is very important, even in a test; to make sure errors are handled so you can close the objects properly in case of an error.

```
Module Module1

    Public Sub HttpChannel()
        Dim dblNumber As Double
        Dim dblInput As Double
        Try
```

Inside of the try/catch, you create an instance of WebChannelFactory with the Uri of
http://localhost/SquareRoot/Web. This allows you to call the service over HTTP. Actually, while
the HTTP channel is open you can open a browser and navigate to http://localhost/
SquareRoot/Web/getsquareroot?dblnumber=16 (see Figure 21-7) and see the service in action via
HTTP in your browser. To make more sense of this, take a look at the main procedure. You create the
HTTP service endpoint at the same Uri. You will see that in detail later.

Figure 21-7

```
        Dim wcfSquareRootHTTP As New WebChannelFactory(Of ISquareRoot) _
    (New Uri("http://localhost/SquareRoot/Web"))
```

You create the channel next. This channel allows you to call any public methods available at the other
end of the channel.

```
        Dim channelHTTP As ISquareRoot = wcfSquareRootHTTP.CreateChannel()
```

Next, you add the interaction with the user through the console application. In the midst of the
interaction, you call channelHTTP.GetSquareRoot(dblInput) to run the method and return the
square root from the service. That one line of code is where the actual work was completed.

```
        Console.WriteLine("Enter a number to get the square root via http? ")
        dblInput = Console.ReadLine()
        Console.WriteLine("Calling GetSquareRoot over http:")
        dblNumber = channelHTTP.GetSquareRoot(dblInput)
        Console.WriteLine("The square root of " + dblInput.ToString + " is " _
+ dblNumber.ToString)

        Console.WriteLine("Press enter to continue and close the HTTP channel")
        Console.ReadLine()
```

At the end of the procedure, you add code that closes the HTTP channel and handles errors. The error handler you add gracefully passes the error to the caller to be handled.

```
        wcfSquareRootHTTP.Close()
    Catch ex As Exception
        Throw ex
    End Try
End Sub
```

The second subroutine you add is `SoapChannel`. This procedure sets up the service to be called over SOAP, hooks the client up and makes the communication work. To start, you declare a couple of storage variables `dblNumber` and `dblInput` for use later. Then, you start a `try/catch`:

```
Public Sub SoapChannel()
    Dim dblNumber As Double
    Dim dblInput As Double
    Try
```

Inside of the `try/catch`, you create an instance `ChannelFactory` with the Uri of `http://localhost/SquareRoot/Soap`. This allows you to call the service SOAP. Take a look back at where you created the `webChannelFactory`. The code you created is almost identical. That is part of the design of WCF. No matter how you communicate using WCF, the code will be very similar.

```
        Dim wcfSquareRootSoap As New ChannelFactory(Of ISquareRoot) _
(New BasicHttpBinding(), "http://localhost/SquareRoot/Soap")
```

You create the channel next. This channel allows you to call any public methods available at the other end of the channel.

```
    Dim channelSoap As ISquareRoot = wcfSquareRootSoap.CreateChannel()
```

Next, you add the interaction with the user through the console application. In the midst of the interaction, you call `channelSoap.GetSquareRoot(dblInput)` to run the method and return the square root from the service. That one line of code is where the actual work is completed:

```
        Console.WriteLine("Enter a number to get the square root via soap? ")
        dblInput = Console.ReadLine()
        Console.WriteLine("Calling GetSquareRoot over soap:")
        dblNumber = channelSoap.GetSquareRoot(dblInput)
        Console.WriteLine("The square root of " + dblInput.ToString + " is " _
+ dblNumber.ToString)
        Console.WriteLine("Press enter to continue and close the SOAP channel")
        Console.ReadLine()
        Console.WriteLine("")
```

At the end of the procedure, you add code that closes the HTTP channel and handles errors. The error handler you add gracefully passes the error to the caller to be handled:

```
        wcfSquareRootSoap.Close()
    Catch ex As Exception
        Throw ex
    End Try
End Sub
```

Finally, you add code to `Sub Main`.

```
    Sub Main()
```

To begin `Sub Main`, you created a WCF service host. The service host allowes you to configure a service and expose it for consumption by client applications.

```
        Dim shSquareRoot As New ServiceHost(GetType(SquareRoot), _
    New Uri("http://localhost/SquareRoot"))
```

Next, you create the end points. For this application, you need two end points. One is for the HTTP `Get` and one is for SOAP requests. To set up the end points, you pass in parameters to specify the contract, the bindings, and the address.

```
        Dim epSquareRoot As ServiceEndpoint
            epSquareRoot = shSquareRoot.AddServiceEndpoint(GetType(ISquareRoot), _
    New WebHttpBinding(), "Web")
            epSquareRoot.Behaviors.Add(New WebHttpBehavior())

        shSquareRoot.AddServiceEndpoint(GetType(ISquareRoot), _
    New BasicHttpBinding(), "Soap")

        Try
```

Now that you have set up the service host, you add one line of code to open the host.

```
        shSquareRoot.Open()
```

Finally, you call the sub procedures to interact with the user and the service method to get the square root. After those procedures complete, you tell the user that the application is done, close the host, and handle any errors that occurred:

```
            SoapChannel()
            HttpChannel()

            Console.WriteLine("Done.  Press any key to exit and close the host")
            Console.ReadLine()
            shSquareRoot.Close()

        Catch ex As Exception
            Console.WriteLine("Application Error: " + ex.Message)
            Console.ReadLine()
            shSquareRoot.Abort()
        End Try

    End Sub
End Module
```

Summary

In this chapter, you were introduced to web services and .NET Remoting. Web services work by allowing a developer to expose an object that is accessible through a web server. Web services are based on open standards such as SOAP and WSDL and are based on tried and tested technologies such as HTTP and XML.

You started this chapter by building a basic web service that could return some information and also do something useful — namely, return the square root of a number that you gave it. Then you jumped into WCF and built some services. Inside WCF, you saw how to use channels and end points to make a service available to clients. With WCF, you were able to call the same code two different ways. This provided the baseline you needed to understand the basics of WCF.

In addition to having a basic understanding of WCF, you should know:

❏   How to use SOAP, the method used to exchange data with web services

❏   How to build a web service

❏   How to build WCF services and how to consume them

Exercises

1.   Create a web service that returns information about the web server. Add three methods that return the web server date, web server time, and web server name, respectively. Run the project to test the three methods.

2.   Add more math functions to the WCF service you created in the last Try It Out. Create methods to add two numbers, subtract two numbers, multiply two numbers and divide two numbers. To make this work, you have to add code to two places.

Building a Sequential Workflow Using the Windows Workflow Foundation

According to Wikipedia (http://en.wikipedia.org/wiki/Workflow): "A workflow is a reliably repeatable pattern of activity enabled by a systematic organization of resources, defined roles and mass, energy and information flows, into a work process that can be documented and learned. Workflows are always designed to achieve processing intents of some sort, such as physical transformation, service provision, or information processing." That sounds like workflow is pretty important stuff. In today's business world you will hear the term *workflow* over and over again.

As you build programs, you will need to integrate some type of workflow support. For example, when a new customer signs up for an account you may want the program to handle some type of workflow. In Windows Workflow Foundation (WF), there are two basic types of workflows: sequential (also referred to as system) and state machine (also known as human/event-driven). A *sequential* workflow is designed in a manner where one process happens after another until the workflow is complete. A *state machine* workflow is designed to handle external events; it does not typically have a set start and end. Take a look at two scenarios, each involving processes used by a cell phone.

Here's a breakdown of some of the phone events and states of a cell phone:

- ❑ Letter key pressed
- ❑ Function key pressed
- ❑ Phone call received
- ❑ Text message received
- ❑ Battery critically low

❑ No service found

❑ Dialing

❑ Call in progress

First, consider a process that would be a good candidate for a state machine workflow: entering a series of key presses into your cell phone. If you have a phone that can text message and e-mail, the phone probably goes through many decisions as you start pressing the keys.

As you press keys, the phone responds to the events. Imagine you have a smartphone with a qwerty keypad and the number pad is mixed into the keys, so when you type *DE* it could also be *52*. The phone will make decisions as you type. If the phone finds a match in your address book for Dennis Smith, it might display that as a choice along with Dennis' phone number. As you keep typing, you move off of the number pad by typing *DENNI* and now the phone selects Dennis Smith for you and gives you a menu of items. Would you like to call, email, or text? Then, as an incoming call interrupts the flow, the screen goes blank, and the phone rings. You answer the phone. In this case, the workflow to place a call was stopped by the incoming call. A process that can be interrupted by an external event is not a good choice for a sequential workflow, so this process calls for a state machine workflow.

Now consider a scenario that's a better candidate for implementing a sequential workflow: using speed dial. To make a call using speed dial, you hold down the 1 key for several seconds. Once the key press has lasted two seconds, the speed dial sequential flow is started. The process flow and decisions might look like these for a complete speed dial call:

1. Number 1 key pressed and held for two seconds.

2. Start speed dial process.

3. Does phone have service?

4. If yes, set phone in dialing state (this locks phone from external interruptions).

5. Retrieve number stored for speed dial key pressed.

6. Dial number.

7. Connect call.

Why is this a good candidate for a sequential workflow? First, the process does not accept interruptions from external sources. Therefore, this process must complete once started. A speed dial call will always start when a key is held for two seconds, even if an incoming call attempts to come through. This means that a speed dial call has a defined start and end. These two items make it a good candidate for a sequential workflow.

In these simple examples, the two workflows are very similar. As you design and lay out the events, processes, and states of an application, you should be able to see if it is a good candidate for a sequential or state machine workflow. Remember the rules:

❑ When you have a workflow that has a well-defined start and end and that does not have to respond to external events, you should choose a sequential workflow implementation.

❑ When the steps of a workflow can happen in any order and external applications can change the state of the workflow then use a state machine workflow.

In this chapter, you will work with sequential workflows.

WF includes a graphical designer that enables you to lay out the workflow visually. The designer allows you to lay out your code as in a Visio program. When you are satisfied with the layout, you can then place the logic into the code pages to finish the workflow. It is a very intuitive design and easy to use.

One of the key pieces to WF is the built-in ability to create long-running transactions. You can create workflows that wait for decisions from people and systems, taking into account possible waits from systems being down or message delivery that is delayed. WF also includes the capability to roll back these long-running workflows if errors occur. In this chapter, you will:

❑   Look at a basic overview of sequential workflows

❑   Review the different workflow project types

❑   Take a look at workflow activities

❑   Create sequential workflows

Now, let's take a look at some pieces, start putting them together, and build a couple of workflows.

> *Error handling has been omitted from all of the Try It Out exercises in this chapter to save space. You should always add the appropriate error handling to your code. Review Chapter 10 for error-handling techniques.*

Visual Studio Workflow Templates

When starting your workflow project, you first have to choose the type of project you want to create. Visual Studio 2008 includes eight project templates for workflows. Figure 22-1 shows the Workflow Templates Form in Visual Studio with the template choices:

❑   **Empty Workflow Project:** An empty project for all of your custom workflow needs.

❑   **Sequential Workflow Console Application:** A project to build a sequential workflow with a console application interface or host.

❑   **Sequential Workflow Library:** A project to create a sequential workflow assembly to host in a .NET application such as a WinFom or WebForm application.

❑   **SharePoint 2007 Sequential Workflow:** A sequential workflow to host inside of SharePoint.

❑   **SharePoint 2007 State Machine Workflow:** A state workflow to host inside of SharePoint.

❑   **State Machine Workflow Console Application:** A project to build a state machine workflow with a console application interface.

❑   **State Machine Workflow Library:** A project to create a state machine workflow assembly to host in a .NET application such as a Windows Forms or Web Forms application.

❑   **Workflow Activity Library:** A project to create your own custom activities to use in any workflow.

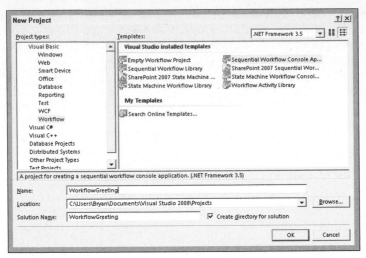

Figure 22-1

In the Try It Out exercises in this chapter, you will use the Sequential Workflow Console Application template.

Workflow Foundation Components

Windows Workflow is made up of many components. Putting these components together into a cohesive unit allows you to create robust and flexible workflow applications. Some of the main components include:

❑ **Activity:** A base unit of work. An activity can range from custom code, a web service call, or delay you add to the processing. Programmers can create custom activities and add them to a workflow. WF includes many pre-built activities (as detailed in the following section); you will be able to complete most if not all of your work using these components.

❑ **Workflow:** Activities that are grouped together to complete a specific process.

❑ **WF designers:** Tools programmers can use to graphically create workflows and activities.

❑ **WF runtime engine:** The runtime engine executes workflows and provides services, such as communicating with external programs.

❑ **Host process:** An application that hosts the runtime and manages the process used in the workflows like transactions and state.

Sequential Workflow Activities

Visual Studio 2008 includes many pre-built activities for use in your workflow. These activities are the building blocks to your workflows. In the visual designer, you can drag activities onto the designer and configure the sequential workflow. The following list describes some of the common activities. If these activities do not give you what you need, you can always create your own custom versions.

- ❏ **IfElse:** Tests multiple conditions and execute only the path where the condition is true. The activity defaults to two conditions, called branches. You can add as many branches as you need for your workflow.

- ❏ **While:** Loops until a condition is met to break out of the loop. The while loop is one of a few controls that can host only one other activity for your custom code or logic. For activities like this one, you can use the Sequential activity, which itself can host multiple activities that process in a sequential nature.

- ❏ **Code:** Executes custom logic written in the workflow.

- ❏ **Listen:** Causes the workflow to wait for an external event to happen and then execute code or activities based on the event.

- ❏ **Delay:** Causes the workflow to wait or sleep for a specified time period.

- ❏ **InvokeMethod:** Calls code (a method) in this project.

- ❏ **InvokeWorkflow:** Calls a different workflow.

- ❏ **InvokeWebService:** Calls a web service method.

- ❏ **Terminate:** Workflow execution is stopped by this activity.

- ❏ **Sequential:** Acting as a single activity, this control can host many other activities and still be viewed as a single activity.

Creating a Sequential Worklow

Now that you have learned about workflows and activities, it's time to put that knowledge to use. Creating workflows using the Visual Designer is straightforward. In the following Try It Out, you will create a simple workflow.

Try It Out   **Basic Sequential Workflow — Greeting**

In this Try It Out, you will create a Hello World type of workflow. A console application will receive text input from a user, evaluate it, and possibly return a greeting to the user based on the input received.

1. Choose File ➪ New Project. Choose Workflow as the project type and Sequential Workflow Console Application as the template. Name the project **WorkflowGreeting**. Click OK to create the project.

2. When the project opens, you will see the designer for a sequential workflow, as shown in Figure 22-2. If you do not see this, choose Designer from the View menu to show it.

Figure 22-2

3. Now, drag a code activity (named Code) from the toolbox to the workflow. Your workflow will look like Figure 22-3.

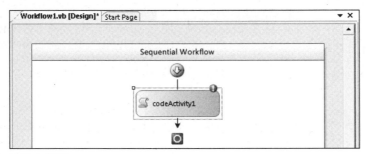

Figure 22-3

4. To insert the code, double-click the codeActivity1 activity. In the `codeActivity1_ExecuteCode` subroutine, add the following code:

```
Dim strInput As String
Console.WriteLine("Welcome ...")
strInput = Console.ReadLine()

Select Case strInput.ToUpper
    Case "HELLO"
        Console.WriteLine("Hi")
    Case "BYE"
        Console.WriteLine("Good Bye")
End Select

Console.WriteLine("Done ...")
Console.ReadLine()
```

5. That is it. You have created the simplest workflow ever. Now press F5 and see it run. Type **hello** or **bye** to see the workflow respond with the appropriate greeting. Figure 22-4 displays the console application that hosts the workflow.

Figure 22-4

How It Works

This is a very simple example of the console application for a sequential workflow. Note that the designer has a similar interface to other projects in Visual Studio. The designer is mainly a visual way to design the workflow in the same way you would design your Windows Form. You drag controls onto the workspace and organize them in structured fashion just like you do in a web or Windows application.

Using a simple control to run custom code, you are able to evaluate input and respond in an appropriate fashion. At the beginning of the following code you see the class and event handler declarations. Note that the code generated for WorkFlow1 inherits SequentialWorkflowActivity. The event handler for the code control named codeActivity1_ExecuteCode is what handles all of the work in the code activity you added.

```
Public class Workflow1
    Inherits SequentialWorkflowActivity
    Private Sub codeActivity1_ExecuteCode(ByVal sender As System.Object, _
        ByVal e As System.EventArgs)
```

To do the work, you create a string variable to accept the input from the console application. Next, you call the WriteLine method for a console application. This displays the Welcome note to the screen. After that, you call the ReadLine method to read input from the console application and store that input in the string variable you created.

```
Dim strInput As String
Console.WriteLine("Welcome ...")
strInput = Console.ReadLine()
```

Next, you write a Case statement to evaluate the input and respond to the console application.

```
Select Case strInput.ToUpper
    Case "HELLO"
         Console.WriteLine("Hi")
    Case "BYE"
         Console.WriteLine("Good Bye")
End Select
```

Finally, you complete the workflow by passing the text output to the console application and calling ReadLine to have the console application wait for the user before closing the application. This last ReadLine call gives you time to review the output and test for any logic errors.

```
        Console.WriteLine("Done ...")
        Console.ReadLine()
    End Sub
End Class
```

The workflow foundation and designer can be be really useful. Next, you'll implement a workflow of a possible business process.

———————

Property Tax Listing Form Workflow

In this example, you design the workflow using a sequential workflow. The project revolves around annual property taxes. In this situation, the taxing authority (TA) receives thousands of property listing forms at the beginning of each year. These forms are scanned and named based on where changes were made to the form. There are three possible places on the form where changes can be made. The scanned form can take on any of the following states: Property Sold, Address Change, New Property Added, or No Change.

The TA receives scanned PDF documents with file names that can be parsed to retrieve form changes and an ID to identify the property owner on the form. The forms are delivered to a folder via FTP and a Windows service. The service picks up the file and then passes the location and filename into the workflow.

When activated, the workflow first moves the file. Next, the file name is parsed. In the file name, the types of changes are evaluated and the appropriate workflow item(s) are added to the database. The final process is to assign the new item(s) to the appropriate user, and then the process is complete. Figure 22-5 displays a diagram from the TA to define the rough workflow. You will convert this diagram into WF workflow in the next Try It Out.

Figure 22-5

Now that you have a little background you will build this using a console application as the host. You will leave out calls to the database, calls to the file system processes, and other items not essential to understanding WF. You will gain the base knowledge of how to put this all together and when you are done you will be ready to explore this new technology on your own.

Try It Out   **Listing Form Sequential Workflow**

In this Try It Out, you will program the workflow diagram just presented, using a console application.

> *As you are working with the controls, be sure to name them such that they can be identified easily. If you leave the default names, controls like IfElse1 and IfElse2 are very difficult to manage on more complex applications. Creating self-documenting names is always a good practice.*

1.   To start, create a new sequential workflow console application. Name it **WorkflowPropertyListing**.

2.   Add the following declaration and public property named `strFileName` to the code. This code goes into the class `Workflow1`.

```
Private _strFileName As String

Public Property strFileName() As String
    Get
        Return _strFileName
    End Get
    Set(ByVal value As String)
        _strFileName = value
    End Set
End Property
```

3. On the workflow designer, place a code control to create a codeActivity activity. Name this **CodePickUpPDF.**

4. Double-click the control to create a `CodePickUpPDF_ExecuteCode` subroutine. In this subroutine, you write the code to pick up a PDF file in a specified directory from the configuration file. For this example, you will use console writes for these code blocks so you can see the workflow's path in the host application.

```
Private Sub CodePickUpPDF_ExecuteCode(ByVal sender As System.Object, _
ByVal e As System.EventArgs)

    Console.WriteLine("What is the file name?")
    'Set the file name property
    'This could be done by an external application
    strFileName = Console.ReadLine()

End Sub
```

5. On the workflow designer, place a second code control after CodePickUpPDF. Name this control **CodeMoveFile.**

6. Double-click the CodeMoveFile and add the following code to the execute code subroutine.

```
    'This is where you would move the file to the network share for storage
    Console.WriteLine("File has been moved successfully")
```

7. On the workflow designer, add a third code control and place it in line after CodeMoveFile. Name this control **CodeParseFileName.**

8. Now that you have the hang of adding the controls to your design, refer to Figure 22-6 to complete the workflow. Just drag the controls onto the workflow and change the control names to match Figure 22-6. The visual designer makes it easy to create a workflow from a visual image since they are so similar. When you finish, you will have a complete sequential workflow design.

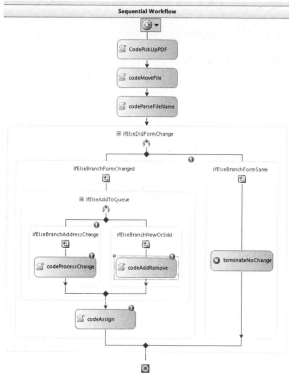

Figure 22-6

9. After completing the diagram, add the following code. This code will display the activity and path of the workflow in the host application.

When you double-click the code activities, a property is wired to the subroutine created. If you enter the procedures for _ExecuteCode, you will need to manually set the code activities property ExecuteCode *to the procedure you create.*

```
Private Sub codeParseFileName_ExecuteCode(ByVal sender As System.Object, _
ByVal e As System.EventArgs)
    Console.WriteLine("File name has been parsed successfully")
End Sub

Private Sub codeProcessChange_ExecuteCode(ByVal sender As System.Object, _
ByVal e As System.EventArgs)
    Console.WriteLine("File address change found")
    Console.WriteLine("Address change workflow item added")
End Sub

Private Sub codeAddRemove_ExecuteCode(ByVal sender As System.Object, _
ByVal e As System.EventArgs)
    Console.WriteLine("File item added or removed found")
    Console.WriteLine("Address change workflow item added")

End Sub
```

```
        Private Sub codeAssign_ExecuteCode(ByVal sender As System.Object, _
    ByVal e As System.EventArgs)
            Console.WriteLine("Workflow item assigned")
            Console.WriteLine("")
            Console.WriteLine("Workflow complete")
            Console.ReadLine()
        End Sub
```

10. Add the last two procedures (`AnyChange` and `WasAddressChange`) that you will wire to the ifElseBranch with the following code:

```
        Private Sub AnyChange(ByVal sender As System.Object, _
    ByVal e As System.Workflow.Activities.ConditionalEventArgs)
            If strFileName.ToUpper.Contains("_ADDRESS") _
                    Or strFileName.ToUpper.Contains("_NEW") _
                    Or strFileName.ToUpper.Contains("_REMOVE") Then
                e.Result = True
            End If
        End Sub
        Private Sub WasAddressChange(ByVal sender As System.Object, _
    ByVal e As System.Workflow.Activities.ConditionalEventArgs)
            If strFileName.ToUpper.Contains("_ADDRESS") Then
                e.Result = True
            End If
        End Sub
```

11. Next, you will wire up the left side of the ifElseBranches. Click ifElseBranchFormChanged and change the condition property to `Code Condition`. Expand the property and you will be able to select from procedures that can handle this event. In this case, the drop-down under `Code Condition` should contain the last two procedures you added: `AnyChange` and `WasAddressChange`. Select `AnyChange`.

12. Select ifElseBranchAddressChange and repeat step 11, this time selecting `WasAddressChange`.

13. That is all. Go ahead and run the application. Enter some file names and review the output to see the flow and test if it is correct or not. Enter names like `1990_NEW.PDF`, `0001_REMOVE.PDF`, `9878_ADDRESS.PDF`, `88877_NO.PDF` and then just enter random text. Those will take you through each path of the workflow. On the no change path, the workflow will terminate and that will cause the console application to exit. See Figure 22-7 for a sample of the output you will see when you run the application.

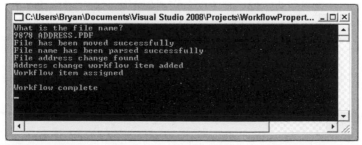

Figure 22-7

How It Works

This example shows a more complex workflow. You are able to use some of the most used activities in the WF toolbox: ifElse and Code. Figure 22-8 shows the ifElse control you add. In this control, you could copy and paste more ifElseBranches into the ifElse. This flexibility would make a workflow easier to see visually, so you create the branches to use only yes/no or true/false answers. Imagine if inside the ifElse you had five `case` statements with different code running for each. That code would be hidden on the visual designer and hard to see. By adding five ifEsleBranches, you could see on the designer that there was special code for each of the five conditions. In a large workflow, that would make maintaining and changing the workflow much easier. Now, let's review in more detail how this works.

Figure 22-8

First, look at the public property. For enterprise workflows, you would normally have a more robust host application than this console application. Think about a forms application that creates an instance of the workflow and needs to pass in data. This is where the property would normally be used, and the forms application would set the `strFileName` property and then start the workflow.

```
Public Property strFileName() As String
    Get
        Return _strFileName
    End Get
    Set(ByVal value As String)
        _strFileName = value
    End Set
End Property
```

All of the rest of the code can be considered event handlers for the controls you added. Figure 22-9 shows the first three activities in the workflow.

Figure 22-9

Now look at the activity to pick up the PDF file. Here you ask for the file name and set the property for file name to the input from the user. This requires some file I/O logic to grab the file from the file system. To test the flow, you add output to the console application using the writeline method.

```
Private Sub CodePickUpPDF_ExecuteCode(ByVal sender As System.Object, _
ByVal e As System.EventArgs)
    Console.WriteLine("What is the file name?")
    'Set the file name property
    'This could be done by an external application
    strFileName = Console.ReadLine()
End Sub
```

The next code activity is to move the file. In this activity, you add code to move the file to the appropriate file server. To test the flow, output is added again:

```
Private Sub codeMoveFile_ExecuteCode(ByVal sender As System.Object, _
ByVal e As System.EventArgs)
    'This is where you would move the file to the network share for
storage
    Console.WriteLine("File has been moved successfully")
End Sub
```

The third activity is similar to the first two. Here you add the logic to output the workflow activity. In a true workflow application, this would have probably parsed the file name and set a property.

```
Private Sub codeParseFileName_ExecuteCode(ByVal sender As System.Object, _
ByVal e As System.EventArgs)
    Console.WriteLine("File name has been parsed successfully")
End Sub
```

Next up is the activity you create for an address change. In this handler, you write code to output the flow to the console application. This activity only handles one true condition. You could easily use a code activity to handle all of the if conditions at once. That would mean that all the conditions would be hidden from you in the Visual Basic code. Try to remember not to hide many conditions in one activity. You should code your conditions using ifElse branches that handle just one case each, so that you will be able to see the true flow visually.

```
Private Sub codeProcessChange_ExecuteCode(ByVal sender As System.Object, _
ByVal e As System.EventArgs)
    Console.WriteLine("File address change found")
    Console.WriteLine("Address change workflow item added")
End Sub
```

Next, the workflow steps into the if/else conditions. Figure 22-10 shows the conditions you add.

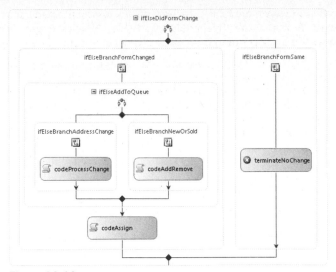

Figure 22-10

At this point, the workflow evaluates whether or not a change was made. The first branch you created calls the handler named `AnyChange`. The properties on ifElseBranchFormChanged look like Figure 22-11. The condition drop-down displays all procedures that can handle ifElseBranches.

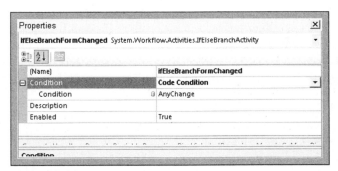

Figure 22-11

Inside the procedure, `AnyChange`, you write the code to determine whether a change was made. To determine a change, the file name is tested for the characters _ADDRESS, _NEW, or _REMOVE. When you test strings, you should use forced upper or lower case unless case sensitivity is required. Here, the magic happens by setting the result property of e to `true`. The parameter e is what the ifElse branch uses to determine the outcome of the code and is of type `System.Workflow.Activities`
`.ConditionalEventArgs`. When setting `e.Result = True` you tell ifElse to proceed down the current path and not evaluate the other branches. Note that for the branches, you only test the condition. You could have put the code here for the `true` condition, but it is much cleaner to keep everything separated by using the code activity on the path to handle the actions of the workflow.

```
        Private Sub AnyChange(ByVal sender As System.Object, _
    ByVal e As System.Workflow.Activities.ConditionalEventArgs)
        If strFileName.ToUpper.Contains("_ADDRESS") _
                Or strFileName.ToUpper.Contains("_NEW") _
                Or strFileName.ToUpper.Contains("_REMOVE") Then
            e.Result = True
        End If
    End Sub
```

For ifElseBranches, the last one does not need a handler as it is considered the `else` clause. Compare the properties for ifElseBranchFormSame to ifElseBranchFormChanged. Figure 22-12 shows the properties window of ifElseBranchFormSame. Notice no condition is set for the last branch, ifElseBranchFormSame.

Figure 22-12

If the workflow finds no change, it travels down the same branch to a terminator. The terminator ends the process. In the console application, you need to look quickly to see the message displayed before the console application closes.

If the workflow finds a change, another ifElse branch is encountered. Again, there are two conditions: one for an address change and one for an insert/delete. For this ifElse, first you test for an address change. If found, you set `e.Result` to `true` to tell the workflow to proceed:

```
        Private Sub WasAddressChange(ByVal sender As System.Object, _
    ByVal e As System.Workflow.Activities.ConditionalEventArgs)
        If strFileName.ToUpper.Contains("_ADDRESS") Then
            e.Result = True
        End If
    End Sub
```

If the change was not an address change you knew that it was a new record or sold record, so the catch `all else` branch ifElseBranchNewOrSold determined what to do next. You write output to the console application so you could see the flow was followed correctly when the workflow runs.

```
        Private Sub codeAddRemove_ExecuteCode(ByVal sender As System.Object, _
    ByVal e As System.EventArgs)
        Console.WriteLine("File item added or removed found")
        Console.WriteLine("New or removed workflow item added")

    End Sub
```

Finally, when the workflow has a change it will eventually go to the codeAssign activity. The code you write here is for the console application. The final `readline` pauses the console application so you can review the results. In a production workflow, this most likely would have interacted with the database to assign the new work to users.

```
    Private Sub codeAssign_ExecuteCode(ByVal sender As System.Object, _
ByVal e As System.EventArgs)
        Console.WriteLine("Workflow item assigned")
        Console.WriteLine("")
        Console.WriteLine("Workflow complete")
        Console.ReadLine()
    End Sub
```

Summary

This chapter showed how to set up a workflow and map the application code to follow the flow. You saw how to use some activities: Terminators, ifElse, and code activities. There are many more activities for you to explore, along with other types of hosts for the workflows. As a beginner, you most likely will not be asked to create many workflows, but now you know that you can use the technology to add functionality to your other applications.

Using workflows, you will be able to accomplish many complex tasks easily. You may want to set up your workflow to have a web service interface, for example. That way other applications can easily call into the workflow and start it from just about anywhere. Workflow Foundation can already be integrated in SharePoint, and soon you will be able to easily integrate with BizTalk Server and Office applications. Just remember to create your workflow so that it is visually represented correctly before adding the code. Try not to hide many complex pieces of logic inside one activity. And most importantly, keep it simple by having one test per ifElse branch. You should be able to tell what is happening in the process just by looking at the visual designer.

You should know how to:

❑   Create sequential workflows

❑   Determine which type of workflow project to use

❑   Use code activities and ifElse logic

❑   Set properties to be used inside the workflow

Exercises

1.   Add a third ifElseBranch to the WorkflowPropertyListing Try It Out. Split the branch for NewOrSold into two branches.

Figure 22-13 shows what your workflow should look like.

Figure 22-13

2. In the WorkflowPropertyListing project, add a while activity before the first ifElse activity. You will need to create a code condition handler and then set the code condition property. This is where the `while` loop determines if it should continue or not. Next, add a code activity that tests for a change found and then asks the user to enter a new file name if no change is found. The `while` loop will continue if `e.result = true` in the condition handler.

23

Building Mobile Applications

Mobile devices — more specifically, personal digital assistants (PDAs) — are being shipped to more and more people around the world. A market once owned by Palm's Operating System is now a market full of devices running Microsoft Windows CE. According to a report published November 12, 2004, by the Associated Press, Windows CE first took the top place over Palm in number of PDAs shipped in the third quarter 2004. Of the 2.8 million PDAs shipped worldwide, Windows CE was the operating system on 48.1 percent. According to a summary of the Gartner PDA Report for Q1 2006 (www.palminfocenter.com/news/8564/gartner-pda-report-for-q1-2006/), Windows Mobile OS is now running on over 50 percent of the PDA's shipped. This represents over 1.8 million devices shipped in that three-month period. The demand for applications to make PDAs and other smart devices valuable to companies is growing with the number of PDAs in use by corporations. As you build skills in Visual Studio 2008, know that building applications for smart devices is definitely a skill many employers are and will be looking for in their developers.

Designing mobile applications for Windows CE, Pocket PC, and Smartphone devices is simplified using Visual Studio 2008. This chapter focuses on applications built for PDAs running Microsoft Windows Mobile operating system.

In this chapter you learn:

- ❑ The differences between the full .NET framework and the Compact Framework
- ❑ How to use ActiveSync and Windows Mobile Device Center to connect to smart devices
- ❑ How to create mobile applications
- ❑ How to use the built-in emulator to test mobile applications

Understanding the Environment

If you have never used a PDA, it is a small version of a stripped-down PC. A typical Pocket PC may have 64 MB of internal memory and a 312-MHz processor. It weighs less than a pound and has a 3.5 inch screen that supports 240 × 320 pixels and 65K colors. Compare that to a desktop computer. A normal PC may have a spec sheet like this: 3 GHz processor, 120 GB hard drive, 1 GB RAM and a 19-inch monitor that supports 1600×1200 pixels and 32-bit color (over 4 billion colors). Another important difference is that the screen on a Pocket PC is tall, whereas a desktop monitor is wide. One more issue to consider is that when the battery dies, you lose all data and applications stored in memory. The user must add a storage device, such as a compact Flash card, to avoid having to reinstall applications when the battery loses power. Keep these differences in mind as you build applications for mobile devices.

Now that you know the basics of a PDA, I will try to outline what Visual Studio 2008 has for you to work with when you create mobile applications. To start, you have the .NET Compact Framework (CF). The best part of the CF is that it is a subset of the .NET Framework you know about from earlier chapters. Most of what you know is part of the CF, and this knowledge will allow you to start creating mobile applications with a small learning curve. Just like the parent Framework, the CF is based on the Common Language Runtime (CLR) and executes Microsoft Intermediate Language (MSIL) to maintain platform independence. The greatest difference you will see is the number of controls that are missing and the number of overloaded methods, properties, and constructors that are not present for controls. Application deployment is different also. Deploying applications to a PDA is not going to be done via CD or floppy disk. You will use Microsoft ActiveSync to facilitate deploying applications to a Pocket PC. Next, we elaborate on what you need to know before you create your first mobile application.

Common Language Runtime

One goal of the CLR, also known as the *execution engine*, is to allow multiple languages to run side by side. The CLR manages the following items:

- ❑ Memory and garbage collection
- ❑ Platform independence via Microsoft Intermediate Language
- ❑ Common type system
- ❑ Exception handling
- ❑ Just-In-Time compilation

ActiveSync and Windows Mobile Device Center

To connect your mobile device to your desktop, you will most likely use ActiveSync for Windows XP or Windows Mobile Device Center (version 6.1 was the latest version at time of writing) for Windows Vista. The software quickly connects you to your PC, your network resources, and even a shared Internet connection. You can use the software connection to synchronize your application data, access web services, or even replicate data to an SQL Server machine on your network. All you need is to download the latest software and connect your device to your desktop. The interface for Windows Mobile Device Center is shown in Figure 23-1. When you are connected using ActiveSync, you have options such as those shown in Figure 23-2.

Figure 23-1

Figure 23-2

Since most of you do not have Pocket PCs, I will briefly explain the ease of deploying a smart device application to a Pocket PC. To deploy a smart device application, Visual Studio 2008 includes a smart device .cab file template under setup and deployment projects. For deploying, add the .cab file project to your device application project. When you build the project, just copy the output to the device using your mobile device software. Next, double-click the .cab file using the device, and it installs the application. That is all it takes to deploy your applications.

You can download the latest version of Microsoft ActiveSync from Microsoft. The .exe for ActiveSync version 3.7.1, used here, was a 3.77MB download. Search for ActiveSync at the Microsoft download site www.microsoft.com/downloads/).

You can download version 6.1 of Windows Mobile Device Center for Vista at www.microsoft.com/downloads/details.aspx?familyid=46F72DF1-E46A-4A5F-A791-09F07AAA1914&displaylang=en.

Common Types in the Compact Framework

The type of system available in the Compact Framework should look familiar to you when you start to program mobile applications. The following table lists the types available in the CF. As you allocate memory with variables in your applications, remember this chapter and the fact that you are working with very limited resources. Refer to this table for a quick reference to ensure you use the smallest data type possible to store data.

VB type	CLR type	Size	Value range
Boolean	Boolean	Depends	True or False
Byte	Byte	1 byte	0 through 255 (unsigned)
Char	Char	2 bytes	Single unicode character
Date	DateTime	8 bytes	0:00:00 (midnight) on January 1, 0001 through 11:59:59 PM on December 31, 9999
Decimal	Decimal	16 bytes	0 through +/−79,228,162,514,264,337,593,543,950,335 (+/−7.9... E+28) with no decimal point; 0 through +/−7.9228162514264337593543950335 with 28 places to the right of the decimal; smallest nonzero number is +/−0.0000000000000000000000000001 (+/−1E-28)
Double	Double	8 bytes	−1.79769313486231570E+308 through −4.94065645841246544E-324 for negative values; 4.94065645841246544E-324 through 1.79769313486231570E+308 for positive values
Integer	Int32	4 bytes	−2,147,483,648 through 2,147,483,647 (signed)
Long	Int64	8 bytes	−9,223,372,036,854,775,808 through 9,223,372,036,854,775,807 (9.2 ... E+18) (signed)
Object	Object	4 bytes	Any type can be stored in a variable of type Object
SByte	SByte	1 byte	−128 through 127 (signed)
Short	Int16	2 bytes	−32,768 through 32,767 (signed)
Single	Single	4 bytes	−3.4028235E+38 through −1.401298E-45 for negative values; 1.401298E-45 through 3.4028235E+38 for positive values

VB type	CLR type	Size	Value range
String	String	Depends	0 to approximately 2 billion Unicode characters
UInteger	UInt32	4 bytes	0 through 4,294,967,295 (unsigned)
ULong	UInt64	8 bytes	0 through 18,446,744,073,709,551,615 (1.8. . . E+19) (unsigned)
UShort	UInt16	2 bytes	0 through 65,535 (unsigned)

The Compact Framework Classes

The .NET Compact Framework classes are a subset of the .NET Framework classes plus a few inclusions that you do not need for desktop applications. Overall, you will not be surprised by the controls you find in the CF.

The .NET Compact Framework is approximately 12 percent of the size of the full framework. That makes it easy to see that, although many of the common controls and namespaces are included, the functionality has been greatly reduced. You will notice quickly that controls like the Label control are missing properties. Take a look at Figure 23-3 to see the differences between label properties available in both frameworks. The Properties window on the right is smaller and that represents the Compact Framework.

Figure 23-3

Two other missing pieces are method overrides and events. Figure 23-4 compares the events of the Button control in both frameworks. The events listed from the full framework on the right of Figure 23-4 are just a partial list and represent about half of the available events.

Figure 23-4

How many overloaded methods have been removed? Based on the size of the CF, you can estimate that more than 75 percent are missing. When you look at the System.IO.FileStream constructors, you will see that the full Framework boasts 15 overloaded constructors, while the CF has been whittled down to only five. When you write applications that will be used on smart devices and desktops, you will have to adjust certain parts of your code to address these differences.

The following table shows a partial list of the default controls available to a Pocket PC application.

Name	Name
Button	NumericUpDown
CheckBox	OpenFileDialog
ComboBox	Panel
ContextMenu	PictureBox

Name	Name
DataGrid	ProgressBar
DateTimePicker	RadioButton
DocumentList	SaveFileDialog
DomainUpDown	Splitter
HScrollBar	StatusBar
ImageList	TabControl
InputPanel	TextBox
Label	Timer
LinkLabel	ToolBar
ListBox	TrackBar
ListView	TreeView
MainMenu	VScrollBar
MonthCalendar	WebBrowser
Notification	

Building a Pocket PC Game

For your first mobile application, you build a simple game of tic-tac-toe. You will see how different the screen is and design a user interface that is simple for the user.

Try It Out   **Tic Tac Toe**

1. In Visual Studio 2008, select the File ⇨ New Project menu. This displays the New Project dialog box.

2. Select Visual Basic from the Project Types pane on the left. Next, expand the Visual Basic label and then select Smart Device. In the templates pane on the right, choose Smart Device Project. Change the project name to **TicTacToe** and click the OK button (Figure 23-5 shows the dialog box). After clicking OK you see a screen for selecting the target device and the CF version. On this screen, shown in Figure 23-6, choose Windows Mobile 5.0 Pocket PC SDK for version 3.5 of the Compact Framework and select the template for Device Application.

Figure 23-5

Figure 23-6

3. The project opens to a view of a Pocket PC, as shown in Figure 23-7. This is the design environment. As you build the application, you will see the screen and be able to design the graphical interface on a replica of the actual device screen. You will know exactly how the application will look when the user installs it.

Figure 23-7

4. Build the user interface. Add 10 buttons to the form as shown in Figure 23-8. The three rows of three buttons represent the tic-tac-toe board. Set the Size to **40, 40** for the nine buttons that make up the board. Starting with the button in the upper left of the board, move left to right, down a row, left to right, down a row, and then left to right again, and name the buttons on the board **btn00, btn01, btn02, btn10, btn11, btn12, btn20, btn21, btn22**. The name begins with *btn* followed by the row (0, 1 or 2) and column (0, 1 or 2) of the button. So btn02 is on the first row (Row 0) and the third column (Column 2). When you use these names in code, you will know the location on the board. Next, set the Font for all of the board buttons to **Tahoma**, **24pt**, **Bold**. Finally, set the Text property to **X** and the Anchor property to **None** for the board buttons. The final button is the New Game button. Set the Name to **btnNewGame** and the Text to **&New Game**. Below the board, add a label named **lblMessages**. Make the label tall enough to display two lines of text. Now, change the Text property of Form1 to **TicTacToe**, and the user interface is complete.

Figure 23-8

5.   Switch to the code behind view and add the following highlighted code to the `Form1` class:

```
Public Class Form1
```

```
'Get the game ready to start again
Sub ResetGame()
    Dim ctrl As Control
    'Loop through the board controls and set them to ""
    For Each ctrl In Me.Controls
        If TypeOf (ctrl) Is Button And ctrl.Name <> "btnNewGame" Then
            ctrl.Text = String.Empty
        End If
    Next
    lblMessages.Text = ""
    'Enable the board buttons
    CorrectEnabledState(True)
End Sub

Private Sub CorrectEnabledState(ByVal ButtonEnabledState As Boolean)
    Dim ctrl As Control
    For Each ctrl In Me.Controls
        If TypeOf (ctrl) Is Button And ctrl.Name <> "btnNewGame" Then
            ctrl.Enabled = ButtonEnabledState
        End If
    Next
End Sub
```

```vb
Private Sub CorrectEnabledState()
   Dim ctrl As Control
   For Each ctrl In Me.Controls
      If TypeOf (ctrl) Is Button And ctrl.Name <> "btnNewGame" Then
         If ctrl.Text = String.Empty Then
            ctrl.Enabled = True
         Else
            ctrl.Enabled = False
         End If
      End If
   Next
End Sub

Sub ComputerPlay()
   Dim RandomGenerator As New Random()
   Dim intRandom As Integer
   Dim intCount As Integer = 0
   Dim ctrl As Control
   intRandom = RandomGenerator.Next(20, 100)
   While intCount < intRandom
      For Each ctrl In Me.Controls
         If TypeOf (ctrl) Is Button And ctrl.Name <> "btnNewGame" Then
            If ctrl.Text = String.Empty Then
               intCount += 1
               If intCount = intRandom Then
                  ctrl.Text = "O"
                  ctrl.Enabled = False
                  Exit For
               End If
            End If
         End If
      Next
   End While
End Sub

Private Sub TicTacToe_Click(ByVal sender As Object, ByVal e As _
System.EventArgs)    Handles btn00.Click, btn20.Click, btn10.Click, _
btn01.Click, btn21.Click, btn11.Click, btn02.Click, btn22.Click, btn12.Click
   CorrectEnabledState(False)
   Application.DoEvents() 'Allows the screen to refresh
   CType(sender, Button).Text = "X"
   If IsGameOver() Then
      MsgBox("Game Over")
   Else
      lblMessages.Text = "Computer selecting ..."
      Application.DoEvents() 'Allows the screen to refresh
      ComputerPlay()
      If IsGameOver() Then
         MsgBox("Game Over")
      Else
         lblMessages.Text = "Select your next position ..."
         CorrectEnabledState()
      End If
   End If
End Sub
```

```
Sub Winner(ByVal strWinner As String)
    Dim strMessage As String
    If strWinner = "X" Then
        strMessage = "You win!!"
    ElseIf strWinner = "O" Then
        strMessage = "Computer wins!!"
    Else
        strMessage = strWinner
    End If
    lblMessages.Text = strMessage
End Sub

Function IsGameOver() As Boolean
    If btn00.Text = btn01.Text And btn01.Text = btn02.Text And _
    btn02.Text <> String.Empty Then
        'Winner on top Row
        Call Winner(btn00.Text)
            Return True
    End If

    If btn10.Text = btn11.Text And btn11.Text = btn12.Text And _
    btn12.Text <> String.Empty Then
        'Winner on middle Row
        Call Winner(btn10.Text)
        Return True
    End If

    If btn20.Text = btn21.Text And btn21.Text = btn22.Text And _
    btn22.Text <> String.Empty Then
        'Winner on bottom Row
        Call Winner(btn20.Text)
        Return True
    End If

    If btn00.Text = btn10.Text And btn10.Text = btn20.Text And _
    btn20.Text <> String.Empty Then
        'Winner on first column
        Call Winner(btn00.Text)
        Return True
    End If

    If btn01.Text = btn11.Text And btn11.Text = btn21.Text And _
    btn21.Text <> String.Empty Then
        'Winner on second column
        Call Winner(btn01.Text)
        Return True
    End If

    If btn02.Text = btn12.Text And btn12.Text = btn22.Text And _
    btn22.Text <> String.Empty Then
        'Winner on third column
        Call Winner(btn02.Text)
        Return True
    End If
```

```
    If btn00.Text = btn11.Text And btn11.Text = btn22.Text And _
    btn22.Text <> String.Empty Then
        'Winner on diagonal top left to bottom right
        Call Winner(btn00.Text)
        Return True
    End If

    If btn20.Text = btn11.Text And btn11.Text = btn02.Text And _
    btn02.Text <> String.Empty Then
        'Winner on diagonal bottom left to top right
        Call Winner(btn20.Text)
        Return True
    End If

    'Test for a tie, all square full
    Dim ctrl As Control
    Dim intOpenings As Integer = 0
    For Each ctrl In Me.Controls
        If TypeOf (ctrl) Is Button And ctrl.Name <> "btnNewGame" Then
            If ctrl.Text = String.Empty Then
                intOpenings = intOpenings + 1
            End If
        End If
    Next
    If intOpenings = 0 Then
        Call Winner("It's a tie.")
        Return True
    End If
    Return False
End Function
End Class
```

6. Add the highlighted code to the `Form1_Load` event handler:

```
Private Sub Form1_Load(ByVal sender As Object, ByVal e As _
System.EventArgs) Handles
Me.Load
    CorrectEnabledState(False)
    lblMessages.Text = "Click new game to begin."
End Sub
```

7. Add the following highlighted code to the `btnNewGame_Click` event handler:

```
Private Sub btnNewGame_Click(ByVal sender As System.Object, ByVal e As _
System.EventArgs) Handles btnNewGame.Click
    ResetGame()
End Sub
```

8. Run the program in debug mode to see how it works. You will be asked how to deploy the application. Choose one of the emulators to use for testing and click the Deploy button shown in Figure 23-9. Be patient, because it takes some time to start the entire process. In the release process, the emulator displays very quickly and then the software takes time to deploy so you might think it is not working.

Figure 23-9

9. When the application starts, the Pocket PC emulator displays, and the TicTacToe program will be running. Wait for the application to start. The emulator will look like Figure 23-10. You may be prompted with an Establishing Connection dialog box. Choose Internet to continue.

Figure 23-10

10. Click New Game and play against the computer. The computer player chooses a random play and is easy to defeat.

How It Works

This game gives you a basic understanding of smart device development. It is relatively the same as the work you completed in earlier chapters. The first thing you may notice is the screen size. You have limited real estate to design the user interface. The screen is the perfect size for a simple game of tic-tac-toe.

To start, you create the user interface. When you add the buttons and labels, it is just like building a desktop application. The controls have many of the same properties you are familiar with from previous chapters. You should have no problem with the user interface.

Most of the work you did for the game was with code. Again, everything you learned earlier in the book applies to smart device applications. You saw the functions and subroutines created to run the game, and you should have remembered most of this logic from previous chapters. We will go through the code one routine at a time to explain what happened.

After a game ends, you need a standard way to get the board and screen ready for a new game. This is accomplished with the `ResetGame` procedure. This procedure uses the collection of controls on the form and iterates through each control that is a button. If the button is a part of the board, the text property will be reset to an empty string. After all buttons have been reset, the message label text is set to blank and all board buttons are enabled.

```
'Get the game ready to start again
Sub ResetGame()
    Dim ctrl As Control
    'Loop through the board controls and set them to ""
    For Each ctrl In Me.Controls
        If TypeOf (ctrl) Is Button And ctrl.Name <> "btnNewGame" Then
            ctrl.Text = String.Empty
        End If
    Next
    lblMessages.Text = ""
    'Enable the board buttons
    CorrectEnabledState(True)
End Sub
```

The `CorrectEnabledState` subroutine has two signatures. This is an example of an overloaded method. When you call `CorrectEnabledState` with one `Boolean` argument, the procedure sets the `Enabled` property of all buttons on the board to the value of the parameter you pass. The other method signature expects no parameters. So when it is called, that procedure tests every button on the board. If a button is blank, it is enabled. Otherwise, the button is disabled.

```
Private Sub CorrectEnabledState(ByVal ButtonEnabledState As Boolean)
    Dim ctrl As Control
    For Each ctrl In Me.Controls
        If TypeOf (ctrl) Is Button And ctrl.Name <> "btnNewGame" Then
            ctrl.Enabled = ButtonEnabledState
        End If
    Next
End Sub
Private Sub CorrectEnabledState()
    Dim ctrl As Control
    For Each ctrl In Me.Controls
        If TypeOf (ctrl) Is Button And ctrl.Name <> "btnNewGame" Then
```

```
            If ctrl.Text = String.Empty Then
                ctrl.Enabled = True
            Else
                ctrl.Enabled = False
            End If
        End If
    Next
End Sub
```

Another procedure that is created is `ComputerPlay`. This procedure enables play for the computer. At the top of the code, declarations are made for local variables. The meat of the logic started before the `while` loop. The `Next` method of the `Random` class generated a random number between 20 and 100. The program loops through every open square on the board, counting each one, until the lucky random number square is found and it is marked with an O.

```
Sub ComputerPlay()
    Dim RandomGenerator As New Random()
    Dim intRandom As Integer
    Dim intCount As Integer = 0
    Dim ctrl As Control
    intRandom = RandomGenerator.Next(20, 100)
    While intCount < intRandom
        For Each ctrl In Me.Controls
            If TypeOf (ctrl) Is Button And ctrl.Name <> "btnNewGame" Then
                If ctrl.Text = String.Empty Then
                    intCount += 1
                    If intCount = intRandom Then
                        ctrl.Text = "O"
                        ctrl.Enabled = False
                    Exit For
                End If
            End If
        End If
    Next
    End While
End Sub
```

When you click any square, the `TicTacToe_Click` procedure is called. Take a look at the `Handles` keyword in the declaration of the subroutine. The `Click` event from every button on the board has been added to the comma-delimited list. So when you click any square, this procedure handles the event. The first step of the procedure disables all squares, followed by a call to `Application.DoEvents`. The `DoEvents` method allowes all waiting events in the queue to complete. This is placed here to avoid the problems associated with clicking more than one button in a turn. If you remove these two lines of code, you can quickly click three squares in a row before the computer made one pick. Next, the button that is clicked, the `sender`, is marked with an X. After the square is marked, the board is checked for a winner. If no winner is found, the computer makes the next move. Again, the board is checked for a winner. If no winner is found, the player is asked to select again.

```
Private Sub TicTacToe_Click(ByVal sender As Object, ByVal e As _
    System.EventArgs)    Handles btn00.Click, btn20.Click, btn10.Click, _
    btn01.Click, btn21.Click, btn11.Click, btn02.Click, btn22.Click, btn12.Click
    CorrectEnabledState(False)
    Application.DoEvents() 'Allows the screen to refresh
```

```
            CType(sender, Button).Text = "X"
            If IsGameOver() Then
                MsgBox("Game Over")
            Else
                lblMessages.Text = "Computer selecting ..."
                Application.DoEvents() 'Allows the screen to refresh
                ComputerPlay()
                If IsGameOver() Then
                    MsgBox("Game Over")
                Else
                    lblMessages.Text = "Select your next position ..."
                    CorrectEnabledState()
                End If
            End If
        End Sub
```

The `Winner` procedure is called when a winner is found. The outcome of the game is displayed on the message label.

```
        Sub Winner(ByVal strWinner As String)
            Dim strMessage As String
            If strWinner = "X" Then
                strMessage = "You win!!"
            ElseIf strWinner = "O" Then
                strMessage = "Computer wins!!"
            Else
                strMessage = strWinner
            End If
            lblMessages.Text = strMessage
        End Sub
```

After every move, `IsGameOver` is called to look for a winner. Every possible combination of squares is tested. If three squares in a row are marked by the same player, the `Winner` procedure is called and `True` is returned from the function. If no winner is found, the board is tested to see whether all squares are marked. When all squares are marked, the game is a tie.

```
        Function IsGameOver() As Boolean
            If btn00.Text = btn01.Text And btn01.Text = btn02.Text And _
            btn02.Text <> String.Empty Then
                'Winner on top Row
                Call Winner(btn00.Text)
                    Return True
            End If

            If btn10.Text = btn11.Text And btn11.Text = btn12.Text And _
            btn12.Text <> String.Empty Then
                'Winner on middle Row
                Call Winner(btn10.Text)
                Return True
            End If

            If btn20.Text = btn21.Text And btn21.Text = btn22.Text And _
            btn22.Text <> String.Empty Then
                'Winner on bottom Row
```

```vb
            Call Winner(btn20.Text)
            Return True
        End If

        If btn00.Text = btn10.Text And btn10.Text = btn20.Text And _
        btn20.Text <> String.Empty Then
            'Winner on first column
            Call Winner(btn00.Text)
            Return True
        End If

        If btn01.Text = btn11.Text And btn11.Text = btn21.Text And _
        btn21.Text <> String.Empty Then
            'Winner on second column
            Call Winner(btn01.Text)
            Return True
        End If

        If btn02.Text = btn12.Text And btn12.Text = btn22.Text And _
        btn22.Text <> String.Empty Then
            'Winner on third column
            Call Winner(btn02.Text)
            Return True
        End If

        If btn00.Text = btn11.Text And btn11.Text = btn22.Text And _
        btn22.Text <> String.Empty Then
            'Winner on diagonal top left to bottom right
            Call Winner(btn00.Text)
            Return True
        End If

        If btn20.Text = btn11.Text And btn11.Text = btn02.Text And _
        btn02.Text <> String.Empty Then
            'Winner on diagonal bottom left to top right
            Call Winner(btn20.Text)
            Return True
        End If

        'Test for a tie, all square full
        Dim ctrl As Control
        Dim intOpenings As Integer = 0
        For Each ctrl In Me.Controls
            If TypeOf (ctrl) Is Button And ctrl.Name <> "btnNewGame" Then
                If ctrl.Text = String.Empty Then
                    intOpenings = intOpenings + 1
                End If
            End If
        Next
        If intOpenings = 0 Then
            Call Winner("It's a tie.")
            Return True
        End If
        Return False
    End Function
```

The remaining code is part of the handlers for the form's Load event and the New Game button Click event. On form load, the overloaded method CorrectEnabledState is called and all buttons are disabled. When you click the New Game button, ResetGame is called to set up the board to start a new game.

```
Private Sub Form1_Load(ByVal sender As Object, ByVal e As System.EventArgs) _
Handles Me.Load
    CorrectEnabledState(False)
    lblMessages.Text = "Click new game to begin."
End Sub

Private Sub btnNewGame_Click(ByVal sender As System.Object, ByVal e As _
System.EventArgs) Handles btnNewGame.Click
    ResetGame()
End Sub
```

Summary

Visual Studio 2008 and the Compact Framework make developing mobile applications very similar to desktop application development. This small learning curve for .NET developers is one of the reasons more PDAs are shipping with a Windows operating system than with any other competitor. The trend has been growing, and companies are starting to value the developer with mobile application skills. Take advantage of your knowledge and leverage it to start developing mobile applications.

In this chapter, you learned the basics of mobile development. You saw what is similar and what is different between the full version of the .NET Framework and the Compact Framework. You were shown examples of the missing pieces that explain how the CF has been shrunk by over 80 percent. Finally, you built your first application, tic-tac-toe.

You should know how to:

❑   Find differences between the full .NET framework and the Compact Framework

❑   Use ActiveSync and Windows Mobile Device Center to connect to smart devices

❑   Create mobile applications

❑   Use the built-in emulator to test mobile applications

Exercise

1.   The computer player is a random picker. Give the computer player some brains. Add at least one function named ComputerPlayToWin to the application. When the computer moves, call ComputerPlayToWin and check for a spot on the board that will create a win for the computer. If it exists, the computer should play that move rather than a random move. You can add other procedures if needed.

Deploying Your Application

Deploying an application can be a complicated process, especially when dealing with large, complex applications. A wealth of knowledge is required on nearly every aspect of a development. A large software installation for Windows requires knowledge ranging from Registry settings, MIME types, and configuration files to database creation and manipulation. Companies tend to rely on dedicated deployment software for these large installations, together with key people who understand the processes involved. However, Visual Studio 2008 does provide some basic deployment functionality, which is tremendously helpful for the standard developer and smaller installations.

Under the Visual Studio 2008 banner, you can create many different types of applications, from desktop to web applications and services. All of these have varying degrees of complexity or peculiarities when it comes to installation time.

Since this is a beginner's guide, this chapter will not go into depth on specifics regarding the deployment of the different applications; rather, it provides an overview of deployment.

In this chapter, you will:

❑ Learn concepts and terminology

❑ Deploy a ClickOnce Application with Visual Studio 2008

❑ Create a setup program with Visual Studio 2008

❑ Edit the installer user interface

What Is Deployment?

Deployment is the activity of delivering copies of an application to other machines so that the application runs in the new environment. It is the larger, architectural view for what you may know as installation or setup. There is a subtle difference between deployment and installation.

Deployment is the art of distribution. In other words, deployment is the way in which software is delivered.

The installation or setup is a process, where you load, configure, and install the software. So an *installation* is what you do to configure the software, and *deployment* is how you get it where you want it.

With this terminology, a CD is a deployment mechanism, as is the Internet. The two deployment mechanisms may have different installation requirements. For example, if an installation is on a CD, you may have all the additional dependent software on that CD. Delivery of the same application via the Internet might require users to visit additional sites to gather all the dependent software. Another example that may affect the installation option is where you may have written an installation in JavaScript. This may work fine when executed on a machine by the user having the correct Windows User Rights, but would not work through Internet Explorer. These kinds of considerations are important when deciding upon your best deployment option. The type of installations you require could also be different per application.

Now that you have an understanding of the terminology, let me show you how to deploy applications using Visual Studio 2008.

ClickOnce Deployment

ClickOnce deployment is the concept of sending an application or its referenced assemblies to the client in a way that allows self-updating applications. You have three distribution options for a ClickOnce application: file share, web page, or external media (CD, DVD, and so on). ClickOnce deployment has benefits with limitations. It is a useful deployment option for small- to medium-sized applications.

The benefits of ClickOnce deployment include three major factors. First, using this deployment option allows for self-updating Windows applications. You can post the latest version of the application at the original location, and the next time the user runs the application, it will install the latest version and run it. Next, any user can install most ClickOnce applications with only basic user security. With other technologies, administrator privileges are required. Finally, the installation has little impact on the user's computer. The application is run from a secure per-user cache and adds entries only to the Start menu and the Add/Remove Programs list. For programs that can run in the Internet or intranet zones that do not need to access the Global Assembly Cache (GAC), this is a terrific deployment solution for distribution via the web or a file share. If you distribute the ClickOnce application through external media, the application will be run with full trust.

In the following Try It Out, you learn how to deploy a ClickOnce application from the Web.

Try It Out   Deploying a ClickOnce Application from the Web

1. Create a new Windows Forms Application named **ClickOnce**.

2. On Form1, add a button and label. Change the button's Name property to **btnVersion** and Text to **Version**. Change the label Name to **lblVersion** and set Text to *""*.

3. Add the following highlighted code to the `Click` event for `btnVersion`:

```
Private Sub btnVersion_Click(ByVal sender As System.Object, ByVal e As _
    System.EventArgs) Handles btnVersion.Click
    lblVersion.Text = "Version 1.0"
End Sub
```

4. Test the form. When the user clicks the button, the label should display Version 1.0. Your form should look like Figure 24-1. Next, build the project. To build the project, click the Build menu and choose Build ClickOnce in the submenu.

Figure 24-1

5. Now, publish the assembly to the Web. If you do not have IIS installed, you can publish the file to a local or network drive. Just remember how you chose to publish the assembly. You will need to be running Visual Studio with elevated privileges to complete this. You may need to close Visual Studio, right-click the shortcut, and choose Run as administrator to launch the software.

6. Right-click the ClickOnce project in the Solution Explorer and choose Publish from the context menu. The Publish Wizard opens (see Figure 24-2). Choose a location to publish the file. In this example, we chose the default location for IIS.

Figure 24-2

7. Click Next. In this step you can choose whether to install a shortcut on the Start menu and add a listing in Add/Remove Programs. Select Yes as shown in Figure 24-3.

Figure 24-3

8. Next, you will see the summary of your choices. Click Finish to complete the wizard. This wizard will complete and open the default web page that users will use to install the application. Click Install to install the application (see Figure 24-4).

Figure 24-4

9. When you run the install from the Web, you may see a few security warnings (see Figure 24-5). If you see this, just click Install to continue. The form you created will open. Click the Version button and you will see Version 1.0. You can close the form.

Figure 24-5

10. Check the Program Files directory, and you will see firsthand that no files were added. A new shortcut has been added to the Start menu.

    Now, you will update the application and see the self-updating capabilities in action.

11. Go back to the ClickOnce Windows application in Visual Studio and change the button `Click` event to update the label to **Version 1.1**. Your `Click` event handler should look like this:

```
Private Sub btnVersion_Click(ByVal sender As System.Object, ByVal e As _
    System.EventArgs) Handles btnVersion.Click
    lblVersion.Text = "Version 1.1"
End Sub
```

12. Test and build the application.

13. Right-click the project in Solution Explorer and choose Properties from the context menu. This time you will not use the wizard to publish the assembly. Click the Publish tab on the left side of the main window.

14. Take a look at the options. You can see all the choices you made using the wizard. Make sure to set the action for updates. To do this, click the Updates button and select the check box for The application should check for updates. Click the radio button to check before the application starts. All you have to do is scroll down to the bottom right of the Publish window and click Publish Now.

15. The Install page will be displayed, but do not click Install. Just close the window.

16. Now, run the application using the shortcut on the Start menu. You will be prompted to update the application. Click OK (see Figure 24-6). After the form opens, click the Version button, and you will see by the text of the label that the application is updated.

Figure 24-6

How It Works

That was easy, but what happened? After a few clicks, you deployed a Windows Forms application that was self-updating. Behind the scenes, Visual Studio completed many tasks that make this deployment strategy easy to implement.

First, you chose the location to publish the assembly. `http://localhost/ClickOnce` was created as a virtual directory to host the deployment files for you. If you open the IIS MMC to investigate the virtual directory, you will see what was published. Your console will look like Figure 24-7. Note that each version of the assembly has its own directory. By default, the .NET Framework would be installed if the user does not have the correct version of the Framework. The installer would download it from Microsoft. Feel free to browse around the web directory. We will discuss the other files later.

Figure 24-7

The next step of the wizard allows you to specify whether offline access is allowed. A shortcut is added to Add/Remove Program files and the Start menu based on your choice to allow offline access. The application also installed to a secure cache on your computer. If you decide not to allow offline access, the user must return to the publishing location to launch the application on each use. In this case, the user would be required to have access to the web site to launch the application.

That's it. When you click Finish, Visual Studio 2008 goes to work. What happens behind the scenes is not magic. Actually, you could manually complete everything without Visual Studio if you ever needed to do so.

Now, take another look at IIS (see Figure 24-7). Here's what happened: First, a virtual directory was added to IIS. This is where the application was deployed. Then a subdirectory was created for the current version's files. Also, required manifest files were generated and placed under the root and version subdirectory.

Other files were part of the deployment. A web page (publish.htm) was created for the user interface. Finally, a setup.exe file for deployment was created. Both the setup.exe and publish .htm files were added to the root virtual directory.

To install the application, you navigated to the publish.htm web page. Each time you launched the installed application, a check was made to see whether a newer version was available. When a new version was available, you were notified and presented with the option to install the update. ClickOnce deployment has an almost unlimited number of deployment options. You just scratched the surface in this exercise.

XCOPY Deployment

XCOPY deployment gets its name from the MS DOS XCOPY command. XCOPY is a copy procedure that simply copies a directory and all files including subfolders. This is commonly associated with web applications, but with Visual Studio 2008 it can also apply to a desktop application. Since a standard .NET assembly does not need any form of registration, it fully supports this option. XCOPY does not work with shared assemblies because they require installation (if they are used from the Global Assembly Cache). You learn more about shared assemblies later in this chapter. When you use XCOPY for desktop applications, you will have to create any shortcuts or menu items via a script or manually. You would typically use XCopy for web site deployment and for testing and prototypes of Windows Forms applications.

Creating a Visual Studio 2008 Setup Application

Visual Studio 2008 supports the Windows Installer. But what is it? The Windows Installer service, which gets installed with Visual Studio 2008, is a general platform for installing applications in Windows. It provides a lot of functionality, such as uninstall capabilities and transactional installation options (the ability to roll back if something fails) as well as other general features. Many of these features either are built in (so that you do not have to do anything) or are configurable or extensible or both.

The Visual Studio 2008 Windows Installer support has made it easier to create a simple installation. Visual Studio has provided templates in the New Project dialog box for this purpose.

Visual Studio 2008 exposes four main templates for creating Windows installer projects:

❑ Setup Project for desktop or general setup

❑ Web Setup Project for web applications or web services

❑ Merge Module, a package that can only be merged into another setup

❑ Cab Project, which creates a package that can be used as a type of install

Finally, Visual Studio 2008 also has a Setup Wizard Project, which aids you in creating one of the Windows Installer templates listed here.

When you are creating setup applications, always be aware of the user. All of the applications you will create with Visual Studio 2008 require version 3.5 of the .NET Framework on the installation system. For internal applications, you will know what prerequisites are installed on each computer, but in many cases you will deliver your application to users with no idea of the target system configuration. When you are not sure of the user's configuration, it is up to you to make all required components available.

Visual Studio 2008 makes the process of including prerequisites easy. Most common requirements can be included (bootstrapping) by selecting a check box. By default, the .NET Framework is automatically bootstrapped. Any setup application that is created with the default settings will prompt the end user to install the Version 3.5 of the Framework if it is not installed prior to setup.

In the following Try It Out, you create a setup application.

Try It Out   Creating a Setup Application

1. Open Visual Studio and create a New Windows Forms Application named **Prerequisite**. You will not make any changes to the form design or code.

2. Save All and then build the project.

3. Add a setup project to the solution, named **Installer** as shown in Figure 24-8. To add a new project, choose File ⇨ Add ⇨ New Project from the main menu bar.

Figure 24-8

When Visual Studio creates the project, it adds a Designer. There are three main folders in the left pane of the Designer: Application Folder, User's Desktop, and User's Program Menu (see Figure 24-9).

Figure 24-9

4. In the Solution Explorer, right-click the Installer project and choose Properties.

5. Find the Prerequisite button to the right and click it. You will see the Prerequisite form as shown in Figure 24-10. Notice that, by default, the .NET Framework 3.5 is selected, along with Windows Installer 3.1.

Figure 24-10

6. Select the check box beside Microsoft Data Access Components 2.8 and click OK twice to both dialog boxes. Note that by default, the components are set to download from the vendor's web site.

7. Right-click the Application Folder node in the Designer (left pane) and select Add ⇨ Project Output. The form will look like Figure 24-11.

Figure 24-11

8. Next, select Primary output from the Add Project Output Group form and click OK.

9. Right-click Primary output from Prerequisite, which you just added. From the context menu, select Create a Shortcut to Primary Output from Prerequisite. Rename the shortcut **Prerequisite**. Right-click the newly created shortcut and select Cut from the context menu. On the left pane, right-click User's Program Menu and click Paste.

10. Save and build the Installer project.

11. Right-click the Installer project in the Solution Explorer and select Install. A Windows Installer will be loaded. This is the Setup project you have just created. Remember the shortcut you added to the user's program menu. Take a peek at your menu, and you will see the shortcut.

How It Works

When you create the setup application, Visual Studio creates a Windows Installer application. Changes you make, such as adding the ClickOnce program to the project, are included in the Installer database file.

In this example, you add one executable. It is also possible to add many other types of files including text files, help files, and other assemblies.

When you build the project, two files are created:

- ❑ The `msi` file
- ❑ An installation loader named `setup.exe`

When you look, you see these files in your `<solution directory>\Installer\Release` folder. You can find the path by selecting the Solution and looking at the `Path` property in the Properties window of Visual Studio. If the user does not have MDAC 2.8 or the correct version of the .NET Framework (3.5), it will be downloaded from the vendor. You can change that under the settings where you add the dependency for MDAC 2.8.

User Interface Editor

Installations can be configured to meet almost any need with Visual Studio 2008. One of the easiest ways to make your installation look professional is to customize the interface the user sees during installation. A tool, User Interface Editor, is available to do just this.

With the User Interface Editor, you can configure the installation to do just about anything you want. You can add prebuilt dialog boxes such as a license agreement. Also, a number of customizable dialog boxes are available. You can even add a custom dialog box to ensure that a valid serial number is entered during installation.

In the following Try It Out, you will customize the installation of a setup application. We will show you some of the options, but know that almost every aspect of the installation is customizable.

Try It Out   Customizing the User Interface

1. Open Visual Studio and create a New Setup Project. Name the project **UserInterface**.

2. Now, select View ➪ Editor ➪ User Interface from the menu.

3. The editor will open as shown in Figure 24-12.

Figure 24-12

4. You will see two main items. Install and Administrative Install both have customizable interfaces. The administrative install is for a special type of installation that we will not explain in detail; it is used when an administrator installs an application image to a network share.

5. Under the Install node at the top, right-click Start and choose Add Dialog from the context menu (see Figure 24-13).

Figure 24-13

6. Select the License Agreement dialog box and click OK. By default, the dialog box will be added as the last dialog box under the Start node. You will make the dialog box the second window the user will see by moving it up the tree node. Right-click the License Agreement dialog box and choose Move Up until it is the second dialog box. Your project will look similar to Figure 24-14.

Figure 24-14

7. This is where you would normally add a license agreement file using the `LicenseFile` property. The only requirement is that is it must be in Rich Text Format (RTF). For this example, leave this property blank.

8. Next, add a Customer Information dialog box and make it the third step under the Start process. Change the `SerialNumberTemplate` property to **%%-###-%%%** and the `ShowSerialNumber` to `True`.

9. That is all it takes. Just build the application and install. You will see the license agreement dialog box as the second screen of the installation. The third step is the customer information screen.

10. The third step is the customer information screen. Enter **77-000-777** for the serial number (see Figure 24-15).

Figure 24-15

11. Now, complete the installation by clicking Next through the rest of the steps.

How It Works

Wow. How easy is that? You customize the installation package with just a few clicks of the mouse. Visual Studio makes this easy. You have complete control over the installation interface.

The second step of the installation is the license agreement you add. You are forced to agree to install the application. Visual Studio adds the dialog boxes in the order you choose.

The third dialog box is the customer information screen. Without a valid serial number, the installation would abort. You create a valid serial number based on the `SerialNumberTemplate` property you changed to `%%-###-%%%`. The `%` character signifies that a required digit is included in the algorithm, and the `#` character is entered for digits that are not included. The serial number algorithm sums up all required digits and then divides the sum by 7. If the remainder is 0, the serial number entered passed validation. So, the first two and the last three digits are added together for a total of 35. Then 35 is divided by 7 for a remainder of 0, and you are allowed to install the application.

Deploying Different Solutions

Deploying applications is actually a large and complex task, made easier by various tools. However, if you consider a large suite of applications such as Microsoft Office, you will notice that there can be a vast number of files. All these files require explicit locations or Registry entries. They all tie together to make the application work. In addition to size, there can also be many other complexities, such as database creation: What happens if the database already exists? What happens with the data that is already there? This kind of activity, commonly referred to as *migration*, could potentially mean a lot of work for an installation expert.

Having multiple application types can also make an installation complex, and detailed knowledge of the different applications is required for a successful installation. The following sections discuss some items related to different deployment scenarios surrounding the different types of applications that can be created with Visual Studio 2008.

Private Assemblies

Private assemblies are installed in a directory named `bin` located under the application directory. These files are private to the application. There are a few benefits in using private assemblies:

❑ No versioning is required, as long as it is the same version as the one with which the application was built.

❑ The private assembly is not a shared assembly, and therefore it cannot be updated by another application (at least it is not meant to be).

❑ You can manually replace the assembly as long as it is the same version.

❑ It enables XCOPY deployment (the ability simply to copy and paste files to a location and have it work).

❑ You can make changes to the assembly, and if two different applications use it, you could update one independently from the other.

❑ There is no configuration or signing (see the following section) to do. It just works.

❑ It is great for small utility assemblies or application-specific code.

Private assemblies have the following negatives:

❑ When you have multiple applications using one assembly, you have to deploy the assembly to the `bin` directory of each application.

❑ You would normally have to include the assembly in each setup project where it is used.

❑ Versioning is not enforced as it is in a shared assembly.

❑ It is not strongly named, which means someone could spoof your assembly.

Spoofing *an assembly is when someone creates an assembly that looks identical to yours and replaces yours with the spoof copy. This spoof copy could behave in malicious ways.*

Shared Assemblies

Shared assemblies are actually more stable than private assemblies, and they have a thorough approach to assembly deployment. A shared assembly can also behave like a private assembly, so all the benefits of that approach apply here too. The traditional shared assembly is different because of the extra work you need to do and the extra capabilities it then gains.

A shared assembly is like going back in time. In Windows 3.1, the main deployment location for these kinds of DLLs was the `Windows\System` directory. Then you were advised to have these files in the local application path, because it made for easier installation and uninstallation. Today, the System directory concept returns in a new guise named the Global Assembly Cache (GAC). However, the strong naming of assemblies is a definite step up.

To install a shared assembly, you have to add the file to a new folder named `Global Assembly Cache`. By default, this folder is not visible in the three default folders that are listed. To add the GAC folder you must right-click the node named File System on Target Machine and select Add Special Folder ➪ Global Assembly Cache.

Note that any project type can use a shared assembly, including a web application.

The following is a list of the main benefits of a shared assembly:

❑ It is signed and cannot be spoofed.

❑ It has strong versioning support and configuration options.

❑ It is stored in one central location and does not need to be copied to the `bin` directory of every application that uses it.

❑ You can have many different versions running side by side.

Shared assemblies have the following negatives:

❑ You have to sign the assembly.

❑ You have to be careful not to break compatibility with existing applications, or else you have to configure the different versions.

❑ Configuration can be a nightmare depending on the requirements.

Deploying Desktop Applications

In the second project, you created a setup for a desktop application. All that you installed was the one executable. It had no dependencies other than the .NET Framework, which is always required. In a more complete application, you may have various assemblies, WinForm controls, or other files that you created for the application. Installing a private assembly with the Setup project means that you include the file by adding it to the setup application.

Deploying Web Applications

A web application, when using private assemblies, can be simple to deploy. You can use the Visual Studio 2008 Web Application setup project to create a simple web setup. The setup creates a virtual directory and copies the files you specify to the physical directory location.

Deploying XML Web Services

A web service is deployed in much the same way as a web application. It also has a virtual directory. The files that it requires are somewhat different, though. You need to deploy the `asmx` and `discovery` files together with the assembly.

Useful Tools

There are a few tools that either come with .NET or are in Windows already for you to use. This section briefly points to these tools. When creating an installation, you need to test it by installing it on various machines. Sometimes, when things do not go according to plan, you may need to do some or all of the activities by hand to see which one was the cause of the problem. As an example, perhaps you suspect that the ASPNET_WP.dll process has become unstable or broken in some fashion and has affected the installation. In this scenario, you may want to restart IIS before you run the install. In a similar vein, perhaps an assembly that was supposed to be registered in the GAC as a shared assembly cannot be found by the client; you may want to register it manually to check whether there was a problem with the registration. The following list briefly describes the tools you may need to use:

❑ **ASPNET_RegIIS:** The aspnet_regiis.exe command line tool can be found in the `<sysdir>\Microsoft.NET\Framework\<version>` directory. This tool makes it an easy task to reinstall various aspects of the ASP.NET runtime.

❑ **IISReset:** IISReset simply restarts IIS without requiring you to open the IIS management console. Simply open a DOS prompt and type IISReset, and it will immediately restart IIS.

❑ **ILDasm:** If you want to inspect the metadata of an assembly, ILDASM is the tool for the job. With the tool, you can inspect everything from the Namespaces to the version. Start ILDasm by typing ILDasm at a Visual Studio command prompt.

❑ **GACUtil:** This is a Visual Studio command line tool for registering/unregistering assemblies from the Global Assembly Cache. The /I option is for registering the assembly, and the /u option is for unregistering.

❑ **RegAsm:** This Visual Studio command line utility is used for creating the necessary Component Object Model (COM) information from an assembly. This is used when you need to expose an assembly for COM Interop. The regasm tool includes switches for registering/unregistering type libraries.

❑ **InstallUtil:** This is a Visual Studio command line tool for executing the Installer classes within an assembly. This can execute the InstallerHelper sample you did earlier in this chapter.

❑ **MageUI (Manifest Generation and Editing Tool):** This is a graphical tool for generating, editing, and signing the application and deployment manifest for ClickOnce applications. Run MageUI from a Visual Studio command prompt to start the tool. A command line tool is available if you prefer to not have the user interface. Mage.exe is the command line version of the tool.

Summary

We hope you enjoyed looking at some general aspects of deployment. In the first section of this chapter, you were introduced to some terminology, and then you saw how to create a ClickOnce Application and a simple Setup application inside Visual Studio. You also learned the positives and negatives of private versus shared assemblies. Ultimately, we hope you learned that there is potentially a lot to learn in this area, from getting to know more about the features of the Windows Installer templates to learning how to do more with ClickOnce deployment.

Now that you have finished this chapter, you should know how to:

❑ Create a ClickOnce deployment application

❑ Create a Visual Studio 2008 setup application

❑ Use general deployment terms such as XCOPY, shared versus private assemblies

❑ Edit the installer user interface

Exercises

1. Create a setup project for Notepad and install the program. You should be able to find the `notepad.exe` file in your Windows System directory. *Hint:* You will need to add the file to a setup project. Have the setup application add a shortcut to the Start menu. Deploy the `notepad.exe` file to the Program Files directory. For extra work, change the `Manufacturer` property of the project from Default Company Name to **Wrox**. Also, change the `Author` property to your name.

2. Using the setup application created in Exercise 1, add a splash screen dialog box that is displayed first during the installation. We have included a bitmap in the code for the book named `Wrox_Logo.bmp`. This bitmap is the correct size, 480 × 320, and you can use this image for the dialog box. *Hint:* You have to add the image you use to the setup application before you can add it to the splash dialog box.

25

Where to Now?

Now that you have come to the end of this book, you should have a relatively good idea of how to write code using Visual Basic 2008. The topics and example code covered in this book have been designed to provide you with a firm foundation, but that foundation is just the beginning of your journey. In fact, this book is just one of the many steps you are going to take on your road to becoming a full-fledged Visual Basic 2008 programmer. Although you have come a long way, there is still a lot farther to go, and you will certainly have many more questions on the way.

Where will you get these questions answered? And then, what next?

This appendix offers you some advice on what your possible next steps could be. As you can imagine, a number of different routes are open to any one person. The path you choose will probably depend on what your goals are, and what you are being asked to do by your employer. Some will want to continue at a more general level with some knowledge about all aspects of Visual Basic 2008, while others may want to drill down into more specific areas.

Well, it is extremely important not to take a long break before carrying on with Visual Basic 2008. If you do so, you will find that you will quickly forget what you have learned. The trick is to practice. You can do this in a number of ways:

❑   Continue with the examples from this book. Try to add more features and more code to extend the examples. Try to merge and blend different samples together.

❑   You may have an idea for a new program. Go on and write it.

❑   Try to get a firm understanding of the terminology.

❑   Read as many articles as you can. Even if you do not understand them at first, bits and pieces will come together.

❑   Make sure you communicate your knowledge. If you know other programmers, get talking and ask questions.

❑   Consult our online and offline resources for more information.

The rest of this chapter lists available resources, both online and offline, to help you decide where to go next.

Online Resources

Basically, there are thousands of places you can go online for help with any problems you may have. The good news is that many of them are free. Whenever you come across a problem — and, unfortunately, you will — there are always loads of people out there willing to help. These unknown souls include others who were at the same stage as you and may have had a similar problem, or experts with a great deal of knowledge. The key is not to be intimidated and to use these resources as much as you like. Remember, everyone was a complete beginner at some point and has had many of the same experiences as you.

In this section, we begin by examining the P2P site provided by Wrox and then follow on with some of the more general sites around. If you can't find what you want through any of the sites listed here or if you have some time and want to explore, just search for Visual Basic 2008 and you will be on your way!

P2P.Wrox.com

P2P provides programmer-to-programmer support on mailing lists, forums, and newsgroups in addition to a one-to-one e-mail system. You can join any of the mailing lists for author and peer support in Visual Basic 2008 (plus any others you may be interested in).

You can choose to join the mailing lists, and you can receive a weekly digest of the list. If you don't have the time or facilities to receive mailing lists, you can search the online archives using subject areas or keywords.

Should you wish to use P2P for online support, go to `http://p2p.wrox.com`. On P2P, you can view the groups without becoming a member. These lists are moderated, so you can be confident of the information presented. Also, junk mail and spam are deleted, and your e-mail is protected by the unique Lyris system from web-bots, which can automatically cover up newsgroup mailing list addresses.

Microsoft Resources

Probably one of the first sites you'll intuitively turn to is the Microsoft site (`www.microsoft.com`). That makes sense, because it is full of information, including support, tips, hints, downloads, and newsgroups (`news://msnews.microsoft.com/microsoft.public.dotnet.languages.vb`). To see more newsgroups, navigate to `http://communities2.microsoft.com/communities/newsgroups/en-us/default.aspx`.

There are also a number of sites on MSDN that you may find to be very helpful, including the following:

- ❑ **Visual Studio:** `http://msdn2.microsoft.com/en-us/vstudio/`
- ❑ **Classic MSDN Library:** `http://msdn.microsoft.com/library/`
- ❑ **MSDN Library(2005):** `http://msdn2.microsoft.com/en-us/library/`
- ❑ **MSDN Library(2008):** `http://msdn2.microsoft.com/en-us/library/52f3sw5c(vs.90).aspx`
- ❑ **Microsoft Developer Network:** `http://msdn.microsoft.com`
- ❑ **Microsoft Visual Basic:** `http://msdn2.microsoft.com/en-us/vbasic/`
- ❑ **.NET Framework download site:** `http://msdn.microsoft.com/netframework/downloads/`

❏ **Microsoft CodePlex:** www.codeplex.com

❏ **ASP .NET 2.0:** www.asp.net

Other Resources

As mentioned earlier, there are hundreds of sites online that discuss both Visual Basic .NET and Visual Basic 2008. These sites give everything from news on moving from Visual Basic .NET to Visual Basic 2008, to listings of up and coming conferences worldwide. Although you can do a search for Visual Basic 2008, the number of sites returned can be extremely overwhelming. Let's look at two of these possible sites, one for the United Kingdom and another for the United States.

In the United Kingdom, www.vbug.co.uk offers a wealth of information on Visual Basic. This is the web site for the Visual Basic Users Group (VBUG), which you can join. Besides the web site, this group holds meetings and an annual conference, plus provides a magazine. There is a listing of further links on the web site, and you may want to use this to start your search over the Internet.

In the United States you can get a journal, *The Visual Studio Magazine*, from a similar user group. Again, this journal is backed by meetings and four yearly conferences along with a web site, www.devx.com/vb/, which can give e-mail updates. On the web site, you have access to a number of different areas both in Visual Basic and other related and nonrelated Visual Studio areas.

Of course, these are just two among the many out there to try to get you started. Remember, however, that the Internet is not the only place to find information, so we will go on to look at some resources not found on the Web.

Offline Resources (Books)

Wrox Press is committed to providing books that will help you develop your programming skills in the direction that you want. We have a selection of tutorial-style books that build on the Visual Basic 2008 knowledge gained here. These will help you to specialize in particular areas. Here are the details of a couple of key titles.

Professional Visual Basic 2008

(Wrox Press, ISBN 978-0-470-19136-1)

This book is different than other Visual Basic books because it explains intermediate to advanced topics in an easily understood and concise model. The comprehensive coverage provides detailed information on how to use Visual Basic in the ever-expanding .NET world, using not only explanations of the topics, but demonstrations of code. It effectively shows developers how to get tasks accomplished. This book is written to show readers what they need to know to take their abilities to new levels. The book shows developers exactly how to build everything from traditional console applications, ASP.NET applications, and XML web services. Along with these various applications, the book deals with the issues of security, data access (ADO.NET), and the latest Visual Studio .NET IDE, as well as introducing developers to everything they need to know to fully understand the new .NET 3.5 Framework. Topics include the following:

❏ Visual Studio 2008

❏ Web services and .NET remoting

- ❑ Deploying applications
- ❑ Windows Workflow Foundation
- ❑ Windows Presentation Foundation
- ❑ Windows Communication Foundation.
- ❑ .NET 3.5 Framework
- ❑ Common Language Runtime
- ❑ Applying objects and components
- ❑ Namespaces
- ❑ Error handling and debugging
- ❑ XML with VB.NET
- ❑ ASP.NET advanced features and much more!

Visual Basic 2008 Programmer's Reference

(Wrox Press, 978-0-470-18262-8)

Visual Basic 2008 Programmer's Reference is a language tutorial and a reference guide to the 2008 release of Visual Basic. The tutorial provides basic material suitable for beginners but also includes in-depth content for more advanced developers.

The second part of the book is a reference that quickly allows programmers to locate information for specific language features. The entries in these appendixes allow the reader to quickly review the details of important programming, objects, properties, methods, and events.

Visual Basic 2008 Programmer's Reference covers the latest features of the 2008 release, including:

- ❑ Changes to variable declaration and initialization
- ❑ XLinq support for XML data types; query comprehensions for using SQL-like syntax to extract data from arrays and other data structures
- ❑ Extension methods for adding new features to existing classes
- ❑ Nested subroutines and functions
- ❑ Anonymous subroutines and functions (lambda expressions)
- ❑ Nullable types
- ❑ Relaxed delegates
- ❑ Dynamic interfaces
- ❑ Dynamic identifiers

Exercise Solutions

Chapter 1

1. Create a Windows Application with a Textbox and Button control that will display whatever is typed in the text box when the user clicks on the button.

A. To display the text from a text box on a form when the user clicks the button, you add code as highlighted here to the button's `Click` event handler:

```
Private Sub btnDisplay_Click(ByVal sender As System.Object, _
    ByVal e As System.EventArgs) Handles btnDisplay.Click

        'Display the contents of the text box
        MessageBox.Show(txtInput.Text, "Exercise 1")
    End Sub
```

Chapter 3

1. Create a Windows application with two button controls. In the `Click` event for the first button, declare two `Integer` variables and set their values to any number that you like. Perform any math operation on these variables and display the results in a message box.

In the `Click` event for the second button, declare two `String` variables and set their values to anything that you like. Perform a string concatenation on these variables and display the results in a message box.

A. The first part of this exercise requires you to declare two `Integer` variables and set their values and then to perform a math operation of these variables and display the results in a message box. The variables can be declared and set as:

```
'Declare variables and set their values
Dim intX As Integer = 5
Dim intY As Integer = 10
```

To perform a math operation and display the results can be performed as:

```
'Multiply the numbers and display the results
MessageBox.Show("The sum of " & intX.ToString & " * " & _
    intY.ToString & " = " & intX * intY, "Exercise 1")
```

The second part of this exercise requires you to declare two String variables and set their values and then to concatenate the variables and display the results in a message box. The String variables can be declared and set as:

```
'Declare variables and set their values
Dim strOne As String = "Visual Basic "
Dim strTwo As String = "2008"
```

To concatenate the variables and display the results, you could write code such as:

```
'Concatenate the strings and display the results
MessageBox.Show(strOne & strTwo, "Exercise 1")
```

2. Create a Windows application with a text box and a button control. In the button's Click event, display three message boxes. The first message box should display the length of the string that was entered into the text box. The second message box should display the first half of the string, and the third message box should display the last half of the string.

A. This exercise requires you to display the length of the string entered into a text box and then to display the first half of the string and the last half of the string. To display the length of the string, you can use the Length property of the Text property of the text box as shown here:

```
'Display the length of the string from the TextBox
MessageBox.Show("The length of the string in the TextBox is " & _
    txtInput.Text.Length, "Exercise 2")
```

To display the first half of the string, you need to use the Substring method with a starting index of 0 and for the length you use the length of the string divided by 2 as shown here. Don't forget that with the Option Strict option turned on, you must convert the results of a division operation to an Integer data type for use in the SubString method:

```
'Display the first half of the string from the TextBox
MessageBox.Show(txtInput.Text.Substring(0, _
    CType(txtInput.Text.Length / 2, Integer)), "Exercise 2")
```

To display the last half of the string you again use the Substring method but this time you simply give it a starting index of the length of the string divided by 2 as shown here:

```
'Display the last half of the string from the TextBox
MessageBox.Show(txtInput.Text.Substring( _
    CType(txtInput.Text.Length / 2, Integer)), "Exercise 2")
```

Chapter 4

1. Create a Windows Forms Application with a text box and a Button control. In the `Click` event of the Button, extract the number from the text box and use a `Select Case` statement with the numbers 1 through 5. In the `Case` statement for each number, display the number in a message box. Ensure that you provide code to handle numbers that are not in the range of 1 through 5.

A. This exercise requires you to create a `Select Case` statement to select and display the numbers 1 through 5 from the text box on the form. The code to do this is shown here:

```
'Determine which number was entered
Select Case CType(txtNumber.Text, Integer)
    Case 1
        MessageBox.Show("The number 1 was entered", "Exercise 1")
    Case 2
        MessageBox.Show("The number 2 was entered", "Exercise 1")
    Case 3
        MessageBox.Show("The number 3 was entered", "Exercise 1")
    Case 4
        MessageBox.Show("The number 4 was entered", "Exercise 1")
    Case 5
        MessageBox.Show("The number 5 was entered", "Exercise 1")
```

To handle numbers other than 1 through 5 you need to provide a `Case Else` statement as shown here:

```
    Case Else
        MessageBox.Show("A number other that 1 - 5 was entered", _
            "Exercise 1")
End Select
```

2. Create a Windows Forms Application that contains a ListBox control and a Button control. In the `Click` event for the button, create a `For...Next` loop that will count from 1 to 10 and display the results in the list box. Then create another `For...Next` loop that will count backwards from 10 to 1 and also display those results in the list box.

A. In this exercise, you are tasked with creating two `For...Next` loops. The first loop should count from 1 to 10 and display the numbers in a list box. The code to execute this loop is shown here:

```
'Count from 1 to 10
For intCount As Integer = 1 To 10
    lstData.Items.Add(intCount)
Next
```

The second `For ... Next` loop should count backward from 10 to 1 and display those numbers in the same list box. The code to execute this loop is shown here:

```
'Count backwards from 10 to 1
For intCount As Integer = 10 To 1 Step -1
    lstData.Items.Add(intCount)
Next
```

Chapter 5

1. Create a Windows Forms Application that contains three buttons. Add an enumeration of three names to your code. For the Click event for each button, display a message box containing a member name and value from the enumeration.

A. This exercise requires you to create an enumeration of three names and to display the member string value as well as the numeric value when a button was clicked. To create an enumeration of names you would use code similar to this:

```
Public Class Form1

    Private Enum Names As Integer
        Jeannie = 1
        Delinda = 2
        Harry = 3
    End Enum
```

In order to display the member names and values from the enumeration, you would use code like this:

```
Private Sub btnName1_Click(ByVal sender As System.Object, _
    ByVal e As System.EventArgs) Handles btnName1.Click

    MessageBox.Show(Names.Jeannie.ToString & " = " & Names.Jeannie, _
        "Exercise 1")
End Sub

Private Sub btnName2_Click(ByVal sender As System.Object, _
    ByVal e As System.EventArgs) Handles btnName2.Click

    MessageBox.Show(Names.Delinda.ToString & " = " & Names.Delinda, _
        "Exercise 1")
End Sub

Private Sub btnName3_Click(ByVal sender As System.Object, _
    ByVal e As System.EventArgs) Handles btnName3.Click

    MessageBox.Show(Names.Harry.ToString & " = " & Names.Harry, _
        "Exercise 1")
End Sub
```

2. Create a Windows Forms Application that contains a TextBox control and a Button control. At the form level, create a names array initialized with a single name. In the Click event for the button control, add the code to redimension the array by one element while preserving the existing data, add the new name from the text box to the array, and display the last name added to the array in a message box.

Hint: To determine the upper boundary of the array, use the GetUpperBound(0) method.

A. You are tasked with creating an application that would redimension an array, preserving its current elements, add a new element to the array, and display the new element in a message box. To create and initialize an array at the form level with just one name, you would code like this:

```
Public Class Form1

    Private strNames() As String = {"Jeannie"}
```

To redimension the array preserving the existing data you would use code like this. Notice that you use the GetUpperBound(0) method to get the upper boundary of the array and then add 1 to it to increase the array by one element:

```
ReDim Preserve strNames(strNames.GetUpperBound(0) + 1)
```

To add the new name from the text box you would use code like this. Again you are using GetUpperBound(0) to determine the upper boundary of the array:

```
strNames(strNames.GetUpperBound(0)) = txtName.Text
```

Finally, to display the last name added to the array in a message box you would use code like this:

```
MessageBox.Show(strNames(strNames.GetUpperBound(0)), "Exercise 2")
```

Chapter 6

1. Add code to the Credit Card application to display a message box containing the user's state selection when they select a state in the State combo box.

Hint: to access a control's default event handler, double-click the control in the Forms Designer.

A. This exercise requires you to create an event handler when the user makes a selection in the State combo box using the default event handler. To create this event handler, you should have double-clicked on the cboState control in the Forms Designer to create the SelectionChanged event handler.

The code that you added to this event handler should resemble the highlighted code shown following. Here you display a simple message box that displays the text Selected state: and then the selected state contained in the combo box's SelectedItem property.

```
Private Sub cboState_SelectionChanged(ByVal sender As System.Object, _
    ByVal e As System.Windows.Controls.SelectionChangedEventArgs) _
    Handles cboState.SelectionChanged

    MessageBox.Show("Selected state: " & cboState.SelectedItem)
End Sub
```

Chapter 7

1. Create a Windows Forms application with two buttons. Add code to the MouseUp event for the first button to display a MessageBox with a message that the event has fired. Add code to the LostFocus event for the first button to also display a MessageBox with a message that the button has lost focus.

A. For this exercise, you are required to create a Windows Forms application with two button controls. You were to wire up the `MouseUp` and `LostFocus` events for the first button. The code for the `MouseUp` event should look similar to this:

```
Private Sub btnMouseEvents_MouseUp(ByVal sender As Object, _
    ByVal e As System.Windows.Forms.MouseEventArgs) _
    Handles btnMouseEvents.MouseUp

    'Display a MessageBox
    MessageBox.Show("The MouseUp event has been fired.", "Exercise 1")
End Sub
```

And the code for the `LostFocus` event should look similar to this:

```
Private Sub btnMouseEvents_LostFocus(ByVal sender As Object, _
    ByVal e As System.EventArgs) Handles btnMouseEvents.LostFocus

    'Display a MessageBox
    MessageBox.Show("Mouse Events button has lost focus.", "Exercise 1")
End Sub
```

When you ran this application, you may have noticed some unexpected behavior when you clicked the first button. As soon as you let the mouse button up, you saw the message box indicating that the button had lost focus, and then immediately after that, you saw the message box indicating that the `MouseUp` event had been fired.

What has actually happened here is that the code in the `MouseUp` event was fired, but the code in that event causes a message box to be displayed. In the course of seeing that code, Visual Basic 2008 has determined that the Button control will lose focus and has fired the `LostFocus` event, which displays the message box in that event handler first.

2. Create a Windows Forms application with a toolbar and status bar. Right-click the ToolStrip control and select the Insert Standard Items menu item from the context menu to have the standard buttons added to the control. For the Click event for each of the ToolStripButton controls, display a message in the status bar indicating which button was clicked.

A. This exercise tasks you with creating an application that has a toolbar and status bar. You were to insert the standard buttons for the toolbar, create event handlers for the `Click` event of each button, and display a message in the status bar when any of the buttons was clicked. Here is the code for the event handlers:

```
Private Sub NewToolStripButton_Click(ByVal sender As System.Object, _
    ByVal e As System.EventArgs) Handles NewToolStripButton.Click

    'Update the status bar
    sslStatus.Text = "The New button was clicked."
End Sub

Private Sub OpenToolStripButton_Click(ByVal sender As System.Object, _
    ByVal e As System.EventArgs) Handles OpenToolStripButton.Click

    'Update the status bar
    sslStatus.Text = "The Open button was clicked."
```

```
    End Sub

    Private Sub SaveToolStripButton_Click(ByVal sender As System.Object, _
        ByVal e As System.EventArgs) Handles SaveToolStripButton.Click

        'Update the status bar
        sslStatus.Text = "The Save button was clicked."
    End Sub

    Private Sub PrintToolStripButton_Click(ByVal sender As System.Object, _
        ByVal e As System.EventArgs) Handles PrintToolStripButton.Click

        'Update the status bar
        sslStatus.Text = "The Print button was clicked."
    End Sub

    Private Sub CutToolStripButton_Click(ByVal sender As System.Object, _
        ByVal e As System.EventArgs) Handles CutToolStripButton.Click

        'Update the status bar
        sslStatus.Text = "The Cut button was clicked."
    End Sub

    Private Sub CopyToolStripButton_Click(ByVal sender As System.Object, _
        ByVal e As System.EventArgs) Handles CopyToolStripButton.Click

        'Update the status bar
        sslStatus.Text = "The Copy button was clicked."
    End Sub

    Private Sub PasteToolStripButton_Click(ByVal sender As System.Object, _
        ByVal e As System.EventArgs) Handles PasteToolStripButton.Click

        'Update the status bar
        sslStatus.Text = "The Paste button was clicked."
    End Sub

    Private Sub HelpToolStripButton_Click(ByVal sender As System.Object, _
        ByVal e As System.EventArgs) Handles HelpToolStripButton.Click

        'Update the status bar
        sslStatus.Text = "The Help button was clicked."
    End Sub
```

Chapter 8

1. Create a simple Windows application with a TextBox control and two Button controls. Set the buttons to open a file and to save a file. Use the `OpenFileDialog` class (not the control) and the `SaveFileDialog` class to open and save your files.

    Hint: To use the corresponding classes for the controls use the following statements:

    ```
    Dim objOpenFileDialog As New OpenFileDialog
    Dim objSaveFileDialog As New SaveFileDialog
    ```

A. The exercise requires you to create a simple application that uses the OpenFileDialog and SaveFileDialog classes.

The code for the Open button starts by declaring an object using the OpenFileDialog class:

```
Private Sub btnOpen_Click(ByVal sender As System.Object, _
    ByVal e As System.EventArgs) Handles btnOpen.Click

    'Declare a OpenFileDialog object
    Dim objOpenFileDialog As New OpenFileDialog
```

The bulk of the code to display the contents of the file in your text box remains the same as the code in the Dialogs project but uses the objOpenFileDialog object versus the OpenFileDialog control:

```
    'Set the Open dialog properties
    With objOpenFileDialog
        .Filter = "Text Documents (*.txt)|*.txt|All Files (*.*)|*.*"
        .FilterIndex = 1
        .Title = "Exercise 1 Open File Dialog"
    End With

    'Show the Open dialog and if the user clicks the Open button,
    'load the file
    If objOpenFileDialog.ShowDialog = Windows.Forms.DialogResult.OK Then
        Try
            'Save the file path and name
            strFileName = objOpenFileDialog.FileName

            Dim fileContents As String
            fileContents = My.Computer.FileSystem.ReadAllText(strFileName)

            'Display the file contents in the text box
            txtFile.Text = fileContents
        Catch ex As Exception
            MessageBox.Show(ex.Message, My.Application.Info.Title, _
                MessageBoxButtons.OK, MessageBoxIcon.Error)
        End Try
    End If
```

Since you are using an object, you need to perform the necessary cleanup to have the object you created release its resources. You do this by calling the Dispose method on your object, and then you release your reference to the object by setting it to Nothing:

```
    'Clean up
    objOpenFileDialog.Dispose()
    objOpenFileDialog = Nothing
End Sub
```

The code for the Save button starts by declaring an object using the `SaveFileDialog` class, and the rest of the code is pretty much the same as the code in the Dialogs project. The code at the end of this procedure also performs the necessary cleanup of your object:

```
Private Sub btnSave_Click(ByVal sender As System.Object, _
    ByVal e As System.EventArgs) Handles btnSave.Click

        'Declare a SaveFileDialog object
        Dim objSaveFileDialog As New SaveFileDialog

        'Set the Save dialog properties
        With objSaveFileDialog
            .DefaultExt = "txt"
            .FileName = strFileName
            .Filter = "Text Documents (*.txt)|*.txt|All Files (*.*)|*.*"
            .FilterIndex = 1
            .OverwritePrompt = True
            .Title = "Exercise 1 Save File Dialog"
        End With

        'Show the Save dialog and if the user clicks the Save button,
        'save the file
        If objSaveFileDialog.ShowDialog = Windows.Forms.DialogResult.OK Then
            Try
                'Save the file path and name
                strFileName = objSaveFileDialog.FileName

                My.Computer.FileSystem.WriteAllText(strFileName, txtFile.Text, _
                    False)
            Catch ex As Exception
                MessageBox.Show(ex.Message, My.Application.Info.Title, _
                    MessageBoxButtons.OK, MessageBoxIcon.Error)
            End Try
        End If

        'Clean up
        objSaveFileDialog.Dispose()
        objSaveFileDialog = Nothing
    End Sub
```

2. Create a simple Windows application with a Label control and a Button control. Set the button to display the Browse For Folder dialog box with the Make New Folder button displayed. Use My Documents as the root folder at which the dialog starts browsing. Use the `FolderBrowserDialog` class (not the control) and display the selected folder in the label on your form.

A. This exercise requires you to display the Browse For Folder dialog box with the Make New Folder button displayed and to set My Documents as the root folder for the browse operation. You start your procedure off by declaring an object using the `FolderBrowserDialog` class:

```
Private Sub btnBrowse_Click(ByVal sender As System.Object, _
    ByVal e As System.EventArgs) Handles btnBrowse.Click

        'Declare a FolderBrowserDialog object
        Dim objFolderBrowserDialog As New FolderBrowserDialog
```

Next, you set the various properties of your `objFolderBrowserDialog` object to customize the Browse For Folder dialog box. Note that you need to use the `Personal` constant to have the dialog start browsing at the My Documents root folder:

```
'Set the Folder Browser dialog properties
With objFolderBrowserDialog
    .Description = "Select your favorite folder:"
    .RootFolder = Environment.SpecialFolder.MyDocuments
    .ShowNewFolderButton = True
End With
```

You then display the dialog box, and when the user clicks the OK button in the dialog box, you display the folder chosen in the label control on your form:

```
'Show the Folder Browser dialog and if the user clicks the
'OK button, display the selected folder
If objFolderBrowserDialog.ShowDialog = Windows.Forms.DialogResult.OK Then
    lblFolder.Text = objFolderBrowserDialog.SelectedPath
End If
```

You end this procedure by performing the necessary cleanup of your object:

```
    'Clean up
    objFolderBrowserDialog.Dispose()
    objFolderBrowserDialog = Nothing
End Sub
```

Chapter 9

1. To give your Menus project the standard look of a typical Windows application, add a StatusStrip control to the form and add the necessary code to display a message when text is cut, copied, or pasted.

A. This exercise asks you to complete your Menus application by adding a StatusStrip control and writing the necessary code to display a message when text was cut, copied, and pasted in your text boxes. If you followed the same basic procedures to add a StatusStrip control as you did in the Windows Forms Text Editor project in Chapter 7, you will have added the control and added one panel named `sspStatus`. You will also have added the `StatusText` property in code to set the text in the label on the StatusStrip control.

All that is required at this point is to add code to the procedures that actually perform the cut, copy, and paste operations. Starting with the `CutToolStripMenuItem_Click` procedure, you should have added a single line of code similar to the following:

```
Private Sub CutToolStripMenuItem_Click(ByVal sender As Object, _
    ByVal e As System.EventArgs) Handles CutToolStripMenuItem.Click

    'Copy the text to the clipboard and clear the field
    If TypeOf Me.ActiveControl Is TextBox Then
        CType(Me.ActiveControl, TextBox).Cut()
```

```
        End If

        'Display a message in the status bar
        StatusText = "Text Cut"
    End Sub
```

And the code for the `CopyToolStripMenuItem_Click` procedure should be similar to this:

```
Private Sub CopyToolStripMenuItem_Click(ByVal sender As Object, _
    ByVal e As System.EventArgs) Handles CopyToolStripMenuItem.Click

        'Copy the text to the clipboard
        If TypeOf Me.ActiveControl Is TextBox Then
            CType(Me.ActiveControl, TextBox).Copy()
        End If

        'Display a message in the status bar
        StatusText = "Text Copied"
    End Sub
```

And finally, the code for the `PasteToolStripMenuItem_Click` procedure should be similar to this:

```
Private Sub PasteToolStripMenuItem_Click(ByVal sender As Object, _
    ByVal e As System.EventArgs) Handles PasteToolStripMenuItem.Click

        'Copy the text from the clipboard to the text box
        If TypeOf Me.ActiveControl Is TextBox Then
            CType(Me.ActiveControl, TextBox).Paste()
        End If

        'Display a message in the status bar
        StatusText = "Text Pasted"
    End Sub
```

Chapter 10

1. Using your Debugging project, add a `Try...Catch` block to the `ListCustomer` procedure to handle an `Exception` error. In the `Catch` block, add code to display a message box with the error message.

A. The `Try...Catch` block that you add is very simple, as shown here:

```
Private Sub ListCusto mer(ByVal customerToList As Customer)
    Try
        lstData.Items.Add(customerToList.CustomerID & _
            " - " & customerToList.CustomerName)
    Catch ExceptionErr As Exception
        MessageBox.Show(ExceptionErr.Message, "Debugging", _
            MessageBoxButtons.OK, MessageBoxIcon.Error)
    End Try
End Sub
```

2. The `Try...Catch` block that you added in Exercise 1 should never throw an error. However, you can throw your own error so that you can test your code in the `Catch` block. Add a `Throw` statement as the first line of code in the `Try` block. Consult the online help for the syntax of the `Throw` statement.

A. Your modified `Try` block should look similar to the following code. When you run your project and click the Start button, you should see a message box with the message that you added to your `Throw` statement.

```
Try
    Throw New Exception("Customer object not initialized.")
    lstData.Items.Add(customerToList.CustomerID & _
        " - " & customerToList.CustomerName)
Catch ExceptionErr As Exception
    MessageBox.Show(ExceptionErr.Message, "Debugging", _
        MessageBoxButtons.OK, MessageBoxIcon.Error)
End Try
```

Chapter 11

1. Modify your `Car` class to implement the `IDisposable` interface. In the `Main` procedure in Module1, add code to dispose of the `objCar` object after calling the `DisplaySportsCarDetails` procedure.

A. After you add the `Implements` statement highlighted as follows and press Enter, the rest of the following code shown it is automatically inserted by Visual Studio 2008 to handle disposing of your class.

```
Namespace CarPerformance
    Public Class Car
        Implements IDisposable

        .
        .
        .

        Private disposedValue As Boolean = False   ' To detect redundant calls

        ' IDisposable
        Protected Overridable Sub Dispose(ByVal disposing As Boolean)
            If Not Me.disposedValue Then
                If disposing Then
                    ' TODO: free other state (managed objects).
                End If

                ' TODO: free your own state (unmanaged objects).
                ' TODO: set large fields to null.
            End If
            Me.disposedValue = True
        End Sub

#Region " IDisposable Support "
        ' This code added by Visual Basic to correctly implement the disposable pattern.
```

```
        Public Sub Dispose() Implements IDisposable.Dispose
' Do not change this code. Put cleanup code in Dispose(ByVal disposing As
' Boolean) above.
            Dispose(True)
            GC.SuppressFinalize(Me)
        End Sub
#End Region

    End Class
End Namespace
```

The code modifications needed in the Main procedure in Module1 are shown in the highlighted section that follows. Even though you did not implement the IDisposable interface in the SportsCar class, it is available to this class through inheritance. Remember that the SportsCar class inherits from the Car class; thus, all of the methods available in the Car class are available to the SportsCar class.

```
        'Display the details of the car
        DisplayCarDetails(objCar)
        DisplaySportsCarDetails(objCar)

        'Dispose of the object
        objCar.Dispose()
        objCar = Nothing

        'Wait for input from the user
        Console.ReadLine()
```

2. Modify the code in the Main procedure in Module1 to encapsulate the declaration and usage of the SportsCar class in a Using...End Using statement. Remember that the Using...End Using statement automatically handles disposal of objects that implement the IDisposable interface.

A. This exercise requires you to encapsulate the declaration and usage of the SportsCar class in a Using...End Using statement. Keeping in mind that the Using...End Using statement automatically handles disposal of objects that implement the IDisposable interface; the code can be implemented as highlighted here:

```
Sub Main()
    Using objCar As New SportsCar
        'Set the horsepower and weight(kg)
        objCar.HorsePower = 240
        objCar.Weight = 1085

        'Display the details of the car
        DisplayCarDetails(objCar)
        DisplaySportsCarDetails(objCar)
    End Using

    'Wait for input from the user
    Console.ReadLine()
End Sub
```

Chapter 12

1. Modify the Favorites Viewer project to select the first favorite in the ListView control automatically after it has been loaded so that the LinkLabel control displays the first item when the form is displayed.

You also need to modify the Load event in Form1, and ensure that the ListView control contains one or more items before proceeding. You do this by querying the Count property of the Items property of the ListView control. Then you select the first item in the ListView control using the lstFavorites.Items(0).Selected property and call the Click event for the ListBox control to update the LinkLabel control.

A. You should have added code similar to this at the end of the Viewer_Load event after the Try...Catch block. First you use the Count property of the Items property to ensure that one or more items exist in the list view control before proceeding. Then you select the first item in the list view control by setting the Selected property to True for the first item in the Items collection. Finally, you call the Click event of the list view control, passing it a value of Nothing for the Object and System.EventArgs parameters.

```
'If one or more items exist...
If lvwFavorites.Items.Count > 1 Then
    'Select the first item
    lvwFavorites.Items(0).Selected = True
    lvwFavorites_Click(Nothing, Nothing)
End If
```

Chapter 13

1. Modify the Favorites Viewer project to use the compiled InternetFavorites.dll instead of the Internet Favorites project.

A. Modifying the Favorites Viewer project requires two steps. First, you right-click the Internet Favorites project in the Solution Explorer and choose Remove from the context menu. Then you right-click the Favorites Viewer project in the Solution Explorer and choose Add Reference from the context menu. You scroll down the list of components in the .NET tab, select Internet Favorites, and then click OK. Then you run your project as normal with no code changes required.

Chapter 14

1. Add a property to the MyNamespace control called SuppressMsgBox, which contains a Boolean value. Add code to the Click event handlers for each of the buttons on this control to show the message box when the SuppressMsgBox property is False and to suppress the message box when this property is True.

A. You start by adding a PrivateBoolean variable to hold the value that determines whether a message box is shown. Since this is a Boolean variable, you also provide a default value of True so that when the control is dragged onto a form, the SuppressMsgBox property will have a default value set.

```
Public Class MyNamespace
    'Private members
    Private strApplicationName As String = String.Empty
    Private blnSuppressMsgBox As Boolean = True
```

Next, you add a `Public` property to get and set the private variable `blnSuppressMsgBox`. This property will be exposed by the MyNamespace control in the Properties Window.

```
Public Property SuppressMsgBox() As Boolean
    Get
        Return blnSuppressMsgBox
    End Get
    Set(ByVal value As Boolean)
        blnSuppressMsgBox = value
    End Set
End Property
```

Now you add code to each of the button to show the message box if the property is not set to `True`.

```
Private Sub btnApplicationCopyright_Click(ByVal sender As System.Object, _
    ByVal e As System.EventArgs) Handles btnApplicationCopyright.Click

    RaiseEvent ApplicationCopyrightChanged( _
        My.Application.Info.Copyright)

    If Not blnSuppressMsgBox Then
        MessageBox.Show(My.Application.Info.Copyright, _
            strApplicationName)
    End If
End Sub

Private Sub btnScreenBounds_Click(ByVal sender As Object, _
    ByVal e As System.EventArgs) Handles btnScreenBounds.Click

    RaiseEvent ScreenBoundsChanged(My.Computer.Screen.Bounds)

    If Not blnSuppressMsgBox Then
        MessageBox.Show(My.Computer.Screen.Bounds.ToString, _
            strApplicationName)
    End If
End Sub

Private Sub btnScreenWorkingArea_Click(ByVal sender As Object, _
    ByVal e As System.EventArgs) Handles btnScreenWorkingArea.Click

    RaiseEvent ScreenWorkingAreaChanged(My.Computer.Screen.WorkingArea)

    If Not blnSuppressMsgBox Then
        MessageBox.Show(My.Computer.Screen.WorkingArea.ToString, _
            strApplicationName)
    End If
End Sub
```

Next, you need to rebuild the control so that it can pick up the code changes in order to display the `SuppressMsgBox` property in the Properties window. After that, you switch to the Controls project and can select a `True/False` value for the `SuppressMsgBox` property in the Properties window.

Chapter 16

1. Create a new query in your Northwind database to select FirstName, LastName, and Title from the Employees table. Order the results by the LastName column and save your query as **EmployeeQuery**. Then create a Windows application with a DataGridView control that uses the EmployeeQuery.

A. The SQL statements for your EmployeeQuery should look like this:

```
SELECT Employees.FirstName, Employees.LastName, Employees.Title
FROM Employees
ORDER BY Employees.LastName;
```

You should have followed most of the steps in the "Binding Data to a DataGridView Control" Try It Out exercise and used the EmployeeQuery above in the Choose Your Database Objects screen of the Data Source Configuration Wizard. Your results should look similar to those shown in Figure A-1.

Figure A-1

2. Using the query created in Exercise 1, create a new Windows application that uses the BindingNavigator control and bind the fields from your query to text boxes on your form.

A. To create this application, you should have followed most of the steps in the "Binding Data to TextBox Controls" Try It Out exercise. Your completed form should look similar to the one shown in Figure A-2, and you should be able to navigate through the records in the database.

Figure A-2

Chapter 17

1. Create a Windows Forms application that will display data to the user from the Authors table in the Pubs database. Use a DataGridView object to display the data. Use the simple select statement here to get the data:

```
Select * From Authors
```

A. To complete this exercise, use a DataGridView object to display the data from the Pubs database. First, you create a Windows application and add two references, one to the System.Data namespace and one to the System.XML namespace. Next, you need to add a DataGridView control to your form. That is all you need to do before adding the code listed here:

```
Imports System.Data
Imports System.Data.SqlClient
Public Class Form1
    Dim strConnectionString As String = "server=bnewsome;" & _
        "database=pubs;uid=sa;pwd=!p@ssw0rd!"
    Dim cnnAuthors As New SqlConnection(strConnectionString)
    Dim daAuthors As New SqlDataAdapter
    Dim dsAuthors As New DataSet

    Private Sub Form1_Load(ByVal sender As Object, _
            ByVal e As System.EventArgs) Handles Me.Load
        daAuthors.SelectCommand = New SqlCommand
        daAuthors.SelectCommand.Connection = cnnAuthors
        daAuthors.SelectCommand.CommandText = "Select * From Authors"
        daAuthors.SelectCommand.CommandType = CommandType.Text

        cnnAuthors.Open()

        daAuthors.Fill(dsAuthors, "authors")

        cnnAuthors.Close()

        dgvAuthors.AutoGenerateColumns = True
        dgvAuthors.DataSource = dsAuthors
```

```
               dgvAuthors.DataMember = "authors"

            daAuthors = Nothing
            cnnAuthors = Nothing
        End Sub
    End Class
```

2.   Looking at the DataGridView, it is not very user-friendly. Update the column headings to make more sense. If you know SQL, you can give each column an alias. The current column header names are au_id, au_lname, au_fname, phone, address, city, state, zip, and contract. The solution to this exercise will give each column an alias in SQL.

A.   To complete this exercise, use a DataGridView object to display the data from the Pubs database. First, you create a Windows application and add two references, one to the System.Data namespace and one to the System.XML namespace. Next, you need to add a DataGridView control to your form. Now you can add the code listed here. You will notice the difference from the first solution is just the SQL.

```
Imports System.Data
Imports System.Data.SqlClient
Public Class Form1
    Dim strConnectionString As String = "server=bnewsome;" & _
        "database=pubs;uid=sa;pwd=!p@ssw0rd!"
    Dim cnnAuthors As New SqlConnection(strConnectionString)
    Dim daAuthors As New SqlDataAdapter
    Dim dsAuthors As New DataSet

    Private Sub Form1_Load(ByVal sender As Object, _
            ByVal e As System.EventArgs) Handles Me.Load
        Dim strSQL As String
        strSQL = "Select au_id as ID, au_lname as [Last Name], " & _
            "au_fname as [First Name], Phone, Address, City, State, " & _
            "Zip, Contract From Authors"
        daAuthors.SelectCommand = New SqlCommand
        daAuthors.SelectCommand.Connection = cnnAuthors
        daAuthors.SelectCommand.CommandText = strSQL
        daAuthors.SelectCommand.CommandType = CommandType.Text

        cnnAuthors.Open()

        daAuthors.Fill(dsAuthors, "authors")

        cnnAuthors.Close()

        dgvAuthors.AutoGenerateColumns = True
        dgvAuthors.DataSource = dsAuthors
        dgvAuthors.DataMember = "authors"

        daAuthors = Nothing
        cnnAuthors = Nothing
    End Sub
End Class
```

3. Create a Windows Forms Application. On form1, add a ListBox named ListBox1. On form load, create a dictionary object with key/value pairs of names and states of your friends. Now, write a query to return all of your friends in a certain state. Take your result and bind it to the ListBox using a for each loop. You may need to add a reference to System.Data.Linq.

A. To complete this exercise, you need to bind a ListBox to a result from a LINQ to Object query. The query is basically the same as in the try it out. On the form, add a ListBox named ListBox1.

First, create a dictionary object of your friends like the one here in your form load sub.

```
Dim objFriends As New Dictionary(Of String, String)
objFriends.Add("Bryan Newsome", "CA")
objFriends.Add("Jennifer Newsome", "CA")
objFriends.Add("Latelyn Newsome", "CA")
objFriends.Add("Chuck Owens", "NC")
objFriends.Add("Tim Moris", "NC")
objFriends.Add("Valan Burgess", "NC")
objFriends.Add("Holly Keeler", "NC")
objFriends.Add("Bill Money", "CA")
objFriends.Add("Bernie Perry", "CA")
objFriends.Add("Richard Clark", "CA")
objFriends.Add("Naresh Clegg", "CA")
```

Next, write the LINQ statement to filter the results based on who lives in CA.

```
Dim authors = From dictKey In objFriends _
            Where dictKey.Value.ToString = "NC"
```

Finally, bind the results to the ListBox by addng each item returned.

```
For Each selectedItem In authors
    ListBox1.Items.Add(selectedItem)
Next
```

Chapter 18

1. Create a new web site, name it **ExerciseOne**, and create it as a local site using the file system and ASP.NET Development Server. Run the web site to make sure it is running in ASP.NET Development Server.

A. When you create your site and run it using F5, you should notice the ASP.NET Development Server start up and then stay in the task bar. When you double-click the icon in the taskbar, you should see a dialog box similar to Figure A-3.

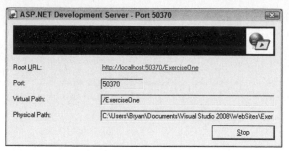

Figure A-3

2. Create a new web site, name it **ExerciseTwo**, and create it as a local IIS. Run the Web site to make sure it is *not* running in ASP.NET Development Server. (You will need IIS on your local machine to complete this exercise.) Note that Vista requires you to run Visual Studio as an administrator for this to work.

A. To create a site on your local IIS, you must run as administrator first. Then, you have to click the Create New Virtual Directory icon or the icon to create a new site. It is typical to use virtual directories on local IIS sites. You would see Figure A-4 when you click Create New Virtual Directory and enter the name and location.

Figure A-4

Your web site location in the New Web Site dialog box should look like Figure A-5.

Figure A-5

Chapter 19

1. Change the font to appear red for an `asp:label` control using the `Main.skin` page (created in TheClub site already) for every page under the Members directory. To do this, you can change the theme attribute on every page or change the `web.config` file for the directory. For this exercise, change the `web.config` file. You have not seen the `web.config` file syntax for this, so I will show it to you. Add the change to the `web.config` file that will apply the theme to the Web Forms under the Members folder. Use the code snippet here as a guide:

```
<configuration>
    <system.web>
        <pages theme="MainTheme" />
        <authorization>
            <deny users="?" />
        </authorization>
    </system.web>
</configuration>
```

A. Your `web.config` file in the `Members` folder should look like this:

```
<configuration>
    <system.web>
        <pages theme="MainTheme" />
        <authorization>
            <deny users="?" />
        </authorization>
    </system.web>
</configuration>
```

The `Main.skin` file should look like this (only one line of code in file):

```
<asp:Label runat="server" ForeColor="Red" />
```

2. The `Login` controls you use in this chapter are fully customizable. In this exercise, you will make some a change to the look of the login control on the `Login.aspx` page. Change the font color of the `Login` control to red by adding the tag and font color properties to the `Main.skin` file. Point the `web.config` file under the root folder to use the `MainTheme`. (You did this in Exercise 1 under a different directory.)

A. Your `web.config` file in the `Root` folder should look like this (although you will find some additional items and comments):

```
<?xml version="1.0" encoding="utf-8"?>
<configuration>
    <system.web>
        <pages theme="MainTheme" />
        <roleManager enabled="true" />
        <authentication mode="Forms" />
    </system.web>
</configuration>
```

The `Main.skin` file should look like this:

```
<asp:Label runat="server" ForeColor="Red" />
<asp:Login runat="server" ForeColor="Red" />
```

Chapter 20

1. Create an XML document that describes a table lamp. You can describe the lamp using a number of different attributes. You should describe items such as shade, bulbs and base. You can validate your XML at a site such as www.w3schools.com/dom/dom_validate.asp that offers a free validator.

A. For this exercise, you are required to create an XML document that described a table lamp. There are a number of ways to correctly describe a lamp. You could have used child elements and no attributes. Or, you could have used different language to describe a lamp. Either way, you should have used the same case and closed your elements.

You can validate your XML at a site like http://www.w3schools.com/dom/dom_validate.asp that offers a free validator. The code for the document should look similar to this:

```
<?xml version="1.0" encoding="utf-8"?>
<lamps xmlns:xsi="http://www.w3.org/2001/XMLSchema-instance"
xmlns:xsd="http://www.w3.org/2001/XMLSchema">
 <lamp type="table" desing="modern" price="269">
        <base shape="square" color="black" height_inches="24"></base>
        <bulbs max_watts="60" number_of_bulbs="3" type="soft white"></bulbs>
        <shade color="white" shape="oval" size_inches="18 X 8"></shade>
 </lamp>
</lamps>
```

2. Expand on what you learned in the chapter by investigating how to place comments in an XML file. As a beginner, one of the most important tasks you can learn is how to research and find answers to questions. For this exercise, search the Web using your favorite search engine and try to find the syntax for inserting comments in XML Once you find the answer, test the comment in the same XML validator you used to test Exercise 1.

A. For this exercise, you have to find the syntax for a valid XML comment. The comment is like a HTML comment and starts with `<!--` and ends with `-->`. Your comment should look similar to this:

```
<!-- This is a valid XML comment -->
```

Chapter 21

1. Create a web service that returns information about the web server. Add three methods that return the web server date, web server time, and web server name, respectively. Run the project to test the three methods.

A. For this exercise, you are required to create a web service with three methods. The three methods should have individually returned the server date, time, and name. First, you had to create a new web site project and then add the web service methods. The code for the methods should look similar to these:

```vb
Imports System.Web
Imports System.Web.Services
Imports System.Web.Services.Protocols

<WebService(Namespace := "http://tempuri.org/")> _
<WebServiceBinding(ConformsTo:=WsiProfiles.BasicProfile1_1)> _
Public Class WebService
    Inherits System.Web.Services.WebService

    Public Sub WebService

    End Sub

    <WebMethod()> _
    Public Function ServerName() As String
        Return My.Computer.Name
    End Function

    <WebMethod()> _
    Public Function ServerDate() As Date
        Return Now().Date
    End Function

    <WebMethod()> _
    Public Function ServerTime() As String
        Return Now().ToShortTimeString
    End Function

End Class
```

When you run the web service, you may be asked to add a `web.config` file for debugging. You could choose either to add the file or to continue without debugging. When you tested each method, you should have seen the date, time, and name of your server.

2. Add more math functions to the WCF service you created in the last Try It Out. Create methods to add two numbers, subtract two numbers, multiply two numbers, and divide two numbers. To make this work, you have to add code to two places.

A. To complete exercise 2, you need to add code to the interface and class. The new code should be similar to this:

```
<ServiceContract()> _
Public Interface ISquareRoot
    <OperationContract()> _
    <WebGet()> _
    Function GetSquareRoot(ByVal dblNumber As Double) As Double
    Function Add(ByVal dblNumber1 As Double, ByVal dblNumber2 As Double) _
As Double
    Function Subtract(ByVal dblNumber1 As Double, ByVal dblNumber2 As Double) _
As Double
    Function Multiply(ByVal dblNumber1 As Double, ByVal dblNumber2 As Double) _
As Double
    Function Divide(ByVal dblNumber1 As Double, ByVal dblNumber2 As Double) _
As Double
End Interface


Public Class SquareRoot
    Implements ISquareRoot
    Public Function GetSquareRoot(ByVal dblNumber As Double) As Double _
Implements ISquareRoot.GetSquareRoot
        Return Math.Sqrt(dblNumber)
    End Function
Public Function Add(ByVal dblNumber1 As Double, ByVal dblNumber2 As Double) _
As Double Implements ISquareRoot.Add
        Return dblNumber1 + dblNumber2
    End Function
    Public Function Subtract(ByVal dblNumber1 As Double, ByVal dblNumber2 _
As Double) As Double Implements ISquareRoot.Subtract
        Return dblNumber1 - dblNumber2
    End Function
    Public Function Multiply(ByVal dblNumber1 As Double, ByVal dblNumber2 _
As Double) As Double Implements ISquareRoot.Multiply
        Return dblNumber1 * dblNumber2
    End Function
    Public Function Divide(ByVal dblNumber1 As Double, ByVal dblNumber2 _
As Double) As Double Implements ISquareRoot.Divide
        Return dblNumber1 / dblNumber2
    End Function
End Class
```

Chapter 22

1. Add a third ifElseBranch to the "WorkflowPropertyListing" Try It Out. Split the branch for NewOrSold into two branches.

Figure A-6 shows what your workflow should look like.

Figure A-6

A. In the project, start by clicking the ifElseBranchNewOrSold or selecting it in the Properties window and copying it. Next, select the ifElseAddToQueue activity and paste the branch into it. This action will create a third branch. Next, update the code to function correctly as the newly added branch is the third one and should be considered the else branch. Also, notice that a code activity was added and that a red circle with an exclamation point was added to show that you must set the condition property of the second branch.

2. In the WorkflowPropertyListing project, add a while activity before the first ifElse activity. You will need to create a code condition handler and then set the code condition property. This is where the while loop determines if it should continue or not. Next, add a code activity that tests for a change found and then asks the user to enter a new file name if no change is found. The while loop will continue if e.result = true in the condition handler.

A. To complete Exercise 2 you need to add the following controls to the project, set the properties as shown, and add the following code. Figures A-7, A-8, A-9, and A-10 show you what the visual designer and output will look like.

For later projects, remember that the while activity allows only one activity to be executed during the loop. When using this activity, it is common to use the Sequence activity to host multiple activities. The while activity can accept a Sequence activity, so you might use it to get around this limitation.

Figure A-7

Figure A-8

Figure A-9

```
C:\Users\Bryan\Documents\Visual Studio 2008\Projects\WorkflowPropertyListing\WorkflowP...  _□×
What is the file name?
sdkf
File has been moved successfully
File name has been parsed successfully
No Change Found
What is the file name?
lkafj
while loop executed codeActivityWhileNoChangeFound_ExecuteCode
No Change Found
What is the file name?
_new
while loop executed codeActivityWhileNoChangeFound_ExecuteCode
File item added or removed found
New or removed workflow item added
Workflow item assigned

Workflow complete
```

Figure A-10

```
      Private Sub codeActivityWhileNoChangeFound_ExecuteCode(ByVal _
sender As System.Object, ByVal e As System.EventArgs)

            Console.WriteLine("while loop executed" & _
                    "codeActivityWhileNoChangeFound_ExecuteCode")
      End Sub
      Private Sub WhileLoop(ByVal sender As System.Object, ByVal e As _
                System.Workflow.Activities.ConditionalEventArgs)
            If strFileName.ToUpper.Contains("_ADDRESS") _
                    Or strFileName.ToUpper.Contains("_NEW") _
                    Or strFileName.ToUpper.Contains("_REMOVE") Then
                e.Result = False
            Else
                Console.WriteLine("No Change Found")
                Console.WriteLine("What is the file name?")
                strFileName = Console.ReadLine()
                e.Result = True
            End If
      End Sub
```

Chapter 23

1. The computer player is a random picker. Give the computer player some brains. Add at least one function named ComputerPlayToWin to the application. When the computer moves, call ComputerPlayToWin and check for a spot on the board that will create a win for the computer. If it exists, the computer should play that move rather than a random move. You can add other procedures if needed.

A. This exercise has numerous correct answers. If you ask 10 programmers to complete it, you will get 10 different answers. So, if your changes work, you have a valid answer. The following is what we came up with to solve the problem.

You need to add a call to the new function, ComputerPlayToWin, from ComputerPlay. It should be the first call in the procedure. If you find a win here and make a move, you can exit the subroutine without allocating any of the local variables in ComputerPlay.

```
Sub ComputerPlay()
    If ComputerPlayToWin() Then Exit Sub
```

Your solution will look different from ours. Compare your solution to ours and think about which one is better and why. The first function, CheckForWin, allows you to check an entire row or column of buttons for a chance to win. If two squares are marked and the third is empty, the computer will make this move by changing the text for all buttons. This is done by passing the buttons ByRef to the function. ComputerPlayToWin calls this function for every row, column, or diagonal win possibility on the board.

```
Private Function CheckForWin(ByRef btnFirst As Windows.Forms.Button, _
    ByRef btnSecond As Windows.Forms.Button, ByRef btnThird As _
    Windows.Forms.Button, ByVal stringToFind As String, _
    ByVal strOpponentsMark As String) As Boolean
```

```
        Dim intSum As Int16 = 0S

        'Check to see if we can win on this row
        'We can win if we have two marks and no opponent marks on the row
        'If there is an opponents mark we are blocked so return false

        If btnFirst.Text = stringToFind Then
            intSum += 1S
        ElseIf btnFirst.Text = strOpponentsMark Then
            Return False
        End If

        If btnSecond.Text = stringToFind Then
            intSum += 1S
        ElseIf btnSecond.Text = strOpponentsMark Then
            Return False
        End If

        If btnThird.Text = stringToFind Then
            intSum += 1S
        ElseIf btnThird.Text = strOpponentsMark Then
            Return False
        End If

        'We will win on this turn
        'so just mark the entire row to save some resources

        If intSum = 2 Then
            btnFirst.Text = stringToFind
            btnSecond.Text = stringToFind
            btnThird.Text = stringToFind
            Return True
        Else
            Return False
        End If
    End Function
```

All that the `ComputerPlayToWin` function does is pass the buttons and strings to check `CheckForWin` for each possible win. If a win is found, the game is over. The computer will not make a random play if it can win.

```
    Private Function ComputerPlayToWin() As Boolean
        If CheckForWin(btn00, btn01, btn02, "O", "X") Then
            'Winner on top Row
            Call Winner("O")
            Return True
        End If
        If CheckForWin(btn10, btn11, btn12, "O", "X") Then
            'Winner on middle Row
            Call Winner("O")
            Return True
        End If
        If CheckForWin(btn20, btn21, btn22, "O", "X") Then
            'Winner on third Row
```

```
            Call Winner("O")
            Return True
        End If
        If CheckForWin(btn00, btn10, btn20, "O", "X") Then
            'Winner on first column
            Call Winner("O")
            Return True
        End If
        If CheckForWin(btn01, btn11, btn21, "O", "X") Then
            'Winner on second column
            Call Winner("O")
            Return True
        End If
        If CheckForWin(btn02, btn12, btn22, "O", "X") Then
            'Winner on third column
            Call Winner("O")
            Return True
        End If

        If CheckForWin(btn00, btn11, btn22, "O", "X") Then
            'Winner on diagonal top left to bottom right
            Call Winner("O")
            Return True
        End If
        If CheckForWin(btn20, btn11, btn02, "O", "X") Then
            'Winner on diagonal bottom left to top right
            Call Winner("O")
            Return True
        End If
    End Function
```

Chapter 24

1. Create a setup project for Notepad and install the program. You should be able to find the notepad.exe file in your Windows System directory. *Hint:* You will need to add the file to a setup project. Have the setup application add a shortcut to the Start menu. Deploy the notepad.exe file to the Program Files directory. For extra work, change the Manufacturer property of the project from Default Company Name to **Wrox**. Also, change the Author property to your name.

A. For this example, you create a setup project for Notepad. You create a new setup project named **Chapter24Exercise1.** Under the Application folder, you browse for and add the notepad.exe file. After adding the file, you create a shortcut to the executable and moved the shortcut to User's Program. Menu. Next, you select the project in Solution Explorer and then find and change the Author and Manufacturer properties in the Properties window. Finally, you build and then run the setup.exe file.

You may be asking why we asked you to change the Author and Manufacturer properties. The manufacturer is used to determine the default location for the installed application. When you installed the application, C:\Program Files\Wrox\Chapter24Exercise1\ was the default installation directory. Without updating the manufacturer, the default directory would have been `C:\Program Files\Default Company Name\Chapter24Exercise1\`. The second reason to change the manufacturer is the support info screen under Add/Remove Programs. When you look at your application's support info screen, you'll see that the publisher is Wrox.

2. Using the setup application created in Exercise 1, add a splash screen dialog box that is displayed first during the installation. We have included a bitmap in the code for the book named `Wrox_Logo.bmp`. This bitmap is the correct size, 480 × 320, and you can use this image for the dialog box.

Hint: You have to add the image you use to the setup application before you can add it to the splash dialog box.

A. In the completed exercise, you add a bitmap image to the application. You add the image to the application folder or a subfolder of the application folder. Next, you add a splash screen via the user interface editor. The `SplashBitmap` property of the Splash dialog box is changed to the bitmap you added, and the dialog box is moved up to the first screen shown. When you run the installation, you see the splash screen as the first dialog box.

Using the Microsoft Solutions Framework

So here you are, ready to go out into the world and build applications with Visual Basic 2008. Congratulate yourself; you should be excited at having worked your way through all the chapters of the book. Soon, creating applications will become second nature to you. As you work in IT, you will play many roles on teams. In some cases, your manager will only ask you to write code. The main portion of this book provides a strong understanding of what you will need to do in that situation. Other times, management will ask you to wear many hats on a project and be responsible for delivering an entire solution. This appendix introduces you to what it takes to create a successful solution.

Let's start with a basic question. How is a solution different from an application? A solution is the entire process of creating a system for a customer. The solution includes planning, documenting, testing, releasing, training, and supporting the application. The application is just one part of the solution.

Microsoft has a set of processes and models that to some is the standard for solution delivery in the IT industry: Microsoft Solutions Framework (MSF). Software developers around the globe apply this framework to internal strategies to ensure best practices when building software. The MSF is a recent interpretation of the classic software development life cycle and provides guidance to project management. In this appendix, you will

- ❑ Learn about the software development life cycle.
- ❑ Get an overview of the MSF and how it relates to the software development life cycle.
- ❑ See how to manage trade-offs.
- ❑ Learn how to define success for a project.

A detailed explanation of the Framework would take two or three hundred pages. This appendix is just a concise summary. Keep this in mind as you begin to explore this tool. To get more info online, you can visit www.microsoft.com/technet/solutionaccelerators/msf/ default.mspx.

Software Development Life Cycle

The software development life cycle (SDLC) is a set of building blocks for software design. Microsoft and others in the industry continue to develop methodologies to interpret the SDLC into a set of steps or milestones. Depending on whom you ask, you may get five steps or even seven steps in an SDLC implementation. Here is one interpretation of the SDLC steps:

- ❑ Defining the problem
- ❑ Gathering requirements
- ❑ Analysis and design
- ❑ Development
- ❑ Testing
- ❑ Installation
- ❑ Maintenance

Theoretically, the work progresses in a linear fashion from each of these steps to the next. In practice, it is often the case that the need for further design work, more specific requirements, or a clearer definition of the problem is discovered during development or testing, and the process loops back to the earlier stage.

Microsoft Solutions Framework

The Microsoft Framework Solution is built for the implementation of large software projects. Two distinct models (Team Model and Process Model) define the entire framework. To set up a large project team, you will need to use the Team Model. As you begin your career, you will most likely work on smaller projects. Because of this, we will not go into detail about the Team Model. The Process Model defines how to successfully complete the solutions using a specific sequence of activities. In this appendix, we will show you how to use the principles of the Process Model in smaller projects.

In the Team Model, a developer is only one role in a large project and generally works on only one task: developing the application code. As you work on small solutions, be aware that you will take on many roles. One day you may be gathering requirements, and the next week you may be developing code for the application. You need to recognize that it is difficult to write the code and simultaneously take on other project roles. As a developer, it will be easy to focus your efforts on the code writing and put the analysis, testing, and documentation on the back burner. This will almost always result in an unsuccessful project. Although the code may work, the documentation may not be good enough to maintain or change the application. You may not understand this concept yet, but in my opinion writing the code is the easy part of the solution. When your manager asks you to play many roles on a project, remember that in most cases you will need to spend more time designing, testing, and documenting code than writing it.

The Process Model, consisting of five phases, is the portion of the MSF that puts the SDLC into practice. It describes the order in which you should complete each phase of the SDLC. Also, this model involves iterations of all phases, known as *versions*. If you are familiar with MS software, you know that Microsoft updates software via new versions. The Process Model is a continuous loop of milestones that incorporates deploying multiple versions of software. Each version of the software will go through all phases of the Framework:

- Envisioning
- Planning
- Developing
- Testing
- Deploying

The following sections lead you through each of these phases in turn.

The Envisioning Phase

To start the MSF, you begin in the envisioning phase. The success of the project starts here. Make sure you take the time to nail down all loose ends before moving forward with the project. Your customers expect and deserve to understand how the project is going to proceed and the scope document at the end of this phase will do that. After completing the envisioning phase, everyone with a stake in the project will be on the same page. There are five goals of the envisioning phase that you need to accomplish before moving on to the planning phase.

Problem Statement

Why is the customer willing to spend $80,000 on a new system? Although there is an obvious answer this question, don't take this step lightly — all of your decisions will be driven by the problem statement. Here is an example of a problem definition:

> As government regulations change, the current system cannot meet the time requirements to implement changes and stay in compliance. To compete in our industry, we must have a system that is flexible enough to make changes easily so as to maintain governmental compliance.

Goals

You need to agree on measurable goals with the customer. These will be used to help define the success of the project. The keyword is *measurable*. The following statements express the same goal, but the second version offers a measurable standard:

- The system should improve customer service by being able to complete a phone order quickly.
- The system will improve customer service by allowing a phone order to be completed in less than 60 seconds.

The first goal is vague and is not measurable. If you base the system on goals like the first one, it is easy for the customer to believe the system is not fast enough at the end, when you feel the system is much faster than it had been. You may think the system is a success, but the customer thinks it is a failure. Remember to make sure that you can measure system goals.

Define Roles

Here is an easy one. On smaller projects, only a few people will be working on the project. You will need to determine who is responsible for planning, development, testing, documentation, and releasing the system. For large projects, you would use the Team Model to define roles.

Create a Scope Document

The scope document will be a blueprint of the solution. All stakeholders in the project should sign off on the final version of the scope document. Sections of the scope document include the following:

- ❑ An initial list of user requirements
- ❑ The problem statement
- ❑ Definition of team roles
- ❑ A set of measurable goals
- ❑ A brief statement defining the upcoming planning process

Risk Analysis

Your customer will need to know any risks that may cause problems for the project. These risks may be that you are working with new, unproven technologies, that system bandwidth requirements may exceed available network resources, that legacy data may not import correctly, or new technology coming out may make the new software obsolete.

The Planning Phase

During the planning stage, you will create documents to validate that the project can succeed. The documents you create will be transformed through feedback from the customer and project stakeholders. Make sure that all project stakeholders have time to review and validate each document. Even for a small project, this process can take many rounds of changes to gain sign-off from all parties. Finally, you will create a project schedule and cost estimate before moving to the developing stage. Listed here are the documents you need to create.

- ❑ Conceptual, logical, and physical design documents
- ❑ Use cases and usage scenarios
- ❑ System specification
- ❑ Project schedule
- ❑ Cost estimate

The Developing Phase

This is the stage you are most familiar with. The MSF encapsulates everything from actually building the development environment to completing documentation into the development stage. The milestone for this phase is a complete application ready for testing.

Setup: *Building Staging Areas for Development and Testing*

For any project, you need a development and test environment that matches the production environment. Take precautions to build the staging areas so that they are the same as the production environment. Something as simple as different printer drivers between test staging and production areas can cause unanticipated results during release of the application.

Completing the Prototype

You must allow the customer to approve a prototype. Do not underestimate the value of this. Imagine you were building a car. Without proper models, how hard is it to determine the proper location of the steering wheel or how to add six inches of leg room for rear passengers? Take this time to let the customer make changes to the design. You will find that it is easy to change a prototype. Once you have three months of coding under way, changes to the user interface can be costly.

Completing the Code

The application is ready for testing. Validate modules through unit testing.

Supply Application Documentation

The documentation from prior phases is compiled and included with a user manual and system documentation. The test team will rely on this data for testing.

The Testing Phase

As a beginner, you may not understand the importance of this phase. There is no better way to make a small project over budget and late than to find 500 bugs while testing. Make sure you have adequate time in your schedule to test and make test plans. Like everything else in the MSF, testing is an iterative process. You will need test plans that you can repeat and validate after bug fixes. After each round of testing, complete your test plans. Remember to document your result. When bugs arise in the application after release, you will want to see why the test plan did not uncover the bug and then adjust the test plan. After the customer has signed off on the test results, complete any documentation changes and package all files for deployment.

You should plan for the following subphases during the testing process:

- ❑ Application tier testing
- ❑ Security testing
- ❑ Performance testing
- ❑ User acceptance testing
- ❑ System integration testing

The Deployment Phase

Now, you are ready for production. If you are on time and within budget, your customer will be happy with the project. With all of the planning and customer interaction, there will be few surprises at this point. You will put the solution into production and have a small team available to train and support the users. After the agreed-upon amount of time, the application will be turned over to the support staff. You will need to train them and turn over system documentation. That is it. You have managed a successful implementation of a project.

There is one item left: How to handle changes using tradeoffs. To have any chance of getting to the end of a project successfully, you must be able to manage tradeoffs. The following section explains this in more detail.

Managing Tradeoffs

To complete a successful project, you must be able to manage tradeoffs. You will find very quickly that your customer will ask you questions of the form " . . . Can you do that?" And your answer should be in almost every instance, "Yes, we can." You will find that you *can* do just about anything. The problem is that it takes a certain amount of time and money for every project or change request. What your customer means to say is, "Can you do that for $50,000 by the end of this year?" So when you answer the "can it be done" question, make sure the customer knows that you can do it for the right price with enough time.

When you work with clients, internal or external, you have to make them aware of project tradeoffs. There are three tradeoff values to consider: budget, deadlines, and functionality. A fourth tradeoff could be quality. You should not consider reducing quality to lower price, finish sooner, or add features to make a project successful. Although you define the project scope, make sure that the project team and customers understand the priorities of tradeoffs. As you make changes involving one of the tradeoff values, you will have to compensate by adjusting at least one of the others.

For example, suppose you are working with the marketing department on a small application. You are the only resource available to work on the solution for the next two weeks during planning. While you are gathering the system requirements, you speak to the marketing vice-president, Tina, about the priorities of the solution. Very quickly she makes it clear that she needs the application by the end of the year and for a cost of under $50,000. As you pry more, you find that Tina cannot spend more than $50,000 this year. She wants the system to be live in three months with at least the core functionality in the first version. Next year, she may be able free up more money in her budget to finish the lower-priority features.

You quickly write down the tradeoffs and the priorities. In order of priority, you write budget, deadline, and features. Take a look at the project priorities listed in the following table. You and Tina sign off on the tradeoff priorities, and now you know how to make the solution a success. Meeting the budget and deadline are required for success. For example, some functionality will be moved to the next version if the project gets behind schedule.

Tradeoff	Priority
Under Budget	First
Meet Deadline	Second
Deliver Functionality	Third

Halfway through the project, Tina wants to add more core functionality to the system. You look at the budget and see that if you add more functionality to this release, you will need more resources to make the deadline. Adding another developer to meet the deadline will cost an extra $10,000. Looking back at the project priorities, you see that Tina cannot spend more than $50,000. You have set aside the entire $50,000 budget, and $10,000 more is too much. It is time to call Tina and explain the situation.

While talking to Tina, you explain the top priority for the project is budget. Adding the extra functionality will cost an additional $10,000, bringing the budget estimate to $60,000. During the discussion, you mention that the only way to add more functionality without increasing the deadline or budget is to drop some of the functionality already planned. After 30 minutes, she agrees that $50,000 is all she can spend, and the additional functionality can be part of a later version.

By understanding and agreeing on tradeoff priorities, you are able to work with customers to manage change. If a customer wants to change any of the tradeoff priorities, you will have to adjust one or both of the others.

Defining Success with the MSF

A successful project is hard to achieve. If you follow the framework, success can be achieved more easily. It all comes down to customer satisfaction and one simple question: Did you make the customer happy? This simple question can be hard to answer. Let me clarify how to find the answer to this question. To make the customer happy, you must succeed in most of these four areas: achieve system goals, meet the release date, stay within budget, and manage tradeoffs.

With the Framework implementation, you will find defining success possible. The two milestones that are straightforward are meeting the budget and release date. Take a look at the project plan and make sure these milestones were met. System goals are also straightforward if you defined measurable goals. Test the system against the project goals to verify the system meets the standards agreed upon. The final milestone is change or tradeoff management. Pull out the final tradeoff chart and review it. For the project to be successful, you must have met the top priority of your customer. Changes may have caused you to miss the other milestones, but if you managed tradeoffs with the customer, the project will still be successful. Success can be that simple if you follow the game plan.

Summary

As you grow in the information technology field, you will work on larger projects and have more responsibility. Use this appendix as a basis for further study. Always keep in mind how many steps you have to take to be successful managing a project. When you do get into a position to lead a project, take the time to plan and test, and always work toward making the customer happy. You will not always be successful by following the framework, so take misfortunes in stride and learn from them. As you complete projects, you will come up with your own interpretation of the SDLC or the MSF, and you will be a success.

An Introduction to Code Security and SSL

In today's electronic world, consumers are bombarded with scams via the Internet and e-mail. If you plan to write applications that take advantage of these technologies, you must be aware of fraudulent activity of others. The most rampant activity today is a tactic known as *phishing*. In this scam, a fraudulent e-mail or pop-up message lures a user to a fake web site on the pretext that a breach in bank security or unwanted account activity has made it necessary to verify the user's account information. Tricked users will see a site that looks like their bank's site but is actually being hosted by criminals in an attempt to bait users into entering their personal and financial information. In these schemes, it is easy for concerned customers to be tricked and enter their card number, social security number, or PIN into the web forms to avoid their accounts being frozen. Little do they know they are giving away their private information to thieves.

Phishing is not the only scam consumers must deal with, but it is one of the most prevalent. As a developer, it is your job to make applications safe. The use of certain features in your application can make it easier for criminals to impersonate you. If your application avoids asking for personal information that you do not need over e-mail or the Web, users may be more alert to a scam when it occurs. You can never assume that e-mail will not be intercepted over the Internet. Make sure you never treat e-mail as a secure means of data transmission.

You must also be aware of security for your Windows applications and assemblies. It seems as though a new hole is found every week in some browser or operating system that allows a hacker to run code on a user's machine. One way in which this type of attack is commonly accomplished is by a *buffer overflow*. To give a simple explanation, hackers discover that a program has memory allocated to store data only up to a certain size. The attacker sends a larger object than the memory allocated. The extra data is not discarded, but instead it gets written to adjacent areas of memory that are intended to store code or the addresses of code. This may corrupt valid allocations of memory, but more important, it installs the attacker's malicious code in memory. The victim's program runs the attacker's code as if it were its own, and the damage is done. The root cause of this problem is not one most Visual Basic developers will encounter, but it should make you aware that people may use your functions in ways you did not intend including malicious ways.

Take a look at another example of a software bug that might be a security risk. Say you write an assembly or web service that would upload files to your company's web site. This application is for salespeople to upload comma-separated files of current sales data each night. The code allows the path and file name to be passed as parameters, and it can be used by numerous departments because of this flexibility. The problem is that this same flexibility allows a hacker to upload a Web page, place it into the root web directory, and do almost anything to the server or network. You should change this web service to store files in a locked-down directory and modify the file name so that an attacker would not be able to access the file by name. Functions like this one are prevalent in many companies' code libraries and create most of the security holes these companies will face.

In this appendix you will learn about security issues and how to handle them within the following topics:

❑   Understanding code access security

❑   Secure Sockets Layer (SSL)

❑   Where to look for security answers

Code Access Security

The goal of code access security (CAS) is simple: Stop unwanted code from running or accessing resources. This is accomplished by the runtime's security system. When an assembly needs access to a resource, all assemblies on the call stack should have permission to access that resource. Take a look at the following example.

An assembly is run from the Internet. By default, it is granted access to a *permission set* (explained in the next subsection) based on the Internet zone. The application has no access to the local file system. If that assembly were to call a public method on an assembly that did have access to the file system, the runtime would throw a security exception. When the permissions of each assembly on the stack are tested, the assembly that was run from the Internet will fail the permission check.

On the other hand, an administrator could grant a signed assembly more permissions. So, if this assembly had the correct digital signature, it could be granted access to a larger set of permissions.

CAS allows the system administrator to apply permissions to code rather than to users. Before CAS, if a hacker could get a user to run code or an attachment that contained a virus, it was granted security based on the *user's* security level. If that user was an administrator on the machine, the virus had full access to do its dirty work. Now, a virus may be stopped by the Common Language Runtime and not have access to corrupt the file system, even if the user has permissions.

The way this works is through permissions, security policy, and evidence. When an assembly requests a file, for example, the runtime makes sure that file is available from a security aspect by checking permissions, security levels, and evidence. Let's start with permissions.

Permissions

Permissions are granted to resources based on trust and origination. Administrators can grant higher or lower levels of access to individual assemblies or zones. Here is a list of four common permissions used by the runtime:

- ❏ `EnvironmentPermission`: Access control for system and user environment variables
- ❏ `FileDialogPermission`: File system access control for file dialogs
- ❏ `FileIOPermission`: File system access control
- ❏ `RegistryPermission`: Control access to the Registry

It would be hard to manage a large group of permissions without a way of grouping them. Grouping permissions is accomplished by using *permission sets*. The .NET Framework has six predefined permission sets. You can use any of the sets in the following list in your code.

- ❏ `Nothing`: This named permission set will not allow code to run.
- ❏ `Execution`: The Execution set allows the code to run, but no access is granted to protected resources.
- ❏ `FullTrust`: The most forgiving permission set. Access to all resources is granted.
- ❏ `Internet`: You can think of this as the access you would permit when browsing. This would be used when running code from the Internet or any nontrusted source.
- ❏ `LocalIntranet`: This is for trusted code running on a trusted network.
- ❏ `Everything`: This is a set of all standard permissions. The permission to skip verification is not granted to this set.

Your code can request any level of permission, and the runtime will verify before running the code that these permissions will be granted.

Security Policy

The runtime enforces policy based on the identity or evidence of the assembly. When loading an assembly, the assembly is inspected for evidence of its origin. Based on the origin, the runtime determines what permissions to grant the assembly.

Evidence

To determine the origin of an assembly, the CLR looks at many attributes of the assembly. This is known as the *evidence*. Table C-1 has a list of evidence types. The runtime may use any or all of these to determine the permissions to grant the assembly.

Table C-1: Types of Evidence

Evidence Type	Description
Application directory	Installation directory
Hash	Assembly hash
Publisher	The Authenticode signature
Site	Web site — for example, wrox.com.
Strong name	Assembly's Strong name
URL	URL of the assembly
Zone	Origination zone

When permissions are tested, an intersection of zones and permissions is evaluated to verify that all permissions for every zone and assembly on the stack are met. If permission is not granted to the code, the zone, or the user, an exception is thrown and access is denied.

Secure Sockets Layer

The Secure Sockets Layer (SSL) protocol was developed to secure communication between a web server and a browser. Today, 128-bit SSL encryption is the standard for secure data transmission over the Internet. If you need to secure parts of a Web site, your customers will expect this type of encryption. To promote the level of security to the end user, Internet Explorer and Firefox display a lock similar to Figure C-1 at the bottom of the browser window.

Figure C-1

Another way users know a site is secure is by the URL. The URL of an SSL site shows https:// instead of the standard http://. The user can also look at details of the certificate by double-clicking the lock icon or viewing the page's properties or info. Figure C-2 is an actual certificate info screen from a large web site. We have removed the company's name from the image.

Figure C-2

Two of the largest companies that issue SSL certificates are Thawte and VeriSign. They are both well respected in the industry and offer free trial certificates for you to test.

Trial certificates can be found at the following sites:

- ❑ `verisign.com/products-services/security-services/ssl/index.html`: Click the Try link for the certificate type you wish to try.

- ❑ `thawte.com/`: Click the link for a 21-day trial.

You should keep in mind that encryption slows down the experience for the user and creates more load for the server. Keep marketing and nonessential areas of your site unencrypted. Only encrypt pages that communicate data that would be considered private.

Finding Information and Answers

This appendix offers only a brief introduction to the vast topic of security. The following list offers some web sites that may help you with further research and finding answers to your security-related questions.

- ❑ `microsoft.com/security/`: Microsoft's security home page. Read the latest in security notes about Microsoft products.

- ❑ `www.microsoft.com/technet/security/default.mspx/`: Microsoft's TechNet Security Center. Here you can get info on the latest security bulletins and security help from Microsoft.

❑   `ftc.gov`: The Federal Trade Commission Web site. Here you can see what types of scams are being reported.

❑   `owasp.org`: Open Web Application Security Project (OWASP). This site offers free tools, documentation, and standards.

❑   `sans.org/rr/`: The SANS Institute Information Security Reading Room. Read thousands of white papers on security issues.

❑   `webappsec.org`: The Web Application Security Consortium. Read white papers on the latest news about web site security.

Summary

Security is the hottest topic in the information technology industry. Making applications 100 percent secure is not possible with the openness of the Internet, but minimizing risks to vital data should be a top priority in application design. As you build applications with VS 2008, know that you have the best tool available to create secure Windows applications, but it is your responsibility to maintain the security of the applications you write.

Administrators will be able to use CAS to stop many types of attacks. Being able to apply permissions to assemblies and validate the origination of the code makes implementing a secure network easier. The widespread use of certificates and code signing will make spoofing applications more difficult and keep users' computers safer.

The world of application security is by no means perfect. You will probably have to design your applications around security risks forever. But you can win by keeping security at the top of the priority list in your application design. Soon you will begin to develop applications for wireless access, and more security implications will need to be understood. Keeping applications secure in a world where information access is expanding will continue to be a challenge.

Just make sure you keep your head up and pay attention. Security holes are announced throughout the media, and, as a developer, you should pay attention and learn from the mistakes of the past. One of your applications may one day be under attack.

An Introduction to Windows CardSpace

Microsoft has added a new feature to the .NET Framework 3.0: Windows CardSpace. (Formerly, this software was known as InfoCard.) This is a new type of identity management system that removes the old user name and password you are used to on the Web. The overall idea is that the users creates your cards and then you can choose which cards to assign to different sites. These cards can contain varying amounts of personal info, so for a very public site you can use a card that includes the minimum requirement for that site. For more personal information like a banking site, you can create a card with more data or even have a card issued to you from a bank that is a card provider. For some users, this will be a great solution.

Using CardSpace

To use CardSpace, there are some limitations for both the web site and user. First, the web site you are registering with must support it. For this emerging technology, that will mean that limited sites support it for now. But you should expect more sites to begin to offer this type of identity technology soon. On the user side, you will be required to use IE 7 or Firefox 2.0 (with a plug-in) as your browser. If you have Microsoft Vista, the CardSpace feature is included with the OS. If not, you can install the .NET Framework 3.0 on Windows XP or Windows Server 2003 to get the client tools needed to use CardSpace.

CardSpace is a very easy way to log into sites on the Internet. When you go to a site that accepts Windows CardSpace, just click the button or link to create an account or log in with a card. If this is your first time at the site, create an account. You may be asked if you want to send a card to this site, and may be shown site information so you can verify the site identity (see Figure D-1).

Figure D-1

Next, you will see all of the cards stored on your computer. Here you will be able to see cards that meet the site requirements and cards you have sent to this site before (see Figure D-2). This makes it easy to keep sending the same card to each site.

Figure D-2

Before sending a card, you can preview the data on the card. To do this, just click preview. Figure D-3 shows you this interface.

Figure D-3

The next time you go to log into the same site, CardSpace will show that you used this card before so you can easily see which card you should send. You will see a screen similar to Figure D-4.

Figure D-4

That is it. Every time you need to log into the same site, just send the card you have assigned to it. You can assign this card to many sites and you will not need to keep up with the user name and password for the site.

Inside of the CardSpace interface in Windows you can manage your cards. You can add, edit and delete cards by going to the CardSpace program in the Control Panel. Be careful about deleting cards. Unless you have a backup, a deleted card is not replaceable. Figure D-5 shows the card editing screen.

Figure D-5

You can go to the Control Panel and run the Windows CardSpace program to handle all of your card maintenance tasks, including backing up and restoring. It is easy to back up and restore your cards. To create a backup, go to the Control Panel and run the Windows CardSpace program. Choose the link to back up your cards. Next, enter a location to store the encrypted backup file. On the next screen, enter a password for the card. You will need this to restore the card on a computer later. Now you can put the file on a CD or thumb drive and store it. Also, you can take the file on the road and use your cards on another computer after you restore them.

If you delete a card or lose your hard drive it is easy to restore your cards. To restore a card, just go to the main Windows CardSpace program and choose Restore Cards. You will have to pick the backup file, enter a password, and that's all. Your cards are back. This is the same process you will use when you travel and take your card files with you.

Some financial web sites and other trusted Internet businesses may become card providers. In this case, your bank can send you a card. This is known as a *managed card*. Here, your personal information is stored at the card provider and not on your computer. These cards come with expiration dates and will either be replaced or eventually expire. Managed cards will be seen in the same interfaces you have seen before for Personal Cards.

Although this is a great idea and for the average user, and a huge security benefit, there are a couple of things to remember. The cards are stored on your computer so if you travel without your computer, you will need to export your cards and take them with you. Then, on a public computer, you will need to import them, use them, and remember to delete them. The cards must be backed up or they cannot be replaced if deleted. If your computer crashes, you can only recover your cards if you backed them up. If you do export your cards, you must find a computer with Windows CardSpace and a compatible browser before you can use them. These are minor issues in the overall scheme of Identity Management and Security. You will most likely see this type of technology throughout the Internet in the very near future.

What about the Linux and MacIntosh operating systems? This technology is not Microsoft-specific. There is documentation available from Microsoft on how to provide this on other platforms and you can bet if it gains any traction at all you will see plug-ins for other browsers and client programs for other operating systems. There are rumors that a plug-in for Firefox on the Mac exists already, although this could not be confirmed at the time of writing.

As you can see, this is a huge improvement over having to remember many user name and password combinations. For the average user, this will be an easy way to secure and manage Internet accounts. This type of technology will be the big push in the future to help users build trust in the Internet. As a developer, you will have to choose if you want to support this technology. If you use the free controls, you may be able to add this to your own sites in a matter of minutes. This is something you should consider when designing your next site.

Adding Cardspace to Your Site

To include support for Cardspace, just download the server controls from Microsoft at http://cardspace.netfx3.com/files/folders/tools-july-ctp/entry12065.aspx and add them to your site. You just have to set the properties to wire them up and go. The controls, created by Microsoft Gold partner Quality Data are free to use. If you don't want to use the pre-built controls, you can create your own controls to manage cards. To host a site that accepts cards, you will need to provide SSL transmission. You will also need to provide read access to the private key for your SSL Certificate to the appropriate security account.

To use the pre-built controls, download and install CardSpaceSetup.msi. A dll is added to your machine with the installation. Next, open Visual Studio, right-click on the toolbox, and click Choose Items. In the Choose Toolbox Items dialog box, browse to the install folder and choose QualityData.CardSpace.dll. It will be in the directory where you told the installer to install the files. Five new controls will be in your toolbox. Figure D-6 shows the five new controls added to a new tab in the toolbox.

Figure D-6

After adding the controls, just drag the appropriate control onto your page, set the properties, and you have added support for CardSpace to your site. Figure D-7 shows the CardSpace Control at the top and the Login Control below. After dragging the controls to the page, you can run the site and pull up the CardSpace screen to select a card.

Figure D-7

Info on the Internet

For more information on this new technology, see CardSpace info on the following sites:

❑   CardSpace Controls for ASP.NET (`http://cardspace.netfx3.com/files/folders/ tools-july-ctp/entry12065.aspx`): This site contains free ASP.NET controls to make your web site able to consume cards from Windows CardSpace. These controls have been tested and are from a trusted source so you can speed up your implementation by using them. As of this writing, you can get the following controls from this site: CardSpace Control, CardSpace Button, CardSpace Login and CardSpace Manage. Soon they will be adding a CardSpace New Account control. *Note:* To use these tools, you may need to update permissions to allow the decrypting of information.

❑ The NetFx3.com Sandbox (`https://sandbox.netfx3.com/`): Here, you can create an account and see CardSpace in action. When you have met all of the requirements, give it a try.

❑ Wikipedia (`http://en.wikipedia.org/wiki/Windows_CardSpace`): Wikipedia provides broad info on CardSpace and where it is going along with information on competing and complementary identity solutions.

❑ Channel 9: Watch a great 20-minute video explaining CardSpace (`http://channel9.msdn.com/Showpost.aspx?postid=291878`), or see an hour-long version with much more detail (`http://channel9.msdn.com/showpost.aspx?postid=181080`).

Summary

CardSpace and similar technologies are being supported by huge corporations like Microsoft and IBM. You might even assume that information cards are the next big thing in the web development world. If you create programs for sites that allow users to log in, you should investigate this technology and see how hard it would be to integrate into your current site security. To keep your skills ahead of the game, you should understand what CardSpace is and how to integrate it into your site.

.NET Framework Differences

In this appendix we discuss two new versions of the .NET Framework: versions 3.0 and 3.5. Visual Studio 2005 was based on version 2.0 of the .NET Framework. Visual Studio 2008 is based on the .NET Framework 3.5. With the release of Vista, .NET Framework 3.0 was released. Version 3.0 included broad new features to support Vista and version 3.5 included smaller incremental changes.

What's New in the .NET Framework: Major Additions since Version 2.0

The .NET Framework 3.0 introduces four main features. These features are discussed in detail in Chapter 6, Chapter 21, Chapter 22, and Appendix D of the book. Here is a brief summary of each.

- ❏ **Windows Presentation Foundation (WPF):** Introduced with Vista, WPF is the latest graphical subsystem that is used with Visual Studio 2008 WPF applications. With WPF, you can build richer applications with true separation between user interfaces and business and data logic layers. Technologies like 3D graphics, video, audio and animation are greatly improved in WPF applications.

- ❏ **Windows Communication Foundation (WCF):** This messaging subsystem allows programs to interface similar to web services. WCF was designed to support service-oriented architecture (SOA). As a developer, this means that now .NET Remoting, web services, message queues, and others can now be built with a single SOA programming model.

- ❏ **Windows Workflow Foundation (WWF):** This feature introduces the ability to manage task using workflows in any application. WWF includes a workflow engine and designer to build workflow applications in .NET.

- ❏ **Windows CardSpace (WCS):** This is a client-side application for securely managing electronic identities. WCF adds the ability to interact with these identities on the Internet. Users would not need to keep up with user names and passwords if this technology takes hold.

What's New in the .NET Framework: Minor Additions since Version 2.0

Released with Visual Studio 2008, version 3.5 of the Framework introduces many new features and improvements. Version 3.0 was introduced alongside of Vista. Here is a list of many of these changes. Some of the changes were available in .NET Framework 3.0 and some not until 3.5:

❑ New ASP.NET ListView control

❑ Language Integrated Query (LINQ) is a new query language for C# and VB.NET. With LINQ, developers can query and transform data in many different types of data sources.

❑ Paging support for ADO.NET

❑ Support for RSS

❑ ASP.NET AJAX controls and support built-in

❑ ClickOnce deployment, which provides improved support for more browsers and XCopy publishing.

❑ Access to ASP.NET authentication information from WPF and Windows Forms applications.

❑ Common file dialog boxes offer support for Windows Vista appearance.

❑ Hosting for WPF controls on a Windows Form and WPF windows from a Windows Form.

What's New in Visual Studio 2008

The release of Visual Studio 2005 a few years ago represented perhaps the largest leap forward in the way a Visual Basic programmer writes code. In November 2007, the bar was raised even higher with the release of Visual Studio 2008. Visual Studio 2008 provides the Visual Basic developer with more tools than ever to increase productivity, reduce errors, and integrate with a team to produce high quality software. Here are a few reasons why you should upgrade and write VB code using Visual Studio 2008.

❑ Project Designer Multitargeting Support allows you to set up VS to be configured to target different versions of the Framework. The IDE allows you to use only controls included in that version.

❑ Windows Installer Deployment provides improved features for smoother release on Vista machines.

❑ IntelliSense added for JavaScript.

❑ Integrated support for AJAX and Office development

❑ Support for LINQ

❑ A better web designer includes split view, improved CSS support and support of nested master pages.

Info on the Internet

Here is a list of sites to get more information on the .NET Framework.

❑ **MSDN — .NET Framework** (`http://msdn2.microsoft.com/en-us/netframework/default.aspx`): MSDN, short for Microsoft Developer Network, is one of the best places for beginning developers. This is a great place to start when working with a new Microsoft Technology or if you are having a problem getting your program to work and need some examples.

❑ **Microsoft .NET Framework 3.0 Community** (`http://netfx3.com/default.aspx`): A new site for info on WPF, WCF, WWF, WCS and other features added to .NET Framework 3.0.

❑ **Wikipedia, the Free Encyclopedia** (`http://en.wikipedia.org/wiki/.NET_Framework`): Wikipedia provides broad info on the .NET Framework versions both previously released and future releases.

Index

P

Get more from Wrox.

978-0-470-18757-9   978-0-470-19137-8   978-0-470-19136-1

wrox™
An Imprint of WILEY

Available wherever books are sold or visit wrox.com